Tammy Kestler

CHAPTER 5   Simple harmonic motion
Damped motion
Forced motion
Resonance
Series electrical and torsional systems
Airplane wings

CHAPTER 7   Current in a circuit
Integrodifferential equations

CHAPTER 8   Coupled springs
Networks
Mixtures

CHAPTER 10   Heat equation
Temperature in a rod
Insulated boundaries
Wave equation
The vibrating string
Laplace's Equation
Temperature in a plate

Dennis G. Zill

Loyola Marymount University

A First Course in
Differential Equations
with Applications

 Prindle, Weber & Schmidt

Boston, Massachusetts

Prindle, Weber & Schmidt is a division of Wadsworth, Inc.
Third printing: January 1980

Library of Congress Cataloging in Publication Data

Zill, Dennis G.,
    A first course in differential equations with applications.

    Includes index.
    1. Differential equations.   I. Title.
QA372.Z54   515'.35   78-21260
ISBN 0-87150-266-6

This book was typeset in monophoto Times Roman by Technical Filmsetters Europe Ltd. Text and cover design by John Servideo and the staff of Prindle, Weber & Schmidt. Technical art by Phil Carver & Friends. Printing and binding by Halliday Lithograph Corp.

PREFACE

This text is intended for a first course in the methods of solution, applications, and theory of ordinary differential equations. Since it has been my experience that the majority of students enrolled in a course in differential equations represents the major areas of science and engineering, the emphasis of the text is on both how to solve differential equations and how to interpret these equations in a physical setting. However, an attempt has been made to strike a balance between methodology, applications, and the theoretical foundations of the subject. Students are encouraged to look beyond merely finding an answer and to think in terms of possible applications as well as problems concerning existence and uniqueness of solutions. Detailed proofs of the more difficult theorems are omitted in favor of additional examples or a plausibility argument. At times intuition is favored over rigor. The style of the text is straightforward, no nonsense, readable, and we hope, understandable.

It has long been my opinion that students in most courses in mathematics use the text primarily as a source of problems and additional illustrations to supplement the class lecture. Thus this text contains an abundance of examples which, for the most part, reflect the typical problems that the student will encounter in the exercises. Occasionally, additional new material and examples appear in the exercises. All examples are set off by three-sided boxes and important formulas are enclosed in boxes to clearly delineate them from the textual discussion and for easy reference. The exercises contain an extensive number of drill problems as well as problems of the more challenging variety. Chapter summaries and review exercises are included at the end of each chapter. The answers to all the odd-numbered problems are given at the end of the book. Even-numbered problems marked with a star are worked out in detail in a student solutions manual that accompanies this text.

The prerequisite for a course in differential equations is the successful completion of a course in calculus. A good working knowledge of ordinary and partial differentiation, integration by parts and use of partial fractions is assumed throughout this text.

The topics covered and the order of the chapters reflect a course in differential equations as taught by the author for the last several years. At this university a good number of students majoring in mathematics and engineering elect to take courses in numerical analysis and partial differential equations. Therefore the material in chapters 9 and 10 is usually omitted. Since many universities with engineering curricula teach a separate course in the theory of the Laplace transform, Chapter 7 and Section 8.2 can be deleted without loss of continuity. In this case a typical one-semester course might consist of Chapters 1 to 6 and Sections 8.1 and 8.3 to 8.6. Those wishing to move quickly into the methods of solution could omit Section 1.3 on the geometric and physical origins of differential equations. Optional sections are marked [O]. In addition, some longer sections are divided into subsections (such as 1.3.1 and 1.3.2) to facilitate coverage in two or more lectures. All chapters after Chapter 4 are sufficiently independent of one another to enable an instructor to rearrange or delete topics in the design of his or her course.

In conclusion, I would like to thank the following reviewers for their helpful comments and criticisms: J. Perryman (Univ. of Texas at Arlington), R.G. Bradshaw (Clarkson College), James Draper (Univ. of Florida), K. Rager (Metropolitan State College), G.E. Latta (Univ. of Virginia), F.W. Stallard (Georgia Institute of Technology), A. Peressini (Univ. of Illinois, Urbana-Champaign), J. Keener (Univ. of Arizona), T. Chow (California State Univ., Sacramento), J.K. Oddson (Univ. of California, Riverside), R. Pruitt (San Jose State Univ.), W.E. Fitzgibbon (Univ. of Houston), F.B. Reis (Northeastern Univ.), and M.B. Tamburro (Georgia Institute of Technology).

While the reviewers have contributed many good ideas that appear in the final version of this text, the author takes full responsibility for whatever weaknesses that remain. The author is indebted also to Warren S. Wright for his help in obtaining the numerical solutions in Chapter 9, and to John Kimmel, editor at Prindle, Weber, and Schmidt, for his cooperation and encouragement. A special word of thanks goes to my faithful typist Erianne Aichner for another job well done.

Dennis G. Zill
Los Angeles

CONTENTS

PREFACE   iii

CHAPTER 1   **An Introduction to Differential Equations**

         1.1   Basic Definitions and Terminology   **1**
         1.2   Existence and Uniqueness, Initial- and Boundary-Value Problems   **13**
         1.3   Origins of Differential Equations   **25**
                1.3.1   The Differential Equation of a Family of Curves   **26**
                1.3.2   Some Physical Origins of Differential Equations   **32**
         Chapter Summary   **43**
         Review Exercises   **44**

CHAPTER 2   **First-Order Differential Equations**

         2.1   Separable Variables   **47**
         2.2   Homogeneous Equations   **56**
         2.3   Exact Equations   **62**
         2.4   Linear Equations   **72**
         2.5   Miscellaneous Equations   **82**
   [O]   2.6   Substitutions   **87**
         Chapter Summary   **91**
         Review Exercises   **92**

CHAPTER 3   **Applications of First-Order Differential Equations**

         3.1   Orthogonal Trajectories   **95**
         3.2   Applications of Linear Equations   **102**
                3.2.1   Growth and Decay   **102**
                3.2.2   Cooling, Circuits, and Chemical Mixtures   **108**

Chapter Summary   **128**
Review Exercises   **128**

CHAPTER 4   **Linear Equations of Higher Order**

4.1   Preliminary Theory   **131**
    4.1.1   Linear Dependence and Linear Independence   **131**
    4.1.2   The Wronskian   **136**
4.2   Constructing a Second Solution from a Known Solution   **148**
4.3   Homogeneous Linear Equations with Constant Coefficients   **154**
4.4   Undetermined Coefficients   **162**
4.5   Variation of Parameters   **173**
Chapter Summary   **181**
Review Exercises   **183**

CHAPTER 5   **Applications of Second-Order Differential Equations: Vibrational Models**

5.1   Simple Harmonic Motion   **185**
5.2   Damped Motion   **194**
5.3   Forced Motion   **205**
[O]   Analogous Systems   **215**
Chapter Summary   **217**
Review Exercises   **219**

CHAPTER 6   **Differential Equations with Variable Coefficients**

Introduction   **223**
6.1   The Cauchy-Euler Equation   **224**
6.2   Power Series Solutions   **232**
    6.2.1   The Procedure   **232**
    6.2.2   Solutions Around Ordinary Points   **234**
6.3   Solutions Around Singular Points   **243**
6.4   Two Special Equations   **264**
    6.4.1   Solution of Bessel's Equation   **265**
    6.4.2   Solution of Legendre's Equation   **268**
Chapter Summary   **277**
Review Exercises   **279**

CHAPTER 7   The Laplace Transform

7.1 The Laplace Transform   **281**
    7.1.1 The Basic Definition   **281**
    7.1.2 The Inverse Transform   **289**
7.2 Operational Properties   **296**
7.3 Applications   **312**
Chapter Summary   **323**
Review Exercises   **325**

CHAPTER 8   Linear Systems of Differential Equations

8.1 The Operator Method   **327**
8.2 The Laplace Transform Method   **340**
8.3 Linear First-Order Systems   **349**
8.4 Preliminary Theory   **358**
8.5 Homogeneous Linear Systems   **376**
8.6 Nonhomogeneous Linear Systems   **391**
    8.6.1 Undetermined Coefficients   **391**
    8.6.2 Variation of Parameters   **396**
[O] 8.7 The Fundamental Matrix and Variation of Parameters Revisited   **402**
Chapter Summary   **411**
Review Exercises   **414**

CHAPTER 9   Numerical Methods

Introduction   **417**
9.1 Direction Fields   **418**
9.2 The Euler Methods   **423**
    9.2.1 Euler's Method   **423**
    9.2.2 The Improved Euler Method   **427**
9.3 The Three-Term Taylor Method   **433**
9.4 The Runge-Kutta Method   **438**
[O] 9.5 Milne's Method, Second-Order Equations, Errors   **444**
Chapter Summary   **447**
Review Exercises   **449**

CHAPTER 10   Partial Differential Equations

Introduction   **451**
10.1 Orthogonal Functions   **452**
10.2 Trigonometric Series   **457**
    10.2.1 Fourier Series   **457**
    10.2.2 Cosine and Sine Series   **461**
10.3 Separable Partial Differential Equations   **468**
10.4 Boundary-Value Problems   **474**
    10.4.1 The Heat Equation   **475**
    10.4.2 The Wave Equation   **477**
    10.4.3 Laplace's Equation   **480**
Chapter Summary   **483**
Review Exercises   **485**

APPENDIX   Answers to Odd-Numbered Problems   A-1
INDEX   I-1

1

An Introduction to Differential Equations

1.1 Basic Definitions and Terminology

In calculus you learned that when we are given a function $y = f(x)$, then the derivative

$$\frac{dy}{dx} = f'(x),$$

itself a function of x, can be found by some appropriate rule. For example, if $y = e^{x^2}$ then its derivative is

$$\frac{dy}{dx} = 2xe^{x^2}$$

or

$$\frac{dy}{dx} = 2xy. \tag{1}$$

The problem that we face in this course is not: given a function $y = f(x)$, find its derivative; but rather our problem is: if we are given an expression such as $dy/dx = 2xy$, to somehow find $y = f(x)$ which satisfies this equation.

1

Any equation, such as (1), containing the derivative or derivatives of an unknown function, is said to be a **differential equation**.

Classification by type

A differential equation containing only ordinary derivatives is naturally called an **ordinary differential equation**, whereas an equation involving the partial derivatives of an unknown function of two or more variables is called a **partial differential equation**. For example,

$$\frac{d^2y}{dx^2} - 2\frac{dy}{dx} + 6y = 0 \tag{2}$$

and

$$a^2\frac{\partial^2 u}{\partial x^2} = \frac{\partial^2 u}{\partial t^2} - 2k\frac{\partial u}{\partial t} \tag{3}$$

are, respectively, ordinary and partial differential equations. The study of partial differential equations depends heavily on the study of ordinary differential equations. In the first nine chapters of this text we shall confine our attention to ordinary differential equations.

Classification by order

The order of the highest derivative in a differential equation is called the **order of the equation**. For example,

$$\frac{d^2y}{dx^2} + 5\left(\frac{dy}{dx}\right)^3 - 4y = x \tag{4}$$

is a second-order ordinary differential equation. Since the differential expression

$$x^2\,dy + y\,dx = 0 \tag{5}$$

can be put into the form

$$x^2\frac{dy}{dx} + y = 0 \tag{6}$$

by dividing by the differential dx, it is an example of a first-order ordinary differential equation.

Classification as linear or nonlinear

A differential equation is said to be **linear** if it has the form

$$a_n(x)\frac{d^ny}{dx^n} + a_{n-1}(x)\frac{d^{n-1}y}{dx^{n-1}} + \cdots + a_1(x)\frac{dy}{dx} + a_0(x)y = g(x). \tag{7}$$

It should be observed that linear differential equations are thus characterized by two properties: (a) y and all its derivatives are of the first degree (that is, the power of each term involving y is 1), and (b) each coefficient depends only on the variable x.

Because of the first property, equation (4) is said to be **nonlinear**. The equations

$$x\,dy + y\,dx = 0 \tag{8}$$

$$y'' - 2y' + y = 0 \tag{9}$$

and

$$x^3\frac{d^3y}{dx^3} - x^2\frac{d^2y}{dx^2} + 3x\frac{dy}{dx} + 5y = e^x \tag{10}$$

are linear first-, second-, and third-order ordinary differential equations, respectively. On the other hand,

$$\frac{dy}{dx} = xy^{1/2} \tag{11}$$

and

$$yy'' - 2y' = x + 1 \tag{12}$$

are nonlinear first- and second-order equations, respectively.

Solutions

Any function $y = f(x)$ defined on some interval $a < x < b$, which when substituted into a differential equation reduces the equation to an identity, is said to be **solution** of the equation on the interval. Of course we must assume that a solution possesses at least as many derivatives as the order of the equation. We have already seen that $y = e^{x^2}$ is a solution of $dy/dx = 2xy$.

EXAMPLE

$y = xe^x$ is a solution of equation (9) since

$$y' = xe^x + e^x$$

$$y'' = xe^x + 2e^x$$

$$y'' - 2y' + y = (xe^x + 2e^x) - 2(xe^x + e^x) + xe^x$$

$$= 0.$$

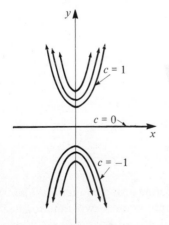

The student should become accustomed to the fact that a given differential equation will usually possess an infinite number of solutions. By direct substitution, we can prove that any curve, that is, function, in the one-parameter family $y = ce^{x^2}$, where c is any arbitrary constant, also satisfies equation (1). As indicated in Figure 1.1, even the trivial function $y \equiv 0$,* obtained by setting $c = 0$, is a solution of the equation. Also, it is easily verified that $y = cxe^x$ is a solution of equation (9) for every value of the constant c.

Figure 1.1

---
* That is, $y = 0$ for every real number x.

EXAMPLES

(a) The functions $y = c_1 \cos 4x$ and $y = c_2 \sin 4x$, where c_1 and c_2 are arbitrary constants, are solutions of the differential equation

$$y'' + 16y = 0. \tag{13}$$

For $y = c_1 \cos 4x$ the first and second derivatives are

$$y' = -4c_1 \sin 4x$$

$$y'' = -16c_1 \cos 4x$$

and so

$$y'' + 16y = -16c_1 \cos 4x + 16(c_1 \cos 4x) = 0.$$

Similarly, for $y = c_2 \sin 4x$

$$y'' + 16y = -16c_2 \sin 4x + 16(c_2 \sin 4x) = 0.$$

(b) The functions

$$y = c_1 \cos 4x + c_2 \sin 4x \qquad \text{and} \qquad y = c_1 \sin 2x \cos 2x$$

can also be shown to be solutions of equation (13).

A solution of a differential equation may be defined **implicitly**, that is, by a relation $G(x, y) = 0$.

EXAMPLE

For $-2 < x < 2$ the relation $x^2 + y^2 - 4 = 0$ is an implicit solution of the differential equation

$$\frac{dy}{dx} = -\frac{x}{y}. \tag{14}$$

By implicit differentiation it follows that

$$\frac{d}{dx}(x^2) + \frac{d}{dx}(y^2) = 0$$

$$2x + 2y\frac{dy}{dx} = 0$$

or

$$\frac{dy}{dx} = -\frac{x}{y}.$$

Recall that a relation $G(x, y) = 0$ need not define a single function. The relation $x^2 + y^2 - 4 = 0$ in the preceding example defines two functions: $y = \sqrt{4 - x^2}$ and $y = -\sqrt{4 - x^2}$ on the interval $-2 < x < 2$. Also note that any relation of the form $x^2 + y^2 - c = 0$ will *formally* satisfy equation (14) for any constant c. However, it is naturally understood that the relation should always make sense in the real number system; thus we cannot say that $x^2 + y^2 + 1 = 0$ is a solution of (14).

EXAMPLE   The functions $y \equiv 0$ and $y = x^4/16$ are solutions of the nonlinear equation

$$\frac{dy}{dx} = xy^{1/2} \tag{15}$$

The result is obtained immediately for the former function; for the latter we have

$$\frac{dy}{dx} = 4 \cdot \frac{x^3}{16} = \frac{x^3}{4}$$

so that

$$\frac{x^3}{4} = x\left(\frac{x^4}{16}\right)^{1/2} = x\left(\frac{x^2}{4}\right).$$

EXAMPLE   For any value of c the function $y = ce^{-5x} + 1/5$ is a solution of the first-order differential equation

$$\frac{dy}{dx} + 5y = 1. \tag{16}$$

We have $\dfrac{dy}{dx} = c\dfrac{d}{dx}(e^{-5x}) + \dfrac{d}{dx}\left(\dfrac{1}{5}\right) = -5ce^{-5x}$

so that $\dfrac{dy}{dx} + 5y = -5ce^{-5x} + 5\left(ce^{-5x} + \dfrac{1}{5}\right) = 1.$

By choosing c to be any real number we can generate an infinite number of solutions; in particular, for $c = 0$ we obtain a constant solution $y \equiv 1/5$.

EXAMPLE   The differential equation

$$\left(\frac{dy}{dx}\right)^2 = -1 \tag{17}$$

possesses no real solution.

EXAMPLE

The reader should be able to show that

$$y = e^x$$

$$y = e^{-x}$$

$$y = c_1 e^x$$

$$y = c_2 e^{-x}$$

and

$$y = c_1 e^x + c_2 e^{-x}$$

are all solutions of the linear second-order differential equation

$$y'' - y = 0. \tag{18}$$

Note that $y = c_1 e^x$ is a solution for any choice of c_1, but $y = e^x + c_1$, $c_1 \neq 0$, does *not* satisfy the equation since for this latter family of functions we would get $y'' - y = -c_1$.

EXAMPLE

Any function in the one-parameter family $y = cx^4$ is a solution of the differential equation

$$xy' - 4y = 0. \tag{19}$$

We have $xy' - 4y = x(4cx^3) - 4cx^4 = 0$. Similarly, it can be shown that the piecewise-defined function

$$y = \begin{cases} -x^4, & x < 0 \\ x^4, & x \geq 0 \end{cases}$$

is a solution of (19). Observe, however, that this function is not a member of the given family. That is, this function cannot be obtained from $y = cx^4$ by a single selection of the parameter c. See Figure 1.2(c).

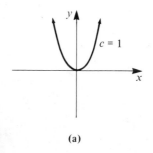

(a)

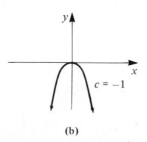

(b)

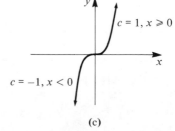

(c)

Figure 1.2

A general solution

If every member of an n-parameter family of curves or functions defined by $G(x, y, c_1, c_2, \ldots, c_n) = 0$ is a solution of an nth-order differential equation, we shall say that the family is a **general solution** of the equation.

EXAMPLES

(a) The one-parameter family $y = ce^x$ is a general solution of the first-order equation $y' - y = 0$.

(b) Although $y = ce^x$ also satisfies the second-order equation $y'' - y = 0$, it is not a general solution since we want a solution that contains *two* arbitrary parameters. The two-parameter family $y = c_1 e^x + c_2 e^{-x}$ not only satisfies the equation for any choice of c_1 and c_2, but, as we shall see, is also a general solution of the differential equation.

(c) The two-parameter family $y = c_1 \cos 4x + c_2 \sin 4x$ is a general solution of $y'' + 16y = 0$. In addition we observe that for any choice of c_1 and c_2 the linear combination

$$y = c_1 \sin 4x + c_2 \sin 2x \cos 2x \tag{20}$$

satisfies the differential equation, but that it is not a general solution since

$$y = c_1 \sin 4x + \tfrac{1}{2}c_2(2 \sin 2x \cos 2x)$$
$$= c_1 \sin 4x + \tfrac{1}{2}c_2(\sin 4x)$$
$$= (c_1 + \tfrac{1}{2}c_2) \sin 4x$$
$$= c_3 \sin 4x.$$

Essential parameters

In part (c) of the preceding example we note that there was basically only *one* parameter, or constant, in the solution of $y'' + 16y = 0$ defined by (20). When a set of constants in a solution cannot be reduced to a fewer number, the constants are sometimes referred to as **essential parameters**. A general solution of a differential equation contains only essential parameters.

EXAMPLES

The family of functions $y = c_1 + \ln c_2 x$ is a solution of the equation $x^2 y'' + xy' = 0$ on the interval $x > 0$ for any choice of c_1 and $c_2 > 0$. However, c_1 and c_2 are not essential parameters since, by the properties of logarithms, we can write $y = c_1 + \ln c_2 + \ln x$. The combination $c_1 + \ln c_2$ can be replaced with a single constant c.

Particular and singular solutions

The solutions of a differential equation obtained by selecting specific values for the parameters in a general solution are called **particular solutions**. However, a solution of an equation may exist that cannot be obtained by specializing the parameters in a general solution; such solutions are **singular solutions**.

EXAMPLES

(a) We have already seen that

$$y = c_1 e^x + c_2 e^{-x} \tag{21}$$

is a general solution of $y'' - y = 0$. By choosing $c_1 = 5$, $c_2 = 0$ and $c_1 = -3$, $c_2 = 4$, we obtain the particular solutions $y = 5e^x$ and $y = -3e^x + 4e^{-x}$, respectively. The choices $c_1 = c_2 = 1/2$ and $c_1 = 1/2$, $c_2 = -1/2$ yield $y = \cosh x$ and $y = \sinh x$, respectively.* If we assign $c_1 = 0$ and $c_2 = 0$ in (21) the result is the trivial solution $y \equiv 0$.

(b) The linear combination

$$y = c_1 \cosh x + c_2 \sinh x \tag{22}$$

satisfies $y'' = c_1 \cosh x + c_2 \sinh x = y$. Hence (22) is also a solution of $y'' - y = 0$. In fact, this combination is an alternative general solution of the differential equation since c_1 and c_2 are essential parameters. Observe that we recover $y = e^x$ and $y = e^{-x}$ as particular solutions from (22) by selecting $c_1 = c_2 = 1$ and $c_1 = 1$, $c_2 = -1$, respectively.

EXAMPLE

In Section 2.1 we shall prove that a general solution of $y' = xy^{1/2}$ is $y = (x^2/4 + c)^2$. When $c = 0$ the resulting particular solution is $y = x^4/16$. In this case the trivial function $y \equiv 0$ is a singular solution of the equation since it cannot be obtained from the general solution for any choice of the parameter c.

Remark: There are two schools of thought concerning the concept of a "general solution" of a differential equation. One view holds that a general solution of an nth-order differential equation is as we defined it above: a family of solutions containing n essential parameters. On the other hand, some texts demand that *all* solutions on some interval must be obtainable from a general solution through the assignment of appropriate values to the parameters. Admittedly, the former interpretation has a distinct disadvantage in that a general solution does not always tell the complete story; singular solutions may exist. The difference in these opinions is really a distinction between the solutions to linear and nonlinear equations. In solving linear differential equations we shall impose relatively simple restrictions on the coefficients; with these restrictions one can always be assured that not only does a solution exist on an interval but that a general solution will indeed yield all possible solutions. Although there are conditions that are sufficient to tell us when a solution of a nonlinear differential equation exists, it simply may not be possible to exhibit a family of solutions. Even in the circumstance when a family of solutions of a nonlinear equation can be found, there are no simple criteria for deciding whether this family encompasses all solutions of the equation on some interval. Because of this some authors will use the words *general solution* only in the context of solving linear equations.

---

* Recall, the hyperbolic cosine and hyperbolic sine are defined by

$$\cosh x = (e^x + e^{-x})/2 \quad \text{and} \quad \sinh x = (e^x - e^{-x})/2.$$

In the next chapter we shall solve certain kinds of nonlinear first-order equations. When we are finished with the formal manipulations comprising the method of solution our final result will be a one-parameter family of functions. Out of an urge to call this result something, and perhaps as a small reward for obtaining a rather large set of solutions, if not necessarily all of them, we shall proclaim that we have obtained a general solution!

EXERCISES 1.1

Answers to odd-numbered problems begin on page A-1 of the Appendix. In Problems 1–10 state whether the given differential equations are linear or nonlinear. Give the order of each equation.

1. $(1 - x)y'' - 4xy' + 5y = \cos x$

2. $x\dfrac{d^3 y}{dx^3} - 2\left(\dfrac{dy}{dx}\right)^4 + y = 0$

3. $yy' + 2y = 1 + x^2$

★4. $x^2\, dy + (y - xy - xe^x)\, dx = 0$

5. $x^3 y^{(4)} - x^2 y'' + 4xy' - 3y = 0$

6. $\dfrac{d^2 y}{dx^2} + 9y = \sin y$

7. $\dfrac{dy}{dx} = \sqrt{1 + \left(\dfrac{d^2 y}{dx^2}\right)^2}$

8. $\dfrac{d^2 r}{dt^2} = -\dfrac{k}{r^2}$

9. $(\sin x)y''' - (\cos x)y' = 2$

10. $(1 - y^2)\, dx + x\, dy = 0$

In Problems 11–30 verify that the indicated function is a solution of the given differential equation. Where appropriate, c_1 and c_2 denote constants.

11. $y' - \dfrac{1}{x}y = 1;\qquad y = x \ln x, x > 0$

12. $(x^2 + y^2)\, dx + (x^2 - xy)\, dy = 0;\qquad c_1(x + y)^2 = xe^{y/x}$

13. $y' + y = \sin x;\qquad y = \tfrac{1}{2}\sin x - \tfrac{1}{2}\cos x + 10e^{-x}$

14. $y' + 2xy = 1;\qquad y = e^{-x^2}\displaystyle\int e^x\, dx + c_1 e^{-x^2}$

15. $y'' + (y')^2 = 0;\qquad y = \ln|x + c_1| + c_2$

16. $\dfrac{dy}{dx} = \sqrt{\dfrac{y}{x}};\qquad y = (\sqrt{x} + c_1)^2$

17. $\dfrac{dy}{dt} + 20y = 24;\qquad y = \tfrac{6}{5} - \tfrac{6}{5}e^{-20t}$

18. $\dfrac{dP}{dt} = P(a - bP);\qquad P = \dfrac{ac_1 e^{at}}{1 + bc_1 e^{at}},\qquad a \text{ and } b \text{ constants}$

19. $y' = 25 + y^2;\qquad y = 5 \tan 5x$

20. $x^2 y'' - xy' + 2y = 0;\qquad y = x \cos(\ln x)$

21. $y''' - 3y'' + 3y' - y = 0;\qquad y = x^2 e^x$

★22. $y' = 2\sqrt{|y|};\qquad y = x|x|$

23. $y = 2xy' + y(y')^2; \qquad y^2 = c_1(x + \frac{1}{4}c_1)$

24. $y'' + y = \tan x; \qquad y = -\cos x \ln(\sec x + \tan x)$

25. $y'' - 6y' + 13y = 0; \qquad y = e^{3x} \cos 2x$

26. $y''' - y'' + 9y' - 9y = 0; \qquad y = c_1 \sin 3x + c_2 \cos 3x + 4e^x$

27. $x^2\, dy + 2xy\, dx = 0; \qquad y = -\dfrac{1}{x^2}$

28. $\left(\dfrac{x^3}{y} - 6x^2y + 3y^2\right) dy + (3x^2 \ln y - 6xy^2 + 2x)\, dx = 0;$

$$x^3 \ln y - 3x^2y^2 + y^3 + x^2 = c_1$$

29. $\dfrac{dX}{dt} = (2 - X)(1 - X); \qquad \ln\dfrac{2 - X}{1 - X} = t$

30. $x^3\dfrac{d^3y}{dx^3} + 2x^2\dfrac{d^2y}{dx^2} - x\dfrac{dy}{dx} + y = 12x^2; \qquad y = c_1 + c_2 x \ln x + 4x^2, x > 0$

The solutions of the differential equations in Problems 31–34 are denoted symbolically by $y = T_n(x)$, $y = H_n(x)$, $y = L_n(x)$, and $y = P_n(x)$ respectively. Verify that the listed functions are particular solutions of each equation for the indicated values of n.

31. Chebyshev's equation

$$(1 - x^2)y'' - xy' + n^2y = 0,$$

$$T_0 = 1, \quad T_1 = x, \quad T_2 = 2x^2 - 1.$$

32. Hermite's equation

$$y'' - xy' + ny = 0$$

$$H_0 = 1, \quad H_1 = x, \quad H_2 = x^2 - 1$$

33. Laguerre's equation

$$xy'' + (1 - x)y' + ny = 0$$

$$L_1 = 1 - x, \quad L_2 = 1 - 2x + \tfrac{1}{2}x^2, \quad L_3 = 1 - 3x + \tfrac{3}{2}x^2 - \tfrac{1}{6}x^3$$

34. Legendre's equation

$$(1 - x^2)y'' - 2xy' + n(n + 1)y = 0,$$

$$P_0 = 1, \quad P_1 = x, \quad P_2 = \tfrac{1}{2}(3x^2 - 1)$$

35. Determine the values of x for which $xy^2 + 4x = x^2 + 3$ defines a solution of the differential equation

$$2xy\dfrac{dy}{dx} + y^2 = 2x - 4.$$

★**36.** A general solution of

$$y = xy' + (y')^2$$

is $\qquad y = cx + c^2.$

Verify that this latter family satisfies the differential equation for every choice of c. Determine a value of k such that $y = kx^2$ is a singular solution of the differential equation.

37. A general solution of

$$y' = y^2 - 1$$

is $\qquad y = \dfrac{1 + ce^{2x}}{1 - ce^{2x}}.$

Verify that this latter family satisfies the differential equation for every choice of c. Show also that the constant functions $y \equiv 1$ and $y \equiv -1$ are solutions of the equation. Can these latter solutions be obtained from the general solution?

★**38.** On page 4 we have seen that $y = \sqrt{4 - x^2}$ and $y = -\sqrt{4 - x^2}$ are solutions of $\dfrac{dy}{dx} = -\dfrac{x}{y}$ on the interval $-2 < x < 2$. Explain why

$$y = \begin{cases} \sqrt{4 - x^2}, & -2 < x < 0 \\ -\sqrt{4 - x^2}, & 0 \le x < 2 \end{cases}$$

is not a solution of the differential equation.

39. The function $y = f(x)$ defined by $y = c_1 e^{x + c_2}$ is a solution of the differential equation $y'' + 4y' - 5y = 0$ for any choice of c_1 and c_2. Is the function a possible general solution of the equation?

In Problems 40-44 find values of m so that $y = e^{mx}$ is a solution of each differential equation.

EXAMPLE $\qquad\qquad\qquad 2y'' + 5y' - 3y = 0$

Solution: If $y = e^{mx}$ then $y' = me^{mx}$ and $y'' = m^2 e^{mx}$. Therefore

$$2y'' + 5y' - 3y = 2m^2 e^{mx} + 5me^{mx} - 3e^{mx}$$

$$= e^{mx}(2m^2 + 5m - 3)$$

$$= 0.$$

Since $e^{mx} \ne 0$ we must have $2m^2 + 5m - 3 = (m + 3)(2m - 1) = 0$ so that $m = -3$ or $m = 1/2$. Hence two particular solutions of the given differential equation are $y = e^{-3x}$ and $y = e^{\frac{1}{2}x}$

40. $y'' - 5y' + 6y = 0$ **41.** $y'' - 4y = 0$

42. $y'' + 10y' + 25y = 0$ **43.** $y''' + 3y'' + 2y' = 0$

★44. $y''' + y' - 2y = 0$

In Problems 45–47 find values of m so that $y = x^m$ is a solution of each differential equation.

45. $x^2 y'' - y = 0$ **★46.** $x^2 y'' + 6xy' + 4y = 0$

47. $x^3 y''' - 6xy' + 12y = 0$

In Problems 48–52 proceed formally to show that the indicated parametric equations form a solution of the given differential equation.

EXAMPLE

$$4\left(\frac{dy}{dx}\right)^2 = y + 2,$$

$$x = 4t + 1, \qquad y = t^2 - 2.$$

Solution: Recall from elementary calculus that

$$\frac{dy}{dx} = \frac{dy/dt}{dx/dt}$$

$$= \frac{2t}{4}$$

$$= \frac{1}{2}t$$

and so
$$4\left(\frac{dy}{dx}\right)^2 = 4\left(\frac{1}{2}t\right)^2$$

$$= t^2$$

$$= t^2 - 2 + 2$$

$$= y + 2.$$

---

48. $y = xy' + (y')^2;$ $x = -2t, \quad y = -t^2$

49. $y = xy' + (y')^2 - \ln y';$ $x = -2t + \dfrac{1}{t}, \quad y = -t^2 - \ln t + 1$

50. $y[1 + (y')^2] = c;$ $x = \dfrac{c}{2}(2\theta - \sin 2\theta), \quad y = \dfrac{c}{2}(1 - \cos 2\theta)$

51. $\left(\dfrac{dy}{dx}\right)^3 + 2x\dfrac{dy}{dx} = 2y + 1;$ $x = -\dfrac{3}{2}t^2, \quad y = -t^3 - \dfrac{1}{2}$

52. $\left(\dfrac{dy}{dx}\right)^2 + 1 = \left(y - x\dfrac{dy}{dx}\right)^2$; $x = \cos\theta, \quad y = \sin\theta$

53. Show that $y_1 = x^2$ and $y_2 = x^3$ are both solutions of

$$x^2 y'' - 4xy' + 6y = 0.$$

Are the constant multiples $c_1 y_1$ and $c_2 y_2$, with c_1 and c_2 arbitrary, also solutions? Is the sum $y_1 + y_2$ a solution?

54. Show that $y_1 = 2x + 2$ and $y_2 = -x^2/2$ are both solutions of

$$y = xy' + (y')^2/2$$

Are the constant multiples $c_1 y_1$ and $c_2 y_2$, c_1 and c_2 arbitrary, also solutions? Is the sum $y_1 + y_2$ a solution?

1.2   Existence and Uniqueness, Initial- and Boundary-Value Problems

We are often interested in solving a differential equation subject to certain side conditions.

EXAMPLE

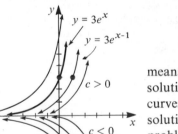

Figure 1.3

The problem

$$y' - y = 0$$

$$y(0) = 3$$

means that out of the infinite number of functions contained in the general solution $y = ce^x$ of the differential equation, we want to find the curve (or curves) passing through the point $(0, 3)$. Substituting $x = 0$ in the general solution gives $3 = ce^0$ hence, $c = 3$. Thus a particular solution to the given problem is

$$y = 3e^x.$$

See Figure 1.3.

Had we demanded that the solution of $y' - y = 0$ pass through the point $(1, 3)$ rather than $(0, 3)$ then $y(1) = 3$ would yield $c = 3e^{-1}$ and so $y = 3e^{x-1}$. The graph of this function is also indicated in Figure 1.3.

EXAMPLE

To solve the differential equation

$$y'' - y = 0$$

subject to the conditions

$$y(0) = 3, \qquad y'(0) = 1$$

means that we are trying to determine a particular function satisfying the equation such that its graph not only passes through the point $(0, 3)$, but as the curve passes through this point its slope is $\left.\dfrac{dy}{dx}\right|_{x=0} = 1$. Using the general solution

$$y = c_1 e^x + c_2 e^{-x}$$

we have

$$y' = c_1 e^x - c_2 e^{-x}.$$

Now from the given conditions we obtain

$$3 = c_1 + c_2$$

and

$$1 = c_1 - c_2$$

which imply

$$c_1 = 2, \quad c_2 = 1.$$

Therefore a solution to the problem is

$$y = 2e^x + e^{-x}.$$

Initial-value problems

The preceding two examples illustrate the concept of an **initial-value problem**. In general, for an nth-order differential equation, an initial-value problem consists of finding a function that satisfies the differential equation subject to the specification of y and its derivatives up to the $(n-1)$st order *at the same value of* x. That is, we must solve some differential equation

$$\frac{d^n y}{dx^n} = f(x, y, y', \dots, y^{(n-1)})* \tag{1}$$

such that $y(x)$ also satisfies the *initial conditions*

$$
\begin{aligned}
y(x_0) &= \gamma_0 \\
y'(x_0) &= \gamma_1 \\
y''(x_0) &= \gamma_2 \\
&\;\;\vdots \qquad \vdots \\
y^{(n-1)}(x_0) &= \gamma_{n-1},
\end{aligned}
\tag{2}
$$

where the γ_i, $i = 0, 1, \dots, n-1$ are constants.

---

* For our purposes, we shall assume that differential equations can be put into this form. As usual there are exceptions. It is not always possible to solve an equation $F(x, y, y', \dots, y^{(n)}) = 0$ for the highest order derivative $y^{(n)}$. Also, if $F(x, y, y', \dots, y^{(n)}) = 0$ can be solved for $y^{(n)}$ we may obtain more than one equation of form (1).

We have seen that the initial-value problems

$$y' - y = 0, \quad y(0) = 3$$

and
$$y'' - y = 0, \quad y(0) = 3, \quad y'(0) = 1$$

yield particular solutions $y = 3e^x$ and $y = 2e^x + e^{-x}$ respectively. One might suspect that since each solution was obtained from a general solution by finding definite constants, it is then the *only* solution to the given problem. While this is a correct conclusion for these specific problems, one should not infer from two examples that solutions to initial-value problems are necessarily unique.

EXAMPLE

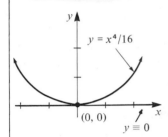

Figure 1.4

As Figure 1.4 shows that the initial-value problem

$$\frac{dy}{dx} = xy^{1/2}$$

$$y(0) = 0$$

has *two* solutions. The graphs of the functions

$$y \equiv 0 \quad \text{and} \quad y = \frac{x^4}{16}$$

both pass through $(0, 0)$.

It is often desirable to know in advance if a solution of an initial-value problem exists and whether it is the only solution of the problem. The following theorem gives sufficient conditions for the existence of a unique solution of the first-order equation

$$\frac{dy}{dx} = f(x, y) \tag{3}$$

subject to
$$y(x_0) = y_0.$$

Theorem 1.1   Suppose R is a region* in the xy-plane, containing the point (x_0, y_0), in which $f(x, y)$ and $\partial f/\partial y$ are continuous. Then there exists a unique function $y(x)$ defined on some interval $x_0 - h \le x \le x_0 + h$, $h > 0$, which satisfies the first-order differential equation

$$\frac{dy}{dx} = f(x, y)$$

and the initial condition $y(x_0) = y_0$.

---

* For those who know and care about such things, R is an open connected set. It is sufficient to consider a rectangular region lying wholly in R with (x_0, y_0) at its center.

EXAMPLE   It might come as a surprise to the reader that there are differential equations for which solutions exist, yet the equation cannot be solved in closed form. That is, no solution can be obtained in terms of elementary functions. The equation

$$\frac{dy}{dx} = x^3 + y^3$$

is one such differential equation. We observe that $f(x, y) = x^3 + y^3$ and $\partial f/\partial y = 3y^2$ are continuous throughout the entire xy-plane, and so through any specified point (x_0, y_0) there passes one and only one solution of the equation. However, the best we can do in this case is to approximate the solution curve (see Chapter 9).

EXAMPLE   We have already seen in a previous example that the differential equation

$$\frac{dy}{dx} = xy^{1/2}$$

possesses at least two solutions whose graphs pass through $(0, 0)$. On the other hand, if the initial condition were $y(0) = 1$, we could conclude from Theorem 1.1 that there is a unique function defined on some interval $-h \leq x \leq h$, which satisfies the differential equation and whose graph passes through $(0, 1)$. This conclusion follows from the fact that

$$f(x, y) = xy^{1/2} \quad \text{and} \quad \frac{\partial f}{\partial y} = \frac{x}{2y^{1/2}}$$

are both continuous in the upper plane defined by $y > 0$.

EXAMPLE   The solution $y = 3e^x$ of the problem

$$y' - y = 0$$
$$y(0) = 3$$

is unique since $f(x, y) = y$ and $\partial f/\partial y = 1$ are continuous throughout the entire xy-plane.

The conditions stated in Theorem 1.1 are *sufficient* but not *necessary*. When $f(x, y)$ and $\partial f/\partial y$ are continuous in a region R it must *always* follow that there exists a unique solution to the differential equation (3) whose graph passes through a given point (x_0, y_0) in R. However, if the conditions stated in the hypothesis of the theorem do not hold, then the initial-value problem may (a) have no solution, (b) have more than one solution, or (c) have a unique solution.

EXAMPLE

Consider the problem

$$xy' = 4y$$

$$y(0) = 0.$$

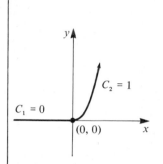

Figure 1.5

We have already seen (page 6) that the function $y = cx^4$ satisfies the differential equation; in addition, it is clear that for any choice of the parameter c, a solution curve must pass through $(0,0)$. Furthermore, a piecewise-defined function such as

$$y = \begin{cases} C_1 x^4, & x < 0, \\ C_2 x^4, & x \geq 0, \end{cases}$$

is also a solution to the problem (see Figure 1.5). Note that for this differential equation, $f(x, y) = 4y/x$ and $\partial f/\partial y = 4/x$ are continuous only in the regions defined by $x > 0$ or $x < 0$.

Linear equations

The next theorem gives conditions sufficient to guarantee the existence and uniqueness of a solution of an initial-value problem associated with a *linear differential equation*.

> **THEOREM 1.2**   Let $a_n(x), a_{n-1}(x), \ldots, a_1(x), a_0(x)$ and $g(x)$ be continuous on an interval $a \leq x \leq b$ (which may be infinite), and let $a_n(x) \neq 0$ for every x in this interval. If x_0 is any point in this interval, then the solution $y(x)$ of the initial-value problem
>
> $$a_n(x)\frac{d^n y}{dx^n} + a_{n-1}(x)\frac{d^{n-1} y}{dx^{n-1}} + \cdots + a_1(x)\frac{dy}{dx} + a_0(x)y = g(x)$$
>
> $$y(x_0) = \gamma_0$$
>
> $$y'(x_0) = \gamma_1$$
>
> $$\vdots \qquad \vdots$$
>
> $$y^{(n-1)}(x_0) = \gamma_{n-1},$$
>
> where the γ_i, $i = 0, 1, \ldots, n - 1$ are constants, exists and is unique.

While we are not in a position to prove the preceding theorem, it is nonetheless interesting to demonstrate the *uniqueness* of the solution in the special case

$$a_2 y'' + a_1 y' + a_0 y = g(x) \tag{4}$$

$$y(0) = \gamma_0$$

$$y'(0) = \gamma_1$$

where a_2, a_1, and a_0 are *positive* constants and $g(x)$ is continuous for all x. We first prove that $y \equiv 0$ is the unique solution of the problem

$$a_2 y'' + a_1 y' + a_0 y = 0 \tag{5}$$

$$y(0) = 0$$

$$y'(0) = 0.$$

Multiplying (5) by y' and integrating over the interval $0 \le x \le t$ gives

$$a_2 \int_0^t y'' y' \, dx + a_1 \int_0^t (y')^2 \, dx + a_0 \int_0^t yy' \, dx = \int_0^t 0 \, dx$$

$$\frac{a_2}{2}[y'(t)^2 - y'(0)^2] + a_1 \int_0^t (y')^2 \, dx + \frac{a_0}{2}[y(t)^2 - y(0)^2] = 0.$$

In view of the imposed initial conditions we find

$$\frac{a_2}{2}(y')^2 + a_1 \int_0^t (y')^2 \, dx + \frac{a_0}{2}y^2 = 0$$

for every t. It follows that the sum of three nonnegative quantities can be zero only when $y \equiv 0$.

To return to the original problem, let us now suppose that y_1 and y_2 are two different solutions of equation (4) and that both solutions satisfy the initial conditions

$$y(0) = \gamma_0$$

$$y'(0) = \gamma_1.$$

If we define the function

$$u = y_1 - y_2$$

then

$$u(0) = y_1(0) - y_2(0) = \gamma_0 - \gamma_0 = 0$$

$$u'(0) = y_1'(0) - y_2'(0) = \gamma_1 - \gamma_1 = 0$$

and

$$a_2 u'' + a_1 u' + a_0 u = a_2[y_1'' - y_2''] + a_1[y_1' - y_2'] + a_0[y_1 - y_2]$$

$$= (a_2 y_1'' + a_1 y_1' + a_0 y_1) - (a_2 y_2'' + a_1 y_2' + a_0 y_2)$$

$$= g(x) - g(x)$$

$$= 0.$$

Hence u satisfies the initial-value problem

$$a_2 u'' + a_1 u' + a_0 u = 0$$

$$u(0) = 0$$

$$u'(0) = 0.$$

From the foregoing discussion we know that the unique solution of this last problem is $u \equiv 0$, thus $y_1 - y_2 \equiv 0$ or $y_1 \equiv y_2$.

EXAMPLE

It follows from Theorem 1.2 that $y = 2e^x + e^{-x}$ is the unique solution of the problem

$$y'' - y = 0$$

$$y(0) = 3, \qquad y'(0) = 1.$$

EXAMPLE

The initial-value problem

$$3y''' + 5y'' - y' + 7y = 0$$

$$y(1) = 0, \qquad y'(1) = 0, \qquad y''(1) = 0$$

possesses the trivial solution $y \equiv 0$. Since the third-order equation is linear with constant coefficients, it follows that all the conditions of Theorem 1.2 are fulfilled. Hence $y \equiv 0$ is the *only* solution.

EXAMPLE

It is easily verified that

$$y = \tfrac{1}{4} \sin 4x$$

is a solution of the problem

$$y'' + 16y = 0$$

$$y(0) = 0, \qquad y'(0) = 1.$$

It follows from Theorem 1.2 that the solution is unique.

The requirements in Theorem 1.2 that $a_i(x)$, $i = 1, 2, \ldots, n$ be continuous and $a_n(x) \neq 0$ for every x in $a \leq x \leq b$ are both important. Specifically, if $a_n(x) = 0$ for some x in the interval $a \leq x \leq b$, then the solution of a linear initial-value problem may not be unique or even exist.

EXAMPLE

The function

$$y = cx^2 + x + 3$$

is a solution of the initial-value problem

$$x^2 y'' - 2xy' + 2y = 6$$

$$y(0) = 3, \qquad y'(0) = 1,$$

for any choice of the parameter c.

Since $y'(x) = 2cx + 1$, $y''(x) = 2c$ it follows that

$$x^2y'' - 2xy' + 2y = x^2(2c) - 2x(2cx + 1) + 2(cx^2 + x + 3)$$
$$= 2cx^2 - 4cx^2 - 2x + 2cx^2 + 2x + 6$$
$$= 6.$$

Also,
$$y(0) = c(0)^2 + 0 + 3 = 3$$
$$y'(0) = 2c(0) + 1 = 1.$$

Although the differential equation in the foregoing example is linear and the coefficients and $g(x) = 6$ are continuous everywhere, the obvious difficulty is that $a_2(x) = x^2$ is zero at $x_0 = 0$.

EXAMPLE   The function

$$y = x^2 - x + 3$$

is the unique solution of the initial-value problem

$$x^2y'' - 2xy' + 2y = 6$$
$$y(1) = 3, \qquad y'(1) = 1$$

on the interval $x > 0$.

Boundary-value problems

Another type of problem consists of solving a differential equation of order two or greater in which the dependent variable y (or its derivatives) is specified at *two different points*. A problem of this sort is called a **boundary-value problem**.

EXAMPLE   The problem:

Solve: $x^2y'' - 2xy' + 2y = 6$

subject to: $y(1) = 0, \qquad y(2) = 3$

is a boundary-value problem.

In the preceding example we want the solution of the differential equation whose graph passes through the two points $(1, 0)$ and $(2, 3)$.

EXAMPLE   We have seen on page 7 that a general solution of the equation $y'' + 16y = 0$ is

$$y = c_1 \cos 4x + c_2 \sin 4x.$$

Suppose we now wish to determine that solution of the equation which further satisfies the boundary conditions

$$y(0) = 0, \qquad y(\pi/2) = 0.$$

Observe that the first condition

$$0 = c_1 \cos 0 + c_2 \sin 0$$

implies $c_1 = 0$ so that

$$y = c_2 \sin 4x$$

But when $x = \pi/2$ we have

$$0 = c_2 \sin 2\pi.$$

Since $\sin 2\pi = 0$ this latter condition is satisfied for any choice of c_2, so it follows that the solution of the problem

$$y'' + 16y = 0$$

$$y(0) = 0, \qquad y\left(\frac{\pi}{2}\right) = 0$$

is the one-parameter family

$$y = c_2 \sin 4x.$$

As Figure 1.6 shows there are an infinite number of functions satisfying the equation whose graphs pass through the two points $(0, 0)$ and $(\pi/2, 0)$.

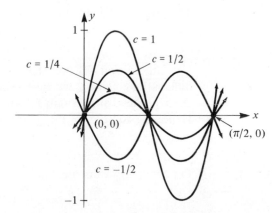

Figure 1.6

As the last example clearly shows, the solution of a boundary-value problem does not have to be unique even when the differential equation is linear.

EXAMPLE   Solve

$$y'' - y = 0$$

subject to

$$y(0) = 0, \qquad y(1) = 1.$$

Solution: In Section 1.1 we saw that a general solution of the differential equation is

$$y = c_1 e^x + c_2 e^{-x}.$$

The boundary conditions give a pair of simultaneous equations for determining c_1 and c_2:

$$0 = c_1 + c_2$$
$$1 = c_1 e + c_2 e^{-1}.$$

The solution is

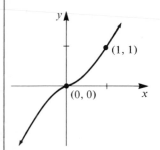

Figure 1.7

$$c_1 = -c_2 = \frac{1}{e - e^{-1}}.$$

Thus a solution of the boundary-value problem is

$$y = \frac{e^x - e^{-x}}{e - e^{-1}}.$$

The graph of this function is given in Figure 1.7.

In Section 4.1 we shall prove that a general solution of a *linear* differential equation, whose coefficients and right-hand member $g(x)$ satisfy the hypothesis of Theorem 1.2, includes *every* possible solution on an interval. Hence the solution of the preceding boundary-value problem is unique.

EXAMPLE   The boundary-value problem

$$y'' + 16y = 0$$

$$y(0) = 0, \qquad y\left(\frac{\pi}{2}\right) = 1$$

has no solution. The condition $y(0) = 0$ still implies that $c_1 = 0$ in the general solution $y = c_1 \cos 4x + c_2 \sin 4x$. Thus $y = c_2 \sin 4x$ so that when $x = \pi/2$ we have $1 = c_2 \sin 2\pi = c_2 \cdot 0 = 0$.

Hence we conclude there is no function in the family of functions constituting the general solution which satisfies the differential equation and both boundary conditions. The obvious question then arises: Could there exist a function, not part of the general solution, which is a solution of the problem? In this case the answer is no; the given linear differential equation has constant coefficients and $g(x) = 0$. As noted in the remark preceding this example, these conditions are sufficient to say that every solution of the differential equation on the interval $-\infty < x < \infty$ can be obtained from its general solution.

As we shall see in Chapter 10, finding solutions of boundary-value problems is of the utmost importance in aspects of applications of partial differential equations.

EXERCISES 1.2   Answers to odd-numbered problems begin on page A-2 of the Appendix.

1. By inspection find at least two solutions of the initial-value problem

$$y' = 3y^{2/3}$$

$$y(0) = 0.$$

2. By inspection find at least two solutions of the initial-value problem

$$x\frac{dy}{dx} = 2y$$

$$y(0) = 0.$$

3. By inspection determine a solution of the nonlinear differential equation $y' = y^3$ satisfying $y(0) = 0$. Is the solution unique?

★4. Explain why the initial-value problem

$$y' = \left(\frac{y-2}{x}\right)^{1/2}$$

$$y(1) = 1$$

possesses no solution.

5. Verify that $y = cx$ is a solution of the differential equation $xy' = y$ for every value of the parameter c including $c = 0$. Observe that the piecewise-defined function

$$y = \begin{cases} 0, & x < 0, \\ x, & x \geq 0 \end{cases}$$

satisfies the condition $y(0) = 0$. Is it a solution of the initial-value problem

$$xy' = y$$

$$y(0) = 0?$$

★6.   By inspection find a solution of the initial-value problem

$$y' = |y - 1|$$
$$y(0) = 1.$$

State why the conditions of Theorem 1.1 do not hold for this differential equation. Although we shall not prove it, the solution to this initial-value problem is unique.

7.   Given that

$$y = c_1 e^{4x} + c_2 e^{-x}$$

is a general solution of the differential equation

$$y'' - 3y' - 4y = 0.$$

Find a solution of the equation satisfying the initial conditions

$$y(0) = 1 \qquad y'(0) = 2.$$

8.   Given that

$$y = c_1 + c_2 \cos x + c_3 \sin x$$

is a general solution of the differential equation

$$y''' + y' = 0.$$

Find a solution of the equation satisfying the initial conditions

$$y(\pi) = 0 \qquad y'(\pi) = 2 \qquad y''(\pi) = -1.$$

9.   Verify that

$$y = c_1 + c_2 x^2$$

is a solution of the linear equation

$$xy'' - y' = 0.$$

Show that constants c_1 and c_2 cannot be found so that $y(x)$ satisfies the initial conditions

$$y(0) = 0 \qquad y'(0) = 1.$$

Explain why this does not violate Theorem 1.2.

★10.   Given that

$$y = c_1 x + c_2 x \ln x$$

is a general solution of the differential equation

$$x^2 y'' - xy' + y = 0$$

on the interval $x > 0$. Find a solution of the equation satisfying the initial conditions

$$y(1) = 3 \qquad y'(1) = -1.$$

11. Given that

$$y = c_1 e^x \cos x + c_2 e^x \sin x$$

is a general solution of the differential equation

$$y'' - 2y' + 2y = 0.$$

Determine whether constants c_1 and c_2 can be found so that $y(x)$ satisfies the conditions

(a) $y(0) = 1, \quad y'(0) = 0$
(b) $y(0) = 1, \quad y(\pi) = -1$
(c) $y(0) = 1, \quad y(\pi/2) = 1$
(d) $y(0) = 0, \quad y(\pi) = 0.$

12. A solution of the differential equation

$$x^2 y'' - 5xy' + 8y = 24$$

is $\qquad y = c_1 x^2 + c_2 x^4 + 3.$

Determine whether constants c_1 and c_2 can be found so that $y(x)$ satisfies the boundary conditions

(a) $y(-1) = 0, \quad y(1) = 4$
(b) $y(0) = 1, \quad y(1) = 2$
(c) $y(0) = 3, \quad y(1) = 0$
(d) $y(1) = 3, \quad y(2) = 15.$

13. Given that $y = c_1 \cos \lambda x + c_2 \sin \lambda x$ is a general solution of the differential equation $y'' + \lambda^2 y = 0$. Determine the values of the parameter λ for which the boundary-value problem

$$y'' + \lambda^2 y = 0, \quad y(0) = 0, \quad y(\pi) = 0$$

has nonzero solutions.

★14. Determine the values of the parameter λ for which the boundary-value problem

$$y'' + \lambda^2 y = 0, \quad y(0) = 0, \quad y(5) = 0$$

has nonzero solutions. (See Problem 13.)

1.3 Origins of Differential Equations

When given an ordinary differential equation, we should immediately classify it as to order, define it as linear or nonlinear, note whether the equation has constant or variable coefficients, whether the equation does or does not equal zero, and so on. We then *try* to put the equation into the form of one of the standard types that we shall study in the succeeding chapters. After the appropriate classification and if necessary, rearrangement, we reach into a bag containing a *limited* number of techniques (and some tricks) and hopefully come up with a method enabling us to find a solution, or if luck holds, a general solution of the equation.*

In Section 1.1 we defined a general solution of an nth-order differential equation as an n-parameter family of curves (that is, functions) that satisfies the equation. Our primary concern in this course is to find a general solution of the equation; thus two important points deserve repeating. If we are fortunate enough to actually obtain a general solution of a nonlinear differential equation, we do not necessarily have all the possible solutions. Also, the reader should not get the impression that we can always find an n-parameter family of solutions for every conceivable nth-order equation. On the other hand, suppose we turn the problem around, starting with an n-parameter family of curves, can we then find an associated nth-order differential equation which is entirely free of arbitrary parameters which represents the given family? In most cases the answer is yes.†

It would be a shame for a student to pass through a course such as this (as some do) and not have a modicum of appreciation for some of the origins of the subject matter. In the discussion that follows we shall see how specific differential equations arise not only out of consideration of families of geometric curves, but also how differential equations result from an attempt to describe, in mathematical terms, physical problems in the sciences and engineering. It would not be overly presumptive to state that differential equations form the backbone of subjects such as physics and electrical engineering, and even provide an important working tool in such diverse areas as biology and economics. Several of the examples and problems in this section will serve as previews of coming attractions for the material in Chapters 3 and 5.

1.3.1   The Differential Equation of a Family of Curves

At the very start of this chapter we saw that each function in the one-parameter family $y = ce^{x^2}$ satisfies the same first-order differential equation $y' = 2xy$. Suppose that we now seek to find the differential equation of the two-parameter family

$$y = c_1 e^{x^2} + c_2.$$

---

* If this sounds a little pessimistic, it is. Don't demand your money back if your instructor tells you that most differential equations cannot be solved in terms of the familiar elementary functions, or that those which can be solved are usually approximations to "reality." But you may be sad or glad to know there is enough material to keep us busy for at least one course.

† See Problem 18 of this section. You should develop a suspicion that exceptions might exist to "general" discussions unless the points under consideration are summarized by means of a theorem. The hypothesis of the theorem sets the conditions under which the conclusion must always follow.

The first two derivatives are

$$\frac{dy}{dx} = 2c_1 x e^{x^2} \tag{1}$$

$$\frac{d^2y}{dx^2} = 4c_1 x^2 e^{x^2} + 2c_1 e^{x^2}$$

$$= c_1(4x^2 e^{x^2} + 2e^{x^2}). \tag{2}$$

Using (1) we can eliminate the parameter c_1 from (2). Since

$$c_1 = \frac{1}{2xe^{x^2}} \frac{dy}{dx}$$

it follows that

$$\frac{d^2y}{dx^2} = \frac{1}{2xe^{x^2}} \frac{dy}{dx}(4x^2 e^{x^2} + 2e^{x^2})$$

or

$$\frac{d^2y}{dx^2} = \left(2x + \frac{1}{x}\right)\frac{dy}{dx}. \tag{3}$$

Multiplying equation (3) by x and rearranging gives the second-order equation

$$x\frac{d^2y}{dx^2} - (2x^2 + 1)\frac{dy}{dx} = 0. \tag{4}$$

EXAMPLE

By taking two derivatives we find that the differential equation of the two-parameter family of straight lines

$$y = c_1 x + c_2$$

is simply

$$\frac{d^2y}{dx^2} = 0.$$

EXAMPLE

Find the differential equation of the family

$$y = cx^3 \tag{5}$$

indicated in Figure 1.8.

Solution: We expect a first-order differential equation since the family contains only one parameter. It follows that

$$\frac{dy}{dx} = 3cx^2,$$

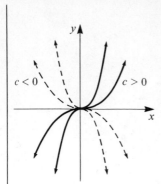

$c < 0$ $c > 0$

Figure 1.8

but from (5) $c = \dfrac{y}{x^3}$ so that

$$\frac{dy}{dx} = 3\left(\frac{y}{x^3}\right)x^2$$

$$= 3\frac{y}{x}.$$

Thus we obtain the linear first-order equation

$$x\frac{dy}{dx} - 3y = 0. \tag{6}$$

First-order differential equations are sometimes written in differential form. Thus equation (6) could also be expressed as

$$x\,dy - 3y\,dx = 0.$$

EXAMPLE

Find the differential equation of the two-parameter family

$$y = c_1 e^{2x} + c_2 e^{-2x}. \tag{7}$$

Solution: Taking two derivatives we obtain

$$\frac{dy}{dx} = 2c_1 e^{2x} - 2c_2 e^{-2x}$$

$$\frac{d^2y}{dx^2} = 4c_1 e^{2x} + 4c_2 e^{-2x}$$

$$= 4[c_1 e^{2x} + c_2 e^{-2x}].$$

Using equation (7) we find

$$\frac{d^2y}{dx^2} = 4y \quad \text{or} \quad y'' - 4y = 0.$$

EXAMPLE

Find the differential equation of the family of circles centered at the origin.

Solution: Concentric circles with center at the origin are described by the one-parameter equation

$$x^2 + y^2 = c^2, \quad c > 0.$$

By implicit differentiation we obtain

$$2x + 2y\frac{dy}{dx} = 0$$

$$\frac{dy}{dx} = -\frac{x}{y}$$

or

$$x\,dx + y\,dy = 0.$$

EXAMPLE

Find the differential equation of the family of circles passing through the origin with center on the *y*-axis.

Solution: This family of circles is characterized by the one-parameter equation

$$x^2 + y^2 = cy. \tag{8}$$

Thus

$$2x + 2y\frac{dy}{dx} = c\frac{dy}{dx}. \tag{9}$$

Substituting $c = (x^2 + y^2)/y$ from (8) into (9) then gives

$$(x^2 - y^2)\frac{dy}{dx} = 2xy \quad\text{or}\quad \frac{dy}{dx} = \frac{2xy}{x^2 - y^2}.$$

EXAMPLE

Find the differential equation of the family of parabolas

$$y = (x + c)^2.$$

Solution: The first derivative is

$$\frac{dy}{dx} = 2(x + c).$$

From the original equation we have $x + c = \pm y^{1/2}$ so that the differential equation representing the family is

$$\frac{dy}{dx} = \pm 2y^{1/2} \quad\text{or}\quad \left(\frac{dy}{dx}\right)^2 = 4y. \tag{10}$$

It should be observed that

$$\frac{dy}{dx} = 2y^{1/2} \tag{11}$$

does not describe the complete family since by convention $y^{1/2} \geq 0$. Equation (11) would give the slope only of a right-hand branch $(x > -c)$ of any particular parabola. Figure 1.9 illustrates the case when $c = 0$. In this case we could say that $y = x^2$ is a solution of (11) on the interval $x > 0$.

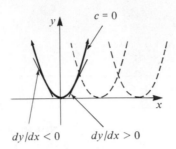

$dy/dx < 0$ $dy/dx > 0$

Figure 1.9

EXAMPLE   Find the differential equation of the family

$$y = \frac{2ce^{2x}}{1 + ce^{2x}}.$$

Solution: By the quotient rule and algebra we find

$$\frac{dy}{dx} = \frac{4ce^{2x}}{(1 + ce^{2x})^2}$$

$$= \frac{y^2 e^{-2x}}{c}.$$

Solving the given equation for c gives

$$c = \frac{e^{-2x}y}{2 - y}$$

and thus we obtain

$$\frac{dy}{dx} = y^2 e^{-2x} \frac{1}{\dfrac{e^{-2x}y}{2 - y}} \qquad \text{or} \qquad \frac{dy}{dx} = y(2 - y). \tag{12}$$

In the preceding two examples the differential equation actually gives a bit more than we bargained for. By inspection we can see that the trivial function $y \equiv 0$ and the constant function $y \equiv 2$ are solutions of (10) and (12), respectively. In neither case are these particular functions a part of the given family.

A two-parameter family of curves can sometimes lead to a rather complicated differential equation.

EXAMPLE

Find the differential equation that describes the family of circles passing through the origin.

Solution: As Figure 1.10 indicates, the general form of the equation of these circles is

$$(x - h)^2 + (y - k)^2 = (\sqrt{h^2 + k^2})^2$$

or

$$x^2 - 2xh + y^2 - 2ky = 0. \tag{13}$$

Using implicit differentiation twice we find

$$x - h + yy' - ky' = 0 \tag{14}$$

and

$$1 + yy'' + (y')^2 - ky'' = 0 \tag{15}$$

We then use the original equation of the family (13) to solve for h:

$$h = \frac{x^2 + y^2 - 2ky}{2x}$$

and substitute in (14),

$$x - \frac{x^2 + y^2 - 2ky}{2x} + yy' - ky' = 0. \tag{16}$$

Now solving (16) for k gives

$$k = \frac{x^2 - y^2 + 2xyy'}{2(xy' - y)}. \tag{17}$$

Substituting this latter value in (15) and simplifying yields the nonlinear equation

$$1 + yy'' + (y')^2 - \frac{x^2 - y^2 + 2xyy'}{2(xy' - y)} y'' = 0$$

or

$$(x^2 + y^2)y'' + 2[(y')^2 + 1](y - xy') = 0. \tag{18}$$

Alternatively, we can obtain equation (18) directly by differentiating (17) by the quotient rule.

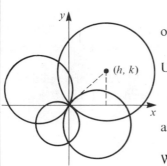

Figure 1.10

1.3.2   Some Physical Origins of Differential Equations

EXAMPLE

It is well known that free-falling objects close to the surface of the earth accelerate at a rate $g = 32$ ft/sec^2. From calculus we also know that acceleration is the derivative of velocity, and this in turn, is the derivative of distance s. Thus if we assume that the upward direction is positive, the statement

$$\frac{d^2s}{dt^2} = -32$$

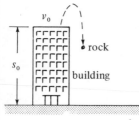

Figure 1.11

is the differential equation governing the vertical distance that the falling body travels. The minus sign is used since the weight of the body is a force directed opposite to the positive direction.

If we further suppose that a rock is tossed off the roof of a building of height s_0 (see Figure 1.11) with an initial upward velocity of, say, v_0 ft/sec, then we must solve the initial-value problem

$$\frac{d^2s}{dt^2} = -32, \qquad 0 < t < t_1,$$

$$s(0) = s_0, \qquad s'(0) = v_0.$$

Here $t = 0$ is taken to be the initial time when the rock leaves the roof of the building and t_1 is the time required to hit the ground. Since the rock is thrown upward it would naturally be assumed that $v_0 > 0$. Now it is easy to see that the solution to this particular problem is

$$s(t) = -16t^2 + v_0t + s_0, \qquad 0 \le t \le t_1.^*$$

Of course this formulation of the problem ignores other forces such as air resistance acting on the body.

EXAMPLE

Consider the single loop series circuit containing an inductor, resistor, and capacitor, shown in Figure 1.12. Kirchoff's second law states that the *sum* of the voltage drops across each part of the circuit is the same as the impressed voltage $E(t)$. If $q(t)$ denotes the charge of the capacitor at any time, then the

---

* In this case you should be able to solve the differential equation directly by integrating twice and using the initial conditions to determine the two resulting constants.

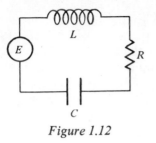

Figure 1.12

current $i(t)$ is given by $i = dq/dt$. Now it is known that the voltage drops across an

$$\text{inductor} = L\frac{di}{dt}$$

$$= L\frac{d^2q}{dt^2}$$

$$\text{capacitor} = \frac{1}{C}q$$

$$\text{resistor} = iR$$

$$= R\frac{dq}{dt}$$

where L, C, and R are constants called the inductance, capacitance, and resistance respectively. To determine $q(t)$ we must therefore solve the second-order differential equation

$$L\frac{d^2q}{dt^2} + R\frac{dq}{dt} + \frac{1}{C}q = E(t) \tag{19}$$

In the previous example, initial conditions $q(0)$ and $q'(0)$ represent the charge on the capacitor and the current in the circuit, respectively, at $t = 0$.

EXAMPLE   To find the vertical displacement $x(t)$ of a weight W attached to a spring we use two different empirical laws: Newton's second law of motion and Hooke's law. The former law states that the net force acting on a weight in motion is $F = ma$ where m is the mass and a is acceleration. Hooke's law states that the restoring force of a stretched spring is proportional to the elongation $s + x$. That is, the restoring force is $k(s + x)$ where $k > 0$ is a constant. As shown in Figure 1.13b, s is the elongation of the spring after the weight has been attached and the

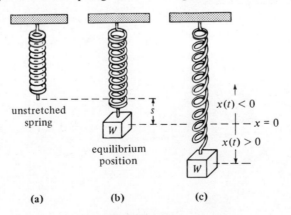

Figure 1.13

system hangs at rest in the *equilibrium position*. When the system is in motion, the variable x represents a directed distance of the weight beyond the equilibrium position. In Chapter 5 we shall prove that when the system is in motion the *net force* acting on the weight is simply $F = -kx$. Thus in the absence of damping and other external forces which might be impressed on the system, the differential equation of the vertical motion through the weight's center of gravity can be obtained by equating:

$$m\frac{d^2x}{dt^2} = -kx.$$

Here the minus sign means that the restoring force of the spring acts opposite to the direction of motion, that is, toward the equilibrium position. In practice this second-order differential equation is often written as

$$\frac{d^2x}{dt^2} + \omega^2 x = 0 \tag{20}$$

where $\omega^2 = k/m$. We can also convert from units of weight (pounds in the engineering system) to units of mass (slugs) by using $W = mg$.

The mathematics of the motion of weights attached to springs will be studied in greater detail in Chapter 5.

A differential equation is often only a close approximation to the description of the actual physical situation.

EXAMPLE

A weight W is suspended from the end of a rod of constant length l. For motion in a vertical plane, we would like to determine the displacement angle θ, measured from the vertical, as a function of time t (we consider $\theta > 0$ to the right of OP and $\theta < 0$ to the left of OP). Recall, an arc s of a circle of radius l is related to the central angle θ through the formula

$$s = l\theta.$$

Hence the angular acceleration is

$$a = \frac{d^2s}{dt^2}$$

$$= l\frac{d^2\theta}{dt^2}.$$

From Newton's second law we then have

$$F = ma$$

$$= ml\frac{d^2\theta}{dt^2}$$

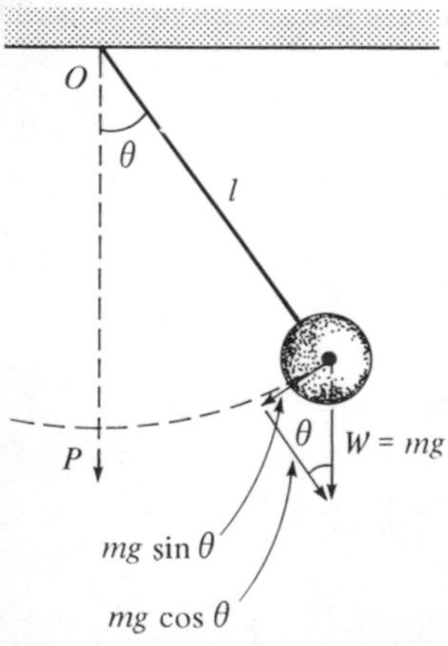

Figure 1.14

where $W = mg$.

Now from Figure 1.14 we see that the tangential component of the force due to the weight W is $mg \sin \theta$. When the mass of the rod is ignored we equate the two different formulations of the tangential force to obtain

$$ml\frac{d^2\theta}{dt^2} = -mg \sin \theta$$

or
$$\frac{d^2\theta}{dt^2} + \frac{g}{l}\sin \theta = 0. \tag{21}$$

Unfortunately the nonlinear equation (21) of the preceding example cannot be solved in terms of the familiar elementary functions, so usually a further simplifying assumption is made. If the angular displacements θ are not too large we can use the approximation $\sin \theta \approx \theta *$ so that (21) can be replaced with the linear second-order differential equation

$$\frac{d^2\theta}{dt^2} + \frac{g}{l}\theta = 0. \tag{22}$$

If we set $\omega^2 = g/l$, observe that equation (22) has the exact same structure as the differential equation governing the free vibrations of a weight on a spring (equation (20)). The fact that one basic differential equation can describe many diverse physical, or even economic, phenomena is a common occurrence in the study of applicable mathematics.

EXAMPLE   It seems plausible to expect that the rate at which a population P expands is proportional to the population that is present at any time. Roughly put, the more people there are, the more there are going to be. Thus one model for population growth is given by the differential equation

$$\frac{dP}{dt} = kP \tag{23}$$

where k is a constant of proportionality. Since we also expect the population to expand we must have $dP/dt > 0$ and thus $k > 0$.

EXAMPLE   In the spread of a contagious disease, for example a flu virus, it is reasonable to assume that the rate, dx/dt, at which the disease spreads is proportional not only to the number of people, $x(t)$, who have contracted the disease, but also to the number of people, $y(t)$, who have not yet been exposed. That is,

$$\frac{dx}{dt} = kxy \tag{24}$$

---

* It is worth a minute of your time to inspect a table of trigonometric values and compare the numerical values of $\sin \theta$ with the values of θ in radians.

where k is the usual constant of proportionality. If one infected person is introduced into a fixed population of n people then x and y are related by

$$x + y = n + 1. \tag{25}$$

Using equation (25) to eliminate y in equation (24) then gives

$$\frac{dx}{dt} = kx(n + 1 - x). \tag{26}$$

The obvious initial condition accompanying equation (26) is $x(0) = 1$.

The logistic equation

The nonlinear first-order equation (26) is a particular example of a more general equation

$$\frac{dP}{dt} = P(a - bP), \qquad a \text{ and } b \text{ constants}, \tag{27}$$

known as the **logistic equation** (see Section 3.3). The solution of this equation is very important in ecological, sociological, and even managerial sciences.

EXAMPLE

Newton's law of cooling states that the time rate at which a body cools is proportional to the difference between the temperature of the body and the temperature of the surrounding medium. If $T(t)$ denotes the temperature of the body at any time t, and T_0 is the constant temperature of the outside medium, it follows that

$$\frac{dT}{dt} = k(T - T_0) \tag{28}$$

where k is the constant of proportionality. Note that when $T_0 = 0$ equation (28) reduces to (23). However in this case $T(t)$ is decreasing so we want $k < 0$.

Equation (23) also appears in a different context in the next example.

EXAMPLE

When interest is compounded **continuously** the rate at which an amount of money S grows is proportional to the amount of money present at any time. That is,

$$\frac{dS}{dt} = rS \tag{29}$$

where r is the annual rate of interest.* This is analogous to the population

---

* Both dS/dt and r are rates. A ratio such as $(dS/dt)/S$ is often called the *growth rate, specific growth rate, relative growth rate,* or *average growth rate.*

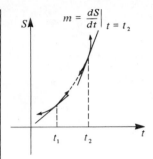

$$m = \frac{dS}{dt}\Big|_{t=t_2}$$

Figure 1.15

growth of an earlier example. The rate of growth is large when the amount of money present in the account is also large. Translated geometrically, this means the tangent line is steep when S is large (see Figure 1.15).

The definition of a derivative provides an interesting derivation of equation (29). Suppose $S(t)$ is the amount accrued in a savings account after t years when the annual rate of interest r is compounded continuously. If h denotes an increment in t then the interest obtained in the time span $(t + h) - t$ is the difference in amounts accrued:

$$S(t + h) - S(t). \tag{30}$$

Since interest is given by

$$(\text{rate}) \times (\text{time}) \times (\text{principal}) \tag{31}$$

we can approximate the interest earned in this same time period by either

$$rhS(t) \tag{32}$$

or

$$rhS(t + h). \tag{33}$$

Intuitively (32) and (33) are lower and upper bounds, respectively, for the actual interest (30), that is,

$$rhS(t) \le S(t + h) - S(t) \le rhS(t + h)$$

or

$$rS(t) \le \frac{S(t + h) - S(t)}{h} \le rS(t + h). \tag{34}$$

Taking the limit of (34) as $h \to 0$ gives

$$rS(t) \le \lim_{h \to 0} \frac{S(t + h) - S(t)}{h} \le rS(t),$$

and so it must follow that

$$\lim_{h \to 0} \frac{S(t + h) - S(t)}{h} = rS(t) \qquad \text{or} \qquad \frac{dS}{dt} = rS.$$

EXAMPLE

Suppose a suspended wire hangs under its own weight. As Figure 1.16(a) shows this could be a long telephone wire between two posts. Our goal here is to determine the differential equation governing the shape that the hanging wire assumes.

Let us examine only a portion of the wire between the lowest point P_1 and any arbitrary point P_2. See Figure 1.16(b). Three forces are acting on the wire: the weight of the segment $P_1 P_2$, and the tensions $\mathbf{T}_1$ and $\mathbf{T}_2$ in the wire at P_1 and P_2 respectively. If w is the linear density (measured, say, in lb/ft) and s is the length of the segment $P_1 P_2$, its weight is necessarily ws.

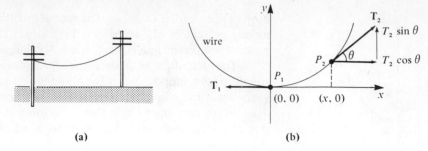

$$(a) \qquad\qquad\qquad\qquad (b)$$

Figure 1.16

Now the tension $\mathbf{T}_2$ resolves into horizontal and vertical components (scalar quantities) $T_2 \cos\theta$ and $T_2 \sin\theta$. Because of equilibrium we can write

$$|\mathbf{T}_1| = T_1 = T_2 \cos\theta,$$

and

$$ws = T_2 \sin\theta.$$

Dividing the last two equations we then find

$$\tan\theta = \frac{ws}{T_1}$$

or

$$\frac{dy}{dx} = \frac{ws}{T_1}. \tag{35}$$

Now since the length of the arc between points P_1 and P_2 is

$$s = \int_0^x \sqrt{1 + \left(\frac{dy}{dx}\right)^2}\, dx$$

it follows from one form of the fundamental theorem of calculus that

$$\frac{ds}{dx} = \sqrt{1 + \left(\frac{dy}{dx}\right)^2}. \tag{36}$$

Differentiating (35) with respect to x and using (36) leads to

$$\frac{d^2y}{dx^2} = \frac{w}{T_1}\frac{ds}{dx}$$

or

$$\frac{d^2y}{dx^2} = \frac{w}{T_1}\sqrt{1 + \left(\frac{dy}{dx}\right)^2}. \tag{37}$$

One might conclude from Figure 1.16 that the shape which the hanging wire assumes is parabolic. However, this is not the case; a wire or heavy rope hanging only under its own weight takes on the shape of a hyperbolic cosine (see Problem 12, Exercises 3.3). Recall that the graph of the hyperbolic cosine is called a **catenary** which stems from the Latin word *catena* meaning "chain." The Romans used the catena as a dog leash. Probably the most graphic example of the shape of a catenary is the 630-ft-high Gateway arch in St. Louis, Missouri.

It may take more than one differential equation to describe a physical situation. The following mechanical system is said to have *two degrees of freedom.*

EXAMPLE

Two weights W_1 and W_2 are connected to two springs A and B having spring constants k_1 and k_2, respectively. In turn, the two springs are attached as shown in Figure 1.17. Let $x_1(t)$ and $x_2(t)$ denote the vertical displacements of the weights from their equilibrium positions. When the system is in motion spring B is subject to both an elongation and a compression, hence its net elongation is $x_2 - x_1$. Therefore it follows from Hooke's law that springs A and B exert forces

$$-k_1 x_1 \quad \text{and} \quad k_2(x_2 - x_1),$$

respectively, on W_1. The net force acting on W_1 is then

$$-k_1 x_1 + k_2(x_2 - x_1).$$

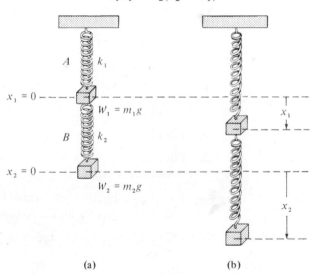

(a)   (b)

Figure 1.17

By Newton's second law we can write

$$m_1 \frac{d^2 x_1}{dt^2} = -k_1 x_1 + k_2(x_2 - x_1). \tag{38}$$

Similarly, the net force exerted on weight W_2 is due solely to the net elongation of B, that is,

$$-k_2(x_2 - x_1).$$

Thus it follows that

$$m_2 \frac{d^2 x_2}{dt^2} = -k_2(x_2 - x_1). \tag{39}$$

In other words, the motion of the coupled system is represented by the *simultaneous* second-order differential equations

$$m_1 x_1'' = -k_1 x_1 + k_2(x_2 - x_1)$$
$$m_2 x_2'' = -k_2(x_2 - x_1). \tag{40}$$

In the derivation of the coupled differential equations given in (40) we have made the usual simplifying assumptions; we assume that no external force is impressed on the system (for example, no one is shaking the system), that there are no damping forces, and that the masses of the two springs are negligible.

EXERCISES 1.3

[1.3.1]

Answers to odd-numbered problems begin on page A-3 of the Appendix. In Problems 1–11 find the differential equation of the given family of curves.

1. $y = cx + 2$
2. $y = c_1 x + c_2 x^2$
3. $y = c_1 + c_2 e^x$
4. $y = c_1 e^x \cos x + c_2 e^x \sin x$
5. $y = c_1 e^{4x} + c_2 x e^{4x}$
6. $y = c_1 e^x + c_2 e^{2x} + c_3 e^{3x}$
7. $cy^2 + 4y = 2x^2$
★8. $cx^2 - y^2 = 1$
9. $y = c_1 \sin \omega t + c_2 \cos \omega t$,   where ω is a constant not to be eliminated
10. $y = c_1 \sinh 3t + c_2 \cosh 3t$
11. $y = c_1 x + c_2 x \ln x$

12. Find the differential equation of the family of straight lines passing through the origin.

13. Find the differential equation of the family of circles passing through the origin with centers on the x-axis.

14. Find the differential equation of the family of circles with centers on the y-axis.

15. Find the differential equation of the family of circles passing through $(0, -3)$ and $(0, 3)$, whose centers are on the x-axis.

★16. Find the differential equation of the family of tangent lines to the parabola $y^2 = 2x$.

17. Find the differential equation of the family of parabolas whose vertex is at the origin but whose focus is on the x-axis.

★18. Show that each curve in the two-parameter family

$$y^2 = 2c_1 x^2 y + c_2 x^4$$

satisfies the first-order differential equation

$$x\frac{dy}{dx} = 2y.$$

[**1.3.2**]   In Problems 19–29, derive the appropriate differential equation(s) describing the given physical situation.

EXAMPLE

Under some circumstances a falling weight w (such as a man hanging from a parachute) encounters air resistance proportional to its instantaneous velocity, $v(t)$. Use Newton's second law to find the differential equation for the velocity of the weight at any time.

Solution: Assuming that the downward direction is positive, the sum of the forces acting on the weight is

$$mg - kv \qquad (41)$$

where k is a constant of proportionality, and the minus sign indicates that the resistance acts in a direction opposite to the motion. Newton's second law can be written as

$$ma = m\frac{dv}{dt} \qquad (42)$$

Figure 1.18

where a represents acceleration. Equating (41) and (42) then gives

$$m\frac{dv}{dt} = mg - kv \qquad \text{or} \qquad \frac{dv}{dt} + \frac{k}{m}v = g.$$

---

19. What is the differential equation for the velocity v of a weight w falling vertically downward through a medium offering a resistance proportional to the square of the instantaneous velocity.

★20. Determine the differential equation governing the height h, at any time, of water flowing through an orifice at the bottom of a cylindrical tank. See Figure 1.19. Use the fact that the decrease in the volume of the water $-A_1 \Delta h$ ($\Delta h < 0$) is the same as the volume of the element of length Δx in a time Δt. Also use the fact that an object falling from rest acquires a velocity $\sqrt{2gh}$ ft/sec, $g = 32$, in h feet. (Where did this come from?)

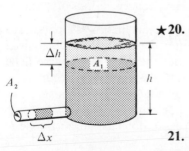

Figure 1.19

21. A man M, starting at the origin moves in the direction of the positive x-axis pulling a weight along the curve C (called a **tractrix**) indicated in Figure 1.20. The weight, initially located on the y-axis at $(0, s)$, is pulled by a rope of constant length s which is kept taut throughout the motion. Find the differential equation of the path of motion. [*Hint:* The rope is always tangent to C; consider the angle of inclination θ as shown in Figure 1.20, page 42.]

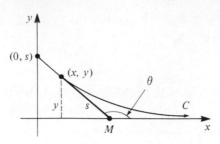

Figure 1.20

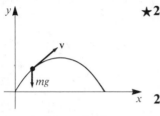

Figure 1.21

★**22.** A projectile shot from a gun has weight $w = mg$ and velocity **v** tangent to its path of motion. Ignoring air resistance and all other forces except its weight, find the system of differential equations which describes the motion. [*Hint:*   Use Newton's second law in the x and y direction. See Figure 1.21.]

23. Determine the equations of motion if the projectile in Problem 22 encounters a retarding force **k** (of magnitude k) acting tangent to the path but opposite to the motion. [*Hint:*   **k** is a multiple of the velocity, say c**v**. See Figure 1.22.]

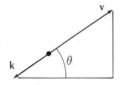

Figure 1.22

24. The rate at which a radioactive substance decays is proportional to the amount of the substance remaining at any time. Determine the differential equation for the amount $A(t)$.

25. A drug is infused into a patient's bloodstream at a constant rate r grams/sec. Simultaneously, the drug is removed at a rate proportional to the amount $x(t)$ of the drug present at any time. Determine the differential equation governing the amount $x(t)$.

26. Two chemicals A and B react to form a new chemical C. Assuming that the concentrations of both A and B decrease by the amount of C formed, find the differential equation governing the concentration $x(t)$ of the chemical C if the rate at which the chemical reaction takes place is proportional to the product of the remaining concentrations of A and B.

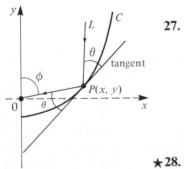

Figure 1.23

27. Light strikes a plane curve C in such a manner that all beams L parallel to the y-axis are reflected to a single point 0. Determine the differential equation for the function $y = f(x)$ describing the shape of the curve. (The fact that the angle of incidence is equal to the angle of reflection is a principle of optics.) [*Hint:*   Inspection of Figure 1.23 shows that the inclination of the tangent line from the horizontal at $P(x, y)$ is $\pi/2 - \theta$ and that we can write $\phi = 2\theta$. (Why?) Also, don't be afraid to use a trigonometric identity.]

★**28.** A cylindrical barrel s feet in diameter of weight w lb is floating in water. After an initial depression the barrel exhibits an up and down bobbing motion along a vertical line. Using Figure 1.24(b), determine the differential equation for the vertical displacements $y(t)$, if the origin is taken to be on the vertical axis at the surface of the water when the barrel is at rest. Use Archimedes' principle that the buoyancy, or upward force of the water on the barrel, is equal to the weight of the water displaced, and the fact that the density of water is 62.4 lb/ft^3. Assume that the downward direction is positive.

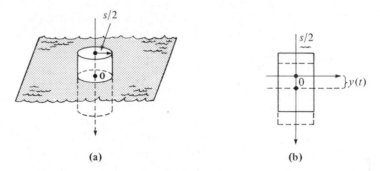

Figure 1.24

29. A rocket is shot vertically upward from the surface of the earth. After all its fuel has been expended the mass of the rocket is a constant m. Use Newton's second law of motion, and the fact that the force of gravity varies inversely as the square of the distance, to find the differential equation for the distance y from the earth's center to the rocket at any time after burnout. State appropriate initial conditions associated with this differential equation.

CHAPTER SUMMARY

In this text we are concerned primarily with **ordinary** differential equations, that is, equations involving a dependent variable y, its ordinary derivatives, and functions of the independent variable x. We classify an ordinary differential equation by its **order** and whether it is **linear** or **nonlinear**. A linear second-order differential equation is any equation having the form

$$a_2(x)\frac{d^2y}{dx^2} + a_1(x)\frac{dy}{dx} + a_0(x)y = g(x). \tag{1}$$

The basic characteristic of linear equations is the fact that the coefficients are functions of x only (including constants), and y and all its derivatives are of the first degree.

A **solution** of a differential equation is any explicit or implicit function, having a sufficient number of derivatives, which satisfies the equation identically on some interval. A solution that contains n arbitrary parameters of an nth-order differential equation is said to be a **general solution**, provided the number of parameters cannot be reduced to a number less than n. A **particular solution** of a differential equation is obtained by assigning specific values to some or all of the constants appearing in a general solution. A **singular solution** of a differential equation is a solution that cannot be obtained from a general

CHAPTER SUMMARY

solution. An **initial-value problem** for a first-order differential equation consists of solving

$$\frac{dy}{dx} = f(x, y) \tag{2}$$

subject to the initial condition $y(x_0) = y_0$. This means we want to find a function satisfying the differential equation such that its graph passes through the point (x_0, y_0). An initial-value problem associated with a linear second-order equation consists of solving an equation of form (1) subject to

$$y(x_0) = \gamma_0 \qquad y'(x_0) = \gamma_1 \tag{3}$$

where γ_0 and γ_1 are constants. Here we want the solution of the differential equation whose graph passes through the point (x_0, y_0) such that the slope of the curve at that point is $m = y'(x_0) = \gamma_1$.

A solution to an initial-value problem does not have to be unique in the sense of being the *only* solution to the problem. However, we can state sufficient conditions which will guarantee uniqueness. In the case of a first-order equation (2) these conditions are the continuity of $f(x, y)$ and $\partial f/\partial y$ throughout some region in the xy-plane containing the point (x_0, y_0). For the second-order equation (1) subject to the conditions (3) we can say that the solution will be unique when the $a_i(x)$ and $g(x)$ are continuous and $a_2(x) \neq 0$ on an interval containing x_0.

A **boundary-value problem** for a second-order differential equation usually consists of finding a solution $y(x)$ which satisfies $y(x_0) = y_0, y(x_1) = y_1$. Geometrically this means a solution curve passes through the two points (x_0, y_0) and (x_1, y_1). The solution of a problem of this kind may not be unique or may not exist.

Starting with an n-parameter family of curves in the plane, we can, in *most* cases, find an nth-order differential equation representing the family. In the analysis of physical problems, many differential equations can be obtained by equating two different empirical formulations of the same situation. For example, a differential equation of motion can sometimes be obtained by simply equating Newton's second law of motion with the net forces acting on a body.

REVIEW EXERCISES   [1.1]

Answers to odd-numbered problems begin on page A-3 of the Appendix.

1. By inspection determine at least one solution for each of the following differential equations.

   (a) $y' = 2x$ **(b)** $y'' = 1$ **(c)** $y'' = y'$

   (d) $\dfrac{dy}{dx} = 5y$ **(e)** $y' = y^3 - 8$ **(f)** $2y\dfrac{dy}{dx} = 1$

2. Verify that $y^3 = c(x^4 - y^3 \ln x)$ is a solution of $3x^5(dy/dx) = y(4x^4 - y^3)$ for any choice of the constant c.

3. Verify that $y = x + \tan x$ is a solution of $y' + 2xy = 2 + x^2 + y^2$.

★**4.** Explain why the differential equation

$$\left(\frac{dy}{dx}\right)^2 = \frac{4 - y^2}{4 - x^2}$$

possesses no real solutions for $|x| < 2, |y| > 2$. Are there other regions in the xy-plane for which the equation has no solutions?

5. Determine an interval for which $y^2 - 2y = x^2 - x - 1$ defines a solution of $2(y - 1)\,dy + (1 - 2x)\,dx = 0$.

6. Each of the following differential equations possesses the given general solution. Verify that each family satisfies the differential equation for every choice of the constants c_1, c_2, and c_3.

(a) $x^2 y'' + xy' + y = 0;\quad y = c_1 \cos(\ln x) + c_2 \sin(\ln x),\quad x > 0$

(b) $y''' - 2y'' - y' + 2y = 6;\quad y = c_1 e^x + c_2 e^{-x} + c_3 e^{2x} + 3$

[**1.2**] **7.** Determine constants c_1 and c_2 so that $y = c_1 \cos(\ln x) + c_2 \sin(\ln x)$, $x > 0$ is a solution of the initial-value problem

$$x^2 y'' + xy' + y = 0 \qquad y(1) = -1 \qquad y'(1) = 4.$$

8. Determine constants c_1, c_2, and c_3 so that $y = c_1 e^x + c_2 e^{-x} + c_3 e^{2x} + 3$ is a solution of the initial-value problem

$$y''' - 2y'' - y' + 2y = 6$$

$$y(0) = 3, \qquad y'(0) = 0, \qquad y''(0) = 1.$$

9. Given that $y = 1 + 1/(c - x)$ is a general solution of the differential equation $y' = (y - 1)^2$. Determine a solution of the equation passing through the point $(0, 1)$.

★**10.** Given that $y = e^{2x}[c_1 \cos 2x + c_2 \sin 2x]$ is a general solution of $y'' - 4y' + 8y = 0$. Determine, if possible, solutions of the equation which satisfy

(a) $y(\pi/2) = 0$ (b) $y(0) = 1$ (c) $y(0) = 0$ (d) $y(0) = 1$
 $y(\pi) = 0$ $y(\pi/4) = 0$ $y(\pi) = 1$ $y(\pi/4) = 1$

[**1.3**] **11.** Find a third-order differential equation representing the three-parameter family of curves

$$y = \frac{c_1 x + c_2}{x + c_3}.$$

★**12.** Find the differential equation representing the family of circles passing through the origin, with centers on the line $y = x$.

13. Find the differential equation which represents the family of straight lines passing through the point $(2, 1)$.

★**14.** A weight of 96 lb slides down an incline making a 30° angle with the horizontal. If the coefficient of sliding friction is μ, determine the differential equation for the velocity $v(t)$ of the weight at any time. Use the fact that the force of friction opposing the motion is μN, where N is the normal component of the weight. (See Figure 1.25.)

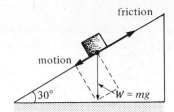

Figure 1.25

15. The conical tank shown in Figure 1.26 loses water out of an orifice at its bottom. If the cross-sectional area of the orifice is $(1/4)\,\text{ft}^2$, find the differential equation representing the height of the water h at any time. (See Problem 20, Exercises 1.3.)

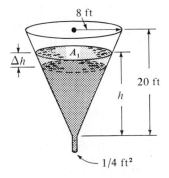

Figure 1.26

CHAPTER 2

First-Order Differential Equations

2.1 Separable Variables

The method of solution   A first-order differential equation of the form $dy/dx = f(x, y)$ where $f(x, y) = g(x)/h(y)$ is said to be **separable**. The variables can be separated in the sense that when the equation is written in differential form, the coefficient of dx depends only on x, and the coefficient of dy depends only on the variable y:

$$\frac{dy}{dx} = \frac{g(x)}{h(y)}$$

or
$$h(y)\,dy = g(x)\,dx. \qquad (1)$$

The general solution can then be obtained by integrating both sides of equation (1). We have

$$\int h(y)\,dy = \int g(x)\,dx$$

or
$$H(y) = G(x) + c \qquad (2)$$

where $\qquad \dfrac{d}{dx}G(x) = g(x) \qquad$ and $\qquad \dfrac{d}{dx}H(y) = h(y)\dfrac{dy}{dx}.$

Constants

Note that there is no need to use two constants in the integration of (1) since

$$H(y) + c_1 = G(x) + c_2$$

$$H(y) = G(x) + c_2 - c_1$$

$$= G(x) + c,$$

where c is completely arbitrary. In many instances throughout the following chapters, we shall not hesitate to relabel constants in a manner which may prove convenient for a given equation. For example, multiples of constants or combinations of constants can sometimes be replaced by one essential constant.

EXAMPLE

Solve

$$xy^4\,dx + (y^2 + 2)e^{-3x}\,dy = 0.$$

Solution: By multiplying the given equation by e^{3x} and dividing by y^4 we obtain the alternative form

$$xe^{3x}\,dx + \frac{y^2 + 2}{y^4}\,dy = 0 \qquad \text{or} \qquad xe^{3x}\,dx + (y^{-2} + 2y^{-4})\,dy = 0.$$

Using integration by parts on the first term yields

$$\tfrac{1}{3}xe^{3x} - \tfrac{1}{9}e^{3x} - y^{-1} - \tfrac{2}{3}y^{-3} = c_1.{}^*$$

The solution can also be written as

$$e^{3x}(3x - 1) = \frac{9}{y} + \frac{6}{y^3} + c$$

or $\qquad\qquad\qquad e^{3x}(3x - 1)y^3 = 9y^2 + 6 + cy^3$

where the constant $9c_1$ is rewritten as c. Unless it is important or convenient, there is no need to solve for y explicitly in terms of x.

EXAMPLE

Solve

$$(1 + x)\,dy - y\,dx = 0.$$

---

* Recall from calculus that $\int u\,dv = uv - \int v\,du$. In this case we let $u = x$ and $dv = e^{3x}\,dx$. You are encouraged to *work* through examples and supply any missing steps.

Solution: Dividing by $(1 + x)y$ we can write $dy/y = dx/(1 + x)$ from which it follows

$$\int \frac{dy}{y} = \int \frac{dx}{1 + x}.$$

Since each indefinite integral results in a logarithm, we shall use $\ln c$ rather than simply the constant c. We have

$$\ln y = \ln (1 + x) + \ln c$$

or

$$\ln y = \ln c(1 + x)$$

so that

$$y = c(1 + x).$$

Even if not *all* the indefinite integrals are logarithms, it may still be advantageous to use $\ln c$. Unfortunately, no firm rule can be given.

Alternative solution:
$$\int \frac{dy}{y} = \int \frac{dx}{1 + x}$$

$$\ln y = \ln (1 + x) + c_1$$

$$y = e^{\ln(1+x)+c_1}$$

$$= e^{\ln(1+x)} \cdot e^{c_1}$$

$$= (1 + x)e^{c_1}$$

Since c_1 is arbitrary so is e^{c_1}, and thus we can relabel it as c. Hence $y = c(1 + x)$.

Notice that although the solution of the preceding example does not contain a logarithm, nonetheless some care should be exercised when dealing with an integral of the form $\int du/u$. Recall that

$$\int \frac{du}{u} = \ln |u| + c, \qquad u \neq 0.$$

For example, $\int \cot x \, dx = \int \frac{\cos x}{\sin x} dx = \ln |\sin x| + c$. As a rule, if a logarithm remains in the solution of a differential equation, then the absolute value should be used unless we are certain that $u > 0$ for the values of x with which we are concerned.

EXAMPLE

Solve the initial-value problem

$$\frac{dy}{dx} = \frac{x - 4}{x - 3}$$

with $y(1) = 2$.

Solution: The right side of the equation can be written as

$$\frac{dy}{dx} = 1 - \frac{1}{x-3}$$

by long division. Integrating the last equation gives

$$y = x - \ln|x-3| + c.$$

When $x = 1$, $y = 2$, we have

$$2 = 1 - \ln|-2| + c$$

so $c = 1 + \ln 2.$

Thus $y = x - \ln|x-3| + 1 + \ln 2$

$$= x + 1 + \ln\frac{2}{|x-3|}, \qquad x \neq 3.$$

EXAMPLE   Solve the initial-value problem

$$\frac{dy}{dx} = -\frac{x}{y}$$

with $y(4) = 3$.

Solution: We saw in Chapter 1 that the differential equation of the family of concentric circles $x^2 + y^2 = c^2$ was $dy/dx = -x/y$. We now are in a position of being able to work "backwards." Obviously $y\,dy = -x\,dx$ and so

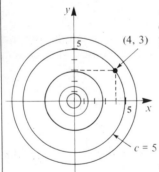

$$\int y\,dy = -\int x\,dx$$

$$\frac{y^2}{2} = -\frac{x^2}{2} + c_1$$

or $x^2 + y^2 = c^2$

Figure 2.1

where the constant $2c_1$ is replaced by c^2.

Now when $x = 4$, $y = 3$ so that $16 + 9 = 25 = c^2$. Thus the initial-value problem determines the solution $x^2 + y^2 = 25$ which is the only circle of the family passing through the point $(4, 3)$. See Figure 2.1.

Note: Observe that it does not matter whether the general solution is written as $x^2 + y^2 = 2c_1$, $x^2 + y^2 = c_2$ or $x^2 + y^2 = c^2$. In the former case the initial condition gives the value $2c_1 = 25$. We do not care about the value of c_1 but rather $2c_1$.

One should never become too complacent when solving differential equations. Even though the so-called general solution of a first-order equation contains an arbitrary constant, we have seen previously that we may not be able to find all solutions by simply assigning different values to this parameter. A solution may get lost in the shuffle of solving the problem.

EXAMPLE

Solve

$$\frac{dy}{dx} = y^2 - 4$$

subject to $y(0) = -2$.

Solution: We put the equation into the form

$$\frac{dy}{y^2 - 4} = dx \tag{3}$$

and use partial fractions on the left side. We have

$$\left[\frac{-\frac{1}{4}}{y + 2} + \frac{\frac{1}{4}}{y - 2} \right] dy = dx \tag{4}$$

so that $-\frac{1}{4}\ln|y + 2| + \frac{1}{4}\ln|y - 2| = x + c_1. \tag{5}$

Thus $\ln\left|\frac{y - 2}{y + 2}\right| = 4x + c_2 \qquad [c_2 = 4c_1]$

and $\frac{y - 2}{y + 2} = ce^{4x} \qquad [c = e^{c_2}]$

from which we finally obtain

$$y = 2\frac{1 + ce^{4x}}{1 - ce^{4x}}. \tag{6}$$

Substituting $x = 0$, $y = -2$ leads to the somewhat embarrassing dilemma

$$-2 = 2\frac{1 + c}{1 - c}$$

$$-1 + c = 1 + c \qquad \text{or} \qquad -1 = 1.$$

Let us consider the differential equation a little more carefully. The fact is, the equation

$$\frac{dy}{dx} = (y + 2)(y - 2)$$

is satisfied by two constant functions, namely, $y \equiv -2$ and $y \equiv 2$.

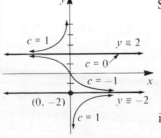

Figure 2.2

When we separated variables we did so under the assumption that the denominators are not zero, and inspection of equations (3), (4), and (5) clearly indicates we must preclude $y = -2$ and $y = 2$ at those steps in our solution. But it is interesting to observe that we can subsequently recover the solution $y \equiv 2$ by setting $c = 0$ in equation (6). However there is no finite value of c which will ever yield the solution $y \equiv -2$. This latter constant function is the only solution to the original initial-value problem. See Figure 2.2.

If, in the preceding example, had we used $\ln c$ for the constant of integration, then the form of the general solution would be

$$y = 2\frac{c + e^{4x}}{c - e^{4x}}. \tag{7}$$

Now when $x = 0$, $y = -2$ we find $c = 0$, but we note further that no finite value of c will give the constant solution $y \equiv 2$.

EXAMPLE

In the first example of this section we saw that the general solution of the equation

$$xy^4\,dx + (y^2 + 2)e^{-3x}\,dy = 0$$

was

$$e^{3x}(3x - 1)y^3 = 9y^2 + 6 + cy^3.$$

Observe that $y \equiv 0$ is a perfectly good solution of the given differential equation but is not a member of the set of solution curves defined by the general solution.

If an initial condition leads to a particular solution by finding a specific value of the parameter c in a general solution of a differential equation, it is a natural inclination of most students (and instructors) to relax and be content. In Chapter 1 we saw, however, that a solution of an initial-value problem may not be unique. For example, the problem

$$\frac{dy}{dx} = xy^{1/2}$$

$$y(0) = 0 \tag{8}$$

has at least two solutions, namely, $y \equiv 0$ and $y = x^4/16$. We are now in a position to solve the equation. By separation of variables

$$y^{-1/2}\,dy = x\,dx \tag{9}$$

$$2y^{1/2} = \frac{x^2}{2} + c_1$$

or
$$y = \left(\frac{x^2}{4} + c\right)^2. \tag{10}$$

When $x = 0$, $y = 0$ so necessarily $c = 0$. Therefore, $y = x^4/16$. The trivial solution $y \equiv 0$ was lost in (9) by dividing by $y^{1/2}$. In addition, the initial-value problem (8) possesses infinitely more solutions, since for any choice of the parameter $a > 0$ the piecewise defined function

$$y = \begin{cases} 0, & x < a \\ \dfrac{(x^2 - a^2)^2}{16}, & x \geq a \end{cases} \tag{11}$$

satisfies both the differential equation and the initial condition.

EXERCISES 2.1   Answers to odd-numbered problems begin on page A-4 of the Appendix. In Problems 1–26 solve the given differential equation by separation of variables.

1. $xy' = 4y$

2. $e^x y\, dy - (e^{-y} + e^{-2x-y})\, dx = 0$

3. $\dfrac{dx}{dy} = \dfrac{x^2 y^2}{1 + x}$

4. $\dfrac{dy}{dx} + 2xy = 0$

5. $y \ln x \dfrac{dx}{dy} = \left(\dfrac{y+1}{x}\right)^2$

6. $\sec^2 x\, dy + \csc y\, dx = 0$

7. $x^2(1 + y^3)\, dx + y^2(1 + x^3)\, dy = 0$

8. $\dfrac{dy}{dx} = \left(\dfrac{2y+3}{4x+5}\right)^2$

9. $x(x + 1)\, dy + (y^2 - 1)\, dx = 0$

★**10.** $e^y \sin 2x\, dx + \cos x(e^{2y} - y)\, dy = 0$

11. $2y(x + 1)\, dy = x\, dx$

12. $\sin 3x\, dx + 2y \cos^3 3x\, dy = 0$

13. $x\sqrt{1 - y^2}\, dx = dy$

14. $\dfrac{dS}{dr} = kS$

15 $t^2 y \dfrac{dy}{dt} = t^2 + 1$

★**16.** $2\dfrac{dy}{dx} - \dfrac{1}{y} = \dfrac{2x}{y}$

Ask   **17.** $x(1 + 2y)\dfrac{dy}{dx} = \ln x$

18. $\dfrac{dy}{dx} = e^{3x + 2y}$

19. $\dfrac{dP}{dt} = P(1 - P)$

20. $\dfrac{y}{x}\dfrac{dy}{dx} = (1 + x^2)^{-1/2}(1 + y^2)^{1/2}$

21. $(e^y + 1)^2 e^{-y}\, dx + (e^x + 1)^3 e^{-x}\, dy = 0$

22. $\dfrac{dN}{dt} + N = Nte^{t+2}$

23. $\dfrac{dy}{dx} = \dfrac{xy + 3x - y - 3}{xy - 2x + 4y - 8}$

★**24.** $\sec y \dfrac{dy}{dx} + \sin(x - y) = \sin(x + y)$

25. $(y + 1)dy - y \ln x \, dx = 0$

26. $(xy^2 + x + y^2 + 1)\, dx + y(x^2 + 4x + 4)\, dy = 0$

In Problems 27–33 solve each differential equation subject to the given initial condition.

EXAMPLE

Solve

$$x \sin x \, e^{-y} dx - y \, dy = 0$$

subject to $y(0) = 1$.

Solution: After dividing by e^{-y} the equation becomes

$$x \sin x \, dx = y e^y \, dy.$$

Using integration by parts on both sides of the equality gives

$$-x \cos x + \sin x = y e^y - e^y + c.$$

Since $y = 1$ when $x = 0$ it follows that

$$0 = e - e + c \qquad \text{or} \qquad c = 0.$$

Thus,

$$-x \cos x + \sin x = y e^y - e^y.$$

---

27. $\sin x(e^{-y} + 1)\, dx = (1 + \cos x)\, dy; \qquad y(0) = 0$

★**28.** $(1 + x^4)\, dy + x(1 + 4y^2)\, dx = 0; \qquad y(1) = 0$

29. $y \, dy = 4x(y^2 - 1)^{1/2}\, dx; \qquad y(0) = 1$

30. $\dfrac{dy}{dt} + ty = y; \qquad y(1) = 3$

31. $\dfrac{dx}{dy} = 4(x^2 + 1); \qquad x\!\left(\dfrac{\pi}{4}\right) = 1$

32. $\dfrac{dy}{dx} = \dfrac{y^2 - 1}{x^2 - 1}; \qquad y(2) = 2$

33. $\dfrac{dy}{dx} - y^2 = -9; \qquad y(0) = 3$

An equation of the form $dy/dx = f(ax + by + c)$, $b \neq 0$, can always be reduced to an equation with separable variables by means of the substitution $w = ax + by + c$. Use this procedure to solve Problems 34–38.

EXAMPLE

Solve

$$\frac{dy}{dx} = \frac{1}{x + y + 1}.$$

Solution: Let $w = x + y + 1$ so that

$$\frac{dw}{dx} = 1 + \frac{dy}{dx}.$$

The given equation then becomes

$$\frac{dw}{dx} - 1 = \frac{1}{w}$$

$$\frac{dw}{dx} = \frac{1}{w} + 1$$

$$= \frac{1 + w}{w}.$$

Therefore

$$\frac{w\,dw}{1 + w} = dx$$

$$\left(1 - \frac{1}{1 + w}\right) dw = dx$$

so that

$$w - \ln|1 + w| = x + c$$

$$x + y + 1 - \ln|x + y + 2| = x + c$$

$$y + 1 - \ln|x + y + 2| = c \qquad \text{or} \qquad x + y + 2 = c_1 e^y$$

where we have replaced e^{1-c} by c_1.

---

34. $\dfrac{dy}{dx} = \tan^2(x + y)$ **35.** $\dfrac{dy}{dx} = (x + \dot{y} + 1)^2$

36. $\dfrac{dy}{dx} = \dfrac{1 - x - y}{x + y}$ [*Hint:*   Let $w = x + y$.]

37. $\dfrac{dy}{dx} = 2 + \sqrt{y - 2x + 3}$ **38.** $\dfrac{dy}{dx} = \sin(x + y)$

2.2   Homogeneous Equations

If an equation in the differential form

$$M(x, y) \, dx + N(x, y) \, dy = 0$$

has the property that

$$M(tx, ty) = t^n M(x, y)$$

and

$$N(tx, ty) = t^n M(x, y)$$

we then say it has **homogeneous coefficients**, or is a **homogeneous equation**. The important point in the subsequent discussion is the fact that a homogeneous first-order differential equation *can always be reduced to a separable equation* through an appropriate algebraic substitution. Before pursuing the method of solution for this type of differential equation let us closely examine the nature of homogeneous functions.

> **DEFINITION 2.1**   If $f(tx, ty) = t^n f(x, y)$, for some real number n, then $f(x, y)$ is said to be a homogeneous function of *degree n*.

EXAMPLES

(a) $f(x, y) = x - 3\sqrt{xy} + 5y$

$$f(tx, ty) = (tx) - 3\sqrt{(tx)(ty)} + 5(ty)$$

$$= tx - 3\sqrt{t^2 xy} + 5ty$$

$$= t[x - 3\sqrt{xy} + 5y]$$

$$= t f(x, y).$$

The function is homogeneous of degree one.

(b) $f(x, y) = \sqrt{x^3 + y^3}$

$$f(tx, ty) = \sqrt{t^3 x^3 + t^3 y^3}$$

$$= t^{3/2} \sqrt{x^3 + y^3}$$

The function is homogeneous of degree 3/2.

(c) $f(x, y) = x^2 + y^2 + 1$

$$f(tx, ty) = t^2 x^2 + t^2 y^2 + 1$$

$$\neq t^2 f(x, y)$$

since $t^2 f(x, y) = t^2 x^2 + t^2 y + t^2$. The function is not homogeneous.

(d) $\quad f(x, y) = \dfrac{x}{2y} + 4$

$$f(tx, ty) = \frac{tx}{2ty} + 4$$

$$= \frac{x}{2y} + 4$$

$$= f(x, y)$$

The function is homogeneous of degree zero.

As parts (c) and (d) of the above example show, a constant added to a function destroys homogeneity, unless the function is homogeneous of degree zero. Also, in many instances a homogeneous function can be recognized by examining the total degree of each term.

EXAMPLES

(a) $\quad f(x, y) = 4xy^3 - x^2y^2$

degree 1, degree 3 } degree 4

degree 2, degree 2 } degree 4

The function is homogeneous of degree 4.

(b) $\quad f(x, y) = x^2 - y$

degree 2

degree 1

The function is not homogeneous.

If $f(x, y)$ is a homogeneous function of degree n, notice that we can write

$$f(x, y) = x^n f\left(1, \frac{y}{x}\right) \qquad \text{and} \qquad f(x, y) = y^n f\left(\frac{x}{y}, 1\right)$$

where $f(1, y/x)$ and $f(x/y, 1)$ are both of degree zero.

EXAMPLE

$$f(x, y) = x^2 + 3xy + y^2$$

$$= x^2\left[1 + 3\left(\frac{y}{x}\right) + \left(\frac{y}{x}\right)^2\right]$$

$$= x^2 f\left(1, \frac{y}{x}\right)$$

$$f(x, y) = y^2 \left[\left(\frac{x}{y} \right)^2 + 3 \left(\frac{x}{y} \right) + 1 \right]$$

$$= y^2 f \left(\frac{x}{y}, 1 \right).$$

The method of solution

An equation of the form $M(x, y) \, dx + N(x, y) \, dy = 0$ where M and N have the same degree of homogeneity can be reduced to separable variables by *either* the substitution $y = ux$ or $x = vy$, where u and v are new dependent variables. In particular if we choose $y = ux$ then $dy = u \, dx + x \, du$. Hence the differential equation becomes

$$M(x, ux) \, dx + N(x, ux) \, [u \, dx + x \, du] = 0.$$

Now by homogeneity of M and N we can write

$$x^n M(1, u) \, dx + x^n N(1, u) \, [u \, dx + x \, du] = 0$$

or

$$[M(1, u) + uN(1, u)] \, dx + xN(1, u) \, du = 0$$

which gives

$$\frac{dx}{x} + \frac{N(1, u) \, du}{M(1, u) + uN(1, u)} = 0.$$

We hasten to point out that the preceding formula should not be memorized; rather, *the procedure should be worked through each time.*

A homogeneous differential equation can always be expressed in the alternative form

$$\frac{dy}{dx} = F \left(\frac{y}{x} \right).$$

To see this suppose we write the equation $M(x, y) \, dx + N(x, y) \, dy = 0$ as $dy/dx = f(x, y)$ where

$$f(x, y) = -\frac{M(x, y)}{N(x, y)}.$$

The function $f(x, y)$ must necessarily be homogeneous of degree zero when M and N are homogeneous of degree n. Using homogeneity it follows that

$$f(x, y) = -\frac{x^n M\left(1, \dfrac{y}{x}\right)}{x^n N\left(1, \dfrac{y}{x}\right)} = -\frac{M\left(1, \dfrac{y}{x}\right)}{N\left(1, \dfrac{y}{x}\right)}.$$

The last ratio is recognized as a function of the form $F(y/x)$. We leave it as an exercise to demonstrate that a homogeneous differential equation can also be written as $dy/dx = G(x/y)$. See Problem 26.

EXAMPLE   Solve

$$(x^2 + y^2)\,dx + (x^2 - xy)\,dy = 0.$$

Solution: Both $M(x, y)$ and $N(x, y)$ are homogeneous of degree 2. If we let $y = ux$ it follows that

$$(x^2 + u^2 x^2)\,dx + (x^2 - ux^2)\,[u\,dx + x\,du] = 0$$

$$x^2(1 + u)\,dx + x^3(1 - u)\,du = 0$$

$$\frac{1 - u}{1 + u}\,du + \frac{dx}{x} = 0$$

$$\left[-1 + \frac{2}{1 + u}\right]du + \frac{dx}{x} = 0$$

$$-u + 2\ln|1 + u| + \ln|x| + \ln c = 0$$

$$-\frac{y}{x} + 2\ln\left|1 + \frac{y}{x}\right| + \ln|x| + \ln c = 0.$$

Using the properties of logarithms the above can be written in the alternative form

$$c(x + y)^2 = xe^{y/x}.$$

The student may be asking by now when should the substitution $x = vy$ be used? Theoretically it could be used for every homogeneous differential equation. However, in practice we try $x = vy$ whenever the function $N(x, y)$ is simpler in structure than $M(x, y)$. In the preceding example there is no appreciable difference between M and N so either $y = ux$ or $x = vy$ can be used. Also, it could happen that after using one substitution we may encounter indefinite integrals that are difficult or impossible to evaluate in closed form; switching substitutions may result in an easier problem.

EXAMPLE   Solve

$$2x^3 y\,dx + (x^4 + y^4)\,dy = 0.$$

Solution: Each coefficient is a homogeneous function of degree four. If we try the substitution $y = ux$ then

$$2x^4 u\,dx + (x^4 + u^4 x^4)\,[u\,dx + x\,du] = 0$$

$$x^4(u^5 + 3u)\,dx + x^5(u^4 + 1)\,du = 0$$

$$\frac{dx}{x} + \frac{u^4 + 1}{u^5 + 3u}\,du = 0.$$

Since the integral of the second term presents a slight problem, we now try $x = vy$.* It follows that

$$2v^3y^4[v\,dy + y\,dv] + (v^4y^4 + y^4)\,dy = 0$$

$$2v^3y^5\,dv + y^4(3v^4 + 1)\,dy = 0$$

$$\frac{2v^3\,dv}{3v^4 + 1} + \frac{dy}{y} = 0$$

$$\frac{1}{6}\ln(3v^4 + 1) + \ln|y| = \ln c_1$$

$$y^6\left[3\left(\frac{x}{y}\right)^4 + 1\right] = c$$

$$3x^4y^2 + y^6 = c.$$

EXAMPLE

Solve

$$x\frac{dy}{dx} = y + xe^{y/x}$$

subject to $y(1) = 1$.

Solution: In the form

$$\frac{dy}{dx} = \frac{y + xe^{y/x}}{x}$$

We see that the function to the right of the equality is homogeneous of degree zero. It occasionally pays to be clever with the algebra before substituting. We write the equation as

$$\frac{dy}{dx} = \frac{y}{x} + e^{y/x}$$

and then use $u = y/x$. Now by the product rule the derivative of $y = ux$ is

$$\frac{dy}{dx} = u + x\frac{du}{dx}$$

so that the equation becomes

$$u + x\frac{du}{dx} = u + e^u$$

$$e^{-u}\,du = dx/x.$$

---

*If you are good at partial fractions the problem is not too difficult.

Hence
$$-e^{-u} + c = \ln|x|$$
$$-e^{-y/x} + c = \ln|x|.$$

Since $x = 1$, $y = 1$, we get

$$-e^{-1} + c = 0 \qquad \text{or} \qquad c = e^{-1}.$$

Therefore the solution to the initial-value problem is

$$e^{-1} - e^{-y/x} = \ln|x|.$$

EXAMPLES

(a) The equation $y\,dx + x\,dy = 0$ is both separable and homogeneous.

(b) The equation $(x + y)\,dx + (x - y)\,dy = 0$ is homogeneous but not separable.

(c) The equation $(y^2 + 1)\,dx + (x^2 + 1)\,dy = 0$ is separable but not homogeneous.

(d) The equation $dy/dx + (1/x)y = xe^x$ is neither separable nor homogeneous.

EXERCISES 2.2

Answers to odd-numbered problems begin on page A-4 of the Appendix. In Problems 1–12 solve the given equation by an appropriate substitution.

1. $(y^2 + yx)\,dx - x^2\,dy = 0$

2. $(y^2 + yx)\,dx + x^2\,dy = 0$

3. $x\,dx + (y - 2x)\,dy = 0$

4. $-y\,dx + (x + \sqrt{xy})\,dy = 0$

5. $y\,dy - \dfrac{y^2}{x}\,dx = xe^{-y/x}\,dx$

★6. $x\dfrac{dy}{dx} - y = \sqrt{x^2 + y^2}$

7. $y^2\,dy = (y\,dx - x\,dy)x\ln\dfrac{x}{y}$

8. $(x^2 + xy - y^2)\,dx + xy\,dy = 0$

9. $y\,dx = 2(x + y)\,dy$

10. $\left(2\left(\dfrac{y}{x}\right) + 3\left(\dfrac{y}{x}\right)^3\right)\left(x\dfrac{dy}{dx} - y\right) = x$

11. $\dfrac{dy}{dx} = \dfrac{y - x}{y + x}$

12. $2x^2y\,dx = (3x^3 + y^3)\,dy$

In Problems 13–22 solve the given initial-value problems.

13. $xy^2\dfrac{dy}{dx} = y^3 - x^3; \quad y(1) = 2$

14. $(x^2 + 2y^2)\,dx = xy\,dy; \quad y(-1) = 1$

15. $2x^2\dfrac{dy}{dx} = 3xy + y^2; \quad y(1) = -2$

16. $xy\,dx - x^2\,dy = y\sqrt{x^2 + y^2}\,dy; \quad y(0) = 1$

17. $(x + ye^{y/x})\,dx - xe^{y/x}\,dy = 0; \quad y(1) = 0$

★18. $y\,dx + \left(y\cos\dfrac{x}{y} - x\right)dy = 0; \quad y(0) = 2$

19. $(y^2 + 3xy)\,dx = (4x^2 + xy)\,dy; \quad y(1) = 1$

20. $y^3\,dx = 2x^3\,dy - 2x^2y\,dx; \quad y(1) = \sqrt{2}$

21. $(x + \sqrt{xy})\dfrac{dy}{dx} + x - y = x^{-1/2}y^{3/2}; \quad y(1) = 1$

★22. $y\,dx + x(\ln x - \ln y - 1)\,dy = 0; \quad y(e) = 1$

In Problems 23 and 24 reduce each equation to one with homogeneous coefficients by means of the given substitutions. Solve.

23. $\dfrac{dy}{dx} = \dfrac{x - y - 3}{x + y - 1}; \quad x = u + 2, \, y = v - 1$

★24. $\dfrac{dy}{dx} = \dfrac{x + y - 6}{x - y}; \quad x = u + 3, \, y = v + 3$

25. Suppose $M(x,y)\,dx + N(x,y)\,dy = 0$ is a homogeneous equation. Show that the substitution $x = vy$ reduces the equation to one with separable variables.

26. Suppose $M(x,y)\,dx + N(x,y)\,dy = 0$ is a homogeneous equation. Show that the equation has the alternative form $\dfrac{dy}{dx} = G\!\left(\dfrac{x}{y}\right)$.

2.3 Exact Equations

While the simple equation

$$y\,dx + x\,dy = 0 \tag{1}$$

is both separable and homogeneous, we should also recognize that it is also equivalent to the differential of the product of x and y. That is,

$$y\,dx + x\,dy = d(xy) = 0.$$

By integrating we immediately obtain the implicit solution $xy = c$.

From calculus you might remember that if $z = f(x,y)$ is a function of two variables then its *total differential* is defined to be

$$dz = \frac{\partial f}{\partial x}\,dx + \frac{\partial f}{\partial y}\,dy. \tag{2}$$

Now if $f(x, y) = c$, we have

$$\frac{\partial f}{\partial x}dx + \frac{\partial f}{\partial y}dy = 0. \tag{3}$$

In other words, given an implicit function $f(x, y) = c$ we can generate a first-order differential equation by computing the total differential.

EXAMPLES

(a)   If $x^2 - 5xy + y^3 = c$ then

$$(2x - 5y)\,dx + (-5x + 3y^2)\,dy = 0 \qquad \text{or} \qquad \frac{dy}{dx} = \frac{5y - 2x}{-5x + 3y^2}.$$

(b)   If $y - \cos x^2 y = 2$ then

$$2xy \sin x^2 y\,dx + (1 + x^2 \sin x^2 y)\,dy = 0.$$

For our purposes, it is more important to turn the problem around, namely, given an equation such as

$$\frac{dy}{dx} = \frac{5y - 2x}{-5x + 3y^2}, \tag{4}$$

can we identify the equation as being equivalent to the statement

$$d(x^2 - 5xy + y^3) = 0?$$

Notice that equation (4) is neither separable nor homogeneous.

Exact equations

We shall say that a differential expression

$$M(x, y)\,dx + N(x, y)\,dy$$

is an **exact differential** if it corresponds to the total differential of some function $f(x, y)$. For example, $x^2 y^3\,dx + x^3 y^2\,dy$ is an exact differential since $d(\frac{1}{3}x^3 y^3) = x^2 y^3\,dx + x^3 y^2\,dy$. An equation

$$M(x, y)\,dx + N(x, y)\,dy = 0 \tag{5}$$

is said to be **exact** if the expression on the left side is an exact differential. The following theorem is often studied in calculus as a test for an exact differential.

THEOREM 2.1   Let M and N be continuous and have continuous first partial derivatives in some region of the xy plane. Then a necessary and sufficient condition that

$$M(x, y)\,dx + N(x, y)\,dy$$

be an exact differential is

$$\frac{\partial M}{\partial y} = \frac{\partial N}{\partial x}. \tag{6}$$

For simplicity let us assume that M and N have continuous first partial derivatives for all (x, y). The necessity is fairly obvious since if the expression $M\,dx + N\,dy$ were exact then

$$M\,dx + N\,dy \equiv \frac{\partial f}{\partial x}\,dx + \frac{\partial f}{\partial y}\,dy$$

for some function f. Therefore

$$M = \frac{\partial f}{\partial x} \quad \text{and} \quad N = \frac{\partial f}{\partial y}.$$

Thus
$$\frac{\partial M}{\partial y} = \frac{\partial}{\partial y}\left(\frac{\partial f}{\partial x}\right) = \frac{\partial^2 f}{\partial y\,\partial x} = \frac{\partial}{\partial x}\left(\frac{\partial f}{\partial y}\right) = \frac{\partial N}{\partial x}.$$

The equality of the mixed partials is a consequence of the continuity of the first partial derivatives of M and N. Now the proof of the sufficiency of condition (6) actually reflects the basic procedure for solving exact equations.

The method of solution   Given the equation

$$M(x, y)\,dx + N(x, y)\,dy = 0$$

first show

$$\frac{\partial M}{\partial y} = \frac{\partial N}{\partial x}.$$

Then assume that

$$\frac{\partial f}{\partial x} = M(x, y)$$

So we can formally find f by integrating M with respect to x while holding y constant. We write

$$f = \int M(x, y)\,dx + g(y) \tag{7}$$

where the arbitrary function $g(y)$ is the "constant" of integration. Now differentiate (7) with respect to y and assume $\partial f/\partial y = N$,

$$\frac{\partial f}{\partial y} = \frac{\partial}{\partial y}\int M(x, y)\,dx + g'(y)$$

$$= N(x, y).$$

This gives

$$g'(y) = N(x, y) - \frac{\partial}{\partial y} \int M(x, y)\, dx.^* \tag{8}$$

Integrate (8) with respect to y and substitute the result in (7). The general solution of the equation is then $f(x, y) = c$.

Note: In the foregoing procedure we could just as well start out with the assumption that $\partial f/\partial y = N(x, y)$. The analogues of equation (7) and (8) would then be respectively

$$f = \int N(x, y)\, dy + h(x) \tag{9}$$

and
$$h'(x) = M(x, y) - \frac{\partial}{\partial x} \int N(x, y)\, dy. \tag{10}$$

In either case *none of these formulas should be memorized.*

EXAMPLE   Solve

$$2xy\, dx + (x^2 - 1)\, dy = 0. \qquad \textit{Not homogenous}$$

Solution: Although the equation is separable it also exact since

$$\frac{\partial M}{\partial y} = 2x = \frac{\partial N}{\partial x}.$$

Now by Theorem 2.1 there exists a function $f(x, y)$ such that

$$\frac{\partial f}{\partial x} = 2xy \qquad \text{and} \qquad \frac{\partial f}{\partial y} = x^2 - 1.$$

From the first of these equations we obtain

$$f = x^2 y + g(y). \tag{11}$$

Taking the partial derivative of the last expression with respect to y and setting the result equal to N gives

$$\frac{\partial f}{\partial y} = x^2 + g'(y)$$

$$= x^2 - 1.$$

---

* It is important to observe that the expression $N - (\partial/\partial y) \int M\, dx$ is independent of x since

$$\frac{\partial}{\partial x}\left[N - \frac{\partial}{\partial y} \int M\, dx \right] = \frac{\partial N}{\partial x} - \frac{\partial}{\partial y}\left(\frac{\partial}{\partial x} \int M\, dx \right)$$

$$= \frac{\partial N}{\partial x} - \frac{\partial M}{\partial y} = 0.$$

It follows that

$$g'(y) = -1$$

and so
$$g(y) = -y. \tag{12}$$

The constant of integration need not be included in the preceding line since the general solution is $f(x, y) = c$. Some of the family of curves $x^2 y - y = c$ are given in Figure 2.3.

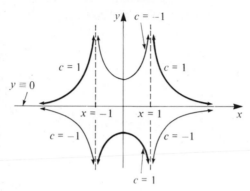

Figure 2.3

Note: The solution of the equation is *not* $f(x, y) = x^2 y - y$, rather it is $f(x, y) = c$ or $f(x, y) = 0$ if a constant is used in equation (12).

EXAMPLE   Solve

$$(e^{2y} - y \cos xy) \, dx + (2xe^{2y} - x \cos xy + 2y) \, dy = 0$$

Solution: The equation is neither separable nor homogeneous, but is exact since

$$\frac{\partial M}{\partial y} = 2e^{2y} + xy \sin xy - \cos xy = \frac{\partial N}{\partial x}.$$

Thus we know that there exists a function $f(x, y)$ such that

$$M = \frac{\partial f}{\partial x} \quad \text{and} \quad N = \frac{\partial f}{\partial y}.$$

For variety we shall start with the assumption that $\partial f / \partial y = N$, that is

$$\frac{\partial f}{\partial y} = 2xe^{2y} - x \cos xy + 2y$$

$$f = 2x \int e^{2y} \, dy - x \int \cos xy \, dy + 2 \int y \, dy.$$

Remember, the reason that x can come out in front of the symbol $\int$ is that in the integration with respect to y, x is treated as an ordinary constant. It follows

$$f = xe^{2y} - \sin xy + y^2 + h(x)$$

$$\frac{\partial f}{\partial x} = e^{2y} - y\cos xy + h'(x)$$

$$= e^{2y} - y\cos xy,$$

so that

$$h'(x) = 0 \quad \text{or} \quad h(x) = c.$$

We can then write the solution as

$$xe^{2y} - \sin xy + y^2 + c = 0.$$

EXAMPLE

Solve

$$(\cos x \sin x - xy^2)\,dx + y(1 - x^2)\,dy = 0$$

subject to $y(0) = 2$.

Solution: The equation is exact since

$$\frac{\partial M}{\partial y} = -2xy = \frac{\partial N}{\partial x}.$$

Now

$$\frac{\partial f}{\partial y} = y(1 - x^2)$$

$$f = \frac{y^2}{2}(1 - x^2) + h(x)$$

$$\frac{\partial f}{\partial x} = -xy^2 + h'(x)$$

$$= \cos x \sin x - xy^2$$

which implies

$$h'(x) = \cos x \sin x$$

$$h(x) = -\int (\cos x)(-\sin x\,dx)$$

$$= -\tfrac{1}{2}\cos^2 x.$$

Thus
$$\frac{y^2}{2}(1 - x^2) - \frac{1}{2}\cos^2 x = c_1$$

or
$$y^2(1 - x^2) - \cos^2 x = c. \qquad (c = 2c_1)$$

The initial condition $x = 0$, $y = 2$ demands that $4(1) - \cos^2(0) = c$ or that $c = 3$. The particular solution is then

$$y^2(1 - x^2) - \cos^2 x = 3.$$

EXAMPLE   The equation

$$x\frac{dy}{dx} + (1 - x)y = 2 \qquad \text{or} \qquad (y - xy - 2)\,dx + x\,dy = 0$$

is neither separable, homogeneous nor exact. We observe

$$\frac{\partial M}{\partial y} = 1 - x \qquad \text{and} \qquad \frac{\partial N}{\partial x} = 1.$$

EXAMPLE   Solve

$$2y(y - 1)\,dx + x(2y - 1)\,dy = 0 \tag{13}$$

Solution: The equation is not exact since if

$$M(x, y) = 2y(y - 1), \qquad N(x, y) = x(2y - 1)$$

then
$$\frac{\partial M}{\partial y} = 4y - 2 \qquad \frac{\partial N}{\partial x} = 2y - 1.$$

It is interesting to note that if we simply multiply the given equation by x we then obtain

$$2xy(y - 1)\,dx + x^2(2y - 1)\,dy = 0 \tag{14}$$

so that
$$M(x, y) = 2xy(y - 1), \qquad N(x, y) = x^2(2y - 1)$$

and
$$\frac{\partial M}{\partial y} = 4xy - 2x \qquad \frac{\partial N}{\partial x} = 4xy - 2x.$$

Since the new equation is exact we can use the above method of solution. It is easily shown that $x^2(y^2 - y) = c$ satisfies both equations (13) and (14).

The function $\mu(x) = x$ in the preceding example is called an **integrating factor** of the differential equation. We shall consider the notion of integrating factors in greater detail in the next section.

EXERCISES 2.3   Answers to odd-numbered problems begin on page A-5 of the Appendix. In Problems 1–20 determine whether the given equation is exact. If exact, solve.

1 $(2y^2x - 3) dx + (2yx^2 + 4) dy = 0$

2. $\left(2y - \dfrac{1}{x} + \cos 3x\right)\dfrac{dy}{dx} + \dfrac{y}{x^2} - 4x^3 + 3y \sin 3x = 0$

3. $(x + y)(x - y) dx + x(x - 2y) dy = 0$

★4. $\left(1 + \ln x + \dfrac{y}{x}\right) dx = (1 - \ln x) dy$

5. $(y^3 - y^2 \sin x - x) dx + (3xy^2 + 2y \cos x) dy = 0$

6. $(x^3 + y^3) dx + 3xy^2 \, dy = 0$

7. $(y \ln y - e^{-xy}) dx + \left(\dfrac{1}{y} + x \ln y\right) dy = 0$

8. $\dfrac{2x}{y} dx - \dfrac{x^2}{y^2} dy = 0$

9. $x\dfrac{dy}{dx} = 2xe^x - y + 6x^2$

10. $(3x^2y + e^y) dx + (x^3 + xe^y - 2y) dy = 0$

11. $\left(1 - \dfrac{3}{x} + y\right) dx + \left(1 - \dfrac{3}{y} + x\right) dy = 0$

★12. $(e^y + 2xy \cosh x)y' + xy^2 \sinh x + y^2 \cosh x = 0$

13. $\left(x^2y^3 - \dfrac{1}{1 + 9x^2}\right) dx + x^3y^2 \, dy = 0$

14. $(5y - 2x)y' - 2y = 0$

15. $(\tan x - \sin x \sin y) dx + \cos x \cos y \, dy = 0$

16. $(3x \cos 3x + \sin 3x - 3) dx + (2y + 5) dy = 0$

17. $(1 - 2x^2 - 2y)\dfrac{dy}{dx} = 4x^3 + 4xy$

★18. $(2y \sin x \cos x - y + 2y^2e^{xy^2}) dx = (x - \sin^2 x - 4xye^{xy^2}) dy$

19. $(4x^3y - 15x^2 - y) dx + (x^4 + 3y^2 - x) dy = 0$

20. $\left(\dfrac{1}{x} + \dfrac{1}{x^2} - \dfrac{y}{x^2 + y^2}\right) dx + \left(ye^y + \dfrac{x}{x^2 + y^2}\right) dy = 0$

In Problems 21–24 solve each differential equation subject to the given initial condition.

21. $(4y + 2x - 5) dx + (6y + 4x - 1) dy = 0; \quad y(-1) = 2$

22. $\left(\dfrac{3y^2 - x^2}{y^5}\right)\dfrac{dy}{dx} + \dfrac{x}{2y^4} = 0; \quad y(1) = 1$

23. $(y^2 \cos x - 3x^2 y - 2x) dx + (2y \sin x - x^3 + \ln y) dy = 0; \quad y(0) = 1$

24. $\left(\dfrac{1}{1 + y^2} + \cos x - 2xy\right)\dfrac{dy}{dx} = y(y + \sin x); \quad y(0) = 1$

25. Determine a function $M(x, y)$ such that

$$M(x, y) dx + \left(xe^{xy} + 2xy + \dfrac{1}{x}\right) dy = 0$$

is an exact differential equation.

★**26.** Determine a function $N(x, y)$ such that

$$\left(y^{1/2}x^{-1/2} + \dfrac{x}{x^2 + y}\right) dx + N(x, y) dy = 0$$

is an exact differential equation.

27. We have seen in the last example of this section that the expression $M(x, y) dx + N(x, y) dy = 0$ may not be exact, but there could exist a function $\mu(x, y)$ such that $\mu(x, y)M(x, y) dx + \mu(x, y)N(x, y) dy = 0$ is exact. Show that a $\mu M\, dx + \mu N\, dy = 0$ is exact if and only if $\mu(x, y)$ satisfies the partial differential equation

$$N(x, y)\dfrac{\partial \mu}{\partial x} - M(x, y)\dfrac{\partial \mu}{\partial y} = \left[\dfrac{\partial M}{\partial y} - \dfrac{\partial N}{\partial x}\right]\mu(x, y).$$

The function $\mu(x, y)$ is called an **integrating factor**.

In Problems 28–32 solve the equation by verifying that the given $\mu(x, y)$ is an appropriate integrating factor. Unfortunately Problem 27 is not of great value in determining μ since we are in no position to solve a partial differential equation.

EXAMPLE

Solve

$$(x + y) dx + x \ln x \, dy = 0, \qquad \mu(x, y) = \dfrac{1}{x}.$$

Solution: Let $M(x, y) = x + y$ and $N(x, y) = x \ln x$ so that $\partial M/\partial y = 1$ and $\partial N/\partial x = 1 + \ln x$. The equation is not exact. However, if we multiply the equation by $\mu = 1/x$ we obtain

$$\left(1 + \dfrac{y}{x}\right) dx + \ln x \, dy = 0.$$

From this latter form we make the identifications:

$$M(x, y) = 1 + y/x, \quad N(x, y) = \ln x, \quad \partial M/\partial y = 1/x, \quad \partial N/\partial x = 1/x.$$

Therefore the second differential equation is exact. It follows

$$\frac{\partial f}{\partial x} = 1 + \frac{y}{x} = M$$

$$f = x + y \ln x + g(y)$$

$$\frac{\partial f}{\partial y} = 0 + \ln x + g'(y) = N$$

$$= \ln x$$

which implies
$$g'(y) = 0$$

$$g(y) = c.$$

Hence $f(x, y) = x + y \ln x + c$ and so the solution of the problem is either

$$x + y \ln x + c = 0 \quad \text{or} \quad x + y \ln x = c_1.$$

---

28. $(2y^2 + 3x) \, dx + 2xy \, dy = 0; \quad \mu = x$

29. $(-xy \sin x + 2y \cos x) \, dx + 2x \cos x \, dy = 0; \quad \mu = xy$

30. $y(x + y + 1) \, dx + (x + 2y) \, dy = 0; \quad \mu = e^x$

31. $6xy \, dx + (4y + 9x^2) \, dy = 0; \quad \mu = y^2$

32. $-y^2 \, dx + (x^2 + xy) \, dy = 0; \quad \mu = 1/x^2 y$

33. Verify that $\mu = (x + y)^{-2}$ is an integrating factor for the equation $(x^2 + 2xy - y^2) \, dx + (y^2 + 2xy - x^2) \, dy = 0$. Solve the resulting equation.

34. The equation $M \, dx + N \, dy = 0$ and $\mu M \, dx + \mu N \, dy = 0$, where μ is an integrating factor, are not necessarily equivalent in the sense that a solution of one is also a solution of the other.

    Show that $y \equiv 0$ is a solution of the non-exact equation

    $$y(2y^2 - 3x^2) \, dx + 2x^3 \, dy = 0$$

    but is not a solution of the exact equation

    $$\left(2 - 3\frac{x^2}{y^2}\right) dx + 2\frac{x^3}{y^3} \, dy = 0.$$

    Here the original equation was multiplied by y^{-3}.

35. A differential equation can have more than one integrating factor. Show that $\mu_1(x, y) = 1/xy$, $\mu_2(x, y) = 1/y^2$, and $\mu_3(x, y) = 1/(x^2 + y^2)$ are all integrating factors of the equation $y \, dx - x \, dy = 0$. Show that the solutions are formally equivalent.

36. Suppose $M\,dx + N\,dy = 0$ has an integrating factor $\mu(x,y)$ such that $df = \mu M\,dx + \mu N\,dy$ is an exact differential. Show that the equation has an infinite number of integrating factors by demonstrating that the product $\mu G(f)$, where G is an arbitrary function, is also an integrating factor.

EXAMPLE

We have seen in Problem 35 that $\mu = 1/y^2$ is an integrating factor of $y\,dx - x\,dy = 0$. The equation

$$\frac{y\,dx - x\,dy}{y^2} = 0$$

is equivalent to

$$d\left(\frac{x}{y}\right) = 0$$

so that we can make the identification $f = x/y$. If we now simply make up a function, say $G(u) = u^{-2}$ then another integrating factor is necessarily

$$\mu_1(x,y) = \frac{1}{y^2}G\left(\frac{x}{y}\right)$$

$$= \frac{1}{y^2}\left(\frac{x}{y}\right)^{-2}$$

$$= \frac{1}{x^2}.$$

The differential equation is then

$$\frac{x\,dy - y\,dx}{x^2} = 0 \qquad \text{(after multiplying by } -1\text{)}$$

or

$$d\left(\frac{y}{x}\right) = 0.$$

---

37. Find three more integrating factors of $y\,dx - x\,dx = 0$ and write down the resulting differential equations.

2.4 Linear Equations

In Chapter 1 we defined the general form of a *linear* differential equation of order n to be

$$a_n(x)\frac{d^n y}{dx^n} + a_{n-1}(x)\frac{d^{n-1}y}{dx^{n-1}} + \cdots + a_1(x)\frac{dy}{dx} + a_0(x)y = g(x).$$

We remind the student that linearity means that all coefficients are functions of

x only, and that y and all its derivatives are raised to the first power. Now when $n = 1$ we obtain the linear first-order equation

$$a_1(x)\frac{dy}{dx} + a_0(x)y = g(x).$$

Dividing by $a_1(x)$ gives the more useful form

$$\frac{dy}{dx} + P(x)y = f(x). \tag{1}$$

We seek the general solution of (1) on an interval $a \leq x \leq b$ for which P and f are continuous.

Solution when $f(x) = 0$ If $f(x) = 0$ a linear first-order equation can always be solved by separation of variables. In this case the equation

$$\frac{dy}{dx} + P(x)y = 0$$

can be written as

$$\frac{dy}{y} = -P(x)\,dx.$$

Thus we get

$$\ln|y| = -\int P(x)\,dx + c_1$$

or

$$\boxed{y = c\,e^{-\int P(x)\,dx}.} \tag{2}$$

EXAMPLE   From (2) we see that the general solution of $\dfrac{dy}{dx} - 3y = 0$ is

$$y = c\,e^{-\int(-3)\,dx}$$
$$= c\,e^{3x}.$$

EXAMPLE   The general solution of $\sin x\,\dfrac{dy}{dx} + (\cos x)y = 0$ or

$$\frac{dy}{dx} + (\cot x)y = 0$$

is
$$y = c\,e^{-\int \cot x \, dx}$$
$$= c\,e^{-\ln|\sin x|}$$
$$= \frac{c}{|\sin x|}$$

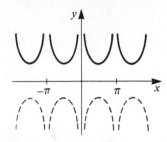

Figure 2.4

on any interval for which $\sin x \neq 0$. An analysis of the graphs in Figure 2.4 should convince the reader that we could just as well write the solution of the equation as $y = c_1/\sin x = c_1 \csc x$. For example, the solution of the initial-value problem

$$\frac{dy}{dx} + (\cot x)y = 0$$

$$y\left(-\frac{\pi}{2}\right) = 1$$

is $y = 1/|\sin x|$ or $y = -1/\sin x = -\csc x$ on $-\pi < x < 0$.

The particular case when $f(x) = 0$ is subsumed in the following discussion.

An integrating factor   Suppose equation (1) is written in the differential form

$$dy + [P(x)y - f(x)]\,dx = 0. \tag{3}$$

Can we find a function $\mu(x)$ such that the multiple of (3)

$$\mu(x)\,dy + \mu(x)\,[P(x)y - f(x)]\,dx = 0 \tag{4}$$

is an exact differential equation? The answer is yes, and not too surprisingly $\mu(x)$ has the same basic form as the exponential function in (2). By Theorem 2.1

we know that the left side of equation (4) will be an exact differential if

$$\frac{\partial}{\partial x}\mu(x) = \frac{\partial}{\partial y}\mu(x)[P(x)y - f(x)] \tag{5}$$

or
$$\frac{d\mu}{dx} = \mu P(x). \tag{6}$$

This is a separable equation from which we can determine μ. We have

$$\frac{d\mu}{\mu} = P(x)\,dx$$

$$\ln|\mu| = \int P(x)\,dx \tag{7}$$

so that
$$\boxed{\mu = e^{\int P(x)\,dx}} \;. \tag{8}$$

The function $\mu(x)$ defined in (8) is called an **integrating factor** for the linear equation. Note that we need not use a constant of integration in (7) since (4) is unaffected by a constant multiple.

It is interesting to observe that equation (4) is still an exact differential equation even when $f(x) = 0$. In fact, $f(x)$ plays no part in determining $\mu(x)$ since we see from (5) that $\frac{\partial}{\partial y}\mu(x)f(x) = 0$. Thus both

$$e^{\int P(x)\,dx}\,dy + e^{\int P(x)\,dx}[P(x)y - f(x)]\,dx$$

and
$$e^{\int P(x)\,dx}\,dy + e^{\int P(x)\,dx}P(x)y\,dx$$

are exact differentials. We now write (4) in the form

$$e^{\int P(x)\,dx}\,dy + e^{\int P(x)\,dx}P(x)y\,dx = e^{\int P(x)\,dx}f(x)\,dx$$

and recognize that we can write the equation as

$$d[e^{\int P(x)\,dx}y] = e^{\int P(x)\,dx}f(x)\,dx.$$

Integrating the last equation gives

$$e^{\int P(x)\,dx}y = \int e^{\int P(x)\,dx}f(x)\,dx + c$$

or
$$\boxed{y = e^{-\int P(x)\,dx}\int e^{\int P(x)\,dx}f(x)\,dx + ce^{-\int P(x)\,dx}.} \tag{9}$$

Equation (9) represents the general solution of equation (1). Again no attempt should be made to memorize (9). The procedure should be followed each time, so for convenience we summarize the results.

The method of solution

To solve a linear first-order differential equation first put it into the form

$$\frac{dy}{dx} + P(x)y = f(x).$$

Then multiply the entire equation by the integrating factor:

$$e^{\int P(x)\,dx}.$$

Now the left side of

$$e^{\int P(x)\,dx}\frac{dy}{dx} + P(x)\,e^{\int P(x)\,dx}y = e^{\int P(x)\,dx}f(x)$$

is the derivative of the product of the integrating factor and the dependent variable, $e^{\int P(x)\,dx}y$. Write the equation in the form

which is

$$\frac{d}{dx}\left[e^{\int P(x)\,dx}y\right] = e^{\int P(x)\,dx}f(x)$$

and finally, integrate both sides.

Note: This procedure can also be used in the case $f(x) = 0$.

EXAMPLE

Solve

$$x\frac{dy}{dx} - 4y = x^6 e^x.$$

Solution: Write the equation as

$$\frac{dy}{dx} - \frac{4}{x}y = x^5 e^x. \tag{10}$$

and determine the integrating factor

$$e^{-4\int dx/x} = e^{-4\ln|x|} = e^{\ln x^{-4}} = x^{-4}.$$

Here we have used the basic identity $b^{\log_b N} = N$. Now multiply by this term

$$x^{-4}\frac{dy}{dx} - 4x^{-5}y = x e^x \tag{11}$$

and obtain
$$\frac{d}{dx}[x^{-4}y] = x\,e^x.*$$
(12)

It follows from integration by parts that

$$x^{-4}y = x\,e^x - e^x + c$$

or
$$y = x^5\,e^x - x^4\,e^x + cx^4.$$

EXAMPLE   Solve

$$\frac{dy}{dx} + 2xy = x$$ *linear*

subject to $y(0) = -3$.

Solution: The integrating factor is

$$e^{2\int x\,dx} = e^{x^2}$$

so that
$$e^{x^2}\frac{dy}{dx} + 2x\,e^{x^2}y = x\,e^{x^2}$$

$$\frac{d}{dx}[e^{x^2}y] = xe^{x^2}$$

$$e^{x^2}y = \int x\,e^{x^2}\,dx$$

$$= \frac{1}{2}\int e^{x^2}(2x\,dx)$$

$$= \frac{1}{2}e^{x^2} + c$$

and thus
$$y = \frac{1}{2} + c\,e^{-x^2}.$$

The initial condition $y(0) = -3$ gives $c = -7/2$ and hence the solution is

$$y = \frac{1}{2} - \frac{7}{2}e^{-x^2}.$$

See Figure 2.5.

---

* The student should perform the indicated differentiations a few times in order to be convinced that all equations, such as (10), (11) and (12), are formally equivalent.

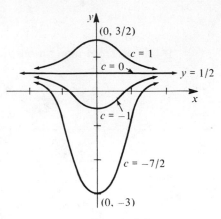

Figure 2.5

EXAMPLE   Solve

$$(x^2 + 9)\frac{dy}{dx} + xy = 0$$

Solution: We write

$$\frac{dy}{dx} + \frac{x}{x^2 + 9}y = 0.$$

Now admittedly $f(x) = 0$ in this case so we could formally solve the problem by applying formula (2). However the discussion of this particular case should perhaps be reread at this time with the hope that everyone can see the connection between formula (2) and the concept of the integrating factor. We have

$$e^{\int x\,dx/(x^2+9)} = e^{\frac{1}{2}\int 2x\,dx/(x^2+9)} = e^{\frac{1}{2}\ln(x^2+9)} = \sqrt{x^2 + 9}$$

so that

$$\sqrt{x^2 + 9}\frac{dy}{dx} + \frac{x}{\sqrt{x^2 + 9}}$$

$$\frac{d}{dx}[\sqrt{x^2 + 9}\,y] = 0$$

$$\sqrt{x^2 + 9}\,y = c$$

$$y = \frac{c}{\sqrt{x^2 + 9}}.$$

EXAMPLE   Solve

$$\frac{dy}{dx} = \frac{1}{x + y^2}$$

subject to $x = -2$, $y = 0$.

Solution: The equation

$$\frac{dy}{dx} = \frac{1}{x + y^2}$$

is neither separable, homogeneous, exact, nor linear in the variable y. However if we take the reciprocal we obtain

$$\frac{dx}{dy} = x + y^2 \qquad \text{or} \qquad \frac{dx}{dy} - x = y^2.$$

This latter equation is *linear in x* so the corresponding integrating factor is $e^{-\int dy} = e^{-y}$. Therefore it follows

$$\frac{d}{dy}[e^{-y}x] = y^2 e^{-y}$$

$$e^{-y}x = \int y^2 e^{-y}\, dy$$

$$= -y^2 e^{-y} - 2y e^{-y} - 2e^{-y} + c$$

$$x = -y^2 - 2y - 2 + c\, e^{y}$$

When $x = -2$, $y = 0$ we find $c = 0$, and so $x = -y^2 - 2y - 2$. The graph of this solution curve is given in Figure 2.6.

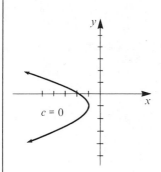

Figure 2.6

$c = 0$

EXERCISES 2.4   Answers to odd-numbered problems begin on page A-5 of the Appendix. In Problems 1–25 find the general solution of the given equation.

1. $2\dfrac{dy}{dx} + 10y = 1$ \qquad **★2.** $\dfrac{dy}{dx} = y + e^x$

3. $y' + 3x^2 y = x^2$ \qquad **4.** $y' + 2xy = x^3$

5. $x^2 y' + xy = 1$ \qquad **6.** $\dfrac{dx}{dy} = x + y$

7. $(x + 4y^2)\, dy + 2y\, dx = 0$

★8. $(1 + x^2)\, dy + (xy + x^3 + x)\, dx = 0$

9. $x\, dy = (x \sin x - y)\, dx$ \qquad **10.** $(1 + e^x)\dfrac{dy}{dx} + e^x y = 0$

11. $\cos x \dfrac{dy}{dx} + y \sin x = 1$ **12.** $\dfrac{dy}{dx} = 2y + x^2 + 5$

13. $x \dfrac{dy}{dx} + 4y = x^3 - x$ **★14.** $(1 + x)y' - xy = x + x^2$

15. $(x + 2)^2 \dfrac{dy}{dx} = 5 - 8y - 4xy$ **16.** $xy' + (1 + x)y = e^{-x} \sin 2x$

17. $\cos^2 x \sin x \, dy + (y \cos^3 x - 1) \, dx = 0$

18. $y \, dx + (xy + 2x - y e^y) \, dy = 0$ **19.** $\dfrac{dy}{dx} = x(x^2 - 2y)$

20. $(x^2 + x) \, dy = (x^5 + 3xy + 3y) \, dx$

21. $\dfrac{dy}{dt} + 2ty = y + 4t - 2$

22. $(1 - \cos x) \, dy + (2y \sin x - \tan x) \, dx = 0$

23. $y \, dx - 4(x + y^6) \, dy = 0$ **★24.** $xy' + 2y = e^x + \ln x$

25. $\dfrac{dy}{dx} + y = \dfrac{1 - e^{-2x}}{e^x + e^{-x}}$

In Problems 26–32 solve each differential equation subject to the given initial condition.

★26. $y' = 2y + x(e^{3x} - e^{2x}); \quad y(0) = 2$

27. $L \dfrac{di}{dt} + Ri = E; \quad L, R, \text{ and } E \text{ constants}; \quad i(0) = i_0$

28. $y \dfrac{dx}{dy} - x = 2y^2; \quad y(1) = 5$

29. $y' + (\tan x)y = \cos^2 x; \quad y(0) = -1$

30. $\dfrac{dy}{dx} = 5x^4 y; \quad y(0) = -7$

31. $(x + 1) \dfrac{dy}{dx} + y = \ln x; \quad y(1) = 10$

32. $xy' + y = e^x; \quad y(1) = 2$

In Problems 33–38 use an appropriate substitution to reduce each equation to linear form and solve.

EXAMPLE   Solve

$$2xy \dfrac{dy}{dx} + 2y^2 = 3x - 6.$$

Solution: The equation as given is not linear in either x or y. However, the presence of the term $2y\dfrac{dy}{dx}$ prompts us to try $w = y^2$ since

$$\frac{dw}{dx} = 2y\frac{dy}{dx}.$$

Now

$$x\frac{dw}{dx} + 2w = 3x - 6$$

has the linear form

$$\frac{dw}{dx} + \frac{2}{x}w = 3 - \frac{6}{x}$$

so that multiplication by the integrating factor $e^{\int(2/x)\,dx} = e^{\ln x^2} = x^2$ then gives

$$\frac{d}{dx}[x^2 w] = 3x^2 - 6x$$

$$x^2 w = x^3 - 3x^2 + c$$

or

$$x^2 y^2 = x^3 - 3x^2 + c.$$

---

33. $x^4 y^2 y' + x^3 y^3 = 2x^3 - 3$ **34.** $x e^y y' - 2e^y = x^2$

35. $y' + 1 = e^{-(x+y)} \sin x$

36. $\sin y \sinh x \, dx + \cos y \cosh x \, dy = 0$

37. $y\dfrac{dx}{dy} + 2x \ln x = xe^y$ **★38.** $x \sin y \dfrac{dy}{dx} + \cos y = -x^2 e^x$

When $f(x)$ in equation (1) is not continuous Theorem 1.1 does not necessarily guarantee the existence of a unique solution of an initial-value problem. In Problems 39–42 find a continuous solution satisfying each equation and the given initial condition.

EXAMPLE   Solve

$$\frac{dy}{dx} + y = f(x) \qquad \text{where } f(x) = \begin{cases} 1, & 0 \le x \le 1 \\ 0, & x > 1 \end{cases}$$

subject to $y(0) = 0$.

Solution: We solve the equation in two parts. For $0 \le x \le 1$ we have

$$\frac{dy}{dx} + y = 1$$

$$\frac{d}{dx}[e^x y] = e^x$$

$$y = 1 + c_1 e^{-x}.$$

Since $y(0) = 0$, we must have $c_1 = -1$, and therefore

$$y = 1 - e^{-x}, \qquad 0 \le x \le 1.$$

For $x > 1$ we then have

$$\frac{dy}{dx} + y = 0$$

which leads to

$$y = c_2 e^{-x}.$$

Hence we can write

$$y = \begin{cases} 1 - e^{-x}, & 0 \le x \le 1 \\ c_2 e^{-x}, & x > 1. \end{cases}$$

Now in order that y be a continuous function we certainly want $\lim_{x \to 1^+} y(x) = y(1)$. This latter requirement is equivalent to $c_2 e^{-1} = 1 - e^{-1}$ or $c_2 = e - 1$. As Figure 2.7 shows, the function

$$y = \begin{cases} 1 - e^{-x}, & 0 \le x \le 1 \\ (e - 1)e^{-x}, & x > 1 \end{cases}$$

is continuous but not differentiable at $x = 1$.

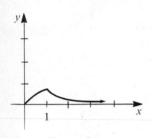

Figure 2.7

---

39. $\dfrac{dy}{dx} + 2y = f(x), \qquad f(x) = \begin{cases} 1, & 0 \le x \le 3 \\ 0, & x > 3, \end{cases}$

$y(0) = 0$

40. $\dfrac{dy}{dx} + y = f(x), \qquad f(x) = \begin{cases} 1, & 0 \le x \le 1 \\ -1, & x > 1 \end{cases}$

$y(0) = 1$

41. $\dfrac{dy}{dx} + 2xy = f(x), \qquad f(x) = \begin{cases} x, & 0 \le x < 1 \\ 0, & x \ge 1 \end{cases}$

$y(0) = 2$

42. $(1 + x^2)\dfrac{dy}{dx} + 2xy = f(x), \qquad f(x) = \begin{cases} x, & 0 \le x < 1 \\ -x, & x \ge 1 \end{cases}$

$y(0) = 0$

2.5   Miscellaneous Equations

In this section we are not going to study any one particular type of differential equation. Rather, we are going to consider a collection of classical equations which, in some instances, can be transformed into equations we have already studied.

The student should not get the impression that we have exhausted all the theory of first-order differential equations. The preceding types of equations: separable, homogeneous, exact, and linear, are, of course, important in many physical and geometric applications. However, the fact that these four basic types of equations are studied in such detail in texts on differential equations is perhaps attributable to the fact that these equations are among the few types of first-order equations that can be readily solved. In fact, one should not expect that for any given differential equation there must necessarily exist a corresponding method of solution. In many cases the best we can do is to obtain an approximate solution. (See Chapter 9.)

EXERCISES 2.5

Answers to odd-numbered problems begin on page A-6 of the Appendix.

1. The equation

$$\frac{dy}{dx} + P(x)y = f(x)y^n,$$

where n is any real number, is called **Bernoulli's equation** after the Swiss mathematician, Jakob Bernoulli (1654–1705). For $n \neq 0$ and $n \neq 1$ show that the substitution $w = y^{1-n}$ leads to the linear equation

$$\frac{dw}{dx} + (1-n)P(x)w = (1-n)f(x).$$

In Problems 2–6 solve the given Bernoulli equation.

EXAMPLE

Solve

$$\frac{dy}{dx} + \frac{1}{x}y = xy^2.$$

Solution: With $n = 2$, the substitution $w = y^{-1}$ gives

$$\frac{dw}{dx} - \frac{1}{x}w = -x. \tag{1}$$

The integrating factor for this linear equation is

$$e^{-\int dx/x} = e^{-\ln x} = e^{\ln x^{-1}} = x^{-1}.$$

so that after multiplication by this factor equation (1) becomes

$$\frac{d}{dx}[x^{-1}w] = -1.$$

Integrating this latter form gives

$$x^{-1}w = -x + c \qquad \text{or} \qquad w = -x^2 + cx.$$

Since $w = y^{-1}$ we obtain

$$y = \frac{1}{w}$$

$$= \frac{1}{-x^2 + cx}$$

2. $\dfrac{dy}{dx} - y = e^x y^2.$ **3.** $x\dfrac{dy}{dx} + y = \dfrac{1}{y^2}.$

★**4.** $y^{1/2}\dfrac{dy}{dx} + y^{3/2} = 1, \quad y(0) = 4.$

5. $x^2\dfrac{dy}{dx} - 2xy = 3y^4, \quad y(1) = \dfrac{1}{2}.$

6. $x\dfrac{dy}{dx} - (1 + x)y = xy^2.$

7. The **Ricatti equation** is a nonlinear equation

$$\frac{dy}{dx} = P(x) + Q(x)y + R(x)y^2$$

named after an Italian mathematician–philosopher Count Jacobo Francesco Ricatti (1676–1754). In many cases, depending on $P(x)$, $Q(x)$ and $R(x)$, the solution of this equation cannot be expressed in terms of elementary functions. Show, that if y_1 is a known particular solution of the Ricatti equation, then the general solution can be written as $y = y_1 + u$ where u is the general solution of the Bernoulli equation

$$\frac{du}{dx} - (Q + 2y_1 R)u = Ru^2.$$

In turn show that this latter equation can be reduced to the linear equation

$$\frac{dw}{dx} + (Q + 2y_1 R)w = -R$$

by the substitution $w = 1/u$ (see Problem 1). Note that when $P(x) = 0$ the original equation becomes a Bernoulli equation.

In Problems 8–12 solve the given Ricatti equation.

EXAMPLE   Solve

$$\frac{dy}{dx} = 2 - 2xy + y^2.$$

Solution: It is easily verified that a particular solution to this equation is $y_1 = 2x$.* From Problem 7 we first make the identification $P(x) = 2$, $Q(x) = -2x$ and $R(x) = 1$ and then solve

$$\frac{dw}{dx} + (-2x + 4x)w = -1$$

or
$$\frac{dw}{dx} + 2xw = -1 \tag{2}$$

Multiplication of (2) by the integrating factor gives

$$\frac{d}{dx}[e^{x^2}w] = -e^{x^2}.$$

Before integrating both sides of this latter equation, we recall from elementary calculus that indefinite integral $\int e^{x^2}\,dx$ cannot be expressed in terms of elementary functions. Thus, we write

$$e^{x^2}w = -\int e^{x^2}\,dx + c$$

or
$$e^{x^2}\left(\frac{1}{u}\right) = -\int e^{x^2}\,dx + c$$

so that
$$u = \frac{e^{x^2}}{c - \int e^{x^2}\,dx}.$$

The general solution is then $y = 2x + u$.

$\bigstar$**8.** $\dfrac{dy}{dx} = 2x^2 + \dfrac{1}{x}y - 2y^2; \quad y_1 = x.$ **9.** $\dfrac{dy}{dx} = -2 - y + y^2; \quad y_1 = 2.$

10. $\dfrac{dy}{dx} = 1 - x - y + xy^2; \quad y_1 = 1.$ **11.** $\dfrac{dy}{dx} = -\dfrac{4}{x^2} - \dfrac{1}{x}y + y^2; \quad y_1 = \dfrac{2}{x}.$

12. $\dfrac{dy}{dx} = \sec^2 x - (\tan x)y + y^2; \quad y_1 = \tan x.$

13. Solve $\dfrac{dy}{dx} = 6 + 5y + y^2.$ **14.** Solve $\dfrac{dy}{dx} = 9 + 6y + y^2.$

* One possible way of solving differential equations is by "inspection." Translated this means we take a good guess and see if it works.

15. When $R(x) = -1$, the Ricatti equation can be written as $y' + y^2 - Q(x)y - P(x) = 0$. Show that the substitution $y = w'/w$ leads to the linear second-order equation $w'' - Q(x)w' - P(x)w = 0$. (When Q and P are also constants there is little difficulty in solving equations of this type.)

16. **Clairaut's equation** is any differential equation of the form

$$y = xy' + f(y').$$

Show that the general solution of this equation is the family of straight lines $y = cx + f(c)$ where c is an arbitrary constant. Also show that the equation may possess a solution in parametric form:

$$x = -f'(t),$$

$$y = f(t) - tf'(t).$$

This latter solution is called a *singular solution* since, if $f''(t) \neq 0$, it cannot be obtained from the general solution. [*Hint:* Differentiate both sides of the Clairaut equation with respect to x and consider two cases. Use parametric differentiation to show

$$dy/dx = (dy/dt)/(dx/dt) = t, \qquad f''(t) \neq 0.$$

Since the slope of the original solution is constant, it follows that the latter solution cannot be obtained from it.]

In Problems 17–21 solve the given Clairaut equation. Obtain the singular solution.

EXAMPLE

Solve

$$y = xy' + \tfrac{1}{2}(y')^2.$$

Solution: We first make the identification $f(y') = (1/2)(y')^2$ so that $f(t) = (1/2)t^2$. It then follows immediately from the preceding problem that the general solution is

$$y = cx + \tfrac{1}{2}c^2.$$

The graph of this particular family is given in Figure 2.8. Since $f'(t) = t$, the singular solution is

$$x = -t$$

$$y = \tfrac{1}{2}t^2 - t \cdot t$$

$$= -\tfrac{1}{2}t^2.$$

After eliminating the parameter we find this latter solution is the same as

$$y = -\tfrac{1}{2}x^2.$$

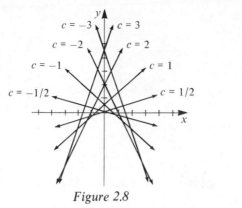

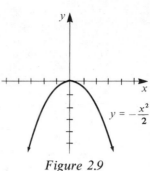

Figure 2.8   *Figure 2.9*

One can readily see that this is not part of the general solution. See Figure 2.9.

17. $y = xy' + 1 - \ln y'$.   ★18. $y = xy' + (y')^{-2}$.

19. $y = x\dfrac{dy}{dx} - \left(\dfrac{dy}{dx}\right)^3$ 20. $y = (x + 4)y' + (y')^2$

21. $xy' - y = e^{y'}$

[O] 2.6 Substitutions

In the preceding sections we often used a substitution to put a particular differential equation into a form that can be solved by one of the standard methods. An equation may look different from any of those that we have just studied, but through a judicious change of variables perhaps an apparently difficult problem may be readily solved. Although we can give no firm rules on what, *if any*, substitution to use, a working axiom might be: Try something! It sometimes pays to be clever.

EXAMPLE   The differential equation

$$y(1 + 2xy)\,dx + x(1 - 2xy)\,dy = 0$$

is neither separable, homogeneous, exact, linear, nor Bernoulli. However, if we stare at the equation long enough we might be prompted to try the substitution

$$u = 2xy \quad \text{or} \quad y = \frac{u}{2x}.$$

Since
$$dy = \frac{x\,du - u\,dx}{2x^2}$$

the equation becomes

$$\frac{u}{2x}(1+u)\,dx + x(1-u)\left(\frac{x\,du - u\,dx}{2x^2}\right) = 0$$

or after simplifying

$$2u^2\,dx + (1-u)x\,du = 0.$$

We recognize the last equation as separable, and so from

$$2\frac{dx}{x} + \frac{1-u}{u^2}\,du = 0$$

we obtain
$$2\ln|x| - u^{-1} - \ln|u| = c$$

$$\ln\left|\frac{x}{2y}\right| = c + \frac{1}{2xy}$$

$$\frac{x}{2y} = c_1 e^{1/2xy} \qquad (c_1 = e^c)$$

$$x = 2c_1 y e^{1/2xy}.$$

Notice again that the general solution in the preceding example does not include the trivial solution, $y \equiv 0$.

EXAMPLE   The differential equation

$$\frac{dy}{dx} + \tan x \tan y \ln(\sin y) = 0 \tag{1}$$

looks somewhat formidable on first inspection. But if we try the substitution

$$u = \ln(\sin y)$$

then
$$\frac{du}{dx} = \frac{1}{\sin y}\cdot\cos y\,\frac{dy}{dx} \qquad \text{or} \qquad \frac{dy}{dx} = \tan y\,\frac{du}{dx}.$$

Thus, equation (1) becomes

$$\frac{du}{dx} + (\tan x)u = 0 \tag{2}$$

which is linear in the variable u. By proceeding formally, we find that the integrating factor is

$$e^{\int \tan x\,dx} = e^{-\ln(\cos x)} = \sec x.$$

Multiplying equation (2) by this factor yields

$$\frac{d}{dx}[(\sec x)u] = 0$$

so that

$$(\sec x)u = c$$

$$u = c \cos x$$

$$\ln(\sin y) = c \cos x.$$

Observe that equation (1) is also separable. The reader is urged to try this method.

EXAMPLE   Solve

$$x\frac{dy}{dx} - y = \frac{x^3}{y}e^{y/x}. \tag{3}$$

Solution: Let

$$u = \frac{y}{x}$$

so that

$$\frac{du}{dx} = \frac{x\dfrac{dy}{dx} - y}{x^2} \quad\text{or}\quad x\frac{dy}{dx} - y = x^2\frac{du}{dx}.$$

Hence equation (3) becomes

$$\frac{du}{dx} = \frac{e^u}{u} \quad\text{or}\quad ue^{-u}\,du = dx.$$

Integration by parts then gives

$$-ue^{-u} - e^{-u} = x + c$$

$$u + 1 = (c_1 - x)e^u \qquad (c_1 = -c)$$

$$\frac{y}{x} + 1 = (c_1 - x)e^{y/x}$$

$$y + x = x(c_1 - x)e^{y/x}.$$

EXERCISES 2.6   Answers to odd-numbered problems begin on page A-6 of the Appendix. In Problems 1–10 solve the given differential equation by using an appropriate substitution.

1. $xe^{2y}\dfrac{dy}{dx} + e^{2y} = \dfrac{\ln x}{x}$ ★2. $y' + y\ln y = ye^x$

3. $y\,dx + (1 + ye^x)\,dy = 0$

4. $(2 + e^{-x/y}) dx + 2 \left(1 - \dfrac{x}{y}\right) dy = 0$

5. $\dfrac{dy}{dx} - \dfrac{4}{x}y = 2x^5 e^{y/x^4}$ **★6.** $\dfrac{dy}{dx} + x + y + 1 = (x + y)^2 e^{3x}$

7. $2yy' + x^2 + y^2 + x = 0$ **8.** $y' = y + x(y + 1)^2 + 1$

9. $2x \csc 2y \dfrac{dy}{dx} = 2x - \ln(\tan y)$

10. $x^2 \dfrac{dy}{dx} + 2xy = x^4 y^2 + 1$

Some higher order differential equations can be reduced to first-order equations by a substitution. In Problems 11–16 solve the given equation.

EXAMPLE   Solve

$$y'' = 2x(y')^2.$$

Solution: If we let $w = y'$ so that $dw/dx = y''$ the equation then reduces to a separable form. We have

$$\frac{dw}{dx} = 2xw^2$$

$$\frac{dw}{w^2} = 2x\, dx$$

$$\int w^{-2}\, dw = \int 2x\, dx$$

$$-w^{-1} = x^2 + c_1^2$$

The constant of integration is written as c_1^2 for convenience. The reason is obvious in the next few steps.

$$-\left(\frac{dy}{dx}\right)^{-1} = x^2 + c_1^2$$

$$\frac{dy}{dx} = -\frac{1}{x^2 + c_1^2}$$

$$dy = -\frac{dx}{x^2 + c_1^2}$$

$$\int dy = -\int \frac{dx}{x^2 + c_1^2}$$

$$y + c_2 = -\frac{1}{c_1} \tan^{-1} \frac{x}{c_1}.$$

Alternatively, the solution can be written in the implicit form $-c_1 \tan(c_2 + c_1 y) = x$ where the product, $c_1 c_2$, has been replaced by c_2.

It should be observed further that had we written $-w^{-1} = x^2 - c_1^2$, then the second integral above could have been written in terms of the inverse hyperbolic tangent or a logarithm.

11. $y'' + (y')^2 + 1 = 0$ **12.** $xy'' = y' + x(y')^2$

13. $xy'' = y' + (y')^3$

★**14.** $y'' + 2y(y')^3 = 0$

$$\left[Hint: \quad \text{Let } w = y' \text{ so that } y'' = \frac{dw}{dx} = \frac{dw}{dy}\frac{dy}{dx} = \frac{dw}{dy}w \right]$$

15. $y' - xy'' - (y')^3 = 1$ ★**16.** $y'' = 1 + (y')^2$

CHAPTER SUMMARY

The method of solution for a first-order differential equation

$$\frac{dy}{dx} = f(x, y) \tag{1}$$

depends on an appropriate classification of the equation. We summarize five cases.

An equation is **separable** if it can be put into the form

$$h(y)\,dy = g(x)\,dx \tag{2}$$

The general solution results from integrating both sides of (2).

If $M(x, y)$ and $N(x, y)$ are **homogeneous functions** of the same degree, then

$$M(x, y)\,dx + N(x, y)\,dy = 0 \tag{3}$$

can be reduced to an equation with separable variables by either the substitution $y = ux$ or $x = vy$. The choice of substitution usually depends on which coefficient is simpler.

The differential equation $M(x, y)\,dx + N(x, y)\,dy = 0$ is said to be **exact** if the form $M\,dx + N\,dy$ is an exact differential. When M and N are continuous and have continuous first partial derivatives, then

$$\frac{\partial M}{\partial y} = \frac{\partial N}{\partial x} \tag{4}$$

is a necessary and sufficient condition that $M\,dx + N\,dy$ be exact. This means there exists some function f for which $M = \partial f/\partial x$ and $N = \partial f/\partial y$. The method of solution for an exact equation starts by integrating either of these latter expressions.

CHAPTER SUMMARY

If a first-order equation can be put into the form

$$\frac{dy}{dx} + P(x)y = f(x) \tag{5}$$

it is said to be **linear** in the variable y. We solve (5) by first finding the **integrating factor**, $e^{\int P(x)\,dx}$, multiplying both sides of the equation by this factor, and then integrating both sides of

$$\frac{d}{dx}\left[e^{\int P(x)\,dx}y\right] = e^{\int P(x)\,dx}f(x). \tag{6}$$

The **Bernoulli equation** is

$$\frac{dy}{dx} + P(x)y = f(x)y^n, \tag{7}$$

where n is any real number. When $n \neq 0$ and $n \neq 1$, Bernoulli's equation can be reduced to a linear equation by the substitution $w = y^{1-n}$.

In certain circumstances a differential equation can be reduced to one of the familiar forms by an appropriate **substitution** or **change of variables**. Of course we already know that this is the procedure when solving a homogeneous or a Bernoulli equation. In the general context, no rule on when to use a substitution can be given.

REVIEW EXERCISES

Answers to odd-numbered problems begin on page A-7 of the Appendix.

1. One can usually deduce that all the problems in the exercise following, say, the discussion on linear equations must involve linear equations. The problem in solving first-order differential equations out of this specific context is then basically one of *recognition*. Knowing the type of equation, we apply the appropriate method. Without solving, classify each of the following equations as to: separable, exact, homogeneous, linear, Bernoulli, Clairaut, or Ricatti.

   (a) $\dfrac{dy}{dx} = \dfrac{1}{y - x}$

   (b) $\dfrac{dy}{dx} = \dfrac{x - y}{x}$

   (c) $\left(\dfrac{dy}{dx}\right)^2 + 2y = 2x\dfrac{dy}{dx}$

   (d) $\dfrac{dy}{dx} = \dfrac{1}{x(x - y)}$

   (e) $\dfrac{dy}{dx} = \dfrac{y^2 + y}{x^2 + x}$

   (f) $\dfrac{dy}{dx} = 4 + 5y + y^2$

   (g) $y\,dx = (y - xy^2)\,dy$

   (h) $x\dfrac{dy}{dx} = ye^{x/y} - x$

   (i) $xyy' + y^2 = 2x$

   (j) $2xyy' + y^2 = 2x^2$

   (k) $\left(x^2 + \dfrac{2y}{x}\right)dx = (3 - \ln x^2)\,dy$

    (l) $y = xy' + (y' - 3)^2$ **(m)** $y' + 5y^2 = 3x^4 - 2xy$

    (n) $\dfrac{y}{x^2}\dfrac{dy}{dx} + e^{2x^3 + y^2} = 0$

[2.1]   **2.**   Solve $(y^2 + 1)\,dx = y \sec^2 x\,dy$

           3.   Solve $\dfrac{y}{x}\dfrac{dy}{dx} = \dfrac{e^x}{\ln y}$ subject to $y(1) = 1.$

[2.2]   ★**4.**   Solve $y(\ln x - \ln y)\,dx = (x \ln x - x \ln y - y)\,dy$

           5.   Solve $xyy' = 3y^2 + x^2$ subject to $y(-1) = 2.$

[2.3]   **6.**   Solve $(6x + 1)y^2\dfrac{dy}{dx} + 3x^2 + 2y^3 = 0$

           7.   Solve $ye^{xy}\dfrac{dx}{dy} + xe^{xy} = 12y^2$ subject to $y(0) = -1.$

[2.4]   ★**8.**   Solve $x\,dy + (xy + y - x^2 - 2x)\,dx = 0$

           9.   Solve $(x^2 + 4)\dfrac{dy}{dx} = 2x - 8xy$ subject to $y(0) = -1.$

         10.   Solve $(2x + y)y' = 1$

[2.5]   **11.**   Solve $x\dfrac{dy}{dx} + 4y = x^4y^2$ subject to $y(1) = 1.$

[2.6]   **12.**   Solve $-xy' + y = (y' + 1)^2$ subject to $y(0) = 0.$

Solve the following by means of a substitution.

         13. $\dfrac{dy}{dx} + xy^3 \sec\dfrac{1}{y^2} = 0$ **14.** $y'' = x - y'$

CHAPTER 3

Applications of First-Order Differential Equations

3.1 Orthogonal Trajectories

Recall from your study of analytic geometry that two lines L_1 and L_2, which are not parallel to the coordinate axes, are perpendicular if and only if their respective slopes satisfy the relationship $m_1 = -1/m_2$. For example, the graph of $y = (-1/2)x + 1$ and $y = 2x + 4$ are obviously perpendicular. Indeed, the line $y = (-1/2)x + 1$ is perpendicular to every line in the family of curves $y = 2x + c_1$. See Figure 3.1(b). In fact, as Figure 3.2 shows, each curve in the family $y = (-1/2)x + c_2$ is perpendicular to every curve in the family $y = 2x + c_1$.

Orthogonal curves   In general, two curves $\mathscr{C}_1$ and $\mathscr{C}_2$ are said to be **orthogonal** at a point if and only if their tangents T_1 and T_2 are perpendicular at the point of intersection. See Figure 3.3. Except for the case when T_1 and T_2 are parallel to the coordinate axes, this means the slopes of the tangents are negative reciprocals of one another.

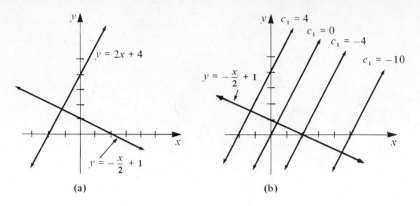

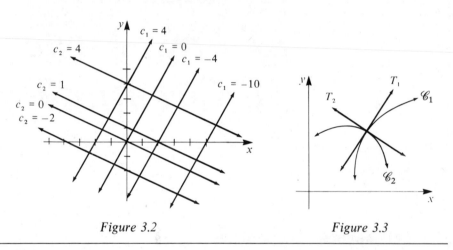

Figure 3.2

Figure 3.3

EXAMPLE   Show that the curves $y = x^3$ and $x^2 + 3y^2 = 4$ are orthogonal at the point(s) of intersection.

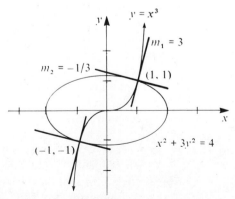

Figure 3.4

Solution: It is easily verified that the points of intersection are $(1, 1)$ and $(-1, -1)$. Now the slope of the tangent line to $y = x^3$ at any point is $dy/dx = 3x^2$. So that

$$\frac{dy}{dx}\bigg|_{x=1} = \frac{dy}{dx}\bigg|_{x=-1} = 3.$$

We use implicit differentiation to obtain dy/dx for the second curve:

$$2x + 6y\frac{dy}{dx} = 0$$

$$\frac{dy}{dx} = -\frac{x}{3y}$$

and therefore $\dfrac{dy}{dx}\bigg|_{(1.1)} = \dfrac{dy}{dx}\bigg|_{(-1.-1)} = -\dfrac{1}{3}.$

Thus, at either $(1, 1)$ or $(-1, -1)$ we have

$$\left(\frac{dy}{dx}\right)_{\mathscr{C}_1} = -\frac{1}{\left(\dfrac{dy}{dx}\right)_{\mathscr{C}_2}}.$$

It is easy to show that any curve $\mathscr{C}_1$ in the family $y = c_1 x^3$ is orthogonal to each curve $\mathscr{C}_2$ in the family $x^2 + 3y^2 = c_2^2$. The differential equation of the first family is:

$$\frac{dy}{dx} = 3c_1 x^2$$

$$= 3\left(\frac{y}{x^3}\right)x^2$$

$$= \frac{3y}{x}$$

since $c_1 = y/x^3$. Now implicit differentiation of $x^2 + 3y^2 = c_2^2$ leads to exactly the same differential equation as for $x^2 + 3y^2 = 4$; namely,

$$\frac{dy}{dx} = -\frac{x}{3y}.$$

Hence, at the point (x, y) on each curve

$$\left(\frac{dy}{dx}\right)_{\mathscr{C}_1} \cdot \left(\frac{dy}{dx}\right)_{\mathscr{C}_2} = \left(\frac{3y}{x}\right)\left(-\frac{x}{3y}\right) = -1.$$

Since the slopes of the tangent lines are negative reciprocals, the curves $\mathscr{C}_1$ and $\mathscr{C}_2$ intersect each other in an orthogonal manner.

This discussion leads to the following definition.

> **DEFINITION 3.1**   When *all* the curves of one family of curves $G(x, y, c_1) = 0$ intersect orthogonally *all* the curves of another family $H(x, y, c_2) = 0$, then the families are said to be **orthogonal trajectories** of each other.

In other words, an orthogonal trajectory is any *one* curve which intersects every curve of another family at right angles.

EXAMPLES

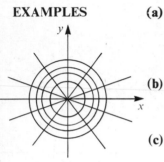

Figure 3.5

(a)   The graph of $y = (-1/2)x + 1$ is an orthogonal trajectory of $y = 2x + c_1$. The families $y = (-1/2)x + c_2$ and $y = 2x + c_1$ are orthogonal trajectories.

(b)   The graph of $y = 4x^3$ is an orthogonal trajectory of $x^2 + 3y^2 = c_2^2$. The families $y = c_1 x^3$ and $x^2 + 3y^2 = c_2^2$ are orthogonal trajectories.

(c)   It is easily seen from Figure 3.5 that the family of straight lines $y = c_1 x$ through the origin and the family $x^2 + y^2 = c_2^2$ of concentric circles with center at the origin are orthogonal trajectories.

Orthogonal trajectories occur naturally in the study of electricity and magnetism. For example, in an electric field the lines of force are perpendicular to the equipotential curves (that is, curves along which the potential is constant).

The general method

To find the orthogonal trajectories of a particular family of curves we first find the differential equation

$$\frac{dy}{dx} = f(x, y)$$

which describes the given family. The differential equation of the second, and orthogonal, family is then

$$\frac{dy}{dx} = \frac{-1}{f(x, y)}.$$

EXAMPLE

Find the orthogonal trajectories of the family of rectangular hyperbolas

$$y = \frac{c_1}{x}.$$

Solution: The derivative of $y = c_1/x$ is

$$\frac{dy}{dx} = \frac{-c_1}{x^2}.$$

Now from the given family we can replace c_1 by $c_1 = xy$:

$$\frac{dy}{dx} = -\frac{xy}{x^2}.$$

Hence, the differential equation of the original family is

$$\frac{dy}{dx} = -\frac{y}{x}.$$

The differential equation of the orthogonal family is then

$$\frac{dy}{dx} = \frac{-1}{(-y/x)} = \frac{x}{y}.$$

We solve this last equation by separation of variables:

$$y\,dy = x\,dx$$

$$\int y\,dy = \int x\,dx$$

$$\frac{y^2}{2} = \frac{x^2}{2} + c_2'$$

or
$$y^2 - x^2 = c_2,$$

where, for convenience we have replaced $2c_2'$ by c_2.

The graphs of the two families, for various values of c_1 and c_2, are given in Figure 3.6.

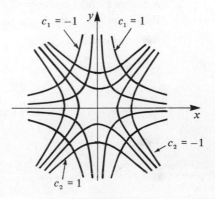

Figure 3.6

EXAMPLE   Find the orthogonal trajectories of

$$y = \frac{c_1 x}{1 + x}.$$

Solution: By the quotient rule

$$\frac{dy}{dx} = \frac{(1 + x)c_1 - c_1 x}{(1 + x)^2}$$

$$= \frac{c_1}{(1 + x)^2}.$$

But $c_1 = y(1 + x)/x$ so that

$$\frac{dy}{dx} = \frac{y}{x(1 + x)}.$$

The differential equation of the orthogonal trajectories is then

$$\frac{dy}{dx} = -\frac{x(1 + x)}{y}.$$

Again by separating variables we have:

$$y\,dy = -x(1 + x)\,dx$$

$$\int y\,dy = -\int (x + x^2)\,dx$$

$$\frac{y^2}{2} = -\frac{x^2}{2} - \frac{x^3}{3} + c_2'$$

or $3y^2 + 3x^2 + 2x^3 = c_2$ ($6c_2'$ replaced by c_2).

EXERCISES 3.1   Answers to odd-numbered problems begin on page A-7 of the Appendix. In Problems 1–15 find the orthogonal trajectories of the given family of curves.

1. $y = c_1 x$ **2.** $3x + 4y = c_1$

3. $y = c_1 x^2$ **4.** $2x^2 + y^2 = c_1^2$

5. $y = c_1 e^{-x}$

6. $y^a = c_1 x^b$, a and b fixed constants

7. $y = \dfrac{x}{1 + c_1 x}$ ★**8.** $x^2 + y^2 = 2c_1 x$

Ask → **9.** $2x^2 + y^2 = 4c_1 x$ **10.** $y^3 + 3x^2 y = c_1$

11. $y = \dfrac{c_1}{1 + x^2}$ **12.** $y = \dfrac{1 + c_1 x}{1 - c_1 x}$

13. $y = \dfrac{1}{\ln c_1 x}$ ★14. $y = -x - 1 + c_1 e^x$

15. $x^{1/3} + y^{1/3} = c_1$

16.   Find the member of the orthogonal trajectories for $3xy^2 = 2 + 3c_1 x$ which passes through $(0, 10)$.

17.   Find the member of the orthogonal trajectories for $x + y = c_1 e^y$ which passes through $(0, 5)$.

18.   In calculus it is shown that for a graph in polar coordinates

$$\tan \psi = r \frac{d\theta}{dr}$$

where ψ is the positive counterclockwise angle between the radius vector and the tangent line. Show that two polar curves $r = f_1(\theta)$ and $r = f_2(\theta)$ are orthogonal if and only if

$$(\tan \psi_1)_{\mathscr{C}_1}(\tan \psi_2)_{\mathscr{C}_2} = -1.$$

In Problems 19–23 find the orthogonal trajectories of the given polar curves. Use the results of Problem 18.

EXAMPLE   Find the orthogonal trajectories of

$$r = c_1(1 - \sin \theta).$$

Solution: For the given curve we can write

$$\frac{dr}{d\theta} = -c_1 \cos \theta$$

$$= \frac{-r \cos \theta}{1 - \sin \theta}$$

so that $$r\frac{d\theta}{dr} = -\frac{1 - \sin \theta}{\cos \theta} = \tan \psi_1.$$

Thus, by Problem 18 the differential equation of the orthogonal trajectories is

$$r\frac{d\theta}{dr} = \frac{\cos \theta}{1 - \sin \theta} = \tan \psi_2.$$

Separating variables then gives

$$\frac{dr}{r} = \frac{1 - \sin \theta}{\cos \theta} d\theta$$

$$= (\sec \theta - \tan \theta)\, d\theta$$

so that $\qquad\ln|r| = \ln|\sec\theta + \tan\theta| + \ln|\cos\theta| + \ln c_2$

$$= \ln|c_2(1 + \sin\theta)|.$$

Hence $\qquad\qquad r = c_2(1 + \sin\theta).$

---

19. $r = 2c_1 \cos\theta$ $\qquad\qquad\qquad$ **20.** $r = c_1(1 + \cos\theta)$

21. $r^2 = c_1 \sin 2\theta$ $\qquad\qquad\qquad$ **22.** $r = \dfrac{c_1}{1 + \cos\theta}$

23. $r = c_1 \sec\theta$

★24. A family of curves can be *self-orthogonal*, in the sense that a member of the orthogonal trajectories is also a member of the original family.
(a) Show that the family of parabolas $y^2 = 2c_1(x + c_1)$ is self-orthogonal.
(b) Show that the family of cardioids $r = c_1(1 + \sin\theta)$ is self-orthogonal.

25. A family of curves that intersects a given family of curves at a specified constant angle $\alpha \neq \pi/2$ is said to be an isogonal family. The two families are said to be **isogonal trajectories** of each other. If $dy/dx = f(x, y)$ is the differential equation of the given family, show that the differential equation of the isogonal family is

$$\frac{dy}{dx} = \frac{f(x, y) \pm \tan\alpha}{1 \mp f(x, y)\tan\alpha}.$$

26. Use the results of Problem 25 to find the isogonal family which intersects the one-parameter family of straight lines $y = c_1 x$ at

(a) $\alpha = 45°,$ $\qquad\qquad\qquad$ (b) $\alpha = 60°.$

3.2   Applications of Linear Equations

3.2.1   Growth and Decay

The simple linear differential equation

$$\frac{dx}{dt} = kx \tag{1}$$

where k is a constant, occurs in many physical theories involving either growth or decay. For example, in biology it is often observed that the rate dx/dt at which certain bacteria grow is proportional to the number of bacteria x present at any time. Also, over short intervals of time the population $P(t)$ of small animals, such as rodents, can be predicted fairly accurately by the solution of the initial-value problem

$$\frac{dP}{dt} = kP \tag{2}$$

$$P(t_0) = P_0$$

where P_0 is an initial population at t_0. The constant k can be determined from the solution of the equation by using a subsequent measurement of the population at a time $t_1 > t_0$. On the other hand, we may simply start out by postulating the value of k. For example, if we assume a population increases, say, by 30% over a unit-time interval, we would then write $k = 0.3$.

In physics an initial-value problem such as (2) provides a model for approximating the remaining amount $A(t)$ of a substance which is disintegrating through radioactivity. Equation (1) could also represent the rate at which the temperature changes in a cooling body, or the rate at which a chemical reaction takes place.

EXAMPLE

A culture initially has N_0 number of bacteria. At $t = 1$ hour the number of bacteria is measured to be $(3/2)N_0$. If the rate of growth is given by (1), determine the time necessary for the number of bacteria to triple.

Solution: We first solve the differential equation

$$\frac{dN}{dt} = kN$$

subject to $N(0) = N_0$.

After we have solved the above problem we then use the empirical condition $N(1) = (3/2)N_0$ to determine the constant of proportionality k.

Now the equation

$$\frac{dN}{dt} = kN$$

is both separable and linear. If put into the form

$$\frac{dN}{dt} - kN = 0$$

we can see by inspection that the integrating factor is e^{-kt}. Multiplying both sides of the equation by this term gives immediately

$$\frac{d}{dt}[e^{-kt}N] = 0.$$

Thus, by integrating both sides of the last equation we obtain

$$e^{-kt}N = c \quad \text{or} \quad N(t) = ce^{kt}.$$

At $t = 0$ it follows that $N_0 = ce^0 = c$ and so $N(t) = N_0 e^{kt}$.
Now at $t = 1$ we have

$$N(1) = \tfrac{3}{2}N_0 = N_0 e^k \qquad \text{or} \qquad e^k = \tfrac{3}{2}$$

from which we get

$$k = \ln\left(\frac{3}{2}\right)$$

$$= 0.4055.$$

Thus, $$N(t) = N_0 e^{0.4055t}.$$

To find the time at which the bacteria have tripled we solve

$$3N_0 = N_0 e^{0.4055t}$$

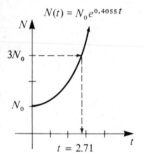

$N(t) = N_0 e^{0.4055t}$

Figure 3.7

for t.
It follows that

$$0.4055t = \ln 3$$

or

$$t = \frac{\ln 3}{0.4055}$$

$$= \frac{1.0986}{0.4055}$$

$$\approx 2.71 \text{ hours.}$$

Note: We can write the function $N(t)$ obtained in the preceding example in an alternative form. From the laws of exponents

$$N(t) = N_0 e^{kt}$$

$$= N_0 (e^k)^t$$

$$= N_0 \left(\frac{3}{2}\right)^t$$

since $e^k = 3/2$. This latter solution provides a convenient method for computing $N(t)$ for small positive integral values of t; it also clearly shows the influence of the subsequent experimental observation at $t = 1$ on the solution for all time. We notice too, that the actual number of bacteria present at time $t = 0$ is quite irrelevant in finding the time required to triple the number in the culture. The necessary time to triple, say, 100, or 10,000 bacteria is still approximately 2.71 hours.

Of course, the exponential function e^{kt} increases as t increases for $k > 0$, and decreases as t increases if $k < 0$. Thus, problems describing growth, such as population, bacteria, or even capital, are characterized by a positive value of k, whereas problems involving decay, as in radioactive disintegration, will yield a negative k value.

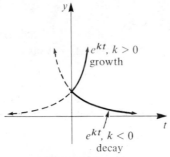

Figure 3.8

Half-life

In physics the half-life is a measure of the stability of a radioactive substance. The half-life is simply the time it takes for one-half of the atoms in an initial amount A_0 to disintegrate. The longer the half-life of a substance the more stable it is. For example, the half-life of highly radioactive radium is approximately 1700 years, whereas the most commonly occurring uranium isotope, U-238, has a half-life of approximately 4,500,000,000 years.

EXAMPLE

A breeder reactor converts the relatively stable uranium 238 into the isotope plutonium 239. After 15 years it is determined that 0.043% of the initial amount A_0 of the plutonium has disintegrated. What is the half-life of this isotope?

Solution: As in the previous example, the solution of the initial value problem

$$\frac{dA}{dt} = kA$$

$$A(0) = A_0$$

is

$$A(t) = A_0 e^{kt}.$$

If 0.043% of the atoms in A_0 have disintegrated then 99.957% of the substance remains. To find k we must therefore solve

$$0.99957 A_0 = A_0 e^{15k}$$

$$e^{15k} = 0.99957$$

Thus,

$$15k = \ln(0.99957)$$

$$= -0.0004301$$

so that

$$k = \frac{-0.0004301}{15}$$

$$= -0.00002867.$$

Hence, for any time t, the amount of the plutonium isotope *remaining* is

$$A(t) = A_0 \, e^{-0.00002867t}.$$

Now the half-life is the corresponding value of time t for which $A(t) = A_0/2$, that is,

$$\frac{A_0}{2} = A_0 \, e^{-0.00002867t} \qquad \text{or} \qquad \frac{1}{2} = e^{-0.00002867t}.$$

It follows that
$$-0.00002867t = \ln\left(\frac{1}{2}\right) = -\ln 2$$

$$= -0.69315$$

and therefore
$$t = \frac{0.69315}{0.00002867}$$

$$\approx 24{,}180 \text{ years}.$$

Carbon dating

About 1950 the chemist Willard Libby devised a method of using radioactive carbon as a means of determining the approximate ages of fossils. The theory is based on the fact that the isotope carbon 14 is produced in the atmosphere by the action of cosmic radiation on nitrogen. The ratio of the amount of C-14 to ordinary carbon in the atmosphere appears to be a constant, and as a consequence the proportionate amount of the isotope present in all living organisms is the same as that in the atmosphere. When an organism dies the absorption of C-14, by either breathing or eating, ceases. Thus, by comparing the proportionate amount of C-14 present, say, in a fossil with the constant ratio found in the atmosphere it is possible to obtain a reasonable estimation of its age. The method is based upon the knowledge that the half-life of the radioactive C-14 is approximately 5600 years. For his work Libby won the Nobel Prize for chemistry in 1960.

EXAMPLE

A fossilized bone is found to contain 1/1000 the original amount of C-14. Determine the age of the fossil.

Solution: We start with the same solution obtained in the preceding example, that is,

$$A(t) = A_0 e^{kt}.$$

When $t = 5600$ years, $A(t) = A_0/2$ from which we can determine the value of k

$$\frac{A_0}{2} = A_0 e^{5600k}$$

$$5600k = \ln\left(\frac{1}{2}\right) = -\ln 2$$

$$k = -\frac{\ln 2}{5600}$$

$$= -\frac{0.69315}{5600}$$

$$= -0.00012378.$$

Therefore $\qquad A(t) = A_0 e^{-0.00012378t}.$

When $\qquad\qquad A(t) = A_0/1000$

we have $\qquad \dfrac{1}{1000}A_0 = A_0 e^{-0.00012378t}$

so that

$$-0.00012378t = \ln\left(\frac{1}{1000}\right) = -\ln 1000$$

$$t = \frac{\ln 1000}{0.00012378}$$

$$= \frac{6.90776}{0.00012378}$$

$$\approx 55{,}800 \text{ years.}$$

Remark: The date found in the preceding example is really at the border of accuracy for this particular method. The usual carbon 14 technique is limited to about 9 half-lives of the isotope or about 50,000 years. The obvious reason is that the chemical analysis needed to obtain an accurate measurement of the remaining C-14 becomes somewhat formidable around the point of $A_0/1000$. Also, this analysis demands the destruction of a rather large sample of the specimen. If this measurement is accomplished indirectly, based on the actual radioactivity of the specimen, then it is very difficult to distinguish between the radiation from the fossil and the normal background radiation. But in recent developments, the use of a particle accelerator has enabled scientists to separate the C-14 from the stable C-12 directly. By computing the precise value of the ratio of C-14 to C-12 the accuracy of this method can be extended to 70,000–100,000 years. Other isotopic techniques such as using potassium 40 and argon 40 can give dates of several million years. Nonisotopic methods based on the use of amino acids are also sometimes possible.

3.2.2   Cooling, Circuits, and Chemical Mixtures

Cooling

Newton's law of cooling states that the rate at which the temperature $T(t)$ changes in a cooling body is proportional to the difference between the temperature in the body and the constant temperature T_0 of the surrounding medium. That is,

$$\frac{dT}{dt} = k(T - T_0) \tag{3}$$

where k is a constant of proportionality.

EXAMPLE

When a cake is removed from a baking oven its temperature is measured at 300°F. Three minutes later its temperature is 200°F. How long will it take to cool off to a room temperature of 70°F?

Solution: We must solve the initial-value problem

$$\frac{dT}{dt} = k(T - 70) \tag{4}$$

$$T(0) = 300$$

and determine the value of k so that $T(3) = 200$.

Equation (3) is both linear and separable; utilizing this latter procedure we have

$$\frac{dT}{T - 70} = k\,dt$$

$$\ln|T - 70| = kt + c_1$$

$$T - 70 = c_2\,e^{kt}$$

$$T = 70 + c_2\,e^{kt}.$$

When $t = 0$, $T = 300$ so that $300 = 70 + c_2$ gives $c_2 = 230$ and therefore $T = 70 + 230\,e^{kt}$.

From $T(3) = 200$ we find

$$e^{3k} = \frac{13}{23}$$

or

$$k = \frac{1}{3}\ln\frac{13}{23}$$

$$= -0.19018.$$

Thus,

$$T(t) = 70 + 230\,e^{-0.19018t} \tag{5}$$

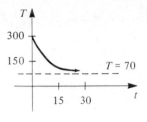

$T(t)$	t (minutes)
75°	20.1
74°	21.3
73°	22.8
72°	24.9
71°	28.6
70.5°	32.3

(a)   (b)

Figure 3.9

Unfortunately (5) furnishes no finite solution to $T(t) = 70$ since $\lim_{t \to \infty} T(t) = 70$. Yet intuitively we expect the cake will assume the room temperature after a reasonably long period of time. How long is long? Of course, we should not be the least bit disturbed by the fact that the model (4) does not quite live up to our physical intuition. Parts (a) and (b) of Figure 3.9 clearly show that the cake will be approximately at room temperature in about one half hour.

An L-R series circuit

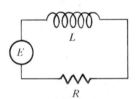

Figure 3.10

In a series circuit containing only a resistor and an inductor, Kirchoff's second law states the sum of the voltage drop across the inductor $(L(di/dt))$ and the voltage drop across the resistor (iR) is the same as the impressed voltage $(E(t))$ on the circuit. See Figure 3.10.

Thus we obtain the linear differential equation for the current $i(t)$,

$$L\frac{di}{dt} + Ri = E(t) \tag{6}$$

where L and R are constants known as the inductance and the resistance, respectively.

EXAMPLE

A 12-volt battery is connected to simple series circuit in which the inductance is 1/2 henry and the resistance is 10 ohms. Determine the current i if the initial current is zero.

Solution: We solve the initial-value problem

$$\frac{1}{2}\frac{di}{dt} + 10i = 12,$$

$$i(0) = 0.$$

First put the equation into standard form by multiplying through by 2 and read off the integrating factor e^{20t}

Hence we find
$$\frac{d}{dt}[e^{20t}i] = 24e^{20t}$$

$$e^{20t}i = \frac{24}{20}e^{20t} + c$$

$$i = \frac{6}{5} + ce^{-20t}.$$

Now $i(0) = 0$ implies
$$0 = \frac{6}{5} + c$$

or $c = 6/5$, and therefore
$$i(t) = \frac{6}{5} - \frac{6}{5}e^{-20t}.$$

Transient and steady-state terms

From equation (9) of Section 2.4 we can write down the general solution of (6),

$$i(t) = \frac{e^{-(R/L)t}}{L} \int e^{(R/L)t}E(t)\,dt + ce^{-(R/L)t}. \tag{7}$$

In particular, when $E(t) = E_0$ is a constant then (7) becomes

$$i(t) = \frac{E_0}{R} + \left(c - \frac{E_0}{R}\right)e^{-(R/L)t}. \tag{8}$$

Note that as $t \to \infty$, the second term in equation (8) approaches zero. Such a term is usually called a **transient term**; the remaining term(s) is called the **steady-state** part of the solution. In this case E_0/R is also called the **steady-state current**; for large time it then appears that the current in the circuit is simply governed by Ohm's law $(E = iR)$. It is also of interest, and some importance (see Section 4.1), to further observe that the **transient current**

$$\left(c - \frac{E_0}{R}\right)e^{-(R/L)t}$$

provides a general solution for the equation

$$L\frac{di}{dt} + Ri = 0,$$

and the steady-state current E_0/R is a solution of

$$L\frac{di}{dt} + Ri = E_0.$$

A mixture problem

The mixing of two fluids sometimes gives rise to a linear first-order differential equation. In the next example we consider the mixture of two salt solutions of different concentrations.

EXAMPLE

Initially 50 pounds of salt is dissolved in a tank holding 300 gallons of water. A brine solution is pumped into the tank at a rate of 3 gallons per minute, and a well-stirred solution is then pumped out at the same rate. If the concentration of the solution entering is 2 pounds per gallon, determine the amount of salt in the tank at any time. How much salt is present after 50 minutes? after a long time?

Solution: Let $A(t)$ be the amount of salt (in pounds) in the tank at any time. For problems of this sort, the net rate at which $A(t)$ changes is given by

$$\frac{dA}{dt} = \text{(rate of substance entering)} - \text{(rate of substance leaving)}$$

$$= R_1 - R_2. \tag{9}$$

Now the rate at which the salt enters the tank is, in pounds per minute,

$$R_1 = (3 \text{ gal/min}) \cdot (2 \text{ lb/gal}) = 6 \text{ lb/min}$$

whereas the rate at which salt is leaving is

$$R_2 = (3 \text{ gal/min}) \cdot \left(\frac{A}{300} \text{ lb/gal}\right) = \frac{A}{100} \text{ lb/min.}$$

Thus equation (9) becomes

$$\frac{dA}{dt} = 6 - \frac{A}{100} \tag{10}$$

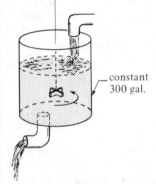

Figure 3.11

which we solve subject to the initial condition $A(0) = 50$.
    Since the integrating factor is $e^{t/100}$ we can write (10) as

$$\frac{d}{dt}[e^{t/100}A] = 6\,e^{t/100}$$

and there

$$e^{t/100}\,A = 600e^{t/100} + c$$

$$A = 600 + c\,e^{-t/100}. \tag{11}$$

When $t = 0$, $A = 50$ so we find that $c = -550$. Finally, we obtain

$$A(t) = 600 - 550\,e^{-t/100}. \tag{12}$$

At $t = 50$ we find $A(50) = 266.41$ lb. Also, as $t \to \infty$ it is obvious from (12) and Figure 3.12 that the steady-state term is $A = 600$.

Of course this is what we would expect in this case; over a long period of time the number of pounds of salt in the solution must be

$$(300 \text{ gal})(2 \text{ lb/gal}) = 600 \text{ lb.}$$

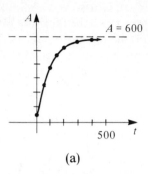

t (minutes)	A (lbs)
50	266.41
100	397.67
150	477.27
200	525.57
300	572.62
400	589.93

(a)

(b)

Figure 3.12

In the preceding example we assumed that the rate at which the solution was pumped in was the same as the rate at which the solution was pumped out. Of course there is no reason why this should hold true in general; the mixed brine solution could be pumped out a rate faster or slower than the rate at which we pump in the other solution. The resulting differential equation in this latter situation is linear with a variable coefficient (see Problems 19 and 20).

EXERCISES 3.2   Answers to odd-numbered problems begin on page A-8 of the Appendix.

[3.2.1]   1. The population of a certain community is known to increase at a rate proportional to the number of people present at any time. If the population has doubled in 5 years, how long will it take to triple? to quadruple?

★2. Suppose it is known that the population of the community in Problem 1 is 10,000 after 3 years. What was the initial population? What will be the population in 10 years?

3. If P_0 is the initial population of a community, show that if P is governed by (2), then

$$\left(\frac{P_1}{P_0}\right)^{t_2} = \left(\frac{P_2}{P_0}\right)^{t_1}$$

where $P_1 = P(t_1)$ and $P_2 = P(t_2)$, $\quad t_1 < t_2$.

4. Use the results of Problem 3 to solve the following. A town has an initial population of 500 that increases by 15% in 10 years. What will be the population in 30 years?

5. In one model of the changing population $P(t)$ of a community it is assumed that

$$\frac{dP}{dt} = \frac{dB}{dt} - \frac{dD}{dt}$$

where dB/dt and dD/dt are the birth and death rates, respectively.
(a) Solve for $P(t)$ if

$$\frac{dB}{dt} = k_1 P \quad \text{and} \quad \frac{dD}{dt} = k_2 P.$$

(b) Analyze the cases $k_1 > k_2$, $k_1 = k_2$, $k_1 < k_2$.

6. Initially there were 100 milligrams of a radioactive substance present. After 6 hours the mass decreased by 3%. If the rate of decay is proportional to the amount of the substance present at any time, find the amount remaining after 24 hours.

7. Determine the half-life of the radioactive substance described in Problem 6.

★8. Show in general that the half-life of a radioactive substance is

$$t = \frac{(t_2 - t_1) \ln 2}{\ln A_1/A_2}$$

where $A_1 = A(t_1)$ and $A_2 = A(t_2)$, $t_1 < t_2$.

9. When a vertical beam of light passes through a transparent substance, the rate at which its intensity I decreases is proportional to $I(t)$, where t represents the thickness of the medium in feet. In clear sea water the intensity 3 feet below the surface is 25% of the initial intensity I_0 of the incident beam. What is the intensity of the beam 15 feet below the surface?

10. Interest compounded continuously means that the amount of money S increases at a rate proportional to the amount present at any time (see Section 1.3).
(a) Find the amount of money accrued at the end of 5 years when $5000 is deposited in a savings account drawing $5\frac{3}{4}\%$ annual interest compounded continuously.
(b) Use a hand calculator to compare the number obtained in part (a) with the value

$$S = 5000\left(1 + \frac{0.0575}{4}\right)^{5(4)}$$

This particular value represents the amount that would be accrued when interest is compounded quarterly.
(c) In how many years will the initial sum deposited be doubled?

11. In a piece of burned wood, or charcoal, it was found that 85.5% of the C-14 has decayed. What is the approximate age of the wood? (It is precisely this data that archaeologists used to date prehistoric paintings in a cave in Lascaux, France.)

[3.2.2]   ★**12.** A thermometer is taken from an inside room to the outside where the air temperature is 5°F. After 1 minute the thermometer reads 55°F and after 5 minutes the reading is 30°F. What is the initial temperature of the room?

13. A thermometer is removed from a room where the air temperature is 70°F to the outside where the temperature is 10°F. After $\frac{1}{2}$ minute the thermometer reads 50°F. What is the reading at $t = 1$ minute? How long will it take for the thermometer to reach 15°F?

14. Formula (3) also obtains when an object absorbs heat from the surrounding medium. If a small metal bar, whose initial temperature is 100°F, is dropped into a container of boiling water, how long will it take for the bar to reach 200°F if it is known that its temperature increased 3° in 1 second? How long will it take the bar to reach 210°F?

15. A 30-volt electromotive force is applied to a series circuit in which the inductance is 0.1 henry and the resistance is 50 ohms. Find the current $i(t)$ if $i(0) = 0$. Determine the behavior of the current for large time.

16. Solve the general equation (6) under the assumption that

$$E(t) = E_0 \sin \omega t$$

$$i(0) = i_0.$$

17. A tank contains 200 gallons of brine in which 30 lb of salt is dissolved. Brine containing 1 lb of salt per gallon is then pumped into the tank at a rate of 4 gallons per minute; the well-mixed solution is pumped out at the same rate. Find the number of pounds of salt $A(t)$ in the tank at any time.

★**18.** Solve problem 17 under the assumption that pure water is pumped into the tank.

19. A large tank is partially filled with 100 gallons of brine in which 10 lb of salt is dissolved. Brine containing $\frac{1}{2}$ lb of salt per gallon is pumped into the tank at a rate of 6 gallons per minute; the well-mixed solution is then pumped out at a slower rate of 4 gallons per minute. Find the number of pounds of salt in the tank after 30 minutes.

20. Beer containing 6% alcohol per gallon is pumped into a vat which initially contains 400 gallons of beer at 3% alcohol. The rate at which the beer is pumped in is 3 gallons per minute, whereas the mixed liquid is pumped out at a rate of 4 gallons per minute. Find the number of gallons of alcohol $A(t)$ in the tank at any time. What is the percentage of alcohol in the tank after 60 minutes? When is the tank empty?

21. The differential equation governing the velocity v of a falling weight w subjected to air resistance proportional to the instantaneous velocity is

$$m\frac{dv}{dt} = mg - kv$$

where k is a positive constant of proportionality. Solve the equation subject to the initial condition $v(0) = v_0$ and determine the limiting velocity of the weight. If distance s is related to velocity by $ds/dt = v$, find an explicit expression for s if it is further known that $s(0) = s_0$.

22. The rate at which a drug disseminates into the bloodstream is governed by the differential equation

$$\frac{dX}{dt} = A - BX$$

where A and B are positive constants. The function $X(t)$ describes the concentration of the drug in the bloodstream at any time t. Find the time that $X(t)$ is one-half the steady-state concentration. Assume that $X(0) = 0$.

3.3   Applications of Nonlinear Equations

We have seen that if a population $P(t)$ is described by the initial-value problem

$$\frac{dP}{dt} = kP, k > 0$$

$$P(0) = P_0 \tag{1}$$

then P exhibits unbounded exponential growth. In many instances (1) provides an unrealistic model of the growth of a population, that is, what is actually observed differs substantially from what is predicted.

Around 1840, the Belgian mathematician-biologist P. F. Verhulst was concerned with mathematical formulations for predicting the human populations of various countries. One of the equations he studied was

$$\frac{dP}{dt} = P(a - bP) \tag{2}$$

where a and b are positive constants. Equation (2) came to be known as the **logistic equation** and its solution is called the **logistic function** (the graph of which is naturally called a logistic curve).

Equation (1) does not provide a very accurate model for population growth when the population itself is very large. Overcrowded conditions with the resulting detrimental effects on the environment, such as pollution, excessive and competitive demands for food and fuel, can have an inhibitive effect on the population growth. If $a, a > 0$, is a constant average birthrate, let us assume that the average death rate is proportional to the population $P(t)$ at any time. Thus, if $\dfrac{1}{P}\dfrac{dP}{dt}$ is the rate of growth per individual in a population, then

$$\frac{1}{P}\frac{dP}{dt} = \text{(average birthrate)} - \text{(average death rate)}$$

$$= a - bP \tag{3}$$

where b is a positive constant of proportionality. Cross multiplying (3) by P immediately gives

$$\frac{dP}{dt} = P(a - bP).$$

As we shall now see, the solution of (2) is bounded as $t \to \infty$. If we rewrite (2) as

$$\frac{dP}{dt} = aP - bP^2 \tag{4}$$

the term $-bP^2$, $b > 0$, can therefore be interpreted as an "inhibition" or "competition" term. Also, in most applications the positive constant a is much larger than the constant b.

Logistic curves have proved to be quite accurate in predicting the growth patterns, in a limited space, of certain types of bacteria, protozoa, water fleas (*Daphnia*), and fruit flies (*Drosophila*). We have already seen equation (2) in the form

$$\frac{dx}{dt} = kx(n + 1 - x) \qquad k > 0.$$

This particular differential equation provides a reasonable model for describing the spread of an epidemic brought about by initially introducing an infected individual into a static population. The solution $x(t)$ represents the number of individuals infected with the disease at any time. (See Section 1.3, Equation 26.) Sociologists, and even the business world, have borrowed this latter model to study the spread of information and the impact of advertising in certain centers of population.

The general solution

One method for solving equation (2) is separation of variables.* By partial fractions we can write

---

* In the form

$$\frac{dP}{dt} - aP = bP^2$$

you might recognize the logistic equation as a special case of Bernoulli's equation (see Section 2.5).

$$\frac{dP}{P(a - bP)} = dt$$

$$\left[\frac{1/a}{P} + \frac{b/a}{a - bP} \right] dP = dt$$

$$\frac{1}{a} \frac{dP}{P} - \frac{1}{a} \frac{(-b\,dP)}{a - bP} = dt$$

$$\frac{1}{a} \ln |P| - \frac{1}{a} \ln |a - bP| = t + c$$

$$\ln \left| \frac{P}{a - bP} \right| = at + ac$$

$$\frac{P}{a - bP} = c_1 e^{at}. \qquad [c_1 = e^{ac}]$$

It follows from the last equation that

$$P(t) = \frac{ac_1 e^{at}}{1 + bc_1 e^{at}} \qquad \text{[divide numerator and denominator by } e^{at}\text{]}$$

$$= \frac{ac_1}{bc_1 + e^{-at}}. \tag{5}$$

Now if we are given the initial condition $P(0) = P_0$, $P_0 \neq a/b$,* equation (5) implies

$$P_0(1 + bc_1) = ac_1$$

$$c_1(bP_0 - a) = -P_0$$

$$c_1 = \frac{P_0}{a - bP_0}$$

and therefore

$$P(t) = \frac{aP_0/(a - bP_0)}{[bP_0/(a - bP_0)] + e^{-at}}$$

or

$$\boxed{P(t) = \frac{aP_0}{bP_0 + (a - bP_0)e^{-at}}.} \tag{6}$$

Graphs of $P(t)$

The basic shape of the graph of the logistic function $P(t)$ can be obtained without too much effort. Although the variable t usually represents time and we are seldom concerned with applications in which $t < 0$, it is nonetheless of some interest to include this interval when displaying the various graphs of P.

---

* Notice that $P = a/b$ is a singular solution of equation (2).

From (6) we see for $t > 0$ that

$$P(t) \to \frac{aP_0}{bP_0} = \frac{a}{b} \qquad \text{as } t \to \infty;$$

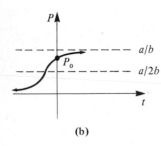

and for $t < 0$ $\qquad\qquad P(t) \to 0 \qquad \text{as } t \to -\infty.$

Now differentiating (2) by the product rule gives

$$\frac{d^2 P}{dt^2} = P\left(-b\frac{dP}{dt}\right) + (a - bP)\frac{dP}{dt}$$

$$= \frac{dP}{dt}(a - 2bP)$$

$$= P(a - bP)(a - 2bP)$$

$$= 2b^2 P\left(P - \frac{a}{b}\right)\left(P - \frac{a}{2b}\right). \tag{7}$$

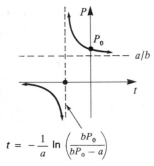

From calculus recall that the points where $d^2P/dt^2 = 0$ are possible points of inflection, but $P = 0$ and $P'' = a/b$ can obviously be ruled out. Hence, $P = a/2b$ is the only possible ordinate value at which the concavity of the graph can change. For $0 < P < a/2b$ it follows from (7) that $P'' > 0$, and $a/2b < P < a/b$ implies $P'' < 0$. Thus, reading from left to right, the graph changes from concave up to concave down at the point corresponding to $P = a/2b$. When the initial value satisfies $0 < P_0 < a/2b$ Figure 3.13(a) shows the graph of $P(t)$ assumes the shape of an S. For $a/2b < P_0 < a/b$ the graph is still S-shaped but the point of inflection occurs at a negative, and therefore, physically meaningless value of t.

If $P_0 > a/b$ equation (7) shows $P'' > 0$ for all t in the domain of $P(t)$ for which $P > 0$; when $P < 0$ equation (7) implies $P'' < 0$. However, $P = 0$ is not a point of inflection since, whenever $a - bP_0 < 0$, a close inspection of (6) reveals a vertical asymptote at

$$t = -\frac{1}{a}\ln\left(\frac{bP_0}{bP_0 - a}\right).$$

The graph of $P(t)$ in this case is as shown in Figure 3.14. It is of interest to note this particular case apparently has no significant physical applicability.

Figure 3.13

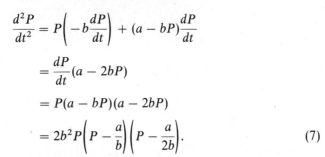

$$t = -\frac{1}{a}\ln\left(\frac{bP_0}{bP_0 - a}\right)$$

Figure 3.14

EXAMPLE

Suppose a student carrying a flu virus returns to an isolated college campus of 1000 students. If it is assumed that the rate at which the virus spreads is proportional not only to the number x of infected students but also to the number of students not infected (see Section 1.3, Page 35), determine the number of infected students after 6 days if it is further observed that after 4 days $x(4) = 50$.

Solution: Assuming that no one leaves the campus throughout the duration of the disease, we must then solve the initial-value problem

$$\frac{dx}{dt} = kx(1000 - x)$$

$$x(0) = 1.$$

By making the identifications $a = 1000k$, $b = k$ we have immediately from (6) that

$$x(t) = \frac{1000k}{k + 999ke^{-1000kt}}$$

$$= \frac{1000}{1 + 999e^{-1000kt}} \tag{8}$$

Now using the information $x(4) = 50$ we can determine k:

$$50 = \frac{1000}{1 + 999e^{-4000k}}$$

$$50 + 49{,}950\,e^{-4000k} = 1000$$

$$e^{-4000k} = \frac{19}{999}$$

$$k = \frac{-1}{4000}\ln\frac{19}{999}$$

$$= 0.0009906$$

Thus, (8) becomes

$$x(t) = \frac{1000}{1 + 999e^{-0.9906t}}.$$

Finally we find

$$x(6) = \frac{1000}{1 + 999e^{-5.9436}}$$

$$= \frac{1000}{3.61995}$$

$$= 276 \text{ students.}$$

Additional calculated values of $x(t)$ are given in the table in Figure 3.15.

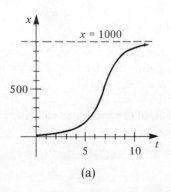

(a)

t days	x (number infected)
4	50 (observed)
5	124
6	276
7	507
8	735
9	882
10	953

(b)

Figure 3.15

Gompertz curves

A modification of the logistic equation is

$$\frac{dP}{dt} = P(a - b \ln P) \tag{9}$$

where a and b are constants. It is readily shown by separation of variables (see Problem 5) that the general solution of (1) is

$$P(t) = e^{a/b} e^{-ce^{-bt}} \tag{10}$$

where c is an arbitrary constant. We note when $b > 0$, $P \to e^{a/b}$ as $t \to \infty$, whereas for $b < 0, c > 0, P \to 0$ as $t \to \infty$. The graph of the function (10), called a **Gompertz curve**,* is quite similar to the graph of the logistic function. Figure 3.16 shows two possibilities for the graph of $P(t)$.

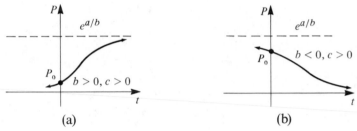

(a)   (b)

Figure 3.16

Functions such as (10) are encountered in studies of the growth, or decline, of certain populations, in actuarial predictions, and for example, in the study of growth of revenue in the sale of a commercial product.

Chemical reactions

The disintegration of a radioactive substance, governed by equation (1) of the preceding section, is said to be a **first-order reaction**. In chemistry a few reactions follow the same empirical law: If the molecules of a substance A decompose into smaller molecules it is a natural assumption to suppose that the rate at which this decomposition takes place is proportional to the amount of the first substance which has not undergone conversion. That is, if $X(t)$ is the amount of substance A remaining at any time, then

$$\frac{dX}{dt} = kX, \tag{11}$$

where k is negative since X is decreasing. An example of a first-order chemical reaction is the conversion of *tert*-butyl chloride into *tert*-butyl alcohol

$$(CH_3)_3CCl + NaOH \quad \to \quad (CH_3)_3COH + NaCl.$$

Only the concentration of the *tert*-butyl chloride controls the rate of reaction.
Now in the reaction

$$CH_3Cl + NaOH \quad \to \quad CH_3OH + NaCl$$

---

* Named after Benjamin Gompertz (1779–1865), an English mathematician.

for every molecule of methyl chloride, one molecule of sodium hydroxide is consumed, thus forming one molecule of methyl alcohol and one molecule of sodium chloride. In this case the rate at which the reaction proceeds is proportional to the product of the remaining concentrations of CH_3Cl and of $NaOH$. If X denotes the amount of CH_3OH formed and α and β are the given amounts of the first two chemicals A and B, then the instantaneous amounts not converted to chemical C are α-X and β-X, respectively. Hence, the rate of formation of C is given by

$$\frac{dX}{dt} = k(\alpha - X)(\beta - X) \tag{12}$$

where k is a constant of proportionality. A reaction described by equation (12) is said to be of **second-order**.

EXAMPLE

A compound C is formed when two chemicals A and B are combined. The resulting reaction between the two chemicals is such that for each gram of A, 4 grams of B are used. It is observed that 30 grams of the compound C are formed in 10 minutes. Determine the amount of C at any time if the rate of the reaction is proportional to the amounts of A and B remaining and that initially there are 50 grams of A and 32 grams of B. How much of the compound C is present at 15 minutes? Interpret the solution as $t \to \infty$.

Solution: Let $X(t)$ denote the number of grams of the compound C present at any time. Clearly $X(0) = 0$ and $X(10) = 30$.

Now for example, if there are 2 grams of compound C then we must have used, say, a grams of A and b grams of B so that

$$a + b = 2$$
$$b = 4a.$$

Thus we must use $a = 2/5 = 2(1/5)$ grams of chemical A and $b = 8/5 = 2(4/5)$ grams of B. In general, for X grams of C then we must use

$$\frac{X}{5} \text{ grams of } A \qquad \text{and} \qquad \frac{4}{5}X \text{ grams of } B.$$

The amounts of A and B remaining at any time are then

$$50 - \frac{X}{5} \qquad \text{and} \qquad 32 - \frac{4}{5}X,$$

respectively.

Now we know that the rate at which chemical C is formed satisfies

$$\frac{dX}{dt} \propto \left(50 - \frac{X}{5}\right)\left(32 - \frac{4}{5}X\right).$$

To simplify the subsequent algebra, we factor $1/5$ from the first term and $4/5$ from the second, and then introduce the constant of proportionality,

$$\frac{dX}{dt} = k(250 - X)(40 - X).$$

By separation of variables and partial fractions we can write

$$\frac{dX}{(250 - X)(40 - X)} = k\,dt$$

$$-\frac{1/210}{250 - X}dX + \frac{1/210}{40 - X}dX = k\,dt$$

$$\ln\frac{250 - X}{40 - X} = 210kt + c_1$$

$$\frac{250 - X}{40 - X} = c_2 e^{210kt}.$$

When $t = 0$, $X = 0$, so it follows at this point that $c_2 = 25/4$. Also when $t = 10$, $X = 30$, hence we find

$$k = \frac{1}{2100}\ln\frac{88}{25}$$

$$= 0.0005993$$

$$210k = 0.1258.$$

Using this information we solve for X

$$X(t) = 1000\frac{1 - e^{-0.1258t}}{25 - 4e^{-0.1258t}}. \tag{13}$$

The behavior of X as a function of time is displayed in Figure 3.17. It is clear, not only from the accompanying table, but also from equation (13) that $X \rightarrow 40$ as $t \rightarrow \infty$. This means there are 40 grams of compound C formed, leaving

$$50 - \tfrac{1}{5}(40) = 42 \text{ grams}$$

of chemical A and

$$32 - \tfrac{4}{5}(40) = 0 \text{ grams}$$

of chemical B.

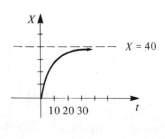

t (minutes)	X (grams)
10	30 (measured)
15	34.78
20	37.25
25	38.54
30	39.22
35	39.59

(a)

(b)

Figure 3.17

The general equation

The preceding example can be generalized in the following manner. Suppose that a grams of substance A are combined with b grams of substance B. If there are M and N parts of A and B, respectively, in the compound formed, then

$$a - \frac{M}{M+N}X(t)$$

represents the amount of substance A remaining at any time and

$$b - \frac{N}{M+N}X(t)$$

is the amount of substance B remaining at any time. Thus

$$\frac{dX}{dt} \propto \left[a - \frac{M}{M+N}X\right]\left[b - \frac{N}{M+N}X\right]. \tag{14}$$

Proceeding as before, if we factor out $M/(M+N)$ from the first term and $N/(M+N)$ from the second term, the resulting differential equation is the same as (12)

$$\frac{dX}{dt} = k(\alpha - X)(\beta - X) \tag{15}$$

where $\alpha = \dfrac{a(M+N)}{M}$ and $\beta = \dfrac{b(M+N)}{N}.$

Chemists refer to reactions described by equation (15) as the **law of mass action**.
    When $\alpha \neq \beta$, it is readily shown (see Problem 9) that a general solution of (15) is

$$\frac{1}{\alpha - \beta}\ln\frac{\alpha - X}{\beta - X} = kt + c. \tag{16}$$

Assuming the natural initial condition $X(0) = 0$ equation (16) yields the explicit solution

$$X(t) = \frac{\alpha\beta[1 - e^{(\alpha - \beta)kt}]}{\beta - \alpha e^{(\alpha - \beta)kt}}. \tag{17}$$

Without loss of generality we assume in (17) that $\beta > \alpha$ or $\alpha - \beta < 0$. Since $X(t)$ is an increasing function we expect $k > 0$ and so it follows immediately from (17) that $X(t) \rightarrow \alpha$ as $t \rightarrow \infty$.

EXERCISES 3.3

Answers to odd-numbered problems begin on page A-8 of the Appendix.

1. The number of supermarkets $C(t)$ throughout the country that are using a computerized checkout system is described by the initial-value problem

$$\frac{dC}{dt} = C(1 - 0.0005C), \qquad t > 0$$

$$C(0) = 1.$$

How many supermarkets are using the computerized method when $t = 10$? How many companies are estimated to adopt the new procedure over a long period of time?

★2. The number of people $N(t)$ in a community who are exposed to a particular advertisement is governed by the logistic equation. Initially $N(0) = 500$, and it is observed that $N(1) = 1000$. If it is predicted that the limiting number of people in the community that will see the advertisement is 50,000, determine $N(t)$ at any time.

3. The population $P(t)$ at any time in a suburb of a large city is governed by the initial-value problem

$$\frac{dP}{dt} = P(10^{-1} - 10^{-7}P)$$

$$P(0) = 5000,$$

where t is measured in months. What is the limiting value of the population? At what time will the population be equal to one-half of this limiting value?

4. Find a general solution of the *modified logistic equation*

$$\frac{dP}{dt} = P(a - bP)(1 - cP^{-1}), \qquad a, b, c > 0.$$

5. (a) Solve equation (9):
$$\frac{dP}{dt} = P(a - b \ln P).$$

(b) If $P(0) = P_0$, then determine the value of c in equation (10).

6. Assuming $0 < P_0 < e^{a/b}$, and $a > 0$, use equation (9) to find the ordinate of the point of inflection for a Gompertz curve.

7. Two chemicals A and B are combined to form a chemical C. The rate or velocity of the reaction is proportional to the product of the instantaneous amounts of A and B not converted to chemical C. Initially there are 40 grams of A and 50 grams of B, and for each gram of B, 2 grams of A are used. It is observed that 10 grams of C are formed in 5 minutes. How much is formed in 20 minutes? What is the limiting amount of C after a long time? How much of chemicals A and B remain after a long time?

8. Solve the preceding problem if there are 100 grams of chemical A present initially. At what time is chemical C half-formed?

9. Obtain a general solution of the equation

$$\frac{dX}{dt} = k(\alpha - X)(\beta - X)$$

governing second-order reactions in the two cases $\alpha \neq \beta$ and $\alpha = \beta$.

10. In a third-order chemical reaction the number of grams X of a compound obtained by combining three chemicals is governed by

$$\frac{dX}{dt} = k(\alpha - X)(\beta - X)(\gamma - X).$$

Solve the equation under the assumption $\alpha \neq \beta \neq \gamma$.

EXAMPLE

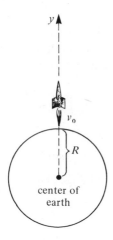

Figure 3.18

A rocket is shot vertically upward from the ground with an initial velocity v_0 (see Figure 3.18). If the positive direction is taken to be upward, the student might recall from Section 1.3 (Problem 29) that in the absence of air resistance, the differential equation of motion after fuel burnout is

$$\frac{d^2y}{dt^2} = -\frac{k}{y^2}$$

where k is a positive constant. While this is not a first-order equation, we note that if we write the acceleration as

$$\frac{d^2y}{dt^2} = \frac{dv}{dt} = \frac{dv}{dy}\frac{dy}{dt} = v\frac{dv}{dy}$$

then the given equation becomes first-order in v. That is,

$$v\frac{dv}{dy} = -\frac{k}{y^2}.$$

Separating variables and integrating then gives

$$\frac{v^2}{2} = \frac{k}{y} + c.$$

Since $v = v_0$ at $y = R$ we obtain

$$\frac{v^2}{2} = \frac{k}{y} - \frac{k}{R} + \frac{v_0^2}{2}.$$

---

11. The reader might object that in the preceding example we really have not solved the original equation for y. Actually, the solution gives quite a bit of information. If $k = gR^2$ show that the "escape velocity" for a rocket is $v_0 = 25,000$ mi/hr. Use a hand calculator and the value $R = 4000$ miles.

12. In the discussion of Section 1.3 we saw that the differential equation describing the shape of a wire of constant density w hanging under its own weight is

$$\frac{d^2y}{dx^2} = \frac{w}{T_1}\sqrt{1 + \left(\frac{dy}{dx}\right)^2}$$

where T_1 is the horizontal tension in the wire at its lowest point. Using the substitution $p = dy/dx$ solve this equation subject to the initial conditions

$$y(0) = 1 \qquad \left.\frac{dy}{dx}\right|_{x=0} = 0.$$

13.   An equation similar to that given in the preceding problem is

$$x\frac{d^2y}{dx^2} = \frac{v_1}{v_2}\sqrt{1 + \left(\frac{dy}{dx}\right)^2}$$

In this case the equation arises in the study of the shape of the path that a pursuer, travelling at a speed v_2, must take in order to intercept a prey travelling at speed v_1. Use the same substitution as in Problem 12 and the initial conditions

$$y(1) = 0 \qquad \left.\frac{dy}{dx}\right|_{x=1} = 0$$

to solve the equation. Consider the two cases: $v_1 = v_2$ and $v_1 \neq v_2$.

★14.   According to **Stefan's law** of radiation, the rate of change of temperature from a body at absolute temperature T is

$$\frac{dT}{dt} = k(T^4 - T_0^4)$$

where T_0 is the absolute temperature of the surrounding medium. Find a general solution of this differential equation. It can be shown that when $T - T_0$ is small compared to T_0 that this particular equation is closely approximated by Newton's law of cooling (Equation (3), Section 3.2).

15.   The height h of water which is flowing through an orifice at the bottom of a cylindrical tank is given by

$$\frac{dh}{dt} = -\frac{A_2}{A_1}\sqrt{2gh}, \qquad g = 32\,\text{ft/sec}^2,$$

where A_1 and A_2 are the cross-sectional areas of the tank and orifice, respectively. (See Problem 20, Exercise 1.3). Solve the equation if the initial height of the water is 20 ft and $A_1 = 50\,\text{ft}^2$ and $A_2 = 1/4\,\text{ft}^2$. At what time is the tank empty?

★16.   The nonlinear differential equation

$$\left(\frac{dr}{dt}\right)^2 = \frac{2\mu}{r} + 2h,$$

where μ and h are nonnegative constants, arises in the study of the two-body problem of celestial mechanics. Here the variable r represents the distance between the two masses. Solve the equation in the two cases $h = 0$ and $h > 0$.

17. Solve the differential equation of the **tractrix**

$$\frac{dy}{dx} = -\frac{y}{\sqrt{s^2 - y^2}}.$$

(See Problem 21, Exercise 1.3.) Assume that the initial point on the y-axis is $(0, 10)$ and the length of rope is $s = 10\,\text{ft}$.

18. A body of mass m falling through a viscous medium encounters a resisting force proportional to the square of its instantaneous velocity. In this situation the differential equation for the velocity $v(t)$ at any time is

$$m\frac{dv}{dt} = mg - kv^2$$

where k is a positive constant of proportionality. Solve the equation subject to $v(0) = v_0$. What is the limiting velocity of the falling body?

19. The equation

$$x\left(\frac{dx}{dy}\right)^2 + 2y\frac{dx}{dy} = x,$$

where $x = x(y)$, occurs in the study of optics. The equation describes the type of plane curve that will reflect all incoming light rays to the same point. (See Problem 27, Exercise 1.3.) Show that the curve must be a parabola. [*Hint:* Use the substitution $w = x^2$ and then re-examine Section 2.5.]

★20. Solve the equation of Problem 19 with the aid of the quadratic formula.

21. The equations of Lotka and Volterra*

$$\frac{dy}{dt} = y(\alpha - \beta x)$$

$$\frac{dx}{dt} = x(-\gamma + \delta y)$$

where α, β, γ and δ are positive constants, occur in the analysis of the biological balance of two species of animals such as a predator and its prey (for example, foxes and rabbits). Here $x(t)$ and $y(t)$ denote the populations of the two species at any time. Although no explicit solutions of the system exist, solutions can be found relating the two populations at

---

*A. J. Lotka (1880–1949) an Austrian-American biomathematician. Vito Volterra (1860–1940) an Italian mathematician.

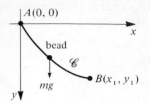

Figure 3.19

any time. Divide the first equation by the second and solve the resulting nonlinear first-order differential equation.

22.   A classical problem in the calculus of variations is to find the shape of a curve $\mathscr{C}$ (see Figure 3.19) such that a bead, under the influence of gravity, will slide from $A(0,0)$ to $B(x_1, y_1)$ in the least time. It can be shown that the differential equation for the shape of the path is $y[1 + (y')^2] = k$ where k is a constant. First solve for dx in terms of y and dy, and then use the substitution $y = k \sin^2 \theta$ to obtain the parametric form of the solution. The curve $\mathscr{C}$ turns out to be a cycloid.

CHAPTER SUMMARY

If every curve in a one-parameter family of curves $G(x, y, c_1) = 0$ is orthogonal to every curve in a second one-parameter family $H(x, y, c_2) = 0$, we say that the two families are **orthogonal trajectories**. Two curves are orthogonal if their tangent lines are perpendicular at a point of intersection. When given a particular family, we find its differential equation

$$\frac{dy}{dx} = f(x, y)$$

by differentiating the equation $G(x, y, c_1) = 0$ and eliminating the parameter c_1. The differential equation of the second, and orthogonal family, is then

$$\frac{dy}{dx} = \frac{-1}{f(x, y)}.$$

We solve this latter equation by the methods of Chapter 2.

In the mathematical analysis of population growth, radioactive decay, or chemical mixtures, we often encounter **linear** differential equations such as

$$\frac{dx}{dt} = kx \qquad \text{and} \qquad \frac{dx}{dt} = a + bx$$

or **nonlinear** differential equations such as

$$\frac{dx}{dt} = x(a - bx) \qquad \text{and} \qquad \frac{dx}{dt} = k(\alpha - x)(\beta - x).$$

The student should be able to find general solutions of these particular equations without hesitation. It is never a good idea simply to memorize solutions of differential equations.

REVIEW EXERCISES

Answers to odd-numbered problems begin on page A-9 of the Appendix.

[**3.1**]   **1.**   Find the orthogonal trajectories of the family of curves $y^3 = c_1 x^2$.

2.   Find the orthogonal trajectory to the family $y = 4x + 1 + c_1 e^{4x}$ passing through the point $(0, 0)$.

3. Find the orthogonal trajectories of the family of parabolas opening in the y-direction with vertex at $(1, 2)$.

[3.2] 4. If a population expands at a rate proportional to the number of people present at any time, show that the doubling time of the population is then

$$T = \frac{1}{k} \ln 2$$

where k is the positive growth rate. This is known as the **Law of Malthus.***

5. In March of 1976 the world population reached 4 billion. A popular news magazine has predicted that with an average yearly growth rate of 1.8%, the world population will be 8 billion in 45 years. How does this value compare with that predicted by the model which says that the rate of increase is proportional to the population at any time?

★6. Air containing 0.06% carbon dioxide is pumped into a room whose volume is 8000 ft^3. The rate at which the air is pumped in is 2000 ft^3/min, and the circulated air is then pumped out at the same rate. If there is an initial concentration of 0.2% carbon dioxide, determine the subsequent amount in the room at any time. What is the concentration at 10 minutes? What is the steady-state or equilibrium concentration of carbon-dioxide?

[3.3] 7. The populations of two competing species of animals are described by the nonlinear system of first-order differential equations

$$\frac{dx}{dt} = k_1 x(\alpha - x) \qquad \frac{dy}{dt} = k_2 xy.$$

Solve for x and y in terms of t.

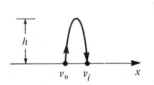

Figure 3.20

★8. A projectile is shot vertically into the air with an initial velocity of v_0 ft/sec. Assuming that air resistance is proportional to the square of the instantaneous velocity, the motion is described by the pair of differential equations:

$$m\frac{dv}{dt} = -mg - kv^2, \qquad k > 0,$$

positive y-axis up, origin at ground level so that $v = v_0$ at $y = 0$,

$$m\frac{dv}{dt} = mg - kv^2, \qquad k > 0,$$

positive y-axis down, origin at the maximum height so that $v = 0$ at $y = h$. The first and second equations describe the motion of the projectile when rising and falling, respectively. Prove that the impact velocity v_i of the projectile is less than the initial velocity v_0. It can also be shown that the time t_1 needed to attain its maximum height h is less than the time t_2 that it takes to fall from this height. See Figure 3.20

---

* Thomas R. Malthus (1766–1834) an English clergyman and economist.

CHAPTER 4

Linear Differential Equations of Higher Order

4.1 Preliminary Theory

4.1.1 Linear Dependence and Linear Independence

Homogeneous equations Recall from discussion in Section 1.2 that a linear nth-order differential equation has the form

$$a_n(x)y^{(n)} + a_{n-1}(x)y^{(n-1)} + \cdots + a_1(x)y' + a_0(x)y = g(x) \tag{1}$$

where the coefficients are functions of x only and $y^{(n)}$ means $d^n y/dx^n$. When $g(x) \neq 0$ we further say that the equation is **nonhomogeneous**, whereas an equation of the form

$$a_n(x)y^{(n)} + a_{n-1}(x)y^{(n-1)} + \cdots + a_1(x)y' + a_0(x)y = 0 \tag{2}$$

is said to be **homogeneous**. Note here that the word "homogeneous" does *not* mean the coefficients are homogeneous functions (see Section 2.2).

131

EXAMPLE   The equation

$$x^3 y'' - 2xy' + 5y = \sin x$$

is nonhomogeneous, while

$$x^3 y'' - 2xy' + 5y = 0$$

is a homogeneous linear second-order ordinary differential equation.

We shall see in the latter part of this section, as well as in the subsequent sections of this chapter, that in order to solve a nonhomogeneous equation (1) we must first solve the associated homogeneous equation (2).

THEOREM 4.1   If $y = y_1(x)$ is a solution of the homogeneous linear equation (2) then so is

$$y = c_1 y_1(x)$$

for any constant c_1.

The preceding theorem should be familiar to you from our discussion of linear first-order equations in Section 2.4. Theorem 4.1 merely says that any constant multiple of a solution is also a solution.

EXAMPLE   Theorem 4.1 need not be true when the equation is nonlinear. The function $y = 1/x$ is a solution of $y'' = 2y^3$ but $y = c/x$, $c \neq 0, \pm 1$, does not satisfy the equation since

$$y' = -\frac{c}{x^2}$$

$$y'' = \frac{2c}{x^3}$$

but

$$\frac{2c}{x^3} \neq \frac{2c^3}{x^3}.$$

EXAMPLE   It is easily verified that $y = x^2$ is a solution of the linear equation

$$x^2 y'' - 3xy' + 4y = 0.$$

Hence $y = cx^2$ is also a solution. For various values of c we see that $y = 3x^2$, $y = ex^2$, $y \equiv 0, \dots$ are all solutions of the equation.

The superposition principle

Observe that Theorem 4.1 implies that a homogeneous linear equation always possesses the trivial solution $y \equiv 0$. Also, Theorem 4.1 is just a special case of the following theorem known as the **superposition principle**.

THEOREM 4.2 If $y_1, y_2, \ldots, y_k$ are all solutions of the homogeneous linear differential equation (2) on an interval $a \leq x \leq b$, then the linear combination

$$y = c_1 y_1(x) + c_2 y_2(x) + \cdots + c_k y_k(x), \tag{3}$$

where the $c_i, i = 1, 2, \ldots, k$ are constants, is also a solution, on the interval.

Proof: We prove the case when $n = k = 2$. Let $y_1(x)$ and $y_2(x)$ be solutions of

$$a_2(x)y'' + a_1(x)y' + a_0(x)y = 0.$$

If we define $\qquad y = c_1 y_1(x) + c_2 y_2(x)$

then

$$a_2(x)[c_1 y_1'' + c_2 y_2''] + a_1(x)[c_1 y_1' + c_2 y_2'] + a_0(x)[c_1 y_1 + c_2 y_2]$$
$$= c_1 \underbrace{[a_2(x)y_1'' + a_1(x)y_1' + a_0(x)y_1]}_{\text{zero}} + c_2 \underbrace{[a_2(x)y_2'' + a_1(x)y_2' + a_0(x)y_2]}_{\text{zero}}$$

$$= c_1 \cdot 0 + c_2 \cdot 0$$

$$= 0.$$

EXAMPLE

The functions

$$y_1 = x^2 \qquad \text{and} \qquad y_2 = x^2 \ln x$$

both are solutions of the third-order equation

$$x^3 y''' - 2xy' + 4y = 0$$

for $x > 0$. By the superposition principle the linear combination

$$y = c_1 x^2 + c_2 x^2 \ln x$$

is also a solution of the equation for $x > 0$.

EXAMPLE

The functions $y_1 = e^x$, $y_2 = e^{2x}$ and $y_3 = e^{3x}$ all satisfy

$$\frac{d^3 y}{dx^3} - 6\frac{d^2 y}{dx^2} + 11\frac{dy}{dx} - 6y = 0.$$

By Theorem 4.2 another solution is

$$y = c_1 e^x + c_2 e^{2x} + c_3 e^{3x}.$$

Linear independence

In Chapter 1 we stipulated that a general solution of an nth-order differential equation should be an n-parameter family of functions. Specifically, we want a general solution of a linear differential equation to be a superposition of a set of **linearly independent** solutions. We first need the following definitions.

DEFINITION 4.1   A set of functions $f_1(x), f_2(x), \ldots, f_n(x)$ is said to be **linearly dependent** on some interval $a \leq x \leq b$, if and only if there exist constants $c_1, c_2, \ldots, c_n$, not all zero, such that

$$c_1 f_1(x) + c_2 f_2(x) + \cdots + c_n f_n(x) = 0 \qquad (4)$$

for every x in the interval.

DEFINITION 4.2   A set of functions $f_1(x), f_2(x), \ldots, f_n(x)$ is said to be **linearly independent** on some interval $a \leq x \leq b$, if and only if it is not linearly dependent on the interval.

In other words, a set of functions is linearly independent on an interval if the only constants for which

$$c_1 f_1(x) + c_2 f_2(x) + \cdots + c_n f_n(x) = 0,$$

for every x in the interval, are $c_1 = c_2 = \cdots = c_n = 0$.

It is easy to understand these definitions in the case of two functions $f_1(x)$ and $f_2(x)$. If the functions are linearly dependent on some interval then there exist constants c_1 and c_2 which are not both zero such that for every x in the interval

$$c_1 f_1(x) + c_2 f_2(x) = 0.$$

Therefore, if we assume that $c_1 \neq 0$, it then follows that

$$f_1(x) = -\frac{c_2}{c_1} f_2(x).$$

That is, *if two functions are linearly dependent then one is simply a constant multiple of the other.* Conversely, if $f_1(x) = c_2 f_2(x)$, for some constant c_2, then

$$1 \cdot f_1(x) + c_2 f_2(x) = 0$$

for every x on some interval. Hence the functions are linearly dependent since at least one of the constants (namely, $c_1 = 1$) is not zero. We conclude that two functions are linearly independent if and only if *neither* is a constant multiple of the other on some interval.

EXAMPLE

The functions $f_1(x) = \sin 2x$ and $f_2(x) = \sin x \cos x$ are linearly dependent on $-\infty < x < \infty$ since

$$c_1 \sin 2x + c_2 \sin x \cos x = 0$$

is satisfied for every real x if we choose $c_1 = 1/2$ and $c_2 = -1$. (Recall the trigonometric identity $\sin 2x = 2 \sin x \cos x$.)

EXAMPLE

Note that the functions $f_1(x) = 2$ and $f_2(x) = e^x$ satisfy at $x = 0$

$$f_1(0) = 2 \cdot f_2(0)$$

or

$$1 \cdot f_1(0) - 2 \cdot f_2(0) = 0.$$

This does not change the fact that f_1 and f_2 are linearly independent on $-\infty < x < \infty$ since the combination

$$c_1 f_1(x) + c_2 f_2(x)$$

cannot be made *identically zero* (that is, zero for every x) except by choosing $c_1 = 0$ and $c_2 = 0$.

EXAMPLE

The functions $f_1(x) = x$ and $f_2(x) = |x|$ are linearly dependent on $x \geq 0$ since on this interval

$$c_1 x + c_2 |x| = c_1 x + c_2 x = 0$$

is satisfied for any nonzero choice of c_1 and c_2 for which $c_1 = -c_2$.

EXAMPLE

The functions $f_1(x) = x$ and $f_2(x) = |x|$ are linearly independent on $-\infty < x < \infty$. Inspection of Figure 4.1 should convince the reader that neither function is a constant multiple of the other. Thus in order to have $c_1 f_1(x) + c_2 f_2(x) = 0$ for every real x we must choose $c_1 = 0$ and $c_2 = 0$.

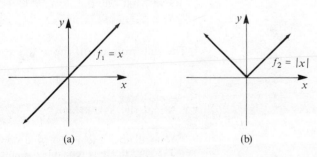

(a)   (b)

Figure 4.1

A set of functions $f_1(x)$, $f_2(x),\ldots,f_n(x)$ are linearly dependent on an interval if at least one function can be expressed as a nontrivial linear combination of the remaining functions.

EXAMPLE

The functions $f_1(x) = \sqrt{x} + 5$, $f_2(x) = \sqrt{x} + 5x$, $f_3(x) = x - 1$, $f_4(x) = x^2$ are linearly dependent on the interval $x \geq 0$ since

$$f_2(x) = 1 \cdot f_1(x) + 5 \cdot f_3(x) + 0 \cdot f_4(x)$$

for every x on the interval.

EXAMPLE

The functions $f_1(x) = \sin^2 x$, $f_2(x) = \cos^2 x$, $f_3(x) = \sec^2 x$, and $f_4(x) = \tan^2 x$ are linearly dependent on the interval $-\pi/2 < x < \pi/2$ since

$$c_1 \cos^2 x + c_2 \sin^2 x + c_3 \sec^2 x + c_4 \tan^2 x = 0$$

is obtained when $c_1 = c_2 = 1$, $c_3 = -1$, $c_4 = 1$. We note that $\cos^2 x + \sin^2 x = 1$ and $1 + \tan^2 x = \sec^2 x$.

4.1.2   The Wronskian

The following theorem provides a sufficient condition for the linear independence of n functions on an interval. Each function is assumed to be differentiable at least $n - 1$ times.

> **THEOREM 4.3**   Suppose $f_1(x)$, $f_2(x),\ldots,f_n(x)$ possess at least $n - 1$ derivatives. If
>
> $$\begin{vmatrix} f_1 & f_2 & \cdots & f_n \\ f'_1 & f'_2 & \cdots & f'_n \\ \vdots & \vdots & \vdots & \vdots \\ f_1^{(n-1)} & f_2^{(n-1)} & \cdots & f_n^{(n-1)} \end{vmatrix} \neq 0 \tag{5}$$
>
> for at least one point in the interval $a \leq x \leq b$, then the functions $f_1(x)$, $f_2(x),\ldots,f_n(x)$ are linearly independent on the interval.

The determinant in the above theorem is denoted by

$$W(f_1(x), f_2(x),\ldots,f_n(x))$$

and is called the **Wronskian*** of the functions.

---

* Named after the Polish philosopher-mathematician Josef M. H. Wronski (1778–1853). He is remembered solely because his name is associated with the above determinant.

Proof We prove Theorem 4.3 by contradiction for the case when $n = 2$. Assume that $W(f_1(x_0), f_2(x_0)) \neq 0$ for a fixed x_0 in the interval $a \leq x \leq b$ and that $f_1(x)$ and $f_2(x)$ are linearly dependent on the interval. The fact that the functions are linearly dependent means there exist constants c_1 and c_2, not both zero, for which

$$c_1 f_1(x) + c_2 f_2(x) = 0$$

for every x in $a \leq x \leq b$. Differentiating this combination then gives

$$c_1 f'_1(x) + c_2 f'_2(x) = 0.$$

Thus we obtain the system of linear equations

$$c_1 f_1(x) + c_2 f_2(x) = 0$$
$$c_1 f'_1(x) + c_2 f'_2(x) = 0. \tag{6}$$

But the linear dependence of f_1 and f_2 implies that (6) possesses a nontrivial solution for each x in the interval. Hence

$$W(f_1(x), f_2(x)) = \begin{vmatrix} f_1(x) & f_2(x) \\ f'_1(x) & f'_2(x) \end{vmatrix} = 0$$

for every x in $a \leq x \leq b$.* This contradicts the assumption that $W(f_1(x_0), f_2(x_0)) \neq 0$. We conclude that f_1 and f_2 are linearly independent.

COROLLARY If $f_1(x), f_2(x), \ldots, f_n(x)$ possess at least $n - 1$ derivatives and are linearly dependent on $a \leq x \leq b$ then the Wronskian of the functions is zero for every x in the interval. That is,

$$W(f_1(x), f_2(x), \ldots, f_n(x)) \equiv 0$$

on the interval.

---

* Recall, a system

$$ax + by = 0$$
$$cx + dy = 0$$

has nontrivial solutions for x and y if and only if the determinant of the coefficients is zero.

EXAMPLE   The functions $f_1(x) = \sin^2 x$ and $f_2(x) = 1 - \cos 2x$ are linearly dependent on $-\infty < x < \infty$. Hence

$$W(\sin^2 x, 1 - \cos 2x) = \begin{vmatrix} \sin^2 x & 1 - \cos 2x \\ 2 \sin x \cos x & 2 \sin 2x \end{vmatrix}$$

$$= 2 \sin^2 x \sin 2x - 2 \sin x \cos x + 2 \sin x \cos x \cos 2x$$

$$= \sin 2x [2 \sin^2 x - 1 + \cos 2x]$$

$$= \sin 2x [2 \sin^2 x - 1 + \cos^2 x - \sin^2 x]$$

$$= \sin 2x [\sin^2 x + \cos^2 x - 1]$$

$$\equiv 0.$$

EXAMPLE   For $f_1(x) = e^{m_1 x}, f_2(x) = e^{m_2 x}, m_1 \neq m_2$

$$W(e^{m_1 x}, e^{m_2 x}) = \begin{vmatrix} e^{m_1 x} & e^{m_2 x} \\ m_1 e^{m_1 x} & m_2 e^{m_2 x} \end{vmatrix}$$

$$= (m_2 - m_1) e^{(m_1 + m_2)x}$$

$$\neq 0$$

for every real value of x. Thus f_1 and f_2 are linearly independent on any interval of the x-axis.

EXAMPLE   If α and β are real numbers, $\beta \neq 0$, then $y_1 = e^{\alpha x} \cos \beta x$ and $y_2 = e^{\alpha x} \sin \beta x$ are linearly independent on the x-axis since

$$W(e^{\alpha x} \cos \beta x, e^{\alpha x} \sin \beta x) = \begin{vmatrix} e^{\alpha x} \cos \beta x & e^{\alpha x} \sin \beta x \\ -\beta e^{\alpha x} \sin \beta x + \alpha e^{\alpha x} \cos \beta x & \beta e^{\alpha x} \cos \beta x + \alpha e^{\alpha x} \sin \beta x \end{vmatrix}$$

$$= \beta e^{2\alpha x} (\cos^2 \beta x + \sin^2 \beta x)$$

$$= \beta e^{2\alpha x}$$

$$\neq 0.$$

Notice when $\alpha = 0$ we see that $\cos \beta x$ and $\sin \beta x$, $\beta \neq 0$, are also linearly independent on any interval of the x-axis.

EXAMPLE

The functions $f_1(x) = e^x$, $f_2(x) = xe^x$, and $f_3(x) = x^2 e^x$ are linearly independent on any interval of the x-axis since

$$W(e^x, xe^x, x^2 e^x) = \begin{vmatrix} e^x & xe^x & x^2 e^x \\ e^x & xe^x + e^x & x^2 e^x + 2xe^x \\ e^x & xe^x + 2e^x & x^2 e^x + 4xe^x + 2e^x \end{vmatrix} = 2e^{3x}$$

is not zero for any real value of x.

EXAMPLE

On page 135 we have seen that $f_1(x) = x$ and $f_2(x) = |x|$ are linearly independent on $-\infty < x < \infty$, however, we cannot compute the Wronskian since f_2 is not differentiable at $x = 0$.

EXAMPLE

$$W(x, xe^x) = \begin{vmatrix} x & xe^x \\ 1 & xe^x + e^x \end{vmatrix} = x^2 e^x.$$

Although $W = 0$ at $x = 0$, it is sufficient to observe that $W \neq 0$ for *at least one* other value of x on $-\infty < x < \infty$. Thus $f_1(x) = x$ and $f_2(x) = xe^x$ are linearly independent on the x-axis.

We leave it as an exercise (see Problem 4) to show that a set of functions could be linearly independent on some interval and yet have a vanishing Wronskian. In other words, $W(f_1(x), f_2(x), \ldots, f_n(x)) \equiv 0$ does not necessarily mean the functions are linearly dependent.

Solutions of linear equations

In particular we are interested in determining when n solutions, $y_1, y_2, \ldots, y_n$, of the *homogeneous* linear nth-order differential equation (2) are linearly independent. Surprisingly the nonvanishing of the Wronskian of a set of n such solutions on an interval $a \leq x \leq b$ is both necessary and sufficient for linear independence.

To avoid needless repetition throughout the remainder of this text we shall make the following important assumptions when referring to and proving theorems about linear equations. On some interval $a \leq x \leq b$

(A) the coefficients $a_i(x)$, $i = 1, 2, \ldots, n$ are continuous;
(B) the right-hand member $g(x)$ is continuous;
(C) and $a_n(x) \neq 0$ for every x in the interval.

THEOREM 4.4   Let $y_1, y_2, \ldots, y_n$ be n solutions of the homogeneous linear equation (2) on an interval $a \leq x \leq b$. Then the set of solutions is linearly independent on $a \leq x \leq b$ if and only if

$$W(y_1, y_2, \ldots, y_n) \neq 0$$

for every x in the interval.

Proof   We prove Theorem 4.4 for the case when $n = 2$. First, if $W(y_1, y_2) \neq 0$ for every x in $a \leq x \leq b$ it follows immediately from Theorem 4.3 that y_1 and y_2 are linearly independent. Next, we must show that if y_1 and y_2 are linearly independent solutions of a homogeneous linear second-order differential equation for which conditions A and C hold, then $W(y_1, y_2) \neq 0$ for every x in $a \leq x \leq b$. To show this, let us suppose y_1 and y_2 are linearly independent and there is some fixed x_0 in $a \leq x \leq b$ for which $W(y_1(x_0), y_2(x_0)) = 0$. Hence there must exist c_1 and c_2, not both zero, such that

$$c_1 y_1(x_0) + c_2 y_2(x_0) = 0$$
$$c_1 y_1'(x_0) + c_2 y_2'(x_0) = 0. \tag{7}$$

If we define

$$y(x) = c_1 y_1(x) + c_2 y_2(x)$$

then in view of (7), $y(x)$ must also satisfy

$$y(x_0) = 0$$
$$y'(x_0) = 0. \tag{8}$$

But the identically zero function satisfies both the differential equation and the initial conditions (8), and thus by Theorem 1.2 it is the unique solution. In other words $y \equiv 0$ or

$$c_1 y_1(x) + c_2 y_2(x) = 0$$

for every x in $a \leq x \leq b$. This contradicts the assumption that y_1 and y_2 are linearly independent on the interval.

From the foregoing discussion we conclude that when $y_1, y_2, \ldots, y_n$ are n solutions of (2) on an interval $a \leq x \leq b$, either the Wronskian is identically zero or is never zero on the interval.

DEFINITION 4.3   Let $y_1, y_2, \ldots, y_n$ be linearly independent solutions of the homogeneous linear differential equation (2) on an interval $a \leq x \leq b$. We define the **general solution** of the equation on the interval to be

$$y = c_1 y_1(x) + c_2 y_2(x) + \cdots + c_n y_n(x),$$

where the $c_i, i = 1, 2, \ldots, n$ are arbitrary constants.

EXAMPLE   The functions $y_1 = e^x, y_2 = e^{2x}$, and $y_3 = e^{3x}$ satisfy the equation

$$\frac{d^3 y}{dx^3} - 6\frac{d^2 y}{dx^2} + 11\frac{dy}{dx} - 6y = 0.$$

Since

$$W(e^x, e^{2x}, e^{3x}) = \begin{vmatrix} e^x & e^{2x} & 3^{3x} \\ e^x & 2e^{2x} & 3e^{3x} \\ e^x & 4e^{2x} & 9e^{3x} \end{vmatrix}$$

$$= e^x(18e^{5x} - 12e^{5x}) - e^{2x}(9e^{4x} - 3e^{4x}) + e^{3x}(4e^{3x} - 2e^{3x})$$

$$= 2e^{6x}$$

$$\neq 0$$

for every real value of x, the combination

$$y = c_1 e^x + c_2 e^{2x} + c_3 e^{3x}$$

is the general solution of the differential equation on $-\infty < x < \infty$.

EXAMPLE

We have seen that $W(\cos \beta x, \sin \beta x) = \beta$. Since $y_1 = \cos \beta x$ and $y_2 = \sin \beta x$, $\beta \neq 0$, satisfy the linear equation

$$y'' + \beta^2 y = 0$$

its general solution on $-\infty < x < \infty$ must be

$$y = c_1 \cos \beta x + c_2 \sin \beta x.$$

The preceding definition is, of course, consistent with the definition used in Section 1.1. It also reflects what one would intuitively expect from a "general" solution: it includes *every* possible solution of a homogeneous linear equation on the interval $a \leq x \leq b$ for which conditions A and C hold. With these conditions in mind we can prove the following:

THEOREM 4.5   Let $y_1, y_2, \ldots, y_n$ be linearly independent solutions of the homogeneous linear differential (2) on an interval $a \leq x \leq b$. If $Y(x)$ is any solution of the equation on the interval we can find constants $C_1, C_2, \ldots, C_n$ such that

$$Y = C_1 y_1(x) + C_2 y_2(x) + \cdots + C_n y_n(x).$$

Proof   We prove the case when $n = 2$. Let Y be a solution, and let y_1 and y_2 be linearly independent solutions of

$$a_2(x)y'' + a_1(x)y' + a_0(x)y = 0$$

on an interval $a \leq x \leq b$ for which conditions A and C hold. Suppose $x = t$ is a point in this interval for which $W(y_1(t), y_2(t)) \neq 0$. Suppose also that the values of $Y(t)$ and $Y'(t)$ are given by

$$Y(t) = k_1$$
$$Y'(t) = k_2.$$

If we now examine the system of equations

$$C_1 y_1(t) + C_2 y_2(t) = k_1$$
$$C_1 y_1'(t) + C_2 y_2'(t) = k_2,$$

it follows that we can determine C_1 and C_2 uniquely provided the determinant of the coefficients satisfies

$$\begin{vmatrix} y_1(t) & y_2(t) \\ y_1'(t) & y_2'(t) \end{vmatrix} \neq 0.$$

But this latter determinant is simply the Wronskian evaluated at $x = t$, and by assumption $W \neq 0$. If we now define the function

$$G(x) = C_1 y_1(x) + C_2 y_2(x)$$

we then observe:

(i) $G(x)$ satisfies the differential equation since it is the superposition of two known solutions y_1 and y_2,

(ii) $G(x)$ satisfies the initial conditions

$$G(t) = C_1 y_1(t) + C_2 y_2(t) = k_1$$
$$G'(t) = C_1 y_1'(t) + C_2 y_2'(t) = k_2,$$

(iii) $Y(x)$ satisfies the *same* linear equation and the *same* initial conditions.

Since the solution of this linear initial-value problem is unique (Theorem 1.2) we have

$$Y(x) \equiv G(x)$$
$$= C_1 y_1(x) + C_2 y_2(x).$$

EXAMPLE   The equation

$$y'' - 9y = 0$$

possesses two linearly independent solutions

$$y_1 = e^{3x}, \qquad y_2 = e^{-3x}.$$

The function $y = 4 \sinh 3x - 5e^{-3x}$ also satisfies the equation. By choosing $c_1 = 2$, $c_2 = -7$ in the general solution

$$y = c_1 e^{3x} + c_2 e^{-3x}$$

we obtain

$$y = 2e^{3x} - 7e^{-3x}$$

$$= 2e^{3x} - 2e^{-3x} - 5e^{-3x}$$

$$= 4\left(\frac{e^{3x} - e^{-3x}}{2}\right) - 5e^{-3x}$$

$$= 4 \sinh 3x - 5e^{-3x}.$$

Particular solutions

We now turn our attention to defining the general solution of a *nonhomogeneous* linear equation. Any function y_p, free of arbitrary parameters, which satisfies equation (1) is said to be a **particular solution** (sometimes also called a *particular integral*).

EXAMPLES

(a)   A particular solution of

$$y'' + 9y = 27$$

is $y_p = 3$ since $y_p'' = 0$, and $0 + 9y_p = 9(3) = 27$.

(b) $y_p = x^3 - x$ is a particular solution of

$$x^2 y'' + 2xy' - 8y = 4x^3 + 6x$$

since $y_p' = 3x^2 - 1$, $y_p'' = 6x$, and

$$x^2 y_p'' + 2x y_p' - 8y_p = x^2(6x) + 2x(3x^2 - 1) - 8(x^3 - x)$$

$$= 4x^3 + 6x.$$

(c)   We leave it as an exercise to verify that

$$y_p = x \sin x + (\cos x) \ln |\cos x|$$

is a particular solution of the equation

$$y'' + y = \sec x.$$

Complementary function

If $y_1, y_2, \ldots, y_n$ are linearly independent solutions of the *homogeneous equation* (2), we shall then say that the linear combination

$$y_c = c_1 y_1(x) + c_2 y_2(x) + \cdots + c_n y_n(x)$$

is the **complementary function** of the *nonhomogeneous equation* (1). We are now in a position to make the following definition.

> **DEFINITION 4.4**   For $g(x) \neq 0$ we define the **general solution** of equation (1) on an interval, $a \leq x \leq b$ to be
>
> $$y = y_c + y_p.$$

EXAMPLE   The function

$$y_p = -\frac{11}{12} - \frac{1}{2}x$$

satisfies the equation

$$\frac{d^3y}{dx^3} - 6\frac{d^2y}{dx^2} + 11\frac{dy}{dx} - 6y = 3x.$$

In order to write down the general solution of the above equation we must also be able to solve the associated homogeneous equation

$$\frac{d^3y}{dx^3} - 6\frac{d^2y}{dx^2} + 11\frac{dy}{dx} - 6y = 0.$$

But on page 141 we saw that the general solution of this latter equation was

$$y_c = c_1e^x + c_2e^{2x} + c_3e^{3x}.$$

Hence the general solution of the given equation on $-\infty < x < \infty$ is

$$y = y_c + y_p$$

$$= c_1e^x + c_2e^{2x} + c_3e^{3x} - \frac{11}{12} - \frac{1}{2}x.$$

We note that the function y_p is a particular solution of equation (1) in the same sense that we defined this term in Chapter 1. By choosing all constants c_i to be zero in the general solution $y = y_c + y_p$ we necessarily recover y_p.

Under conditions A, B, and C we can prove the following analogue of Theorem 4.5.

> **THEOREM 4.6**   Let $Y(x)$ be any solution of the nonhomogeneous equation (1) on an interval $a \leq x \leq b$. Then we can always find constants $C_1, C_2, \ldots, C_n$ such that
>
> $$Y = C_1y_1(x) + C_2y_2(x) + \cdots + C_ny_n(x) + y_p(x)$$
>
> where the y_i, $i = 1, 2, \ldots, n$ are the linearly independent solutions of the associated homogeneous equation.

Proof We prove the case when $n = 2$. Suppose Y and y_p are both solutions of

$$a_2(x)y'' + a_1(x)y' + a_0(x)y = g(x).$$

If we define a function u by

$$u(x) = Y(x) - y_p(x)$$

then $a_2(x)u'' + a_1(x)u' + a_0(x)u$

$$= a_2(x)[Y'' - y_p''] + a_1(x)[Y' - y_p'] + a_0(x)[Y - y_p]$$

$$= a_2(x)Y'' + a_1(x)Y' + a_0(x)Y - [a_2(x)y_p'' + a_1(x)y_p' + a_0(x)y_p]$$

$$= g(x) - g(x)$$

$$= 0.$$

Therefore, in view of Definition 4.3 and Theorem 4.5 we can write

$$u(x) = C_1y_1(x) + C_2y_2(x) + \cdots + C_ny_n(x)$$

$$Y(x) - y_p(x) = C_1y_1(x) + C_2y_2(x) + \cdots + C_ny_n(x)$$

or $\qquad Y(x) = C_1y_1(x) + C_2y_2(x) + \cdots + C_ny_n(x) + y_p(x).$

EXERCISES 4.1

Answers to odd-numbered problems begin on page A-9 of the Appendix.

[4.1.1]

1. Determine whether the following functions are linearly independent or dependent on $-\infty < x < \infty$.

   (a) $f_1(x) = x$, $\ f_2(x) = x^2$, $\ f_3(x) = 4x - 3x^2$
   (b) $f_1(x) = 0$, $\ f_2(x) = x$, $\ f_3(x) = e^x$
   (c) $f_1(x) = 5$, $\ f_2(x) = \cos^2 x$, $\ f_3(x) = \sin^2 x$
   (d) $f_1(x) = \cos 2x$, $\ f_2(x) = \sin 2x$, $\ f_3(x) = \sin^2 x$
   (e) $f_1(x) = x$, $\ f_2(x) = x - 1$, $\ f_3(x) = x + 3$
   (f) $f_1(x) = 2 + x$, $\ f_2(x) = 2 + |x|$
   (g) $f_1(x) = 1 + x$, $\ f_2(x) = x$, $\ f_3(x) = x^2$
   (h) $f_1(x) = e^{ix}$, $\ f_2(x) = -e^{-ix}$, $\ i^2 = -1$
   (i) $f_1(x) = e^x$, $\ f_2(x) = e^{-x}$, $\ f_3(x) = \sinh x$

2. Show that $y = x^2$ is a solution of the differential equation

$$y'' - 2x^2y^{-1} = 0$$

but that $y = cx^2$ is not a solution for $c \neq 1$.

3. Given $y_1 = e^{2x}$, $y_2 = e^{-2x}$, and $y_3 = e^x$ are linearly independent solutions of the differential equation

$$\frac{d^3y}{dx^3} - \frac{d^2y}{dx^2} - 4\frac{dy}{dx} + 4y = 0$$

on $-\infty < x < \infty$.

(a)   Explain   why $y_4 = -10e^{2x}$, $y_5 = 8e^x$, $y_6 = 4e^{-2x} + 6e^x$,
       $y_7 = \cosh 2x$, and $y_8 = \sinh 2x$ are also solutions of the equation.

(b)   Use Definitions 4.1 and 4.2 to determine which of the following sets
       of solutions are linearly dependent or linearly independent on
       $-\infty < x < \infty$:

Dependent

(i) y_3, y_5 (ii) y_3, y_6 (iii) y_1, y_2, y_4
(iv) y_1, y_2, y_8 (v) y_2, y_3, y_6 (vi) y_4, y_5, y_6.

[4.1.2]   ★**4.**   (a)   Show graphically that

$$f_1(x) = x^2 \quad \text{and} \quad f_2(x) = x|x|$$

are linearly independent on $-\infty < x < \infty$.

(b)   Show that

$$W(f_1(x), f_2(x)) \equiv 0,$$

that is, $W = 0$ for every real value of x.

5.   (a)   Verify that

$$y_1 = x^3 \quad \text{and} \quad y_2 = |x|^3$$

are linearly independent solutions of the differential equation
$x^2 y'' - 3xy' + 3y = 0$ on $-\infty < x < \infty$.

(b)   Show that $W(y_1, y_2) \equiv 0$.
(c)   Does the result of part (b) violate Theorem 4.4?

★**6.**   (a)   Verify that

$$Y_1 = x^3 \quad \text{and} \quad Y_2 = x$$

are linearly independent solutions of $x^2 y'' - 3xy' + 3y = 0$ on
$-\infty < x < \infty$.

(b)   If y_1 and y_2 are linearly independent functions defined in Problem 5,
       is

$$y = c_1 y_1 + c_2 y_2 \quad \text{or} \quad y = c_1 Y_1 + c_2 Y_2,$$

both, or neither the general solution of the given differential
equation?

7.   Verify that

$$y_1 = x^4 \cos(3 \ln x) \quad \text{and} \quad y_2 = x^4 \sin(3 \ln x)$$

are linearly independent solutions of $x^2 y'' - 7xy' + 25y = 0$ for $x > 0$.
[*Hint:* Rather than expanding the determinant (5) for every x, recall it is
sufficient to show that $W \neq 0$ for, say, $x = 1$.]

★**8.** Prove that the indicated function is the general solution of the given differential equation.

(a) $y'' - y' - 12y = 0$;
$y = c_1 e^{4x} + c_2 e^{-3x}$, $-\infty < x < \infty$

(b) $y'' - 2y' + 5y = 0$;
$y = c_1 e^x \cos 2x + c_2 e^x \sin 2x$, $-\infty < x < \infty$

(c) $4y'' - 4y' + y = 0$;
$y = c_1 e^{x/2} + c_2 x e^{x/2}$, $-\infty < x < \infty$

(d) $y^{(4)} + y'' = 0$;
$y = c_1 + c_2 x + c_3 \cos x + c_4 \sin x$, $-\infty < x < \infty$

(e) $x^2 y'' - 6xy' + 12y = 0$;
$y = c_1 x^3 + c_2 x^4$, $x > 0$

(f) $x^3 y''' + 6x^2 y'' + 4xy' - 4y = 0$;
$y = c_1 x + c_2 x^{-2} + c_3 x^{-2} \ln x$, $x > 0$

(g) $x^2 y'' + xy' + y = 0$;
$y = c_1 \cos(\ln x) + c_2 \sin(\ln x)$, $x > 0$

9. Let y_1 and y_2 be two solutions of

$$a_2(x)y'' + a_1(x)y' + a_0(x)y = 0$$

where $a_2(x)$, $a_1(x)$, $a_0(x)$ are continuous, and $a_2(x) \neq 0$ for every x in some interval $a \leq x \leq b$.

(a) If $W(y_1, y_2)$ is the Wronskian of y_1 and y_2, show that

$$a_2(x)\frac{dW}{dx} + a_1(x)W = 0.$$

(b) Derive **Abel's formula***

$$W = ce^{-\int [a_1(x)/a_2(x)]\,dx}$$

where c is a constant.

(c) Using an alternative form of Abel's formula

$$W = ce^{-\int_{x_0}^x [a_1(t)/a_2(t)]\,dt},$$

for x_0 in $a \leq x \leq b$, show that

$$W(y_1, y_2) = W(x_0)e^{-\int_{x_0}^x [a_1(t)/a_2(t)]\,dt}.$$

---

* Niels Henrik Abel (1802–1829) a brilliant Norwegian mathematician whose tragic death at age 26 was an unestimable loss for mathematics.

(d) Show that if $W(x_0) = 0$, then $W = 0$ for every x in $a \leq x \leq b$; whereas if $W(x_0) \neq 0$, then $W \neq 0$ for every x in the interval.

In Problems 10 and 11 use the results of Problem 9.

10. If y_1 and y_2 are two solutions of

$$(1 - x^2)y'' - 2xy' + n(n + 1)y = 0$$

on $-1 < x < 1$, show that

$$W(y_1, y_2) = \frac{c}{1 - x^2}$$

where c is a constant.

11. In Chapter 6 we shall see that the solutions y_1 and y_2 of $xy'' + y' + xy = 0$, for $x > 0$, are infinite series. Suppose we consider initial conditions

$$y_1(x_0) = k_1 \qquad\qquad y_2(x_0) = k_3$$
$$\text{and}$$
$$y_1'(x_0) = k_2 \qquad\qquad y_2'(x_0) = k_4$$

for $x_0 > 0$. Show that

$$W(y_1, y_2) = \frac{(k_1 k_4 - k_2 k_3)x_0}{x}.$$

12. Verify that the indicated function is a particular solution of the given differential equation.
    (a) $y'' + 6y' - 4y = 10$; $y_p = -5/2$
    (b) $y''' - 5y'' + 6y' = 12x - 10$; $y_p = x^2$
    (c) $x^2 y''' + 3xy'' + 4y' = 3x^{-1}$; $y_p = \ln x, x > 0$
    (d) $3y'' - 2y' - 4y = -8x^2 + 8x + 16$; $y_p = 2x^2 - 4x + 1$
    (e) $y'' - 4y' + 4y = 2e^{2x} + 4x - 12$; $y_p = x^2 e^{2x} + x - 1$
    (f) $y'' + y = \sec x$; $y = x \sin x + (\cos x) \ln |\cos x|$

13. Determine which of the following functions is the general solution of the nonhomogeneous equation $y''' + 4y' = 4x + 12$ on $-\infty < x < \infty$.
    (a) $y = c_1 + c_2 \cos 2x + c_3 \sin 2x + \frac{1}{2}x^2 + 3x$
    (b) $y = c_1 + c_2 \sin 2x + c_3 \sin^2 x + \frac{1}{2}x^2 + 3x$
    (c) $y = c_1 + c_2 \cos 2x + c_3 \sin x \cos x + \frac{1}{2}x^2 + 3x + 5$
    (d) $y = c_1 + c_2 \cos 2x + c_3 \sin^2 x + \frac{1}{2}x^2 + 3x$
    (e) $y = c_1 + c_2 e^{2ix} + c_2 e^{-2ix} + \frac{1}{2}x^2 + 3x,\quad i^2 = -1$

4.2 Constructing a Second Solution from a Known Solution

Reduction of order

It is one of the more interesting, as well as important, facts of life in the study of linear second-order differential equations that we can construct a second, and linearly independent, solution from a *known* solution. Suppose $y_1(x)$ is a nontrivial solution of the equation

$$a_2(x)y'' + a_1(x)y' + a_0(x)y = 0. \tag{1}$$

The process we shall use to find a second solution $y_2(x)$ consists of **reducing the order** of equation (1) to a first-order equation. For example, it is easily verified that $y_1 = e^x$ satisfies the differential equation $y'' - y = 0$. If we try to determine a solution of the form $y = u(x)e^x$ then

$$y' = ue^x + e^x u'$$

$$y'' = ue^x + 2e^x u' + e^x u''$$

and so

$$y'' - y = e^x(u'' + 2u') = 0.$$

Since $e^x \neq 0$ this last equation requires that $u'' + 2u' = 0$.

If we let $w = u'$, then the latter equation is recognized as a linear first-order equation in w: $w' + 2w = 0$. Using the integrating factor e^{2x} we can write

$$\frac{d}{dx}[e^{2x}w] = 0$$

and thus

$$w = c_1 e^{-2x}$$

$$\frac{du}{dx} = c_1 e^{-2x}$$

$$u = -\frac{c_1}{2}e^{-2x} + c_2.$$

Hence we obtain

$$y = u(x)e^x$$

$$= -\frac{c_1}{2}e^{-x} + c_2 e^x.$$

By picking $c_2 = 0$ and $c_1 = -2$, we obtain the second solution $y_2 = e^{-x}$. Since $W(e^x, e^{-x}) \neq 0$ for every x the solutions are linearly independent on $-\infty < x < \infty$ and thus the expression for y is actually the general solution of the given equation.

The general case   Suppose we divide* by $a_2(x)$ in order to put equation (1) in the form

$$y'' + P(x)y' + Q(x)y = 0. \tag{2}$$

---

* We naturally assume, as we did in the preceding section, that the coefficients in (1) are continuous and $a_2(x) \neq 0$ for every x in some interval $a \leq x \leq b$.

Let us suppose further that $y_1(x)$ is a known solution of (2) on some interval and that $y_1(x) \neq 0$ for every x in the interval. If we define $y = u(x)y_1(x)$, then it follows that

$$y' = uy'_1 + y_1u'$$

$$y'' = uy''_1 + 2y'_1u' + y_1u''$$

$$y'' + Py' + Qy = u\underbrace{[y''_1 + Py'_1 + Qy_1]}_{\text{zero}} + y_1u'' + (2y'_1 + Py_1)u' = 0.$$

This implies we must have

$$y_1u'' + (2y'_1 + Py_1)u' = 0$$

or
$$y_1w' + (2y'_1 + Py_1)w = 0 \qquad (3)$$

where we have let $w = u'$. Observe that equation (3) is both linear and separable. Applying the latter technique we obtain

$$\frac{dw}{w} + 2\frac{y'_1}{y_1}dx + P\,dx = 0$$

$$\ln|w| + 2\ln|y_1| = -\int P\,dx + c$$

$$\ln|wy_1^2| = -\int P\,dx + c$$

$$wy_1^2 = c_1e^{-\int P\,dx}$$

$$w = c_1\frac{e^{-\int P\,dx}}{y_1^2}$$

$$\frac{du}{dx} = c_1\frac{e^{-\int P\,dx}}{y_1^2}$$

$$u = c_1\int\frac{e^{-\int P\,dx}}{y_1^2}dx + c_2.$$

And finally we have

$$y = u(x)y_1(x)$$

$$= c_1y_1(x)\int\frac{e^{-\int P(x)\,dx}}{y_1^2(x)}dx + c_2y_1(x)$$

By choosing $c_2 = 0$ and $c_1 = 1$, we find that a second solution of equation (2) is

$$\boxed{y_2 = y_1(x)\int\frac{e^{-\int P(x)\,dx}}{y_1^2(x)}dx.} \qquad (4)$$

It makes a good review exercise in differentiation to start with equation (4) and actually verify that equation (2) is satisfied.

Now $y_1(x)$ and $y_2(x)$ are linearly independent since

$$W(y_1(x), y_2(x)) = \begin{vmatrix} y_1 & y_1 \int \dfrac{e^{-\int P\,dx}}{y_1^2}\,dx \\[4mm] y_1' & \dfrac{e^{-\int P\,dx}}{y_1} + y_1' \int \dfrac{e^{-\int P\,dx}}{y_1^2}\,dx \end{vmatrix} = e^{-\int P\,dx}$$

which is not zero on any interval that $y_1(x)$ is not zero.*

EXAMPLE   The function

$$y_1 = x^2$$

is a solution of $x^2 y'' - 3xy' + 4y = 0$. Find the general solution.

Solution: Since the equation has the alternative form

$$y'' - \frac{3}{x}y' + \frac{4}{x^2}y = 0$$

we find

$$y_2 = x^2 \int \frac{e^{3\int dx/x}}{x^4}\,dx$$

$$= x^2 \int \frac{dx}{x}$$

$$= x^2 \ln|x|.$$

The general solution is

$$y = c_1 y_1 + c_2 y_2$$

$$= c_1 x^2 + c_2 x^2 \ln|x|.$$

In the foregoing example keep in mind we are working on an interval for which $y_1 \neq 0$; in this case $x > 0$ or $x < 0$ will suffice.

EXAMPLE   It can be verified that

$$y_1 = \frac{\sin x}{\sqrt{x}}$$

is a solution of $x^2 y'' + xy' + (x^2 - \frac{1}{4})y = 0$ on $0 < x < \pi$. Find a second solution.

---

* Alternatively, if $y_2 = u(x)y_1$ then $W(y_1, y_2) = u'(y_1)^2 \neq 0$, since $y_1 \neq 0$ for every x on some interval. If $u' = 0$, then $u = $ constant.

Solution: First put the equation into the form

$$y'' + \frac{1}{x}y' + \left(1 - \frac{1}{4x^2}\right)y = 0.$$

Then by formula (4) we have

$$y_2 = \frac{\sin x}{\sqrt{x}} \int \frac{e^{-\int dx/x}}{\left(\dfrac{\sin x}{\sqrt{x}}\right)^2} dx$$

$$= \frac{\sin x}{\sqrt{x}} \int \csc^2 x \, dx \qquad [e^{-\int dx/x} = e^{\ln x^{-1}} = x^{-1}]$$

$$= \frac{\sin x}{\sqrt{x}}(-\cot x)$$

$$= -\frac{\cos x}{\sqrt{x}}.$$

Since the differential equation is homogeneous, we can disregard the negative sign and take the second solution to be $y_2 = \cos x/\sqrt{x}$.

Observe that $y_1(x)$ and $y_2(x)$ of the previous example are linearly independent solutions of the given differential equation on the larger interval $x > 0$.

EXERCISES 4.2

Answers to odd-numbered problems begin on page A-11 of the Appendix. In Problems 1-15 use formula (4) to find a second linearly independent solution of each differential equation.

1. $y'' + 4y' = 0$; $y_1 = 1$ **2.** $y'' + 2y' + y = 0$; $y_1 = xe^x$

3. $y'' - 4y' + 4y = 0$; $y_1 = e^{2x}$ **4.** $y'' + 9y = 0$; $y_1 = \sin 3x$

5. $y'' - y = 0$; $y_1 = \cosh x$

6. $6y'' + y' - y = 0$; $y_1 = e^{x/3}$

7. $9y'' - 12y' + 4y = 0$; $y_1 = e^{2x/3}$

8. $x^2 y'' + 2xy' - 6y = 0$; $y_1 = x^2$

9. $x^2 y'' - 7xy' + 16y = 0$; $y_1 = x^4$

★10. $4x^2 y'' + y = 0$; $y_1 = x^{1/2} \ln x$

11. $(1 - 2x - x^2)y'' + 2(1 + x)y' - 2y = 0$; $y_1 = x + 1$

12. $(1 - x^2)y'' - 2xy' = 0$; $y_1 = 1$

13. $x^2 y'' - xy' + 2y = 0$; $y_1 = x \sin(\ln x)$

★**14.** $(1 + x)y'' + xy' - y = 0;$ $y_1 = x$

15. $(1 + 2x)y'' + 4xy' - 4y = 0;$ $y_1 = e^{-2x}$

In Problems 16–21 use the substitution $y_2 = u(x)y_1(x)$, where $y_1(x)$ is a known solution, to reduce the order of each differential equation. Solve for $y_2(x)$.

EXAMPLE

$$x^2 y'' - 6y = 0;   y_1 = x^3$$

Solution: Define

$$y_2 = u(x)x^3$$

so that

$$y_2' = 3x^2 u + x^3 u'$$

$$y_2'' = 3x^2 u' + 6xu + x^3 u'' + 3x^2 u'$$

$$= x^3 u'' + 6x^2 u' + 6xu$$

$$x^2 y_2'' - 6y_2 = x^2(x^3 u'' + 6x^2 u' + 6xu) - 6ux^3$$

$$= x^5 u'' + 6x^4 u'$$

$$= 0$$

provided $u(x)$ is a solution of

$$x^5 u'' + 6x^4 u' = 0   \text{or}   u'' + \frac{6}{x}u' = 0.$$

If we let $w = u'$, we then obtain the linear first-order equation

$$w' + \frac{6}{x}w = 0$$

which possesses the integrating factor $e^{6 \int dx/x} = e^{6 \ln x} = x^6$. It follows that

$$\frac{d}{dx}[x^6 w] = 0$$

$$x^6 w = c$$

$$w = \frac{c}{x^6}$$

$$u' = \frac{c}{x^6}$$

$$u = -\frac{c}{5x^5}.$$

Since in this case a constant multiple of a solution is also a solution we may disregard $-c/5$ and simply write

$$y_2 = u(x)x^3$$

$$= \left(\frac{1}{x^5}\right)x^3$$

$$= x^{-2}.$$

16. $x^2y'' - 20y = 0$; $\quad y_1 = x^{-4}$ **17.** $x^2y'' - xy' + y = 0$; $\quad y_1 = x$

18. $x^2y'' + xy' + y = 0$; $\quad y_1 = \cos(\ln x)$

19. $x^2y'' - 4xy' + 6y = 0$; $\quad y_1 = x^2 + x^3$

20. $xy'' - (x + 1)y' + y = 0$; $\quad y_1 = e^x$

21. $y'' - 3(\tan x)y' = 0$; $\quad y_1 = 1$

★**22.** By direct substitution verify that formula (4) satisfies equation (2).

4.3 Homogeneous Linear Equations with Constant Coefficients

We have seen that the linear first-order equation $dy/dx + ay = 0$, where a is a constant, has the exponential solution $y = c_1 e^{-ax}$ on $-\infty < x < \infty$. Therefore it is natural to seek to determine whether exponential solutions exist on $-\infty < x < \infty$ for higher order equations such as

$$a_n y^{(n)} + a_{n-1} y^{(n-1)} + \cdots + a_2 y'' + a_1 y' + a_0 y = 0, \tag{1}$$

where the $a_i, i = 0, 1, \ldots, n$ are constants. The surprising fact is that *all* solutions of (1) are exponential functions or constructed out of exponential functions. We shall begin by considering the special case of the second-order equation

$$ay'' + by' + cy = 0. \tag{2}$$

The auxiliary equation   If we try a solution of the form $y = e^{mx}$, then $y' = me^{mx}$ and $y'' = m^2 e^{mx}$ so that equation (2) becomes

$$am^2 e^{mx} + bme^{mx} + ce^{mx} = 0 \quad \text{or} \quad e^{mx}[am^2 + bm + c] = 0.$$

Because e^{mx} is never zero for real values of x, it is apparent that the only way that this exponential function can satisfy the differential equation is to choose m so that it is a root of the quadratic equation

$$am^2 + bm + c = 0. \tag{3}$$

This latter equation is called the **auxiliary equation** or **characteristic equation** of the differential equation (2). We shall consider three cases, namely, the solutions corresponding to real distinct roots, real but equal roots, and lastly, complex conjugate roots.

CASE I   Under the assumption that the auxiliary equation (3) has two unequal real roots m_1 and m_2 we find two solutions

$$y_1 = e^{m_1 x} \quad \text{and} \quad y_2 = e^{m_2 x}.$$

We have already seen that these functions are linearly independent on $-\infty < x < \infty$ (see page 138) and thus from the superposition principle it follows that the general solution of (2) on this interval is

$$y = c_1 e^{m_1 x} + c_2 e^{m_2 x}. \tag{4}$$

CASE II   When $m_1 = m_2$ we necessarily obtain only one exponential solution $y_1 = e^{m_1 x}$. However, it follows immediately from the discussion of Section 4.2 that a second solution is

$$y_2 = e^{m_1 x} \int \frac{e^{-(b/a)x}}{e^{2m_1 x}} \, dx \tag{5}$$

But from the quadratic formula we have

$$m = \frac{-b \pm \sqrt{b^2 - 4ac}}{2a} = -\frac{b}{2a}$$

since the only way to have $m_1 = m_2$ is to have $b^2 - 4ac = 0$. Therefore (5) becomes

$$y_2 = e^{m_1 x} \int \frac{e^{2m_1 x}}{e^{2m_1 x}} dx = e^{m_1 x} \int dx$$

$$= x e^{m_1 x}.$$

The general solution is then

$$y = c_1 e^{m_1 x} + c_2 x e^{m_1 x}. \tag{6}$$

CASE III   If m_1 and m_2 are complex then we can write

$$m_1 = \alpha + i\beta \quad \text{and} \quad m_2 = \alpha - i\beta$$

where α and β are real and $i^2 = -1$. Formally there is no difference between this case and Case I, and hence the general solution is

$$y = C_1 e^{(\alpha + i\beta)x} + C_2 e^{(\alpha - i\beta)x}. \tag{7}$$

However, in practice we would prefer to work with real functions instead of complex exponentials. Now we can rewrite (7) in a more practical form by using Euler's formula*

$$\boxed{e^{i\theta} = \cos\theta + i\sin\theta,}$$

where θ is any real number. From this result we can write

$$e^{i\beta x} = \cos\beta x + i\sin\beta x \qquad \text{and} \qquad e^{-i\beta x} = \cos\beta x - i\sin\beta x,$$

where we have used $\cos(-\beta x) = \cos\beta x$ and $\sin(-\beta x) = -\sin\beta x$. Thus (7) becomes

$$y = e^{\alpha x}[C_1 e^{i\beta x} + C_2 e^{-i\beta x}]$$
$$= e^{\alpha x}[C_1\{\cos\beta x + i\sin\beta x\} + C_2\{\cos\beta x - i\sin\beta x\}]$$
$$= e^{\alpha x}[(C_1 + C_2)\cos\beta x + (C_1 i - C_2 i)\sin\beta x].$$

Since $e^{\alpha x}\cos\beta x$ and $e^{\alpha x}\sin\beta x$ are themselves linearly independent solutions of the given differential equation on $-\infty < x < \infty$ we can simply relabel $C_1 + C_2$ as c_1 and $C_1 i - C_2 i$ as c_2 and use the superposition principle to write the general solution

$$\boxed{\begin{aligned} y &= c_1 e^{\alpha x}\cos\beta x + c_2 e^{\alpha x}\sin\beta x \\ &= e^{\alpha x}[c_1\cos\beta x + c_2\sin\beta x]. \end{aligned}} \tag{8}$$

EXAMPLES   Solve the following equations.

(a) $2y'' - 5y' - 3y = 0,$
(b) $y'' - 10y' + 25y = 0,$
(c) $y'' + y' + y = 0.$

Solutions: **(a)** $2m^2 - 5m - 3 = 0$

$$(2m + 1)(m - 3) = 0$$

$$m_1 = -\frac{1}{2}, \qquad m_2 = 3$$

$$y = c_1 e^{-x/2} + c_2 e^{3x}.$$

---

* In case you have never seen this result before, it is worth going through the formal proof at least once. Write down the MacLaurin series for e^x and then substitute $x = i\theta$. Separate the real and imaginary parts and look closely at the resulting two series.

(b) $m^2 - 10m + 25 = 0$

$$(m - 5)^2 = 0$$

$$m_1 = m_2 = 5$$

$$y = c_1 e^{5x} + c_2 x e^{5x}.$$

(c) $m^2 + m + 1 = 0$

$$m = \frac{-1 \pm \sqrt{-3}}{2}$$

$$m_1 = -\frac{1}{2} + \frac{\sqrt{3}}{2}i, \qquad m_2 = -\frac{1}{2} - \frac{\sqrt{3}}{2}i$$

$$y = e^{-x/2}\left[c_1 \cos \frac{\sqrt{3}}{2}x + c_2 \sin \frac{\sqrt{3}}{2}x \right].$$

EXAMPLE

The two equations

$$y'' + k^2 y = 0 \tag{9}$$

and $\qquad\qquad\qquad y'' - k^2 y = 0 \tag{10}$

are frequently encountered in the study of applied mathematics. For the former equation the auxiliary equation $m^2 + k^2 = 0$ has imaginary roots $m_1 = ki$ and $m_2 = -ki$. It follows from (8) that the general solution of (9) is

$$y = c_1 \cos kx + c_2 \sin kx. \tag{11}$$

The latter equation has the auxiliary equation $m^2 - k^2 = 0$ with real roots $m_1 = k$ and $m_2 = -k$, so that its general solution is

$$y = c_1 e^{kx} + c_2 e^{-kx} \tag{12}$$

Notice that if we choose $c_1 = c_2 = 1/2$ in (12), then,

$$y = \frac{e^{kx} + e^{-kx}}{2}$$

$$= \cosh kx$$

is also a solution of (10). Furthermore, when $c_1 = 1/2$, $c_2 = -1/2$ then (12) becomes

$$y = \frac{e^{kx} - e^{-kx}}{2}$$

$$= \sinh kx.$$

Since $\cosh kx$ and $\sinh kx$ are linearly independent on any interval of the x-axis we obtain an alternative form for the general solution of (10):

$$y = c_1 \cosh kx + c_2 \sinh kx. \tag{13}$$

Higher order equations   In general, to solve an nth-order differential equation

$$a_n y^{(n)} + a_{n-1} y^{(n-1)} + \cdots + a_2 y'' + a_1 y' + a_0 y = 0, \tag{14}$$

where the $a_i, i = 0, 1, \ldots, n$ are real constants, we must solve an nth-degree polynominal equation

$$a_n m^n + a_{n-1} m^{n-1} + \cdots + a_2 m^2 + a_1 m + a_0 = 0. \tag{15}$$

If all the roots of (15) are real and distinct, then the general solution of (14) is

$$y = c_1 e^{m_1 x} + c_2 e^{m_2 x} + \cdots + c_n e^{m_n x}. \tag{16}$$

It is somewhat harder to summarize the analogues of Case II and Case III because the roots of an auxiliary equation of degree greater than two can occur in many combinations. For example, a fifth degree equation would have five distinct real roots, three distinct real and two complex roots, one real and four complex roots, five real but equal roots, five real roots but two of them equal, and so on. When, say, k roots of the nth-degree auxiliary equation are equal to m_1, then it can be shown that the linearly independent solutions are

$$e^{m_1 x}, xe^{m_1 x}, x^2 e^{m_1 x}, \ldots, x^{k-1} e^{m_1 x},$$

and the general solution must contain the combination

$$c_1 e^{m_1 x} + c_2 x e^{m_1 x} + c_3 x^2 e^{m_1 x} + \cdots + c_k x^{k-1} e^{m_1 x}.$$

Lastly, it should be remembered that when the coefficients are real, complex roots of an auxiliary equation will always appear in pairs. Thus for example, a cubic polynomial equation can have at most two complex roots.

EXAMPLE   Solve $y''' + 3y'' - 4y = 0.$

Solution: It should be apparent from inspection of

$$m^3 + 3m^2 - 4 = 0$$

that one root is $m_1 = 1$. Now if we divide* $m^3 + 3m^2 - 4$ by $m - 1$ we find

$$m^3 + 3m^2 - 4 = (m - 1)(m^2 + 4m + 4)$$

$$= (m - 1)(m + 2)^2,$$

and so the other roots are $m_2 = m_3 = -2$. Thus the general solution is

$$y = c_1 e^x + c_2 e^{-2x} + c_3 x e^{-2x}.$$

Of course, the most difficult aspect of solving constant-coefficient equations is finding the roots of auxiliary equations of degree greater than two. As illustrated in the preceding example, one way to solve an equation is to guess† a root m_1 and then divide by $m - m_1$ to obtain the factorization $(m - m_1)q(m)$. We then try to find the roots of $q(m)$.

EXAMPLE

Solve $3y''' - 19y'' + 36y' - 10y = 0.$

Solution: It is easily verified that $m_1 = 1/3$ is one root of

$$3m^3 - 19m^2 + 36m - 10 = 0.$$

By division we find that

$$3m^3 - 19m^2 + 36m - 10 = \left(m - \frac{1}{3}\right)(3m^2 - 18m + 30)$$

$$= (3m - 1)(m^2 - 6m + 10).$$

---

* Synthetic division provides a quick way of testing for roots. In the above case

$$
\begin{array}{rrr|r}
1 & 3 & 0 & -4 \ \underline{\,1} \\
 & 1 & 4 & 4 \\
\hline
1 & 4 & 4 & \underline{\,0} = R
\end{array}
$$

If $R \neq 0$ the number tested is not a root. For example, dividing by $m + 1$ is equivalent to

$$
\begin{array}{rrr|r}
1 & 3 & 0 & -4 \ \underline{\,-1} \\
 & -1 & -2 & 2 \\
\hline
1 & 2 & -2 & \underline{\,-2} = R.
\end{array}
$$

Therefore $m = -1$ is not a root and so $m + 1$ is not a factor.

† If the equation $a_n m^n + \cdots + a_1 m + a_0 = 0$ has a *rational* real root $m_1 = p/q$, where p and q are integers, then q must be a factor of a_n and p must be a factor of a_0. We can test all the possible ratios by synthetic division.

From the quadratic formula we find $m_2 = 3 + i$ and $m_3 = 3 - i$. Thus the general solution is

$$y = c_1 e^{x/3} + e^{3x}[c_2 \cos x + c_3 \sin x].$$

EXAMPLE   Solve $\dfrac{d^4y}{dx^4} + 2\dfrac{d^2y}{dx^2} + y = 0.$

Solution: The auxiliary equation

$$m^4 + 2m^2 + 1 = 0$$

is equivalent to $(m^2 + 1)^2 = 0.$

Therefore, the roots are $m_1 = m_3 = i$ and $m_2 = m_4 = -i$. From Case II the formal solution would be

$$y = C_1 e^{ix} + C_2 e^{-ix} + C_3 x e^{ix} + C_4 x e^{-ix}.$$

By Euler's formula the grouping $C_1 e^{ix} + C_2 e^{-ix}$ can be rewritten as $c_1 \cos x + c_2 \sin x$ after a relabeling of constants. Similarly, $x(C_3 e^{ix} + C_4 e^{-ix})$ can be expressed as $x(c_3 \cos x + c_4 \sin x)$. Hence the general solution is

$$y = c_1 \cos x + c_2 \sin x + c_3 x \cos x + c_4 x \sin x.$$

EXERCISES 4.3   Answers to odd-numbered problems begin on page A-11 of the Appendix. In Problems 1–20 find the general solution of the given differential equation.

1. $3y'' - y' = 0$ 2. $2y'' + 5y' = 0$

3. $y'' + 9y = 0$ ★4. $y'' - 8y = 0$

5. $\dfrac{d^2y}{dx^2} + 8\dfrac{dy}{dx} + 16y = 0$ 6. $y'' - 10y' + 25y = 0$

7. $y'' + 3y' - 5y = 0$ 8. $2y'' - 3y' + 4y = 0$

9. $y'' - y' - 42y = 0$ 10. $12y'' - 5y' - 2y = 0$

11. $y'' - 4y' + 5y = 0$ ★12. $y''' + y'' - 2y = 0$

13. $y''' - 4y'' - 5y' = 0$ ★14. $4y''' + 4y'' + y' = 0$

15. $\dfrac{d^4y}{dx^4} + \dfrac{d^3y}{dx^3} + \dfrac{d^2y}{dx^2} = 0$ ★16. $y''' + 3y'' - 4y' - 12y = 0$

17. $2\dfrac{d^3y}{dx^3} - 7\dfrac{d^2y}{dx^2} + 12\dfrac{dy}{dx} + 8y = 0$

18. $\dfrac{d^4y}{dx^4} - 7\dfrac{d^2y}{dx^2} - 18y = 0$ 19. $16\dfrac{d^4y}{dx^4} + 24\dfrac{d^2y}{dx^2} + 9y = 0$

20. $\dfrac{d^5y}{dx^5} + 5\dfrac{d^4y}{dx^4} - 2\dfrac{d^3y}{dx^3} - 10\dfrac{d^2y}{dx^2} + \dfrac{dy}{dx} + 5y = 0$

21.   The roots of the auxiliary equation are

$$m_1 = 4, \quad m_2 = m_3 = -5.$$

What is the corresponding differential equation?

★22.   The roots of the auxiliary equation are

$$m_1 = -\frac{1}{2}, \quad m_2 = 3 + i, \quad m_3 = 3 - i.$$

What is the corresponding differential equation?

In Problems 23–35 solve the given initial-value problem.

EXAMPLE

Solve $y'' - 4y' + 13y = 0$

subject to $y(0) = -1, \quad y'(0) = 2.$

Solution: The roots of the auxiliary equation

$$m^2 - 4m + 13 = 0$$

are $m_1 = 2 + 3i$

$$m_2 = 2 - 3i$$

so that $y = e^{2x}[c_1 \cos 3x + c_2 \sin 3x]$

The condition $y(0) = -1$ implies

$$-1 = e^0[c_1 \cos 0 + c_2 \sin 0]$$

$$= c_1$$

from which we can write

$$y = e^{2x}[-\cos 3x + c_2 \sin 3x].$$

Differentiating this latter expression and using the second condition gives

$$y' = e^{2x}[3 \sin 3x + 3c_2 \cos 3x] + 2e^{2x}[-\cos 3x + c_2 \sin 3x]$$

$$2 = 3c_2 - 2$$

so that $c_2 = 4/3$. Hence

$$y = e^{2x}\left[-\cos 3x + \frac{4}{3}\sin 3x\right].$$

23. $y'' + 16y = 0$, $y(0) = 2$, $y'(0) = -2$

24. $y'' - y = 0$, $y(0) = y'(0) = 1$

25. $y'' + 6y' + 5y = 0$, $y(0) = 0$, $y'(0) = 3$

26. $y'' - 8y' + 17y = 0$, $y(0) = 4$, $y'(0) = -1$

27. $2y'' - 2y' + y = 0$, $y(0) = -1$, $y'(0) = 0$

28. $\dfrac{d^4y}{dx^4} = 0$, $y(0) = 2$, $y'(0) = 3$, $y''(0) = 4$, $y'''(0) = 5$

29. $y''' + 12y'' + 36y' = 0$, $y(0) = 0$, $y'(0) = 1$, $y''(0) = -7$

30. $y''' + 2y'' - 5y' - 6y = 0$, $y(0) = y'(0) = 0$, $y''(0) = 1$

31. $\dfrac{d^4y}{dx^4} - 3\dfrac{d^3y}{dx^3} + 3\dfrac{d^2y}{dx^2} + \dfrac{dy}{dx} = 0$, $y(0) = y'(0) = 0$,

$y''(0) = y'''(0) = 1$

★32. $y''' - 8y = 0$, $y(0) = 0$, $y'(0) = -1$, $y''(0) = 0$

33. $y'' + y' + 2y = 0$, $y(0) = y'(0) = 0$

34. $4y'' - 4y' - 3y = 0$, $y(0) = 1$, $y'(0) = 5$

35. $y'' - 3y' + 2y = 0$, $y(1) = 0$, $y'(1) = 1$

★36. Use the fact that

$$i = \left(\frac{\sqrt{2}}{2} + \frac{\sqrt{2}}{2}i\right)^2 \qquad \text{and} \qquad -i = \left(\frac{\sqrt{2}}{2} - \frac{\sqrt{2}}{2}i\right)^2$$

to solve the differential equation

$$\frac{d^4y}{dx^4} + y = 0.$$

[*Hint:* Write the auxiliary equation $m^4 + 1 = 0$ as $(m^2 + 1)^2 - 2m^2 = 0$. See what happens when you factor.]

4.4   Undetermined Coefficients

To obtain the general solution of a nonhomogeneous differential equation with constant coefficients

$$a_ny^{(n)} + a_{n-1}y^{(n-1)} + \cdots + a_2y'' + a_1y' + a_0y = g(x) \tag{1}$$

we must do two things: find the complementary function y_c, and then find *any* particular solution y_p of the nonhomogeneous equation. Recall from the discussion of Section 4.1 that a particular solution is any function, free of arbitrary constants, which satisfies the equation identically. The general solution of a nonhomogeneous equation is the sum of y_c and y_p.

$g(x)$ is constant

When $g(x)$ is a constant, say $g(x) = k$ and $a_0 \neq 0$, we can readily find a constant particular solution. Write (1) in the form

$$a_n y^{(n)} + a_{n-1} y^{(n-1)} + \cdots + a_1 y' + a_0 \left[y - \frac{k}{a_0} \right] = 0 \qquad (2)$$

and define $Y(x) = y - k/a_0$. Since $Y^{(n)} = y^{(n)}, n \geq 1$, (2) becomes

$$a_n Y^{(n)} + a_{n-1} Y^{(n-1)} + \cdots + a_1 Y + a_0 Y = 0. \qquad (3)$$

Equation (3) is homogeneous and so its general solution can be written as

$$Y(x) = c_1 y_1 + c_2 y_2 + \cdots + c_n y_n$$

where $y_1, y_2, \ldots, y_n$ are linearly independent on $-\infty < x < \infty$. Therefore we have

$$y = Y + \frac{k}{a_0}$$

$$= c_1 y_1 + c_2 y_2 + \cdots + c_n y_n + \frac{k}{a_0} \qquad (4)$$

$$= y_c + y_p.$$

EXAMPLE

The general solution of

$$y'' + 9y = 18$$

is

$$y = c_1 \cos 3x + c_2 \sin 3x + 2$$

where $y_c = c_1 \cos 3x + c_2 \sin 3x$ is the solution of $y'' + 9y = 0$ and $y_p = 18/9 = 2$.

Restrictions on $g(x)$

Unfortunately, it is not always quite so easy to obtain a particular solution when $g(x)$ is nonconstant. In fact, we shall limit the discussion in this section to the cases where $g(x)$ is either

(a)   a polynomial in x,
(b)   an exponential function e^{ax},   (5)
(c) $\sin kx, \cos kx,$ $[A \sin kx + B \cos kx]$

or a finite sum or product of these functions.

Consider, for example, the problem of finding y_p for the equation

$$\frac{d^2y}{dx^2} + 3\frac{dy}{dx} + 2y = 4x^2. \tag{6}$$

It seems reasonable to expect that y_p is a polynomial because differentiation of a polynomial yields a polynomial. Now observe that we can make equation (6) homogeneous by taking three derivatives of each side of the equation. That is,

$$\frac{d^5y}{dx^5} + 3\frac{d^4y}{dx^4} + 2\frac{d^3y}{dx^3} = 0 \tag{7}$$

since $\frac{d^3}{dx^3}(4x^2) = 0$. Now the auxiliary equation of (7) is

$$m^5 + 3m^4 + 2m^3 = 0 \quad \text{or} \quad m^3(m^2 + 3m + 2) = 0$$

$$m^3(m + 1)(m + 2) = 0,$$

so that its general solution must be

$$y = \underbrace{c_1 e^{-x} + c_2 e^{-2x}}_{y_c} + \underbrace{c_3 + c_4 x + c_5 x^2}_{y_p}. \tag{8}$$

Formally we can then argue that every solution of equation (6) should also be a solution of equation (7). Since we recognize $c_1 e^{-x} + c_2 e^{-2x}$ as the complementary function of (6), it follows that y_p must have the basic structure

$$y_p = Ax^2 + Bx + C, \tag{9}$$

where we have replaced c_5, c_4, and c_3 in (8) by A, B, and C, respectively. In order that y_p be a particular solution of (6) it is now necessary to find *specific* coefficients A, B, and C. Differentiating (9) and substituting in (6) gives

$$y_p'' + 3y_p' + 2y_p = 2A + 3(2Ax + B) + 2(Ax^2 + Bx + C)$$

$$= 2Ax^2 + (6A + 2B)x + 2A + 3B + 2C$$

$$= 4x^2.$$

By equating coefficients in the last identity we obtain the system of equations

$$2A = 4$$

$$6A + 2B = 0 \tag{10}$$

$$2A + 3B + 2C = 0.$$

Solving (10) gives $A = 2, B = -6$, and $C = 7$. Thus, $y_p = 2x^2 - 6x + 7$ and the general solution of (6) is

$$y = c_1 e^{-x} + c_2 e^{-2x} + 2x^2 - 6x + 7.$$

Undetermined coefficients   In theory we could always render a nonhomogeneous equation homogeneous by differentiation whenever $g(x)$ is any finite combination of the functions listed in (5). However, in practice it is useful to state two general rules governing the formation of a particular solution. The procedure is called the **method of undetermined coefficients**.

> **RULE I**   Form a linear combination of $g(x)$ and all its linearly independent derivatives. If no part of this combination duplicates a part of the complementary function y_c, then this combination may be used as the assumption for y_p.

Let us elaborate on the phrase "a combination of $g(x)$ and all its linearly independent derivatives."

EXAMPLE   The right side of

$$y'' + 3y' + 2y = 8x^2 + 3xe^x$$

can be written as

$$g(x) = f_1(x) + f_2(x)$$

where $f_1(x) = 8x^2$ and $f_2(x) = 3xe^x$. The first function f_1, and its first two derivatives $f_1' = 16x, f_1'' = 16$, yield the linearly independent set of functions $x^2, x, 1$.*

Differentiation of the second function f_2 produces only one new function, namely, e^x. Hence associated with f_2 we have another linearly independent set xe^x, e^x.

Since no function in either of the above two sets appears in

$$y_c = c_1 e^{-x} + c_2 e^{-2x}$$

we then form the linear combination

$$y_p = Ax^2 + Bx + C + Dxe^x + Ee^x.$$

Again, we must now find the values of A, B, C, D, and E such that this combination is a particular solution of the original equation.

In practice, it is not really necessary to formally write $g(x)$ in terms of $f_1, f_2, \ldots$, and so on. All we need do is to form a combination of the various parts of $g(x)$ with any new function discovered through differentiation.

---

* Note $f_1''' = 0$ is nothing new since it is a constant as is f_1''. Also, when taking derivatives we are concerned only with the *basic functions generated* by this operation and so we ignore constant multiples.

EXAMPLE

For the equation $y'' + 3y' + 2y = 6x^3$ we note that $g(x) = 6x^3$, $g'(x) = 18x^2$, $g''(x) = 36x$, and $g'''(x) = 36$. We assume that y_p consists of a combination of the basic functions

$$x^3, x^2, x, 1.$$

That is,

$$y_p = Ax^3 + Bx^2 + Cx + D.$$

From our earlier discussion of equation (6), we can verify that no part of this assumption is contained in y_c. The reason for making this crucial observation will become clear shortly.

Now

$$y_p' = 3Ax^2 + 2Bx + C$$

$$y_p'' = 6Ax + 2B$$

so that the differential equation becomes

$$y_p'' + 3y_p' + 2y_p = 6Ax + 2B + 3(3Ax^2 + 2Bx + C)$$

$$+ 2(Ax^3 + Bx^2 + Cx + D)$$

$$= 2Ax^3 + (9A + 2B)x^2 + (6A + 6B + 2C)x$$

$$+ 2B + 3C + 2D$$

$$= 6x^3.$$

This last equality will hold identically provided

$$2A = 6$$

$$9A + 2B = 0$$

$$6A + 6B + 2C = 0$$

$$2B + 3C + 2D = 0.$$

Solving the system gives $A = 3$, $B = -27/2$, $C = 63/2$, $D = -135/4$ and so

$$y_p = 3x^3 - \frac{27}{2}x^2 + \frac{63}{2}x - \frac{135}{4}.$$

Thus the general solution is

$$y = y_c + y_p$$

$$= c_1e^{-x} + c_2e^{-2x} + 3x^3 - \frac{27}{2}x^2 + \frac{63}{2}x - \frac{135}{4}.$$

EXAMPLE   Solve $$y'' + 8y = 2e^{-x} + 5x.$$

Solution: Since $m^2 + 8 = 0$ has the roots $m_1 = 2\sqrt{2}i$ and $m_2 = -2\sqrt{2}i$ we have

$$y_c = c_1 \cos 2\sqrt{2}x + c_2 \sin 2\sqrt{2}x.$$

The only new function resulting from differentiating $g(x) = 2e^{-x} + 5x$ is a constant function. Thus we assume

$$y_p = Ae^{-x} + Bx + C$$

since no part of this assumption is contained in y_c. Differentiating this latter expression and substituting into the equation gives

$$y_p'' + 8y_p = 9Ae^{-x} + 8Bx + 8C$$
$$= 2e^{-x} + 5x.$$

This implies $A = 2/9$, $B = 5/8$, and $C = 0$ so that the general solution is

$$y = c_1 \cos 2\sqrt{2}x + c_2 \sin 2\sqrt{2}x + \frac{2}{9}e^{-x} + \frac{5}{8}x.$$

EXAMPLE   Solve $$y''' + 4y'' + 4y' = -3xe^x + \sin x.$$

Solution: The roots of $m^3 + 4m^2 + 4m = m(m + 2)^2 = 0$ are $m_1 = 0$, $m_2 = m_3 = -2$ so that

$$y_c = c_1 + c_2 e^{-2x} + c_3 xe^{-2x}.$$

Differentiation of $g(x)$ results in two additional functions: e^x and $\cos x$. Neither of these functions, nor any part of $g(x)$ is contained in y_c. Thus we can write

$$y_p = Axe^x + Be^x + C\sin x + D\cos x.$$

After taking the first three derivatives we have

$$y_p''' + 4y_p'' + 4y_p' = 9Axe^x + (15A + 9B)e^x + (-4C - 3D)\sin x$$
$$+ (3C - 4D)\cos x$$
$$= -3xe^x + \sin x.$$

The last equation is an identity and so it follows that

$$9A = -3$$
$$15A + 9B = 0$$
$$-4C - 3D = 1$$
$$3C - 4D = 0.$$

We find $A = -1/3$, $B = 5/9$, $C = -4/25$, and $D = -3/25$. Therefore

$$y = c_1 + c_2 e^{-2x} + c_3 x e^{-2x} - \frac{1}{3} x e^x + \frac{5}{9} e^x - \frac{4}{25} \sin x - \frac{3}{25} \cos x.$$

Rule I is not directly applicable when $g(x)$, or some linearly independent derivative of $g(x)$, is duplicated in the complementary function y_c. For example, for $y'' - y = e^x$ we have $y_c = c_1 e^{-x} + c_2 e^x$, and since $g(x) = e^x$ does not generate any new functions we would naturally try $y_p = Ae^x$. However this choice leads to the impossible situation $Ae^x - Ae^x = 0 = e^x$.

To discover the correct form of y_p in this case, we differentiate

$$y'' - y = e^x \tag{11}$$

and obtain

$$y''' - y' = e^x. \tag{12}$$

Subtracting (11) from (12) we find y satisfies

$$y''' - y'' + y' - y = 0. \tag{13}$$

The solution of (13) is

$$y = \underbrace{c_1 e^{-x} + c_2 e^x}_{y_c} + \underbrace{c_3 x e^x}_{y_p}. \tag{14}$$

Formally arguing as before, every solution of (11) should also be a solution of (13) so that we are led to try

$$y_p = Axe^x. \tag{15}$$

Now
$$\begin{aligned} y_p'' - y_p &= (Axe^x + 2Ae^x) - Axe^x \\ &= 2Ae^x \\ &= e^x \end{aligned}$$

immediately gives $A = 1/2$. Thus the general solution of (11) is

$$y = c_1 e^{-x} + c_2 e^x + \frac{1}{2} x e^x.$$

The general procedure is summarized in the following:

> **RULE II** Form a linear combination of $g(x)$ and all its linearly independent derivatives. If any part of this combination is duplicated in y_c, then the entire corresponding portion of the combination should be multiplied by the lowest positive integral power of x which will eliminate the duplications. Make this new assumption the function y_p.

Admittedly this rule is somewhat difficult to understand on first reading. By "corresponding portion" we mean that unit of the linear combination consisting of those basic functions in $g(x)$, and their linearly independent derivatives, which actually result in the duplication.

EXAMPLE

The complementary function for the equation

$$y'' - 2y' + y = 5x^2 - 6x + 3x^2 e^x$$

is

$$y_c = c_1 e^x + c_2 x e^x.$$

For the sake of illustration let us write the function g as

$$g(x) = f_1(x) + f_2(x)$$

where $f_1(x) = 5x^2 - 6x$ and $f_2(x) = 3x^2 e^x$. Now these basic functions and their derivatives lead us to form the linear combination

$$Ax^2 + Bx + C + Dx^2 e^x + Exe^x + Fe^x.$$

Notice that although there are no duplications between the terms in g and y_c, there are two functions in y_c which are also contained in the set of derivatives of f_2 (namely, xe^x and e^x). Thus, according to Rule II we must multiply the *unit*

$$Dx^2 e^x + Exe^x + Fe^x \qquad (16)$$

by some positive integral power of x which will eliminate all the duplications between this unit and y_c. We observe that simply multiplying (16) by x will not suffice since the last term in

$$Dx^3 e^x + Ex^2 e^x + Fxe^x$$

is still to be found in y_c. Hence we must multiply (16) by x^2 and use the assumption

$$y_p = Ax^2 + Bx + C + Dx^4 e^x + Ex^3 e^x + Ex^3 e^x + Fx^2 e^x.$$

EXAMPLES

In parts **(a)** and **(b)** determine the form of y_p.

(a)
$$\frac{d^3 y}{dx^3} - 4\frac{d^2 y}{dx^2} = x + 5e^{2x}$$

$$y_c = \underline{c_1 + c_2 x} + c_3 e^{4x}$$

$$\uparrow$$

Form:
$$\underline{Ax + B} + Ce^{2x}$$
$$\text{multiply}$$
$$\text{by } x^2$$

Use: $y_p = Ax^3 + Bx^2 + Ce^{2x}$.

(b) $\dfrac{d^3y}{dx^3} - 4\dfrac{d^2y}{dx^2} = 8 + 3e^{4x} - e^x \sin x$

$$y_c = \underbrace{c_1 + c_2x} + \underbrace{c_3e^{4x}}$$

Form: $\underbrace{A}_{\substack{\text{multiply}\\\text{by } x^2}} + \underbrace{Be^{4x}}_{\substack{\text{multiply}\\\text{by } x}} + Ce^x \sin x + De^x \cos x$

Use: $y_p = Ax^2 + Bxe^x + Ce^x \sin x + De^x \cos x$.

EXAMPLE

Solve

$$y'' + y = x\cos x - \cos x.$$

Solution:

$$y_c = c_1 \cos x + c_2 \sin x$$

Form:

$$\underbrace{Ax \cos x + Bx \sin x + C \cos x + D \sin x}_{\text{multiply by } x} \tag{17}$$

Use: $y_p = Ax^2 \cos x + Bx^2 \sin x + Cx \cos x + Dx \sin x$ (18)

$$
\begin{aligned}
y_p'' + y_p &= [-Ax^2 \cos x - 4Ax \sin x + 2A \cos x \\
&\quad - Bx^2 \sin x + 4Bx \cos x + 2B \sin x \\
&\quad - Cx \cos x - 2C \sin x - Dx \sin x + 2D \cos x] \\
&\quad + [Ax^2 \cos x + Bx^2 \sin x + Cx \cos x + Dx \sin x] \\
&= -4Ax \sin x + 4Bx \cos x + (2A + 2D) \cos x \\
&\quad + (2B - 2C) \sin x \\
&= x \cos x - \cos x.
\end{aligned}
$$

Equating coefficients gives

$$
\begin{aligned}
-4A &= 0 \\
4B &= 1 \\
2A + 2D &= -1 \\
2B - 2C &= 0
\end{aligned}
$$

from which it follows $A = 0$, $B = 1/4$, $C = 1/4$, $D = -1/2$. Thus, the general solution is

$$
\begin{aligned}
y &= y_c + y_p \\
&= c_1 \cos x + c_2 \sin x + \frac{1}{4}x^2 \sin x + \frac{1}{4}x \cos x - \frac{1}{2}x \sin x.
\end{aligned}
$$

In the preceding example an observant reader might have noticed that had we multiplied only the grouping $C \cos x + D \sin x$ by x in the linear combination (16) we would have eliminated the duplications between this assumption and y_c. Of course the new assumption would then have been equivalent to

$$A' x \cos\ x + B' x \sin x. \tag{19}$$

We need only try this assumption to see that it is impossible to determine the coefficients A' and B'. Keep in mind that Rule II demands that we not only multiply the duplicated portion, but also that part of $g(x)$ and *all* its derivatives which give rise to the duplication. Successive derivatives of $x \cos x$ generate the terms $x \sin x$, $\cos x$, and $\sin x$. Thus, all four of these terms must be multiplied by an appropriate power of x. Notice that the form of the assumptions (17) and (18) would have been unchanged had g been any one of the following types of functions:

$$g(x) = x \cos x, \qquad\qquad g(x) = x \sin x,$$

$$g(x) = x \cos x + \sin x, \qquad g(x) = x \cos x + \cos x + \sin x,$$

and so on.

EXAMPLE

Solve
$$y''' + 2y'' + y' = xe^{-x} + x^2.$$

Solution: Since the auxiliary equation is $m(m + 1)^2 = 0$ we have

$$y_c = c_1 + c_2 e^{-x} + c_3 x e^{-x}.$$

Form:
$$\underbrace{Axe^{-x} + Be^{-x}}_{\substack{\text{multiply} \\ \text{by } x^2}} + \underbrace{Cx^2 + Dx + E}_{\substack{\text{multiply} \\ \text{by } x}}$$

Use: $y_p = Ax^3 e^{-x} + Bx^2 e^{-x} + Cx^3 + Dx^2 + Ex.$

Now

$$y_p''' + 2y_p'' + y_p' = -6Axe^{-x} + (-2B + 6A)e^{-x} + 3Cx^2 + (2D + 12C)x$$
$$+ 6C + 4D + E$$
$$= xe^{-x} + x^2$$

which gives

$$-6A = 1$$
$$-2B + 6A = 0$$
$$3C = 1$$
$$2D + 12C = 0$$
$$6C + 4D + E = 0.$$

Solving the system yields $A = -1/6$, $B = -1/2$, $C = 1/3$, $D = -2$, and $E = 6$.

Thus the general solution is

$$y = c_1 + c_2 e^{-x} + c_3 x e^{-x} - \frac{1}{6} x^3 e^{-x} - \frac{1}{2} x^2 e^{-x} + \frac{1}{3} x^3 - 2x^2 + 6x.$$

We have confined our attention to the kinds of functions listed in (5) since only these functions, when combined in finite sums and products, have a finite number of linearly independent derivatives. The method of undetermined coefficients becomes formidable or even impossible to apply to equations for which $g(x)$ has an infinite number of independent derivatives. For example, we could not readily solve either $y'' + y = e^{1/x}$ or $y'' + y = \sec x$ by the above procedures. In the next section we shall study a technique for solving nonhomogeneous equations with no restrictions on $g(x)$. Unfortunately, this new procedure has a practical (but not theoretical) limitation; namely, it is most conveniently applied only to second-order equations.

EXERCISES 4.4   Answers to odd-numbered problems begin on page A-11 of the Appendix. In Problems 1–5 set up the correct form of y_p but do not solve the equation.

EXAMPLE $$y''' - 4y'' + 4y' = x^3 e^{2x} - x + 9$$

Solution: The solution of the homogeneous equation $y''' - 4y'' + 4y' = 0$ is

$$y_c = c_1 e^{2x} + c_2 x e^{2x} + c_3.$$

Repeated differentiations of $g(x) = x^3 e^{2x} - x + 9$ yield the following basic functions: $x^3 e^{2x}$, $x^2 e^{2x}$, $x e^{2x}$, e^{2x}, x, and a constant. Therefore we

Form: $\underbrace{Ax^3 e^{2x} + Bx^2 e^{2x} + Cx e^{2x} + De^{2x}}_{\substack{\text{multiply} \\ \text{by } x^2}} + \underbrace{Ex + F}_{\substack{\text{multiply} \\ \text{by } x}}$

but

Use: $y_p = Ax^5 e^{2x} + Bx^4 e^{2x} + Cx^3 e^{2x} + Dx^2 e^{2x} + Ex^2 + Fx.$

---

1. $y'' + 9y = x \sin 3x$

2. $y''' + y' = \cos^2 x$ [*Hint:* Use an identity for $\cos^2 x$].

3. $y^{(4)} - y'' = e^{-x} + 2e^{2x} - x^2$

★4. $y^{(4)} + 9y'' = x^2(e^x - 1) + (x - 3)\sin 3x + x^2 \cos 3x$

5. $y'' + 4y = (x + 1)e^x \sin x$

In Problems 6–26 solve the given differential equation.

★6. $2y'' - 7y' + 5y = -29$ 7. $y'' + y = x^2$

8. $y'' - 2y' + y = e^x - 3x + 1$ 9. $y'' - 2y' + y = x^3 + 4x$

10. $y'' + 4y = 3 \sin x + 4 \cos x - 8$

11. $y'' + 4y = \sin x \cos x$ 12. $y'' + 3y' + 2y = e^{-2x} - xe^{-x}$

13. $y''' - 3y'' = 4x^3 + 2x^2$ ★14. $y^{(4)} - 5y'' + 4y = 2 \cosh x - 6$

15. $y''' + 4y'' + 4y' = xe^{-x} + \cos x$ 16. $y'' - 2y' + 5y = e^x \sin x$

17. $y'' + y' = (x + 1)^3$ 18. $y'' + y' + y = x \sin x$

19. $y'' - 4y' + 3y = -x^2 + 2x - 3e^x$

20. $2y''' - 3y'' - 3y' + 2y = (e^x + e^{-x})^2$

21. $16y^{(4)} - y = e^{x/2}$

22. $y^{(4)} - 4y'' = 8e^{-2x} + 2e^x - x + 5$

23. $y'' + 6y' + 9y = x^2 e^{-x} + 4x$ 24. $y'' - y' = e^x(1 - e^{-x})^2$

25. $y''' - 3y'' + 3y' - y = e^x - x + 16$

26. $y''' - y'' + y' - y = xe^x - e^{-x} + 7$

In Problems 27–31 solve the given initial-value problem.

27. $y'' - 5y' = x - 2;$ $y(0) = 0, y'(0) = 2$

28. $y'' + 5y' - 6y = 10e^{2x};$ $y(0) = 1, y'(0) = 1$

29. $y'' + y = 8 \cos 2x - 4 \sin x;$ $y(\pi/2) = -1, y'(\pi/2) = 0$

30. $y''' - 2y'' + y' = xe^x + 5;$ $y(0) = 2, y'(0) = 2,\ y''(0) = -1$

31. $y'' - 4y' + 8y = x^3;$ $y(0) = 2, y'(0) = 4$

32. Find a particular solution for

$$y'' + 2y' + 5y = 13 \cos 3x$$

by considering the equation

$$u'' + 2u' + 5u = 13e^{i3x}.$$

[*Hint:*   Recall Euler's formula and use the fact that $\cos 3x$ is the real part of e^{i3x}.]

4.5   Variation of Parameters

The linear first-order equation revisisted

In Chapter 2 we have seen that the general solution of the linear equation

$$\frac{dy}{dx} + P(x)y = f(x), \tag{1}$$

where P and f are continuous on an interval $a \le x \le b$, is

$$y = e^{-\int P(x)\,dx} \int e^{\int P(x)\,dx} f(x)\,dx + c_1 e^{-\int P(x)\,dx} \tag{2}$$

Now it is easily verified that the solution (2) has the form

$$y = y_c + y_p$$

where
$$y_c = c_1 e^{-\int P(x)\,dx}$$

is a solution of

$$\frac{dy}{dx} + P(x)y = 0 \tag{3}$$

and
$$y_p = e^{-\int P(x)\,dx} \int e^{\int P(x)\,dx} f(x)\,dx$$

is a particular solution of equation (1). As a means of *motivating* an additional method for solving nonhomogeneous second-order linear equations we shall rederive equation (2) by a method known as **variation of parameters**. The basic procedure is similar to that employed in Section 4.1. For second-order equations we shall see that variation of parameters has the distinct advantage that it will always yield a particular solution y_p, provided the related homogeneous equation can be solved. Also, there are no special cases which need be considered.

Suppose y_1 is a known solution of equation (3), that is,

$$\frac{dy_1}{dx} + P(x)y_1 = 0.$$

We have already proved in Section 2.4 that $y_1 = e^{-\int P(x)\,dx}$ is a solution, and since the differential equation is linear its general solution is

$$y = c_1 y_1(x). \tag{4}$$

Variation of parameters consists of finding a function u_1 such that $y = u_1(x)y_1(x)$ is a particular solution of (1). In other words, we replace the parameter c_1 in (4) by a variable u_1.

Substituting $y = u_1 y_1$ into equation (1) gives

$$\frac{d}{dx}[u_1 y_1] + P(x)u_1 y_1 = f(x)$$

$$u_1 \frac{dy_1}{dx} + y_1 \frac{du_1}{dx} + P(x)u_1 y_1 = f(x)$$

$$u_1 \underbrace{\left[\frac{dy_1}{dx} + P(x)y_1\right]}_{\text{zero}} + y_1 \frac{du_1}{dx} = f(x)$$

so that

$$y_1 \frac{du_1}{dx} = f(x).$$

By separating variables we find

$$du_1 = \frac{f(x)}{y_1(x)} dx \quad \text{and} \quad u_1 = \int \frac{f(x)}{y_1(x)} dx + c_1$$

from which it follows that

$$y = u_1 y_1 = y_1 \int \frac{f(x)}{y_1(x)} dx + c_1 y_1. \tag{5}$$

From the definition of y_1 we see that (5) is identical to (2).

Second-order equations   Throughout this discussion we shall put the linear second-order equation

$$a_2(x)y'' + a_1(x)y' + a_0(x)y = g(x)$$

into the form

$$y'' + P(x)y' + Q(x)y = f(x) \tag{6}$$

by dividing through by $a_2(x)$. Here we shall assume that P, Q and f are continuous on some interval $a \le x \le b$. Equation (6) is the analogue of (1). As we know, when P and Q are constants there is absolutely no difficulty in writing down y_c. Although at this time we shall confine our attention to second-order equations with constant coefficients, it should be noted that the method of variation of parameters can be generalized to higher order equations as well as equations with variable coefficients. (See Problems 21 and 24.)

Suppose y_1 and y_2 are two linearly independent solutions on $a \le x \le b$ of the associated homogeneous form of (6). That is,

$$y_1'' + P(x)y_1' + Q(x)y_1 = 0 \quad \text{and} \quad y_2'' + P(x)y_2' + Q(x)y_2 = 0.$$

Now can we find two functions u_1 and u_2 such that

$$y_p = u_1(x)y_1(x) + u_2(x)y_2(x)$$

is a particular solution of (1)? Notice our assumption for y_p is the same as $y_c = c_1 y_1 + c_2 y_2$, but we have replaced c_1 and c_2 by the "variable parameters" u_1 and u_2. Now

$$y_p' = u_1 y_1' + y_1 u_1' + u_2 y_2' + y_2 u_2'. \tag{7}$$

If we make the further demand that u_1 and u_2 be functions for which

$$y_1 u_1' + y_2 u_2' = 0 \qquad (8)$$

then (7) becomes

$$y_p' = u_1 y_1' + u_2 y_2'.$$

Continuing, we find

$$y_p'' = u_1 y_1'' + y_1' u_1' + u_2 y_2'' + y_2' u_2'$$

and hence

$$\begin{aligned}
y_p'' + P y_p' + Q y_p &= u_1 y_1'' + y_1' u_1' + u_2 y_2'' + y_2' u_2' \\
&\quad + P u_1 y_1' + P u_2 y_2' + Q u_1 y_1 + Q u_2 y_2 \\
&= u_1 \underbrace{[y_1'' + P y_1' + Q y_1]}_{\text{zero}} + u_2 \underbrace{[y_2'' + P y_2' + Q y_2]}_{\text{zero}} \\
&\quad + y_1' u_1' + y_2' u_2'. \\
&= f(x).
\end{aligned}$$

In other words, u_1 and u_2 must be functions which also satisfy the condition

$$y_1' u_1' + y_2' u_2' = f(x). \qquad (9)$$

Equations (8) and (9) constitute a set of simultaneous equations for determining the derivatives u_1' and u_2'. That is, we must solve

$$y_1 u_1' + y_2 u_2' = 0$$
$$y_1' u_1' + y_2' u_2' = f(x).$$

By Cramer's rule we obtain

$$u_1' = \frac{\begin{vmatrix} 0 & y_2 \\ f(x) & y_2' \end{vmatrix}}{\begin{vmatrix} y_1 & y_2 \\ y_1' & y_2' \end{vmatrix}} = -\frac{y_2 f(x)}{W}$$

$$\qquad (10)$$

and

$$u_2' = \frac{\begin{vmatrix} y_1 & 0 \\ y_1' & f(x) \end{vmatrix}}{\begin{vmatrix} y_1 & y_2 \\ y_1' & y_2' \end{vmatrix}} = \frac{y_1 f(x)}{W}$$

where we recognize the determinant in the denominator as the Wronskian W of y_1 and y_2. By linear independence of y_1 and y_2 on $a \le x \le b$ we know that $W(y_1(x), y_2(x)) \neq 0$ for every x in the interval.

A summary of the method

Usually it is not a good idea to memorize formulas in lieu of understanding a procedure. However, the foregoing procedure is much too long and complicated to use each time we wish to solve a differential equation. In this case it is more efficient to simply use the formulas in (10). Thus to solve $ay'' + by' + cy = g(x)$ where a, b and c are constants, first find the complementary function $y_c = c_1 y_1 + c_2 y_2$, and then compute the Wronskian

$$W = \begin{vmatrix} y_1 & y_2 \\ y_1' & y_2' \end{vmatrix}.$$

By dividing by a we put the equation into the form $y'' + Py' + Qy = f(x)$ to determine $f(x)$. Find u_1 and u_2 by integrating

$$u_1' = -\frac{y_2 f(x)}{W} \quad \text{and} \quad u_2' = \frac{y_1 f(x)}{W}.$$

Finally, form the particular solution

$$y_p = u_1 y_1 + u_2 y_2.$$

EXAMPLE

Solve
$$y'' - 4y' + 4y = (x + 1)e^{2x}.$$

Solution: Since the auxiliary equation is $m^2 - 4m + 4 = (m - 2)^2 = 0$ we have
$$y_c = c_1 e^{2x} + c_2 x e^{2x}.$$

In addition
$$W(e^{2x}, xe^{2x}) = \begin{vmatrix} e^{2x} & xe^{2x} \\ 2e^{2x} & 2xe^{2x} + e^{2x} \end{vmatrix} = e^{4x}.$$

Because the coefficient of y'' is already unity we can then write
$$u_1' = -\frac{xe^{2x}(x + 1)e^{2x}}{e^{4x}}$$

$$= -x^2 - x$$

and
$$u_2' = \frac{e^{2x}(x + 1)e^{2x}}{e^{4x}}$$

$$= x + 1.$$

It follows that
$$u_1 = -\frac{x^3}{3} - \frac{x^2}{2}$$

$$u_2 = \frac{x^2}{2} + x$$

and therefore

$$y_p = \left(-\frac{x^3}{3} - \frac{x^2}{2}\right)e^{2x} + \left(\frac{x^2}{2} + x\right)xe^{2x}$$

$$= \left(\frac{x^3}{6} + \frac{x^2}{2}\right)e^{2x}.$$

Thus we have

$$y = y_c + y_p$$

$$= c_1 e^{2x} + c_2 xe^{2x} + \left(\frac{x^3}{6} + \frac{x^2}{2}\right)e^{2x}.$$

EXAMPLE

Solve
$$4y'' + 36y = \csc 3x.$$

Solution: We first write the equation in the form

$$y'' + 9y = \frac{1}{4}\csc 3x.$$

Since the roots of the auxiliary equation $m^2 + 9 = 0$ are $m_1 = 3i$ and $m_2 = -3i$ we have

$$y_c = c_1 \cos 3x + c_2 \sin 3x.$$

and

$$W(\cos 3x, \sin 3x) = \begin{vmatrix} \cos 3x & \sin 3x \\ -3\sin 3x & 3\cos 3x \end{vmatrix} = 3.$$

Therefore

$$u_1' = -\frac{(\sin 3x)(\frac{1}{4}\csc 3x)}{3}$$

$$= -\frac{1}{12} \qquad\qquad \left[\csc 3x = \frac{1}{\sin 3x}\right]$$

$$u_2' = \frac{(\cos 3x)(\frac{1}{4}\csc 3x)}{3}$$

$$= \frac{1}{12}\frac{\cos 3x}{\sin 3x}$$

from which we obtain

$$u_1 = -\frac{1}{12}x$$

$$u_2 = \frac{1}{36}\ln|\sin 3x|.$$

Hence

$$y_p = -\frac{1}{12}x\cos 3x + \frac{1}{36}(\sin 3x)\ln|\sin 3x|$$

and $y = y_c + y_p$

$$= c_1\cos 3x + c_2\sin 3x - \frac{1}{12}x\cos 3x + \frac{1}{36}(\sin 3x)\ln|\sin 3x|.$$

Constants of integration   When computing the indefinite integrals of u'_1 and u'_2 we need not introduce any constants. This is because

$$y = y_c + y_p$$

$$= c_1 y_1 + c_2 y_2 + (u_1 + a_1)y_1 + (u_2 + b_1)y_2$$

$$= (c_1 + a_1)y_1 + (c_2 + b_2)y_2 + u_1 y_1 + u_2 y_2$$

$$= C_1 y_1 + C_2 y_2 + u_1 y_1 + u_2 y_2.$$

EXERCISES 4.5   Answers to odd-numbered problems begin on page A-12 of the Appendix. In Problems 1–16 solve each differential equation by variation of parameters.

EXAMPLE   Solve $y'' - y = \dfrac{1}{x}.$

Solution: $m^2 - 1 = 0$

$$m_1 = 1, \qquad m_2 = -1$$

$$y_c = c_1 e^x + c_2 e^{-x}$$

$$W(e^x, e^{-x}) = \begin{vmatrix} e^x & e^{-x} \\ e^x & -e^{-x} \end{vmatrix} = -2$$

$$u'_1 = -\frac{e^{-x}(1/x)}{-2}, \qquad u_1 = \frac{1}{2}\int\frac{e^{-x}}{x}\,dx$$

$$u'_2 = \frac{e^x(1/x)}{-2}, \qquad u_2 = -\frac{1}{2}\int\frac{e^x}{x}\,dx.$$

It is well known that the integrals defining u_1 and u_2 cannot be expressed in terms of elementary functions. Hence we write

$$y_p = \frac{1}{2}e^x\int\frac{e^{-x}}{x}\,dx - \frac{1}{2}e^{-x}\int\frac{e^x}{x}\,dx$$

and therefore

$$y = y_c + y_p$$

$$= c_1 e^x + c_2 e^{-x} + \frac{1}{2} e^x \int \frac{e^{-x}}{x} dx - \frac{1}{2} e^{-x} \int \frac{e^x}{x} dx.$$

1. $y'' + y = \sec x$ 2. $y'' + y = \tan x$

3. $y'' + y = \sin x$ ★4. $y'' + y = \sec x \tan x$

5. $y'' + y = \cos^2 x$ 6. $y'' - y = \cosh x$

7. $y'' - 4y = e^{2x}/x$ ★8. $y'' - 3y' + 2y = e^{3x}/(1 + e^x)$

9. $y'' + 3y' + 2y = \sin e^x$ 10. $y'' - 2y' + y = e^x \arctan x$

11. $y'' - 2y' + y = e^x/(1 + x^2)$ 12. $y'' - 2y' + 2y = e^x \sec x$

13. $y'' + 2y' + y = e^{-x} \ln x$ 14. $y'' + 10y' + 25y = e^{-10x}/x^2$

15. $4y'' - 4y' + y = 8e^{-x} + x$ ★16. $4y'' - 4y' + y = e^{x/2}\sqrt{1 - x^2}$

In Problems 17–20 solve each differential equation by variation of parameters subject to the initial conditions $y(0) = 1$, $y'(0) = 0$.

17. $y'' - y = xe^x$ ★18. $2y'' + y' - y = x + 1$

19. $y'' + 2y' - 8y = 2e^{-2x} - e^{-x}$

20. $y'' - 4y' + 4y = (12x^2 - 6x)e^{2x}$

21. Given that $y_1 = x$ and $y_2 = x \ln x$ are known solutions of

$$x^2 y'' - xy' + y = 0$$

for $x > 0$. Find the general solution of

$$x^2 y'' - xy' + y = 4x \ln x.$$

22. Solve the third-order equation

$$y''' + 4y' = \sin x \cos x.$$

[*Hint:* $(d/dx)\,(y'' + 4y) = y''' + 4y'$, integrate and then use variation of parameters.]

23. Solve $y''' - y' = xe^x$ by the method outlined in Problem 22.

★24. The complementary function for

$$y''' - 2y'' - y' + 2y = e^{3x}$$

is

$$y_c = c_1 e^{-x} + c_2 e^x + c_3 e^{2x}.$$

Find variable parameters u_1, u_2, and u_3 such that

$$y_p = u_1(x)e^{-x} + u_2(x)e^x + u_3(x)e^{2x}$$

is a particular solution of the differential equation.

CHAPTER SUMMARY

We summarize here the salient information for the important case of solving a linear second-order differential equation with constant coefficients:

$$ay'' + by' + cy = g(x) \tag{1}$$

where g is continuous on an interval $a \leq x \leq b$. We first solve the **homogeneous** equation

$$ay'' + by' + cy = 0. \tag{2}$$

Equation (2) possesses two solutions y_1 and y_2 which are **linearly independent** on $-\infty < x < \infty$. In a general context, two functions f_1 and f_2 are linearly independent on an interval if and only if neither function is a constant multiple of the other on the interval. Also, if the **Wronskian**

$$W(f_1, f_2) = \begin{vmatrix} f_1 & f_2 \\ f_1' & f_2' \end{vmatrix} \neq 0$$

for at least one point in an interval then the functions are linearly independent on the interval. The Wronskian of two solutions of a homogeneous linear second-order differential equation on an interval $a \leq x \leq b$ is either identically zero or is never zero on the interval.* The solutions are then linearly dependent or linearly independent, respectively.

By the **superposition principle** we know that the sum of two solutions of a homogeneous linear equation is also a solution. Thus for the linearly independent solutions y_1 and y_2 we define the **general solution** of (2) to be

$$y = c_1 y_1 + c_2 y_2 \tag{3}$$

where c_1 and c_2 are arbitrary constants.

To find y_1 and y_2 we must solve the **auxiliary equation**

$$am^2 + bm + c = 0. \tag{4}$$

There are three forms of the general solution depending on the three possible ways in which the roots of (4) may occur.

---

* When the coefficients of the equation are not constant we assume conditions A and C of Section 4.1 hold.

CHAPTER SUMMARY

	Roots	General Solution
1.	m_1 and m_2: real and distinct	$y = c_1 e^{m_1 x} + c_2 e^{m_2 x}$
2.	m_1 and m_2: real but $m_1 = m_2$	$y = c_1 e^{m_1 x} + c_2 x e^{m_1 x}$
3.	m_1 and m_2: complex	
	$m_1 = \alpha + i\beta$	$y = e^{\alpha x}[c_1 \cos \beta x + c_2 \sin \beta x]$
	$m_2 = \alpha - i\beta$	

To solve the **nonhomogeneous** equation (1) we write down the **complementary function** y_c (equation (3)) and then find a **particular solution** y_p by either (a) **undetermined coefficients**, or (b) **variation of parameters**.

The former procedure is limited to the cases where $g(x)$ is a polynomial, an exponential function e^{ax}, the trigonometric functions $\cos kx$ or $\sin kx$, or finite sums and products of these functions. The method consists of assuming y_p is a linear combination of $g(x)$ and its linearly independent derivatives. When any part of this combination duplicates a part of y_c then some portion of the assumption must be multiplied by x^n, where n is some positive integer. Variation of parameters is a procedure which always yields a particular solution provided the homogeneous equation can be solved. This method consists of finding a solution of the form

$$y_p = u_1(x)y_1(x) + u_2(x)y_2(x)$$

where y_1 and y_2 are the linearly independent solutions of (2) and u_1 and u_2 are functions determined from the equations

$$u_1' = -\frac{y_2 f(x)}{W}$$

$$u_2' = \frac{y_1 f(x)}{W}.$$

W is the Wronskian of y_1 and y_2, and $f(x) = g(x)/a$.

The general solution of the nonhomogeneous equation (1) is then

$$y = y_c + y_p$$

$$= c_1 y_1 + c_2 y_2 + y_p. \tag{5}$$

In the case of constant coefficients, we can say that *every* solution of the homogeneous equation (2) can be obtained from its general solution (3). In addition, if we make the natural assumption that $g(x)$ is continuous on an interval $a \le x \le b$, then this is sufficient to guarantee that every solution of the nonhomogeneous equation (1) on the interval, can be obtained from its general solution (5).

**REVIEW
EXERCISES**

Answers to odd-numbered problems begin on page A-12 of the Appendix.

[4.1]   1.   Which of the following sets of functions are linearly independent on $0 < x < \infty$?

(a) $f_1(x) = x^2$, $f_2(x) = x|x|$

(b) $f_1(x) = 2x + 8$, $f_2(x) = 2x$

(c) $f_1(x) = x^2 + 1$, $f_2(x) = 1 - x^2$, $f_3(x) = 5$

(d) $f_1(x) = 1$, $f_2(x) = \cosh x$, $f_3(x) = e^x$

(e) $f_1(x) = \cos^2 x$, $f_2(x) = \cos 2x$, $f_3(x) = 2$

(f) $f_1(x) = e^x$, $f_2(x) = xe^x$, $f_3(x) = x^2 e^x$

2.   Prove that

$$y = c_1 \frac{\sin x}{\sqrt{x}} + c_2 \frac{\cos x}{\sqrt{x}}$$

is the general solution of

$$x^2 y'' + xy' + \left(x^2 - \frac{1}{4}\right) y = 0$$

on the interval $0 < x < \infty$.

[4.2]   In Problems 3 and 4 use formula (4) of Section 4.2 to find a second solution for the differential equation given that $y_1(x)$ is a known solution.

3. $y'' + 4y = 0$; $y_1 = \cos 2x$

★4. $xy'' - 2(x + 1)y' + (x + 2)y = 0$; $y_1 = e^x$

[4.3]   In Problems 5–10 find the general solution of each differential equation.

5. $y'' - 2y' - 2y = 0$

6. $2y'' + 2y' + 3y = 0$

7. $y''' + 10y'' + 25y' = 0$

★8. $2\dfrac{d^4 y}{dx^4} + 3\dfrac{d^3 y}{dx^3} + 2\dfrac{d^2 y}{dx^2} + 6\dfrac{dy}{dx} - 4y = 0$

9. $3y''' + 10y'' + 15y' + 4y = 0$

10. $2y''' + 9y'' + 12y' + 5y = 0$

[4.4]   In Problems 11–13 solve each differential equation by the method of undetermined coefficients.

11. $y'' - 3y' + 5y = 4x^3 - 2x$

★12. $y'' - 2y' + y = x^2 e^x$

13. $y''' - 5y'' + 6y' = 2 \sin x + 8$

[4.5]   In Problems 14 and 15 solve each differential equation by the method of variation of parameters.

★**14.** $y'' - y = 2e^x/(e^x + e^{-x})$

15. $y'' - 2y' + 2y = e^x \tan x$

CHAPTER 5

Applications of Second-Order Differential Equations: Vibrational Models

5.1 Simple Harmonic Motion

Hooke's law

When different weights are attached to a flexible spring suspended from a rigid support (such as a ceiling), the amount of stretch, or elongation, will of course be different in each case.

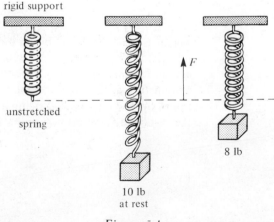

rigid support

unstretched
spring

F

10 lb
at rest

8 lb

Figure 5.1

185

By Hooke's law, the spring itself exerts a restoring force F (in lbs) opposite to the direction of elongation and proportional to the amount of elongation s (in ft). Simply stated, $F = ks$ where k is a constant of proportionality. Although different weights stretch a spring by different amounts, the spring is essentially characterized by the number k. For example, if a 10-lb weight stretches a spring by 1/2 ft then

$$10 = k(\tfrac{1}{2})$$

$$k = 20 \, \text{lb/ft.} \tag{1}$$

Necessarily then an 8-lb weight stretches the same spring 2/5 ft.

Newton's second law

After a weight is attached to a spring it will stretch the spring by an amount s and attain a position of equilibrium at which the weight W is balanced by the restoring force ks. Recall from elementary physics that in the *fps* (ft-lb-sec) system weight is defined by

$$W = mg \tag{2}$$

where the mass m is measured in slugs and $g = 32 \, \text{ft/sec}^2$. As indicated in Figure 5.2(b) the condition of equilibrium is $mg = ks$ or $mg - ks = 0$. If the

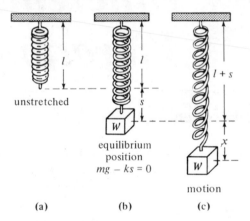

unstretched

equilibrium
position
$mg - ks = 0$

motion

(a)   (b)   (c)

Figure 5.2

weight is now displaced by an amount x from its equilibrium position and released the net force F in this dynamic case is given by **Newton's second law of motion** $F = ma$ where a is the acceleration d^2x/dt^2. Assuming that there are no retarding forces acting on the system and assuming that the weight vibrates free of other external influencing forces (*free motion*), we can then equate F to the resultant force of the weight and the restoring force:

$$m\frac{d^2x}{dt^2} = -k(s + x) + mg$$

$$= -kx + \underbrace{mg - ks}_{\text{zero}}$$

$$= -kx. \tag{3}$$

The negative sign in (3) indicates that the restoring force of the spring acts opposite to the direction of motion. Furthermore, we shall adopt the convention that displacements measured *below* the equilibrium position are *positive*. See Figure 5.3.

Equation of free undamped motion

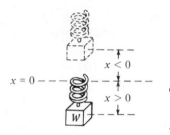

Figure 5.3

By dividing (3) by the mass m we obtain the second-order differential equation

$$\frac{d^2x}{dt^2} + \frac{k}{m}x = 0 \tag{4}$$

or

$$\frac{d^2x}{dt^2} + \omega^2 x = 0 \tag{5}$$

where $\omega^2 = k/m$. Equation (5) is said to describe **simple harmonic motion**, or **free undamped motion**. Associated with equation (5) there are two obvious initial conditions:

$$x(0) = \alpha \qquad \frac{dx}{dt}\bigg|_{t=0} = \beta \tag{6}$$

representing the amount of initial displacement and the initial velocity, respectively. For example, if $\alpha > 0$, $\beta < 0$, the weight would start from a point *below* the equilibrium position with an imparted *upward* velocity. If $\alpha < 0$, $\beta = 0$, the weight would be released from *rest* from a point $|\alpha|$ units *above* the equilibrium position, and so on.

The solution

To solve equation (5) we note that the solutions of the auxiliary equation $m^2 + \omega^2 = 0$ are the complex numbers

$$m_1 = \omega i \qquad m_2 = -\omega i.$$

Thus, from equation (8) of Section 4.3 we can write

$$x(t) = c_1 \cos \omega t + c_2 \sin \omega t. \tag{7}$$

The period of oscillations for a function such as (7) is $T = 2\pi/\omega$ and the frequency of free vibrations is $f = 1/T = \omega/2\pi$.† For example, for $x(t) = 2\cos 3t - 4\sin 3t$, the period is $2\pi/3$ and the frequency is $3/2\pi$. The former number means that the graph of $x(t)$ repeats every $2\pi/3$ units; the latter number means that 3 cycles of the graph are completed every 2π units, or equivalently, the weight undergoes $3/2\pi$ oscillations per unit time.

---

† Sometimes the number ω is also called the frequency of vibrations.

EXAMPLE   Solve and interpret the initial-value problem

$$\frac{d^2x}{dt^2} + 16x = 0$$

$$x(0) = 10 \qquad \frac{dx}{dt}\bigg|_{t=0} = 0.$$

Solution: The problem is equivalent to pulling a weight on a spring down 10 units below the equilibrium position, holding it until $t = 0$, and then releasing it from rest. Applying the initial conditions to the solution

$$x(t) = c_1 \cos 4t + c_2 \sin 4t$$

gives

$$x(0) = 10 = c_1 \cdot 1 + c_2 \cdot 0$$

so that $c_1 = 10$, and therefore

$$x(t) = 10 \cos 4t + c_2 \sin 4t$$

$$\frac{dx}{dt} = -40 \sin 4t + 4c_2 \cos 4t$$

$$\frac{dx}{dt}\bigg|_{t=0} = 0 = 4c_2 \cdot 1.$$

The latter equation implies $c_2 = 0$ so therefore $x(t) = 10 \cos 4t$.

The solution clearly shows that once the system is set in motion, it stays in motion with the weight bouncing back and forth 10 units on either side of the equilibrium position $x = 0$. As shown in Figure 5.4(b), the period of oscillation is $2\pi/4 = \pi/2$.

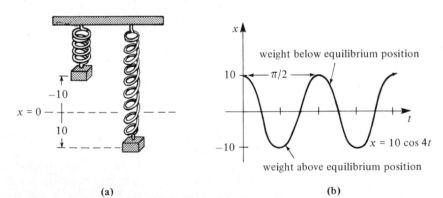

(a)   (b)

Figure 5.4

EXAMPLE

A 2-lb weight stretches a spring 6 inches. It is then released from a point 8 inches below the equilibrium position with an upward velocity of 4/3 ft/sec. Determine the function $x(t)$ which describes the subsequent free motion.

Solution: Before solving the problem, we note that the measures given in terms of inches must be converted to feet: 6 inches = 6/12 = 1/2 foot; 8 inches = 8/12 = 2/3 foot. In addition we must convert the units of weight given in pounds to units of mass. Since $W = mg$ and $m = W/g$ it follows that

$$m = \frac{2}{32} = \frac{1}{16} \text{ slug.}$$

Also from Hooke's law

$$2 = k \cdot \frac{1}{2}$$

we find

$$k = 4 \text{ lb/ft.}$$

Hence the analogue of equation (3) is

$$\frac{1}{16} \frac{d^2x}{dt^2} = -4x$$

or

$$\frac{d^2x}{dt^2} + 64x = 0. \tag{8}$$

The initial displacement and initial velocity are given by

$$x(0) = \frac{2}{3} \qquad \frac{dx}{dt}\bigg|_{t=0} = -\frac{4}{3}$$

where the negative sign in the last condition is a consequence of the fact that the weight is given an initial velocity in the negative or upward direction.

Now $\omega^2 = 64$ or $\omega = 8$ so that the general solution of (8) is

$$x(t) = c_1 \cos 8t + c_2 \sin 8t. \tag{9}$$

Applying the initial conditions to (9) we obtain

$$x(0) = \frac{2}{3} = c_1 \cdot 1 + c_2 \cdot 0,$$

$c_1 = 2/3$,

$$x(t) = \frac{2}{3} \cos 8t + c_2 \sin 8t$$

$$x'(t) = -\frac{16}{3} \sin 8t + 8c_2 \cos 8t$$

$$x'(0) = -\frac{4}{3} = -\frac{16}{3} \cdot 0 + 8c_2 \cdot 1,$$

$c_2 = -\dfrac{1}{6}$. Thus the equation of motion is

$$x(t) = \frac{2}{3}\cos 8t - \frac{1}{6}\sin 8t \qquad (10)$$

Alternative form of
x(t)

When $c_1 \neq 0$ and $c_2 \neq 0$, the actual amplitude A of free vibrations is not obvious from inspection of equation (7). For example, although the weight in the preceding example is initially displaced $2/3$ ft beyond the equilibrium position, the amplitude of vibrations is a number larger than $2/3$. Hence it is often convenient to convert a solution of form (7) to the simpler form

$$\boxed{x(t) = A\sin(\omega t + \phi).} \qquad (11)$$

Here

$$\boxed{A = \sqrt{c_1^2 + c_2^2}}$$

and ϕ is a **phase angle** defined by

$$\left.\begin{array}{l} \sin\phi = \dfrac{c_1}{A} \\[2ex] \cos\phi = \dfrac{c_2}{A} \end{array}\right\} \quad \phi = \tan^{-1}\left(\dfrac{c_1}{c_2}\right). \qquad (12)$$

To verify this we expand (11) by the addition formula for the sine function

$$A\sin\omega t\cos\phi + A\cos\omega t\sin\phi = (A\sin\phi)\cos\omega t + (A\cos\phi)\sin\omega t. \quad (13)$$

It follows from Figure 5.5 that if ϕ is defined by

$$\sin\phi = \frac{c_1}{\sqrt{c_1^2 + c_2^2}} = \frac{c_1}{A}, \qquad \cos\phi = \frac{c_2}{\sqrt{c_1^2 + c_2^2}} = \frac{c_2}{A}$$

then (13) becomes

$$A\frac{c_1}{A}\cos\omega t + A\frac{c_2}{A}\sin\omega t = c_1\cos\omega t + c_2\sin\omega t$$

$$= x(t).$$

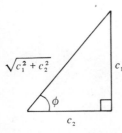

Figure 5.5

EXAMPLE   In view of the foregoing discussion, we can write the solution to the preceding example

$$x(t) = \frac{2}{3}\cos 8t - \frac{1}{6}\sin 8t$$

alternatively as $x(t) = A\sin(8t + \phi).$

The amplitude is given by

$$A = \sqrt{\left(\frac{2}{3}\right)^2 + \left(-\frac{1}{6}\right)^2}$$

$$= \sqrt{\frac{4}{9} + \frac{1}{36}}$$

$$= \frac{\sqrt{17}}{6} \approx 0.69.$$

One should exercise some care when finding the phase angle ϕ since a formal computation of

$$\tan^{-1}\left(\frac{2/3}{-1/6}\right) = \tan^{-1}(-4)$$

on a scientific hand calculator would give

$$\tan^{-1}(-4) = -1.326 \text{ radians.}$$

Unfortunately, this particular angle is located in the fourth quadrant and therefore contradicts the fact that $\sin\phi > 0$ and $\cos\phi < 0$ (recall, $c_1 > 0$ and $c_2 < 0$). Hence we must take ϕ to be the second quadrant, or supplementary, angle

$$\phi = \pi + (-1.326)$$

$$= 1.816 \text{ radians.}$$

Thus we have

$$x(t) = \frac{\sqrt{17}}{6}\sin(8t + 1.816). \tag{14}$$

Form (11) is very useful since it is easy to find the values of time for which the graph of $x(t)$ crosses the positive t-axis (the line $x = 0$). We observe that $\sin(\omega t + \phi) = 0$ when

$$\omega t + \phi = n\pi$$

where n is a nonnegative integer.

EXAMPLE   For motion described by $x(t) = (\sqrt{17}/6) \sin(8t + 1.816)$ find the first value of time for which the weight passes through the equilibrium position heading downward.

Solution: The values of t for which $\sin(8t + 1.816) = 0$ are determined from

$$8t + 1.816 = \pi, \quad 8t + 1.816 = 2\pi, \quad 8t + 1.816 = 3\pi, \ldots$$

and so $t_1 = 0.166$, $t_2 = 0.558$, $t_3 = 0.951, \ldots$, respectively.

Inspection of Figure 5.6 shows that the weight passes through $x = 0$ heading downward (namely, toward $x > 0$) the first time at $t_2 = 0.558$.

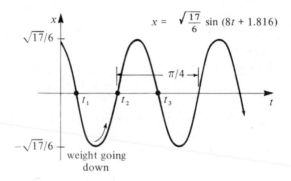

Figure 5.6

Remark: One differential equation can serve as a model for many different physical phenomena. We have already seen equation (5) in the form

$$\frac{d^2\theta}{dt^2} + \frac{g}{l}\theta = 0. \tag{15}$$

In this case the corresponding solution

$$\theta(t) = c_1 \cos\sqrt{g/l}\,t + c_2 \sin\sqrt{g/l}\,t \tag{16}$$

describes small angular displacements of a plane pendulum (see Section 1.3).

EXERCISES 5.1   Answers to odd-numbered exercises begin on page A-12 of the Appendix. In Problems 1–4 write the solution of the given initial-value problem in form (11).

1. $x'' + 25x = 0$
    $x(0) = -2, \quad x'(0) = 10$

★2. $\frac{1}{2}x'' + 8x = 0$
    $x(0) = 1, \quad x'(0) = -2$

3. $x'' + 2x = 0$

    $x(0) = -1, \quad x'(0) = -2\sqrt{2}.$

4. $\dfrac{1}{4}x'' + 16x = 0$

    $x(0) = 4, \quad x'(0) = 16$

5. State in words a possible physical interpretation of the problem:

    $$\frac{1}{8}x'' + 3x = 0$$

    $$x(0) = -3, \quad x'(0) = -2$$

★6. A 4-lb weight is attached to a spring whose spring constant is 16 lb/ft. What is the period of simple harmonic motion?

7. The period of free undamped oscillations of a weight on a spring is $\pi/4$ sec. If the spring constant is 16 lb/ft, what is the numerical value of the weight?

★8. Show that any linear combination $x(t) = c_1 \cos \omega t + c_2 \sin \omega t$ can also be written in the form

    $$x(t) = A \cos(\omega t + \phi)$$

    where $$A = \sqrt{c_1^2 + c_2^2}$$

    and $$\sin \phi = -\frac{c_2}{A} \qquad \cos \phi = \frac{c_1}{A}.$$

9. Express the solution of Problem 1 in the form of the cosine function given in Problem 8.

10. If x_0 and v_0 are the initial position and velocity, respectively, of a weight exhibiting simple harmonic motion, show that the amplitude of oscillations is

    $$A = \sqrt{x_0^2 + \left(\frac{v_0}{\omega}\right)^2}$$

11. A 24-lb weight, attached to the end of a spring, stretches it 4 in. Find the equation of subsequent motion if the weight is released from rest from a point 3 in. above the equilibrium position.

★12. Determine the equation of motion if the weight in Problem 11 is released from the equilibrium position with an initial downward velocity of 2 ft/sec.

13. A 20-lb weight stretches a spring 6 in. If the weight is released from rest 6 in. below the equilibrium position,

    (a) find the position of the spring at $t = \pi/12, \pi/8, \pi/6, \pi/4, 9\pi/32$ sec.

(b) What is the velocity of the weight when $t = 3\pi/16$ sec? In which direction is the weight heading at this instant?

(c) At what times does the weight pass through the equilibrium position?

★**14.** A 32-lb weight stretches a spring 2 ft. Determine the amplitude and period of motion if the weight is released 1 ft above the equilibrium position with an initial upward velocity of 2 ft/sec. How many complete cycles will the weight have completed at the end of 4π sec?

15. An 8-lb weight attached to a spring exhibits simple harmonic motion. Determine the equation of motion if the spring constant is 1 lb/ft and if the weight is released 6 in. below the equilibrium position with a downward velocity of 3/2 ft/sec. Express the solution in form (11).

16. A 64-lb weight attached to the end of a spring stretches it 0.32 ft. From a position 8 in. above the equilibrium position the weight is given a downward velocity of 5 ft/sec.

(a) Find the equation of motion.

(b) What is the amplitude and period of motion?

(c) How many complete cycles will the weight have completed at the end of 3π sec?

(d) At what time does the weight pass through the equilibrium position heading downward for the second time?

(e) At what times does the weight attain its maximum displacement on either side of the equilibrium position?

(f) What is the position of the weight at $t = 3$ sec?

(g) What is the instantaneous velocity at $t = 3$ sec?

(h) What is the instantaneous velocity at the times when the weight passes through the equilibrium position?

(i) At what times is the weight 5 in. below the equilibrium position?

(j) At what times is the weight 5 in. below the equilibrium position heading in the upward direction?

17. A weight of mass 1 slug is suspended from a spring whose characteristic spring constant is 9 lb/ft. Initially the weight starts from a point 1 ft above the equilibrium position with an upward velocity of $\sqrt{3}$ ft/sec. Find the times for which the weight is heading downward at a velocity of 3 ft/sec.

18. Prove that when a weight attached to a spring exhibits simple harmonic motion the maximum value of the speed (that is, $|v(t)|$) occurs when the weight is passing through the equilibrium position.

5.2 Damped Motion

The discussion of free harmonic motion is somewhat unrealistic since the motion described by equation (5) of Section 5.1 assumes that no retarding forces are acting on the moving weight. Unless the weight is suspended in a perfect vacuum, there will be at least a resisting force due to the surrounding medium. For example, as Figure 5.7 shows, the weight could be suspended in a viscous medium or connected to a dashpot damping device.

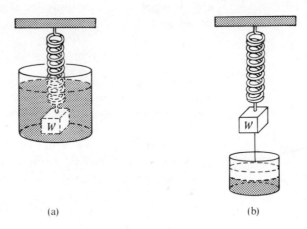

(a)　　　　　　　　　　　　　　(b)

Figure 5.7

Equation of motion with damping

In the study of mechanics, damping forces acting on a body are considered to be proportional to a power of the *instantaneous velocity*; in particular we shall assume throughout the subsequent discussion that this force is given by a constant multiple of dx/dt.† When no other external forces are impressed on the system it follows from Newton's second law that

$$m\frac{d^2x}{dt^2} = -kx - \beta\frac{dx}{dt} \tag{1}$$

where β is a positive constant and the negative sign is a consequence of the fact that the damping force acts in a direction opposite to the motion.

Dividing (1) by the mass m, the differential equation of *free, damped motion* then is

$$\boxed{\frac{d^2x}{dt^2} + \frac{\beta}{m}\frac{dx}{dt} + \frac{k}{m}x = 0} \tag{2}$$

or

$$\frac{d^2x}{dt^2} + 2\lambda\frac{dx}{dt} + \omega^2x = 0. \tag{3}$$

† In many instances, such as problems in hydrodynamics, the damping force is proportional to $(dx/dt)^2$.

In equation (3) we make the identification

$$2\lambda = \frac{\beta}{m} \qquad \omega^2 = \frac{k}{m}. \qquad (4)$$

The symbol 2λ is used only for algebraic convenience since the auxiliary equation is $m^2 + 2\lambda m + \omega^2 = 0$ and the corresponding roots are then

$$m_1 = -\lambda + \sqrt{\lambda^2 - \omega^2} \qquad m_2 = -\lambda - \sqrt{\lambda^2 - \omega^2}.$$

We can now distinguish three possible cases depending on the algebraic sign of $\lambda^2 - \omega^2$. Since each solution will contain the factor $e^{-\lambda t}, \lambda > 0$, the displacements of the weight will become negligible for large time .

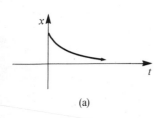

(a)

CASE I $\lambda^2 - \omega^2 > 0$. In this situation the system is said to be **overdamped** since the damping coefficient β is large when compared to the spring constant k. The corresponding solution of (3) is

$$x(t) = c_1 e^{m_1 t} + c_2 e^{m_2 t}$$

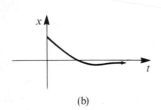

(b)

Figure 5.8

or

$$x(t) = e^{-\lambda t}[c_1 e^{\sqrt{\lambda^2 - \omega^2}\, t} + c_2 e^{-\sqrt{\lambda^2 - \omega^2}\, t}]. \qquad (5)$$

This equation represents a smooth and nonoscillatory motion. Figure 5.8 shows two possible graphs of $x(t)$.

CASE II $\lambda^2 - \omega^2 = 0$. The system is said to be **critically damped** since any slight decrease in the damping force would result in oscillatory motion. The general solution of (3) is

$$x(t) = c_1 e^{m_1 t} + c_2 t e^{m_1 t}$$

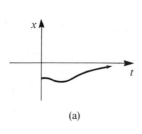

(a)

or

$$x(t) = e^{-\lambda t}[c_1 + c_2 t]. \qquad (6)$$

Some graphs of typical motion are given in Figure 5.9. Notice that the motion is quite similar to that of an overdamped system.

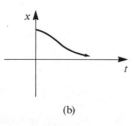

(b)

Figure 5.9

CASE III $\lambda^2 - \omega^2 < 0$. In this case the system is said to be **underdamped** since the damping coefficient is small compared to the spring constant. The roots m_1 and m_2 are now complex,

$$m_1 = -\lambda + \sqrt{\omega^2 - \lambda^2}\, i \qquad m_2 = -\lambda - \sqrt{\omega^2 - \lambda^2}\, i,$$

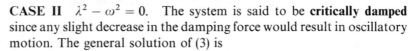

and so the general solution of equation (3) is

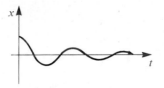

Figure 5.10

$$x(t) = e^{-\lambda t}[c_1 \cos \sqrt{\omega^2 - \lambda^2}\, t + c_2 \sin \sqrt{\omega^2 - \lambda^2}\, t]. \qquad (7)$$

As indicated in Figure 5.10 the motion is oscillatory but because of the coefficient $e^{-\lambda t}$ the amplitudes of vibration $\to 0$ as $t \to \infty$.

EXAMPLE

It is readily verified that the solution of the initial-value problem

$$\frac{d^2 x}{dt^2} + 5\frac{dx}{dt} + 4x = 0$$

$$x(0) = 1 \qquad \frac{dx}{dt}\bigg|_{t=0} = 1$$

is

$$x(t) = \frac{5}{3}e^{-t} - \frac{2}{3}e^{-4t}. \qquad (8)$$

The problem can be interpreted as representing the overdamped motion of a weight on a spring. The weight starts from a position 1 unit *below* the equilibrium position with a *downward* velocity of 1 ft/sec.

To graph $x(t)$ it is important to find the value of t for which the displacement is a maximum, that is, the value of time for which the first derivative (velocity) is zero. We have

$$x'(t) = -\frac{5}{3}e^{-t} + \frac{8}{3}e^{-4t}$$

so that $x'(t) = 0$ implies

$$\frac{5}{3}e^{-t} = \frac{8}{3}e^{-4t}$$

$$e^{3t} = \frac{8}{5}$$

$$3t = \ln\frac{8}{5}$$

$$t = \frac{1}{3}\ln\frac{8}{5} = 0.157.$$

It follows from the first derivative test, as well as our physical intuition, that $x(0.157) = 1.069\,\text{ft}$ is actually a maximum.

We should also check to see whether the graph crosses the t-axis, that is, whether the weight passes through the equilibrium position. This cannot happen since the equation $x(t) = 0$, or

$$\frac{5}{3}e^{-t} = \frac{2}{3}e^{-4t}$$

$$e^{3t} = \frac{2}{5}$$

$$3t = \ln\frac{2}{5}$$

$$t = \frac{1}{3}\ln\frac{2}{5}$$

has the physically irrelevant solution $t = -0.305$.

The graph of $x(t)$, along with some other pertinent data, is given in Figure 5.11.

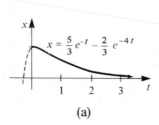

t	$x(t)$
1	0.601
1.5	0.370
2	0.225
2.5	0.137
3	0.083

(a)   (b)

Figure 5.11

EXAMPLE

An 8-lb weight stretches a spring 2 ft. Assuming a damping force numerically equal to two times the instantaneous velocity acts on the system, determine the equation of motion if the weight is released from the equilibrium position with an upward velocity of 3 ft/sec.

Solution: From Hooke's law we have

$$8 = k(2)$$

$$k = 4\,\text{lb/ft}$$

and from $m = W/g$

$$m = \frac{8}{32} = \frac{1}{4}\,\text{slug.}$$

Thus, the differential equation of motion is

$$\frac{1}{4}\frac{d^2x}{dt^2} = -4x - 2\frac{dx}{dt} \qquad \text{or} \qquad \frac{d^2x}{dt^2} + 8\frac{dx}{dt} + 16x = 0. \tag{9}$$

The initial conditions are

$$x(0) = 0 \qquad \frac{dx}{dt}\bigg|_{t=0} = -3.$$

Now the auxiliary equation for (9) is

$$m^2 + 8m + 16 = (m + 4)^2 = 0$$

so that $m_1 = m_2 = -4$. Hence the system is critically damped and

$$x(t) = c_1 e^{-4t} + c_2 t e^{-4t}. \tag{10}$$

The initial condition $x(0) = 0$ immediately demands that $c_1 = 0$, whereas using $x'(0) = -3$ gives $c_2 = -3$. Thus, the equation of motion is

$$x(t) = -3t e^{-4t}. \tag{11}$$

To graph $x(t)$ we proceed as in the preceding example:

$$x'(t) = -3(-4t e^{-4t} + e^{-4t})$$
$$= -3e^{-4t}(1 - 4t).$$

Clearly $x'(t) = 0$ when $t = 1/4$. At this value the vertical displacement

$$x\left(\frac{1}{4}\right) = -3\left(\frac{1}{4}\right)e^{-1} = -0.276 \,\text{ft}$$

is a maximum. The graph of $x(t)$ is given in Figure 5.12.

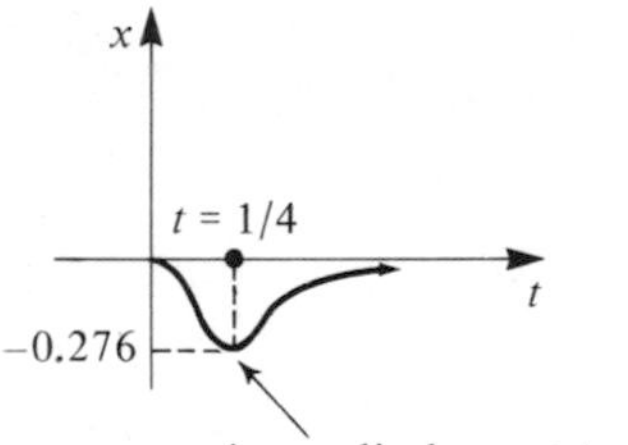

$t = 1/4$

-0.276

maximum displacement
above equilibrium position

Figure 5.12

EXAMPLE

A 16-lb weight is attached to a 5-ft-long spring. At equilibrium the spring then measures 8.2 ft. If the weight is pushed up and released from rest at a point 2 ft above the equilibrium position, find the displacements $x(t)$ if it is further known that the surrounding medium offers a resistance numerically equal to the instantaneous velocity.

Solution: The elongation of the spring after the weight is attached is $8.2 - 5 = 3.2$ ft so it follows from Hooke's law that

$$16 = k(3.2)$$
$$k = 5 \,\text{lb/ft}.$$

In addition we have

$$m = \frac{16}{32} = \frac{1}{2} \,\text{slug},$$

so that the differential equation of motion is given by

$$\frac{1}{2}\frac{dx^2}{dt^2} = -5x - \frac{dx}{dt}$$

or
$$\frac{d^2x}{dt^2} + 2\frac{dx}{dt} + 10x = 0. \tag{12}$$

This latter equation is solved subject to the conditions

$$x(0) = -2 \qquad \frac{dx}{dt}\bigg|_{t=0} = 0.$$

Proceeding, we find that the roots of $m^2 + 2m + 10 = 0$ are $m_1 = -1 + 3i$ and $m_2 = -1 - 3i$ which then implies the system is underdamped and

$$x(t) = e^{-t}[c_1 \cos 3t + c_2 \sin 3t]. \tag{13}$$

Now

$$x(0) = -2 = c_1$$
$$x(t) = e^{-t}[-2\cos 3t + c_2 \sin 3t]$$
$$x'(t) = e^{-t}[6 \sin 3t + 3c_2 \cos 3t] - e^{-t}[-2\cos 3t + c_2 \sin 3t]$$
$$x'(0) = 0 = 3c_2 + 2$$

which gives $c_2 = -2/3$. Thus we finally obtain

$$x(t) = e^{-t}\left[-2\cos 3t - \frac{2}{3}\sin 3t\right]. \tag{14}$$

Alternative form of the solution

In a manner identical to the procedure used in Section 5.1 we can write any solution of form (7)

$$x(t) = e^{-\lambda t}[c_1 \cos \sqrt{\omega^2 - \lambda^2}\,t + c_2 \sin \sqrt{\omega^2 - \lambda^2}\,t]$$

in the alternative form

$$\boxed{x(t) = Ae^{-\lambda t} \sin [\sqrt{\omega^2 - \lambda^2}\,t + \phi]} \tag{15}$$

where the phase angle ϕ is determined from the equations

$$\phi = \tan^{-1}\left(\frac{c_1}{c_2}\right) \qquad \sin \phi = \frac{c_1}{A} \qquad \cos \phi = \frac{c_2}{A}.$$

To graph an equation such as (15), we first find the intercepts $t_1, t_2, \ldots, t_k, \ldots$. That is, for some integer n we must solve

$$\sqrt{\omega^2 - \lambda^2}\, t + \phi = n\pi$$

for t. It follows

$$\boxed{t = \frac{n\pi - \phi}{\sqrt{\omega^2 - \lambda^2}}.}$$

In addition, we note that $|x(t)| \le Ae^{-\lambda t}$ since

$$|\sin\,[\sqrt{\omega^2 - \lambda^2}\, t + \phi]| \le 1.$$

Indeed, the graph of (15) touches the graphs of $\pm Ae^{-\lambda t}$ at the values $t_1^*, t_2^*, \ldots, t_k^*, \ldots$ for which

$$\sin\,[\sqrt{\omega^2 - \lambda^2}\, t + \phi] = \pm 1.$$

This means $\sqrt{\omega^2 - \lambda^2}\, t + \phi$ must be an odd multiple of $\pi/2$,

$$\sqrt{\omega^2 - \lambda^2}\, t + \phi = (2n + 1)\frac{\pi}{2},$$

$$\boxed{t = \frac{(2n + 1)\pi/2 - \phi}{\sqrt{\omega^2 - \lambda^2}}.}$$

For example, were we asked to graph $x(t) = e^{-0.5t}\sin(2t - \pi/3)$, we find the intercepts on the *positive* t-axis by solving

$$2t - \frac{\pi}{3} = 0, \quad 2t - \frac{\pi}{3} = \pi, \quad 2t - \frac{\pi}{3} = 2\pi, \ldots$$

which gives

$$t_1 = \frac{\pi}{6}, \quad t_2 = \frac{4\pi}{6}, \quad t_3 = \frac{7\pi}{6}, \ldots$$

Notice that even though $x(t)$ is *not periodic*, the difference between the successive roots is $t_k - t_{k-1} = \pi/2$ units. Also, $\sin(2t - \pi/3) = \pm 1$ at the solutions of

$$2t - \frac{\pi}{3} = \frac{\pi}{2}, \quad 2t - \frac{\pi}{3} = \frac{3\pi}{2}, \quad 2t - \frac{\pi}{3} = \frac{5\pi}{2}, \ldots$$

or
$$t_1^* = \frac{5\pi}{12}, \quad t_2^* = \frac{11\pi}{12}, \quad t_3^* = \frac{17\pi}{12}, \ldots .\dagger$$

The graph of $x(t)$ is given in Figure 5.13.

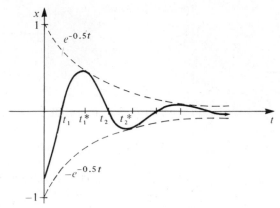

Figure 5.13

EXAMPLE   Using (15) we can write the solution of the preceding example

$$\frac{d^2x}{dt^2} + \frac{dx}{dt} + 10x = 0$$

$$x(0) = -2 \qquad \left.\frac{dx}{dt}\right|_{t=0} = 0$$

in the form $x(t) = Ae^{-t}\sin(3t + \phi)$.
   Now from (14) we have $c_1 = -2$, $c_2 = -2/3$ so that

$$A = \sqrt{4 + \frac{4}{9}} = \frac{2}{3}\sqrt{10}$$

and

$$\tan^{-1}\left(\frac{-2}{-2/3}\right) = \tan^{-1}(3)$$

$$= 1.249 \text{ radians.}$$

---

† It is easily shown that the difference between the successive t_k^* is also $\pi/2$. As a consequence of this phenomenon it is often said that the general formula $e^{-\lambda t}\sin[\sqrt{\omega^2 - \lambda^2}\,t + \phi]$ has a *quasi-period* $2\pi/\sqrt{\omega^2 - \lambda^2}$.
   It should be noted that the values of t for which the graph of $x(t)$ touches the exponential graphs are not the values for which the function attains its relative extrema. Nonetheless, the quasi-period is the difference in times between, say, two successive maxima. See Problems 9 and 11 of Exercise 5.2.

But, since $\sin \phi < 0$ and $\cos \phi < 0$ we take ϕ to be the third quadrant angle $\phi = \pi + 1.249 = 4.391$ radians. Hence

$$x(t) = \frac{2}{3}\sqrt{10}\,e^{-t}\sin(3t + 4.391).$$

The graph of this function is given in Figure 5.14. The values of t_k and t_k^* are the intercepts and the points where the graph of $x(t)$ touches the graphs of $\pm(2/3)\sqrt{10}\,e^{-t}$, respectively. In this example the difference between the successive t_k (and the successive t_k^*) is $\pi/3$ units.

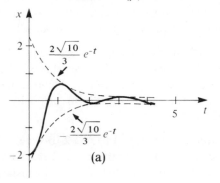

k	t_k	t_k^*	$x(t_k^*)$
1	0.631	1.154	0.665
2	1.678	2.202	−0.233
3	2.725	3.249	0.082
4	3.772	4.296	−0.029

(a)   (b)

Figure 5.14

EXERCISES 5.2   Answers to odd-numbered problems begin on page A-13 of the Appendix.

1. Give a possible physical interpretation of the initial-value problem:

$$\frac{1}{16}x'' + 2x' + x = 0$$

$$x(0) = 0 \qquad \left.\frac{dx}{dt}\right|_{t=0} = -1.5.$$

★2. A 4-ft spring measures 8 ft long after an 8-lb weight is attached to it. The medium through which the weight moves offers a resistance numerically equal to $\sqrt{2}$ times the instantaneous velocity. Find the equation of motion if the weight is released from the equilibrium position with a downward velocity of 5 ft/sec. Find the time for which the weight attains its maximum displacement from the equilibrium position. What is the position of the weight at this instant?

3. A 4-lb weight is attached to a spring whose constant is 2 lb/ft. The medium offers a resistance to the motion of the weight numerically equal to the instantaneous velocity. If the weight is released from a point 1 ft above the equilibrium position with a downward velocity of 8 ft/sec, determine the time that the weight passes through the equilibrium position. Find the time for which the weight attains its maximum displacement from the equilibrium position. What is the position of the weight at this instant?

4. A 2-lb weight is attached to a spring whose constant is 1 lb/ft and the entire system is then submerged in a liquid which imparts a damping force numerically equal to 5/8 times the instantaneous velocity. Determine the equations of motion if

    (a) the weight is released from rest 1 ft below the equilibrium position;
    (b) the weight is released 1 ft below the equilibrium position with an upward velocity of 12 ft/sec.

5. In parts (a) and (b) of Problem 4, determine whether the weight passes through the equilibrium position. In each case, find the time at which the weight attains its maximum displacement from the equilibrium position. What is the position of the weight at this instant?

★6. A 10-lb weight attached to a spring stretches it 2 ft. The weight is then set in motion in a medium which offers a resistance numerically equal to β ($\beta > 0$) times the instantaneous velocity. Determine the values of β so that the motion is (a) overdamped, (b) critically damped, and (c) underdamped.

7. A force of 2 lb stretches a spring 1 ft. A 3.2-lb weight is attached to the spring and the system is then immersed in a medium which imparts a damping force numerically equal to 0.4 times the instantaneous velocity.

    (a) Find the equation of motion if the weight is released from rest 1 ft above the equilibrium position.
    (b) Express the equation of motion in the form given in (15).
    (c) Find the first time for which the weight passes through the equilibrium position heading upward.

★8. A 24-lb weight stretches a spring 4 ft. The subsequent motion takes place in a medium offering a resistance numerically equal to β times the instantaneous velocity. If the weight starts from the equilibrium position with an upward velocity of 2 ft/sec, show that if $\beta > 3\sqrt{2}$, the equation of motion is

$$x(t) = \frac{-3}{\sqrt{\beta^2 - 18}} e^{-2\beta t/3} \sinh \frac{2}{3}\sqrt{\beta^2 - 18}\,t.$$

9. In the case of underdamped motion show that the difference in times between two successive positive maxima is $2\pi/\sqrt{\omega^2 - \lambda^2}$.

10. In the case of underdamped motion show that the ratio between two consecutive maximum (or minimum) displacements is the constant

$$e^{-2\pi\lambda/\sqrt{\omega^2 - \lambda^2}}$$

The number $2\pi\lambda/\sqrt{\omega^2 - \lambda^2}$ is sometimes called the **logarithmic decrement**.

11. We have seen that the intercepts of the graph of $x(t) = Ae^{-\lambda t}\sin(\sqrt{\omega^2 - \lambda^2}\,t + \phi)$ are halfway between the values of t for which the graph of $x(t)$ touches the graphs of $\pm Ae^{-\lambda t}$. The values of t for which $x(t)$ is a maximum or minimum are not located halfway between the intercepts of the graph of $x(t)$. Verify this last statement by considering the function $x(t) = e^{-t}\sin(t + \pi/4)$.

5.3   Forced Motion

With damping

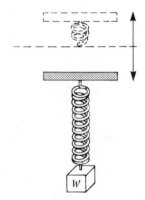

Figure 5.15

Suppose we now take into consideration an external force $f(t)$ acting on the vibrating spring. For example, $f(t)$ could represent a driving force causing an oscillatory vertical motion of the support of the spring (Figure 5.15). The inclusion of f(t) in the formulation of Newton's second law gives

$$m\frac{d^2x}{dt^2} = -kx - \beta\frac{dx}{dt} + f(t), \tag{1}$$

$$\frac{d^2x}{dt^2} + \frac{\beta}{m}\frac{dx}{dt} + \frac{k}{m}x = \frac{f(t)}{m}, \tag{2}$$

or

$$\frac{d^2x}{dt^2} + 2\lambda\frac{dx}{dt} + \omega^2 x = F(t), \tag{3}$$

where, as in the preceding section, $2\lambda = \beta/m$, $\omega^2 = k/m$. To solve the latter nonhomogeneous equation, we can employ either the method of undetermined coefficients or variation of parameters.

EXAMPLE

Solve and interpret the initial-value problem

$$\frac{1}{5}\frac{d^2x}{dt^2} + 1.2\frac{dx}{dt} + 2x = 5\cos 4t \tag{4}$$

$$x(0) = \frac{1}{2} \qquad \frac{dx}{dt}\bigg|_{t=0} = 0.$$

Solution: We can interpret the problem to represent a vibrational system consisting of weight ($m = 1/5$) attached to a spring ($k = 2$). The weight is released from rest 1/2 ft below the equilibrium position. Although the motion is damped ($\beta = 1.2$), the system is also being driven by an external periodic ($T = \pi/2$) force. Intuitively we would expect that even with damping the system will remain in motion until such time as the forcing function is "turned off," in which case the amplitudes would gradually diminish. However, as the problem is given, $f(t) = 5\cos 4t$ will remain "on" forever.

We first multiply (4) by 5 and solve the homogeneous equation

$$\frac{dx^2}{dt^2} + 6\frac{dx}{dt} + 10x = 0$$

by the usual methods. Since $m_1 = -3 + i$, $m_2 = -3 - i$ it follows that

$$x_c(t) = e^{-3t}(c_1 \cos t + c_2 \sin t).$$

Now by Rule I of the method of undetermined coefficients, we assume a particular solution of the form $x_p(t) = A \cos 4t + B \sin 4t$. Now

$$x'_p = -4A \sin 4t + 4B \cos 4t$$
$$x''_p = -16A \cos 4t - 16B \sin 4t$$

so that

$$x''_p + 6x'_p + 10x_p = -16A \cos 4t - 16B \sin 4t - 24A \sin 4t + 24B \cos 4t$$
$$+ 10A \cos 4t + 10B \sin 4t$$
$$= (-6A + 24B) \cos 4t + (-24A - 6B) \sin 4t$$
$$= 25 \cos 4t.$$

The resulting system of equations

$$-6A + 24B = 25$$
$$-24A - 6B = 0$$

yields $A = -25/102$ and $B = 50/51$. It follows that

$$x(t) = e^{-3t}(c_1 \cos t + c_2 \sin t) - \frac{25}{102} \cos 4t + \frac{50}{51} \sin 4t. \tag{5}$$

When we set $t = 0$ in the above equation we immediately obtain $c_1 = 38/51$. By differentiating the expression and then setting $t = 0$ we also find that $c_2 = -86/51$. Therefore,

$$x(t) = e^{-3t}\left(\frac{38}{51} \cos t - \frac{86}{51} \sin t\right) - \frac{25}{102} \cos 4t + \frac{50}{51} \sin 4t. \tag{6}$$

Transient and steady-state terms

Notice that the complementary function

$$x_c(t) = e^{-3t}\left(\frac{38}{51} \cos t - \frac{86}{51} \sin t\right)$$

in the preceding example possesses the property that

$$\lim_{t \to \infty} x_c(t) = 0.$$

Any part of the solution of a differential equation, such as (2), which becomes negligible (namely, →0) as $t \to \infty$ is said to be a **transient term**. Thus, for large time, the displacements of the weight in the preceding problem are closely approximated by the particular solution $x_p(t)$. This latter function is also called the **steady-state solution**.

EXAMPLE

The solution to the initial-value problem

$$\frac{d^2x}{dt^2} + 2\frac{dx}{dt} + 2x = 4\cos t + 2\sin t$$

$$x(0) = 0 \qquad \frac{dx}{dt}\bigg|_{t=0} = 3$$

is readily shown to be

$$x(t) = \underbrace{e^{-t}\sin t}_{\text{transient}} + \underbrace{2\sin t}_{\text{steady-state}}.$$

Inspection of Figure 5.16 shows that the effect of the transient term on the solution is, in this case, negligible for about $t > 2\pi$.

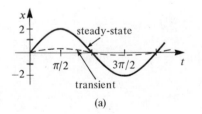
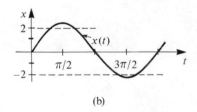

(a)   (b)

Figure 5.16

Without damping

In the absence of a damping force there will be no transient term in the solution of a problem. Also, we shall see that a periodic impressed force with a frequency near, or the same as, the frequency of free, undamped vibrations can cause a severe problem in any oscillatory mechanical system.

EXAMPLE

Solve the initial-value problem

$$\frac{d^2x}{dt^2} + \omega^2 x = F_0 \sin \gamma t, \qquad F_0 = \text{constant}, \tag{7}$$

$$x(0) = 0 \qquad \frac{dx}{dt}\bigg|_{t=0} = 0.$$

Solution: The complementary function is $x_c(t) = c_1 \cos \omega t + c_2 \sin \omega t$.
    To obtain a particular solution we assume $x_p(t) = A \cos \gamma t + B \sin \gamma t$, so that

$$x_p' = -A\gamma \sin \gamma t + B\gamma \cos \gamma t$$

$$x_p'' = -A\gamma^2 \cos \gamma t - B\gamma^2 \sin \gamma t$$

$$x_p'' + \omega^2 x_p = A(\omega^2 - \gamma^2)\cos \gamma t + B(\omega^2 - \gamma^2)\sin \gamma t$$

$$= F_0 \sin \gamma t.$$

It follows

$$A = 0$$

$$B = \frac{F_0}{\omega^2 - \gamma^2} \qquad (\gamma \neq \omega)$$

and therefore

$$x_p(t) = \frac{F_0}{\omega^2 - \gamma^2} \sin \gamma t.$$

Applying the given initial conditions to the general solution

$$x(t) = c_1 \cos \omega t + c_2 \sin \omega t + \frac{F_0}{\omega^2 - \gamma^2} \sin \gamma t$$

yields $c_1 = 0$ and $c_2 = -\gamma F_0 / \omega(\omega^2 - \gamma^2)$. Thus the solution is

$$x(t) = \frac{-\gamma F_0}{\omega(\omega^2 - \gamma^2)} \sin \omega t + \frac{F_0}{\omega^2 - \gamma^2} \sin \gamma t$$

$$= \frac{F_0}{\omega(\omega^2 - \gamma^2)} [-\gamma \sin \omega t + \omega \sin \gamma t] \qquad \gamma \neq \omega. \tag{8}$$

Pure resonance

Although equation (8) is not defined for $\gamma = \omega$, it is interesting to observe that its limiting value as $\gamma \to \omega$ can be obtained by applying L'Hopital's rule. This limiting process is analogous to "tuning in" the frequency of the driving force ($\gamma/2\pi$) to the frequency of free vibrations ($\omega/2\pi$). Intuitively we expect that over a length of time we should be able to substantially increase the amplitudes of vibration.† For $\gamma = \omega$ we define the solution to be

$$x(t) = \lim_{\gamma \to \omega} F_0 \frac{-\gamma \sin \omega t + \omega \sin \gamma t}{\omega(\omega^2 - \gamma^2)}$$

$$= F_0 \lim_{\gamma \to \omega} \frac{\dfrac{d}{d\gamma}[-\gamma \sin \omega t + \omega \sin \gamma t]}{\dfrac{d}{d\gamma}[\omega^3 - \omega\gamma^2]}$$

$$= F_0 \lim_{\gamma \to \omega} \frac{-\sin \omega t + \omega t \cos \gamma t}{-2\omega\gamma}$$

$$= F_0 \frac{-\sin \omega t + \omega t \cos \omega t}{-2\omega^2}$$

$$= \frac{F_0}{2\omega^2}[\sin \omega t - \omega t \cos \omega t]$$

$$= \frac{F_0}{2\omega^2} \sin \omega t - \frac{F_0}{2\omega} t \cos \omega t. \tag{9}$$

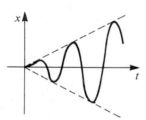

Figure 5.17

As suspected, when $t \to \infty$ the displacements become large, in fact, $|x(t)| \to \infty$. The phenomenon we have just described is known as **pure resonance**. The graph in Figure 5.17 displays typical motion in this case.

In conclusion, it should be noted that there is no actual need to use a limiting process on (8) to obtain the solution for $\gamma = \omega$. Alternatively, equation (9) follows by solving the initial-value problem

$$\frac{d^2x}{dt^2} + \omega^2 x = F_0 \sin \omega t$$

$$x(0) = 0 \qquad \frac{dx}{dt}\bigg|_{t=0} = 0$$

directly by conventional methods.

Remark: If a mechanical system were actually described by a function such as (9) of this section, it would necessarily fail; large oscillations of a weight on a spring would eventually force the spring beyond its elastic limit. One might argue too that the resonating model presented (Figure 5.17) is completely unrealistic since it ignores the retarding effects of ever-present

---

†Forgetting about damping effects of shock absorbers, the situation is roughly equivalent to a number of passengers jumping up and down in the back of a bus in time with the natural vertical motion caused by equally spaced faults (such as cracks) in the road. Theoretically these passengers could upset the bus—assuming they are not kicked off first.

damping forces. While it is true that pure resonance cannot occur when the smallest amount of damping is taken into consideration, nevertheless, large and equally destructive amplitudes of vibration (though bounded as $t \to \infty$) could take place (see Problem 3).

If you have ever looked out a window while in flight you have probably observed that wings on an airplane are not perfectly rigid. A reasonable amount of flutter is not only tolerated but necessary to prevent the wing from snapping like a piece of peppermint stick candy. In late 1959 and early 1960 two commercial plane crashes occurred, with a then relatively new model of prop-jet, which illustrate the destructive effects of large mechanical oscillations.

The unusual aspect of these crashes was that they both happened while the planes were in mid-flight. Barring mid-air collisions, the safest period during any flight is when the plane has attained its cruising altitude. It is well known that a plane is most vulnerable to an accident when it is least manuverable, namely, either during take-off or landing. So having two planes simply fall out of the sky was at least an embarassment to the aircraft industry as well as a thoroughly puzzling problem to aerodynamic engineers. In crashes of this sort, a structural failure of some kind is immediately suspected. After a subsequent and massive technical investigation the problem was eventually traced in each case to an outboard engine and engine housing. Roughly, it was determined that when each plane surpassed a critical speed of approximately 400 mph, a propeller and engine began to wobble, causing a gyroscopic force which could not be quelled or damped by the engine housing. This external vibrational force was then transferred to the already oscillating wing. This in itself need not have been destructively dangerous since the aircraft wings are designed to withstand the stress of unusual and excessive forces. (In fact, the particular wing in question was so incredibly strong that

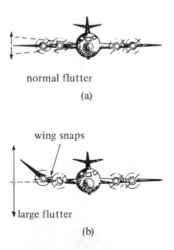

normal flutter

(a)

wing snaps

large flutter

(b)

Figure 5.18

test engineers and pilots, who were deliberately trying, failed to snap a wing under every conceivable flight condition.) Unfortunately, after a short period of time during which the engine wobbled rapidly, the frequency of the impressed force actually slowed to a point where it approached and finally coincided with the maximum frequency of wing flutter (around 3 cycles per second). The resulting resonance situation finally accomplished what the test engineers could not do, namely, the amplitudes of wing flutter became large enough to snap the wing. The problem was solved in two steps. All models of this particular plane were required to fly at speeds substantially below 400 mph until each plane could be modified by considerably strengthening (or stiffening) the engine housings. A strengthened engine housing was shown to be able to impart a damping effect capable of preventing the critical resonance phenomenon even in the unlikely event of a subsequent engine wobble.†

You may be aware that soldiers usually do not march in step across bridges. The reason for breaking stride is simply to avoid any possibility of resonance occuring between the natural vibrations of a bridge and the frequency of the external force of a multitude of feet stomping in unison on the bridge.

Bridges are good examples of vibrating mechanical systems which are constantly being subjected to external forces, either from people walking, cars and trucks driving on them, water pushing against their foundations, or wind blowing against their superstructures. On November 7, 1940, the Tacoma Narrows Bridge at Puget Sound in Washington collapsed. However, the crash came as no surprise, since this particular bridge was famous in the local community for a vertical undulating motion of its roadway which gave many motorists a very exciting crossing. On November 7, only four months after its grand opening, the amplitudes of these undulations became so large that the bridge failed and a substantial portion was sent splashing into the water below. In the investigation that followed, it was found that a poorly designed superstructure caused the wind blowing across it to vortex in a periodic manner. When the frequency of this periodic force approached the natural frequency of the bridge, large upheavals of the road resulted. In a word, the bridge was another victim of the destructive effect of mechanical resonance. Since this disaster developed over a matter of months, there was sufficient opportunity to record on film the strange and frightening phenomenon of a bucking and heaving bridge and its ultimate collapse.‡

Acoustic vibrations can be as equally destructive as large mechanical vibrations. Operatic and jazz singers sometimes take pride in their ability to inflict destruction on the lowly water glass. The sounds from organs and piccolos have been known to crack windows.

---

† For a fascinating nontechnical account of the investigation see Robert J. Serling, *Loud and Clear*, New York: Dell, 1970), Chapter 5.

‡ National Committee for Fluid Mechanics Films, Educational Services, Inc., Watertown, Mass. See also, *American Society of Civil Engineers: Proceedings*, "Failure of The Tacoma Narrows Bridge", Vol. 69, pp. 1555–86, Dec. 1943.

"As the horns blew, the people began to shout. When they heard the signal horn, they raised a tremendous shout. The wall collapsed...."   *Joshua* 6:20

Did the power of acoustic resonance cause the walls of Jericho to tumble down? This is the conjecture of some contemporary scholars.

EXERCISES 5.3   Answers to odd-numbered problems begin on page A-13 of the Appendix.

1. A 16-lb weight stretches a spring 8/3 ft. Initially the weight starts from rest 2 ft below the equilibrium position and the subsequent motion takes place in a medium that offers a damping force numerically equal to 1/2 the instantaneous velocity. Find the equation of motion if the weight is driven by an external force equal to $f(t) = 10 \cos 3t$.

2. In the case of underdamped vibrations show that the general solution of the differential equation

$$\frac{d^2x}{dt^2} + 2\lambda \frac{dx}{dt} + \omega^2 x = F_0 \sin \gamma t$$

is

$$x(t) = Ae^{-\lambda t} \sin \left[\sqrt{\omega^2 - \lambda^2}\, t + \phi\right] + \frac{F_0}{\sqrt{(\omega^2 - \gamma^2)^2 + 4\lambda^2 \gamma^2}} \sin (\gamma t + \theta)$$

where $A = \sqrt{c_1^2 + c_2^2}$ and the phase angles ϕ and θ are respectively defined by

$$\sin \phi = \frac{c_1}{A}$$

$$\cos \phi = \frac{c_2}{A}$$

$$\sin \theta = \frac{-2\lambda \gamma}{\sqrt{(\omega^2 - \gamma^2)^2 + 4\lambda^2 \gamma^2}}$$

$$\cos \theta = \frac{\omega^2 - \gamma^2}{\sqrt{(\omega^2 - \gamma^2)^2 + 4\lambda^2 \gamma^2}}.$$

EXAMPLE   Inspection of Problem 2 shows that $x_c(t)$ is transient when damping is present and hence for large values of time the solution is closely approximated by the steady-state solution

$$x_p(t) = g(\gamma) \sin (\gamma t + \theta)$$

where we define

$$g(\gamma) = \frac{F_0}{\sqrt{(\omega^2 - \gamma^2)^2 + 4\lambda^2 \gamma^2}}. \tag{10}$$

Although the amplitude of x_p is bounded as $t \to \infty$ it is easily shown that the maximum oscillations will occur at the value $\gamma_1 = \sqrt{\omega^2 - 2\lambda^2}$. See Problem 3. Thus when the frequency of the external force is $2\pi/\sqrt{\omega^2 - 2\lambda^2}$ the system is said to be in **resonance**.

In the specific case $k = 4$, $m = 1$, $F_0 = 2$, $g(\gamma)$ becomes

$$g(\gamma) = \frac{2}{\sqrt{(4 - \gamma^2)^2 + \beta^2\gamma^2}}. \tag{11}$$

Figure 5.19(a) shows the graph of (11) for various values of the damping coefficient β. This family of graphs is called the **resonance curve** of the system. Observe the behavior of the amplitudes $g(\gamma)$ as $\beta \to 0$, that is, as the system approaches pure resonance.

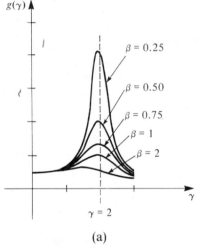

β	γ_1	$g(\gamma_1)$
2	1.41	0.58
1	1.87	1.03
0.75	1.93	1.36
0.50	1.97	2.02
0.25	1.99	4.01

(a) (b)

Figure 5.19

3. **(a)** Prove that $g(\gamma)$ given in (10) of the preceding example has a maximum value at $\gamma_1 = \sqrt{\omega^2 - 2\lambda^2}$. [*Hint:* Differentiate with respect to γ.]

   (b) What is the maximum value of $g(\gamma)$ at resonance?

★4. **(a)** If $k = 3$ lb/ft and $m = 1$ slug, use the information in the above example to show that the system is underdamped when the damping coefficient β satisfies $0 < \beta < 2\sqrt{3}$ but that resonance can occur only if $0 < \beta < \sqrt{6}$.

   (b) Construct the resonance curve of the system when $F_0 = 3$.

5. A mass of 1/2 slug is suspended on a spring whose constant is 6 lb/ft. The system is set in motion in a medium offering a damping force numerically equal to twice the instantaneous velocity. Find the steady-state solution if an external force $f(t) = 40 \sin 2t$ is applied to the system starting at

$t = 0$. Write this solution in the form of a constant multiple of $\sin(2t + \theta)$.

6. Verify that the mechanical system described in Problem 5 is in resonance. Show that the amplitude of the steady-state solution is the maximum value of $g(\gamma)$ described in Problem 3.

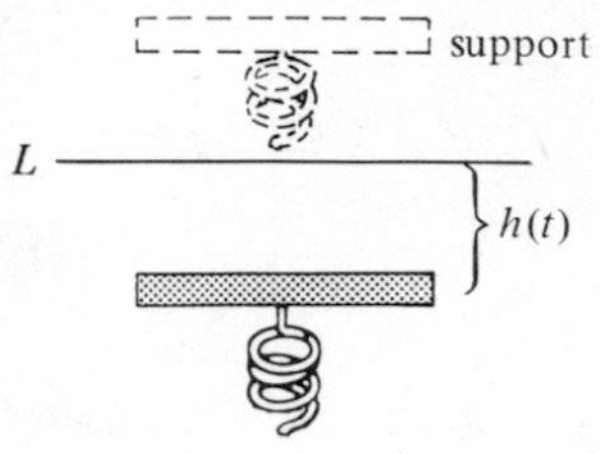

support

L

$h(t)$

Figure 5.20

7. A weight of mass m is attached to the end of a spring whose constant is k. After the weight reaches equilibrium, its support begins to oscillate vertically about a horizontal line L according to a formula $h(t)$. The value of h represents the distance in feet measured from L (see Figure 5.20). Determine the differential equation of motion if the entire system moves through a medium offering a damping force numerically equal to $\beta(dx/dt)$.

★**8.** Solve the differential equation of the preceding problem if the spring is stretched 4 ft by a weight of 16 lb, and $\beta = 2$, $h(t) = 5\cos t$, $x(0) = x'(0) = 0$.

9. **(a)** Show that the solution of the initial-value problem

$$\frac{d^2x}{dt^2} + \omega^2 x = F_0 \cos \gamma t$$

$$x(0) = 0 \qquad \frac{dx}{dt}\bigg|_{t=0} = 0$$

is $$x(t) = \frac{F_0}{\omega^2 - \gamma^2}[\cos \gamma t - \cos \omega t].$$

(b) Evaluate

$$\lim_{\gamma \to \omega} \frac{F_0}{\omega^2 - \gamma^2}[\cos \gamma t - \cos \omega t].$$

10. Compare the result obtained in part (b) of the preceding problem with the solution obtained using variation of parameters when the external force is $F_0 \cos \omega t$.

11. **(a)** Show that $x(t)$ given in part (a) of Problem 9 can be written in the form

$$x(t) = \frac{-2F_0}{\omega^2 - \gamma^2} \sin \frac{1}{2}(\gamma - \omega)t \sin \frac{1}{2}(\gamma + \omega)t.$$

(b) If we define $\varepsilon = \frac{1}{2}(\gamma - \omega)$, show that when ε is small that an *approximate* solution is

$$x(t) = \frac{F_0}{2\varepsilon\gamma} \sin \varepsilon t \sin \gamma t.$$

(c) Evaluate

$$\lim_{\varepsilon \to 0} \frac{F_0}{2\varepsilon\gamma} \sin \varepsilon t \sin \gamma t.$$

EXAMPLE

In part (b) of the preceding problem, when ε is small, the frequency $\gamma/2\pi$ of the impressed force is close to the frequency $\omega/2\pi$ of free vibrations. When this occurs, the motion is as indicated in Figure 5.21. Oscillations of this kind are called *beats* and are due to the fact that the frequency of $\sin \varepsilon t$ is quite small in comparison to the frequency of $\sin \gamma t$. The dotted curves, or *envelope* of the graph of $x(t)$, are obtained from the graphs of $\pm (F_0/2\varepsilon\gamma) \sin \varepsilon t$.

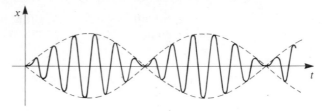

Figure 5.21

12. Show that the solution of

$$\frac{d^2x}{dt^2} + 25x = 10 \cos 7t$$

$$x(0) = 0 \qquad \frac{dx}{dt}\bigg|_{t=0} = 0$$

is $x(t) = \dfrac{5}{6} \sin t \sin 6t$.

13. Solve

$$\frac{d^2x}{dt^2} + 4x = -5 \sin 2t + 3 \cos 2t$$

$$x(0) = -1 \qquad \frac{dx}{dt}\bigg|_{t=0} = 1.$$

[O] 5.4 Analogous Systems

The series circuit analogue

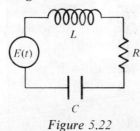

Figure 5.22

You may recall from Section 1.3 that when the various voltage drops in an $L-R-C$ series electrical circuit (Figure 5.22) are added (Kirchoff's second law) we obtain the following differential equation

$$L\frac{d^2q}{dt^2} + R\frac{dq}{dt} + \frac{1}{C}q = E(t) \tag{1}$$

where $q(t)$ is the instantaneous charge on the capacitor and $E(t)$ is the impressed voltage or electromotive force (emf), on the circuit.

EXAMPLE

A series circuit contains only a capacitor and inductor. If the capacitor has an initial charge q_0, determine the subsequent charge $q(t)$.

Solution: From equation (1) we can write

$$L\frac{d^2q}{dt^2} + \frac{1}{C}q = 0$$

subject to $q(0) = q_0$. Assuming that no current flows initially (for example, a switch could be open) then $q'(0) = 0$ since $q'(t) = i(t)$. The general solution of the equation is

$$q(t) = c_1 \cos\frac{1}{\sqrt{LC}}t + c_2 \sin\frac{1}{\sqrt{LC}}t.$$

Now the initial conditions imply $c_1 = q_0$ and $c_2 = 0$ so that

$$q(t) = q_0 \cos\frac{1}{\sqrt{LC}}t.$$

The twisted shaft

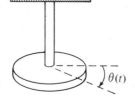

Figure 5.23

Similarly, it can be shown that the differential equation governing the torsional motion of a weight suspended from the end of an elastic shaft is

$$I\frac{d^2\theta}{dt^2} + c\frac{d\theta}{dt} + k\theta = T(t). \tag{2}$$

As shown in Figure 5.23 the function $\theta(t)$ represents the amount of twist of the weight at any time.

By comparing equations (1) and (2) with the general equation of forced motion with damping

$$m\frac{d^2x}{dt^2} + \beta\frac{dx}{dt} + kx = f(t) \tag{3}$$

we see, that with the exception of terminology, there is absolutely no difference between the mathematics of vibrating springs, torsional vibrations, and simple series circuits. The following table gives a comparison of the analogous parts of the three kinds of systems.

Mechanical	Series electrical	Torsional
m (mass)	L (inductance)	I (moment of inertia)
β (damping)	R (resistance)	c (damping)
k (spring constant)	$\dfrac{1}{C}$ (reciprocal of capacitance— called elastance)	k (elastic shaft constant)
$f(t)$ (applied force)	$E(t)$ (impressed voltage)	$T(t)$ (applied torque)

A second-order linear differential equation such as (3) appears in the mathematical analysis of many other problems in physics, engineering, and even chemistry. Although a substantial number of these problems deal directly with classical vibrational phenomena such as oscillations of tuning forks or oscillations of atomic particles, many new and interesting applications are being found in the field of mathematical biology.† Our goal, of course, is not to study all possible applications, but to acquaint the student with the mathematical procedures which are common to these problems.

EXERCISES 5.4   Answers to odd-numbered exercises begin on page A-14 of the Appendix.

1. Show that the current $i(t)$ in a series circuit such as illustrated in Figure 5.22 satisfies the differential equation

$$L\frac{d^2i}{dt^2} + R\frac{di}{dt} + \frac{1}{C}i = E'(t).$$

2. Use undetermined coefficients to find a particular solution of the differential equation in Problem 1 when $L = 1$ farad, $R = 2$ ohms, $C = 0.25$ farad, $E(t) = 50 \cos t$ volts. The particular solution i_p is called the *steady-state current*.

3. Use the differential equation in Problem 1 to find the steady-state current in an L–C circuit when $L = 0.1$ henry, $C = 0.1$ farad, and $E(t) = 120 \sin kt$ volts, $k \neq 10$.

★4. Solve equation (1) of Section 5.4 for $q(t)$ if $L = 5/3$ henry, $R = 10$ ohms, $C = 1/30$ farad, $E = 300$ volts, and $q(0) = 0$, $i(0) = 0$. Determine the current $i(t)$. What is the maximum charge on the capacitor?

5. A series L–R–C circuit contains $L = 1/2$ henry, $R = 10$ ohms, $C = 1/100$ farad, and $E(t) = 150$ volts. Determine the instantaneous charge $q(t)$ on the capacitor for $t > 0$ if $q(0) = 1$ and $i(0) = 0$. After a long period of time what is the charge on the capacitor?

CHAPTER SUMMARY

When a mass is attached to a spring it stretches to a position where the restoring force ks of the spring is balanced by the weight mg. Any subsequent motion is then measured x units (feet in the engineering system) above or below this **equilibrium position**. When the weight is above the equilibrium position, we adopt the convention that $x < 0$, whereas when the weight is below the equilibrium position we take $x > 0$.

The differential equation of motion is obtained by equating Newton's second law $F = ma = m(d^2x/dt^2)$ with the net force acting on the weight at any time. We distinguish three cases.

---

† See M. Braun, *Differential Equations and Their Applications*, (N.Y.: Springer-Verlag, 1975), pp. 257–268, for an application of $x'' + 2\lambda x' + \omega^2 x = 0$ to "A model for the detection of diabetes."

CASE I   The equation

$$m\frac{d^2x}{dt^2} = -kx$$

or

$$\frac{d^2x}{dt^2} + \omega^2 x = 0, \qquad \omega^2 = \frac{k}{m} \tag{1}$$

describes the motion under the assumptions that no damping force and no external impressed forces are acting on the system. The solution of (1) is $x(t) = c_1 \cos \omega t + c_2 \sin \omega t$ and the weight is said to exhibit **simple harmonic motion**. The constants c_1 and c_2 are determined by the initial position $x(0)$ and the initial velocity $x'(0)$ of the weight.

CASE II   When a damping force is present the differential equation becomes

$$m\frac{d^2x}{dt^2} = -kx - \beta\frac{dx}{dt}, \qquad \beta > 0$$

or

$$\frac{d^2x}{dt^2} + 2\lambda\frac{dx}{dt} + \omega^2 x = 0, \qquad 2\lambda = \frac{\beta}{m}, \omega^2 = \frac{k}{m}. \tag{2}$$

The resulting motion is said to be **overdamped**, **critically damped**, or **underdamped** accordingly as $\lambda^2 - \omega^2 > 0$, $\lambda^2 - \omega^2 = 0$, $\lambda^2 - \omega^2 < 0$.
The respective solutions of equation (2) are then

$$x(t) = c_1 e^{m_1 t} + c_2 e^{m_2 t},$$

where $m_1 = -\lambda + \sqrt{\lambda^2 - \omega^2}$, $m_2 = -\lambda - \sqrt{\lambda^2 - \omega^2}$;

$$x(t) = c_1 e^{m_1 t} + c_2 t e^{m_1 t},$$

where $m_1 = -\lambda$; and

$$x(t) = e^{-\lambda t}[c_1 \cos \sqrt{\omega^2 - \lambda^2}\,t + c_2 \sin \sqrt{\omega^2 - \lambda^2}\,t].$$

In each case, the damping force is responsible for the displacements becoming negligible for large time, that is, $x \to 0$ as $t \to \infty$.
The motion described in Cases I and II is said to be **free motion**.

CASE III   When an external force is impressed on the system for $t > 0$, the differential equation becomes

$$m\frac{d^2x}{dt^2} = -kx - \beta\frac{dx}{dt} + f(t)$$

or

$$\frac{d^2x}{dt^2} + 2\lambda\frac{dx}{dt} + \omega^2 x = F(t), \tag{3}$$

where λ and ω^2 are defined in (2). The solution of the nonhomogeneous equation (3) is $x(t) = x_c + x_p$.

Since the complementary function x_c always contains the factor $e^{-\lambda t}$, it will be **transient**, that is, $x_c \to 0$ as $t \to \infty$. The particular solution x_p is called the **steady-state solution**. For practical purposes, the displacements of the weight are given by the steady-state solution for large time.

In the absence of a damping force, an impressed periodic force can cause the amplitudes of vibration to become very large. If the frequency of the external force is the same as the frequency $\omega/2\pi$ of free vibrations, we say that the system is in a state of **pure resonance**. In this case the amplitudes of vibrations become unbounded as $t \to \infty$. In the presence of a damping force, the amplitudes of oscillatory motion are always bounded. However, large and potentially destructive amplitudes can occur.

When a series circuit containing an inductor, resistor, and capacitor is driven by an electromotive force $E(t)$, the resulting differential equations for the charge $q(t)$ or the current $i(t)$ are quite similar in structure to equation (3). Hence the analysis of such circuits is the same as outlined above.

REVIEW EXERCISES

Answers to odd-numbered problems begin on page A-14 of the Appendix.

[5.1]

1. A 20-lb weight stretches a spring 8 in. In the absence of damping, what is the frequency of free vibrations.

★2. A 16-lb weight attached to a spring exhibits simple harmonic motion. If the frequency of oscillations is $3/2\pi$ cycles/sec, what is the spring constant?

3. A 2-lb weight attached to a spring, whose constant is $k = 9$ lb/ft, is released from a point 6 in. above the equilibrium position with a downward velocity of 4 ft/sec. Determine the amplitude of simple harmonic motion.

4. A 12-lb weight stretches a spring 2 ft. The weight is released from a point 1 ft below the equilibrium position with an upward velocity of 4 ft/sec.

   (a) Find the equation describing the resulting simple harmonic motion.
   (b) What is the amplitude, period, and frequency of motion?
   (c) At what times does the weight return to the point 1 ft below the equilibrium position?
   (d) At what times does the weight pass through the equilibrium position moving upward? Moving downward?

    (e)   What is the velocity of weight at $t = 3\pi/16$?

    (f)   At what times is the velocity zero?

[5.2]   **5.**   A force of 2 lb stretches a spring 1 ft. With one end held fixed, an 8-lb weight is attached to the other end and the system lies on a table which imparts a frictional force numerically equal to 3/2 times the instantaneous velocity. Initially the weight is displaced 4 in. above the equilibrium position and released from rest. Find the equation of motion if the motion takes place along a horizontal straight line which is taken as the x-axis.

    6.   A 32-lb weight stretches a spring 6 in. The weight moves through a medium offering a damping force numerically equal to β times the instantaneous velocity. Determine the values of β for which the system will exhibit oscillatory motion.

    7.   A spring with constant $k = 2$ is suspended in a liquid that offers a damping force numerically equal to 4 times the instantaneous velocity. If a mass m is suspended from the spring, determine the values of m for which the subsequent free motion is nonoscillatory.

    ★**8.**   The vertical motion of a weight attached to a spring is described by the initial-value problem

$$\frac{1}{4}\frac{d^2x}{dt^2} + \frac{dx}{dt} + x = 0$$

$$x(0) = 4 \qquad x'(0) = 2.$$

Determine the maximum vertical displacement.

[5.3]   **9.**   A 4-lb weight stretches a spring 18 in. A periodic force equal to $f(t) = \cos \gamma t + \sin \gamma t$ is impressed on the system starting at $t = 0$. In the absence of a damping force, for what value of γ will the system be in a state of pure resonance?

    10.   Find the steady-state solution for

$$\frac{d^2x}{dt^2} + 2\lambda\frac{dx}{dt} + \omega^2x = A,$$

where A is a constant force.

    11.   A 4-lb weight is suspended from a spring whose constant is 3 lb/ft. The entire system is immersed in a fluid offering a damping force numerically equal to the instantaneous velocity. Beginning at $t = 0$, an external force equal to $f(t) = e^{-t}$ is impressed on the system. Determine the equation of motion if the weight is released from rest at a point 2 ft below the equilibrium position.

[5.4]   **12.**   A series circuit contains an inductance of $L = 1$ henry, a capacitance of $C = 10^{-4}$ farad, and an electromotive force of $E(t) = 100 \sin 50t$ volts.

Initially the charge q and current i are zero.

(a)   Find the equation for the charge at any time.
(b)   Find the equation for the current at any time.
(c)   Find the times for which the charge on the capacitor is zero.

CHAPTER 6

Differential Equations with Variable Coefficients

Introduction

The same ease with which we solved differential equations with constant coefficients does not usually carry over to equations with variable coefficients. In fact, we cannot expect to be able to express the solutions of even a simple linear equation such as $y'' - xy = 0$ in terms of the usual sines, cosines, logarithms, exponentials, and other elementary functions. Although it is easily verified that

$$(1 - x^2)y'' - 2xy' + 2y = 0 \qquad \text{and} \qquad x^2y'' + xy' + (x^2 - \tfrac{1}{4})y = 0$$

have elementary solutions

$$y = x \qquad \text{and} \qquad y = \frac{\sin x}{\sqrt{x}}$$

respectively, the best that we can *usually* expect from equations of this sort is an *infinite series solution.* On the other hand, we shall now consider one important type of equation with variable coefficients whose general solution can always be written in terms of elementary functions.

6.1   The Cauchy–Euler Equation

Any differential equation of the form

$$a_n x^n \frac{d^n y}{dx^n} + a_{n-1} x^{n-1} \frac{d^{n-1} y}{dx^{n-1}} + \cdots + a_1 x \frac{dy}{dx} + a_0 y = g(x)$$

where $a_n, a_{n-1}, \ldots, a_0$ are constants is said to be a **Cauchy–Euler equation.**[*]
The obvious characteristic of this type of equation is that the *degree* of the
polynomial coefficients x^k matches the *order* of differentiation in the terms
$d^k y / dx^k$ for $k = 1, 2, \ldots, n$.

For the sake of discussion we shall confine our attention to solving the
homogeneous second-order equation

$$ax^2 \frac{d^2 y}{dx^2} + bx \frac{dy}{dx} + cy = 0.$$

The solution of higher order equations follows analogously. Also, we can solve
the nonhomogeneous equation

$$ax^2 \frac{d^2 y}{dx^2} + bx \frac{dy}{dx} + cy = g(x)$$

by variation of parameters once we have determined the complementary
function $y_c(x)$.

Note that the coefficient of $d^2 y / dx^2$ is zero at $x = 0$. Hence, in order to
guarantee that the fundamental results of Theorem 1.2 are applicable to the
Cauchy–Euler equation, we shall confine our attention to finding its general
solution on the interval $x > 0$. Solutions for $x < 0$ can be obtained by
substituting $t = -x$ in the differential equation.

The method of solution   We try a solution of the form $y = x^m$ where m is to be determined. The first and
second derivatives are

$$\frac{dy}{dx} = mx^{m-1}$$

$$\frac{d^2 y}{dx^2} = m(m-1)x^{m-2},$$

so that the differential equation becomes

$$ax^2 \frac{d^2 y}{dx^2} + bx \frac{dy}{dx} + cy = ax^2 \cdot m(m-1)x^{m-2} + bx \cdot mx^{m-1} + cx^m$$

$$= am(m-1)x^m + bmx^m + cx^m$$

$$= x^m[am(m-1) + bm + c].$$

---

[*] Named after the famous mathematicians Leonhard Euler (Swiss, 1707–1783)
and Augustin Louis Cauchy (French, 1789–1857). The Cauchy–Euler equation
is sometimes referred to as the **equidimensional equation.**

Thus $y = x^m$ will be a solution of the differential equation whenever m is a solution of the **auxiliary equation**

$$am(m-1) + bm + c = 0 \tag{1}$$

or

$$am^2 + (b-a)m + c = 0.$$

There are three different cases to be considered depending on whether the roots of this quadratic equation are real and distinct, real and equal, or complex conjugates.

CASE I   Let m_1 and m_2 be the real roots of (1) such that $m_1 \neq m_2$. Then both

$$y_1 = x^{m_1} \quad \text{and} \quad y_2 = x^{m_2}$$

are solutions of the differential equation. By the superposition principle the general solution is

$$y = c_1 x^{m_1} + c_2 x^{m_2}. \tag{2}$$

EXAMPLE   Solve $\qquad x^2 \dfrac{d^2 y}{dx^2} - 2x \dfrac{dy}{dx} - 4y = 0.$

Solution: Rather than just memorizing equation (1) it is preferable to assume $y = x^m$ as the solution a few times in order to understand the origin and the difference between this new form of the auxiliary equation and that obtained in Chapter 4. Differentiate twice and substitute back into the equation:

$$\frac{dy}{dx} = mx^{m-1}$$

$$\frac{d^2 y}{dx^2} = m(m-1)x^{m-2}$$

$$x^2 \frac{d^2 y}{dx^2} - 2x \frac{dy}{dx} - 4y = x^2 \cdot m(m-1)x^{m-2} - 2x \cdot mx^{m-1} - 4x^m$$

$$= x^m [m(m-1) - 2m - 4]$$

$$= x^m [m^2 - 3m - 4]$$

$$= 0$$

if $m^2 - 3m - 4 = 0.$

Now $(m + 1)(m - 4) = 0$ implies $m_1 = -1$, $m_2 = 4$ so that

$$y = c_1 x^{-1} + c_2 x^4.$$

CASE II   If $m_1 = m_2$ then we obtain only one solution, namely, $y = x^{m_1}$. When the roots of the quadratic equation $am^2 + (b - a)m + c = 0$ are equal, the discriminant of the coefficients is necessarily zero. It follows from the quadratic formula that the root must be $m_1 = -(b - a)/2a$.

Now we can construct a second solution y_2 using formula (4) of Section 4.2. We first write the Cauchy–Euler equation in the form

$$\frac{d^2 y}{dx^2} + \frac{b}{ax} \frac{dy}{dx} + \frac{c}{ax^2} y = 0$$

and make the identification $P(x) = b/ax$. Thus

$$y_2 = x^{m_1} \int \frac{e^{-\int (b/ax) dx}}{(x^{m_1})^2} dx$$

$$= x^{m_1} \int \frac{e^{-(b/a) \ln x}}{x^{2m_1}} dx$$

$$= x^{m_1} \int x^{-b/a} \cdot x^{-2m_1} dx \qquad [\text{since } e^{-(b/a) \ln x} = e^{\ln x^{-b/a}} = x^{-b/a}]$$

$$= x^{m_1} \int x^{-b/a} \cdot x^{(b-a)/a} dx \qquad \left[\text{since } 2m_1 = -\frac{b - a}{a} \right]$$

$$= x^{m_1} \int \frac{dx}{x}$$

$$= x^{m_1} \ln x.$$

The general solution is then

$$y = c_1 x^{m_1} + c_2 x^{m_1} \ln x. \qquad (3)$$

EXAMPLE   Solve

$$4x^2 \frac{d^2 y}{dx^2} + 8x \frac{dy}{dx} + y = 0.$$

Solution: The substitution $y = x^m$ yields

$$4x^2 \frac{d^2 y}{dx^2} + 8x \frac{dy}{dx} + y = [4m(m - 1) + 8m + 1] x^m$$

$$= (4m^2 + 4m + 1) x^m$$

$$= 0$$

when

$$4m^2 + 4m + 1 = 0 \qquad \text{or} \qquad (2m + 1)^2 = 0.$$

Since $m_1 = -1/2$ the general solution is

$$y = c_1 x^{-1/2} + c_2 x^{-1/2} \ln x.$$

CASE III   If m_1 and m_2 are complex conjugates, say,

$$m_1 = \alpha + \beta i \qquad m_2 = \alpha - \beta i$$

then the formal solution would be

$$y = C_1 x^{\alpha + \beta i} + C_2 x^{\alpha - \beta i}.$$

But as in the case of equations with constant coefficients, when the roots of the auxiliary equation are complex we wish to write the solution in terms of real functions only. We note the identity

$$x^{\beta i} = (e^{\ln x})^{\beta i} = e^{i \beta \ln x}$$

which, by Euler's formula, is the same as

$$x^{\beta i} = \cos(\beta \ln x) + i \sin(\beta \ln x).$$

Therefore

$$
\begin{aligned}
y &= C_1 x^{\alpha + \beta i} + C_2 x^{\alpha - \beta i} \\
&= x^\alpha [C_1 x^{\beta i} + C_2 x^{-\beta i}] \\
&= x^\alpha [C_1 \{\cos(\beta \ln x) + i \sin(\beta \ln x)\} + C_2 \{\cos(\beta \ln x) - i \sin(\beta \ln x)\}] \\
&= x^\alpha [(C_1 + C_2) \cos(\beta \ln x) + (C_1 i - C_2 i) \sin(\beta \ln x)].
\end{aligned}
$$

On the interval $x > 0$ it is easily verified that

$$y_1 = x^\alpha \cos(\beta \ln x) \qquad \text{and} \qquad y_2 = x^\alpha \sin(\beta \ln x)$$

are linearly independent solutions of the differential equation, and so it follows that the general solution is

$$\boxed{y = x^\alpha [c_1 \cos(\beta \ln x) + c_2 \sin(\beta \ln x)].} \qquad (4)$$

EXAMPLE   Solve

$$x^2 \frac{d^2 y}{dx^2} + 3x \frac{dy}{dx} + 3y = 0.$$

Solution: We have

$$x^2 \frac{d^2y}{dx^2} + 3x \frac{dy}{dx} + 3y = x^m[m(m-1) + 3m + 3]$$

$$= x^m[m^2 + 2m + 3]$$

$$= 0$$

when $m^2 + 2m + 3 = 0$.

From the quadratic formula we find $m_1 = -1 + \sqrt{2}i$ and $m_2 = -1 - \sqrt{2}i$. If we make the identifications $\alpha = -1$ and $\beta = \sqrt{2}$, we see from (4) that

$$y = x^{-1}[c_1 \cos(\sqrt{2}\ln x) + c_2 \sin(\sqrt{2}\ln x)].$$

EXAMPLE

Solve the third-order Cauchy–Euler equation

$$x^3 \frac{d^3y}{dx^3} + 5x^2 \frac{d^2y}{dx^2} + 7x \frac{dy}{dx} + 8y = 0.$$

Solution: The first three derivatives of $y = x^m$ are

$$\frac{dy}{dx} = mx^{m-1}$$

$$\frac{d^2y}{dx^2} = m(m-1)x^{m-2}$$

$$\frac{d^3y}{dx^3} = m(m-1)(m-2)x^{m-3}$$

so that the given differential equation becomes

$$x^3 \frac{d^3y}{dx^3} + 5x^2 \frac{d^2y}{dx^2} + 7x \frac{dy}{dx} + 8y$$

$$= x^3 m(m-1)(m-2)x^{m-3} + 5x^2 m(m-1)x^{m-2} + 7xmx^{m-1} + 8x^m$$

$$= x^m[m(m-1)(m-2) + 5m(m-1) + 7m + 8]$$

$$= x^m[m^3 + 2m^2 + 4m + 8].$$

In this case we see that $y = x^m$ will be a solution of the differential equation provided m is a root of the cubic equation

$$m^3 + 2m^2 + 4m + 8 = 0$$

or

$$m^2(m+2) + 4(m+2) = 0$$

$$(m+2)(m^2+4) = 0.$$

The roots are: $m_1 = -2$, $m_2 = 2i$, $m_3 = -2i$. Hence the general solution is

$$y = c_1 x^{-2} + c_2 \cos(2 \ln x) + c_3 \sin(2 \ln x).$$

EXAMPLE   Solve the nonhomogeneous equation

$$x^2 y'' - 3xy' + 3y = 2x^4 e^x.$$

Solution: The substitution $y = x^m$ leads to the auxiliary equation

$$m(m - 1) - 3m + 3 = 0 \quad \text{or} \quad m^2 - 4m + 3 = 0$$
$$(m - 1)(m - 3) = 0$$

so that $m_1 = 1$, $m_2 = 3$ and therefore

$$y_c = c_1 x + c_2 x^3.$$

Before using variation of parameters, recall that the formulas $u_1' = -y_2 f(x)/W$ and $u_2' = y_1 f(x)/W$ were derived under the assumption that the differential equation has been put into the form $y'' + P(x)y' + Q(x)y = f(x)$. Therefore we must divide the given equation by x^2 and then make the identification that $f(x) = 2x^2 e^x$.

Now

$$W = \begin{vmatrix} x & x^3 \\ 1 & 3x^2 \end{vmatrix} = 3x^3 - x^3 = 2x^3$$

so that

$$u_1' = -\frac{x^3(2x^2 e^x)}{2x^3} = -x^2 e^x \quad \text{and} \quad u_2' = \frac{x(2x^2 e^x)}{2x^3} = e^x.$$

The indefinite integral of the latter function is immediate, but in the case of u_1' we must integrate by parts twice. The results are

$$u_1 = -x^2 e^x + 2x e^x - 2e^x, \qquad u_2 = e^x.$$

Hence
$$y_p = u_1 y_1 + u_2 y_2$$
$$= (-x^2 e^x + 2x e^x - 2e^x)x + e^x x^3$$
$$= 2x^2 e^x - 2x e^x.$$

Finally we have

$$y = y_c + y_p$$
$$= c_1 x + c_2 x^3 + 2x^2 e^x - 2x e^x.$$

EXERCISES 6.1   Answers to odd-numbered problems begin on page A-14 of the Appendix. In Problems 1–14 solve the given differential equation.

1. $x^2y'' - 2y = 0$ 2. $4x^2y'' + y = 0$

3. $xy'' + y' = 0$ 4. $x^2y'' + 5xy' + 3y = 0$

5. $2x^2y'' + 2xy' + 8y = 0$ ★6. $x^2y'' + 3xy' - 4y = 0$

7. $x^2y'' - xy' + 2y = 0$ 8. $x^2y'' + 8xy' + 6y = 0$

9. $3x^2y'' + 6xy' + y = 0$ ★10. $x^3y''' + xy' - y = 0$

11. $x^3y''' - 6y = 0$

12. $x^3\dfrac{d^3y}{dx^3} - 2x^2\dfrac{d^2y}{dx^2} - 2x\dfrac{dy}{dx} + 8y = 0.$

13. $(x - 1)^2\dfrac{d^2y}{dx^2} - 2(x - 1)\dfrac{dy}{dx} - 4y = 0.$

★14. $(3x + 4)^2y'' + 10(3x + 4)y' + 9y = 0$

The Cauchy–Euler equation can be reduced to an equation with constant coefficients by means of the substitution $x = e^t$. Solve Problems 15–20 using this change of variables.

EXAMPLE   Solve $x^2\dfrac{d^2y}{dx^2} - x\dfrac{dy}{dx} + y = \ln x.$

Solution: With the substitution $x = e^t$ or $t = \ln x$ it follows from the chain rule that

$$\frac{dy}{dx} = \frac{dy}{dt}\frac{dt}{dx}$$

$$= \frac{1}{x}\frac{dy}{dt},$$

$$\frac{d^2y}{dx^2} = \frac{1}{x}\frac{d}{dx}\left(\frac{dy}{dt}\right) + \frac{dy}{dt}\left(-\frac{1}{x^2}\right)$$

$$= \frac{1}{x}\left(\frac{d^2y}{dt^2}\frac{1}{x}\right) + \frac{dy}{dt}\left(-\frac{1}{x^2}\right)$$

$$= \frac{1}{x^2}\left[\frac{d^2y}{dt^2} - \frac{dy}{dt}\right],$$

or $x^2\dfrac{d^2y}{dx^2} = \dfrac{d^2y}{dt^2} - \dfrac{dy}{dt}.$

Therefore the differential equation becomes

$$\frac{d^2y}{dt^2} - 2\frac{dy}{dt} + y = t.$$

Since this last equation has constant coefficients, its auxiliary equation is $m^2 - 2m + 1 = 0$ or $(m-1)^2 = 0$. Thus we obtain

$$y_c = c_1 e^t + c_2 t e^t.$$

By undetermined coefficients we try a particular solution of the form $y_p = A + Bt$.

This assumption leads to $-2B + A + Bt = t$ so that $A = 2$ and $B = 1$. Hence

$$y = y_c + y_p$$
$$= c_1 e^t + c_2 t e^t + 2 + t$$

and so the solution of the original differential equation is

$$y = c_1 x + c_2 x \ln x + 2 + \ln x$$

for $x > 0$.

---

15. $x^2 \dfrac{d^2y}{dx^2} + 10x \dfrac{dy}{dx} + 8y = x^2$

[handwritten: for $x = e^t$ $t = \ln x$]

[handwritten: $\dfrac{dy}{dx} = \dfrac{1}{x}\dfrac{dy}{dt}$]

16. $x^2 y'' - 4xy' + 6y = \ln x^2$

17. $x^2 y'' - 3xy' + 13y = 4 + 3x$

[handwritten: $\dfrac{d^2y}{dt^2} = \dfrac{1}{x^2}\left(\dfrac{d^2y}{dt^2} - \dfrac{dy}{dt}\right)$]

18. $2x^2 y'' - 3xy' - 3y = 1 + 2x + x^2$

19. $x^2 y'' + 9xy' - 20y = 5/x^3$

20. $x^3 \dfrac{d^3y}{dx^3} - 3x^2 \dfrac{d^2y}{dx^2} + 6x \dfrac{dy}{dx} - 6y = 3 + \ln x^3$

Solve Problems 21–25 by variation of parameters.

21. $xy'' + y' = x$

22. $x^2 y'' - 2xy' + 2y = x^4 e^x$

23. $2x^2 y'' + 5xy' + y = x^2 - x$

24. $x^2 y'' - 2xy' + 2y = x^3 \ln x$

25. $x^2 y'' - xy' + y = 2x$

★26. Show that the auxiliary equation for the fourth-order Cauchy–Euler equation

$$x^4 \dfrac{d^4y}{dx^4} + 6x^3 \dfrac{d^3y}{dx^3} + 9x^2 \dfrac{d^2y}{dx^2} + 3x \dfrac{dy}{dx} + y = 0$$

has repeated complex roots. Find the general solution of the equation.

27. By considering $x^2 y'' - 2y = xe^x$, determine what happens when the method of undetermined coefficients is applied directly to the equation.

28. Solve the differential equation $x^2 y'' - 2xy' + 2y = 0$ subject to:

(a) $y(1) = 0$ **(b)** $y(1) = 0$
  $y'(1) = 1$ $y(3) = 6$.

6.2   Power Series Solutions

6.2.1   The Procedure

In Section 1.1 we have seen that the function $y = e^{x^2}$ is an explicit solution of the linear first-order differential equation

$$\frac{dy}{dx} - 2xy = 0. \tag{1}$$

Recall from calculus that a power series representation for e^x is

$$e^x = \sum_{n=0}^{\infty} \frac{x^n}{n!} \tag{2}$$

so that the solution can then be written as

$$y = e^{x^2} = \sum_{n=0}^{\infty} \frac{x^{2n}}{n!}. \tag{3}$$

Both series (2) and (3) converge absolutely for all real values of x.*

In other words, knowing the solution in advance, we were able to find an infinite series solution of the differential equation. We now propose to obtain the power series solution of (1) directly; the method of attack is similar to the technique of undetermined coefficients.

If we assume that

$$y = \sum_{n=0}^{\infty} c_n x^n \tag{4}$$

we pose the question: Can we determine coefficients c_n for which (4) converges to a function satisfying (1)? Term-by-term differentiation† of (4) gives

$$\frac{dy}{dx} = \sum_{n=0}^{\infty} nc_n x^{n-1}$$

$$= \sum_{n=1}^{\infty} nc_n x^{n-1}. \qquad \text{[the first term corresponding to } n = 0 \text{ is zero]}$$

---

* A series $\sum_{n=0}^{\infty} u_n$ converges absolutely when $\sum_{n=0}^{\infty} |u_n|$ converges. A power series $\sum_{n=0}^{\infty} a_n x^n$ converges absolutely for those values of x satisfying

$$\lim_{n \to \infty} \left| \frac{a_{n+1}}{a_n} x \right| = L|x| < 1.$$

This *ratio test* will yield an *interval of convergence*.

† Term-by-term differentiation is possible within the interval of convergence of a power series.

Using this last result and the assumption (4) we find

$$\frac{dy}{dx} - 2xy = \sum_{n=1}^{\infty} nc_n x^{n-1} - \sum_{n=0}^{\infty} 2c_n x^{n+1}. \tag{5}$$

We would formally like to add the two series in (5), but in order to do this we must have both summation indices start at the same value. In addition, it is desirable that the numerical values of the powers of x be "in phase" in each summation. That is, if one series starts with a multiple of, say, x to the first power, then we want the other series to start with this same power. To this end we write (5) as

$$\frac{dy}{dx} - 2xy = 1 \cdot c_1 x^0 + \sum_{n=2}^{\infty} nc_n x^{n-1} - \sum_{n=0}^{\infty} 2c_n x^{n+1} \tag{6}$$

and let $k = n - 1$ in the first series and $k = n + 1$ in the second.* The right side of equation (6) then becomes

$$c_1 + \sum_{k=1}^{\infty} (k+1)c_{k+1} x^k - \sum_{k=1}^{\infty} 2c_{k-1} x^k.$$

By adding the series termwise it follows that

$$\frac{dy}{dx} - 2xy = c_1 + \sum_{k=1}^{\infty} [(k+1)c_{k+1} - 2c_{k-1}] x^k = 0. \tag{7}$$

Hence, in order to have (7) identically zero it is necessary that the coefficients satisfy

$$c_1 = 0$$

and

$$(k+1)c_{k+1} - 2c_{k-1} = 0, \ k = 1, 2, 3 \ldots. \tag{8}$$

Equation (8) provides a *recurrence relation* that determines the c_k. Since $k + 1 \neq 0$ for any of the indicated values of k we can write (8) as

$$c_{k+1} = \frac{2c_{k-1}}{k+1}. \tag{9}$$

---

* Recall the summation index is a "dummy" variable. The fact that $k = n - 1$ in one case and $k = n + 1$ in the other should cause no confusion if you keep in mind that it is the *value* of the summation index which is important. In both cases k takes on the successive values $1, 2, 3, \ldots$ for $n = 2, 3, 4, \ldots$ (for $k = n - 1$) and $n = 0, 1, 2, \ldots$ (for $k = n + 1$) respectively.

Iteration of this last formula then gives

$$k = 1, \quad c_2 = \frac{2}{2}c_0 = c_0$$

$$k = 2, \quad c_3 = \frac{2}{3}c_1 = 0$$

$$k = 3, \quad c_4 = \frac{2}{4}c_2 = \frac{1}{2}c_0 = \frac{1}{2!}c_0$$

$$k = 4, \quad c_5 = \frac{2}{5}c_3 = 0$$

$$k = 5, \quad c_6 = \frac{2}{6}c_4 = \frac{1}{3 \cdot 2!}c_0 = \frac{1}{3!}c_0$$

$$k = 6, \quad c_7 = \frac{2}{7}c_5 = 0$$

$$k = 7, \quad c_8 = \frac{2}{8}c_6 = \frac{1}{4 \cdot 3!}c_0 = \frac{1}{4!}c_0$$

and so on. Thus from the original assumption (4) we find

$$
\begin{aligned}
y &= \sum_{n=0}^{\infty} c_n x^n \\
&= c_0 + c_1 x + c_2 x^2 + c_3 x^3 + c_4 x^4 + c_5 x^5 + \cdots \\
&= c_0 + 0 + c_0 x^2 + 0 + \frac{1}{2!}c_0 x^4 + 0 + \frac{1}{3!}c_0 x^6 + 0 + \cdots \\
&= c_0 \left[1 + x^2 + \frac{1}{2!}x^4 + \frac{1}{3!}x^6 + \cdots \right] \\
&= c_0 \sum_{n=0}^{\infty} \frac{x^{2n}}{n!}
\end{aligned}
\tag{10}
$$

Since the iteration of (9) leaves c_0 completely undetermined, we have actually found the general solution of (1).

6.2.2 Solutions Around Ordinary Points

Ordinary and singular points

Consider the differential equation

$$a_2(x)y'' + a_1(x)y' + a_0(x)y = 0 \tag{11}$$

where $a_2(x)$, $a_1(x)$, and $a_0(x)$ are arbitrary polynomials with no common factors. We make the following definition.

DEFINITION 6.1 Any point $x = x_0$ for which $a_2(x_0) \neq 0$ is said to be an **ordinary point** of equation (11), whereas a point $x = x_0$ for which $a_2(x_0) = 0$ is said to be a **singular point** of the equation.

EXAMPLES

(a) The singular points of the equation $(x^2 - 1)y'' + 2xy' + 6y = 0$ are the solutions of $x^2 - 1 = 0$ or $x = \pm 1$. All other finite values of x are ordinary points.

(b) Singular points need not be real numbers. The equation $(x^2 + 1)y'' + xy' - y = 0$ has singular points at the solutions of $x^2 + 1 = 0$, namely, $x = \pm i$. All other finite values of x, real or complete, are ordinary points.

EXAMPLE

The Cauchy–Euler equation $ax^2 y'' + bxy' + cy = 0$, where a, b, and c are constants has a singular point at $x = 0$. All other finite values of x, real or complex, are ordinary points.

In a more general sense, when a differential equation is written as $y'' + P(x)y' + Q(x)y = 0$ we say that $x = x_0$ is an ordinary point provided the functions P and Q are *analytic* at x_0. That is, both P and Q must possess power series expansions of the form $\sum_{n=0}^{\infty} b_n(x - x_0)^n$.

EXAMPLE

The differential equation $xy'' + (\sin x)y = 0$ has an ordinary point at $x = 0$ since it can be shown that $Q(x) = (\sin x)/x$ possesses the power series expansion

$$Q(x) = 1 - \frac{x^2}{3!} + \frac{x^4}{5!} - \frac{x^6}{7!} + \cdots$$

that converges for all finite values of x.

In the remaining discussion of this section we shall be concerned with finding power series solutions about ordinary points for differential equations of type (11) in which the coefficients are polynomials. Also, for our purposes ordinary points and singular points will always be finite. It is possible for a differential equation to have, say, a singular point at infinity (see Exercise 6.3). We state the following theorem without proof.

THEOREM 6.1 If $x = x_0$ is an ordinary point of equation (11), we can always find two distinct power series solutions of the form

$$y = \sum_{n=0}^{\infty} c_n(x - x_0)^n.$$

A series solution is guaranteed to converge at least on an interval defined by $|x - x_0| < R$, where R is the distance to the closest singular point.*

To solve an equation such as (11) we must find two different sets of coefficients c_n so that we have two distinct linearly independent power series $y_1(x)$ and $y_2(x)$, both expanded about the same ordinary point $x = x_0$. On a common interval of convergence not containing the origin the general solution of the equation is then $y = C_1 y_1(x) + C_2 y_2(x)$. The procedure used to solve a second-order equation is the same as illustrated in solving $y' - 2xy = 0$, namely, we assume a solution $y = \sum_{n=0}^{\infty} c_n(x - x_0)^n$ and then determine the c_n. In fact, we shall find that $C_1 = c_0$ and $C_2 = c_1$ where c_0 and c_1 are arbitrary. Also, for the sake of simplicity we shall assume an ordinary point is always located at $x = 0$, since, if not, the substitution $t = x - x_0$ translates the value $x = x_0$ to $t = 0$.

EXAMPLE

Solve the second-order equation

$$y'' - 2xy = 0.$$

Solution: Since $x = 0$ is an ordinary point of the equation we assume $y = \sum_{n=0}^{\infty} c_n x^n$. Proceeding formally we write

$$y' = \sum_{n=0}^{\infty} n c_n x^{n-1} = \sum_{n=1}^{\infty} n c_n x^{n-1}$$

$$y'' = \sum_{n=1}^{\infty} n(n-1) c_n x^{n-2} = \sum_{n=2}^{\infty} n(n-1) c_n x^{n-2}$$

where we have used the fact that the first term in each series, corresponding to $n = 0$ and $n = 1$, respectively, is zero. Therefore

$$y'' - 2xy = \sum_{n=2}^{\infty} n(n-1) c_n x^{n-2} - \sum_{n=0}^{\infty} 2 c_n x^{n+1}$$

$$= 2 \cdot 1 c_2 x^0 + \underbrace{\sum_{n=3}^{\infty} n(n-1) c_n x^{n-2} - \sum_{n=0}^{\infty} 2 c_n x^{n+1}}_{\text{both series start with } x^1.}$$

Letting $k = n - 2$ in the first series and $k = n + 1$ in the second gives

$$y'' - 2xy = 2 c_2 + \sum_{k=1}^{\infty} (k+2)(k+1) c_{k+2} x^k - \sum_{k=1}^{\infty} 2 c_{k-1} x^k$$

$$= 2 c_2 + \sum_{k=1}^{\infty} [(k+2)(k+2) c_{k+2} - 2 c_{k-1}] x^k = 0.$$

---

* For example, there could exist polynomial solutions in which case the solution is valid for all finite values of x.

We must then have

$$2c_2 = 0$$

and $$(k + 2)(k + 1)c_{k+2} - 2c_{k-1} = 0.$$

The last expression is the same as

$$c_{k+2} = \frac{2c_{k-1}}{(k + 2)(k + 1)}, \quad k = 1, 2, 3 \ldots.$$

Iterating

$$c_3 = \frac{2c_0}{3 \cdot 2}$$

$$c_4 = \frac{2c_1}{4 \cdot 3}$$

$$c_5 = \frac{2c_2}{5 \cdot 4} = 0$$

$$c_6 = \frac{2c_3}{6 \cdot 5} = \frac{2^2}{6 \cdot 5 \cdot 3 \cdot 2}c_0$$

$$c_7 = \frac{2c_4}{7 \cdot 6} = \frac{2^2}{7 \cdot 6 \cdot 4 \cdot 3}c_1$$

$$c_8 = \frac{2c_5}{8 \cdot 7} = 0$$

$$c_9 = \frac{2c_6}{9 \cdot 8} = \frac{2^3}{9 \cdot 8 \cdot 6 \cdot 5 \cdot 3 \cdot 2}c_0$$

$$c_{10} = \frac{2c_7}{10 \cdot 9} = \frac{2^3}{10 \cdot 9 \cdot 7 \cdot 6 \cdot 4 \cdot 3}c_1$$

$$c_{11} = \frac{2c_8}{11 \cdot 10} = 0$$

and so on. It should be apparent that both c_0 and c_1 are arbitrary.

Now

$$y = c_0 + c_1 x + c_2 x^2 + c_3 x^3 + c_4 x^4 + c_5 x^5 + c_6 x^6 + c_7 x^7 + c_8 x^8$$
$$+ c_9 x^9 + c_{10} x^{10} + c_{11} x^{11} + \cdots$$

$$= c_0 + c_1 x + 0 + \frac{2}{3 \cdot 2} c_0 x^3 + \frac{2}{4 \cdot 3} c_1 x^4 + 0 + \frac{2^2}{6 \cdot 5 \cdot 3 \cdot 2} c_0 x^6$$

$$+ \frac{2^2}{7 \cdot 6 \cdot 4 \cdot 3} c_1 x^7 + 0 + \frac{2^3}{9 \cdot 8 \cdot 6 \cdot 5 \cdot 3 \cdot 2} c_0 x^9$$

$$+ \frac{2^3}{10 \cdot 9 \cdot 7 \cdot 6 \cdot 4 \cdot 3} c_1 x^{10} + 0 + \cdots$$

$$= c_0 \left[1 + \frac{2}{3 \cdot 2} x^3 + \frac{2^2}{6 \cdot 5 \cdot 3 \cdot 2} x^6 + \frac{2^3}{9 \cdot 8 \cdot 6 \cdot 5 \cdot 3 \cdot 2} x^9 + \cdots \right]$$

$$+ c_1 \left[x + \frac{2}{4 \cdot 3} x^4 + \frac{2^2}{7 \cdot 6 \cdot 4 \cdot 3} x^7 + \frac{2^3}{10 \cdot 9 \cdot 7 \cdot 6 \cdot 4 \cdot 3} x^{10} + \cdots \right]$$

where each series converges for $|x| < \infty$ since the equation has no finite singular points.

Although the pattern of the coefficients in the preceding example should be clear it is sometimes useful to write the solutions in terms of summation notation. By using the properties of the factorial it is easily verified that

$$y_1(x) = c_0 \left[1 + \sum_{k=1}^{\infty} \frac{2^k [1 \cdot 4 \cdot 7 \cdots (3k - 2)]}{(3k)!} x^{3k} \right]$$

and

$$y_2(x) = c_1 \left[x + \sum_{k=1}^{\infty} \frac{2^k [2 \cdot 5 \cdot 8 \cdots (3k - 1)]}{(3k + 1)!} x^{3k+1} \right].$$

In this form the ratio test can be used to verify that each series converges for $|x| < \infty$.

EXAMPLE   Solve $$(x^2 + 1)y'' + xy' - y = 0$$

Solution: Since the singular points are $x = \pm i$ a power series solution will converge at least for $|x| < 1$.* The assumption $y = \sum_{n=0}^{\infty} c_n x^n$ leads to

---

* The modulus or magnitude of the complex number $x = i$ is $|x| = 1$. If $x = a + bi$ is a singular point then $|x| = \sqrt{a^2 + b^2}$.

$$(x^2 + 1) \sum_{n=2}^{\infty} n(n-1)c_n x^{n-2} + x \sum_{n=1}^{\infty} nc_n x^{n-1} - \sum_{n=0}^{\infty} c_n x^n$$

$$= \sum_{n=2}^{\infty} n(n-1)c_n x^n + \sum_{n=2}^{\infty} n(n-1)c_n x^{n-2} + \sum_{n=1}^{\infty} nc_x x^n - \sum_{n=0}^{\infty} c_n x^n$$

$$= 2c_2 x^0 - c_0 x^0 + 6c_3 x + c_1 x - c_1 x + \underbrace{\sum_{n=2}^{\infty} n(n-1)c_n x^n}_{k=n}$$

$$+ \underbrace{\sum_{n=4}^{\infty} n(n-1)c_n x^{n-2}}_{k=n-2} + \underbrace{\sum_{n=2}^{\infty} nc_n x^n}_{k=n} - \underbrace{\sum_{n=2}^{\infty} c_n x^n}_{k=n}$$

$$= 2c_2 - c_0 + 6c_3 x$$

$$+ \sum_{k=2}^{\infty} [k(k-1)c_k + (k+2)(k+1)c_{k+2} + kc_k - c_k]x^k$$

$$= 2c_2 - c_0 + 6c_3 x$$

$$+ \sum_{k=2}^{\infty} [(k+1)(k-1)c_k + (k+2)(k+1)c_{k+2}]x^k = 0.$$

Thus we must have

$$2c_2 - c_0 = 0$$

$$c_3 = 0$$

$$(k+1)(k-1)c_k + (k+2)(k+1)c_{k+2} = 0$$

or, after dividing by $k+1$,

$$c_3 = 0$$

$$c_2 = \frac{1}{2}c_0$$

$$c_{k+2} = \frac{k-1}{k+2}c_k, \quad k = 2, 3, 4 \ldots.$$

Iteration of the last formula gives

$$c_4 = \frac{1}{4}c_2 = \frac{1}{2 \cdot 4}c_0 = \frac{1}{2^2 2!}c_0$$

$$c_5 = \frac{2}{5}c_3 = 0$$

$$c_6 = \frac{3}{6}c_4 = \frac{3}{2 \cdot 4 \cdot 6}c_0 = \frac{1 \cdot 3}{2^3 3!}c_0$$

$$c_7 = \frac{4}{7}c_5 = 0$$

$$c_8 = \frac{5}{8}c_6 = \frac{3 \cdot 5}{2 \cdot 4 \cdot 6 \cdot 8}c_0 = \frac{1 \cdot 3 \cdot 5}{2^4 4!}c_0$$

$$c_9 = \frac{6}{9}c_7 = 0$$

$$c_{10} = \frac{7}{10}c_8 = \frac{3 \cdot 5 \cdot 7}{2 \cdot 4 \cdot 6 \cdot 8 \cdot 10}c_0 = \frac{1 \cdot 3 \cdot 5 \cdot 7}{2^5 5!}c_0$$

and so on. Therefore

$$y = c_0 + c_1 x + c_2 x^2 + c_3 x^3 + c_4 x^4 + c_5 x^5 + c_6 x^6 + c_7 x^7 + c_8 x^8 + \cdots$$

$$= c_1 x + c_0 \left[1 + \frac{1}{2}x^2 + \frac{1}{2^2 2!}x^4 \right.$$

$$\left. + \frac{1 \cdot 3}{2^3 3!}x^6 + \frac{1 \cdot 3 \cdot 5}{2^4 4!}x^8 + \frac{1 \cdot 3 \cdot 5 \cdot 7}{2^5 5!}x^{10} + \cdots \right].$$

The solutions are

$$y_1(x) = c_0 \left[1 + \frac{1}{2}x^2 + \sum_{n=2}^{\infty} \frac{1 \cdot 3 \cdot 5 \cdots (2n-3)}{2^n n!}x^{2n} \right], \qquad |x| < 1,$$

$$y_2(x) = c_1 x.$$

EXERCISES 6.1

[6.2.1]   Answers to odd-numbered problems begin on page A-15 of the Appendix. In Problems 1–5 solve each differential equation in the manner of the previous chapters and then compare the results with the solutions obtained by assuming a power series solution $y = \sum_{n=0}^{\infty} c_n x^n$.

1. $y' + y = 0$ ★2. $y' - x^2 y = 0$

3. $y'' - y = 0$ 4. $y'' + 2y' - 3y = 0$

5. $y'' + y = 0$

[6.2.2]   In Problems 6–18 for each differential equation find two linearly independent power series solutions about the ordinary point $x = 0$.

EXAMPLE   If we seek a solution $y = \sum_{n=0}^{\infty} c_n x^n$ for the equation

$$y'' - (1 + x)y = 0$$

we obtain $c_2 = c_0/2$ and the three-term recurrence relation

$$c_{k+2} = \frac{c_k + c_{k-1}}{(k+1)(k+2)}, \qquad k = 1, 2, 3 \ldots .$$

To simplify the iteration we can first choose $c_0 \neq 0$, $c_1 = 0$; this will yield one solution. The other solution follows from next choosing $c_0 = 0$, $c_1 \neq 0$. With the first assumption we find

$$c_2 = \frac{1}{2}c_0$$

$$c_3 = \frac{c_1 + c_0}{2 \cdot 3} = \frac{c_0}{2 \cdot 3} = \frac{1}{6}c_0$$

$$c_4 = \frac{c_2 + c_1}{3 \cdot 4} = \frac{c_0}{2 \cdot 3 \cdot 4} = \frac{1}{24}c_0$$

$$c_5 = \frac{c_3 + c_2}{4 \cdot 5} = \frac{c_0}{4 \cdot 5}\left[\frac{1}{2 \cdot 3} + \frac{1}{2}\right] = \frac{1}{30}c_0$$

and so on. Thus one solution is

$$y_1(x) = c_0\left[1 + \frac{1}{2}x^2 + \frac{1}{6}x^3 + \frac{1}{24}x^4 + \frac{1}{30}x^5 + \cdots\right].$$

Similarly if we choose $c_0 = 0$ then

$$c_2 = 0$$

$$c_3 = \frac{c_1 + c_0}{2 \cdot 3} = \frac{c_1}{2 \cdot 3} = \frac{1}{6}c_1$$

$$c_4 = \frac{c_2 + c_1}{3 \cdot 4} = \frac{c_1}{3 \cdot 4} = \frac{1}{12}c_1$$

$$c_5 = \frac{c_3 + c_2}{4 \cdot 5} = \frac{c_1}{2 \cdot 3 \cdot 4 \cdot 5} = \frac{1}{120}c_1$$

and so on. Hence another solution is

$$y_2(x) = c_1\left[x + \frac{1}{6}x^3 + \frac{1}{12}x^4 + \frac{1}{120}x^5 + \cdots\right].$$

Each series converges for all finite values of x.

6. $y'' - xy' + 2y = 0$

7. $y'' - 2xy' + y = 0$

8. $y'' + 2xy' + 2y = 0$

9. $y'' + x^2y' + xy = 0$

10. $y'' + x^2y = 0$

11. $(x - 1)y'' + y' = 0$

12. $(x + 2)y'' + xy' - y = 0$ **13.** $y'' - (x + 1)y' - y = 0$

14. $(x^2 + 1)y'' - 6y = 0$ **15.** $(x^2 - 1)y'' + 4xy' + 2y = 0$

16. $(x^2 - 1)y'' + xy' - y = 0$ **17.** $(x^2 + 2)y'' + 3xy' - y = 0$

★**18.** $y'' - xy' - (x + 2)y = 0$

EXAMPLE

The series method of this section can sometimes be used when the coefficients are not polynomials. Solve $y'' + (\cos x)y = 0$.

Solution: Since $\cos x = 1 - \dfrac{x^2}{2!} + \dfrac{x^4}{4!} - \dfrac{x^2}{6!} + \cdots$ we see that $x = 0$ is an ordinary point. Thus the assumption $y = \sum_{n=0}^{\infty} c_n x^n$ leads to

$$y'' + (\cos x)y = \sum_{n=2}^{\infty} n(n-1)c_n x^{n-2} + \left(1 - \frac{x^2}{2!} + \frac{x^4}{4!} + \cdots\right)\sum_{n=0}^{\infty} c_n x^n$$

$$= (2c_2 + 6c_3 x + 12c_4 x^2 + 20c_5 x^3 + \cdots)$$

$$+ \left(1 - \frac{x^2}{2} + \frac{x^4}{24} + \cdots\right)(c_0 + c_1 x + c_2 x^2 + c_3 x^3 + \cdots)$$

$$= 2c_2 + c_0 + (6c_3 + c_1)x + \left(12c_4 + c_2 - \frac{1}{2}c_0\right)x^2$$

$$+ \left(20c_5 + c_3 - \frac{1}{2}c_1\right)x^3 + \cdots.$$

Since the last line is to be identically zero we must have

$$2c_2 + c_0 = 0$$

$$6c_3 + c_1 = 0$$

$$12c_4 + c_2 - \frac{1}{2}c_0 = 0$$

$$20c_5 + c_3 - \frac{1}{2}c_1 = 0$$

and so on. Since c_0 and c_1 are arbitrary we find *, by solving for all other c_j in terms of c_0 and c_1:*

$$y_1(x) = c_0\left[1 - \frac{1}{2}x^2 + \frac{1}{12}x^4 + \cdots\right]$$

and

$$y_2(x) = c_1\left[x - \frac{1}{6}x^3 + \frac{1}{30}x^5 + \cdots\right].$$

Both series converge for all finite values of x.

In Problems 19–21 for each differential equation find two power series solutions about the ordinary point $x = 0$.

19. $y'' + e^{-x}y = 0$ **20.** $y'' + (\sin x)y = 0$

21. $y'' + e^x y' - y = 0$

★22. Solve: $y'' - 4xy' - 4y = e^x$ [*Hint:* Expand e^x in a power series about $x = 0$.]

23. Solve: $y'' - xy = 1$

6.3   Solutions Around Singular Points

We saw in the preceding section that there is no basic problem in finding a power series solution of

$$a_2(x)y'' + a_1(x)y' + a_0(x)y = 0 \tag{1}$$

about a point $x = x_0$ which is not a root of the polynomial $a_2(x)$. However, when $a_2(x_0) = 0$ it is not always possible to find a solution of the form $y = \sum_{n=0}^{\infty} c_n(x - x_0)^n$; it turns out that we may be able to find a solution of the form $y = \sum_{n=0}^{\infty} c_n(x - x_0)^{n+r}$ where r is a constant that must be determined.

Regular and irregular singular points

Recall that when $a_2(x)$, $a_1(x)$, and $a_0(x)$ are polynomials with no common factors we say that $x = x_0$ is a singular point of the differential equation if $a_2(x_0) = 0$. Singular points are further classified as either **regular** or **irregular**.

DEFINITION 6.2   Suppose equation (1) is written in the form

$$y'' + P(x)y' + Q(x)y = 0 \tag{2}$$

where $P(x)$ and $Q(x)$ are rational functions formed by reducing $a_1(x)/a_2(x)$ and $a_0(x)/a_2(x)$ to *lowest terms*. If the factor $(x - x_0)$ appears *at most* to the first power in the denominator of $P(x)$ and *at most* to the second power in the denominator of $Q(x)$ then $x = x_0$ is said to be a **regular singular point.*** A singular point which is not regular is said to be **irregular**.

EXAMPLE

It should be clear that $x = -2$ and $x = 2$ are singular points of the equation

$$(x^2 - 4)^2 y'' + (x - 2)y' + y = 0.$$

---

* When $a_2(x)$, $a_1(x)$ and $a_0(x)$ are not polynomials, then a singular point $x = x_0$ is said to be regular if both functions $(x - x_0)P(x)$ and $(x - x_0)^2 Q(x)$ possess power series expansions about $x = x_0$.

Dividing the equation by $(x^2 - 4)^2 = (x - 2)^2(x + 2)^2$ we find that

$$P(x) = \frac{1}{(x - 2)(x + 2)^2} \quad \text{and} \quad Q(x) = \frac{1}{(x - 2)^2(x + 2)^2}.$$

We now test P and Q at each singular point.

In order that $x = -2$ be a regular singular point, the factor $x + 2$ can appear at most to the first power in the denominator of $P(x)$, and can appear at most to the second power in the denominator of $Q(x)$. Inspection of P and Q shows that the first condition does not obtain, and so we conclude that $x = -2$ is an irregular singular point.

In order that $x = 2$ be a regular singular point, the factor $x - 2$ can appear at most to the first power in the denominator of $P(x)$, and can appear at most to the second power in the denominator of $Q(x)$. Further inspection of P and Q shows that both these conditions are satisfied, so $x = 2$ is a regular singular point.

EXAMPLE

Both $x = 0$ and $x = -1$ are singular points of the differential equation

$$x^2(x + 1)^2 y'' + (x^2 - 1)y' + 2y = 0.$$

Inspection of

$$P(x) = \frac{x - 1}{x^2(x + 1)} \quad \text{and} \quad Q(x) = \frac{2}{x^2(x + 1)^2}.$$

shows that $x = 0$ is an irregular singular point since $(x - 0)$ appears to the second power in the denominator of $P(x)$. Note however that $x = -1$ is a regular singular point.

EXAMPLES

(a) $x = 1$ and $x = -1$ are regular singular points of

$$(1 - x^2)y'' - 2xy' + 30y = 0$$

(b) $x = 0$ is an irregular singular point of

$$x^3 y'' - 2xy' + 5y = 0$$

since

$$Q(x) = 5/x^3$$

(c) $x = 0$ is a regular singular point of

$$xy'' - 2xy' + 5y = 0$$

since

$$P(x) = -2 \quad \text{and} \quad Q(x) = 5/x.$$

In part **(c)** of the preceding example notice that $(x - 0)$ and $(x - 0,^2$ do not even appear in the denominators of P and Q. Remember Definition 6.2 states that these factors can appear *at most* in this fashion. For a singular point $x = x_0$, any nonnegative power of $(x - x_0)$ less than one (namely, zero) and nonnegative power less than two (namely, zero and one) in the denominators of $P(x)$ and $Q(x)$, respectively, implies x_0 is a regular singular point.

Also, recall that singular points could be complex numbers. It should be apparent that both $x = 3i$ and $x = -3i$ are regular singular points of the equation $(x^2 + 9)y'' - 3xy' + (1 - x)y = 0$ since

$$P(x) = \frac{-3x}{(x - 3i)(x + 3i)} \quad \text{and} \quad Q(x) = \frac{1 - x}{(x - 3i)(x + 3i)}$$

EXAMPLE

From our discussion of the Cauchy–Euler equation in Section 6.1, we can easily show that $y_1 = x^2$ and $y_2 = x^2 \ln x$ are solutions of the equation $x^2 y'' - 3xy + 4y = 0$ for $x > 0$. If the procedure of Theorem 6.1 is formally attempted at the regular singular point $x = 0$ (that is, an assumed solution of the form $y = \Sigma_{n=0}^{\infty} c_n x^n$) we would succeed in obtaining only the solution $y_1 = x^2$. The fact that we would not obtain the second solution is not really surprising since $y_2 = x^2 \ln x$ does not possess a Taylor series expansion about $x = 0$.

EXAMPLE

The differential equation

$$6x^2 y'' + 5xy' + (x^2 - 1)y = 0$$

has a regular singular point at $x = 0$, but does not possess *any* solution of the form $y = \Sigma_{n=0}^{\infty} c_n x^n$. By the procedure that we shall now consider it can be shown, however, that there exist two series solutions of the form

$$y = \sum_{n=0}^{\infty} c_n x^{n+1/2} \quad \text{and} \quad y = \sum_{n=0}^{\infty} c_n x^{n-1/3}.$$

The method of Frobenius

To solve a differential equation such as (1) about a regular singular point we employ the following theorem due to Georg Frobenius.*

---

* Frobenius, a German mathematician (1848–1917), published this method in 1873.

THEOREM 6.2 If $x = x_0$ is a regular singular point of equation (1) then there exists at least one series solution of the form

$$y = (x - x_0)^r \sum_{n=0}^{\infty} c_n(x - x_0)^n$$

$$= \sum_{n=0}^{\infty} c_n(x - x_0)^{n+r} \tag{3}$$

where the number r is a constant which must be determined.* The series will converge at least on some interval $0 < x - x_0 < R$.

As an example, we note that $x = 0$ is a regular singular point of the equation

$$3xy'' + y' - y = 0 \tag{4}$$

so we try a solution of the form

$$y = \sum_{n=0}^{\infty} c_n x^{n+r}$$

Now

$$y' = \sum_{n=0}^{\infty} (n + r)c_n x^{n+r-1}$$

$$y'' = \sum_{n=0}^{\infty} (n + r)(n + r - 1)c_n x^{n+r-2}$$

so that

$$3xy'' + y' - y = 3 \sum_{n=0}^{\infty} (n + r)(n + r - 1)c_n x^{n+r-1}$$

$$+ \sum_{n=0}^{\infty} (n + r)c_n x^{n+r-1} - \sum_{n=0}^{\infty} c_n x^{n+r}$$

$$= \sum_{n=0}^{\infty} (n + r)(3n + 3r - 2)c_n x^{n+r-1} - \sum_{n=0}^{\infty} c_n x^{n+r}$$

$$= x^r \Bigg[r(3r - 2)c_0 x^{-1} +$$

$$+ \underbrace{\sum_{n=1}^{\infty} (n + r)(3n + 3r - 2)c_n x^{n-1}}_{k = n - 1} - \underbrace{\sum_{n=0}^{\infty} c_n x^n}_{k = n} \Bigg]$$

$$= x^r \Bigg[r(3r - 2)c_0 x^{-1} +$$

$$+ \sum_{k=0}^{\infty} [(k + r + 1)(3k + 3r + 1)c_{k+1} - c_k] x^k \Bigg] = 0$$

---

* As noted in the foregoing section, for the sake of simplicity we shall always assume $x_0 = 0$.

which implies

$$r(3r - 2)c_0 = 0$$

$$(k + r + 1)(3k + 3r + 1)c_{k+1} - c_k = 0, \quad k = 0, 1, 2 \ldots . \tag{5}$$

Since nothing is gained by taking $c_0 = 0$ we must then have

$$r(3r - 2) = 0 \tag{6}$$

and

$$c_{k+1} = \frac{c_k}{(k + r + 1)(3k + 3r + 1)}, \quad k = 0, 1, 2 \ldots . \tag{7}$$

The two values of r that satisfy (6), $r_1 = 2/3$ and $r_2 = 0$, when substituted in (7) gives two different recurrence relations

$$r_1 = \frac{2}{3}, \qquad c_{k+1} = \frac{c_k}{(3k + 5)(k + 1)}, \tag{8}$$

and

$$r_2 = 0, \qquad c_{k+1} = \frac{c_k}{(k + 1)(3k + 1)}. \tag{9}$$

Iteration of (8) gives

$$c_1 = \frac{c_0}{5 \cdot 1}$$

$$c_2 = \frac{c_1}{8 \cdot 2} = \frac{c_0}{2!5 \cdot 8}$$

$$c_3 = \frac{c_2}{11 \cdot 3} = \frac{c_0}{3!5 \cdot 8 \cdot 11}$$

$$c_4 = \frac{c_3}{14 \cdot 4} = \frac{c_0}{4!5 \cdot 8 \cdot 11 \cdot 14}$$

$$\vdots$$

$$c_n = \frac{c_0}{n!5 \cdot 8 \cdot 11 \cdots (3n + 2)}, \qquad n = 1, 2, 3 \ldots,$$

whereas iteration of (9) yields

$$c_1 = \frac{c_0}{1 \cdot 1}$$

$$c_2 = \frac{c_1}{2 \cdot 4} = \frac{c_0}{2!1 \cdot 4}$$

$$c_3 = \frac{c_2}{3 \cdot 7} = \frac{c_0}{3!1 \cdot 4 \cdot 7}$$

$$c_4 = \frac{c_3}{4 \cdot 10} = \frac{c_0}{4!1 \cdot 4 \cdot 7 \cdot 10}$$

$$\vdots$$

$$c_n = \frac{c_0}{n!1 \cdot 4 \cdot 7 \cdots (3n - 2)}, \qquad n = 1, 2, 3 \ldots .$$

Thus we obtain two series solutions

$$y_1 = c_0 x^{2/3} \left[1 + \sum_{n=1}^{\infty} \frac{1}{n! 5 \cdot 8 \cdot 11 \cdots (3n + 2)} x^n \right] \qquad (10)$$

and

$$y_2 = c_0 x^0 \left[1 + \sum_{n=1}^{\infty} \frac{1}{n! 1 \cdot 4 \cdot 7 \cdots (3n - 2)} x^n \right]. \qquad (11)$$

By the ratio test it is readily demonstrated that both (10) and (11) converge for all finite values of x. Also, it should be clear from the form of (10) and (11) that neither series is a constant multiple of the other and therefore $y_1(x)$ and $y_2(x)$ are linearly independent solutions on the x-axis. Hence, by the superposition principle

$$y = C_1 y_1(x) + C_2 y_x(x)$$

$$= C_1 \left[x^{2/3} + \sum_{n=1}^{\infty} \frac{1}{n! 5 \cdot 8 \cdot 11 \cdots (3n + 2)} x^{n + 2/3} \right]$$

$$+ C_2 \left[1 + \sum_{n=1}^{\infty} \frac{1}{n! 1 \cdot 4 \cdot 7 \cdots (3n - 2)} x^n \right], \qquad |x| < \infty,$$

is another solution of (4). On any interval not containing the origin (such as, $x > 0$) this combination represents the general solution of the equation on the interval.

Although the foregoing example illustrates the general procedure for using the method of Frobenius, we hasten to point out that we may not always be able to find two solutions so readily, or for that matter, that we can find two solutions which are infinite series consisting entirely of powers of x.

Indicial equation   Equation (6) is called the **indicial equation** of the problem and the values $r_1 = 2/3$ and $r_2 = 0$ are called the **indicial roots** or **exponents** of the singularity ($x = 0$). In general, when using the assumption $y = \sum_{n=0}^{\infty} c_n x^{n+r}$ in an attempt to solve a linear second-order differential equation, the indicial equation is a quadratic equation in r resulting from equating to zero the *total coefficient of the lowest power of x*. We then solve for the two values of the exponents and substitute these values into a corresponding recurrence relation such as (7). Theorem 6.2 guarantees that we can always find at least one solution of the assumed series form.

EXAMPLE   Were we to try the method of Frobenius on the slightly different equation

$$xy'' + 3y' - y = 0 \qquad (12)$$

we would find

$$xy'' + 3y' - y = x^r \left[r(r + 2)c_0 x^{-1} + \right.$$

$$\left. + \sum_{k=0}^{\infty} [(k + r + 1)(k + r + 3)c_{k+1} - c_k] x^k \right] = 0$$

so that the indicial equation and exponents are $r(r + 2) = 0$ and $r_1 = 0$, $r_2 = -2$ respectively.

Since

$$(k + r + 1)(k + r + 3)c_{k+1} - c_k = 0, \quad k = 0, 1, 2\dots \tag{13}$$

it follows that when $r_1 = 0$

$$c_{k+1} = \frac{c_k}{(k + 1)(k + 3)}$$

$$c_1 = \frac{c_0}{1 \cdot 3}$$

$$c_2 = \frac{c_1}{2 \cdot 4} = \frac{2c_0}{2!4!}$$

$$c_3 = \frac{c_2}{3 \cdot 5} = \frac{2c_0}{3!5!}$$

$$c_4 = \frac{c_3}{4 \cdot 6} = \frac{2c_0}{4!6!}$$

$$\vdots$$

$$c_n = \frac{2c_0}{n!(n + 2)!}, \quad n = 1, 2, 3\dots.$$

Thus one series solution is

$$y_1 = c_0 x^0 \left[1 + \sum_{n=1}^{\infty} \frac{2}{n!(n + 2)!} x^n \right].$$

$$= c_0 \sum_{n=0}^{\infty} \frac{2}{n!(n + 2)!} x^n, \quad |x| < \infty. \tag{14}$$

Now when $r_2 = -2$, (13) becomes

$$(k - 1)(k + 1)c_{k+1} - c_k = 0, \tag{15}$$

but note here that we *do not divide* by $(k - 1)(k + 1)$ immediately since this term is zero for $k = 1$. However, we use the recurrence relation (15) directly for the cases $k = 0$ and $k = 1$:

$$-1 \cdot 1 c_1 - c_0 = 0 \quad \text{and} \quad 0 \cdot 2 c_2 - c_1 = 0.$$

The latter equation implies that $c_1 = 0$ and so the former equation implies $c_0 = 0$. Continuing we find

$$c_{k+1} = \frac{c_k}{(k - 1)(k + 1)}, \quad k = 2, 3, \dots$$

and so

$$c_3 = \frac{c_2}{1 \cdot 3}$$

$$c_4 = \frac{c_3}{2 \cdot 4} = \frac{2c_2}{2!4!}$$

$$c_5 = \frac{c_4}{3 \cdot 5} = \frac{2c_2}{3!5!}$$

$$\vdots$$

$$c_n = \frac{2c_2}{(n-2)!n!}, \qquad n = 2, 3, 4, \ldots.$$

Thus we can formally write

$$y_2 = c_2 x^{-2} \sum_{n=2}^{\infty} \frac{2}{(n-2)!n!} x^n. \tag{16}$$

However, close inspection of (16) reveals that y_2 is simply a constant multiple of (14). To see this, let $k = n - 2$ in (16). We conclude that the method of Frobenius gives only one series solution of equation (12).

Cases of indicial roots

When using the method of Frobenius we usually distinguish three possible cases corresponding to the nature of the indicial roots. For the sake of discussion let us suppose that r_1 and r_2 are the real solutions of the indicial equation and that, when appropriate, r_1 *denotes the largest root.*

CASE I   If r_1 and r_2 are distinct and *do not* differ by an integer, then there exist two linearly independent solutions of equation (1) of the form

$$y_1 = \sum_{n=0}^{\infty} c_n x^{n+r_1}, \qquad c_0 \neq 0 \tag{17a}$$

$$y_2 = \sum_{n=0}^{\infty} b_n x^{n+r_2}, \qquad b_0 \neq 0. \tag{17b}$$

CASE II   If $r_1 - r_2 = N$, where N is a positive integer, then there exist two linearly independent solutions of the form

$$y_1 = \sum_{n=0}^{\infty} c_n x^{n+r_1}, \qquad c_0 \neq 0 \tag{18a}$$

$$y_2 = Cy_1(x) \ln x + \sum_{n=0}^{\infty} b_n x^{n+r_2}, \qquad b_0 \neq 0, \tag{18b}$$

where C is a constant that could be zero.

CASE III If $r_1 = r_2$ there always exist two linearly independent solutions of the form

$$y_1 = \sum_{n=0}^{\infty} c_n x^{n+r_1}, \qquad c_0 \neq 0, \tag{19a}$$

$$y_2 = y_1(x) \ln x + \sum_{n=1}^{\infty} b_n x^{n+r_1}. \tag{19b}$$

When the roots of the indicial equation differ by a positive integer we may or may not be able to find two solutions of the form (3). If not, then one solution, corresponding to the smaller root, contains a logarithmic term. When the exponents are equal a second solution will *always* contain a logarithm. This latter situation is analogous to the solutions of the Cauchy–Euler differential equation when the roots of the auxiliary equation are equal.

CASE I   Roots Not Differing by an Integer

EXAMPLE

Solve
$$2xy'' + (1 + x)y' + y = 0 \tag{20}$$

Solution: If $y = \sum_{n=0}^{\infty} c_n x^{n+r}$ then

$$2xy'' + (1 + x)y' + y = 2 \sum_{n=0}^{\infty} (n + r)(n + r - 1)c_n x^{n+r-1}$$

$$+ \sum_{n=0}^{\infty} (n + r)c_n x^{n+r-1}$$

$$+ \sum_{n=0}^{\infty} (n + r)c_n x^{n+r} + \sum_{n=0}^{\infty} c_n x^{n+r}$$

$$= \sum_{n=0}^{\infty} (n + r)(2n + 2r - 1)c_n x^{n+r-1}$$

$$+ \sum_{n=0}^{\infty} (n + r + 1)c_n x^{n+r}$$

$$= x^r \Bigg[r(2r - 1)c_0 x^{-1}$$

$$+ \underbrace{\sum_{n=1}^{\infty} (n + r)(2n + 2r - 1)c_n x^{n-1}}_{k = n - 1} +$$

$$+ \underbrace{\sum_{n=0}^{\infty} (n + r + 1)c_n x^n}_{k = n} \Bigg]$$

$$= x^r \Bigg[r(2r - 1)c_0 x^{-1}$$

$$+ \sum_{k=0}^{\infty} [(k + r + 1)(2k + 2r + 1)c_{k+1} +$$

$$+ (k + r + 1)c_k] x^k \Bigg] = 0$$

which implies
$$r(2r - 1) = 0 \tag{21}$$

$$(k + r + 1)(2k + 2r + 1)c_{k+1} + (k + r + 1)c_k = 0, 1, 2 \ldots. \tag{22}$$

For $r_1 = 1/2$ we can divide by $k + 3/2$ in (22) to obtain

$$c_{k+1} = \frac{-c_k}{2(k + 1)}$$

$$c_1 = \frac{-c_0}{2 \cdot 1}$$

$$c_2 = \frac{-c_1}{2 \cdot 2} = \frac{c_0}{2^2 \cdot 2!}$$

$$c_3 = \frac{-c_2}{2 \cdot 3} = \frac{-c_0}{2^3 \cdot 3!}$$

$$\vdots$$

$$c_n = \frac{(-1)^n c_0}{2^n n!}, \qquad n = 1, 2, 3 \ldots.$$

Thus we have

$$y_1 = c_0 x^{1/2} \left[1 + \sum_{n=1}^{\infty} \frac{(-1)^n}{2^n n!} x^n \right]$$

$$= c_0 \sum_{n=0}^{\infty} \frac{(-1)^n}{2^n n!} x^{n+1/2} \tag{23}$$

which converges for $x \geq 0$. As given, the series is not meaningful for $x < 0$ because of the presence of $x^{1/2}$.

Now for $r_2 = 0$, formula (22) becomes

$$c_{k+1} = \frac{-c_k}{2k + 1}$$

$$c_1 = \frac{-c_0}{1}$$

$$c_2 = \frac{-c_1}{3} = \frac{c_0}{1 \cdot 3}$$

$$c_3 = \frac{-c_2}{5} = \frac{-c_0}{1 \cdot 3 \cdot 5}$$

$$c_4 = \frac{-c_3}{7} = \frac{c_0}{1 \cdot 3 \cdot 5 \cdot 7}$$

$$\vdots$$

$$c_n = \frac{(-1)^n c_0}{1 \cdot 3 \cdot 5 \cdot 7 \cdots (2n - 1)}, \qquad n = 1, 2, 3 \ldots.$$

We conclude that a second solution to (20) is

$$y_2 = c_0 \left[1 + \sum_{n=1}^{\infty} \frac{(-1)^n}{1 \cdot 3 \cdot 5 \cdot 7 \cdots (2n-1)} x^n \right], \qquad |x| < \infty. \qquad (24)$$

On $x > 0$ the general solution is $y = C_1 y_1(x) + C_2 y_2(x)$.

CASE II Roots Differing by a Positive Integer

EXAMPLE

Solve

$$xy'' + (x - 6)y' - 3y = 0. \qquad (25)$$

Solution: The assumption $y = \sum_{n=0}^{\infty} c_n x^{n+r}$ leads to

$$xy'' + (x - 6)y' - 3y$$

$$= \sum_{n=0}^{\infty} (n + r)(n + r - 1)c_n x^{n+r-1}$$

$$- 6 \sum_{n=0}^{\infty} (n + r)c_n x^{n+r-1} + \sum_{n=0}^{\infty} (n + r)c_n x^{n+r} - 3 \sum_{n=0}^{\infty} c_n x^{n+r}$$

$$= x^r \left[r(r-7)c_0 x^{-1} + \underbrace{\sum_{n=1}^{\infty} (n+r)(n+r-7)c_n x^{n-1}}_{k = n-1} \right.$$

$$\left. + \underbrace{\sum_{n=0}^{\infty} (n+r-3)c_n x^n}_{k = n} \right]$$

$$= x^r \left[r(r-7)c_0 x^{-1} + \sum_{k=0}^{\infty} [(k+r+1)(k+r-6)c_{k+1} \right.$$

$$\left. + (k+r-3)c_k] x^k \right] = 0.$$

Thus $r(r-7) = 0$ so that $r_1 = 7$, $r_2 = 0$, $r_1 - r_2 = 7$, and

$$(k + r + 1)(k + r - 6)c_{k+1} + (k + r - 3)c_k = 0, \quad k = 0, 1, 2 \ldots . \qquad (26)$$

For the smaller root $r_2 = 0$, (26) becomes

$$(k + 1)(k - 6)c_{k+1} + (k - 3)c_k = 0. \qquad (27)$$

Since $k - 6 = 0$ when $k = 6$ we do not divide by this term until $k > 6$. We find

$$1 \cdot (-6)c_1 + (-3)c_0 = 0$$

$$2 \cdot (-5)c_2 + (-2)c_1 = 0$$

$$3 \cdot (-4)c_3 + (-1)c_2 = 0$$

$$4 \cdot (-3)c_4 + 0 \cdot c_3 = 0$$

$$5 \cdot (-2)c_5 + 1 \cdot c_4 = 0 \qquad \text{implies } c_4 = c_5 = c_6 = 0$$

$$6 \cdot (-1)c_6 + 2 \cdot c_5 = 0 \qquad \text{but } c_0 \text{ and } c_7 \text{ can be}$$

$$7 \cdot 0 c_7 + 3 \cdot c_6 = 0 \qquad \text{chosen arbitrarily.}$$

Thus

$$c_1 = -\frac{1}{2}c_0$$

$$c_2 = -\frac{1}{5}c_1 = \frac{1}{10}c_0 \tag{28}$$

$$c_3 = -\frac{1}{12}c_2 = -\frac{1}{120}c_0$$

and for $k \geq 7$

$$c_{k+1} = \frac{-(k-3)c_k}{(k+1)(k-6)}$$

$$c_8 = \frac{-4}{8 \cdot 1}c_7$$

$$c_9 = \frac{-5}{9 \cdot 2}c_8 = \frac{4 \cdot 5}{2! 8 \cdot 9}c_7$$

$$c_{10} = \frac{-6}{10 \cdot 3}c_9 = \frac{-4 \cdot 5 \cdot 6}{3! 8 \cdot 9 \cdot 10}c_7$$

$$\vdots$$

$$c_n = \frac{(-1)^{n+1} 4 \cdot 5 \cdot 6 \cdots (n-4)}{(n-7)! 8 \cdot 9 \cdot 10 \cdots n}c_7, \qquad n = 8, 9, 10 \ldots . \tag{29}$$

If we choose $c_7 = 0$ and $c_0 \neq 0$, we obtain the polynomial solution

$$y_1 = c_0 \left[1 - \frac{1}{2}x + \frac{1}{10}x^2 - \frac{1}{120}x^3 \right], \tag{30}$$

but when $c_7 \neq 0$ and $c_0 = 0$, it follows that a second, though infinite series, solution is

$$y_2 = c_7\left[x^7 + \sum_{n=8}^{\infty} \frac{(-1)^{n+1}4 \cdot 5 \cdot 6 \cdots (n-4)}{(n-7)!8 \cdot 9 \cdot 10 \cdots n}x^n\right]$$

$$= c_7\left[x^7 + \sum_{k=1}^{\infty} \frac{(-1)^k 4 \cdot 5 \cdot 6 \cdots (k+3)}{k!8 \cdot 9 \cdot 10 \cdots (k+7)}x^{k+7}\right], \qquad |x| < \infty \qquad (31)$$

Finally, for $x > 0$ the general solution to equation (25) is

$$y = C_1 y_1(x) + C_2 y_2(x)$$

$$= C_1\left[1 - \frac{1}{2}x + \frac{1}{10}x^2 - \frac{1}{120}x^3\right]$$

$$+ C_2\left[x^7 + \sum_{k=1}^{\infty} \frac{(-1)^k 4 \cdot 5 \cdot 6 \cdots (k+3)}{k!8 \cdot 9 \cdot 10 \cdots (k+7)}x^{k+7}\right].$$

It is interesting to observe that in the preceding example the larger root $r_1 = 7$ was not used. Had we done so, we would have obtained a series solution of the form*

$$\sum_{n=0}^{\infty} c_n x^{n+7} \qquad (32)$$

where the c_n are defined by the formula (equation (26) with $r_1 = 7$)

$$c_{k+1} = \frac{-(k+4)}{(k+8)(k+1)}c_k, \qquad k = 0, 1, 2 \ldots.$$

Iteration of this latter recurrence relation then would yield only *one* solution, namely, the solution given by (31).

When the roots of the indicial equation differ by a positive integer the second solution *may* contain a logarithm. In practice this is something we do not know in advance, but is determined after we have found the indicial roots and have carefully examined the recurrence relation which defines the coefficients c_n. As the foregoing example shows, we just may be lucky enough to find two solutions which involve only powers of x. On the other hand, if we fail to find a second series-type solution, we can always formally use the fact that

$$y_2 = y_1(x)\int \frac{e^{-\int P(x)\,dx}}{y_1^2(x)}\,dx \qquad (33)$$

is also a solution of the equation $y'' + P(x)y' + Q(x)y = 0$ whenever y_1 is a known solution (see Section 4.2).

---

* Observe that both (31) and (32) start with the power x^7. In Case II it is always a good idea to work with the smaller root first.

EXAMPLE   Find the general solution of

$$xy'' + 3y' - y = 0$$

Solution: Recall from page 249 that the method of Frobenius provides only one solution to this particular equation, namely,

$$y_1 = \sum_{n=0}^{\infty} \frac{2}{n!(n+2)!} x^n$$

$$= 1 + \frac{1}{3}x + \frac{1}{24}x^2 + \frac{1}{360}x^3 + \cdots. \qquad (34)$$

From (33) we obtain a second solution

$$y_2 = y_1(x) \int \frac{e^{-\int (3/x)dx}}{y_1^2(x)} dx$$

$$= y_1(x) \int \frac{dx}{x^3 \left(1 + \frac{1}{3}x + \frac{1}{24}x^2 + \frac{1}{360}x^3 + \cdots\right)^2}$$

$$= y_1(x) \int \frac{dx}{x^3 \left(1 + \frac{2}{3}x + \frac{7}{36}x^2 + \frac{1}{30}x^3 + \cdots\right)} \qquad \text{(squaring)}$$

$$= y_1(x) \int \frac{1}{x^3} \left[1 - \frac{2}{3}x + \frac{1}{4}x^2 - \frac{19}{270}x^3 + \cdots \right] dx \qquad \text{(long division)}$$

$$= y_1(x) \int \left[\frac{1}{x^3} - \frac{2}{3x^2} + \frac{1}{4x} - \frac{19}{270} + \cdots \right] dx$$

$$= y_1(x) \left[-\frac{1}{2x^2} + \frac{2}{3x} + \frac{1}{4}\ln x - \frac{19}{270}x + \cdots \right]$$

or $$y_2 = \frac{1}{4}y_1(x)\ln x + y_1(x)\left[-\frac{1}{2x^2} + \frac{2}{3x} - \frac{19}{270}x + \cdots \right]. \qquad (35)$$

Hence, for $x > 0$, the general solution is

$$y = C_1 y_1(x) + C_2 \left[\frac{1}{4}y_1(x)\ln x + y_1(x)\left(-\frac{1}{2x^2} + \frac{2}{3x} - \frac{19}{270}x + \cdots \right) \right] \qquad (36)$$

where $y_1(x)$ is defined by (34).

An alternative procedure

There are several alternative procedures to formula (33) when the method of Frobenius fails to provide a second series solution. Although the next method is somewhat tedious, it is nonetheless straightforward. The basic idea is to assume a solution either of the form (18b) or (19b) and determine coefficients b_n in terms of the coefficients c_n which define the known solution $y_1(x)$.

EXAMPLE

The smaller of the two indicial roots for the equation $xy'' + 3y' - y = 0$ is $r_2 = -2$. From (18b) we now assume a second solution

$$y_2 = y_1 \ln x + \sum_{n=0}^{\infty} b_n x^{n-2} \qquad (37)$$

where

$$y_1 = \sum_{n=0}^{\infty} \frac{2}{n!(n+2)!} x^n. \qquad (38)$$

Differentiation of (37) gives

$$y_2' = \frac{y_1}{x} + y_1' \ln x + \sum_{n=0}^{\infty} (n-2)b_n x^{n-3}$$

$$y_2'' = -\frac{y_1}{x^2} + \frac{2y_1'}{x} + y_1'' \ln x + \sum_{n=0}^{\infty} (n-2)(n-3)b_n x^{n-4}$$

so that

$$xy_2'' + 3y_2' - y_2 = \ln x \underbrace{[xy_1'' + 3y_1' - y_1]}_{\text{zero}} + 2y_1' + \frac{2y_1}{x}$$

$$+ \sum_{n=0}^{\infty} (n-2)(n-3)b_n x^{n-3}$$

$$+ 3 \sum_{n=0}^{\infty} (n-2)b_n x^{n-3} - \sum_{n=0}^{\infty} b_n x^{n-2}$$

$$= 2y_1' + \frac{2y_1}{x} + \sum_{n=0}^{\infty} (n-2)nb_n x^{n-3} - \sum_{n=0}^{\infty} b_n x^{n-2} \qquad (39)$$

where we have combined the first two summations and have used the fact that $xy_1'' + 3y_1' - y_1 = 0$.

By differentiating (38) we can write (39) as

$$\sum_{n=0}^{\infty} \frac{4n}{n!(n+2)!} x^{n-1} + \sum_{n=0}^{\infty} \frac{4}{n!(n+2)!} x^{n-1} + \sum_{n=0}^{\infty} (n-2)n b_n x^{n-3} - \sum_{n=0}^{\infty} b_n x^{n-2}$$

$$= 0(-2)b_0 x^{-3} + (-b_0 - b_1)x^{-2}$$

$$+ \underbrace{\sum_{n=0}^{\infty} \frac{4(n+1)}{n!(n+2)!} x^{n-1}}_{k=n} + \underbrace{\sum_{n=2}^{\infty} (n-2)n b_n x^{n-3}}_{k=n-2} - \underbrace{\sum_{n=1}^{\infty} b_n x^{n-2}}_{k=n+1}$$

$$= -(b_0 + b_1)x^{-2} + \sum_{k=0}^{\infty} \left[\frac{4(k+1)}{k!(k+2)!} + k(k+2)b_{k+2} - b_{k+1} \right] x^{k-1} \quad (40)$$

Setting (40) equal to zero then gives $b_1 = -b_0$

$$\frac{4(k+1)}{k!(k+2)!} + k(k+2)b_{k+2} - b_{k+1} = 0, \qquad \text{for } k = 0, 1, 2, \ \ldots. \quad (41)$$

When $k = 0$ in (41) we have $2 + 0 \cdot 2 b_2 - b_1 = 0$ so that $b_1 = 2, b_0 = -2$, but b_2 is arbitrary.

Rewriting (41) as

$$b_{k+2} = \frac{b_{k+1}}{k(k+2)} - \frac{4(k+1)}{k!(k+2)!k(k+2)} \quad (42)$$

and evaluating for $k = 1, 2, \ldots$, gives

$$b_3 = \frac{b_2}{3} - \frac{4}{9}$$

$$b_4 = \frac{1}{8}b_3 - \frac{1}{32} = \frac{1}{24}b_2 - \frac{25}{288}$$

and so on. Thus we can finally write

$$y_2 = y_1 \ln x + b_0 x^{-2} + b_1 x^{-1} + b_2 + b_3 x + \cdots$$

$$= y_1 \ln x - 2x^{-2} + 2x^{-1} + b_2 + \left(\frac{b_2}{3} - \frac{4}{9} \right) x + \cdots \quad (43)$$

where b_2 is arbitrary.

Equivalent solutions

At this point you may be wondering whether (35) and (43) are really equivalent. If we choose $C_2 = 4$ in (36) then

$$y_2 = y_1 \ln x + y_1 \left(-\frac{2}{x^2} + \frac{8}{3x} - \frac{38}{135}x + \cdots \right)$$

$$= y_1 \ln x + \left(1 + \frac{1}{3}x + \frac{1}{24}x^2 + \frac{1}{360}x^3 + \cdots \right)\left(-\frac{2}{x^2} + \frac{8}{3x} - \frac{38}{135}x + \cdots \right)$$

$$= y_1 \ln x - 2x^{-2} + 2x^{-1} + \frac{29}{36} - \frac{19}{108}x + \cdots \tag{44}$$

which is precisely what we obtain from (43) if b_2 is chosen as 29/36.

CASE III   Equal Indicial Roots

EXAMPLE

Find the general solution of

$$xy'' + y' - 4y = 0 \tag{45}$$

Solution: The assumption $y = \sum\limits_{n=0}^{\infty} c_n x^{n+r}$ leads to

$$xy'' + y' - 4y = \sum_{n=0}^{\infty} (n+r)(n+r-1)c_n x^{n+r-1}$$

$$+ \sum_{n=0}^{\infty} (n+r)c_n x^{n+r-1} - 4 \sum_{n=0}^{\infty} c_n x^{n+r}$$

$$= \sum_{n=0}^{\infty} (n+r)^2 c_n x^{n+r-1} - 4 \sum_{n=0}^{\infty} c_n x^{n+r}$$

$$= x^r \left[r^2 c_0 x^{-1} + \underbrace{\sum_{n=1}^{\infty} (n+r)^2 c_n x^{n-1}}_{k=n-1} - \underbrace{4 \sum_{n=0}^{\infty} c_n x^n}_{k=n} \right]$$

$$= x^r \left[r^2 c_0 x^{-1} + \sum_{k=0}^{\infty} [(k+r+1)^2 c_{k+1} - 4c_k] x^k \right] = 0.$$

Therefore, $r^2 = 0$, $r_1 = r_2 = 0$, and

$$(k+r+1)^2 c_{k+1} - 4c_k = 0, \qquad k = 0, 1, 2\ldots. \tag{46}$$

Clearly, the root $r_1 = 0$ will only yield one solution corresponding to the coefficients defined by the iteration of

$$c_{k+1} = \frac{4c_k}{(k+1)^2}, \qquad k = 0, 1, 2 \ldots.$$

The result is

$$y_1 = c_0 \sum_{n=0}^{\infty} \frac{4^n}{(n!)^2} x^n, \qquad |x| < \infty. \tag{47}$$

To obtain the second linearly independent solution we set $c_0 = 1$ in (47) and then use formula (33)

$$y_2 = y_1(x) \int \frac{e^{-\int (1/x)\,dx}}{y_1^2(x)}\, dx$$

$$= y_1(x) \int \frac{dx}{x\left[1 + 4x + 4x^2 + \dfrac{16}{9}x^3 + \cdots\right]^2}$$

$$= y_1(x) \int \frac{dx}{x\left[1 + 8x + 24x^2 + \dfrac{16}{9}x^3 + \cdots\right]}$$

$$= y_1(x) \int \frac{1}{x}\left[1 - 8x + 40x^2 - \frac{1472}{9}x^3 + \cdots\right] dx$$

$$= y_1(x) \int \left[\frac{1}{x} - 8 + 40x - \frac{1472}{9}x^2 + \cdots\right] dx$$

$$= y_1(x)\left[\ln x - 8x + 20x^2 - \frac{1472}{27}x^3 + \cdots\right]. \tag{48}$$

Thus, for $x > 0$, the general solution of (45) is

$$y = C_1 y_1(x) + C_2\left[y_1(x)\ln x + y_1(x)\left(-8x + 20x^2 - \frac{1472}{27}x^3 + \cdots\right)\right] \tag{49}$$

where $y_1(x)$ is defined by (47).

Alternative procedure   As in Case II, we can determine $y_2(x)$ of the preceding example directly from the assumption (19b).

EXAMPLE   For equation (45) we know $r_1 = r_2 = 0$ so that (19b) becomes

$$y_2 = y_1 \ln x + \sum_{n=1}^{\infty} b_n x^n \tag{50}$$

and therefore

$$y_2' = \frac{y_1}{x} + y_1' \ln x + \sum_{n=1}^{\infty} b_n n x^{n-1}$$

$$y_2'' = -\frac{y_1}{x^2} + \frac{2y_1'}{x} + y_1'' \ln x + \sum_{n=1}^{\infty} b_n n(n-1)x^{n-2}$$

$$xy_2'' + y_2' - 4y_2 = \ln x \underbrace{[xy_1'' + y_1' - 4y_1]}_{\text{zero}} + 2y_1' + \sum_{n=1}^{\infty} n(n-1)b_n x^{n-1}$$

$$+ \sum_{n=1}^{\infty} nb_n x^{n-1} - 4 \sum_{n=1}^{\infty} b_n x^n$$

$$= 2y_1' + \sum_{n=1}^{\infty} n^2 b_n x^{n-1} - 4 \sum_{n=1}^{\infty} b_n x^n. \qquad (51)$$

Using the fact that

$$y_1 = \sum_{n=0}^{\infty} \frac{4^n}{(n!)^2} x^n$$

(51) then becomes

$$2 \sum_{n=0}^{\infty} \frac{4^n n}{(n!)^2} x^{n-1} + \sum_{n=1}^{\infty} n^2 b_n x^{n-1} - 4 \sum_{n=1}^{\infty} b_n x^n$$

$$= 8 + b_1 + 2 \underbrace{\sum_{n=2}^{\infty} \frac{4^n n}{(n!)^2} x^{n-1}}_{k = n - 1} + \underbrace{\sum_{n=2}^{\infty} n^2 b_n x^{n-1}}_{k = n - 1} - 4 \underbrace{\sum_{n=1}^{\infty} b_n x^n}_{k = n}$$

$$= 8 + b_1 + \sum_{k=1}^{\infty} \left[\frac{2 \cdot 4^{k+1}(k+1)}{[(k+1)!]^2} + (k+1)^2 b_{k+1} - 4b_k \right] x^k \qquad (52)$$

Equating (52) to zero gives

$$b_1 = -8$$

$$b_{k+1} = \frac{4}{(k+1)^2} b_k - \frac{2 \cdot 4^{k+1}}{(k+1)[(k+1)!]^2}, \qquad k = 1, 2, 3, \ldots, \qquad (53)$$

which implies

$$b_2 = b_1 - 4 = -12$$

$$b_3 = \frac{4}{9} b_2 - \frac{32}{27} = -\frac{176}{27}$$

and so on. Hence, it follows that

$$y_2 = y_1 \ln x - 8x - 12x^2 - \frac{176}{27}x^3 - \cdots . \tag{54}$$

Equivalent solutions

If we examine (48) in a little more detail, we find that

$$y_2 = y_1 \ln x + y_1\left(-8x + 20x^2 - \frac{1472}{27}x^3 + \cdots\right)$$

$$= y_1 \ln x + \left(1 + 4x + 4x^2 + \frac{16}{9}x^3 + \cdots\right)\left(-8x + 20x^2 - \frac{1472}{27}x^3 + \cdots\right)$$

$$= y_1 \ln x - 8x - 12x^2 - \frac{176}{27}x^3 - \cdots$$

which, of course, is the same as (54).

    Remark: We purposely have not considered two further complications when solving a differential equation such as (1) about a point x_0 for which $a_2(x_0) = 0$. When using (3), it is quite possible that the roots of the indicial equation could turn out to be complex numbers. When the exponents r_1 and r_2 are complex, the statement $r_1 > r_2$ is meaningless and must be replaced with $Re(r_1) > Re(r_2)$ (for example, if $r = \alpha + \beta i$, then $Re(r) = \alpha$). In particular, when the indicial equation has real coefficients, the complex roots will be a conjugate pair

$$r_1 = \alpha + \beta i \qquad r_2 = \alpha - \beta i$$

and $r_1 - r_2 = \beta i \neq$ integer. Thus, for $x_0 = 0$, there will always exist two solutions

$$y_1 = \sum_{n=0}^{\infty} c_n x^{n+r_1} \qquad \text{and} \qquad y_2 = \sum_{n=0}^{\infty} b_n x^{n+r_2}.$$

Unfortunately, both solutions will give complex values of y for each real choice of x. This latter difficulty can be surmounted by the superposition principle. Since a combination of solutions is also a solution to the differential equation, we could form appropriate combinations of $y_1(x)$ and $y_2(x)$ to yield real solutions. (See Case III of the solution of the Cauchy–Euler Equation.)

    Lastly, if $x = 0$ is an irregular singular point, it should be noted that we may not be able to find *any* solution of the form $y = \sum_{n=0}^{\infty} c_n x^{n+r}$.

EXERCISES 6.3

Answers to odd-numbered problems begin on page A-16 of the Appendix. In Problems 1–7 determine the singular points of each differential equation. Classify each singular point as regular or irregular.

1. $x^3 y'' + 4x^2 y' + 3y = 0$ ★2. $xy'' - (x + 3)^{-2} y = 0$

3. $(x^2 - 9)^2 y'' + (x + 3)y' + 2y = 0$

4. $y'' - \dfrac{1}{x} y' + \dfrac{1}{(x-1)^3} y = 0$

5. $(x^3 + 4x)y'' - 2xy' + 6y = 0$

6. $x^2(x - 5)^2 y'' + 4xy' + (x^2 - 25)y = 0$

7. $(x^2 + x - 6)y'' + (x + 3)y' + (x - 2)y = 0$

8. Show that $x = 0$ is a regular singular point of the Cauchy–Euler equation

$$x^2 y'' + 3xy' - 8y = 0.$$

Solve the equation by the method of Frobenius.

In Problems 9–18 show that the indicial roots do not differ by an integer. Use the method of Frobenius to obtain two linearly independent series solutions about the regular singular point $x_0 = 0$. Form the general solution for $x > 0$.

9. $2xy'' - y' + 2y = 0$ 10. $2x^2 y'' + 3xy' + (2x - 1)y = 0$

11. $4xy'' + \dfrac{1}{2} y' + y = 0$ 12. $2x^2 y'' - xy' + (x^2 + 1)y = 0$

13. $3xy'' + (2 - x)y' - y = 0$ ★14. $x^2 y'' - \left(x - \dfrac{2}{9}\right)y = 0$

15. $2xy'' - (3 + 2x)y' + y = 0$ 16. $x^2 y'' + xy' + \left(x^2 - \dfrac{4}{9}\right)y = 0$

17. $9x^2 y'' + 9x^2 y' + 2y = 0$ 18. $2xy'' + 5y' + xy = 0$

In Problems 19–30 show that the indicial roots differ by an integer. Use the method of Frobenius to obtain two linearly independent series solutions about the regular singular point $x_0 = 0$. Form the general solution for $x > 0$.

19. $xy'' + 2y' - xy = 0$ 20. $x^2 y'' + xy' + \left(x^2 - \dfrac{1}{4}\right)y = 0$

21. $x(x - 1)y'' + 3y' - 2y = 0$ 22. $y'' + \dfrac{3}{x} y' - 2y = 0$

23. $xy'' + (1 - x)y' - y = 0$ ★24. $xy'' + y = 0$

25. $xy'' + y' + y = 0$ 26. $xy'' - xy' + y = 0$

27. $x^2 y'' + x(x - 1)y' + y = 0$ 28. $xy'' + y' - 4xy = 0$

29. $xy'' + (x - 1)y' - 2y = 0$ 30. $xy'' - y' + x^3 y = 0$

In Problems 31–32 note that $x_0 = 0$ is an irregular singular point of each equation. In each case determine whether the method of Frobenius will yield a solution.

31. $x^3y'' + y = 0$ **★32.** $x^2y'' - y' + y = 0$

A differential equation is said to have a singular point at ∞ if, after the substitution $w = 1/x$, the resulting equation has a singular point at $w = 0$. In Problems 33–35 determine whether the given equation has a singular point at ∞, if so, state whether it is regular or irregular.

EXAMPLE

The equation $y'' + xy = 0$ has no singular points in the finite plane. Using the substitution $w = 1/x$, it follows from the chain rule that

$$\frac{dy}{dx} = \frac{dy}{dw}\frac{dw}{dx}$$

$$= -\frac{1}{x^2}\frac{dy}{dw}$$

$$= -w^2\frac{dy}{dw},$$

$$\frac{d^2y}{dx^2} = -w^2\frac{d}{dx}\left[\frac{dy}{dw}\right] - \frac{dy}{dw}\frac{d}{dx}[w^2]$$

$$= -w^2\frac{d}{dw}\left(\frac{dy}{dw}\right)\frac{dw}{dx} - \frac{dy}{dw}\left(2w\frac{dw}{dx}\right)$$

$$= w^4\frac{d^2y}{dw^2} + 2w^3\frac{dy}{dw}$$

so that the original equation transforms into

$$w^4\frac{d^2y}{dw^2} + 2w^3\frac{dy}{dw} + \frac{1}{w}y = 0.$$

Inspection of

$$P(w) = \frac{2}{w} \quad \text{and} \quad Q(w) = \frac{1}{w^5}$$

clearly indicates that $w = 0$ is an irregular singular point. Hence ∞ is an irregular singular point.

---

33. $x^2y'' - 4y = 0$ **34.** $(1 - x)y'' + xy' - y = 0$

35. $x^3y'' + 2x^2y' + 3y = 0$

6.4 Two Special Equations

The two equations

$$x^2y'' + xy' + (x^2 - v^2)y = 0 \tag{1}$$

$$(1 - x^2)y'' - 2xy' + n(n + 1)y = 0 \tag{2}$$

occur frequently in advanced studies in applied mathematics, physics, and engineering. They are called **Bessel's equation** and **Legendre's equation**, respectively.* In the solution of (1) we shall assume $v \geq 0$, whereas in (2) we shall consider only the case when n is a nonnegative integer. Since we seek series solutions of each equation about $x = 0$, we observe that the origin is a regular singular point of Bessel's equation, but it is an ordinary point of Legendre's equation.

6.4.1 Solution of Bessel's Equation

If we assume $y = \sum_{n=0}^{\infty} c_n x^{n+r}$ then

$$x^2 y'' + xy' + (x^2 - v^2)y = \sum_{n=0}^{\infty} c_n(n+r)(n+r-1)x^{n+r}$$

$$+ \sum_{n=0}^{\infty} c_n(n+r)x^{n+r} + \sum_{n=0}^{\infty} c_n x^{n+r+2} - v^2 \sum_{n=0}^{\infty} c_n x^{n+r}$$

$$= c_0(r^2 - r + r - v^2)x^r$$

$$+ x^r \sum_{n=1}^{\infty} c_n [(n+r)(n+r-1) + (n+r) - v^2]x^n$$

$$+ x^r \sum_{n=0}^{\infty} c_n x^{n+2}$$

$$= c_0(r^2 - v^2)x^r + x^r \sum_{n=1}^{\infty} c_n$$

$$\times [(n+r)^2 - v^2]x^n + x^r \sum_{n=0}^{\infty} c_n x^{n+2} \qquad (3)$$

From (3) we see that the indicial equation is $r^2 - v^2 = 0$ so that the indicial roots are $r = \pm v$. When $r = v$, (3) becomes

$$x^v \sum_{n=1}^{\infty} c_n n(n+2v)x^n + x^v \sum_{n=0}^{\infty} c_n x^{n+2}$$

$$= x^v \left[(1+2v)c_1 x + \underbrace{\sum_{n=2}^{\infty} c_n n(n+2v)x^n}_{k=n-2} + \underbrace{\sum_{n=0}^{\infty} c_n x^{n+2}}_{k=n} \right]$$

$$= x^v \left[(1+2v)c_1 x + \sum_{k=0}^{\infty} [(k+2)(k+2+2v)c_{k+2} + c_k]x^{k+2} \right] = 0.$$

---

* Named after Friedrich Wilhelm Bessel (1784–1846) and Adrien Marie Legendre (1752–1833). Bessel was a German astronomer who was the first to measure the distance to a star. Legendre, a French mathematician, is best remembered for spending almost 40 years of his life studying and calculating elliptic integrals. However, the particular polynomial solutions of the equation which bears his name were encountered in his studies of gravitation.

Therefore by the usual argument we can write

$$(1 + 2v)c_1 = 0$$

$$(k + 2)(k + 2 + 2v)c_{k+2} + c_k = 0$$

or
$$c_{k+2} = \frac{-c_k}{(k + 2)(k + 2 + 2v)}, \qquad k = 0, 1, 2 \ldots. \tag{4}$$

The choice $c_1 = 0$ in (4) implies $c_3 = c_5 = c_7 = \cdots = 0$ so that for $k = 0, 2,$ $4, \ldots$, we find, after letting $k + 2 = 2n$, $n = 1, 2, 3, \ldots$, that

$$c_{2n} = -\frac{c_{2n-2}}{2^2 n(n + v)}. \tag{5}$$

Thus,
$$c_2 = -\frac{c_0}{2^2 \cdot 1 \cdot (1 + v)}$$

$$c_4 = -\frac{c_2}{2^2 \cdot 2(2 + v)} = \frac{c_0}{2^4 \cdot 1 \cdot 2(1 + v)(2 + v)}$$

$$c_6 = -\frac{c_4}{2^2 \cdot 3(3 + v)} = -\frac{c_0}{2^6 \cdot 1 \cdot 2 \cdot 3(1 + v)(2 + v)(3 + v)}$$

$$\vdots$$

$$c_{2n} = \frac{(-1)^n c_0}{2^{2n} n!(1 + v)(2 + v) \cdots (n + v)}, \qquad n = 1, 2, 3 \ldots. \tag{6}$$

It is standard practice to choose c_0 to be a specific value, namely,

$$c_0 = \frac{1}{2^v \Gamma(1 + v)}$$

where $\Gamma(1 + v)$ is the gamma function (see Problem 1). Since this latter function possesses the convenient property $\Gamma(1 + \alpha) = \alpha \Gamma(\alpha)$, we can collapse the indicated product in the denominator of (6) into one term. For example,

$$\Gamma(1 + v + 1) = (1 + v)\Gamma(1 + v)$$

$$\Gamma(1 + v + 2) = (2 + v)\Gamma(2 + v)$$

$$= (2 + v)(1 + v)\Gamma(1 + v).$$

Hence we can write (6) as

$$c_{2n} = \frac{(-1)^n}{2^{2n+v} n!(1 + v)(2 + v) \cdots (n + v)\Gamma(1 + v)}$$

$$= \frac{(-1)^n}{2^{2n+v} n! \Gamma(1 + v + n)}, \qquad n = 0, 1, 2 \ldots.$$

It follows that one solution is then

$$y = \sum_{n=0}^{\infty} c_{2n} x^{2n+v}$$

$$= \sum_{n=0}^{\infty} \frac{(-1)^n}{n!\,\Gamma(1+v+n)} \left(\frac{x}{2}\right)^{2n+v} \tag{7}$$

If $v \geq 0$, the series will converge at least on the interval $x \geq 0$.

Bessel functions

The series given in (7) is usually denoted by $y = J_v(x)$. Also, for the second exponent $r = -v$ we obtain, in exactly the same manner,

$$y = \sum_{n=0}^{\infty} \frac{(-1)^n}{n!\,\Gamma(1-v+n)} \left(\frac{x}{2}\right)^{2n-v} \tag{8}$$

$$= J_{-v}(x).$$

The functions $J_v(x)$ and $J_{-v}(x)$ are called **Bessel functions of the first kind** of order v and $-v$, respectively. When $v \neq$ integer, J_v and J_{-v} are linearly independent on $x > 0$ so that the general solution of equation (1) is given by

$$y = c_1 J_v(x) + c_2 J_{-v}(x), \qquad v \neq \text{integer.} \tag{9}$$

When $v = m =$ nonnegative integer, (9) is no longer the general solution since it can be shown that $J_{-m}(x) = (-1)^m J_m(x)$ (see Problem 2).

The graphs of $y = J_0(x)$ and $y = J_1(x)$ are given in Figure 6.1.

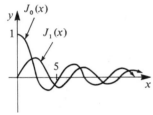

Figure 6.1

EXAMPLE

Find the general solution of the equation

$$x^2 y'' + xy' + (x^2 - 9)y = 0.$$

Solution: Since $v^2 = 9$, we identify $v = 3$, and so one solution is $y_1 = J_3(x)$. Dividing the equation by x^2 yields $P(x) = 1/x$, and hence a second linearly independent solution can be constructed by the method of Section 4.2:

$$y_2 = J_3(x) \int \frac{e^{-\int dx/x}}{J_3^2(x)}\,dx$$

$$= J_3(x) \int \frac{dx}{x J_3^2(x)}.$$

One form of the general solution is then

$$y = c_1 J_3(x) + c_2 J_3(x) \int \frac{dx}{x J_3^2(x)}.$$

6.4.2   Solution of Legendre's Equation

Since $x = 0$ is an ordinary point of equation (2) we assume a solution of the form $y = \sum_{k=0}^{\infty} c_k x^k$. Therefore

$$(1 - x^2)y'' - 2xy' + n(n + 1)y$$

$$= (1 - x^2) \sum_{k=0}^{\infty} c_k k(k - 1)x^{k-2} - 2 \sum_{k=0}^{\infty} c_k k x^k + n(n + 1) \sum_{k=0}^{\infty} c_k x^k$$

$$= \sum_{k=2}^{\infty} c_k k(k - 1)x^{k-2} - \sum_{k=2}^{\infty} c_k k(k - 1)x^k$$

$$\quad - 2 \sum_{k=1}^{\infty} c_k k x^k + n(n + 1) \sum_{k=0}^{\infty} c_k x^k$$

$$= [n(n + 1)c_0 + 2c_2]x^0 + [n(n + 1)c_1 - 2c_1 + 6c_3]x$$

$$\quad + \underbrace{\sum_{k=4}^{\infty} c_k k(k - 1)x^{k-2}}_{j = k - 2} - \underbrace{\sum_{k=2}^{\infty} c_k k(k - 1)x^k}_{j = k}$$

$$\quad - 2 \underbrace{\sum_{k=2}^{\infty} c_k k x^k}_{j = k} + n(n + 1) \underbrace{\sum_{k=2}^{\infty} c_k x^k}_{j = k}$$

$$= [n(n + 1)c_0 + 2c_2] + [(n - 1)(n + 2)c_1 + 6c_3]x$$

$$\quad + \sum_{j=2}^{\infty} [(j + 2)(j + 1)c_{j+2} + (n - j)(n + j + 1)c_j]x^j = 0$$

implies that

$$n(n + 1)c_0 + 2c_2 = 0$$

$$(n - 1)(n + 2)c_1 + 6c_3 = 0$$

$$(j + 2)(j + 1)c_{j+2} + (n - j)(n + j + 1)c_j = 0$$

or

$$c_2 = -\frac{n(n + 1)}{2!}c_0$$

$$c_3 = -\frac{(n - 1)(n + 2)}{3!}c_1$$

$$c_{j+2} = -\frac{(n - j)(n + j + 1)}{(j + 2)(j + 1)}c_j, \qquad j = 2, 3, 4 \ldots. \qquad (10)$$

Iterating (10) gives

$$c_4 = -\frac{(n-2)(n+3)}{4\cdot 3}c_2 = \frac{(n-2)n(n+1)(n+3)}{4!}c_0$$

$$c_5 = -\frac{(n-3)(n+4)}{5\cdot 4}c_3 = \frac{(n-3)(n-1)(n+2)(n+4)}{5!}c_1$$

$$c_6 = -\frac{(n-4)(n+5)}{6\cdot 5}c_4 = -\frac{(n-4)(n-2)n(n+1)(n+3)(n+5)}{6!}c_0$$

$$c_7 = -\frac{(n-5)(n+6)}{7\cdot 6}c_5 = -\frac{(n-5)(n-3)(n-1)(n+4)}{7!}c_1$$

and so on. Thus for at least $|x| < 1$ we obtain two formal linearly independent power series solutions

$$y_1(x) = c_0\left[1 - \frac{n(n+1)}{2!}x^2 + \frac{(n-2)n(n+1)(n+3)}{4!}x^4 \right.$$

$$\left. - \frac{(n-4)(n-2)n(n+1)(n+3)(n+5)}{6!}x^6 + \cdots \right] \tag{11}$$

$$y_2(x) = c_1\left[x - \frac{(n-1)(n+2)}{3!}x^3 + \frac{(n-3)(n-1)(n+2)(n+4)}{5!}x^5 \right.$$

$$\left. - \frac{(n-5)(n-3)(n-1)(n+2)(n+4)}{7!}x^7 + \cdots \right].$$

Notice that if n is an even integer the first series terminates, whereas $y_2(x)$ is an infinite series. For example, if $n = 4$ then

$$y_1(x) = c_0\left[1 - \frac{4\cdot 5}{2!}x_2 + \frac{2\cdot 4\cdot 5\cdot 7}{4!}x^4 \right]$$

$$= c_0\left[1 - 10x^2 + \frac{35}{3}x^4 \right].$$

Similarly, when n is an odd integer the series for $y_2(x)$ terminates with x^n. That is, *when* n *is a nonnegative integer we obtain an* nth *degree polynomial solution* of Legendre's equation.

Since we know that a constant multiple of a solution of Legendre's equation is also a solution, it is traditional to choose specific values for c_0 and c_1 depending on whether n is an even or odd positive integer, respectively.* For $n = 0$ we choose

$$c_0 = 1,$$

---

* The reason for these choices is reflected in the results of Problem 24.

and for $n = 2, 4, 6, \ldots$,

$$c_0 = (-1)^{n/2} \frac{1 \cdot 3 \cdots (n-1)}{2 \cdot 4 \cdots n},$$

whereas for $n = 1$ we choose

$$c_1 = 1,$$

and for $n = 3, 5, 7, \ldots$,

$$c_1 = (-1)^{(n-1)/2} \frac{1 \cdot 3 \cdots n}{2 \cdot 4 \cdots (n-1)}.$$

For example, when $n = 4$ we have

$$y_1(x) = (-1)^{4/2} \frac{1 \cdot 3}{2 \cdot 4} \left[1 - 10x^2 + \frac{35}{3} x^4 \right]$$

$$= \frac{3}{8} - \frac{30}{8} x^2 + \frac{35}{8} x^4$$

$$= \frac{1}{8}(35x^4 - 30x^2 + 3).$$

Legendre polynomials   These specific nth degree polynomial solutions are called **Legendre polynomials** and are denoted by $P_n(x)$. From the series for $y_1(x)$ and $y_2(x)$ and from the above choices of c_0 and c_1, it is easily verified that the first several Legendre polynomials are

$$P_0(x) = 1$$

$$P_1(x) = x$$

$$P_2(x) = \frac{1}{2}(3x^2 - 1)$$ (12)

$$P_3(x) = \frac{1}{2}(5x^3 - 3x)$$

$$P_4(x) = \frac{1}{8}(35x^4 - 30x^2 + 3).$$

Remember, $P_0(x)$, $P_1(x)$, $P_2(x)$, $P_3(x)$, and $P_4(x)$ are *particular solutions* of the differential equations

$$n = 0, \quad (1 - x^2)y'' - 2xy' = 0$$
$$n = 1, \quad (1 - x^2)y'' - 2xy' + 2y = 0$$
$$n = 2, \quad (1 - x^2)y'' - 2xy' + 6y = 0 \qquad (13)$$
$$n = 3, \quad (1 - x^2)y'' - 2xy' + 12y = 0$$
$$n = 4, \quad (1 - x^2)y'' - 2xy' + 20y = 0,$$

respectively.

The graphs of the first four Legendre polynomials on the interval $-1 \le x \le 1$ are given in Figure 6.2.

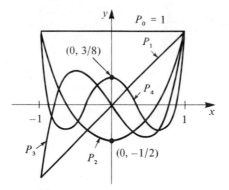

Figure 6.2

EXERCISES 6.4   Answers to odd numbered problems begin on page A-17 of the Appendix.

[6.4.1]   **1.**   One definition of the gamma function is

$$\Gamma(\alpha) = \int_0^\infty t^{\alpha-1} e^{-t}\, dt, \qquad \alpha > 0.*$$

(a) Use this definition to show that $\Gamma(1 + \alpha) = \alpha\Gamma(\alpha)$.
(b) Show that $\Gamma(1) = 1$.
(c) Show that when n is a positive integer $\Gamma(1 + n) = n!$.

2.   Use (8) with $v = m$, where m is a positive integer, and the fact that $1/\Gamma(N) = 0$ when N is a negative integer, to show that

$$J_{-m}(x) = (-1)^m J_m(x).$$

Recurrence formulas are very important in the study of Bessel functions. In Problems 3–7 derive the given formula.

EXAMPLE $xJ'_v(x) = vJ_v(x) - xJ_{v+1}(x)$

Solution: $J_v(x) = \displaystyle\sum_{n=0}^\infty \frac{(-1)^n}{n!\,\Gamma(1 + v + n)} \left(\frac{x}{2}\right)^{2n+v}$

---

* Although this integral converges only for $\alpha > 0$, there are other representations of the gamma function that extend its domain to the set of complex numbers except α equal to a negative integer.

$$xJ_\nu'(x) = \sum_{n=0}^{\infty} \frac{(-1)^n(2n+\nu)}{n!\Gamma(1+\nu+n)}\left(\frac{x}{2}\right)^{2n+\nu}$$

$$= \nu \sum_{n=0}^{\infty} \frac{(-1)^n}{n!\Gamma(1+\nu+n)}\left(\frac{x}{2}\right)^{2n+\nu}$$

$$+ 2 \sum_{n=0}^{\infty} \frac{(-1)^n n}{n!\Gamma(1+\nu+n)}\left(\frac{x}{2}\right)^{2n+\nu}$$

$$= \nu J_\nu(x) + x \underbrace{\sum_{n=1}^{\infty} \frac{(-1)^n}{(n-1)!\Gamma(1+\nu+n)}\left(\frac{x}{2}\right)^{2n+\nu-1}}_{k=n-1}$$

$$= \nu J_\nu(x) - x \sum_{k=0}^{\infty} \frac{(-1)^k}{k!\Gamma(2+\nu+k)}\left(\frac{x}{2}\right)^{2k+\nu+1}$$

$$= \nu J_\nu(x) - x J_{\nu+1}(x).$$

The expression $xJ_\nu'(x) = \nu J_\nu(x) - xJ_{\nu+1}(x)$ is called a *differential recurrence relation*.

---

3. $xJ_\nu'(x) = -\nu J_\nu(x) + xJ_{\nu-1}(x)$ [*Hint:* $2n + \nu = 2(n + \nu) - \nu$]

4. $2J_\nu'(x) = J_{\nu-1}(x) - J_{\nu+1}(x)$ **5.** $2\nu J_\nu(x) = xJ_{\nu+1}(x) + xJ_{\nu-1}(x)$

★6. $\dfrac{d}{dx}[x^\nu J_\nu(x)] = x^\nu J_{\nu-1}(x)$ **7.** $\dfrac{d}{dx}[x^{-\nu}J_\nu(x)] = -x^{-\nu}J_{\nu+1}(x)$

8. Show that

    (a) $J_0'(x) = J_{-1}(x) = -J_1(x)$ **(b)** $\displaystyle\int_0^x rJ_0(r)\,dr = xJ_1(x)$

EXAMPLE

Find an alternative expression for $J_{1/2}(x)$. Use the fact that $\Gamma(\tfrac{1}{2}) = \sqrt{\pi}$.

Solution: With $\nu = 1/2$, we have from (7)

$$J_{1/2}(x) = \sum_{n=0}^{\infty} \frac{(-1)^n}{n!\Gamma(1 + \tfrac{1}{2} + n)}\left(\frac{x}{2}\right)^{2n+\frac{1}{2}}.$$

Now observe that

$$n = 0, \qquad \Gamma\left(1 + \frac{1}{2}\right) = \frac{1}{2}\Gamma\left(\frac{1}{2}\right) = \frac{1}{2}\sqrt{\pi}$$

$$n = 1, \qquad \Gamma\left(1 + \frac{3}{2}\right) = \frac{3}{2}\Gamma\left(\frac{3}{2}\right) = \frac{3}{2^2}\sqrt{\pi}$$

$$n = 2, \qquad \Gamma\left(1 + \frac{5}{2}\right) = \frac{5}{2}\Gamma\left(\frac{5}{2}\right) = \frac{5 \cdot 3}{2^3}\sqrt{\pi} = \frac{5 \cdot 4 \cdot 3 \cdot 2 \cdot 1}{2^3 4 \cdot 2}\sqrt{\pi} = \frac{5!}{2^5 2!}\sqrt{\pi}$$

$$n = 3, \qquad \Gamma\left(1 + \frac{7}{2}\right) = \frac{7}{2}\Gamma\left(\frac{7}{2}\right) = \frac{7 \cdot 5 \cdot 3}{2^4}\sqrt{\pi} = \frac{7 \cdot 6 \cdot 5 \cdot 4 \cdot 3 \cdot 2 \cdot 1}{2^4 6 \cdot 4 \cdot 2}\sqrt{\pi}$$

$$= \frac{7!}{2^7 3!}\sqrt{\pi}.$$

In general,

$$\Gamma\left(1 + \frac{1}{2} + n\right) = \frac{(2n + 1)!}{2^{2n + 1} n!}\sqrt{\pi}.$$

Hence we can write

$$J_{1/2}(x) = \sum_{n=0}^{\infty} \frac{(-1)^n}{n!\dfrac{(2n + 1)!\sqrt{\pi}}{2^{2n+1} n!}}\left(\frac{x}{2}\right)^{2n + \frac{1}{2}}$$

$$= \sqrt{\frac{2}{\pi x}} \sum_{n=0}^{\infty} \frac{(-1)^n}{(2n + 1)!} x^{2n + 1}$$

$$= \sqrt{\frac{2}{\pi x}} \sin x.$$

9. Express $J_{-1/2}(x)$ in terms of $\cos x$ and a power of x.

When $v = $ half an odd integer, $J_v(x)$ can be expressed in terms of $\sin x$, $\cos x$, and powers of x. Such Bessel functions are usually called **spherical Bessel functions**. Use the results of Problems 5 and 9 and the preceding example to write the following in terms of elementary functions.

★**10.** (a) $J_{3/2}(x)$ (b) $J_{-3/2}(x)$
      (c) $J_{5/2}(x)$ (d) $J_{-5/2}(x)$
      (e) $J_{7/2}(x)$

11. Show that the general solution of the **parametric Bessel equation**

$$x^2 y'' + xy' + (\lambda^2 x^2 - v^2)y = 0$$

is

$$y = c_1 J_v(\lambda x) + c_2 J_{-v}(\lambda x), \qquad v \neq \text{integer}.$$

12. Show that the parametric Bessel equation has the alternative form

$$\frac{d}{dx}\left[x\frac{dy}{dx}\right] + \left(\lambda^2 x - \frac{v^2}{x}\right)y = 0.$$

13. Use the change of variables $y = x^{-1/2}v(x)$ to find the general solution of the equation

$$x^2 y'' + 2xy' + \lambda^2 x^2 y = 0.$$

14. Find the general solution of each equation
    (a) $xy'' + y' + xy = 0$
    (b) $x^2 y'' + xy' + (x^2 - 1)y = 0$
    (c) $9x^2 y'' + 9xy' + (9x^2 - 1)y = 0$

15. Verify that the differential equation

$$xy'' + (1 + 2n)y' + xy = 0$$

possesses the particular solution $y = x^{-n}J_n(x)$.

16. Verify that the differential equation

$$xy'' + (1 - 2n)y' + xy = 0$$

possesses the particular solution $y = x^n J_n(x)$.

17. Find a particular solution for each equation
    (a) $xy'' - y' + xy = 0$
    (b) $xy'' + 3y' + xy = 0$
    (c) $xy'' - 5xy' + xy = 0.$

18. If $y_1 = J_0(x)$ is one solution of the zero-order Bessel equation verify that another solution is

$$y_2 = J_0(x)\ln x + \frac{x^2}{4} - \frac{3x^4}{128} + \frac{11x^6}{13,824} - \cdots.$$

[6.4.2] 19. (a) Use the explicit solutions $y_1(x)$ and $y_2(x)$ of Legendre's equation and the appropriate choices of c_0 and c_1 to find the Legendre polynomials $P_5(x)$ and $P_6(x)$.
    (b) Write the explicit differential equations for which $P_5(x)$ and $P_6(x)$ are particular solutions.

★20. Show that Legendre's equation has the alternative form

$$\frac{d}{dx}\left[(1 - x^2)\frac{dy}{dx}\right] + n(n + 1)y = 0$$

21. Show that the equation

$$\sin\theta\frac{d^2 y}{d\theta^2} + \cos\theta\frac{dy}{d\theta} + n(n + 1)(\sin\theta)\,y = 0$$

can be transformed in Legendre's equation by means of the substitution $x = \cos \theta$.

22. The general Legendre polynomial can be written as

$$P_n(x) = \sum_{k=0}^{[n/2]} \frac{(-1)^k (2n - 2k)!}{2^n k! (n - k)! (n - 2k)!} x^{n-2k}$$

where $[n/2]$ is the greatest integer not greater than $n/2$. Verify the results for $n = 0, 1, 2, 3, 4, 5$.

23. Use the binomial theorem to formally show that

$$(1 - 2xt + t^2)^{-1/2} = \sum_{n=0}^{\infty} P_n(x) t^n.$$

The expression $(1 - 2xt + t^2)^{-1/2}$ is called a **generating function** for the Legendre polynomials.

24. Prove that $P_n(1) = 1$ and $P_n(-1) = (-1)^n$.

EXAMPLE

Differentiating the generating function given in Problem 23 with respect to t gives

$$(1 - 2xt + t^2)^{-3/2}(x - t) = \sum_{n=0}^{\infty} nP_n(x) t^{n-1}$$

$$= \sum_{n=1}^{\infty} nP_n(x) t^{n-1}$$

so that after multiplying by $1 - 2xt + t^2$ we have

$$(x - t)(1 - 2xt + t^2)^{-1/2} = (1 - 2xt + t^2) \sum_{n=1}^{\infty} nP_n(x) t^{n-1}$$

or

$$(x - t) \sum_{n=0}^{\infty} P_n(x) t^n = (1 - 2xt + t^2) \sum_{n=1}^{\infty} nP_n(x) t^{n-1}. \qquad (14)$$

Multiply out and rewrite (14) as

$$\sum_{n=0}^{\infty} xP_n(x) t^n - \sum_{n=0}^{\infty} P_n(x) t^{n+1} - \sum_{n=1}^{\infty} nP_n(x) t^{n-1} + 2x \sum_{n=1}^{\infty} nP_n(x) t^n$$

$$- \sum_{n=1}^{\infty} nP_n(x) t^{n+1} = 0$$

or

$$x + x^2 t + \sum_{n=2}^{\infty} xP_n(x) t^n - t - \sum_{n=1}^{\infty} P_n(x) t^{n+1} - x - 2\left(\frac{3x^2 - 1}{2}\right) t$$

$$- \sum_{n=3}^{\infty} nP_n(x) t^{n-1} + 2x^2 t + 2x \sum_{n=2}^{\infty} nP_n(x) t^n - \sum_{n=1}^{\infty} nP_n t^{n+1} = 0$$

Observing the appropriate cancellations, simplifying, and changing the summation indices gives

$$\sum_{k=2}^{\infty} [-(k + 1)P_{k+1}(x) + (2k + 1)xP_k(x) - kP_{k-1}(x)]t^k = 0.$$

Equating the total coefficient of t^k to be zero gives the three term recurrence relation

$$(k + 1)P_{k+1}(x) - (2k + 1)xP_k(x) + kP_{k-1}(x) = 0, \qquad k = 2, 3, 4 \ldots.$$

This formula is also valid when $k = 1$.

25. Use the results of the preceding example and the fact that $P_0(x) = 1$, $P_1(x) = x$ to generate the next three Legendre polynomials.

26. The Legendre polynomials are also generated by **Rodrigues' formula***

$$P_n(x) = \frac{1}{2^n n!} \frac{d^n}{dx^n} (x^2 - 1)^n.$$

Verify the results for $n = 0, 1, 2, 3$.

27. Use the explicit Legendre polynomials $P_0(x)$, $P_1(x)$, $P_2(x)$, and $P_3(x)$ to evaluate $\int_{-1}^{1} P_n^2(x) \, dx$ for $n = 0, 1, 2, 3$. Generalize the results.

28. Use the explicit Legendre polynomials $P_0(x)$, $P_1(x)$, $P_2(x)$, and $P_3(x)$ to evaluate $\int_{-1}^{1} P_n(x)P_m(x) \, dx$ for $n \neq m$. Generalize the results.

29. Find constants $c_0, c_1, c_2,$ and c_3 so that

$$x^3 = c_0 P_0(x) + c_1 P_1(x) + c_2 P_2(x) + c_3 P_3(x)$$

for $-1 \leq x \leq 1$.

★30. We know that $y_1 = x$ is a solution of Legendre's equation when $n = 1$, $(1 - x^2)y'' - 2xy' + 2y = 0$. Show that a second linearly independent solution on the interval $-1 < x < 1$ is

$$y_2 = \frac{x}{2} \ln \left(\frac{1 + x}{1 - x} \right) - 1$$

31. In the study of applied partial differential equations, the equation

$$\frac{\partial}{\partial r} \left[r^2 \frac{\partial u}{\partial r} \right] = -\frac{\partial^2 u}{\partial \theta^2} - \frac{\cos \theta}{\sin \theta} \frac{\partial u}{\partial \theta}$$

---

* Named after a minor French mathematician, O. Rodrigues (1794–1885).

where $u = u(r, \theta)$, occurs in certain problems involving temperatures in a sphere.

(a) If we let $u = R(r)\Theta(\theta)$ show that

$$r^2 \frac{R''}{R} + 2r \frac{R'}{R} = -\frac{\Theta''}{\Theta} - \frac{\cos\theta}{\sin\theta} \frac{\Theta'}{\Theta}$$

(b) If we equate both sides equal to the same constant $n(n + 1)$, show that particular product solutions of the partial differential equation can be found provided we can solve the ordinary differential equations

$$r^2 R'' + 2rR' - n(n + 1)R = 0$$

$$(\sin\theta)\Theta'' + (\cos\theta)\Theta' + n(n + 1)(\sin\theta)\Theta = 0.$$

(c) Solve both ordinary differential equations in part (b), and find particular product solutions $u = R(r)\Theta(\theta)$ of the original partial differential equation. [*Hint:* Review Problem 21 and Section 6.1.]

CHAPTER SUMMARY

The remarkable characteristic of a Cauchy–Euler equation is the fact that even though it is a differential equation with variable coefficients it can be solved in terms of closed form, or elementary functions. A **second-order Cauchy–Euler** equation is any differential equation of the form

$$ax^2 y'' + bxy' + cy = g(x) \tag{1}$$

where a, b, and c are constants. To solve the homogeneous equation we try a solution of the form $y = x^m$ and this in turn leads to an algebraic **auxiliary equation**

$$am(m - 1) + bm + c = 0. \tag{2}$$

Accordingly, when the roots are: real and distinct, real and equal, and complex conjugates, the general solution of the differential equation for $x > 0$ would be

$$y = c_1 x^{m_1} + c_2 x^{m_2}$$

$$y = c_1 x^{m_1} + c_2 x^{m_1} \ln x \tag{3}$$

$$y = x^\alpha [c_1 \cos(\beta \ln x) + c_2 \sin(\beta \ln x)],$$

respectively.

We say that $x = 0$ is an **ordinary point** of the linear second-order differential equation

$$a_2(x)y'' + a_1(x)y' + a_0(x)y = 0 \tag{4}$$

provided $a_2(0) \neq 0$ and $a_2(x)$, $a_1(x)$, $a_0(x)$ are polynomials having no common factors. Every solution of (4) has the form of an expansion about $x = 0$, that is,

$$y = \sum_{n=0}^{\infty} c_n x^n. \tag{5}$$

To find the coefficients c_n we substitute the basic assumption (5) into (4), and after appropriate algebraic manipulations we determine a **recurrence relation** by equating to zero the combined total coefficient of x^k. Iteration of the recurrence relation yields two distinct sets of coefficients, one set containing the arbitrary coefficient c_0 and the other containing c_1. Using each set of coefficients we form two linearly independent solutions $y_1(x)$ and $y_2(x)$. It could happen that $y_1(x)$ or $y_2(x)$ is a polynomial, but generally we expect infinite series solutions. A solution is valid at least on an interval defined by $|x| < R$, where R is the distance to the closest singular point of the equation.

If $a_2(0) = 0$ then $x = 0$ is said to be a **singular point** of (4). Singular points are classified as either **regular** or **irregular**. To determine whether $x = 0$ is a regular singular point, we examine the denominators of the rational functions P and Q that result when equation (4) is written as $y'' + P(x)y' + Q(x)y = 0$. It is understood that the ratios $a_1(x)/a_2(x)$ and $a_0(x)/a_2(x)$ are reduced to lowest terms.

If x appears *at most* to the first power in the denominator of $P(x)$ and *at most* to the second power in the denominator of $Q(x)$, then $x = 0$ is a regular singular point. The **method of Frobenius** guarantees that there exists *at least one* solution, expanded about the regular singular point $x = 0$, of the form

$$y = \sum_{n=0}^{\infty} c_n x^{n+r}. \tag{6}$$

The exponent r is a root of a quadratic **indicial equation**.

When the indicial roots r_1 and r_2 ($r_1 > r_2$) satisfy $r_1 - r_2 \neq$ an integer, then we can always find *two* linearly independent solutions of the assumed form (6). When $r_1 - r_2 =$ positive integer, then we could *possibly* find two solutions of form (6) by working with the smaller root r_2 and the recurrence relation which defines the c_n. If we cannot determine a second series solution, then another solution can be found that contains a logarithm. Lastly, when $r_1 - r_2 = 0$ or $r_1 = r_2$, we can find only one solution of form (6); the second solution is *always* of the form

$$y_2 = y_1(x) \ln x + \sum_{n=1}^{\infty} b_n x^{n+r_1}.$$

Bessel's equation:

$$x^2 y'' + xy' + (x^2 - v^2)y = 0$$

possesses the regular singular point $x = 0$. The method of Frobenius leads to

CHAPTER SUMMARY

the solution

$$J_v(x) = \sum_{n=0}^{\infty} \frac{(-1)^n}{n!\Gamma(1 + v + n)} \left(\frac{x}{2}\right)^{2n+v}$$

known as the **Bessel function of the first kind of order v**.
Legendre's equation:

$$(1 - x^2)y'' - 2xy' + n(n + 1)y = 0$$

possesses the ordinary point $x = 0$. There always exist polynomial solutions when n is a nonnegative integer. For example, when $n = 2$ the equation $(1 - x^2)y'' - 2xy' + 6y = 0$ has a solution $P_2(x) = \frac{1}{2}(3x^2 - 1)$ known as the **Legendre polynomial of degree 2**.

REVIEW EXERCISES

[6.1]   Answers to odd-numbered problems begin on page A-19 of the Appendix. In Problems 1–3 solve the given Cauchy–Euler equation.

1. $2x^3y''' + 19x^2y'' + 39xy' + 9y = 0$

★2. $x^2y'' - xy' + y = x^3$

3. $x^2y'' - 4xy' + 6y = 2x^4 + x^2$

[6.2]   In Problems 5–7 for each equation find two power series solutions about the ordinary point $x_0 = 0$.

4. $y'' - 4y = 0$

5. $y'' + xy = 0$

★6. $y'' - x^2y' + xy = 0$

7. $(x - 1)y'' + 3y = 0$

[6.3]   In Problems 8–13 find two linearly independent solutions of each equation.

8. $2xy'' + y' + y = 0$

9. $2x^2y'' + xy' - (x + 1)y = 0$

10. $x^2y'' - xy' + (x^2 + 1)y = 0$

11. $x(1 - x)y'' - 2y' + y = 0$

12. $x^2y'' - x^2y' + (x^2 - 2)y = 0$

13. $xy'' - (2x - 1)y' + (x - 1)y = 0$

[6.4]   14.   Without referring to Section 6.4, use the method of Frobenius to obtain a solution of the Bessel equation for $v = 0$: $xy'' + y' + xy = 0$.

15.   Show that $y = \sqrt{x}J_v(ax)$ is a solution of the differential equation

$$4x^2y'' + (4a^2x^2 - 4v^2 + 1)y = 0.$$

16. Use the result of Problem 15 to find a solution of the equation

$$x^2 y'' + \left(x^2 + \frac{1}{4}\right) y = 0.$$

17. Write the general solution of the equation $y'' + y = 0$ in terms of Bessel functions.

18. Without referring to Section 6.4, use a power series to find a polynomial solution of the Legendre equation for $n = 2$:

$$(1 - x^2)y'' - 2xy' + 6y = 0.$$

19. Find coefficients $c_0, c_1, c_2,$ and c_3 so that

$$4x^3 - 3x^2 + 5x - 8 = c_0 P_0(x) + c_1 P_1(x) + c_2 P_2(x) + c_3 P_3(x).$$

CHAPTER 7

The Laplace Transform

7.1   The Laplace Transform

7.1.1   Basic Definition

In elementary calculus you have studied the operations of differentiation and integration; recall that

$$\frac{d}{dx}[\alpha f(x) + \beta g(x)] = \alpha \frac{d}{dx}f(x) + \beta \frac{d}{dx}g(x)$$

$$\int [\alpha f(x) + \beta g(x)]\,dx = \alpha \int f(x)\,dx + \beta \int g(x)\,dx.$$

(1)

for any real constants α and β. *Any* operation having the property illustrated in (1) is said to be a **linear operation**. A definite integral of a sum can, of course, be written

$$\int_a^b [\alpha f(x) + \beta g(x)]\,dx = \alpha \int_a^b f(x)\,dx + \beta \int_a^b g(x)\,dx$$

provided each integral exists. Hence definite integration is a linear operation. In this section we are particularly interested in an improper integral for which the integrand contains a parameter s (a constant during integration). That is,

$$\int_0^\infty f(s, t)\, dt = \lim_{b \to \infty} \int_0^b f(s, t)\, dt. \tag{2}$$

If the limit in (2) exists, the integral is said to be convergent.

The Laplace transform   The foregoing linear operations of differentiation and integration *transform* a function into another expression. For example,

$$\frac{d}{dx} x^2 = 2x$$

$$\int x^2\, dx = \frac{x^3}{3} + c$$

$$\int_0^3 x^2\, dx = 9.$$

Specifically we are concerned with an improper integral which transforms a function $f(t)$ into a function of a parameter s. As we shall see in Section 7.3, the following transform is useful in solving certain differential equations connected with problems in physics and engineering.

DEFINITION 7.1   Let $f(t)$ be defined for $t \geq 0$, then the integral

$$\int_0^\infty e^{-st} f(t)\, dt = \lim_{b \to \infty} \int_0^b e^{-st} f(t)\, dt \tag{3}$$

is said to be the **Laplace transform** of f provided the limit exists.*

Symbolically the Laplace transform of f is denoted by $\mathscr{L}\{f(t)\}$, and since the answer depends on s we write $\mathscr{L}\{f(t)\} = F(s)$.

---

* Pierre Simon de Laplace (1749–1827) was a noted French mathematician and astronomer, called by some of his enthusiastic contemporaries the "Newton of France." Although Laplace made use of this particular integral transformation in his work in probability theory, it is likely that the integral was first discovered by Euler.

EXAMPLE   Evaluate $\mathscr{L}\{1\}$.

Solution:
$$\mathscr{L}\{1\} = \int_0^\infty e^{-st}(1)\,dt$$

$$= \lim_{b \to \infty} \int_0^b e^{-st}\,dt$$

$$= \lim_{b \to \infty} \left. \frac{-e^{-st}}{s} \right|_0^b$$

$$= \lim_{b \to \infty} \frac{-e^{-sb} + 1}{s}$$

$$= \frac{1}{s}, \qquad \text{provided } s > 0.$$

The use of the limit sign becomes somewhat tedious, so we shall adopt the notation $\Big|_0^\infty$ as a shorthand to writing

$$\lim_{b \to \infty} (\quad) \bigg|_0^b .$$

For example,

$$\mathscr{L}\{1\} = \int_0^\infty e^{-st}\,dt$$

$$= \left. \frac{-e^{-st}}{s} \right|_0^\infty$$

$$= \frac{1}{s}, \qquad s > 0.$$

Because

$$\int_0^\infty e^{-st}[\alpha f(t) + \beta g(t)]\,dt = \alpha \int_0^\infty e^{-st}f(t)\,dt + \beta \int_0^\infty e^{-st}g(t)\,dt$$

whenever both integrals converge, it follows that

$$\mathscr{L}\{\alpha f(t) + \beta g(t)\} = \alpha\mathscr{L}\{f(t)\} + \beta\mathscr{L}\{g(t)\}$$

$$= \alpha F(s) + \beta G(s). \qquad (4)$$

The integral which defines the Laplace transform does not have to converge. For example, neither $\mathscr{L}\{1/t\}$ nor $\mathscr{L}\{e^{t^2}\}$ exists. We state sufficient conditions which will guarantee the existence of $\mathscr{L}\{f(t)\}$.

THEOREM 7.1   Let $f(t)$ be piecewise continuous for $t \geq 0$.* If

$$|f(t)| \leq Me^{ct}, \qquad t > T \tag{5}$$

for some constant c and $T > 0$, then $\mathscr{L}\{f(t)\}$ exists for $s > c$.

Proof:
$$\mathscr{L}\{f(t)\} = \int_0^\infty e^{-st} f(t)\, dt$$

$$= \int_0^T e^{-st} f(t)\, dt + \int_T^\infty e^{-st} f(t)\, dt$$

$$= I_1 + I_2.$$

Now I_1 exists since it can be written as a sum of integrals over intervals for which f is continuous. I_2 exists since by (5)

$$|I_2| \leq \int_T^\infty |e^{-st} f(t)|\, dt$$

$$\leq M \int_T^\infty e^{-st} e^{ct}\, dt$$

$$= M \int_T^\infty e^{-(s-c)t}\, dt$$

$$= -M \frac{e^{-(s-c)t}}{s-c} \Big|_T^\infty$$

$$= M \frac{e^{-(s-c)T}}{s-c} \qquad \text{for } s > c.$$

Exponential order

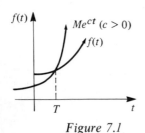

Figure 7.1

If, say, f is an increasing function, then the condition $|f(t)| \leq Me^{ct}$, $t > T$, simply states that its graph on the interval (T, ∞) does not grow faster than the graph of Me^{ct} where c is a positive constant (see Figure 7.1). Functions with this exponential function as an upper bound for $t > T$ are said to be of **exponential order**. For example, $f(t) = t$, $f(t) = e^{-t}$, and $f(t) = 2\cos t$ are all of exponential order for $t > 0$ since on this interval we have respectively

$$|t| \leq e^t$$

$$|e^{-t}| \leq e^t$$

$$|2\cos t| \leq 2e^t$$

(See Figure 7.2.)

---

* In any interval $0 \leq a \leq t \leq b$, the function f possesses at most a finite number of points t_k, $k = 1, 2, \ldots, n$ $(t_{k-1} < t_k)$ at which it has finite discontinuities; it is continuous on each open interval $t_{k-1} < t < t_k$.

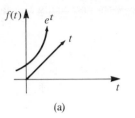

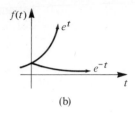

(a)

(b)

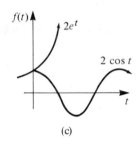

(c)

Figure 7.2

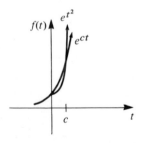

Figure 7.3

A function such as $f(t) = e^{t^2}$ is not of exponential order since, as shown in Figure 7.3, its graph grows faster than any positive linear power of e for $t > c$.

A positive integral power of t is always of exponential order since for $c > 0$

$$|t^n| \le Me^{ct} \qquad \text{or} \qquad \left|\frac{t^n}{e^{ct}}\right| \le M \qquad \text{for } t > T$$

is equivalent to showing that $\lim_{t \to \infty} t^n/e^{ct}$ is a finite limit for $n = 1, 2, 3 \dots$. The result follows by n applications of L'Hôpital's rule.

Throughout this entire chapter we shall be concerned only with functions which are both piecewise continuous and of exponential order. We note, however, that these conditions are sufficient but not necessary for the existence of a Laplace transform. The function $f(t) = t^{-1/2}$ is not piecewise continuous on $t \ge 0$ but its Laplace transform exists (see Problem 16).

EXAMPLE

Evaluate $\mathscr{L}\{t\}$.

Solution: From Definition 7.1 we have

$$\mathscr{L}\{t\} = \int_0^\infty e^{-st} t \, dt.$$

Integrating by parts and using the fact that $\lim_{t \to \infty} te^{-st} = 0$ for $s > 0$, we obtain

$$\mathscr{L}\{t\} = \frac{-te^{-st}}{s}\bigg|_0^\infty + \frac{1}{s}\int_0^\infty e^{-st}\, dt$$

$$= \frac{1}{s}\mathscr{L}\{1\} = \frac{1}{s}\left(\frac{1}{s}\right)$$

$$= \frac{1}{s^2}, \qquad s > 0.$$

EXAMPLE

Evaluate $\mathscr{L}\{e^{-3t}\}$.

Solution: From Definition 7.1

$$\mathscr{L}\{e^{-3t}\} = \int_0^\infty e^{-st}e^{-3t}\, dt$$

$$= \int_0^\infty e^{-(s+3)t}\, dt$$

$$= \frac{-e^{-(s+3)t}}{s+3}\bigg|_0^\infty$$

$$= \frac{1}{s+3}, \qquad s > -3.$$

The last result follows from the fact that $\lim_{t \to \infty} e^{-(s+3)t} = 0$ for $s + 3 > 0$ or $s > -3$.

EXAMPLE

Evaluate $\mathscr{L}\{\sin 2t\}$.

Solution: From Definition 7.1

$$\mathscr{L}\{\sin 2t\} = \int_0^\infty e^{-st} \sin 2t\, dt$$

$$= -\frac{e^{-st}\sin 2t}{s}\bigg|_0^\infty + \frac{2}{s}\int_0^\infty e^{-st}\cos 2t\, dt$$

$$= \frac{2}{s}\int_0^\infty e^{-st}\cos 2t\, dt, \qquad s > 0$$

$$= \frac{2}{s}\left[-\frac{e^{-st}\cos 2t}{s}\bigg|_0^\infty - \frac{2}{s}\int_0^\infty e^{-st}\sin 2t\, dt\right]$$

$$= \frac{2}{s^2} - \frac{4}{s^2}\mathscr{L}\{\sin 2t\}, \qquad s > 0.$$

Now solve for $\mathcal{L}\{\sin 2t\}$,

$$\left[1 + \frac{4}{s^2}\right]\mathcal{L}\{\sin 2t\} = \frac{2}{s^2}$$

$$\mathcal{L}\{\sin 2t\} = \frac{2}{s^2 + 4}, \qquad s > 0.$$

EXAMPLE

Evaluate $\mathcal{L}\{3t - 5\sin 2t\}$.

Solution: From the preceding examples and the linearity property of the Laplace transform we can write

$$\mathcal{L}\{3t - 5\sin 2t\} = 3\mathcal{L}\{t\} - 5\mathcal{L}\{\sin 2t\}$$

$$= 3 \cdot \frac{1}{s^2} - 5 \cdot \frac{2}{s^2 + 4}$$

$$= \frac{-7s^2 + 12}{s^2(s^2 + 4)}, \qquad s > 0.$$

EXAMPLE

Evaluate $\mathcal{L}\{te^{-2t}\}$ and $\mathcal{L}\{t^2 e^{-2t}\}$.

Solution: From Definition 7.1 and integration by parts

$$\mathcal{L}\{te^{-2t}\} = \int_0^\infty e^{-st}(te^{-2t})\,dt$$

$$= \int_0^\infty te^{-(s+2)t}\,dt$$

$$= \frac{-te^{-(s+2)t}}{s+2}\bigg|_0^\infty + \frac{1}{s+2}\int_0^\infty e^{-(s+2)t}\,dt$$

$$= -\frac{1}{(s+2)^2}e^{-(s+2)t}\bigg|_0^\infty \qquad (s > -2)$$

$$= \frac{1}{(s+2)^2} \qquad (s > -2).$$

Again, integration by parts gives

$$\mathcal{L}\{t^2 e^{-2t}\} = \frac{-t^2 e^{-(s+2)t}}{s+2}\bigg|_0^\infty + \frac{2}{s+2}\int_0^\infty t e^{-(s+2)t}\, dt$$

$$= \frac{2}{s+2}\int_0^\infty e^{-st}(te^{-2t})\, dt \qquad (s > -2)$$

$$= \frac{2}{s+2}\mathcal{L}\{te^{-2t}\} = \frac{2}{s+2}\left[\frac{1}{(s+2)^2}\right]$$

$$= \frac{2}{(s+2)^3} \qquad (s > -2).$$

We state the generalizations of some of the preceding examples by means of the next theorem. From this point on we shall also refrain from stating any restrictions on s; it is understood that s is sufficiently restricted to guarantee the convergence of the appropriate Laplace transform.

THEOREM 7.2   (a) $\qquad \mathcal{L}\{t^n\} = \dfrac{n!}{s^{n+1}}, \qquad n = 1, 2, 3, \ldots$

(b) $\qquad \mathcal{L}\{e^{at}\} = \dfrac{1}{s-a}$

(c) $\qquad \mathcal{L}\{\sin kt\} = \dfrac{k}{s^2 + k^2}$

(d) $\qquad \mathcal{L}\{\cos kt\} = \dfrac{s}{s^2 + k^2}$

(e) $\qquad \mathcal{L}\{\sinh kt\} = \dfrac{k}{s^2 - k^2}$

(f) $\qquad \mathcal{L}\{\cosh kt\} = \dfrac{s}{s^2 - k^2}.$

Part (a) can be justified in the following manner. Integration by parts yields

$$\mathcal{L}\{t^n\} = \int_0^\infty e^{-st} t^n\, dt$$

$$= -\frac{1}{s} e^{-st} t^n\bigg|_0^\infty + \frac{n}{s}\int_0^\infty e^{-st} t^{n-1}\, dt$$

$$= \frac{n}{s}\int_0^\infty e^{-st} t^{n-1}\, dt,$$

or

$$\mathcal{L}\{t^n\} = \frac{n}{s}\mathcal{L}\{t^{n-1}\}, \qquad n = 1, 2, 3 \ldots.$$

Now we know that $\mathscr{L}\{1\} = 1/s$, so it follows by iteration that

$$\mathscr{L}\{t\} = \frac{1}{s}\mathscr{L}\{1\} = \frac{1}{s^2},$$

$$\mathscr{L}\{t^2\} = \frac{2}{s}\mathscr{L}\{t\} = \frac{2}{s}\left(\frac{1}{s^2}\right) = \frac{2}{s^3},$$

$$\mathscr{L}\{t^3\} = \frac{3}{s}\mathscr{L}\{t^2\} = \frac{3}{s}\left(\frac{2}{s^3}\right) = \frac{3!}{s^4}.$$

In general, it seems reasonable that

$$\mathscr{L}\{t^n\} = \frac{n}{s}\mathscr{L}\{t^{n-1}\} = \frac{n}{s}\left[\frac{(n-1)!}{s^n}\right] = \frac{n!}{s^{n+1}}.*$$

The justifications of parts (e) and (f) of Theorem 7.2 are left to the student (see Problems 9 and 10).

EXAMPLE

Evaluate $\mathscr{L}\{\sin^2 t\}$.

Solution: With the aid of a trigonometric identity and part (d) of Theorem 7.2, we obtain

$$\mathscr{L}\{\sin^2 t\} = \mathscr{L}\left\{\frac{1 - \cos 2t}{2}\right\}$$

$$= \frac{1}{2}\mathscr{L}\{1\} - \frac{1}{2}\mathscr{L}\{\cos 2t\}$$

$$= \frac{1}{2}\cdot\frac{1}{s} - \frac{1}{2}\cdot\frac{s}{s^2 + 4}$$

$$= \frac{2}{s(s^2 + 4)}.$$

7.1.2 The Inverse Transform

By using the integral definition of the Laplace transform of a function $f(t)$, we determine another function, that is, a function of the transform parameter s. We have denoted this symbolically by $\mathscr{L}\{f(t)\} = F(s)$.

We now turn the problem around, namely, given $F(s)$ find the function $f(t)$ corresponding to this transform. We say $f(t)$ is the **inverse Laplace transform** of $F(s)$ and write $f(t) = \mathscr{L}^{-1}\{F(s)\}$. The analogue of Theorem 7.2 for the inverse transform is the following.

---

*A rigorous proof requires mathematical induction.

THEOREM 7.3   **(a)** $t^n = \mathscr{L}^{-1}\left\{\dfrac{n!}{s^{n+1}}\right\},$ $n = 1, 2, 3, \ldots$

(b) $e^{at} = \mathscr{L}^{-1}\left\{\dfrac{1}{s-a}\right\}$

(c) $\sin kt = \mathscr{L}^{-1}\left\{\dfrac{k}{s^2 + k^2}\right\}$

(d) $\cos kt = \mathscr{L}^{-1}\left\{\dfrac{s}{s^2 + k^2}\right\}$

(e) $\sinh kt = \mathscr{L}^{-1}\left\{\dfrac{k}{s^2 - k^2}\right\}$

(f) $\cosh kt = \mathscr{L}^{-1}\left\{\dfrac{s}{s^2 - k^2}\right\}.$

$\mathscr{L}^{-1}$ is also a linear operation.

We shall assume that the inverse Laplace transform is itself a linear transformation,* that is, for constants α and β

$$\mathscr{L}^{-1}\{\alpha F(s) + \beta G(s)\} = \alpha \mathscr{L}^{-1}\{F(s)\} + \beta \mathscr{L}^{-1}\{G(s)\},$$

where F and G are the transforms of some functions f and g.

Not every arbitrary function of s is a Laplace transform of a piecewise function of exponential order.

THEOREM 7.4   Let $f(t)$ be piecewise continuous for $t \geq 0$ and of exponential order for $t > T$. Then

$$\lim_{s \to \infty} \mathscr{L}\{f(t)\} = 0.$$

Proof: Since $f(t)$ is piecewise continuous on $0 \leq t \leq T$ it is necessarily bounded on this interval:

$$|f(t)| < M_1 = M_1 e^{0t}.$$

Also $$|f(t)| < M_2 e^{\gamma t}$$

for $t > T$. If M denotes the maximum of $\{M_1, M_2\}$ and c denotes the

---

* The inverse Laplace transform is actually another integral. However, evaluation of this integral demands the use of complex variables which is beyond the scope of this text.

maximum of $\{0, \gamma\}$, then

$$|\mathscr{L}\{f(t)\}| \le \int_0^\infty e^{-st} |f(t)| \, dt$$

$$< M \int_0^\infty e^{-st} \cdot e^{ct} \, dt$$

$$= -M \frac{e^{-(s-c)t}}{s-c} \Big|_0^\infty$$

$$= \frac{M}{s-c} \qquad \text{for } s > c.$$

As $s \to \infty$ we have $|\mathscr{L}\{f(t)\}| \to 0$ and so $\mathscr{L}\{f(t)\} \to 0$.

EXAMPLE $F(s) = s^2$ is not the Laplace transform of any piecewise continuous function of exponential order since $F(s) \nrightarrow 0$ as $s \to \infty$. Hence we shall say that $\mathscr{L}^{-1}\{F(s)\}$ does not exist.

It should also be noted that the inverse Laplace transform of a function $F(s)$ may *not* be unique (see Problem 33). However, if $f_1(t)$ and $f_2(t)$ are continuous for $t \ge 0$ and $\mathscr{L}\{f_1(t)\} = \mathscr{L}\{f_2(t)\}$ then necessarily $f_1(t) = f_2(t)$.

EXAMPLE   Evaluate $\mathscr{L}^{-1}\left\{\dfrac{1}{s^5}\right\}$.

Solution: We multiply and divide by 4! and then use part (a) of Theorem 7.3. It follows that

$$\mathscr{L}^{-1}\left\{\frac{1}{s^5}\right\} = \frac{1}{4!} \mathscr{L}^{-1}\left\{\frac{4!}{s^5}\right\} = \frac{1}{24} t^4.$$

EXAMPLE   Evaluate $\mathscr{L}^{-1}\left\{\dfrac{3s+5}{s^2+7}\right\}$.

Solution: Use termwise division and the linearity property of the inverse transform. From parts (c) and (d) of Theorem 7.3 we have

$$\mathscr{L}^{-1}\left\{\frac{3s+5}{s^2+7}\right\} = 3\mathscr{L}^{-1}\left\{\frac{s}{s^2+7}\right\} + \frac{5}{\sqrt{7}} \mathscr{L}^{-1}\left\{\frac{\sqrt{7}}{s^2+7}\right\}$$

$$= 3\cos\sqrt{7}\,t + \frac{5}{\sqrt{7}} \sin\sqrt{7}\,t.$$

Partial fractions

The use of **partial fractions** is very important in evaluating inverse Laplace transforms. Here we review three basic cases of that theory. For example, the denominators of

(a) $F(s) = \dfrac{1}{(s - 1)(s + 2)(s + 4)}$

(b) $F(s) = \dfrac{s + 1}{s^2(s + 2)^3}$

(c) $F(s) = \dfrac{3s - 2}{s^3(s^2 + 4)}$

contain respectively
(a)   only distinct linear factors,
(b)   repeated linear factors,
(c)   a quadratic factor.*

EXAMPLE

Evaluate $\mathscr{L}^{-1}\left\{\dfrac{1}{(s - 1)(s + 2)(s + 4)}\right\}$

Solution: There exist constants A, B, and C so that

$$\frac{1}{(s - 1)(s + 2)(s + 4)} = \frac{A}{s - 1} + \frac{B}{s + 2} + \frac{C}{s + 4}$$

$$= \frac{A(s + 2)(s + 4) + B(s - 1)(s + 4) + C(s - 1)(s + 2)}{(s - 1)(s + 2)(s + 4)}.$$

Since the numerators are identical we must then have

$$1 = A(s + 2)(s + 4) + B(s - 1)(s + 4) + C(s - 1)(s + 2).$$

By comparing coefficients of powers of s on both sides of the equality we know that the last equation is equivalent to a system of three equations in the three unknowns A, B, and C. However, you might recall the following shortcut for determining these unknowns. If we set $s = 1$, $s = -2$, and $s = -4$ [the zeros of the common denominator $(s - 1)(s + 2)(s + 4)$] we obtain, respectively,

$$1 = A(3)(5), \qquad A = 1/15,$$
$$1 = B(-3)(2), \qquad B = -1/6,$$
$$1 = C(-5)(-2), \qquad C = 1/10.$$

---

* Usually irreducible, that is, nonfactorable, over the set of real numbers.

Hence we can write

$$\frac{1}{(s-1)(s+2)(s+4)} = \frac{1/15}{s-1} - \frac{1/6}{s+2} + \frac{1/10}{s+4}$$

and thus

$$\mathscr{L}^{-1}\left\{\frac{1}{(s-1)(s+2)(s+4)}\right\} = \frac{1}{15}\mathscr{L}^{-1}\left\{\frac{1}{s-1}\right\} - \frac{1}{6}\mathscr{L}^{-1}\left\{\frac{1}{s+2}\right\}$$

$$+ \frac{1}{10}\mathscr{L}^{-1}\left\{\frac{1}{s+4}\right\}$$

$$= \frac{1}{15}e^t - \frac{1}{6}e^{-2t} + \frac{1}{10}e^{-4t}.$$

EXAMPLE

Evaluate $\mathscr{L}^{-1}\left\{\dfrac{s+1}{s^2(s+2)^3}\right\}$.

Solution: Assume

$$\frac{s+1}{s^2(s+2)^3} = \frac{A}{s} + \frac{B}{s^2} + \frac{C}{s+2} + \frac{D}{(s+2)^2} + \frac{E}{(s+2)^3}$$

so that

$$s + 1 = As(s+2)^3 + B(s+2)^3 + Cs^2(s+2)^2 + Ds^2(s+2) + Es^2.$$

Setting $s = 0$ and $s = -2$ gives, respectively,

$$1 = B(2)^3, \qquad B = 1/8$$
$$-1 = E(-2)^2, \qquad E = -1/4.$$

By equating coefficients of s^4, s^3, and s, we obtain

$$0 = A + C$$
$$0 = 6A + B + 4C + D$$
$$1 = 8A + 12B$$

from which it follows that $A = -1/16$, $C = 1/16$, $D = 0$. Hence

$$\mathscr{L}^{-1}\left\{\frac{s+1}{s^2(s+2)^3}\right\} = \mathscr{L}^{-1}\left\{-\frac{1/16}{s} + \frac{1/8}{s^2} + \frac{1/16}{s+2} - \frac{1/4}{(s+2)^3}\right\}$$

$$= -\frac{1}{16}\mathscr{L}^{-1}\left\{\frac{1}{s}\right\} + \frac{1}{8}\mathscr{L}^{-1}\left\{\frac{1}{s^2}\right\} + \frac{1}{16}\mathscr{L}^{-1}\left\{\frac{1}{s+2}\right\}$$

$$-\frac{1}{8}\mathscr{L}^{-1}\left\{\frac{2}{(s+s)^3}\right\}$$

$$= -\frac{1}{16} + \frac{1}{8}t + \frac{1}{16}e^{-2t} - \frac{1}{8}t^2e^{-2t}.$$

Here we have used $\mathscr{L}^{-1}\{2/(s+2)^3\} = t^2e^{-2t}$. (See page 288.)

EXAMPLE   Evaluate $\mathscr{L}^{-1}\left\{\dfrac{3s-2}{s^3(s^2+4)}\right\}$.

Solution: Assume $\dfrac{3s-2}{s^3(s^2+4)} = \dfrac{A}{s} + \dfrac{B}{s^2} + \dfrac{C}{s^3} + \dfrac{Ds+E}{s^2+4}$

so that $3s - 2 = As^2(s^2+4) + Bs(s^2+4) + C(s^2+4) + (Ds+E)s^3$.

Setting $s = 0$ gives immediately $C = -1/2$. Now the coefficients of s^4, s^3, s^2, and s are

$$0 = A + D$$
$$0 = B + E$$
$$0 = 4A + C$$
$$3 = 4B$$

from which we obtain $B = 3/4$, $E = -3/4$, $A = 1/8$, $D = -1/8$. Therefore

$$\mathscr{L}^{-1}\left\{\frac{3s-2}{s^3(s^2+4)}\right\} = \mathscr{L}^{-1}\left\{\frac{1/8}{s} + \frac{3/4}{s^2} - \frac{1/2}{s^3} + \frac{-s/8-3/4}{s^2+4}\right\}$$

$$= \frac{1}{8}\mathscr{L}^{-1}\left\{\frac{1}{s}\right\} + \frac{3}{4}\mathscr{L}^{-1}\left\{\frac{1}{s^2}\right\} - \frac{1}{4}\mathscr{L}^{-1}\left\{\frac{2}{s^3}\right\}$$

$$-\frac{1}{8}\mathscr{L}^{-1}\left\{\frac{s}{s^2+4}\right\} - \frac{3}{8}\mathscr{L}^{-1}\left\{\frac{2}{s^2+4}\right\}$$

$$= \frac{1}{8} + \frac{3}{4}t - \frac{1}{4}t^2 - \frac{1}{8}\cos 2t - \frac{3}{8}\sin 2t.$$

EXERCISES 7.1
[7.1.1]

Answers to odd-numbered problems begin on page A-20 of the Appendix. In Problems 1–15 use Definition 7.1 or Theorem 7.2 to evaluate $\mathcal{L}\{f(t)\}$ for the given functions.

EXAMPLE

Find $\mathcal{L}\{f(t)\}$ if

$$f(t) = \begin{cases} 0, & 0 \leq t < 3 \\ 2, & t \geq 3. \end{cases}$$

Solution:

$$\mathcal{L}\{f(t)\} = \int_0^\infty e^{-st} f(t)\, dt$$

$$= \int_0^3 e^{-st} f(t)\, dt + \int_3^\infty e^{-st} f(t)\, dt$$

$$= \int_0^3 e^{-st}(0)\, dt + \int_3^\infty e^{-st}(2)\, dt$$

$$= -\frac{2e^{-st}}{s} \Big|_3^\infty$$

$$= \frac{2e^{-3s}}{s}.$$

---

1. $f(t) = \begin{cases} -1, & 0 < t < 1, \\ 1, & t \geq 1. \end{cases}$

2. $f(t) = \begin{cases} 4, & 0 < t < 2, \\ 0, & t \geq 2. \end{cases}$

3. $f(t) = \begin{cases} t, & 0 < t < 1, \\ 1, & t \geq 1. \end{cases}$

4. $f(t) = t^3 e^{-t}$

5. $f(t) = e^{-t} \sin t$

★6. $f(t) = \cos^2 t$

7. $f(t) = \sin 2t \cos 2t$

8. $f(t) = 10 - e^{t-5}$

9. $f(t) = \sinh kt$

10. $f(t) = \cosh kt$

11. $f(t) = 4t^2 - 5\sin 3t$

12. $f(t) = (t + 1)^3$

13. $f(t) = (e^t - e^{-t})^2$

★14. $f(t) = t \sin t$

15. $f(t) = (\cos^2 t - \sin^2 t)^2$

16. Recall from Exercise 6.4 that the gamma function, or generalized factorial, is defined by the integral

$$\Gamma(\alpha) = \int_0^\infty e^{-t} t^{\alpha-1}\, dt, \qquad \alpha > 0.$$

(a) Show that $\mathcal{L}\{t^\alpha\} = \dfrac{\Gamma(\alpha + 1)}{s^{\alpha+1}}, \qquad \alpha > -1.$

(b) Evaluate $\mathcal{L}\{t^{-1/2}\}$.

17. Evaluate the following
(a) $\mathscr{L}\{\cos t \cos 2t\}$
(b) $\mathscr{L}\{\sin t \sin 2t\}$
(c) $\mathscr{L}\{\sin t \cos 2t\}$
[*Hint:* Examine $\cos(t_1 \pm t_2)$ and $\sin(t_1 \pm t_2)$.]

★**18.** Evaluate $\mathscr{L}\{\sin^3 t\}$. [*Hint:* $\sin^3 t = \sin t \sin^2 t$.]

[**7.1.2**]   In Problems 19–32 evaluate $f(t) = \mathscr{L}^{-1}\{F(s)\}$.

19. $\mathscr{L}^{-1}\left\{\dfrac{(s+1)^3}{s^4}\right\}$ **20.** $\mathscr{L}^{-1}\left\{\dfrac{4}{s} - \dfrac{3}{s+5} + \dfrac{7s}{s^2+6}\right\}$

21. $\mathscr{L}^{-1}\left\{\dfrac{1}{4s+1}\right\}$ **22.** $\mathscr{L}^{-1}\left\{\dfrac{1}{4s^2+1}\right\}$

23. $\mathscr{L}^{-1}\left\{\dfrac{4s}{4s^2+1}\right\}$ ★**24.** $\mathscr{L}^{-1}\left\{\dfrac{2s+5}{s^2+9}\right\}$

25. $\mathscr{L}^{-1}\left\{\dfrac{1}{s^2+3s}\right\}$ **26.** $\mathscr{L}^{-1}\left\{\dfrac{1}{s^2-16}\right\}$

27. $\mathscr{L}^{-1}\left\{\dfrac{2s+4}{(s-2)(s^2+4s+3)}\right\}$ ★**28.** $\mathscr{L}^{-1}\left\{\dfrac{s+1}{(s^2-4s)(s+5)}\right\}$

29. $\mathscr{L}^{-1}\left\{\dfrac{s}{(s-1)(s^2+1)}\right\}$ **30.** $\mathscr{L}^{-1}\left\{\dfrac{s-1}{s^2(s^2+1)}\right\}$

31. $\mathscr{L}^{-1}\left\{\dfrac{s}{(s^2-4)(s+2)}\right\}$ ★**32.** $\mathscr{L}^{-1}\left\{\dfrac{1}{s^4-9}\right\}$

33. The inverse Laplace transform may not be unique. Evaluate $\mathscr{L}\{f(t)\}$ for the given functions.

(a) $f(t) = \begin{cases} 1, & t \geq 0,\, t \neq 1,\, t \neq 2 \\ 3, & t = 1 \\ -3, & t = 2 \end{cases}$

(b) $f(t) = \begin{cases} e^{3t} & 0 \leq t < 5,\, t > 5 \\ 1, & t = 5 \end{cases}$

7.2   Operational Properties

It is not convenient to use Definition 7.1 each time we wish to find the Laplace transform of a function $f(t)$. For example, the integration by parts involved in evaluating, say, $\mathscr{L}\{e^t t^2 \sin 3t\}$ is formidable to say the least. In the discussion that follows, we present several labor saving theorems, and these in turn enable us to build up a more extensive list of transforms without the necessity of using the definition of a Laplace transform. Indeed, we shall see that evaluating transforms such as $\mathscr{L}\{e^{4t}\cos 6t\}$, $\mathscr{L}\{t^3\sin 2t\}$, and $\mathscr{L}\{t^{10}e^{-t}\}$ are fairly easy, provided we know $\mathscr{L}\{\cos 6t\}$, $\mathscr{L}\{\sin 2t\}$, and $\mathscr{L}\{t^{10}\}$, respectively. Though extensive tables can be constructed, and we have included three tables in the Chapter Summary, it is nonetheless a good idea to know the Laplace transforms of basic functions such as t^n, e^{at}, $\sin kt$, $\cos kt$, $\sinh kt$, and $\cosh kt$.

The first translation theorem

THEOREM 7.5 If a is any real number then

$$\mathscr{L}\{e^{at}f(t)\} = F(s-a)$$

where $F(s) = \mathscr{L}\{f(t)\}$.

Proof: The proof is immediate, since by Definition 7.1

$$\mathscr{L}\{e^{at}f(t)\} = \int_0^\infty e^{-st}e^{at}f(t)\,dt$$

$$= \int_0^\infty e^{-(s-a)t}f(t)\,dt$$

$$= F(s-a).$$

Thus if we already know $\mathscr{L}\{f(t)\} = F(s)$, we can compute $\mathscr{L}\{e^{at}f(t)\}$ with no additional effort other than translating, or shifting, $F(s)$ to $F(s-a)$. For emphasis it is also sometimes useful to employ the symbolism

$$\mathscr{L}\{e^{at}f(t)\} = \mathscr{L}\{f(t)\}_{s\to s-a}.$$

Theorem 7.5 is known as the **first translation theorem**.

EXAMPLES

Evaluate **(a)** $\mathscr{L}\{e^{5t}t^3\}$, **(b)** $\mathscr{L}\{e^{-2t}\cos 4t\}$.

Solutions: The results follow from Theorem 7.5.

(a) $\mathscr{L}\{e^{5t}t^3\} = \mathscr{L}\{t^3\}_{s\to s-5}$

$$= \left.\frac{3!}{s^4}\right|_{s\to s-5}$$

$$= \frac{6}{(s-5)^4}.$$

(b) $\mathscr{L}\{e^{-2t}\cos 4t\} = \mathscr{L}\{\cos 4t\}_{s\to s+2}$ [*Note:* $a = -2$, so

$$s - a = s - (-2) = s + 2]$$

$$= \left.\frac{s}{s^2+16}\right|_{s\to s+2}$$

$$= \frac{s+2}{(s+2)^2+16}.$$

EXAMPLE

Evaluate $\mathscr{L}^{-1}\left\{\dfrac{s}{s^2 + 6s + 11}\right\}$.

Solution:

$$\mathscr{L}^{-1}\left\{\frac{s}{s^2 + 6s + 11}\right\} = \mathscr{L}^{-1}\left\{\frac{s}{(s+3)^2 + 2}\right\} \qquad \text{[completion of square]}$$

$$= \mathscr{L}^{-1}\left\{\frac{s + 3 - 3}{(s+3)^2 + 2}\right\} \qquad \text{[adding zero in the numerator]}$$

$$= \mathscr{L}^{-1}\left\{\frac{s + 3}{(s+3)^2 + 2} - \frac{3}{(s+3)^2 + 2}\right\} \qquad \text{[termwise division]}$$

$$= \mathscr{L}^{-1}\left\{\frac{s + 3}{(s+3)^2 + 2}\right\}$$

$$- 3\mathscr{L}^{-1}\left\{\frac{1}{(s+3)^2 + 2}\right\} \qquad \text{[linearity of } \mathscr{L}^{-1}\text{]}$$

$$= \mathscr{L}^{-1}\left\{\frac{s}{s^2 + 2}\bigg|_{s \to s+3}\right\} - \frac{3}{\sqrt{2}}\mathscr{L}^{-1}\left\{\frac{\sqrt{2}}{s^2 + 2}\bigg|_{s \to s+3}\right\}$$

$$= e^{-3t}\cos\sqrt{2}\,t - \frac{3}{\sqrt{2}}e^{-3t}\sin\sqrt{2}\,t. \qquad \text{[Theorem 7.5]}$$

EXAMPLE

Evaluate $\mathscr{L}^{-1}\left\{\dfrac{1}{(s-1)^3} + \dfrac{1}{s^2 + 2s - 8}\right\}$.

Solution:

$$\mathscr{L}^{-1}\left\{\frac{1}{(s-1)^3} + \frac{1}{s^2 + 2s - 8}\right\} = \mathscr{L}^{-1}\left\{\frac{1}{(s-1)^3} + \frac{1}{(s+1)^2 - 9}\right\}$$

$$= \frac{1}{2!}\mathscr{L}^{-1}\left\{\frac{2!}{(s-1)^3}\right\} + \frac{1}{3}\mathscr{L}^{-1}\left\{\frac{3}{(s+1)^2 - 9}\right\}$$

$$= \frac{1}{2!}\mathscr{L}^{-1}\left\{\frac{2!}{s^3}\bigg|_{s \to s-1}\right\} + \frac{1}{3}\mathscr{L}^{-1}\left\{\frac{3}{s^2 - 9}\bigg|_{s \to s+1}\right\}$$

$$= \frac{1}{2}e^t t^2 + \frac{1}{3}e^{-t}\sinh 3t.$$

The unit step function

In engineering one frequently encounters functions which can be either "on" or "off." For example, an external force acting on a mechanical system or a voltage impressed on a circuit can be turned off after a period of time. It is thus convenient to define a special function called the **unit step function**.

DEFINITION 7.2   The function $\mathcal{U}(t - a)$ is defined to be

$$\mathcal{U}(t - a) = \begin{cases} 0, & 0 \le t < a \\ 1, & t \ge a. \end{cases}$$

Notice that we define $\mathcal{U}(t - a)$ only on the nonnegative t-axis since this is all that we are concerned with in the study of Laplace transforms. In a broader sense, $\mathcal{U}(t - a) = 0$ for $t < a$.

EXAMPLES

Graph **(a)** $\mathcal{U}(t)$, **(b)** $\mathcal{U}(t - 2)$.

Solutions: **(a)** $\mathcal{U}(t) = 1,$ $t \ge 0$

(b) $\mathcal{U}(t - 2) = \begin{cases} 0, & 0 \le t < 2 \\ 1, & t \ge 2. \end{cases}$

The respective graphs are given in Figure 7.4.

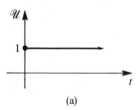

(a)

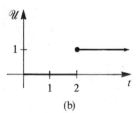

(b)

Figure 7.4

When combined with other functions defined for $t \ge 0$, the unit step function "turns off" a portion of their graphs. For example, Figure 7.5 illustrates the graph of $y = f(t)$ where

$$f(t) = \sin t \, \mathcal{U}(t - 2\pi), \qquad t \ge 0.$$

$$= \begin{cases} 0, & 0 \le t < 2\pi \\ \sin t, & t \ge 2\pi. \end{cases}$$

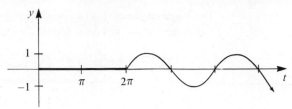

Figure 7.5

EXAMPLE

Consider the function $y = f(t)$ defined by $f(t) = t^3$. Compare the graphs of
(a) $f(t) = t^3$,   **(b)** $f(t) = t^3$, $t \ge 0$,
(c) $f(t-2)$, $t \ge 0$,   **(d)** $f(t-2)\ \mathcal{U}(t-2)$, $t \ge 0$.

Solution: The respective graphs are given in Figure 7.6.

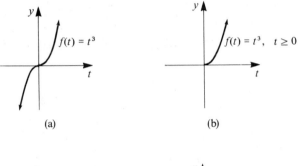

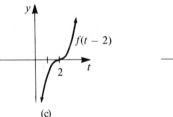

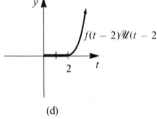

Figure 7.6

We have already seen in Theorem 7.5 that an exponential multiple of $f(t)$ results in a shift or translation of the transform $F(s)$. In the next theorem we see that whenever $F(s)$ is multiplied by an appropriate exponential function, the graph of $f(t)$ is not only translated but a portion of the graph is turned off as well.

Second translation theorem

THEOREM 7.6   If $a > 0$ then

$$\mathcal{L}\{f(t-a)\mathcal{U}(t-a)\} = e^{-as}\mathcal{L}\{f(t)\}$$
$$= e^{-as}F(s).$$

Proof: From Definition 7.1

$$\mathcal{L}\{f(t-a)\mathcal{U}(t-a)\} = \int_0^\infty e^{-st}f(t-a)\mathcal{U}(t-a)\,dt$$

$$= \int_0^a e^{-st}f(t-a)\mathcal{U}(t-a)\,dt$$

zero for $0 \le t < a$

$$+ \int_a^\infty e^{-st}f(t-a)\mathcal{U}(t-a)\,dt$$

one for $t \ge a$

$$= \int_a^\infty e^{-st}f(t-a)\,dt.$$

Now let $v = t - a$, $dv = dt$

$$\mathcal{L}\{f(t-a)\mathcal{U}(t-a)\} = \int_0^\infty e^{-s(v+a)}f(v)\,dv$$

$$= e^{-as} \int_0^\infty e^{-sv}f(v)\,dv$$

$$= e^{-as}\mathcal{L}\{f(t)\}.$$

Theorem 7.6 is known as the **second translation theorem**.

EXAMPLE   Evaluate $\mathcal{L}\{(t-1)^4\mathcal{U}(t-1)\}$.

Solution: From Theorem 7.6 we have

$$\mathcal{L}\{(t-1)^4\mathcal{U}(t-1)\} = e^{-s}\mathcal{L}\{t^4\}$$

$$= e^{-s}\frac{4!}{s^5}$$

$$= \frac{24}{s^5}e^{-s}.$$

Note: This result is equivalent to evaluating the integral

$$\int_1^\infty e^{-st}(t-1)^4\,dt.$$

EXAMPLE   Evaluate $\mathcal{L}^{-1}\left\{\dfrac{e^{-\pi s/2}}{s^2+9}\right\}$

Solution:
$$\mathcal{L}^{-1}\left\{\frac{e^{-\pi s/2}}{s^2 + 9}\right\} = \frac{1}{3}\mathcal{L}^{-1}\left\{\frac{3}{s^2+9}\right\}_{t \to t - \pi/2} \mathcal{U}\left(t - \frac{\pi}{2}\right)$$

$$= \frac{1}{3}\sin 3\left(t - \frac{\pi}{2}\right)\mathcal{U}\left(t - \frac{\pi}{2}\right)$$

$$= \frac{1}{3}\cos 3t\ \mathcal{U}\left(t - \frac{\pi}{2}\right).$$

If $F(s) = \mathcal{L}\{f(t)\}$, and if we assume that interchanging of differentiation and integration is possible, then it follows that

$$\frac{d}{ds}F(s) = \frac{d}{ds}\int_0^\infty e^{-st}f(t)\,dt$$

$$= \int_0^\infty \frac{\partial}{\partial s}\left[e^{-st}f(t)\,dt\right]$$

$$= -\int_0^\infty e^{-st}tf(t)\,dt$$

$$= -\mathcal{L}\{tf(t)\}.$$

That is,
$$\mathcal{L}\{tf(t)\} = -\frac{d}{ds}\mathcal{L}\{f(t)\}.$$

Similarly,
$$\mathcal{L}\{t^2 f(t)\} = \mathcal{L}\{t \cdot tf(t)\}$$

$$= -\frac{d}{ds}\mathcal{L}\{tf(t)\}$$

$$= -\frac{d}{ds}\left(-\frac{d}{ds}\mathcal{L}\{f(t)\}\right)$$

$$= \frac{d^2}{ds^2}\mathcal{L}\{f(t)\}.$$

We have formally justified two cases of the following theorem.

Derivatives of transforms   **THEOREM 7.7**   For $n = 1, 2, 3, \ldots$

$$\mathcal{L}\{t^n f(t)\} = (-1)^n \frac{d^n}{ds^n}\mathcal{L}\{f(t)\}$$

$$= (-1)^n \frac{d^n}{ds^n}F(s).$$

EXAMPLES   Evaluate (a) $\mathcal{L}\{te^{3t}\}$, (b) $\mathcal{L}\{t \sin kt\}$, (c) $\mathcal{L}\{t^2 \sin kt\}$, (d) $\mathcal{L}\{te^{-t}\cos t\}$.

Solutions: The results follow from Theorem 7.7.

(a) $\mathcal{L}\{te^{3t}\} = -\dfrac{d}{ds}\mathcal{L}\{e^{3t}\}$

$$= -\frac{d}{ds}\left(\frac{1}{s-3}\right)$$

$$= \frac{1}{(s-3)^2}.$$

(b) $\mathcal{L}\{t\sin kt\} = -\dfrac{d}{ds}\mathcal{L}\{\sin kt\}$

$$= -\frac{d}{ds}\left(\frac{k}{s^2+k^2}\right)$$

$$= \frac{2ks}{(s^2+k^2)^2}$$

(c) $\mathcal{L}\{t^2\sin kt\} = \dfrac{d^2}{ds^2}\mathcal{L}\{\sin kt\}$

$$= -\frac{d}{ds}\mathcal{L}\{t\sin kt\}$$

$$= -\frac{d}{ds}\left[\frac{2ks}{(s^2+k^2)^2}\right] \qquad \text{[from part (b)]}$$

$$= -\frac{(s^2+k^2)^2 2k - 8ks^2(s^2+k^2)}{(s^2+k^2)^4}$$

$$= \frac{6ks^2 - 2k^3}{(s^2+k^2)^3}.$$

(d) $\mathcal{L}\{te^{-t}\cos t\} = -\dfrac{d}{ds}\mathcal{L}\{e^{-t}\cos t\}$

$$= -\frac{d}{ds}\mathcal{L}\{\cos t\}_{s\to s+1}$$

$$= -\frac{d}{ds}\left[\frac{s+1}{(s+1)^2+1}\right]$$

$$= \frac{(s+1)^2 - 1}{[(s+1)^2+1]^2}$$

The transform of derivatives

We shall, of course, use the Laplace transform to solve certain kinds of differential equations. To that end we need to evaluate quantities such as

$\mathcal{L}\{dy/dt\}$ and $\mathcal{L}\{d^2y/dt^2\}$. For example, if $y = f(t)$ then

$$\mathcal{L}\{f'(t)\} = \int_0^\infty e^{-st} f'(t)\, dt$$

$$= e^{-st} f(t) \Big|_0^\infty + s \int_0^\infty e^{-st} f(t)\, dt$$

$$= -f(0) + s\mathcal{L}\{f(t)\}$$

$$= sF(s) - f(0).$$

Similarly,

$$\mathcal{L}\{f''(t)\} = \int_0^\infty e^{-st} f''(t)\, dt$$

$$= e^{-st} f'(t) \Big|_0^\infty + s \int_0^\infty e^{-st} f'(t)\, dt$$

$$= -f'(0) + s\mathcal{L}\{f'(t)\}$$

$$= s[sF(s) - f(0)] - f'(0)$$

$$= s^2 F(s) - sf(0) - f'(0).$$

We state the general case in the following theorem.

THEOREM 7.8   If $f(t), f'(t), \ldots, f^{(n-1)}(t)$ are continuous for $t \geq 0$ and are of exponential order, and if $f^{(n)}(t)$ is piecewise continuous for $t \geq 0$, then

$$\mathcal{L}\{f^{(n)}(t)\} = s^n F(s) - s^{n-1} f(0) - s^{n-2} f'(0) - \cdots - f^{(n-1)}(0).$$

EXAMPLE   If $\mathcal{L}\{1\} = 1/s$, compute $\mathcal{L}\{t\}$.

Solution: Let $f(t) = t$ so that $f'(t) = 1$ and $f(0) = 0$. By Theorem 7.8 with $n = 1$ we have

$$\mathcal{L}\{1\} = s\mathcal{L}\{t\} - f(0)$$

which implies

$$\mathcal{L}\{t\} = \frac{1}{s}\mathcal{L}\{1\}$$

$$= \frac{1}{s^2}.$$

EXAMPLE   If $\mathcal{L}\{\cos t\} = s/(s^2 + 1)$, compute $\mathcal{L}\{\sin t\}$.

Solution: Let $f(t) = \cos t, \quad f'(t) = -\sin t, \quad f(0) = 1.$ Therefore from Theorem 7.8

$$\mathcal{L}\{\sin t\} = -[s\mathcal{L}\{\cos t\} - \cos 0]$$

$$= \frac{-s^2}{s^2 + 1} + 1$$

$$= \frac{1}{s^2 + 1}.$$

EXAMPLE

$$\mathcal{L}\{kt\cos kt + \sin kt\} = \mathcal{L}\left\{\frac{d}{dt}(t\sin kt)\right\}$$

$$= s\mathcal{L}\{t\sin kt\} \qquad \text{[Theorem 7.8]}$$

$$= s\left[-\frac{d}{ds}\mathcal{L}\{\sin kt\}\right] \qquad \text{[Theorem 7.7]}$$

$$= s\left[\frac{2ks}{(s^2 + k^2)^2}\right]$$

$$= \frac{2ks^2}{(s^2 + k^2)^2}.$$

EXAMPLE   Evaluate $\mathcal{L}\{\cos^2 t\}$.

Solution: Let $f(t) = \cos^2 t$ so that $f(0) = 1$ and

$$f'(t) = -2\cos t\sin t = -\sin 2t.$$

It follows from Theorem 7.8 that

$$-\mathcal{L}\{\sin 2t\} = s\mathcal{L}\{\cos^2 t\} - 1$$

or $$\mathcal{L}\{\cos^2 t\} = -\frac{1}{s}\mathcal{L}\{\sin 2t\} + \frac{1}{s}$$

$$= \frac{-2}{s(s^2 + 4)} + \frac{1}{s}$$

$$= \frac{s^2 + 2}{s(s^2 + 4)}.$$

THEOREM 7.9   Let $f(t)$ be piecewise continuous for $t \geq 0$ and of exponential order.* Then

$$\mathscr{L}\left\{\int_0^t f(\tau)\,d\tau\right\} = \frac{1}{s}\mathscr{L}\{f(t)\}$$

$$= \frac{F(s)}{s}.$$

Proof: We make use of the facts that

$$\int_0^0 f(\tau)\,d\tau = 0 \quad \text{and} \quad \frac{d}{dt}\int_0^t f(\tau)\,d\tau = f(t).$$

Now by Definition 7.1 and integration by parts we have

$$\int_0^\infty e^{-st}\left\{\int_0^t f(\tau)\,d\tau\right\} dt = \int_0^\infty e^{-st}\left\{\int_0^t f(\tau)\,d\tau\right\} dt$$

$$= -\frac{1}{s}e^{-st}\int_0^t f(\tau)\,d\tau\,\Big|_0^\infty + \frac{1}{s}\int_0^\infty e^{-st}f(t)\,dt$$

$$= \frac{1}{s}\int_0^\infty e^{-st}f(t)\,dt$$

$$= \frac{1}{s}\mathscr{L}\{f(t)\}.$$

The convolution theorem

Theorem 7.9 is a special case of the following theorem known as the **convolution theorem**.

THEOREM 7.10   Let $f(t)$ and $g(t)$ be piecewise continuous for $t \geq 0$ and of exponential order. Then

$$\mathscr{L}\left\{\int_0^t f(\tau)g(t-\tau)\,d\tau\right\} = \mathscr{L}\{f(t)\}\mathscr{L}\{g(t)\}$$

$$= F(s)G(s).$$

Proof: Let

$$F(s) = \mathscr{L}\{f(t)\} = \int_0^\infty e^{-s\tau}f(\tau)\,d\tau$$

and

$$G(s) = \mathscr{L}\{g(t)\} = \int_0^\infty e^{-s\beta}g(\beta)\,d\beta.$$

---

* It can be shown that when $f(t)$ is piecewise continuous for $t \geq 0$ and of exponential order, then $\int_0^t f(\tau)\,d\tau$ is also of exponential order.

Proceeding formally we have

$$F(s)G(s) = \left(\int_0^\infty e^{-s\tau}f(\tau)\,d\tau\right)\left(\int_0^\infty e^{-s\beta}g(\beta)\,d\beta\right)$$

$$= \int_0^\infty \int_0^\infty e^{-s(\tau+\beta)}f(\tau)g(\beta)\,d\tau\,d\beta$$

$$= \int_0^\infty f(\tau)\,d\tau \int_0^\infty e^{-s(\tau+\beta)}g(\beta)\,d\beta.$$

Holding τ fixed, we let $t = \tau + \beta$, $dt = d\beta$ so that

$$F(s)G(s) = \int_0^\infty f(\tau)\,d\tau \int_\tau^\infty e^{-st}g(t-\tau)\,dt.$$

In the $t\tau$ plane we are integrating over the shaded region in Figure 7.7. Since f and g are piecewise continuous for $t \geq 0$ and of exponential order, it can be shown that it is possible to interchange the order of integration:

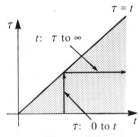

Figure 7.7

$$F(s)G(s) = \int_0^\infty e^{-st}\,dt \int_0^t f(\tau)g(t-\tau)\,d\tau$$

$$= \int_0^\infty e^{-st}\left\{\int_0^t f(\tau)g(t-\tau)\,d\tau\right\}dt$$

$$= \mathscr{L}\left\{\int_0^t f(\tau)g(t-\tau)\,d\tau\right\}.$$

The integral in Theorem 7.10 is called the **convolution** of $f(t)$ and $g(t)$, and it is commonly denoted by

$$f * g = \int_0^t f(\tau)g(t-\tau)\,d\tau.$$

We leave it as an exercise to show that $f * g = g * f$. The convolution theorem is sometimes useful in finding the inverse Laplace transform of a product of two Laplace transforms. That is, if

$$\mathscr{L}\{f * g\} = F(s)G(s)$$

then $f * g = \mathscr{L}^{-1}\{F(s)G(s)\}.$

Also, notice that Theorem 7.10 reduces to Theorem 7.9 when $g(t) = 1$ and $G(s) = 1/s$.

EXAMPLE   Evaluate $\mathscr{L}^{-1}\left\{\dfrac{1}{(s-1)(s+4)}\right\}.$

Solution: Admittedly, we could use partial fractions, but if

$$F(s) = \frac{1}{s-1} \quad \text{and} \quad G(s) = \frac{1}{s+4}$$

then

$$\mathscr{L}^{-1}\{F(s)\} = f(t) = e^t \quad \text{and} \quad \mathscr{L}^{-1}\{G(s)\} = g(t) = e^{-4t}.$$

By the convolution theorem we can write

$$\mathscr{L}^{-1}\left\{\frac{1}{(s-1)(s+4)}\right\} = \int_0^t f(\tau)g(t-\tau)\,d\tau$$

$$= \int_0^t e^\tau e^{-4(t-\tau)}\,d\tau$$

$$= e^{-4t}\int_0^t e^{5\tau}\,d\tau$$

$$= e^{-4t}\frac{1}{5}e^{5\tau}\Big|_0^t$$

$$= \frac{e^{-4t}}{5}[e^{5t} - 1]$$

$$= \frac{1}{5}e^t - \frac{1}{5}e^{-4t}$$

EXAMPLE

Evaluate $\mathscr{L}^{-1}\left\{\dfrac{1}{(s^2+k^2)^2}\right\}$.

Solution: Let

$$F(s) = G(s) = \frac{1}{s^2+k^2}$$

so that

$$f(t) = g(t) = \frac{1}{k}\,\mathscr{L}^{-1}\left\{\frac{k}{s^2+k^2}\right\}$$

$$= \frac{1}{k}\sin kt.$$

Thus

$$\mathscr{L}^{-1}\left\{\frac{1}{(s^2+k^2)^2}\right\} = \frac{1}{k^2}\int_0^t \sin k\tau \sin k(t-\tau)\,d\tau.$$

Now recall from trigonometry that

$$\cos(A+B) = \cos A \cos B - \sin A \sin B$$

and

$$\cos(A-B) = \cos A \cos B + \sin A \sin B.$$

Subtracting the first from the second gives the identity

$$\sin A \sin B = \tfrac{1}{2}[\cos(A - B) - \cos(A + B)].$$

If we set $A = k\tau$ and $B = k(t - \tau)$, it follows that

$$\mathcal{L}^{-1}\left\{\frac{1}{(s^2 + k^2)^2}\right\} = \frac{1}{2k^2}\int_0^t [\cos k(2\tau - t) - \cos kt]\,d\tau$$

$$= \frac{1}{2k^2}\left[\frac{1}{2k}\sin k(2\tau - t) - \tau \cos kt\right]_0^t$$

$$= \frac{1}{2k^2}\left[\frac{1}{2k}\sin kt - \frac{1}{2k}\sin(-kt) - t\cos kt\right]$$

$$= \frac{\sin kt - kt\cos kt}{2k^3}.$$

EXERCISES 7.2

Answers to odd-numbered problems begin on page A-20 of the Appendix. In Problems 1–31 find either $F(s)$ or $f(t)$ as indicated.

1. $\mathcal{L}\{te^{10t}\}$

2. $\mathcal{L}\{t^{10}e^{-7t}\}$

3. $\mathcal{L}\{e^t \sin 3t\}$

4. $\mathcal{L}\{e^{2t}(t - 1)^2\}$

5. $\mathcal{L}\{e^{5t} \sinh 3t\}$

★6. $\mathcal{L}\{e^{-t} \cos^2 t\}$

7. $\mathcal{L}^{-1}\left\{\dfrac{1}{(s + 2)^3}\right\}$

8. $\mathcal{L}^{-1}\left\{\dfrac{1}{s^2 + 2s + 5}\right\}$

9. $\mathcal{L}^{-1}\left\{\dfrac{s}{s^2 + 4s + 5}\right\}$

★10. $\mathcal{L}^{-1}\left\{\dfrac{2s + 5}{s^2 + 6s + 34}\right\}$

11. $\mathcal{L}^{-1}\left\{\dfrac{2s - 1}{s^2(s + 1)^3}\right\}$

12. $\mathcal{L}^{-1}\left\{\dfrac{(s + 1)^2}{(s + 2)^4}\right\}$

13. $\mathcal{L}^{-1}\left\{\dfrac{s}{(s + 1)^2}\right\}$

14. $\mathcal{L}\left\{\displaystyle\int_0^t \tau \sin \tau\,d\tau\right\}$

15. $\mathcal{L}\left\{\displaystyle\int_0^t e^{-\tau} \cos \tau\,d\tau\right\}$

★16. $\mathcal{L}\left\{t\displaystyle\int_0^t \tau e^{-\tau}\,d\tau\right\}$

17. $\mathcal{L}\{e^{2-t}\mathcal{U}(t - 2)\}$

18. $\mathcal{L}\{\sin t\,\mathcal{U}(t - 2\pi)\}$

19. $\mathcal{L}\{t\mathcal{U}(t - 1)\}$

20. $\mathcal{L}\{(t - 1)e^{t-1}\mathcal{U}(t - 1)\}$

21. $\mathcal{L}^{-1}\left\{\dfrac{e^{-2s}}{s^3}\right\}$

22. $\mathcal{L}^{-1}\left\{\dfrac{se^{-\pi s/2}}{s^2 + 4}\right\}$

23. $\mathcal{L}\{t \cos 2t\}$

★24. $\mathcal{L}\{t \sin t \cos t\}$

25. $\mathcal{L}\{t^2 \sinh t\}$

26. $\mathcal{L}\{t \sin^2 t\}$

27. $\mathcal{L}\{t(e^t + e^{2t})^2\}$

★28. $\mathcal{L}\{te^{2t} \sin 6t\}$

29. $\mathcal{L}\{\sin 4t \cos 4t\}$ **30.** $\mathcal{L}^{-1}\left\{\dfrac{s}{(s^2 + 1)^2}\right\}$

31. $\mathcal{L}^{-1}\left\{\dfrac{s + 1}{(s^2 + 2s + 2)^2}\right\}$

In Problems 32–37 use Theorem 7.10 to find $f(t)$.

★32. $\mathcal{L}^{-1}\left\{\dfrac{1}{s(s + 1)}\right\}$ **33.** $\mathcal{L}^{-1}\left\{\dfrac{1}{(s + 1)(s - 2)}\right\}$

34. $\mathcal{L}^{-1}\left\{\dfrac{1}{(s + 1)^2}\right\}$ **35.** $\mathcal{L}^{-1}\left\{\dfrac{1}{s(s^2 + 1)}\right\}$

36. $\mathcal{L}^{-1}\left\{\dfrac{1}{(s^2 + 1)(s^2 + 4)}\right\}$ **37.** $\mathcal{L}^{-1}\left\{\dfrac{s}{(s^2 + 4)^2}\right\}$

·★38. Sketch the graph of the function

$$f(t) = \mathcal{L}^{-1}\left\{\frac{2}{s} - \frac{3e^{-s}}{s^2} + \frac{5e^{-2s}}{s^2}\right\}$$

In Problems 39–41 use Theorem 7.7 in the form $(n = 1)$

$$f(t) = -\frac{1}{t}\mathcal{L}^{-1}\left\{\frac{d}{ds}F(s)\right\}$$

to evaluate the given inverse Laplace transformations.

EXAMPLE   Evaluate $\mathcal{L}^{-1}\left\{\tan^{-1}\dfrac{1}{s}\right\}$.

Solution:

$$f(t) = -\frac{1}{t}\mathcal{L}^{-1}\left\{\frac{d}{ds}\tan^{-1}\frac{1}{s}\right\}$$

$$= -\frac{1}{t}\mathcal{L}^{-1}\left\{\frac{1}{1 + (1/s)^2}\cdot(-s^{-2})\right\}$$

$$= -\frac{1}{t}\mathcal{L}^{-1}\left\{\frac{-1}{s^2 + 1}\right\}$$

$$= \frac{\sin t}{t}.$$

---

39. $\mathcal{L}^{-1}\left\{\ln\dfrac{s - 3}{s + 1}\right\}$ **40.** $\mathcal{L}^{-1}\left\{\ln\dfrac{s^2 + 1}{s^2 + 4}\right\}$

41. $\mathscr{L}^{-1}\left\{\dfrac{\pi}{2} - \tan^{-1}\dfrac{s}{2}\right\}$

42. If $f(t)$ is piecewise continuous and of exponential order and $\lim_{t\to 0} + \dfrac{f(t)}{t}$ exists, show that

$$\mathscr{L}\left\{\frac{f(t)}{t}\right\} = \int_s^\infty F(s)\,ds,$$

where $F(s) = \mathscr{L}\{f(t)\}$.

43. Use the results of Problem 42 to evaluate

$$\mathscr{L}\left\{\frac{e^t - e^{-t}}{t\cdot}\right\}.$$

★44. Show that $f * g = g * f$, that is,

$$\int_0^t f(\tau)g(t-\tau)\,d\tau = \int_0^t g(\tau)f(t-\tau)\,d\tau.$$

45. Find the Laplace transform of
(a) $e^{2t} * \sin t$
(b) $t^2 * t^4$
(c) $e^{-t} * e^t \cos t$

46. If $a > 0$ show that

$$\mathscr{L}\{f(at)\} = \frac{1}{a}F\left(\frac{s}{a}\right).$$

47. If $f(t)$ is a periodic function of period T show that

$$\mathscr{L}\{f(t)\} = \frac{1}{1 - e^{-sT}}\int_0^T e^{-st}f(t)\,dt.$$

48. Use the result of Problem 47 to find the Laplace transform of

$$f(t) = \begin{cases} 2, & 0 \leqslant t < 3/2 \\ 0, & 3/2 \leqslant t < 3, \end{cases} \quad f(t+3) = f(t).$$

In Problems 49–51 write the given function in terms of unit step functions. Find the Laplace transform of each function.

49. $f(t) = \begin{cases} 0, & 0 \leq t < 1, \\ t^2, & t \geq 1. \end{cases}$

★50. $f(t) = \begin{cases} 0, & 0 \leq t < \dfrac{3\pi}{2} \\ \sin t, & t \geq \dfrac{3\pi}{2} \end{cases}$

51. $f(t) = \begin{cases} 0, & 0 \leq t < 2, \\ e^t, & t \geq 2 \end{cases}$

7.3   Applications

Since $\mathcal{L}\{y^{(n)}(t)\}, n > 1$, depends on $y(t)$ and $n - 1$ derivatives at $t = 0$, the Laplace transform is ideally suited to initial-value problems for linear differential equations with constant coefficients. This particular kind of differential equation can be reduced to an algebraic equation in the transformed function $Y(s) = \mathcal{L}\{y(t)\}$.

EXAMPLE

Solve
$$y'' - 6y' + 9y = t^2 e^{3t}$$
subject to $y(0) = 2$ and $y'(0) = 6$.

Solution: By the linearity property of the transform we can write
$$\mathcal{L}\{y''\} - 6\mathcal{L}\{y'\} + 9\mathcal{L}\{y\} = \mathcal{L}\{t^2 e^{3t}\}$$
or
$$s^2 Y(s) - sy(0) - y'(0) - 6[sY(s) - y(0)] + 9Y(s) = \frac{2}{(s-3)^3}.$$

Using the initial conditions and simplifying then gives
$$(s^2 - 6s + 9)Y(s) = 2s - 6 + \frac{2}{(s-3)^3}$$
$$(s-3)^2 Y(s) = 2(s-3) + \frac{2}{(s-3)^3}$$
$$Y(s) = \frac{2}{s-3} + \frac{2}{(s-3)^5}.$$

Thus
$$y(t) = 2\mathcal{L}^{-1}\left\{\frac{1}{s-3}\right\} + \frac{2}{4!}\mathcal{L}^{-1}\left\{\frac{4!}{(s-3)^5}\right\}$$
$$= 2e^{3t} + \frac{1}{12}t^4 e^{3t}.$$

EXAMPLE

Solve
$$y'' + 4y' + 6y = 1 + e^{-t}$$
subject to $y(0) = 0$ and $y'(0) = 0$.

Solution:

$$\mathscr{L}\{y''\} + 4\mathscr{L}\{y'\} + 6\mathscr{L}\{y\} = \mathscr{L}\{1\} + \mathscr{L}\{e^{-t}\}$$

$$s^2 Y(s) - sy(0) - y'(0) + 4[sY(s) - y(0)] + 6Y(s) = \frac{1}{s} + \frac{1}{s+1}$$

$$(s^2 + 4s + 6)Y(s) = \frac{2s+1}{s(s+1)}$$

$$Y(s) = \frac{2s+1}{s(s+1)(s^2+4s+6)}.$$

By partial fractions:

$$\frac{2s+1}{s(s+1)(s^2+4s+6)} = \frac{A}{s} + \frac{B}{s+1} + \frac{Cs+D}{s^2+4s+6},$$

which implies

$$2s + 1 = A(s+1)(s^2+4s+6) + Bs(s^2+4s+6) + (Cs+D)s(s+1).$$

Setting $s = 0$ and $s = -1$ gives, respectively, $A = 1/6$ and $B = 1/3$. Equating the coefficients of s^3 and s gives

$$A + B + C = 0$$

$$10A + 6B + D = 2,$$

so it follows that $C = -1/2$ and $D = -5/3$. Thus,

$$Y(s) = \frac{1/6}{s} + \frac{1/3}{s+1} + \frac{-s/2 - 5/3}{s^2+4s+6}$$

$$= \frac{1/6}{s} + \frac{1/3}{s+1} + \frac{-1/2(s+2) - 2/3}{(s+2)^2 + 2}$$

$$= \frac{1/6}{s} + \frac{1/3}{s+1} - \frac{1}{2}\frac{s+2}{(s+2)^2+2} - \frac{2}{3}\frac{1}{(s+2)^2+2}$$

and therefore

$$y(t) = \frac{1}{6}\mathscr{L}^{-1}\left\{\frac{1}{s}\right\} + \frac{1}{3}\mathscr{L}^{-1}\left\{\frac{1}{s+1}\right\} - \frac{1}{2}\mathscr{L}^{-1}\left\{\frac{s+2}{(s+2)^2+2}\right\}$$

$$- \frac{2}{3\sqrt{2}}\mathscr{L}^{-1}\left\{\frac{\sqrt{2}}{(s+2)^2+2}\right\}$$

$$= \frac{1}{6} + \frac{1}{3}e^{-t} - \frac{1}{2}e^{-2t}\cos\sqrt{2}t - \frac{\sqrt{2}}{3}e^{-2t}\sin\sqrt{2}t.$$

EXAMPLE   Solve
$$x'' + 16x = \cos 4t$$
subject to $x(0) = 0$ and $x'(0) = 1$.

Solution: Recall that this initial value problem could describe the forced, undamped, and resonant motion of a mass on a spring. The mass starts with an initial velocity of one foot per second in the downward direction from the equilibrium position. Now, one could readily solve this problem by, say, variation of parameters, but the use of Laplace transforms obviates the necessity of determining the constants which would naturally occur in the general solution $x = x_c(t) + x_p(t)$.
Transforming the equation gives

$$(s^2 + 16)X(s) = 1 + \frac{s}{s^2 + 16}$$

$$X(s) = \frac{1}{s^2 + 16} + \frac{s}{(s^2 + 16)^2}$$

so that

$$x(t) = \frac{1}{4}\mathscr{L}^{-1}\left\{\frac{4}{s^2 + 16}\right\} + \frac{1}{8}\mathscr{L}^{-1}\left\{\frac{8s}{(s^2 + 16)^2}\right\}$$

$$= \frac{1}{4}\sin 4t + \frac{1}{8}t \sin 4t.$$

EXAMPLE   Solve
$$x'' + 16x = f(t)$$
where

$$f(t) = \begin{cases} \cos 4t, & 0 \le t < \pi, \\ 0, & t \ge \pi, \end{cases}$$

and $x(0) = 0$, $x'(0) = 1$.

Solution: The function $f(t)$ can be interpreted as an external force which is acting on a mechanical system only for a very short period of time and then is removed. While this problem could be solved by conventional means, the procedure is not at all convenient when $f(t)$ is defined in a piecewise manner.

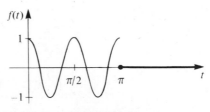

Figure 7.8

Since we can write

$$f(t) = \cos 4t - \cos 4t\, \mathscr{U}(t - \pi)$$

$$= \cos 4t - \cos 4(t - \pi)\, \mathscr{U}(t - \pi) \quad [\text{by periodicity of the cosine}]$$

it follows that

$$\mathscr{L}\{x''\} + 16\mathscr{L}\{x\} = \mathscr{L}\{f(t)\}$$

$$s^2 X(s) - sx(0) - x'(0) + 16X(s) = \frac{s}{s^2 + 16} - \frac{s}{s^2 + 16}e^{-\pi s}$$

$$(s^2 + 16)X(s) = 1 + \frac{s}{s + 16} - \frac{s}{s^2 + 16}e^{-\pi s}$$

$$X(s) = \frac{1}{s^2 + 16} + \frac{s}{(s^2 + 16)^2} - \frac{s}{(s^2 + 16)^2}e^{-\pi s}.$$

Thus

$$x(t) = \frac{1}{4}\mathscr{L}^{-1}\left\{\frac{4}{s^2 + 16}\right\} + \frac{1}{8}\mathscr{L}^{-1}\left\{\frac{8s}{(s^2 + 16)^2}\right\} - \frac{1}{8}\mathscr{L}^{-1}\left\{\frac{8s}{(s^2 + 1)^2}e^{-\pi s}\right\}$$

$$= \frac{1}{4}\sin 4t + \frac{1}{8}t\sin 4t - \frac{1}{8}(t - \pi)\sin 4(t - \pi)\,\mathscr{U}(t - \pi).$$

We have

$$x(t) = \begin{cases} \dfrac{1}{4}\sin 4t + \dfrac{1}{8}t\sin 4t, & 0 \le t < \pi \\[2mm] \dfrac{2 + \pi}{8}\sin 4t, & t \ge \pi. \end{cases}$$

The graph of $x(t)$ is given in Figure 7.9. Notice that the amplitudes of vibration become steady as soon as the external force is turned off.

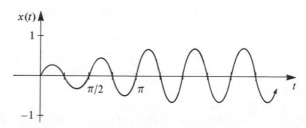

Figure 7.9

An integrodifferential equation

In a single loop or series circuit, *Kirchoff's second law* states that the sum of the voltage drops across an inductor, resistor, and capacitor is equal to the impressed voltage $E(t)$. Now it is known (see Section 1.3) that the

$$\text{voltage drop across the inductor} = L\frac{di}{dt},$$

$$\text{voltage drop across the resistor} = Ri(t),$$

$$\text{voltage drop across the capacitor} = \frac{1}{C}\int_0^t i(\tau)\,d\tau,$$

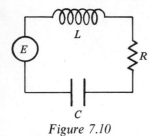

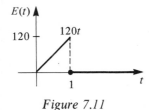

Figure 7.10

where $i(t)$ is the current and L, R, and C are constants. It follows that the current in a circuit, such as that shown in Figure 7.10, is governed by the **integrodifferential equation**

$$L\frac{di}{dt} + Ri + \frac{1}{C}\int_0^t i(\tau)\,d\tau = E(t). \tag{1}$$

EXAMPLE

Determine the current $i(t)$ in a single loop L–R–C circuit when $L = 0.1$ henry, $R = 20$ ohms, $C = 10^{-3}$ farads, $i(0) = 0$, and if the impressed voltage $E(t)$ is as given in Figure 7.11.

Figure 7.11

Solution: Since the voltage is off for $t \geq 1$, we can write

$$E(t) = 120t - 120t\,\mathcal{U}(t - 1). \tag{2}$$

But, in order to use the second translation theorem, we must rewrite (2) as

$$E(t) = 120t - 120(t - 1)\mathcal{U}(t - 1) - 120\mathcal{U}(t - 1) \tag{3}$$

Equation (1) then becomes

$$0.1\frac{di}{dt} + 20i + 10^3\int_0^t i(\tau)\,d\tau = 120t - 120(t - 1)\mathcal{U}(t - 1) - 120\mathcal{U}(t - 1). \tag{4}$$

Now recall from Theorem 7.9 that

$$\mathscr{L}\left\{\int_0^t i(\tau)\,d\tau\right\} = I(s)/s$$

where $I(s) = \mathscr{L}\{i(t)\}$. Thus, the transform of equation (4) is

$$0.1sI(s) + 20I(s) + \frac{10^3}{s}I(s) = 120\left[\frac{1}{s^2} - \frac{1}{s^2}e^{-s} - \frac{1}{s}e^{-s}\right], \tag{5}$$

or after multiplying by 10s,

$$(s + 100)^2 I(s) = 1200\left[\frac{1}{s} - \frac{1}{s}e^{-s} - e^{-s}\right]$$

$$I(s) = 1200\left[\frac{1}{s(s + 100)^2} - \frac{1}{s(s + 100)^2}e^{-s} - \frac{1}{(s + 100)^2}e^{-s}\right].$$

By partial fractions we can write

$$I(s) = 1200\left[\frac{1/10,000}{s} - \frac{1/10,000}{s + 100} - \frac{1/100}{(s + 100)^2}\right.$$

$$- \frac{1/10,000}{s}e^{-s} + \frac{1/10,000}{s + 100}e^{-s} + \frac{1/100}{(s + 100)^2}e^{-s}$$

$$\left. - \frac{1}{(s + 100)^2}e^{-s}\right]$$

from which it follows

$$i(t) = \tfrac{3}{25}[1 - \mathcal{U}(t - 1)] - \tfrac{3}{25}[e^{-100t} - e^{-100(t - 1)}\mathcal{U}(t - 1)]$$

$$- 12te^{-100t} - 1188(t - 1)e^{-100(t - 1)}\mathcal{U}(t - 1).$$

In some circumstances the Laplace transform can be used to solve equations with variable coefficients. However, in this case the transform of the equation does not result in an algebraic expression, but rather in another differential equation in the transformed function $Y(s)$.

EXAMPLE   Solve $ty''(t) + 2(t - 1)y'(t) - 2y(t) = 0$

subject to $y(0) = 0$.

Solution: Since $y'(0)$ is not specified, we expect the solution to contain an arbitrary constant. From Theorem 7.7 we know that

$$\mathcal{L}\{tf(t)\} = -\frac{d}{ds}\mathcal{L}\{f(t)\}$$

from which it follows

$$\mathcal{L}\{ty'(t)\} = -\frac{d}{ds}\mathcal{L}\{y'(t)\}$$

$$= -\frac{d}{ds}[sY(s) - y(0)]$$

$$= -s\frac{dY}{ds} - Y$$

and
$$\mathscr{L}\{ty''(t)\} = -\frac{d}{ds}\mathscr{L}\{y''(t)\}$$

$$= -\frac{d}{ds}[s^2 Y(s) - sy(0) - y'(0)]$$

$$= -s^2\frac{dY}{ds} - 2sY + y(0).$$

Using $y(0) = 0$ we have

$$\mathscr{L}\{ty''\} + 2\mathscr{L}\{ty'\} - 2\mathscr{L}\{y'\} - 2\mathscr{L}\{y\} = \mathscr{L}\{0\}$$

$$-s^2\frac{dY}{ds} - 2sY - 2s\frac{dY}{ds} - 2Y - 2sY - 2Y = 0$$

$$(s^2 + 2s)\frac{dY}{ds} + (4s + 4)Y = 0.$$

This latter equation is separable, so we write

$$\frac{dY}{Y} + \frac{4s + 4}{s(s + 2)}ds = 0$$

$$\frac{dY}{Y} + \left[\frac{2}{s} + \frac{2}{s + 2}\right]ds = 0.$$

Integrating the last equation gives

$$\ln Y + 2\ln s + 2\ln(s + 2) = \ln c$$

$$\ln[s^2(s + 2)^2 Y] = \ln c$$

$$Y = \frac{c}{s^2(s + 2)^2}.$$

By partial fractions:

$$Y = c\left[\frac{-1/4}{s} + \frac{1/4}{s^2} + \frac{1/4}{s + 2} + \frac{1/4}{(s + 2)^2}\right].$$

The common factor of 1/4 can, of course, be absorbed in the arbitrary constant. Writing c_1 for $c/4$ we obtain

$$y(t) = c_1[-1 + t + e^{-2t} + te^{-2t}].$$

However, the Laplace transform does not provide a general method for solving differential equations with variable coefficients.

EXERCISES 7.3   Answers to odd-numbered problems begin on page A-21 of the Appendix. Use the Laplace transform to solve Problems 1–12.

 1. $y'' + 5y' + 4y = 0$, $y(0) = 1$, $y'(0) = 0$

 2. $y'' - 6y' + 13y = 0$, $y(0) = 0$, $y'(0) = -3$

 3. $y'' - 6y' + 9y = t$, $y(0) = 0$, $y'(0) = 1$

★4. $y'' - 4y' + 4y = t^3$, $y(0) = 1$, $y'(0) = 0$

 5. $y'' - 4y' + 4y = t^3 e^{2t}$, $y(0) = 0$, $y'(0) = 0$

 6. $y'' - 2y' + 5y = 1 + t$, $y(0) = 0$, $y'(0) = 4$

 7. $y'' + y = \sin t$, $y(0) = 1$, $y'(0) = -1$

 8. $y'' + 16y = 1$, $y(0) = 1$, $y'(0) = 2$

 9. $y'' - y' = e^t \cos t$, $y(0) = 0$, $y'(0) = 0$

★10. $2y''' + 3y'' - 3y' - 2y = e^{-t}$, $y(0) = 0$, $y'(0) = 0$, $y''(0) = 1$

11. $y^{(4)} - y = 0$, $y(0) = 1$, $y'(0) = 0$, $y''(0) = -1$, $y'''(0) = 0$

12. $y^{(4)} - y = t$, $y(0) = 0$, $y'(0) = 0$, $y''(0) = 0$, $y'''(0) = 0$

In Problems 13–16 use the Laplace transform and Theorem 7.7 to find a solution of the given equation.

13. $ty'' - y' = t^2$, $y(0) = 0$

14. $ty'' + 2ty' + 2y = 0$, $y(0) = 0$

15. $ty'' + y' + ty = 0$ [*Hint:* Expand $[1 + 1/s^2]^{-1/2}$ by the binomial theorem.]

16. $ty'' + (t + 2)y' + y = -1$, $y(0) = 0$

17. Determine whether a Laplace transform could be used to solve a Cauchy–Euler equation such as $t^2 y'' - 2ty' + 2y = 0$.

In Problems 18–22 use the Laplace transform to solve the given equation.

EXAMPLE   Solve

$$y' + 2y = f(t)$$

where

$$f(t) = \begin{cases} 2, & 0 \le t < 1 \\ 0, & t \ge 1 \end{cases}$$

and $y(0) = 1$.

Solution: By the usual operational properties, the transformation of the left-hand side of the equation is

$$sY(s) - y(0) + 2Y(s) = (s + 2)Y(s) - 1.$$

Whereas to transform the right-hand side, we use Definition 7.1

$$\mathcal{L}\{f(t)\} = \int_0^\infty e^{-st} f(t)\, dt$$

$$= 2 \int_0^1 e^{-st}\, dt$$

$$= -2 \frac{e^{-st}}{s} \Big|_0^1$$

$$= \frac{2}{s}[1 - e^{-s}].$$

Hence the differential equation becomes

$$(s + 2)Y(s) - 1 = \frac{2}{s}[1 - e^{-s}]$$

$$Y(s) = \frac{2}{s(s + 2)}[1 - e^{-s}] + \frac{1}{s + 2}$$

$$= \left[\frac{1}{s} - \frac{1}{s + 2}\right][1 - e^{-s}] + \frac{1}{s + 2}$$

$$= \frac{1}{s} - \frac{1}{s}e^{-s} + \frac{1}{s + 2}e^{-s}.$$

Thus from the second translation theorem it follows that

$$y(t) = \mathcal{L}^{-1}\left\{\frac{1}{s}\right\} - \mathcal{L}^{-1}\left\{\frac{1}{s}e^{-s}\right\} + \mathcal{L}^{-1}\left\{\frac{1}{s + 2}e^{-s}\right\}$$

$$= 1 - \mathcal{U}(t - 1) + e^{-2(t-1)}\mathcal{U}(t - 1)$$

$$= \begin{cases} 1, & 0 \le t < 1 \\ e^{-2(t-1)}, & t \ge 1. \end{cases}$$

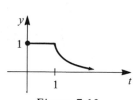

Figure 7.12   The graph of $y(t)$ is given in Figure 7.12.

18. $y' + y = f(t)$ where $f(t) = \begin{cases} 1, & 0 \le t < 1 \\ -1, & t \ge 1 \end{cases}$, $y(0) = 0$

19. $y' + 2y = f(t)$ where $f(t) = \begin{cases} t, & 0 \le t < 1 \\ 0, & t \ge 1 \end{cases}$, $y(0) = 0$

20. $y'' + 4y = f(t)$ where $f(t) = \begin{cases} 1, & 0 \le t < 1 \\ 0, & t \ge 1 \end{cases}$, $y(0) = 0$, $y'(0) = -1$

21. $y'' + 4y = f(t)$ where $f(t) = \sin t\, \mathcal{U}(t - 2\pi)$, $y(0) = 1$, $y'(0) = 0$

★22. $y'' - 5y' + 6y = \mathcal{U}(t - 1)$, $y(0) = 0$, $y'(0) = 1$

In Problems 23–30 use Theorem 7.10 to solve the given integral equations for $f(t)$.

EXAMPLE   Solve for $f(t)$

$$f(t) = 3t^2 - e^{-t} - \int_0^t f(\tau)e^{t-\tau}\,d\tau.$$

Solution: It follows from the convolution theorem that

$$\mathscr{L}\{f(t)\} = 3\mathscr{L}\{t^2\} - \mathscr{L}\{e^{-t}\} - \mathscr{L}\{f(t)\}\mathscr{L}\{e^t\}$$

$$F(s) = 3\cdot\frac{2}{s^3} - \frac{1}{s+1} - F(s)\cdot\frac{1}{s-1}$$

$$\left[1 + \frac{1}{s-1}\right]F(s) = \frac{6}{s^3} - \frac{1}{s+1}$$

$$\frac{s}{s-1}F(s) = \frac{6}{s^3} - \frac{1}{s+1}$$

$$F(s) = \frac{6(s-1)}{s^4} - \frac{s-1}{s(s+1)}$$

$$= \frac{6}{s^3} - \frac{6}{s^4} + \frac{1}{s} - \frac{2}{s+1} \quad\text{[termwise division}$$

$$\text{and partial functions].}$$

Therefore,

$$f(t) = 3\mathscr{L}^{-1}\left\{\frac{2}{s^3}\right\} - \mathscr{L}^{-1}\left\{\frac{6}{s^4}\right\} + \mathscr{L}^{-1}\left\{\frac{1}{s}\right\} - 2\mathscr{L}^{-1}\left\{\frac{1}{s+1}\right\}$$

$$= 3t^2 - t^3 + 1 - 2e^{-t}.$$

23. $f(t) + \displaystyle\int_0^t (t-\tau)f(\tau)\,d\tau = t$

24. $f(t) = 2t - 4\displaystyle\int_0^t \sin\tau f(t-\tau)\,d\tau$

25. $f(t) = te^t + \displaystyle\int_0^t \tau f(t-\tau)\,d\tau$

26. $f(t) + 2\displaystyle\int_0^t f(\tau)\cos(t-\tau)\,d\tau = 4e^{-t} + \sin t$

27. $f(t) + \displaystyle\int_0^t f(\tau)\,d\tau = 1$

28. $f(t) = \cos t + \int_0^t e^{-\tau} f(t - \tau) d\tau$

29. $f(t) = 1 + t - \dfrac{8}{3} \int_0^t (\tau - t)^3 f(\tau) d\tau$

★30. $t - 2f(t) = \int_0^t (e^\tau - e^{-\tau}) f(t - \tau) d\tau$

31. Solve the integrodifferential equation

$$y'(t) = 1 - \sin t - \int_0^t y(\tau) d\tau, \quad y(0) = 0.$$

32. The current $i(t)$ in a series circuit is given by

$$0.005 \frac{di}{dt} + i + 50 \int_0^t i(\tau) d\tau = 100[1 - \mathcal{U}(t - 1)].$$

Use Laplace transforms to solve for $i(t)$ if $i(0) = 0$.

33. Recall that the differential equation for the current $i(t)$ in a series circuit containing an inductor and a resistor is

$$L \frac{di}{dt} + Ri = E(t),$$

where $E(t)$ is the impressed voltage (see Section 3.2). Use the Laplace transform to determine the current $i(t)$ when $L = 1$ henry, $R = 10$ ohms,

$$E(t) = \begin{cases} \sin t, & 0 \le t < \dfrac{3\pi}{2} \\[2mm] 0, & t \ge \dfrac{3\pi}{2} \end{cases}$$

and $i(0) = 0$.

34. Recall that when a series circuit contains an inductor, resistor, and a capacitor, the differential equation for the instantaneous charge $q(t)$ on the capacitor is given by

$$L \frac{d^2 q}{dt^2} + R \frac{dq}{dt} + \frac{1}{C} q = E(t),$$

(see Section 5.4). Use the Laplace transform to determine $q(t)$ when $L = 1$ henry, $R = 20$ ohms, $C = 0.005$ farad, $E(t) = 150$ volts, $t > 0$, and $q(0) = 0$, $i(0) = 0$. What is the current $i(t)$? What is the charge $q(t)$ if the same constant voltage is turned off for $t \ge 2$?

35. Determine the charge $q(t)$ and current $i(t)$ for a series circuit in which $L = 1$ henry, $R = 20$ ohms, $C = 0.01$ farad, $E(t) = 120 \sin 10t$ volts, $q(0) = 0$, and $i(0) = 0$. What is the steady-state current?

★**36.** Suppose a 32-lb weight stretches a spring 2 ft. If the weight is released from rest at the equilibrium position, determine the equation of a motion if an impressed force $f(t) = \sin t$ acts on the system for $0 \le t < 2\pi$ and is then removed. Ignore any damping forces. [*Hint:* Write the impressed force in terms of the unit step function.]

37. A 4-lb weight stretches a spring 2 ft. The weight is released from rest 18 in. above the equilibrium position, and the resulting motion takes place in a medium offering a damping force numerically equal to 7/8 times the instantaneous velocity. Use the Laplace transform to determine the equation of motion.

38. A 16-lb weight is attached to a spring whose constant is $k = 4.5$ lb/ft. Beginning at $t = 0$, a force equal to $f(t) = 4 \sin 3t + 2 \cos 3t$ acts on the system. Assuming that no damping forces are present, use the Laplace transform to find the equation of motion if the weight is released from rest from the equilibrium position.

CHAPTER SUMMARY

The **Laplace transform** of a function $f(t)$, $t \ge 0$, is defined by the integral

$$\mathscr{L}\{f(t)\} = \int_0^\infty e^{-st} f(t) \, dt = F(s).$$

The parameter s is usually restricted in such a manner to guarantee convergence of the integral. When applied to a linear equation with constant coefficients such as $ay'' + by' + cy = g(t)$ there results an algebraic equation

$$a[s^2 Y(s) - sy(0) - y'(0)] + b[sY(s) - y(0)] + cY(s) = G(s)$$

which depends on the initial conditions $y(0)$ and $y'(0)$. When these values are known, we determine $y(t)$ by evaluating $y(t) = \mathscr{L}^{-1}\{Y(s)\}$.

The following tables summarize all of the basic results obtained in this chapter.

Table I. Transforms of Some Basic Functions

$f(t)$	$\mathscr{L}\{f(t)\} = F(s)$
1. 1	$\dfrac{1}{s}$
2. $t^n, \quad n = 1, 2, 3, \ldots$	$\dfrac{n!}{s^{n+1}}$
3. e^{at}	$\dfrac{1}{s-a}$
4. $\sin kt$	$\dfrac{k}{s^2 + k^2}$
5. $\cos kt$	$\dfrac{s}{s^2 + k^2}$

Table I.   *continued*

$f(t)$	$\mathscr{L}\{f(t)\} = F(s)$
6. $\sinh kt$	$\dfrac{k}{s^2 - k^2}$
7. $\cosh kt$	$\dfrac{s}{s^2 - k^2}$

Table II.   Operational Properties

8. $e^{at} f(t)$	$F(s - a)$
9. $f(t - a)\mathscr{U}(t - a),\ a > 0$	$e^{-as} F(s)$
10. $t^n f(t),\quad n = 1, 2, 3, \ldots$	$(-1)^n \dfrac{d^n}{ds^n} F(s)$
11. $f^{(n)}(t),\quad n = 1, 2, 3, \ldots$	$s^n F(s) - s^{n-1} f(0) - \cdots - f^{(n-1)}(0)$
12. $\displaystyle\int_0^t f(\tau)\,d\tau$	$\dfrac{F(s)}{s}$
13. $\displaystyle\int_0^t f(\tau) g(t - \tau)\,d\tau$	$F(s)G(s)$

Table III.   Some Consequences of Tables I and II

14. $t^n e^{at},\quad n = 1, 2, 3, \ldots$	$\dfrac{n!}{(s - a)^{n+1}}$
15. $e^{at} \sin kt$	$\dfrac{k}{(s - a)^2 + k^2}$
16. $e^{at} \cos kt$	$\dfrac{s - a}{(s - a)^2 + k^2}$
17. $t \sin kt$	$\dfrac{2ks}{(s^2 + k^2)^2}$
18. $t \cos kt$	$\dfrac{s^2 - k^2}{(s^2 + k^2)^2}$
19. $\sin kt - kt \cos kt$	$\dfrac{2k^3}{(s^2 + k^2)^2}$
20. $\sin kt + kt \cos kt$	$\dfrac{2ks^2}{(s^2 + k^2)^2}$

REVIEW EXERCISES

[7.1]   Answers to odd-numbered problems begin on page A-22 of the Appendix. In Problems 1–3 use Definition 7.1 to find the Laplace transform of the given function.

1. $f(t) = (t - 1)^2$

2. $f(t) = \begin{cases} 0, & 0 \le t < 2 \\ 1, & 2 \le t < 4 \\ 0, & t \ge 4 \end{cases}$

3. $f(t) = \begin{cases} t, & 0 \le t < 1 \\ 2 - t, & t \ge 1 \end{cases}$

[7.2]   In Problems 4–13 evaluate the given by any means.

4. $\mathcal{L}\{(2t - 5)^2\}$

5. $\mathcal{L}\{\sin 8t - te^{3t} + 4t^2 e^{-2t}\}$

★6. $\mathcal{L}\{te^{t/2} \cosh 2t\}$

7. $\mathcal{L}\{e^{(t-3)}\mathcal{U}(t - 3)\}$

8. $\mathcal{L}^{-1}\left\{\dfrac{2}{s^3} - \dfrac{2}{s^3}e^{-s}\right\}$

9. $\mathcal{L}^{-1}\left\{\dfrac{s}{s^2 - 6s + 25}\right\}$

10. $\mathcal{L}^{-1}\left\{\dfrac{s}{(s - 2)(s^2 + 3s - 10)}\right\}$

11. $\mathcal{L}^{-1}\{\cot^{-1}(s + 4)\}$

★12. $\mathcal{L}^{-1}\left\{\dfrac{1}{(s^2 + 1)^2}\right\}$

13. $\mathcal{L}\{\sin^2 t \cos t\}$

[7.3]   In Problems 14–18 use the Laplace transform to solve the given equation.

14. $y'' - 8y' + 20y = te^t$, $y(0) = 0$, $y'(0) = 0$

15. $y'' - 2y' + y = e^t$, $y(0) = 0$, $y'(0) = 5$

★16. $f(t) = 1 - 2\displaystyle\int_0^t e^{-3\tau} f(t - \tau)\, d\tau$

17. $y'(t) = \cos t + \displaystyle\int_0^t y(\tau) \cos(t - \tau)\, d\tau$, $y(0) = 1$

18. $y' - 5y = f(t)$ where $f(t) = \begin{cases} t^2, & 0 \le t < 1 \\ 0, & t \ge 1 \end{cases}$ $y(0) = 1$.

19. A series circuit contains an inductor, resistor, and capacitor for which $L = 1/2$ henry, $R = 10$ ohms, and $C = 0.01$ farad, respectively. The voltage

$$E(t) = \begin{cases} 10, & 0 \le t < 5, \\ 0, & t \ge 5, \end{cases}$$

is applied to the circuit. Determine the instantaneous charge $q(t)$ on the capacitor for $t > 0$ if $q(0) = 0$ and $q'(0) = 0$.

CHAPTER 8

Linear Systems of Differential Equations

8.1 The Operator Method

Until now we have been considering methods of solution for single ordinary differential equations. However, in practice, a physical situation may demand that more than one differential equation be used in its mathematical description. In Chapter 5, for example, we saw that the vibrations of a weight attached to a spring could be described by one relatively simple equation; were we to attach two such springs we would then need two coupled, or simultaneous, differential equations to represent the motion.

If we suppose x and y are functions of the independent variable t, then the following are examples of simultaneous differential equations:

$$x' - 3x + y' + y = 5$$
$$x + y' + 3y = t,$$

$$4\frac{d^2x}{dt^2} = -5x + y$$

$$2\frac{d^2y}{dt^2} = 3x - y,$$

327

$$\frac{dx}{dt} = x - y$$

$$\frac{dy}{dt} = x + y.$$

Linear systems

Note that each differential equation in the foregoing examples is linear in the dependent variables x and y. Throughout this chapter we shall confine our attention to the solution of systems of linear differential equations, or simply, **linear systems**, in which all coefficients are constants.

Operator notation

The first technique that we shall consider for solving such systems is based on the fundamental principle of systematic algebraic elimination of variables. We shall see that the analogue of *multiplying* an algebraic equation by a constant is *operating* on a differential equation with some combination of derivatives. To facilitate this particular technique let us use the symbol D to represent the operation of differentiation with respect to t, that is,

$$Dx = \frac{dx}{dt}$$

$$D^2x = \frac{d^2x}{dt^2}$$

$$\vdots$$

$$D^nx = \frac{d^nx}{dt^n}.$$

In addition we can rewrite terms such as

$$x'' + 2x \qquad \text{and} \qquad 3y'' - 4y' + y$$

as

$$(D^2 + 2)x \qquad \text{and} \qquad (3D^2 - 4D + 1)y,$$

respectively. Specifically, the symbolism $D^2 + 2$ has the appearance of a *multiple* of x, but in reality means the *operation* of taking two derivatives of x and then adding $2x$ to the result. The symbols D, $D^2, \ldots, D^n$, $D^2 + 2$, $3D^2 - 4D + 1$, and so on, are called **differential operators**.

EXAMPLE

Given

$$x(t) = t^2 + 3e^{-2t}$$

$$y(t) = 5\sin 2t - 4\cos 2t$$

compute

(a) $(D^2 + 4)x$,   and   **(b)** $(D^2 + 4)y$.

Solution:

(a) $(D^2 + 4)x = D^2x + 4x$

$$= \frac{d^2}{dt^2}[t^2 + 3e^{-2t}] + 4[t^2 + 3e^{-2t}]$$

$$= 2 + 12e^{-2t} + 4t^2 + 12e^{-2t}$$

$$= 2 + 4t^2 + 24e^{-2t}$$

(b) $(D^2 + 4)y = D^2y + 4y$

$$= \frac{d^2}{dt^2}[5\sin 2t - 4\cos 2t] + 4[5\sin 2t - 4\cos 2t]$$

$$= -20\sin 2t + 16\cos 2t + 20\sin 2t - 16\cos 2t$$

$$= 0.$$

Properties

In general, a differential equation such as

$$a_ny^{(n)} + a_{n-1}y^{(n-1)} + \cdots + a_1y' + a_0y = g(t) \tag{1}$$

where the $a_i, i = 0, 1, \ldots, n$ are constants, can be written as

$$(a_nD^n + a_{n-1}D^{n-1} + \cdots + a_1D + a_0)y = g(t).$$

If we further denote the differential operator

$$a_nD^n + a_{n-1}D^{n-1} + \cdots + a_1D + a_0$$

by the letter L, we can then write equation (1) simply as

$$Ly = g(t). \tag{2}$$

Before proceeding with the solution of simultaneous differential equations we note the following properties.

1.   The differential operator L is linear. That is, for sufficiently differentiable functions $f(t)$ and $g(t)$ and any constants a and b

$$L\{af(t) + bg(t)\} = aL\{f(t)\} + bL\{g(t)\}. \tag{3}$$

2.   A differential operator can sometimes be factored using real numbers.*

---

* If one is willing to use complex numbers, then a differential operator with constant coefficients can *always* be factored. We are primarily concerned with writing differential equations in operator form with real coefficients.

3.   The factors of a differential operator with constant coefficients always commute. That is, if L has constant coefficients and $L = L_1 L_2$, where L_1 and L_2 are also differential operators, then $L = L_2 L_1$.

We note that if $L = D$, then (3) is merely a statement of the fact that the derivative of a sum is the sum of the derivatives.

EXAMPLES

(a)   The operators $D^2 + D$ and $D^2 - 1$ can be factored as

$$D(D + 1) \quad \text{and} \quad (D + 1)(D - 1),$$

respectively. Factoring a differential operator with constant coefficients is exactly the same as factoring a polynomial.

(b)   The operator $D^2 + 1$ does not factor using real numbers.

EXAMPLE

If $y = f(x)$ possesses a second derivative then

$$(D^2 + 5D + 6)y = (D + 2)(D + 3)y$$
$$= (D + 3)(D + 2)y.$$

To prove this let $w = (D + 3)y = y' + 3y$

$$(D + 2)w = Dw + 2w$$

$$= \frac{d}{dt}[y' + 3y] + 2[y' + 3y]$$

$$= y'' + 3y' + 2y' + 6y$$

$$= y'' + 5y' + 6y.$$

Similarly, if we let $w = (D + 2)y = y' + 2y$ then

$$(D + 3)y = Dw + 3w$$

$$= \frac{d}{dt}[y' + 2y] + 3[y' + 2y]$$

$$= y'' + 2y' + 3y' + 6y$$

$$= y'' + 5y' + 6y.$$

EXAMPLE

The factors of a differential operator with variable coefficients need not commute. The operator $D^3 + tD$ can be written as $(D^2 + t)D$, however, this is not the same as $D(D^2 + t)$. The reader should verify this by comparing the expression $(D^2 + t)Dy$ with $D(D^2 + t)y$.

EXAMPLE	Write the system of differential equations

$$x'' + 2x' + y'' = x + 3y + \sin t$$

$$x' + y' = -4x + 2y + e^{-t}$$

in operator notation.

Solution: Rewrite the given system as

$$x'' + 2x' - x + y'' - 3y = \sin t$$

$$x' + 4x + y' - 2y = e^{-t}$$

so that

$$(D^2 + 2D - 1)x + (D^2 - 3)y = \sin t$$

$$(D + 4)x + (D - 2)y = e^{-t}.$$

Method of solution

Consider the simple system of linear first-order equations

$$Dy = 2x$$
$$Dx = 3y \tag{4}$$

or equivalently

$$2x - Dy = 0$$
$$Dx - 3y = 0.$$

Operating on the first equation by D while multiplying the second by 2 and then subtracting will eliminate x from the system. It follows that

$$-D^2y + 6y = 0 \quad \text{or} \quad D^2y - 6y = 0.$$

Since the roots of the auxiliary equation are $m_1 = \sqrt{6}$ and $m_2 = -\sqrt{6}$ we obtain

$$y(t) = c_1 e^{\sqrt{6}t} + c_2 e^{-\sqrt{6}t}. \tag{5}$$

Whereas multiplying the first equation by -3 while operating on the second by D and then adding gives the differential equation for x, $D^2x - 6x = 0$. It follows immediately that

$$x(t) = c_3 e^{\sqrt{6}t} + c_4 e^{-\sqrt{6}t}. \tag{6}$$

Now (5) and (6) do not satisfy the system (4) for every choice of c_1, c_2, c_3, and c_4. Substituting $x(t)$ and $y(t)$ into the first equation of the original system (4) gives

$$c_1\sqrt{6}e^{\sqrt{6}t} - c_2\sqrt{6}e^{-\sqrt{6}t} = 2c_3 e^{\sqrt{6}t} + 2c_4 e^{-\sqrt{6}t}$$

or

$$(\sqrt{6}c_1 - 2c_3)e^{\sqrt{6}t} + (-\sqrt{6}c_2 - 2c_4)e^{-\sqrt{6}t} = 0.$$

Since the latter expression is to be zero for all values of t we must have

$$\sqrt{6}c_1 - 2c_3 = 0$$

$$-\sqrt{6}c_2 - 2c_4 = 0$$

or $\qquad c_3 = \dfrac{\sqrt{6}}{2}c_1 \qquad c_4 = -\dfrac{\sqrt{6}}{2}c_2.$ $\qquad\qquad$ (7)

Hence we conclude that the solution of the system must be

$$x(t) = \frac{\sqrt{6}}{2}c_1 e^{\sqrt{6}t} - \frac{\sqrt{6}}{2}c_2 e^{-\sqrt{6}t}$$

$$y(t) = c_1 e^{\sqrt{6}t} + c_2 e^{-\sqrt{6}t}.$$

$\qquad\qquad$ (8)

The reader is urged to substitute (5) and (6) into the second equation of (4) and verify that the same relationship (7) between the constants obtains.

Symbolically, if L_1, L_2, L_3, and L_4 denote differential operators with constant coefficients, then a system of linear differential equations in two variables x and y can be written as

$$L_1 x + L_2 y = g_1(t)$$

$$L_3 x + L_4 y = g_2(t).$$

Eliminating variables, as we would for algebraic equations, formally leads to

$$(L_1 L_4 - L_2 L_3)x = f_1(t) \qquad \text{and} \qquad (L_1 L_4 - L_2 L_3)y = f_2(t)$$

where

$$f_1(t) = L_4 g_1(t) - L_2 g_2(t) \qquad \text{and} \qquad f_2(t) = L_1 g_2(t) - L_3 g_1(t).$$

The student should make no attempt to memorize these particular formulas; it is the *procedure* of systematic elimination by *operating* on equations which is important here.

EXAMPLE $\qquad$ Solve

$$Dx + (D + 2)y = 0$$

$$(D - 3)x - \qquad 2y = 0$$

$\qquad\qquad$ (9)

Solution: Operating on the first equation by $D - 3$ and on the second by D and subtracting eliminates x from the system. It follows that the differential equation for y is

$$[(D - 3)(D + 2) + 2D]y = 0$$

or $\qquad\qquad (D^2 + D - 6)y = 0.$ $\qquad\qquad$ (10)

Since the characteristic equation of this last differential equation is $m^2 + m - 6 = (m - 2)(m + 3) = 0$, we obtain the solution

$$y(t) = c_1 e^{2t} + c_2 e^{-3t}. \tag{11}$$

Eliminating y in a similar manner yields $(D^2 + D - 6)x = 0$ from which we find

$$x(t) = c_3 e^{2t} + c_4 e^{-3t}. \tag{12}$$

As we noted in the foregoing discussion, the solution of (9) does not contain four independent constants since the system itself puts a constraint on the actual number which can be chosen arbitrarily. Substituting (11) and (12) into the first equation of the system gives

$$2c_3 e^{2t} - 3c_4 e^{-3t} + 2c_1 e^{2t} - 3c_2 e^{-3t} + 2c_1 e^{2t} + 2c_2 e^{-3t}$$

$$= (4c_1 + 2c_3)e^{2t} + (-c_2 - 3c_4)e^{-3t}$$

$$= 0$$

and so
$$4c_1 + 2c_3 = 0$$
$$-c_2 - 3c_4 = 0$$

or
$$c_3 = -2c_1$$
$$c_4 = -\tfrac{1}{3}c_2.$$

Accordingly, the solution of (9) is

$$x(t) = -2c_1 e^{2t} - \tfrac{1}{3}c_2 e^{-3t}$$
$$y(t) = \quad c_1 e^{2t} + \quad c_2 e^{-3t}. \tag{13}$$

Since we could just as easily solve for c_3 and c_4 in terms of c_1 and c_2, the solution of the preceding example can be written in the alternative form

$$x(t) = c_3 e^{2t} + c_4 e^{-3t}$$
$$y(t) = -\tfrac{1}{2}c_3 e^{2t} - 3c_4 e^{-3t}.$$

Also, it sometimes pays to keep one's eyes open when solving systems. Had we solved for x first, then y, and the relationship between the constants could be determined by simply using the last equation in the form

$$y = \tfrac{1}{2}(D - 3)x$$
$$= \tfrac{1}{2}(Dx - 3x)$$
$$= \tfrac{1}{2}[2c_3 e^{2t} - 3c_4 e^{-3t} - 3c_3 e^{2t} - 3c_4 e^{-3t}]$$
$$= -\tfrac{1}{2}c_3 e^{2t} - 3c_4 e^{-3t}.$$

EXAMPLE   Solve

$$x' - 4x + y'' = t^2$$
$$x' + x + y' = 0. \tag{14}$$

Solution: First write the system in differential operator notation

$$(D - 4)x + D^2 y = t^2$$
$$(D + 1)x + Dy = 0. \tag{15}$$

Then by eliminating x we obtain

$$[(D + 1)D^2 - (D - 4)D]y = (D + 1)t^2 - (D - 4)0$$

or $$(D^3 + 4D)y = t^2 + 2t.$$

Since the roots of the auxiliary equation $m(m^2 + 4) = 0$ are $m_1 = 0$, $m_2 = 2i$, and $m_3 = -2i$, the complementary function is

$$y_c = c_1 + c_2 \cos 2t + c_3 \sin 2t.$$

To determine the particular solution y_p we use Rule II of undetermined coefficients by multiplying the assumption

$$At^2 + Bt + C$$

by t to obtain $$y_p = At^3 + Bt^2 + Ct.$$

Therefore $$y_p' = 3At^2 + 2Bt + C$$
$$y_p'' = 6At + 2B$$
$$y_p''' = 6A,$$
$$y_p''' + 4y_p' = 6A + 12At^2 + 8Bt + 4C$$
$$= 12At^2 + 8Bt + 6A + 4C$$
$$= t^2 + 2t.$$

The last equality implies

$$12A = 1, \qquad 8B = 2, \qquad 6A + 4C = 0$$

and hence $$A = \tfrac{1}{12}, \qquad B = \tfrac{1}{4}, \qquad C = -\tfrac{1}{8}.$$

Thus $$y = y_c + y_p$$
$$= c_1 + c_2 \cos 2t + c_3 \sin 2t + \tfrac{1}{12}t^3 + \tfrac{1}{4}t^2 - \tfrac{1}{8}t. \tag{16}$$

Eliminating y from the system (15) leads to

$$[(D - 4) - D(D + 1)]x = t^2 \qquad \text{or} \qquad (D^2 + 4)x = -t^2.$$

It should be obvious that

$$x_c = c_4 \cos 2t + c_5 \sin 2t$$

and that Rule I of undetermined coefficients can be applied to obtain a particular solution of the form

$$x_p = At^2 + Bt + C.$$

In this case the usual differentiations and algebra yield

$$x_p = -\tfrac{1}{4}t^2 + \tfrac{1}{8}$$

and so

$$x = x_c + x_p$$

$$= c_4 \cos 2t + c_5 \sin 2t - \tfrac{1}{4}t^2 + \tfrac{1}{8}. \tag{17}$$

Now c_4 and c_5 can be expressed in terms of c_2 and c_3 by substituting (16) and (17) into either equation of (14). In particular, by using the second equation we find after combining terms

$$(c_5 - 2c_4 - 2c_2)\sin 2t + (2c_5 + c_4 + 2c_3)\cos 2t = 0$$

so that

$$c_5 - 2c_4 - 2c_2 = 0$$
$$2c_5 + c_4 + 2c_3 = 0.$$

Solving for c_4 and c_5 in terms of c_2 and c_3 gives

$$c_4 = -\tfrac{1}{5}(4c_2 + 2c_3)$$
$$c_5 = \tfrac{1}{5}(2c_2 - 4c_3).$$

Finally, the solution of (14) is found to be

$$x(t) = -\tfrac{1}{5}(4c_2 + 2c_3)\cos 2t + \tfrac{1}{5}(2c_2 - 4c_3)\sin 2t - \tfrac{1}{4}t^2 + \tfrac{1}{8}$$
$$y(t) = c_1 + c_2 \cos 2t + c_3 \sin 2t + \tfrac{1}{12}t^3 + \tfrac{1}{4}t^2 - \tfrac{1}{8}t. \tag{18}$$

Use of determinants

Linear algebraic equations can sometimes be solved by the use of determinants. For example, by Cramer's rule the system of two equations in two unknowns

$$a_1 x + b_1 y = c_1$$
$$a_2 x + b_2 y = c_2 \tag{19}$$

has the solution

$$x = \frac{\begin{vmatrix} c_1 & b_1 \\ c_2 & b_2 \end{vmatrix}}{\begin{vmatrix} a_1 & b_1 \\ a_2 & b_2 \end{vmatrix}}, \qquad y = \frac{\begin{vmatrix} a_1 & c_1 \\ a_2 & c_2 \end{vmatrix}}{\begin{vmatrix} a_1 & b_1 \\ a_2 & b_2 \end{vmatrix}} \tag{20}$$

or

$$\begin{vmatrix} a_1 & b_1 \\ a_2 & b_2 \end{vmatrix} x = \begin{vmatrix} c_1 & b_1 \\ c_2 & b_2 \end{vmatrix}, \qquad \begin{vmatrix} a_1 & b_1 \\ a_2 & b_2 \end{vmatrix} y = \begin{vmatrix} a_1 & c_1 \\ a_2 & c_2 \end{vmatrix} \qquad (21)$$

provided that

$$\begin{vmatrix} a_1 & b_1 \\ a_2 & b_2 \end{vmatrix} \neq 0.$$

While ratios of operators are not defined, the foregoing method can be applied in its modified form (21) to systems of differential equations. For example, we can solve

$$\begin{aligned} 2Dx + (D-1)y &= t \\ Dx + \quad Dy &= t^2 \end{aligned} \qquad (22)$$

for the differential equation of, say, $x(t)$ by writing

$$\begin{vmatrix} 2D & D-1 \\ D & D \end{vmatrix} x = \begin{vmatrix} t & D-1 \\ t^2 & D \end{vmatrix}. \qquad (23)$$

The left-hand determinant can be expanded in the usual algebraic sense, the result then operating on the function $x(t)$. That is,

$$\begin{aligned} \begin{vmatrix} 2D & D-1 \\ D & D \end{vmatrix} x &= [2D^2 - D(D-1)]x \\ &= (D^2 + D)x \\ &= D(D+1)x. \end{aligned}$$

However, some care should be exercised in the expansion of the right-hand determinant of equation (23). We must expand this particular determinant in the sense of the internal differential operators actually operating upon the functions t and t^2. In other words,

$$\begin{aligned} \begin{vmatrix} t & D-1 \\ t^2 & D \end{vmatrix} &= Dt - (D-1)t^2 \\ &= Dt - Dt^2 + t^2 \\ &= t^2 - 2t + 1. \end{aligned}$$

It should be noted carefully that this latter determinant is *not* the same as $tD - (D-1)t^2$ or $tD - t^2(D-1)$. Thus we conclude that the differential equation for $x(t)$ is

$$D(D+1)x = t^2 - 2t + 1.$$

To obtain the equation for $y(t)$ we proceed in the same manner:

$$\begin{vmatrix} 2D & D-1 \\ D & D \end{vmatrix} y = \begin{vmatrix} 2D & t \\ D & t^2 \end{vmatrix},$$

$$(D^2 + D)y = 2Dt^2 - Dt,$$

or
$$D(D+1)y = 4t - 1.$$

EXAMPLE   Solve

$$x' = 3x - y - 1$$

$$y' = x + y + 4e^t. \tag{24}$$

Solution: Write the system in terms of operators

$$(D-3)x + \quad\quad y = -1$$

$$-x + (D-1)y = 4e^t$$

and then use determinants

$$\begin{vmatrix} D-3 & 1 \\ -1 & D-1 \end{vmatrix} x = \begin{vmatrix} -1 & 1 \\ 4e^t & D-1 \end{vmatrix}$$

$$\begin{vmatrix} D-3 & 1 \\ -1 & D-1 \end{vmatrix} y = \begin{vmatrix} D-3 & -1 \\ -1 & 4e^t \end{vmatrix}.$$

After expanding we find that

$$(D-2)^2 x = 1 - 4e^t$$

$$(D-2)^2 y = -1 - 8e^t.$$

By the usual methods it follows that

$$x = x_c + x_p$$

$$= c_1 e^{2t} + c_2 t e^{2t} + \tfrac{1}{4} - 4e^t \tag{25}$$

$$y = y_c + y_p$$

$$= c_3 e^{2t} + c_4 t e^{2t} - \tfrac{1}{4} - 8e^t. \tag{26}$$

Substituting (25) and (26) into the second equation of (24) gives

$$(c_3 - c_1 + c_4)e^{2t} + (c_4 - c_2)t e^{2t} = 0$$

which then implies

$$c_3 - c_1 + c_4 = 0$$

$$c_4 - c_2 = 0,$$

or
$$c_3 = c_1 - c_4$$
$$= c_1 - c_2$$

since $c_4 = c_2$. Thus we obtain

$$x(t) = c_1 e^{2t} + c_2 t e^{2t} + \tfrac{1}{4} - 4e^t$$

$$y(t) = (c_1 - c_2)e^{2t} + c_2 t e^{2t} - \tfrac{1}{4} - 8e^t. \tag{27}$$

EXERCISES 8.1   Answers to odd-numbered problems begin on page A-22 of the Appendix.

1. Prove that $(D + 3)(2D - 1) = (2D - 1)(D + 3)$. [*Hint:* Consider $(D + 3)(2D - 1)y$.]

★2. Determine whether the operator $(tD - 1)(D + 4)$ is the same as the operator $(D + 4)(tD - 1)$.

3. Write the differential equation $(D^6 - 1)y = 0$ in factored operator form.

4. Compute $(D^2 - 4D + 5)y$ for
    (a) $y = te^{-6t} + \cos 3t - 7$ (b) $y = 4e^{2t} \sin t - 10e^{2t} \cos t$.

In Problems 5–22 solve the given system of differential equations by either systematic elimination or the use of determinants.

5. $\dfrac{dx}{dt} = -y + t$ 6. $\dfrac{dx}{dt} = 4x + 7y$

    $\dfrac{dy}{dt} = x - t$ $\dfrac{dy}{dt} = x - 2y$

7. $\dfrac{dx}{dt} = 2x - y$

    $\dfrac{dy}{dt} = x$

8. $(D + 1)x + (D - 1)y = 2$

    $3x + (D + 2)y = -1$

9. $(D^2 + 5)x - \qquad 2y = 0$

    $-2x + (D^2 + 2)y = 0$

★10. $\dfrac{d^2 x}{dt^2} + \dfrac{dy}{dt} = -5x$ 11. $\dfrac{d^2 x}{dt^2} = 4y + e^t$

    $\dfrac{dx}{dt} + \dfrac{dy}{dt} = -x + 4y$ $\dfrac{d^2 y}{dt^2} = 4x - e^t$

12. $\quad D^2x - \quad\quad Dy = t$ 13. $\quad Dx + \quad\quad D^2y = e^{3t}$

$\quad\quad (D + 3)x + (D + 3)y = 2$ $\quad (D + 1)x + (D - 1)y = 4e^{3t}$

14. $(2D^2 - D - 1)x - (2D + 1)y = 1$

$\quad\quad\quad (D - 1)x + \quad\quad\quad Dy = -1$

15. $2\dfrac{dx}{dt} - 5x + \dfrac{dy}{dt} = e^t$ 16. $(D^2 - 1)x - \quad y = 0$

$\quad\quad\quad\quad\quad\quad\quad\quad\quad\quad\quad\quad\quad (D - 1)x + Dy = 0$

$\quad\quad \dfrac{dx}{dt} - \quad x + \dfrac{dy}{dt} = 5e^t$

17. $\quad \dfrac{dx}{dt} + \dfrac{dy}{dt} = e^t$

$\quad -\dfrac{d^2x}{dt^2} + \dfrac{dx}{dt} + x + y = 0$

EXAMPLE

Given the system

$$Dx + \quad\quad\quad\quad Dz = t^2$$

$$2x + D^2y \quad\quad\quad = e^t$$

$$-2Dx - 2y + (D + 1)z = 0$$

find the differential equation for the variable y.

Solution: By determinants we can write

$$\begin{vmatrix} D & 0 & D \\ 2 & D^2 & 0 \\ -2D & -2 & D + 1 \end{vmatrix} y = \begin{vmatrix} D & t^2 & D \\ 2 & e^t & 0 \\ -2D & 0 & D + 1 \end{vmatrix}.$$

In turn, expanding each determinant by cofactors of the first row gives

$$\left\{ D\begin{vmatrix} D^2 & 0 \\ -2 & D + 1 \end{vmatrix} + D\begin{vmatrix} 2 & D^2 \\ -2D & -2 \end{vmatrix} \right\} y = D\begin{vmatrix} e^t & 0 \\ 0 & D + 1 \end{vmatrix} - \begin{vmatrix} 2 & 0 \\ -2D & D + 1 \end{vmatrix} t^2 + D\begin{vmatrix} 2 & e^t \\ -2D & 0 \end{vmatrix}$$

or $\quad\quad\quad\quad\quad\quad\quad\quad D(3D^3 + D^2 - 4)y = 4e^t - 2t^2 - 4t.$

Again, we remind the reader that the D symbol in the left-hand brace is to be treated as an algebraic quantity, but this is not the case on the right-hand side.

★18. $\dfrac{dx}{dt} = -x + z$

$\dfrac{dy}{dt} = -y + z$

$\dfrac{dz}{dt} = -x + y$

19. $Dx = y$

$Dy = z$

$Dz = x$

20. $\quad Dx + \qquad z = e^t$

$(D - 1)x + Dy + Dz = 0$

$x + 2y + Dz = e^t$

21. $\dfrac{dx}{dt} - 6y \qquad = 0$

$x - \dfrac{dy}{dt} + z = 0$

$x + y - \dfrac{dz}{dt} = 0$

★22. $\quad Dx - \qquad 2Dy = t^2$

$(D + 1)x - 2(D + 1)y = 1$

23. Determine, if possible, a system of differential equations having

$$x(t) = c_1 + c_2 e^{2t}$$
$$y(t) = -c_1 + c_2 e^{2t}$$

as its general solution.

8.2 The Laplace Transform Method

When initial conditions are specified, the Laplace transform will reduce a system of linear differential equations with constant coefficients to a set of simultaneous algebraic equations in the transformed functions.

EXAMPLE

Solve

$$2x' + y' - y = t$$
$$x' + y' \qquad = t^2 \tag{1}$$

subject to $x(0) = 1$, $y(0) = 0$.

Solution: If $X(s) = \mathscr{L}\{x(t)\}$ and $Y(s) = \mathscr{L}\{y(t)\}$, then after transforming each equation we obtain

$$2[sX(s) - x(0)] + sY(s) - y(0) - Y(s) = \frac{1}{s^2}$$

$$sX(s) - x(0) + sY(s) - y(0) = \frac{2}{s^3}$$

or
$$2sX(s) + (s-1)Y(s) = 2 + \frac{1}{s^2}$$

$$(2)$$

$$sX(s) + \qquad sY(s) = 1 + \frac{2}{s^3}.$$

Multiplying the second equation of (2) by 2 and subtracting yields

$$(-s-1)Y(s) = \frac{1}{s^2} - \frac{4}{s^3}$$

$$Y(s) = \frac{4-s}{s^3(s+1)}.$$

$$(3)$$

Now by partial fractions

$$\frac{4-s}{s^3(s+1)} = \frac{A}{s} + \frac{B}{s^2} + \frac{C}{s^3} + \frac{D}{s+1}$$

so that

$$4 - s = As^2(s+1) + Bs(s+1) + C(s+1) + Ds^3.$$

Setting $s = 0$ and $s = -1$ in the last line gives $C = 4$ and $D = -5$, respectively; whereas equating the coefficients of s^3 and s^2 on each side of the equality yields

$$A + D = 0 \qquad \text{and} \qquad A + B = 0.$$

It follows that $A = 5$, $B = -5$. Thus (3) becomes

$$Y(s) = \frac{5}{s} - \frac{5}{s^2} + \frac{4}{s^3} - \frac{5}{s+1}$$

and so

$$y(t) = 5\mathcal{L}^{-1}\left\{\frac{1}{s}\right\} - 5\mathcal{L}^{-1}\left\{\frac{1}{s^2}\right\} + 2\mathcal{L}^{-1}\left\{\frac{2!}{s^3}\right\} - 5\mathcal{L}^{-1}\left\{\frac{1}{s+1}\right\}$$

$$= 5 - 5t + 2t^2 - 5e^{-t}.$$

By the second equation of (2)

$$X(s) = -Y(s) + \frac{1}{s} + \frac{2}{s^4}$$

from which it follows that

$$x(t) = -\mathcal{L}^{-1}\{Y(s)\} + \mathcal{L}^{-1}\left\{\frac{1}{s}\right\} + \frac{2}{3!}\mathcal{L}^{-1}\left\{\frac{3!}{s^4}\right\}$$

$$= -4 + 5t - 2t^2 + \tfrac{1}{3}t^3 + 5e^{-t}.$$

Hence we conclude that the solution of the given system (1) is

$$x(t) = -4 + 5t - 2t^2 + \tfrac{1}{3}t^3 + 5e^{-t}$$
$$y(t) = \quad 5 - 5t + 2t^2 - 5e^{-t}.$$

(4)

Applications

Let us turn now to some elementary applications involving systems of differential equations. The solutions of the problems that we shall consider can be obtained either by the method of the preceding section or through the use of the Laplace transformation. We shall confine our attention to the latter method.

Coupled springs

Suppose two weights W_1 and W_2 of masses m_1 and m_2 are attached to two springs A and B having spring constants k_1 and k_2, respectively. In turn the springs are connected and the resulting system is set in motion. Let $x_1(t)$ and $x_2(t)$ represent the vertical displacements of the two weights beyond their equilibrium positions as shown in Figure 8.1. We saw in Section 1.3 that the vertical motion in a straight line through the centers of mass of each weight is described by the system of linear second-order equations

$$m_1 x_1'' = -k_1 x_1 + k_2(x_2 - x_1)$$
$$m_2 x_2'' = -k_2(x_2 - x_1).$$

(5)

Recall that the right side of the first equation is the net force acting on W_1 due to the elongation of spring A and the net elongation of spring B; whereas the right side of the second equation is the force acting on W_2 due only to net elongation of spring B.

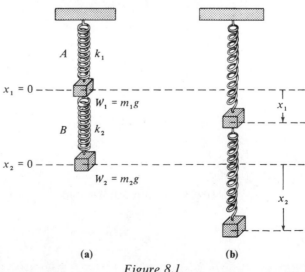

(a)   (b)

Figure 8.1

In the next example we shall solve the system (5) under the assumption

$$k_1 = 6, \qquad k_2 = 4, \qquad m_1 = 1, \qquad m_2 = 1$$

and that the weights start from their equilibrium positions with opposite unit velocities.

EXAMPLE

Solve

$$x_1'' + 10x_1 \qquad - 4x_2 = 0$$
$$-4x_1 + x_2'' + 4x_2 = 0 \tag{6}$$

subject to

$$x_1(0) = 0, \qquad x_1'(0) = 1, \qquad x_2(0) = 0, \qquad x_2'(0) = -1.$$

Solution: The Laplace transform of each equation is

$$s^2 X_1(s) - sx_1(0) - x_1'(0) + 10X_1(s) - 4X_2(s) = 0$$
$$-4X_1(s) + s^2 X_2(s) - sx_2(0) - x_2'(0) + 4X_2(s) = 0$$

where $X_1(s) = \mathscr{L}\{x_1(t)\}$ and $X_2(s) = \mathscr{L}\{x_2(t)\}$. The preceding system is the same as

$$(s^2 + 10)X_1(s) - \qquad 4X_2(s) = 1$$
$$-4X_1(s) + (s^2 + 4)X_2(s) = -1. \tag{7}$$

Eliminating X_2 gives

$$(s^4 + 14s^2 + 24)X_1(s) = s^2$$

or

$$X_1(s) = \frac{s^2}{(s^2 + 2)(s^2 + 12)}.$$

By partial fractions we can write

$$\frac{s^2}{(s^2 + 2)(s^2 + 12)} = \frac{As + B}{s^2 + 2} + \frac{Cs + D}{s^2 + 12}$$

and

$$s^2 = (As + B)(s^2 + 12) + (Cs + D)(s^2 + 2).$$

Comparing coefficients of s on each side of the last equality gives

$$A + C = 0$$
$$B + D = 1$$
$$12A + 2C = 0$$
$$12B + 2D = 0$$

so that $A = 0, \quad C = 0, \quad B = -\frac{1}{5}, \quad D = \frac{6}{5}.$

Hence $$X_1(s) = -\frac{1/5}{s^2 + 2} + \frac{6/5}{s^2 + 12}$$

and therefore

$$x_1(t) = -\frac{1}{5\sqrt{2}}\mathscr{L}^{-1}\left\{\frac{\sqrt{2}}{s^2 + 2}\right\} + \frac{6}{5\sqrt{12}}\mathscr{L}^{-1}\left\{\frac{\sqrt{12}}{s^2 + 12}\right\}$$

$$= -\frac{\sqrt{2}}{10}\sin\sqrt{2}t + \frac{\sqrt{3}}{5}\sin 2\sqrt{3}t.$$

From the first equation of (7) it follows that

$$X_2(s) = -\frac{s^2 + 6}{(s^2 + 2)(s^2 + 12)}.$$

Proceeding as before with partial fractions we find

$$X_2(s) = -\frac{2/5}{s^2 + 2} - \frac{3/5}{s^2 + 12}$$

and so

$$x_2(t) = -\frac{2}{5\sqrt{2}}\mathscr{L}^{-1}\left\{\frac{\sqrt{2}}{s^2 + 2}\right\} - \frac{3}{5\sqrt{12}}\mathscr{L}^{-1}\left\{\frac{\sqrt{12}}{s^2 + 12}\right\}$$

$$= -\frac{\sqrt{2}}{5}\sin\sqrt{2}t - \frac{\sqrt{3}}{10}\sin 2\sqrt{3}t.$$

Finally, the solution to the given system (6) is

$$x_1(t) = -\frac{\sqrt{2}}{10}\sin\sqrt{2}t + \frac{\sqrt{3}}{5}\sin 2\sqrt{3}t$$

$$x_2(t) = -\frac{\sqrt{2}}{5}\sin\sqrt{2}t - \frac{\sqrt{3}}{10}\sin 2\sqrt{3}t$$

(8)

Networks

An electrical network having more than one loop also gives rise to simultaneous differential equations. As shown in Figure 8.2, the current $i_1(t)$ splits in the directions shown at point B_1 called a *branch point* of the network. By *Kirchoff's first law* we can write

$$i_1(t) = i_2(t) + i_3(t).$$

(9)

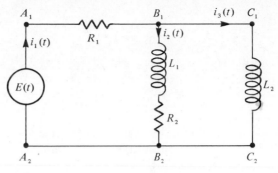

Figure 8.2

In addition, we can also apply *Kirchoff's second law* to each loop. For loop $A_1B_1B_2A_2A_1$, summing the voltage drops across each part of the loop gives

$$E(t) = i_1R_1 + L_1\frac{di_2}{dt} + i_2R_2. \tag{10}$$

Similarly, for loop $A_1B_1C_1C_2B_2A_2A_1$, we find

$$E(t) = i_1R_1 + L_2\frac{di_3}{dt}. \tag{11}$$

Using (9) to eliminate i_1 in (10) and (11) yields two first-order equations for the currents $i_2(t)$ and $i_3(t)$

$$L_1\frac{di_2}{dt} + (R_1 + R_2)i_2 + R_1i_3 = E(t)$$
$$L_2\frac{di_3}{dt} + \qquad R_1i_2 + R_1i_3 = E(t). \tag{12}$$

Given the natural initial conditions $i_2(0) = 0$, $i_3(0) = 0$, the system (12) is amenable to solution by the Laplace transform.

We leave it as an exercise (see Problem 16) to show that the system of differential equations describing the currents $i_1(t)$ and $i_2(t)$ in the network containing a resistor, inductor, and capacitor shown in Figure 8.3 is

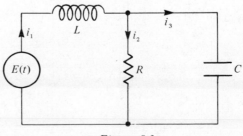

Figure 8.3

$$L\frac{di_1}{dt} + Ri_2 \quad = E(t)$$

$$RC\frac{di_2}{dt} + i_2 - i_1 = 0. \tag{13}$$

EXAMPLE

Solve the system (13) under the conditions $E = 60$ volts, $L = 1$ henry, $R = 50$ ohms, $C = 10^{-4}$ farads, and i_1 and i_2 are initially zero.

Solution: We must solve

$$\frac{di_1}{dt} + 50i_2 \quad = 60$$

$$50(10^{-4})\frac{di_2}{dt} + i_2 - i_1 = 0$$

subject to $i_1(0) = 0$, $i_2(0) = 0$.

Applying the Laplace transform to each equation of the system and simplifying gives

$$sI_1(s) + \qquad 50I_2(s) = \frac{60}{s}$$

$$-200I_1(s) + (s + 200)I_2(s) = 0$$

where $I_1(s) = \mathscr{L}\{i_1(t)\}$ and $I_2(s) = \mathscr{L}\{i_2(t)\}$. Solving the system for I_1 and I_2 yields

$$I_1(s) = \frac{60s + 12{,}000}{s(s + 100)^2}$$

$$I_2(s) = \frac{12{,}000}{s(s + 100)^2}.$$

By partial fractions we can write

$$I_1(s) = \frac{6/5}{s} - \frac{6/5}{s + 100} - \frac{60}{(s + 100)^2}$$

$$I_2(s) = \frac{6/5}{s} - \frac{6/5}{s + 100} - \frac{120}{(s + 100)^2}$$

from which it follows that

$$i_1(t) = \tfrac{6}{5} - \tfrac{6}{5}e^{-100t} - 60te^{-100t}$$

$$i_2(t) = \tfrac{6}{5} - \tfrac{6}{5}e^{-100t} - 120te^{-100t}.$$

Note that both $i_1(t)$ and $i_2(t)$ in the preceding example tend toward the value $E/R = 6/5$ as $t \to \infty$. Furthermore, since the current through the capacitor is $i_3(t) = i_1(t) - i_2(t) = 60te^{-100t}$ we observe $i_3(t) \to 0$ as $t \to \infty$.

EXERCISES 8.2

Answers to odd-numbered problems begin on page A-23 of the Appendix.

In Problems 1–12 use the Laplace transform to solve the given system of differential equations.

1. $\dfrac{dx}{dt} = -x + y$

$\dfrac{dy}{dt} = 2x,$

$x(0) = 0, \quad y(0) = 1$

★2. $\dfrac{dx}{dt} = 2y + e^t$

$\dfrac{dy}{dt} = 8x - t,$

$x(0) = 1, \quad y(0) = 1$

3. $\dfrac{dx}{dt} = x - 2y$

$\dfrac{dy}{dt} = 5x - y,$

$x(0) = -1, \quad y(0) = 2$

4. $\dfrac{dx}{dt} + 3x + \dfrac{dy}{dt} = 1$

$\dfrac{dx}{dt} - x + \dfrac{dy}{dt} - y = e^t,$

$x(0) = 0, \quad y(0) = 0$

5. $2\dfrac{dx}{dt} + \dfrac{dy}{dt} - 2x = 1$

$\dfrac{dx}{dt} + \dfrac{dy}{dt} - 3x - 3y = 2,$

$x(0) = 0, \quad y(0) = 0$

★6. $\dfrac{dx}{dt} + x - \dfrac{dy}{dt} + y = 0$

$\dfrac{dx}{dt} + \dfrac{dy}{dt} + 2y = 0,$

$x(0) = 0, \quad y(0) = 1$

7. $\dfrac{d^2x}{dt^2} + x - y = 0$

$\dfrac{d^2y}{dt^2} + y - x = 0,$

$x(0) = 0, \quad x'(0) = -2, \quad y(0) = 0, \quad y'(0) = 1$

8. $\dfrac{d^2x}{dt^2} + \dfrac{dx}{dt} + \dfrac{dy}{dt} = 0$

$\dfrac{d^2y}{dt^2} + \dfrac{dy}{dt} - 4\dfrac{dx}{dt} = 0,$

$x(0) = 1, \quad x'(0) = 0, \quad y(0) = -1, \quad y'(0) = 5$

9. $\dfrac{d^2x}{dt^2} + \dfrac{d^2y}{dt^2} = t^2$

$\dfrac{d^2x}{dt^2} - \dfrac{d^2y}{dt^2} = 4t,$

$x(0) = 8, \quad x'(0) = 0, \quad y(0) = 0, \quad y'(0) = 0$

10. $\dfrac{dx}{dt} - 4x + \dfrac{d^3y}{dt^3} = 6\sin t$

$\dfrac{dx}{dt} + 2x - 2\dfrac{d^3y}{dt^3} = 0,$

$x(0) = 0, \quad y(0) = 0, \quad y'(0) = 0, \quad y''(0) = 0$

11. $\dfrac{d^2x}{dt^2} + 3\dfrac{dy}{dt} + 3y = 0$

$\dfrac{d^2x}{dt^2} \qquad + 3y = te^{-t},$

$x(0) = 0, \quad x'(0) = 2, \quad y(0) = 0$

★12. $\dfrac{dx}{dt} = 4x - 2y + 2\mathcal{U}(t-1)$

$\dfrac{dy}{dt} = 3x - y + \mathcal{U}(t-1),$

$x(0) = 0, \quad y(0) = \tfrac{1}{2}$

13. Solve system (5) when

$$k_1 = 3, \quad k_2 = 2, \quad m_1 = 1, \quad m_2 = 1$$

and $\qquad\qquad x_1(0) = 0, \qquad x_1'(0) = 1,$

$\qquad\qquad\qquad x_2(0) = 1, \qquad x_2'(0) = 0.$

14. Derive the system of differential equations describing the straight line vertical motion of the coupled springs shown in Figure 8.4. Use the Laplace transform to solve the system when $k_1 = 1$, $k_2 = 1$, $k_3 = 1$, $m_1 = 1$, $m_2 = 1$, and $x_1(0) = 0$, $x_1'(0) = -1$, $x_2(0) = 0$, $x_2'(0) = 1$.

15. Find the current $i_1(t)$ at any time in the network shown in Figure 8.5. Assume $i_2(0) = 0$, $i_3(0) = 0$.

★16. Derive the system of equations (13).

17. Solve (13) when $E = 60$ volts, $L = 1/2$ henry, $R = 50$ ohms, $C = 10^{-4}$ farads, $i_1(0) = 0$, $i_2(0) = 0$.

18. Solve (13) when $E = 60$ volts, $L = 2$ henry, $R = 50$ ohms, $C = 10^{-4}$ farads, $i_1(0) = 0$, $i_2(0) = 0$.

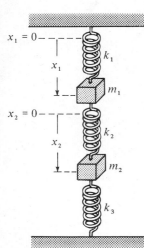

$x_1 = 0$

x_1

k_1

m_1

$x_2 = 0$

x_2

k_2

m_2

k_3

Figure 8.4

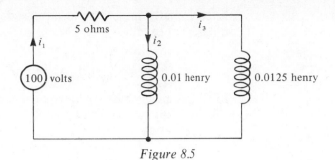

Figure 8.5

19. Solve the system given in (12) when $R_1 = 6\,\text{ohms}$, $R_2 = 5\,\text{ohms}$, $L_1 = 1$ henry, $L_2 = 1$ henry, $E(t) = 50 \sin t$ volts.

20. The system

$$\frac{dx_1}{dt} = -\frac{2}{25}x_1 + \frac{1}{50}x_2$$

$$\frac{dx_2}{dt} = \frac{2}{25}x_1 - \frac{2}{25}x_2$$

results from the analysis of a particular problem that involves the pumping of a well-mixed salt solution between two tanks (see Section 8.3). Use the Laplace transform to solve the system when $x_1(0) = 25$ and $x_2(0) = 0$.

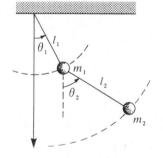

Figure 8.6

21. A double pendulum oscillates in a vertical plane under the influence of gravity (see Figure 8.6). For small displacements $\theta_1(t)$ and $\theta_2(t)$, it can be shown* that the differential equations of motion are

$$(m_1 + m_2)l_1^2\theta_1'' + m_2 l_1 l_2 \theta_2'' + (m_1 + m_2)l_1 g \theta_1 = 0$$

$$m_2 l_2^2 \theta_2'' + m_2 l_1 l_2 \theta_1'' + m_2 l_2 g \theta_2 = 0.$$

Use the Laplace transform to solve the system when $m_1 = 3$, $m_2 = 1$, $l_1 = l_2 = 16$, $\theta_1(0) = 1$, $\theta_2(0) = -1$, $\theta_1'(0) = 0$, $\theta_2'(0) = 0$.

8.3   Linear First-Order Systems

The study of systems of first-order differential equations

$$\frac{dx_1}{dt} = g_1(t, x_1, x_2, \ldots, x_n)$$

$$\frac{dx_2}{dt} = g_2(t, x_1, x_2, \ldots, x_n)$$

$$\vdots$$

$$\frac{dx_n}{dt} = g_n(t, x_1, x_2, \ldots, x_n)$$

(1)

---

* See W. Hauser, *Introduction to the Principles of Mechanics* (Reading, MA: Addison-Wesley, 1965), pp. 268–70.

is particularly important in advanced mathematics since every nth-order differential equation

$$y^{(n)} = F(t, y, y', \ldots, y^{(n-1)})$$

as well as most systems of differential equations can be reduced to form (1). In the preceding two sections we have dealt with linear systems which were of the form

$$P_{11}(D)x_1 + P_{12}(D)x_2 + \cdots + P_{1n}(D)x_n = b_1(t)$$
$$P_{21}(D)x_1 + P_{22}(D)x_2 + \cdots + P_{2n}(D)x_n = b_2(t)$$
$$\vdots \qquad\qquad \vdots \qquad \vdots \qquad\qquad\quad (2)$$
$$P_{n1}(D)x_1 + P_{n2}(D)x_2 + \cdots + P_{nn}(D)x_n = b_n(t)$$

where the P_{ij} are polynomials in the differential operator D. For example, a system such as

$$(D^2 - 2D)x - \qquad 2Dy = 1$$
$$(D - 1)x + (D^2 - 2)y = t$$

obviously is of form (2).

Linear normal form   Of course, a system such as (1) need not be linear and need not have constant coefficients. Consequently, the system may not be readily solvable, if at all. In the remaining sections of this chapter we shall be interested only in a particular, but important, case of (1), namely, those systems having the linear **normal**, or **canonical**, form

$$\frac{dx_1}{dt} = a_{11}x_1 + a_{12}x_2 + \cdots + a_{1n}x_n + f_1(t)$$

$$\frac{dx_2}{dt} = a_{21}x_1 + a_{22}x_2 + \cdots + a_{2n}x_n + f_2(t) \qquad (3)$$

$$\vdots$$

$$\frac{d x_n}{dt} = a_{n1}x_1 + a_{n2}x_2 + \cdots + a_{nn}x_n + f_n(t).$$

Hereafter we shall always assume that the coefficients a_{ij} are constants and that the functions $f_i(t)$ are continuous on some common interval. When $f_i(t) = 0, i = 1, 2, \ldots, n$, the system (3) is said to be **homogeneous**, otherwise it is called **nonhomogeneous**.

We shall now show that every linear nth-order differential equation (see equation (1) of Section 4.1) and most linear systems of form (2) can be reduced to a linear system having the normal form (3).

Equation to a system   Suppose a linear nth-order differential equation with constant coefficients is first written as

$$\frac{d^n y}{dt^n} = -\frac{a_0}{a_n}y - \frac{a_1}{a_n}y' - \cdots - \frac{a_{n-1}}{a_n}y^{(n-1)} + f(t). \tag{4}$$

If we then introduce the variables

$$
\begin{aligned}
y &= x_1 \\
y' &= x_2 \\
y'' &= x_3 \\
&\;\vdots \\
y^{(n-1)} &= x_n
\end{aligned}
\tag{5}
$$

it follows that $y' = x_1' = x_2$, $y'' = x_2' = x_3$, and so on. Hence, with the help of (4), the system (5) becomes

$$
\begin{aligned}
x_1' &= x_2 \\
x_2' &= x_3 \\
x_3' &= x_4 \\
&\;\vdots \\
x_{n-1}' &= x_n \\
x_n' &= -\frac{a_0}{a_n}x_1 - \frac{a_1}{a_n}x_2 - \cdots - \frac{a_{n-1}}{a_n}x_n + f(t).
\end{aligned}
\tag{6}
$$

Inspection of (6) reveals that it has the same form as (3).

EXAMPLE   Reduce the equation

$$2y''' - 6y'' + 4y' + y = \sin t$$

to form (3).

Solution: Write the differential equation as

$$y''' = -\tfrac{1}{2}y - 2y' + 3y'' + \tfrac{1}{2}\sin t$$

and then let $y = x_1, y' = x_2, y'' = x_3$.

Since

$$x_1' = y' = x_2$$
$$x_2' = y'' = x_3$$
$$x_3' = y'''$$

it follows that

$$x_1' = x_2$$
$$x_2' = x_3$$
$$x_3' = -\tfrac{1}{2}x_1 - 2x_2 + 3x_3 + \tfrac{1}{2}\sin t.$$

The requirement that the differential equation have constant coefficients is not necessary; a general linear equation can be reduced to a normal form identical with (6) except that some of the a_{ij} would be functions of t (specifically, the coefficients in the last line of the system). A partial converse is also true; a linear system in normal form that contains n unknowns can be reduced to a single linear nth-order differential equation. Of course, in this case we must make the additional assumption that the $f_i(t)$, $i = 1, 2, \ldots, n$ of (3) are sufficiently differentiable. For example, if we write the homogeneous system

$$\frac{dx}{dt} = a_{11}x + a_{12}y$$

$$\frac{dy}{dt} = a_{21}x + a_{22}y$$

(7)

in operator form

$$(D - a_{11})x - \qquad a_{12}y = 0$$
$$-a_{21}x + (D - a_{22})y = 0$$

it should be fairly obvious that we can use the elimination technique of Section 8.1 to obtain one differential equation in either $x(t)$ or $y(t)$. Knowing, say, $x(t)$, we can find $y(t)$ from the first equation of (7). We note that a system in which either $a_{12} = 0$ or $a_{21} = 0$ can still be reduced to a second-order equation although there is no practical reason to do so, since one of the equations can be solved immediately.

EXAMPLE

Reduce

$$\frac{dx}{dt} = x - y$$

$$\frac{dy}{dt} = 2x - y + t$$

to a single second-order differential equation.

Solution: Differentiating the first equation

$$\frac{d^2x}{dt^2} = \frac{dx}{dt} - \frac{dy}{dt}$$

and then using the second gives

$$\frac{d^2x}{dt^2} = \frac{dx}{dt} - (2x - y + t)$$

$$= \frac{dx}{dt} - 2x + y - t.$$

Using the first differential equation of the system to eliminate y then gives

$$\frac{d^2x}{dt^2} = \frac{dx}{dt} - 2x + \left(x - \frac{dx}{dt}\right) - t$$

or

$$\frac{d^2x}{dt^2} + x = -t.$$

Alternatively, we can write the original system as

$$(D - 1)x + \qquad y = 0$$

$$-2x + (D + 1)y = t$$

and operate on the first equation by $D + 1$ and subtract

$$[(D^2 - 1) + 2]x = -t,$$

$$(D^2 + 1)x = -t.$$

Systems reduced to normal form

Using a procedure similar to that just outlined, we can reduce *most* systems of the linear form (2) to the linear normal form (3). To accomplish this it is necessary to first solve the system for the highest order derivative of each of the unknowns. As we shall see, this may not always be possible.

EXAMPLE   Reduce

$$(D^2 - D + 5)x + \quad 2D^2y = e^t$$
$$-2x + (D^2 + 2)y = 3t^2$$

to the normal form (3)

Solution: Write the system as

$$D^2x + 2D^2y = \quad e^t - 5x + Dx$$
$$D^2y = 3t^2 + 2x - 2y$$

and then eliminate D^2y by multiplying the second equation by 2 and subtracting. We have

$$D^2x = e^t - 6t^2 - 9x + 4y + Dx.$$

Since the second equation of the system already expresses the highest order derivative of y in terms of the remaining functions, we are now in a position to introduce new variables. If we let

$$Dx = u \quad \text{and} \quad Dy = v$$

the expressions for D^2x and D^2y become, respectively,

$$Du = e^t - 6t^2 - 9x + 4y + u$$
$$Dv = 3t^2 + 2x - 2y.$$

Thus the original system can be written in the normal form

$$Dx = u$$
$$Dy = v$$
$$Du = -9x + 4y + u + e^t - 6t^2$$
$$Dv = \quad 2x - 2y + 3t^2.$$

Degenerate systems   Those systems of differential equations of form (2) which cannot be reduced to a linear system in normal form are said to be **degenerate**. For example, the contradictory system

$$x'' + y' = 1$$
$$x'' + y' = -1$$

is degenerate because it is impossible to solve the system for the highest order derivative of each variable. It should be obvious that this system possesses no solution. However, as the next example shows, a system may be degenerate but yet possess a solution.

EXAMPLE

It is a straightforward matter to show that the system

$$(D + 1)x + (D + 1)y = 0$$
$$2Dx + (2D + 1)y = 0$$

cannot be reduced to the normal form (3), and hence is degenerate. However, by the elimination procedure of Section 8.1, it can also be shown that the system possesses the solution

$$x(t) = c_1 e^{-t}$$
$$y(t) = -2c_1 e^{-t}.$$

By this time the reader may be wondering why anyone would want to convert a single differential equation to a system of equations, or for that matter, a system of differential equations to an even larger system. While we are not in a position to completely justify their importance, suffice it to say that these procedures are more than a theoretical exercise. There are times where it is actually desirable to work with a system rather than with one equation. In the numerical analysis of differential equations, almost all computational algorithms are established for first-order equations. Since these algorithms can be generalized directly to systems, to compute numerically, say, a second-order equation, we would reduce it to a system of two first-order equations (see Chapter 9).

A linear system such as (3) arises naturally in some physical applications. The following example illustrates a homogeneous system in two dependent variables.

EXAMPLE

Tank *A* contains 50 gallons of water in which 25 pounds of salt are dissolved. A second tank, *B*, contains 50 gallons of pure water. Liquid is pumped in and out

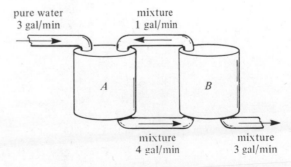

Figure 8.7

of the tanks at rates shown in Figure 8.7. Derive the differential equations which describe the number of pounds $x_1(t)$ and $x_2(t)$ of salt at any time in tanks A and B, respectively.

Solution: By an analysis similar to that used in Section 3.2 we see that the net rate of change in $x_1(t)$ in lb/min is

$$\frac{dx_1}{dt} = \overbrace{(3 \text{ gal/min}) \cdot (0 \text{ lb/gal}) + (1 \text{ gal/min}) \cdot \left(\frac{x_2}{50} \text{ lb/gal}\right)}^{\text{input}} - \overbrace{(4 \text{ gal/min}) \cdot \left(\frac{x_1}{50} \text{ lb/gal}\right)}^{\text{output}}$$

$$= -\frac{2}{25}x_1 + \frac{1}{50}x_2.$$

In addition, we find that the net rate of change in $x_2(t)$ is

$$\frac{dx_2}{dt} = 4 \cdot \frac{x_1}{50} - 3 \cdot \frac{x_2}{50} - 1 \cdot \frac{x}{50}2$$

$$= \frac{2}{25}x_1 - \frac{2}{25}x_2.$$

Thus we must solve the first-order system

$$\frac{dx_1}{dt} = -\frac{2}{25}x_1 + \frac{1}{50}x_2$$

$$\frac{dx_2}{dt} = \frac{2}{25}x_1 - \frac{2}{25}x_2$$

subject to the initial conditions $x_1(0) = 25$, $x_2(0) = 0$.

EXERCISES 8.3

Answers to odd-numbered problems begin on page A-24 of the Appendix.

In Problems 1–5 rewrite the given differential equations as a system in normal form (3).

1. $y'' - 3y' + 4y = \sin 3t$ 2. $2\dfrac{d^2y}{dt^2} + 4\dfrac{dy}{dt} - 5y = 0$

3. $y''' - 3y'' + 6y' - 10y = t^2 + 1$ 4. $4y''' + y = e^t$

5. $\dfrac{d^4y}{dt^4} - 2\dfrac{d^2y}{dt^2} + 4\dfrac{dy}{dt} + y = t$

★6. Show that

$$t^2 y'' + ty' + (t^2 - 4)y = 0$$

can be reduced to form (3) with variable coefficients.

7. Reduce the nonlinear equation

$$y''' - yy'' + y^2 = 2t - 1$$

to a system of first-order differential equations.

8. Reduce the system

$$\frac{dx}{dt} = x + 2y$$
$$\frac{dy}{dt} = -x + y$$

to a single, second-order differential equation in $x(t)$.

9. Reduce the system

$$\frac{dx}{dt} = 3x - y + 1$$
$$\frac{dy}{dt} = x + 4y - t$$

to a single, second-order differential equation in $y(t)$.

★10. Reduce the system

$$\frac{dx}{dt} = x - y$$
$$\frac{dy}{dt} = y - z$$
$$\frac{dz}{dt} = -x + z$$

to a single, third-order differential equation in $z(t)$.

In Problems 11–15 rewrite, if possible, the given systems in the normal form (3).

11. $(D - 1)x - Dy = t^2$
    $x + Dy = 5t - 2$

★12. $x'' - 2y'' = \sin t$
    $x'' + y'' = \cos t$

13. $(2D + 1)x - 2Dy = 4$
    $Dx - Dy = e^t$

14. $m_1 x_1'' = -k_1 x_1 + k_2(x_2 - x_1)$
    $m_2 x_2'' = -k_2(x_2 - x_1)$

15. $\dfrac{d^3 x}{dt^3} = 4x - 3\dfrac{d^2 x}{dt^2} + 4\dfrac{dy}{dt}$

$\dfrac{d^2 y}{dt^2} = 10t^2 - 4\dfrac{dx}{dt} + 3\dfrac{dy}{dt}$

★**16.** Consider the first-order system

$$(a_1D - b_1)x + (a_2D - b_2)y = 0$$
$$(a_3D - b_3)x + (a_4D - b_4)y = 0$$

where the a_i are nonzero constants. Determine a condition on the a_i such that the system is degenerate.

17. Consider two tanks A and B with liquid being pumped in and out at the same rates as given in the last example of this section. What is the system of differential equations if, instead of pure water, a brine solution containing 2 lb of salt per gallon is pumped into tank A?

18. Using the information given in Figure 8.8, derive the system of differential equations describing the number of pounds of salt x_1, x_2, and x_3 at any time in tanks A, B, and C, respectively.

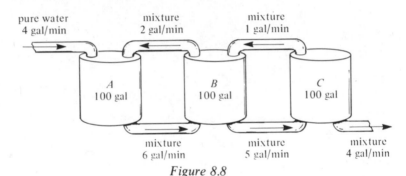

Figure 8.8

8.4   Preliminary Theory

Matrix notation

Before we examine the systematic procedure for solving linear first-order systems in normal form, it is necessary to investigate some of the basic underlying theory. A substantial amount of this theory will be quite similar to that which we considered in Chapter 4. However, we begin with the new and useful concept of a **matrix**.

> **DEFINITION 8.1**   A **matrix A** is any rectangular array of numbers or functions:
>
> $$\mathbf{A} = \begin{pmatrix} a_{11} & a_{12} & \cdots & a_{1n} \\ a_{21} & a_{22} & \cdots & a_{2n} \\ \vdots & & & \vdots \\ a_{m1} & a_{m2} & \cdots & a_{mn} \end{pmatrix}.$$

A matrix with m rows and n columns is usually referred to as an $m \times n$ (m by n) matrix.

Vectors

DEFINITION 8.2   A **column matrix X** is any matrix

$$X = \begin{pmatrix} b_1 \\ b_2 \\ \vdots \\ b_n \end{pmatrix}$$

having n rows, but one column.

A column matrix is also called a **column vector** or simply a **vector**.

Multiples of a matrix

DEFINITION 8.3   A **multiple** of a matrix A is defined to be

$$k\mathbf{A} = \begin{pmatrix} ka_{11} & ka_{12} & \cdots & ka_{1n} \\ ka_{21} & ka_{22} & \cdots & ka_{2n} \\ \vdots & & & \vdots \\ ka_{m1} & ka_{m2} & \cdots & ka_{mn} \end{pmatrix},$$

where k is a constant or a function.

EXAMPLES

(a)
$$5 \begin{pmatrix} 2 & -3 \\ 4 & -1 \\ \frac{1}{5} & 6 \end{pmatrix} = \begin{pmatrix} 10 & -15 \\ 20 & -5 \\ 1 & 30 \end{pmatrix}.$$

(b)
$$e^t \begin{pmatrix} 1 \\ -2 \\ 4 \end{pmatrix} = \begin{pmatrix} e^t \\ -2e^t \\ 4e^t \end{pmatrix}.$$

We note in passing that for any matrix $\mathbf{A}$ the product $k\mathbf{A}$ is the same as $\mathbf{A}k$. For example,

$$e^{-3t} \begin{pmatrix} 2 \\ 5 \end{pmatrix} = \begin{pmatrix} 2e^{-3t} \\ 5e^{-3t} \end{pmatrix} = \begin{pmatrix} 2 \\ 5 \end{pmatrix} e^{-3t}.$$

Addition of vectors

DEFINITION 8.4   Let

$$X_1 = \begin{pmatrix} b_1 \\ b_2 \\ \vdots \\ b_n \end{pmatrix} \quad \text{and} \quad X_2 = \begin{pmatrix} c_1 \\ c_2 \\ \vdots \\ c_n \end{pmatrix}$$

be two column vectors having the same number of entries. The **sum** of X_1 and X_2 is defined to be the column vector

$$X_1 + X_2 = \begin{pmatrix} b_1 + c_1 \\ b_2 + c_2 \\ \vdots \\ b_n + c_n \end{pmatrix}.$$

The **difference** of two column matrices is defined in the usual manner: $X_1 - X_2 = X_1 + (-X_2)$ where $-X_2 = (-1)X_2$.

Subsequently, we are most interested in the sum of vectors whose entries are functions.

EXAMPLE

The single matrix

$$\begin{pmatrix} 3t^2 - 2e^t \\ t^2 + 7t \\ 5t \end{pmatrix}$$

can be written as the sum of three column vectors

$$\begin{pmatrix} 3t^2 - 2e^t \\ t^2 + 7t \\ 5t \end{pmatrix} = \begin{pmatrix} 3t^2 \\ t^2 \\ 0 \end{pmatrix} + \begin{pmatrix} 0 \\ 7t \\ 5t \end{pmatrix} + \begin{pmatrix} -2e^t \\ 0 \\ 0 \end{pmatrix}$$

$$= \begin{pmatrix} 3 \\ 1 \\ 0 \end{pmatrix} t^2 + \begin{pmatrix} 0 \\ 7 \\ 5 \end{pmatrix} t + \begin{pmatrix} -2 \\ 0 \\ 0 \end{pmatrix} e^t.$$

Product of a matrix and a vector

DEFINITION 8.5   Let A be a matrix having m rows and n columns, and X be a column vector having n rows. We define the **product** AX to be the matrix

$$AX = \begin{pmatrix} a_{11} & a_{12} & \cdots & a_{1n} \\ a_{21} & a_{22} & \cdots & a_{2n} \\ \vdots & & & \vdots \\ a_{m1} & a_{m2} & \cdots & a_{mn} \end{pmatrix} \begin{pmatrix} b_1 \\ b_2 \\ \vdots \\ b_n \end{pmatrix}$$

$$= \begin{pmatrix} a_{11}b_1 + a_{12}b_2 + \cdots + a_{1n}b_n \\ a_{21}b_1 + a_{22}b_2 + \cdots + a_{2n}b_n \\ \vdots \\ a_{m1}b_1 + a_{m2}b_2 + \cdots + a_{mn}b_n \end{pmatrix}.$$

Each row of the resulting matrix is formed by multiplying the entries in a given row of **A** with the corresponding entries in the column **X** and then adding all the products. The reader might recognize the entries of the final matrix as being equivalent to the component definition of the inner or dot product of two vectors. Also, we must emphasize that **AX** is a *column matrix*.

EXAMPLES

(a)
$$\begin{pmatrix} 2 & -1 & 3 \\ 0 & 4 & 5 \\ 1 & -7 & 9 \end{pmatrix} \begin{pmatrix} -3 \\ 6 \\ 4 \end{pmatrix} = \begin{pmatrix} 2(-3) + (-1)6 + 3\cdot4 \\ 0(-3) + 4\cdot6 \quad + 5\cdot4 \\ 1(-3) + (-7)6 + 9\cdot4 \end{pmatrix}$$

$$= \begin{pmatrix} 0 \\ 44 \\ -9 \end{pmatrix}$$

(b)
$$\begin{pmatrix} -4 & 2 \\ 3 & 8 \end{pmatrix} \begin{pmatrix} x \\ y \end{pmatrix} = \begin{pmatrix} -4x + 2y \\ 3x + 8y \end{pmatrix}$$

Derivative of a matrix of functions

DEFINITION 8.6

If
$$\mathbf{X} = \begin{pmatrix} x_1(t) \\ x_2(t) \\ \vdots \\ x_n(t) \end{pmatrix}$$

is a column matrix of differentiable functions, we define its derivative **X′** to be the matrix

$$\frac{d\mathbf{X}}{dt} = \begin{pmatrix} \dfrac{dx_1}{dt} \\ \dfrac{dx_2}{dt} \\ \vdots \\ \dfrac{dx_n}{dt} \end{pmatrix}.$$

EXAMPLE

If
$$\mathbf{X} = \begin{pmatrix} \sin 2t \\ -3\cos 2t \end{pmatrix}$$

then
$$\frac{d\mathbf{X}}{dt} = \begin{pmatrix} 2\cos 2t \\ 6\sin 2t \end{pmatrix}.$$

Matrix form of a system   The point of this brief excursion into matrix theory is to provide a convenient notation for writing linear systems and their solutions. Thus if we define

$$\mathbf{X} = \begin{pmatrix} x_1 \\ x_2 \\ \cdot \\ \cdot \\ \cdot \\ x_n \end{pmatrix} = \begin{pmatrix} x_1(t) \\ x_2(t) \\ \cdot \\ \cdot \\ \cdot \\ x_n(t) \end{pmatrix}$$

and

$$\mathbf{A} = \begin{pmatrix} a_{11} & a_{12} & \cdots & a_{1n} \\ a_{21} & a_{22} & \cdots & a_{2n} \\ \cdot & & & \cdot \\ \cdot & & & \cdot \\ a_{n1} & a_{n2} & \cdots & a_{nn} \end{pmatrix}$$

then the homogeneous system

$$\frac{dx_1}{dt} = a_{11}x_1 + a_{12}x_2 + \cdots + a_{1n}x_n$$

$$\frac{dx_2}{dt} = a_{21}x_1 + a_{22}x_2 + \cdots + a_{2n}x_n$$

$$\cdot$$
$$\cdot$$

$$\frac{dx_n}{dt} = a_{n1}x_1 + a_{n2}x_2 + \cdots + a_{nn}x_n$$

(1)

can be written as

$$\frac{d}{dt}\begin{pmatrix} x_1 \\ x_2 \\ \cdot \\ \cdot \\ \cdot \\ x_n \end{pmatrix} = \begin{pmatrix} a_{11} & a_{12} & \cdots & a_{1n} \\ a_{21} & a_{22} & \cdots & a_{2n} \\ \cdot & & & \cdot \\ \cdot & & & \cdot \\ a_{n1} & a_{n2} & \cdots & a_{nn} \end{pmatrix}\begin{pmatrix} x_1 \\ x_2 \\ \cdot \\ \cdot \\ \cdot \\ x_n \end{pmatrix}$$

or simply

$$\frac{d\mathbf{X}}{dt} = \mathbf{A}\mathbf{X}.$$

(2)

Also, if we define

$$\mathbf{F}(t) = \begin{pmatrix} f_1(t) \\ f_2(t) \\ \cdot \\ \cdot \\ \cdot \\ f_n(t) \end{pmatrix}$$

where the $f_i(t)$, $i = 1, 2, \ldots, n$ are continuous on some common interval $a \le t \le b$, then the nonhomogeneous system

$$\frac{dx_1}{dt} = a_{11}x_1 + a_{12}x_2 + \cdots + a_{1n}x_n + f_1(t)$$

$$\frac{dx_2}{dt} = a_{21}x_1 + a_{22}x_2 + \cdots + a_{2n}x_n + f_2(t) \qquad (3)$$

$$\vdots$$

$$\frac{dx_n}{dt} = a_{n1}x_1 + a_{n2}x_2 + \cdots + a_{nn}x_n + f_n(t)$$

can be written as

$$\frac{d\mathbf{X}}{dt} = \mathbf{A}\mathbf{X} + \mathbf{F}(t). \qquad (4)$$

EXAMPLE

The matrix form of the homogeneous system

$$\frac{dx}{dt} = 2x - 3y$$

$$\frac{dy}{dt} = 6x + 5y$$

is

$$\frac{d\mathbf{X}}{dt} = \begin{pmatrix} 2 & -3 \\ 6 & 5 \end{pmatrix} \mathbf{X}$$

where

$$\mathbf{X} = \begin{pmatrix} x \\ y \end{pmatrix}.$$

EXAMPLE

The nonhomogeneous system

$$\frac{dx}{dt} = -2x + 5y + e^t - 2t$$

$$\frac{dy}{dt} = 4x - 3y + 10t$$

can be written as

$$\mathbf{X}' = \begin{pmatrix} -2 & 5 \\ 4 & -3 \end{pmatrix} \mathbf{X} + \begin{pmatrix} e^t - 2t \\ 10t \end{pmatrix}$$

or
$$\mathbf{X}' = \begin{pmatrix} -2 & 5 \\ 4 & -3 \end{pmatrix} \mathbf{X} + \begin{pmatrix} e^t \\ 0 \end{pmatrix} + \begin{pmatrix} -2t \\ 10t \end{pmatrix}$$

$$= \begin{pmatrix} -2 & 5 \\ 4 & -3 \end{pmatrix} \mathbf{X} + \begin{pmatrix} 1 \\ 0 \end{pmatrix} e^t + \begin{pmatrix} -2 \\ 10 \end{pmatrix} t$$

where $\mathbf{X} = \begin{pmatrix} x \\ y \end{pmatrix}$.

Homogeneous systems   In the next several definitions and theorems we are concerned only with homogeneous systems.

> **DEFINITION 8.7** A **solution vector** on an interval $a \le t \le b$ is any column matrix
>
> $$\mathbf{X} = \begin{pmatrix} x_1(t) \\ x_2(t) \\ \vdots \\ x_n(t) \end{pmatrix}$$
>
> whose entries are differentiable functions satisfying the system (2).

EXAMPLE   Both

$$\mathbf{X}_1 = \begin{pmatrix} 1 \\ -1 \end{pmatrix} e^{-2t} = \begin{pmatrix} e^{-2t} \\ -e^{-2t} \end{pmatrix} \quad \text{and} \quad \mathbf{X}_2 = \begin{pmatrix} 3 \\ 5 \end{pmatrix} e^{6t} = \begin{pmatrix} 3e^{6t} \\ 5e^{6t} \end{pmatrix}$$

are solutions of

$$\frac{dx}{dt} = x + 3y$$

$$\frac{dy}{dt} = 5x + 3y. \tag{5}$$

Since
$$\frac{d\mathbf{X}_1}{dt} = \begin{pmatrix} -2e^{-2t} \\ 2e^{-2t} \end{pmatrix}$$

and

$$\mathbf{AX}_1 = \begin{pmatrix} 1 & 3 \\ 5 & 3 \end{pmatrix} \begin{pmatrix} e^{-2t} \\ -e^{-2t} \end{pmatrix} = \begin{pmatrix} e^{-2t} - 3e^{-2t} \\ 5e^{-2t} - 3e^{-2t} \end{pmatrix} = \begin{pmatrix} -2e^{-2t} \\ 2e^{-2t} \end{pmatrix}$$

it is obvious that $\mathbf{X}_1' = \mathbf{AX}_1$.

As an alternative procedure, to say that $\mathbf{X}_2$ is a solution vector we mean that the pair of functions

$$x = 3e^{6t}, \qquad y = 5e^{6t}$$

satisfies the given system. Now

$$x' = 18e^{6t}, \qquad y' = 30e^{6t}$$

so that after substituting in (5) it follows

$$18e^{6t} = 3e^{6t} + 3(5e^{6t})$$

$$30e^{6t} = 5(3e^{6t}) + 3(5e^{6t}).$$

THEOREM 8.1   A constant multiple of any solution vector of the homogeneous system (2) is also a solution.

EXAMPLE   One solution of the system

$$\frac{dx}{dt} = \quad x + z$$

$$\frac{dy}{dt} = \quad x + y \qquad\qquad (6)$$

$$\frac{dz}{dt} = -2x - z$$

is

$$\mathbf{X}_1 = \begin{pmatrix} \cos t \\ -\frac{1}{2}\cos t + \frac{1}{2}\sin t \\ -\cos t - \sin t \end{pmatrix}.$$

For any constant c_1 the vector $\mathbf{X} = c_1\mathbf{X}_1$ is also a solution since

$$\frac{d\mathbf{X}}{dt} = \begin{pmatrix} -c_1\sin t \\ \frac{1}{2}c_1\sin t + \frac{1}{2}c_1\cos t \\ c_1\sin t - c_1\cos t \end{pmatrix}$$

and

$$\mathbf{AX} = \begin{pmatrix} 1 & 0 & 1 \\ 1 & 1 & 0 \\ -2 & 0 & -1 \end{pmatrix} \begin{pmatrix} c_1\cos t \\ -\frac{1}{2}c_1\cos t + \frac{1}{2}c_1\sin t \\ -c_1\cos t - c_1\sin t \end{pmatrix}$$

$$= \begin{pmatrix} -c_1 \sin t \\ \frac{1}{2}c_1 \cos t + \frac{1}{2}c_1 \sin t \\ -c_1 \cos t + c_1 \sin t \end{pmatrix}.$$

Inspection of the resulting matrices shows that $\mathbf{X}' = \mathbf{AX}$.

The superposition principle

Theorem 8.1 is just a special case of the general **superposition principle**.

THEOREM 8.2   If $\mathbf{X}_1, \mathbf{X}_2, \ldots, \mathbf{X}_k$ are solution vectors of the homogeneous system (2), then so is the linear combination

$$\mathbf{X} = c_1 \mathbf{X}_1 + c_2 \mathbf{X}_2 + \cdots + c_k \mathbf{X}_k,$$

where the $c_i, i = 1, 2, \ldots, n$, are arbitrary constants.

EXAMPLE

If

$$\mathbf{X}_2 = \begin{pmatrix} 0 \\ 1 \\ 0 \end{pmatrix} e^t = \begin{pmatrix} 0 \\ e^t \\ 0 \end{pmatrix}$$

then

$$\mathbf{X}_2' = \begin{pmatrix} 0 \\ e^t \\ 0 \end{pmatrix}$$

and

$$\mathbf{AX}_2 = \begin{pmatrix} 1 & 0 & 1 \\ 1 & 1 & 0 \\ -2 & 0 & -1 \end{pmatrix} \begin{pmatrix} 0 \\ e^t \\ 0 \end{pmatrix} = \begin{pmatrix} 0 \\ e^t \\ 0 \end{pmatrix}.$$

Thus we see that $\mathbf{X}_2$ is also a solution vector of the system (6) given in the preceding example. By the superposition principle the sum

$$\mathbf{X} = c_1 \mathbf{X}_1 + c_2 \mathbf{X}_2$$

$$= c_1 \begin{pmatrix} \cos t \\ -\frac{1}{2}\cos t + \frac{1}{2}\sin t \\ -\cos t - \sin t \end{pmatrix} + c_2 \begin{pmatrix} 0 \\ e^t \\ 0 \end{pmatrix}$$

is yet another solution.

Linear independence

We are primarily interested in linearly independent solutions of the homogeneous system (2).

DEFINITION 8.8   Let $X_1, X_2, \ldots, X_k$ be a set of solution vectors of the system (2) on some interval $a \leq t \leq b$. We say that the set is **linearly dependent** on the interval if and only if there exist constants $c_1, c_2, \ldots, c_n$, not all zero, such that

$$c_1 X_1 + c_2 X_2 + \cdots + c_k X_k = 0$$

for every t in the interval. Here 0 denotes a column matrix consisting of all zeros. If the set of vectors is not linearly dependent on the interval, it is said to be **linearly independent**.

The case when $k = 2$ should be clear; two solution vectors X_1 and X_2 are linearly dependent if one is a constant multiple of the other, and conversely. For $k > 2$, a set of solution vectors is linearly dependent if we can express at least one solution vector as a nontrivial linear combination of the remaining vectors.

EXAMPLE

It can be verified that

$$X_1 = \begin{pmatrix} 3 \\ 1 \end{pmatrix} e^t \quad \text{and} \quad X_2 = \begin{pmatrix} 1 \\ 1 \end{pmatrix} e^{-t}$$

are solution vectors of the system

$$X' = \begin{pmatrix} 2 & -3 \\ 1 & -2 \end{pmatrix} X.$$

Now X_1 and X_2 are linearly independent on the t-axis since

$$c_1 X_1 + c_2 X_2 = 0 \quad \text{or} \quad c_1 \begin{pmatrix} 3 \\ 1 \end{pmatrix} e^t + c_2 \begin{pmatrix} 1 \\ 1 \end{pmatrix} e^{-t} = \begin{pmatrix} 0 \\ 0 \end{pmatrix}$$

is equivalent to

$$3c_1 e^t + c_2 e^{-t} = 0$$
$$c_1 e^t + c_2 e^{-t} = 0.$$

Solving this system for c_1 and c_2 immediately yields $c_1 = 0$ and $c_2 = 0$.

EXAMPLE

The vector

$$X_3 = \begin{pmatrix} e^t + \cosh t \\ \cosh t \end{pmatrix}$$

is also a solution of the system of differential equations given in the preceding example. However, $\mathbf{X}_1, \mathbf{X}_2$, and $\mathbf{X}_3$ are linearly dependent since

$$\mathbf{X}_3 = \tfrac{1}{2}\mathbf{X}_1 + \tfrac{1}{2}\mathbf{X}_2.$$

Wronskian

As in our earlier consideration of the theory of a single ordinary differential equation we can introduce the concept of the **Wronskian** determinant as a test for linear independence. We state the following theorem without proof.

THEOREM 8.3   Let

$$\mathbf{X}_1 = \begin{pmatrix} x_{11} \\ x_{21} \\ \vdots \\ x_{n1} \end{pmatrix}, \mathbf{X}_2 = \begin{pmatrix} x_{12} \\ x_{22} \\ \vdots \\ x_{n2} \end{pmatrix}, \ldots, \mathbf{X}_n = \begin{pmatrix} x_{1n} \\ x_{2n} \\ \vdots \\ x_{nn} \end{pmatrix}$$

be n solution vectors of the homogeneous system (2) on some interval $a \leq t \leq b$. A necessary and sufficient condition that the set of solutions be linearly independent is that the Wronskian

$$W(\mathbf{X}_1, \mathbf{X}_2, \ldots, \mathbf{X}_n) = \begin{vmatrix} x_{11} & x_{12} \cdots x_{1n} \\ x_{21} & x_{22} \cdots x_{2n} \\ \vdots \\ x_{n1} & x_{n2} \cdots x_{nn} \end{vmatrix} \neq 0 \tag{7}$$

for every t in $a \leq t \leq b$.

In fact, it can be shown that if $\mathbf{X}_1, \mathbf{X}_2, \ldots, \mathbf{X}_n$ are solution vectors of (2), then either

$$W(\mathbf{X}_1, \mathbf{X}_2, \ldots, \mathbf{X}_n) \neq 0$$

for every t in $a \leq t \leq b$, or

$$W(\mathbf{X}_1, \mathbf{X}_2, \ldots, \mathbf{X}_n) = 0$$

for every t in the interval. Thus if we can show that $W \neq 0$ for some t_0 in $a \leq t \leq b$, then $W \neq 0$ for every t and hence the solutions are linearly independent on the interval.

Notice that, unlike our previous definition of the Wronskian, the determinant (7) does not involve differentiation.

EXAMPLE

We have already seen (page 364) that

$$\mathbf{X}_1 = \begin{pmatrix} 1 \\ -1 \end{pmatrix} e^{-2t} = \begin{pmatrix} e^{-2t} \\ -e^{-2t} \end{pmatrix}$$

and

$$\mathbf{X}_2 = \begin{pmatrix} 3 \\ 5 \end{pmatrix} e^{6t} = \begin{pmatrix} 3e^{6t} \\ 5e^{6t} \end{pmatrix}$$

are solutions of the system

$$\mathbf{X}' = \begin{pmatrix} 1 & 3 \\ 5 & 3 \end{pmatrix} \mathbf{X}.$$

Clearly, $\mathbf{X}_1$ and $\mathbf{X}_2$ are linearly independent on $-\infty < t < \infty$ since neither vector is a constant multiple of the other. In addition, we have

$$W(\mathbf{X}_1, \mathbf{X}_2) = \begin{vmatrix} e^{-2t} & 3e^{6t} \\ -e^{-2t} & 5e^{6t} \end{vmatrix}$$

$$= 8e^{4t}$$

$$\neq 0$$

for all real values of t.

DEFINITION 8.9 Let $\mathbf{X}_1, \mathbf{X}_2, \ldots, \mathbf{X}_n$ be linearly independent solution vectors of (2) on some interval $a \leq t \leq b$. We define the **general solution** of the system to be the sum

$$\mathbf{X} = c_1\mathbf{X}_1 + c_2\mathbf{X}_2 + \cdots + c_n\mathbf{X}_n. \tag{8}$$

Although we shall not pursue the details, it can be shown that, for appropriate choices of the constants, *any* solution of (2) can be obtained from (8).

EXAMPLE

Since the vectors

$$\mathbf{X}_1 = \begin{pmatrix} 1 \\ -1 \end{pmatrix} e^{-2t}, \qquad \mathbf{X}_2 = \begin{pmatrix} 3 \\ 5 \end{pmatrix} e^{6t}$$

are linearly independent solutions of

$$\mathbf{X}' = \begin{pmatrix} 1 & 3 \\ 5 & 3 \end{pmatrix} \mathbf{X}$$

on the interval $-\infty < t < \infty$, the general solution of the system on the interval is

$$\mathbf{X} = c_1\mathbf{X}_1 + c_2\mathbf{X}_2$$

$$= c_1\begin{pmatrix} 1 \\ -1 \end{pmatrix}e^{-2t} + c_2\begin{pmatrix} 3 \\ 5 \end{pmatrix}e^{6t}.$$

EXAMPLE   The vectors

$$\mathbf{X}_1 = \begin{pmatrix} \cos t \\ -\tfrac{1}{2}\cos t + \tfrac{1}{2}\sin t \\ -\cos t - \sin t \end{pmatrix}, \quad \mathbf{X}_2 = \begin{pmatrix} 0 \\ 1 \\ 0 \end{pmatrix}e^{t}, \quad \mathbf{X}_3 = \begin{pmatrix} \sin t \\ -\tfrac{1}{2}\sin t - \tfrac{1}{2}\cos t \\ -\sin t + \cos t \end{pmatrix}$$

are solutions* of the system

$$\mathbf{X}' = \begin{pmatrix} 1 & 0 & 1 \\ 1 & 1 & 0 \\ -2 & 0 & -1 \end{pmatrix}\mathbf{X}.$$

Now

$$W(\mathbf{X}_1,\mathbf{X}_2,\mathbf{X}_3) = \begin{vmatrix} \cos t & 0 & \sin t \\ -\tfrac{1}{2}\cos t + \tfrac{1}{2}\sin t & e^{t} & -\tfrac{1}{2}\sin t - \tfrac{1}{2}\cos t \\ -\cos t - \sin t & 0 & -\sin t + \cos t \end{vmatrix}$$

$$= e^{t}\begin{vmatrix} \cos t & \sin t \\ -\cos t - \sin t & -\sin t + \cos t \end{vmatrix}$$

$$= e^{t}$$

$$\neq 0$$

for all real values of t. We conclude that $\mathbf{X}_1, \mathbf{X}_2$, and $\mathbf{X}_3$ are linearly independent on $-\infty < t < \infty$. Thus the general solution on the interval is

$$\mathbf{X} = c_1\mathbf{X}_1 + c_2\mathbf{X}_2 + c_3\mathbf{X}_3$$

$$= c_1\begin{pmatrix} \cos t \\ -\tfrac{1}{2}\cos t + \tfrac{1}{2}\sin t \\ -\cos t - \sin t \end{pmatrix} + c_2\begin{pmatrix} 0 \\ 1 \\ 0 \end{pmatrix}e^{t} + c_3\begin{pmatrix} \sin t \\ -\tfrac{1}{2}\sin t - \tfrac{1}{2}\cos t \\ -\sin t + \cos t \end{pmatrix}.$$

---

* We have already seen (page 366) that $\mathbf{X}_1$ and $\mathbf{X}_2$ are solutions; we leave it as an exercise to demonstrate that $\mathbf{X}_3$ is also a solution.

Nonhomogeneous systems

For nonhomogeneous systems we have the following.

DEFINITION 8.10   A **particular solution** $\mathbf{X}_p$ on an interval $a \leq t \leq b$ is any vector whose entries are functions satisfying the system (4).

EXAMPLE

The vector

$$\mathbf{X}_p = \begin{pmatrix} 3t - 4 \\ -5t + 6 \end{pmatrix}$$

is a particular solution of the system

$$\mathbf{X}' = \begin{pmatrix} 1 & 3 \\ 5 & 3 \end{pmatrix}\mathbf{X} + \begin{pmatrix} 12t - 11 \\ -3 \end{pmatrix}$$

since

$$\mathbf{X}'_p = \begin{pmatrix} 3 \\ -5 \end{pmatrix}$$

and

$$\begin{pmatrix} 1 & 3 \\ 5 & 3 \end{pmatrix}\mathbf{X}_p + \begin{pmatrix} 12t - 11 \\ -3 \end{pmatrix} = \begin{pmatrix} 1 & 3 \\ 5 & 3 \end{pmatrix}\begin{pmatrix} 3t - 4 \\ -5t + 6 \end{pmatrix} + \begin{pmatrix} 12t - 11 \\ -3 \end{pmatrix}$$

$$= \begin{pmatrix} (3t - 4) + 3(-5t + 6) \\ 5(3t - 4) + 3(-5t + 6) \end{pmatrix} + \begin{pmatrix} 12t - 11 \\ -3 \end{pmatrix}$$

$$= \begin{pmatrix} -12t + 14 \\ -2 \end{pmatrix} + \begin{pmatrix} 12t - 11 \\ -3 \end{pmatrix}$$

$$= \begin{pmatrix} 3 \\ -5 \end{pmatrix}$$

$$= \mathbf{X}'_p.$$

DEFINITION 8.11   Let $\mathbf{X}_p$ be any particular solution vector of (4) on an interval $a \leq t \leq b$, and let

$$\mathbf{X}_c = c_1\mathbf{X}_1 + c_2\mathbf{X}_2 + \cdots + c_n\mathbf{X}_n$$

denote the general solution on the same interval of the corresponding homogeneous system (2). The **general solution** of the nonhomogeneous system (4) is defined to be

$$\mathbf{X} = \mathbf{X}_c + \mathbf{X}_p. \tag{9}$$

EXAMPLE   We have shown previously that the general solution of the homogeneous system

$$X' = \begin{pmatrix} 1 & 3 \\ 5 & 3 \end{pmatrix} X$$

is

$$X_c = c_1 \begin{pmatrix} 1 \\ -1 \end{pmatrix} e^{-2t} + c_2 \begin{pmatrix} 3 \\ 5 \end{pmatrix} e^{6t}$$

and that a particular solution of the nonhomogeneous system

$$X' = \begin{pmatrix} 1 & 3 \\ 5 & 3 \end{pmatrix} X + \begin{pmatrix} 12t - 11 \\ -3 \end{pmatrix} \qquad (10)$$

is

$$X_p = \begin{pmatrix} 3t - 4 \\ -5t + 6 \end{pmatrix}.$$

Hence by Definition 8.11

$$X = X_c + X_p$$

$$= c_1 \begin{pmatrix} 1 \\ -1 \end{pmatrix} e^{-2t} + c_2 \begin{pmatrix} 3 \\ 5 \end{pmatrix} e^{6t} + \begin{pmatrix} 3t - 4 \\ -5t + 6 \end{pmatrix}.$$

is the general solution of (10).

If **X** is *any* solution of the nonhomogeneous system (4) then it is always possible to find appropriate constants $c_1, c_2, \ldots, c_n$ so that **X** can be obtained from the general solution (9).

EXERCISES 8.4   Answers to odd-numbered problems begin on page A-24 of the Appendix. In Problems 1–5 write the indicated sum as a one column matrix.

1. $4\begin{pmatrix} -1 \\ 2 \end{pmatrix} - 2\begin{pmatrix} 2 \\ 8 \end{pmatrix} + 3\begin{pmatrix} -2 \\ 3 \end{pmatrix}$

2. $3t\begin{pmatrix} 2 \\ t \\ -1 \end{pmatrix} + (t-1)\begin{pmatrix} -1 \\ -t \\ 3 \end{pmatrix} - 2\begin{pmatrix} 3t \\ 4 \\ -5t \end{pmatrix}$

3. $\begin{pmatrix} 2 & -3 \\ 1 & 4 \end{pmatrix}\begin{pmatrix} -2 \\ 5 \end{pmatrix} - \begin{pmatrix} -1 & 6 \\ -2 & 3 \end{pmatrix}\begin{pmatrix} -7 \\ 2 \end{pmatrix}$

★4. $\begin{pmatrix} 1 & -3 & 4 \\ 2 & 5 & -1 \\ 0 & -4 & -2 \end{pmatrix}\begin{pmatrix} t \\ 2t - 1 \\ -t \end{pmatrix} + \begin{pmatrix} -t \\ 1 \\ 4 \end{pmatrix} - \begin{pmatrix} 2 \\ 8 \\ -6 \end{pmatrix}$

5. $\dfrac{d}{dt}\begin{pmatrix} 4 & -2 \\ 6 & -5 \end{pmatrix}\begin{pmatrix} 2e^{2t} \\ 3e^{2t} \end{pmatrix} - \begin{pmatrix} 4 \\ -6 \end{pmatrix}e^{2t}$

In Problems 6–9 write the given systems in matrix form.

6. $\dfrac{dx}{dt} = 3x - 5y$

$\dfrac{dy}{dt} = 4x + 8y$

7. $\dfrac{dx}{dt} = \quad x - y$

$\dfrac{dy}{dt} = \quad x + 2z$

$\dfrac{dz}{dt} = -x + z$

8. $\dfrac{dx}{dt} = \quad x - y + z + t - 1$

$\dfrac{dy}{dt} = 2x + y - z - 3t^2$

$\dfrac{dz}{dt} = \quad x + y + z + t^2 - t + 2$

9. $\dfrac{dx}{dt} = -3x + 4y + \quad e^{-t}\sin 2t$

$\dfrac{dy}{dt} = \quad 5x + 9y + 4e^{-t}\cos 2t$

★10. Write the following system without the use of matrices.

$$\frac{d}{dt}\begin{pmatrix} x \\ y \\ z \end{pmatrix} = \begin{pmatrix} 1 & -1 & 2 \\ 3 & -4 & 1 \\ -2 & 5 & 6 \end{pmatrix}\begin{pmatrix} x \\ y \\ z \end{pmatrix} + \begin{pmatrix} 1 \\ 2 \\ 2 \end{pmatrix}e^{-t} - \begin{pmatrix} 3 \\ -1 \\ 1 \end{pmatrix}t$$

In Problems 11–15 verify that the vector **X** is a solution of the given system.

11. $\dfrac{dx}{dt} = 3x - 4y$

$\dfrac{dy}{dt} = 4x - 7y$

$$\mathbf{X} = \begin{pmatrix} 1 \\ 2 \end{pmatrix}e^{-5t}$$

12. $\mathbf{X'} = \begin{pmatrix} 1 & 0 & 1 \\ 1 & 1 & 0 \\ -2 & 0 & -1 \end{pmatrix}\mathbf{X}; \qquad \mathbf{X} = \begin{pmatrix} \sin t \\ -\tfrac{1}{2}\sin t - \tfrac{1}{2}\cos t \\ -\sin t + \cos t \end{pmatrix}$

13. $\dfrac{d\mathbf{X}}{dt} = \begin{pmatrix} 1 & 2 & 1 \\ 6 & -1 & 0 \\ -1 & -2 & -1 \end{pmatrix}\mathbf{X}; \qquad \mathbf{X} = \begin{pmatrix} 1 \\ 6 \\ -13 \end{pmatrix}$

14. $\mathbf{X'} = \begin{pmatrix} 2 & 0 \\ -1 & 0 \end{pmatrix}\mathbf{X}; \qquad \mathbf{X} = \begin{pmatrix} 1 \\ 3 \end{pmatrix}e^{t} + \begin{pmatrix} 4 \\ -4 \end{pmatrix}te^{t}$

15. $\dfrac{dx}{dt} = -2x + 5y$

$$\mathbf{X} = \begin{pmatrix} 5\cos t \\ 3\cos t - \sin t \end{pmatrix} e^{t}$$

$\dfrac{dy}{dt} = -2x + 4y$

In Problems 16–20 verify that the vector $\mathbf{X}_p$ is a particular solution of the given system.

16. $\mathbf{X}' = \begin{pmatrix} 2 & 1 \\ 1 & -1 \end{pmatrix} \mathbf{X} + \begin{pmatrix} -5 \\ 2 \end{pmatrix}$; $\mathbf{X}_p = \begin{pmatrix} 1 \\ 3 \end{pmatrix}$

17. $\dfrac{dx}{dt} = x + 4y + 2t - 7$

$$\mathbf{X}_p = \begin{pmatrix} 2 \\ -1 \end{pmatrix} t + \begin{pmatrix} 5 \\ 1 \end{pmatrix}$$

$\dfrac{dy}{dt} = 3x + 2y - 4t - 18$

18. $\mathbf{X}' = \begin{pmatrix} 1 & 2 & 3 \\ -4 & 2 & 0 \\ -6 & 1 & 0 \end{pmatrix} \mathbf{X} + \begin{pmatrix} -1 \\ 4 \\ 3 \end{pmatrix} \sin 3t$; $\mathbf{X}_p = \begin{pmatrix} \sin 3t \\ 0 \\ \cos 3t \end{pmatrix}$

19. $\mathbf{X}' = \begin{pmatrix} 2 & 1 \\ 3 & 4 \end{pmatrix} \mathbf{X} - \begin{pmatrix} 1 \\ 7 \end{pmatrix} e^{t}$; $\mathbf{X}_p = \begin{pmatrix} 1 \\ 1 \end{pmatrix} e^{t} + \begin{pmatrix} 1 \\ -1 \end{pmatrix} t e^{t}$

20. $\dfrac{dx}{dt} = -x - y + t^2 + 4t - 1$

$$\mathbf{X}_p = \begin{pmatrix} 1 \\ 0 \end{pmatrix} t^2 - \begin{pmatrix} 2 \\ -4 \end{pmatrix} t + \begin{pmatrix} 1 \\ 0 \end{pmatrix}$$

$\dfrac{dy}{dt} = -x + y + t^2 - 6t + 5$

21. Prove that the general solution of

$$\mathbf{X}' = \begin{pmatrix} 0 & 6 & 0 \\ 1 & 0 & 1 \\ 1 & 1 & 0 \end{pmatrix} \mathbf{X}$$

is $\mathbf{X} = c_1 \begin{pmatrix} 6 \\ -1 \\ -5 \end{pmatrix} e^{-t} + c_2 \begin{pmatrix} -3 \\ 1 \\ 1 \end{pmatrix} e^{-2t} + c_3 \begin{pmatrix} 2 \\ 1 \\ 1 \end{pmatrix} e^{3t}.$

In Problems 22–25 the given vectors are solutions of a system $\mathbf{X}' = \mathbf{A}\mathbf{X}$. By computing the Wronskian, determine whether the set is linearly independent on $-\infty < t < \infty$.

22. $\mathbf{X}_1 = \begin{pmatrix} 1 \\ 1 \end{pmatrix} e^{-2t}, \qquad \mathbf{X}_2 = \begin{pmatrix} 1 \\ -1 \end{pmatrix} e^{-6t}$

23. $\mathbf{X}_1 = \begin{pmatrix} 1 \\ 6 \\ -13 \end{pmatrix}, \qquad \mathbf{X}_2 = \begin{pmatrix} 1 \\ -2 \\ -1 \end{pmatrix} e^{-4t}, \qquad \mathbf{X}_3 = \begin{pmatrix} 2 \\ 3 \\ -2 \end{pmatrix} e^{3t}$

★24. $\mathbf{X}_1 = \begin{pmatrix} 1 \\ -1 \end{pmatrix} e^{t}, \qquad \mathbf{X}_2 = \begin{pmatrix} 2 \\ 6 \end{pmatrix} e^{t} + \begin{pmatrix} 8 \\ -8 \end{pmatrix} t e^{t}$

25. $\mathbf{X}_1 = \begin{pmatrix} 1 \\ -2 \\ 4 \end{pmatrix} + t \begin{pmatrix} 1 \\ 2 \\ 2 \end{pmatrix}, \qquad \mathbf{X}_2 = \begin{pmatrix} 1 \\ -2 \\ 4 \end{pmatrix}, \qquad \mathbf{X}_3 = \begin{pmatrix} 3 \\ -6 \\ 12 \end{pmatrix} + t \begin{pmatrix} 2 \\ 4 \\ 4 \end{pmatrix}$

★26. For two 2×2 matrices

$$\mathbf{A} = \begin{pmatrix} a_{11} & a_{12} \\ a_{21} & a_{22} \end{pmatrix}, \qquad \mathbf{B} = \begin{pmatrix} b_{11} & b_{12} \\ b_{21} & b_{22} \end{pmatrix}$$

we define the sum by

$$\mathbf{A} + \mathbf{B} = \begin{pmatrix} a_{11} + b_{11} & a_{12} + b_{12} \\ a_{21} + b_{21} & a_{22} + b_{22} \end{pmatrix}$$

and the product by

$$\mathbf{AB} = \begin{pmatrix} a_{11}b_{11} + a_{12}b_{21} & a_{11}b_{12} + a_{12}b_{22} \\ a_{21}b_{11} + a_{22}b_{21} & a_{21}b_{12} + a_{22}b_{22} \end{pmatrix}.$$

If $\quad \mathbf{A} = \begin{pmatrix} 2 & -3 \\ -5 & 4 \end{pmatrix} \quad$ and $\quad \mathbf{B} = \begin{pmatrix} -1 & 6 \\ 3 & 2 \end{pmatrix}$

find the following matrices.

(a) $\mathbf{A} + \mathbf{B}$

(b) $\mathbf{A} - \mathbf{B} = \mathbf{A} + (-\mathbf{B})$

(c) $\mathbf{AB}$

(d) $\mathbf{BA}$ [*Hint:* Interchange the symbols a and b in the preceding product definition while retaining the same subscripts.]

(e) $\mathbf{A}(\mathbf{A} - 2\mathbf{B})$

(f) $\mathbf{B}(2\mathbf{A} + 3\mathbf{B})$

(g) $\mathbf{A}(\mathbf{AB})$

(h) $\mathbf{B}(\mathbf{BA})$

(i) $\mathbf{A}^2 = \mathbf{AA}$

(j) $\mathbf{B}^2 = \mathbf{BB}$

27. Let $\quad \mathbf{A} = \begin{pmatrix} a_{11} & a_{12} \\ a_{21} & a_{22} \end{pmatrix} \quad$ and $\quad \mathbf{C} = \begin{pmatrix} c_1 \\ c_2 \end{pmatrix}.$

Suppose $\mathbf{AC} = \mathbf{0}$ for *every* column matrix $\mathbf{C}$. Show that the entries of $\mathbf{A}$ must be all zero.

8.5   Homogeneous Linear Systems

We saw in the preceding section that the general solution of the system

$$\frac{dx}{dt} = x + 3y$$

$$\frac{dy}{dt} = 5x + 3y$$

is
$$\mathbf{X} = c_1 \mathbf{X}_1 + c_2 \mathbf{X}_2$$

$$= c_1 \begin{pmatrix} 1 \\ -1 \end{pmatrix} e^{-2t} + c_2 \begin{pmatrix} 3 \\ 5 \end{pmatrix} e^{6t}.$$

Since both solution vectors have the basic form

$$\mathbf{X}_i = \begin{pmatrix} k_1 \\ k_2 \end{pmatrix} e^{\lambda_i t} \qquad i = 1, 2,$$

we are prompted to ask whether we can always find solutions of the form

$$\mathbf{X} = \begin{pmatrix} k_1 \\ k_2 \\ \vdots \\ k_n \end{pmatrix} e^{\lambda t} \tag{1}$$

for the general homogeneous linear first-order system

$$\frac{d\mathbf{X}}{dt} = \mathbf{AX}. \tag{2}$$

Given the discussion of Section 8.4 and the fact that a system such as (2) with constant coefficients can be reduced to a single nth-order differential equation, it should not come as any surprise that there do indeed exist solutions of form (1).

For the sake of discussion and illustration we shall limit our attention principally to the case of systems in two dependent variables $x(t)$ and $y(t)$.

Eigenvalues and eigenvectors

If we make the assumption that

$$\mathbf{X} = \begin{pmatrix} k_1 \\ k_2 \end{pmatrix} e^{\lambda t} \tag{3}$$

is a solution vector of (2) then

$$\frac{d\mathbf{X}}{dt} = \begin{pmatrix} k_1 \\ k_2 \end{pmatrix} \lambda e^{\lambda t}$$

so that the system becomes

$$\begin{pmatrix} k_1 \\ k_2 \end{pmatrix} \lambda e^{\lambda t} = \begin{pmatrix} a_{11} & a_{12} \\ a_{21} & a_{22} \end{pmatrix} \begin{pmatrix} k_1 \\ k_2 \end{pmatrix} e^{\lambda t}.$$

After dividing out $e^{\lambda t}$ and rearranging we obtain

$$\begin{pmatrix} a_{11} & a_{12} \\ a_{21} & a_{22} \end{pmatrix} \begin{pmatrix} k_1 \\ k_2 \end{pmatrix} - \lambda \begin{pmatrix} k_1 \\ k_2 \end{pmatrix} = \begin{pmatrix} 0 \\ 0 \end{pmatrix}$$

$$\begin{pmatrix} (a_{11} - \lambda)k_1 + & a_{12}k_2 \\ a_{21}k_1 + (a_{22} - \lambda)k_2 \end{pmatrix} = \begin{pmatrix} 0 \\ 0 \end{pmatrix} \tag{4}$$

or

$$\begin{pmatrix} a_{11} - \lambda & a_{12} \\ a_{21} & a_{22} - \lambda \end{pmatrix} \begin{pmatrix} k_1 \\ k_2 \end{pmatrix} = \begin{pmatrix} 0 \\ 0 \end{pmatrix}. \tag{5}$$

Equations (4) and (5) are equivalent to the simultaneous algebraic equations

$$
\begin{aligned}
(a_{11} - \lambda)k_1 + & \quad a_{12}k_2 = 0 \\
a_{21}k_1 + & (a_{22} - \lambda)k_2 = 0.
\end{aligned}
\tag{6}
$$

Although an immediate solution to this homogeneous system is $k_1 = 0$ and $k_2 = 0$, we are naturally seeking only nonzero solutions. Recall from algebra, a necessary and sufficient condition for the existence of a nontrivial solution for systems such as (6) is that the determinant of the coefficients must be zero. That is,

$$\begin{pmatrix} k_1 \\ k_2 \end{pmatrix}$$

is a nontrivial solution vector of (5) if and only if λ is a solution of

$$\begin{vmatrix} a_{11} - \lambda & a_{12} \\ a_{21} & a_{22} - \lambda \end{vmatrix} = 0 \tag{7}$$

or, after expanding,

$$\lambda^2 - (a_{11} + a_{22})\lambda + a_{11}a_{22} - a_{12}a_{21} = 0. \tag{8}$$

The values of λ satisfying (8) are said to be **eigenvalues*** of the matrix **A** and the solution vector

$$\begin{pmatrix} k_1 \\ k_2 \end{pmatrix}$$

---

* From the German word *eigenwert* meaning characteristic or particular value.

of (5), corresponding to a specific value of λ, is called an **eigenvector**. Equation (8) is also called the **characteristic equation** of the matrix **A**.

The method of solution

The procedure for solving the homogeneous system

$$\frac{dx}{dt} = a_{11}x + a_{12}y$$

$$\frac{dy}{dt} = a_{21}x + a_{22}y$$

$\qquad(9)$

is outlined as follows.

(1)   Identify the matrix of coefficients

$$\begin{pmatrix} a_{11} & a_{12} \\ a_{21} & a_{22} \end{pmatrix}$$

and form the determinant

$$\begin{vmatrix} a_{11} - \lambda & a_{12} \\ a_{21} & a_{22} - \lambda \end{vmatrix}.$$

Expand, and set it equal to zero. This determines the eigenvalues. Since the resulting equation (8) is a quadratic polynomial equation, we need to distinguish three cases as we did in the discussion of Section 4.3. Namely, the values of λ can be real and distinct, real and equal, or complex.

(2)   For each value of λ, find the corresponding eigenvector by solving the system (6). When the eigenvalues are real and distinct or complex, we can always find two eigenvectors. When the roots of (8) are equal, then the assumption (3) leads to only one solution of (9).* In this latter circumstance we shall have to modify the assumed form of (3).

(3)   Having found two eigenvectors, say,

$$\begin{pmatrix} k_1 \\ k_2 \end{pmatrix} \quad \text{and} \quad \begin{pmatrix} k_1' \\ k_2' \end{pmatrix}$$

corresponding respectively to different eigenvalues λ_1 and λ_2, form the solution vectors

$$\mathbf{X}_1 = \begin{pmatrix} k_1 \\ k_2 \end{pmatrix} e^{\lambda_1 t} \quad \text{and} \quad \mathbf{X}_2 = \begin{pmatrix} k_1' \\ k_2' \end{pmatrix} e^{\lambda_1 t}.$$

---

* There does exist one unexciting case where $\lambda_1 = \lambda_2$ yields two solutions of form (1) with $n = 2$. For systems involving more than two variables we may be able to find two distinct eigenvectors corresponding to equal eigenvalues. See Problems 14 and 15.

The general solution of (9) is the linear combination

$$\mathbf{X} = c_1 \mathbf{X}_1 + c_2 \mathbf{X}_2. \tag{10}$$

We shall see that even when $\lambda_1 = \lambda_2$, the general solution of (9) is still of form (10), but that the entries in one of the solution vectors will be linear polynomials in the variable t rather than simply constants.

CASE I.   Distinct Real Eigenvalues

The preceding three steps are illustrated in detail in the following example.

EXAMPLE   Solve the system

$$\frac{dx}{dt} = 2x + 3y$$

$$\tag{11}$$

$$\frac{dy}{dt} = 2x + \ y.$$

Solution: The assumed solution

$$\mathbf{X} = \begin{pmatrix} x(t) \\ y(t) \end{pmatrix} = \begin{pmatrix} k_1 \\ k_2 \end{pmatrix} e^{\lambda t}$$

leads to the system

$$(2 - \lambda)k_1 + \qquad 3k_2 = 0$$

$$\tag{12}$$

$$2k_1 + (1 - \lambda)k_2 = 0.$$

And so in order to have nontrivial solutions, λ must satisfy

$$\begin{vmatrix} 2 - \lambda & 3 \\ 2 & 1 - \lambda \end{vmatrix} = 0$$

or

$$(2 - \lambda)(1 - \lambda) - 6 = 0$$

$$\lambda^2 - 3\lambda - 4 = 0$$

$$(\lambda + 1)(\lambda - 4) = 0.$$

Thus the eigenvalues are $\lambda_1 = -1$ and $\lambda_2 = 4$. For $\lambda_1 = -1$ the system (12) becomes

$$3k_1 + 3k_2 = 0$$

$$2k_1 + 2k_2 = 0$$

which implies that $k_2 = -k_1$. The related eigenvector is then

$$\begin{pmatrix} k_1 \\ k_2 \end{pmatrix} = k_1 \begin{pmatrix} 1 \\ -1 \end{pmatrix} \tag{13}$$

For $\lambda_2 = 4$ we find

$$-2k_1 + 3k_2 = 0$$
$$2k_1 - 3k_2 = 0$$

so that $k_2 = 2k_1/3$ and, therefore, the corresponding eigenvector is

$$\begin{pmatrix} k_1 \\ k_2 \end{pmatrix} = k_1 \begin{pmatrix} 1 \\ 2/3 \end{pmatrix} \tag{14}$$

We are really interested only in the basic eigenvectors in (13) and (14), hence to avoid confusion and to emphasize the fact that the values of k_1 in (13) and (14) *are not related*, we can choose $k_1 = 1$ in each case. By the superposition principle a linear combination of

$$\mathbf{X}_1 = \begin{pmatrix} 1 \\ -1 \end{pmatrix} e^{-t} \tag{15}$$

and

$$\mathbf{X}_2 = \begin{pmatrix} 1 \\ 2/3 \end{pmatrix} e^{4t} \tag{16}$$

will also be a solution of (11). But (15) and (16) are clearly linearly independent, hence the general solution of (11) is

$$\mathbf{X} = c_1\mathbf{X}_1 + c_2\mathbf{X}_2$$

$$= c_1 \begin{pmatrix} 1 \\ -1 \end{pmatrix} e^{-t} + c_2 \begin{pmatrix} 1 \\ 2/3 \end{pmatrix} e^{4t}. \tag{17}$$

For the sake of review, the reader should keep firmly in mind that a solution of a system of first-order differential equations, when written in terms of matrices, is simply an alternative to the method that we employed in Section 8.1, namely, listing the individual functions and the relationships between the constants. By adding the vectors given in (17) we obtain

$$\begin{pmatrix} x(t) \\ y(t) \end{pmatrix} = \begin{pmatrix} c_1 e^{-t} + c_2 e^{4t} \\ -c_1 e^{-t} + \tfrac{2}{3}c_2 e^{4t} \end{pmatrix}$$

and this in turn yields the more familiar statement

$$\begin{aligned} x(t) &= c_1 e^{-t} + c_2 e^{4t} \\ y(t) &= -c_1 e^{-t} + \tfrac{2}{3}c_2 e^{4t}. \end{aligned} \tag{18}$$

Also, it should be noted that we could just as well choose $k_1 = 1$ in (13) and $k_1 = 3$ in (14) so that an alternative, but equivalent, form of (17) is

$$\mathbf{X} = c_1 \begin{pmatrix} 1 \\ -1 \end{pmatrix} e^{-t} + c_2 \begin{pmatrix} 3 \\ 2 \end{pmatrix} e^{4t}. \tag{19}$$

CASE II. Equal Eigenvalues

So far the theory of linear first-order system in normal form having two dependent variables has paralleled the theory of linear second-order equations with constant coefficients. Consequently, we might expect that when $\lambda_1 = \lambda_2$, one solution would be

$$\mathbf{X}_1 = \begin{pmatrix} k_1 \\ k_2 \end{pmatrix} e^{\lambda_1 t}$$

and that a second linearly independent solution could be obtained by multiplying $\mathbf{X}_1$ by t:

$$\mathbf{X}_2 = \begin{pmatrix} k_1 \\ k_2 \end{pmatrix} t e^{\lambda_1 t}.$$

Unfortunately, this latter assumption does *not*, in general, lead to a second solution.

For example, the characteristic equation for the system

$$\frac{dx}{dt} = 3x - 18y$$

$$\frac{dy}{dt} = 2x - 9y$$

is

$$\begin{vmatrix} 3 - \lambda & -18 \\ 2 & -9 - \lambda \end{vmatrix} = (3 - \lambda)(-9 - \lambda) + 36$$

$$= \lambda^2 + 6\lambda + 9$$

$$= (\lambda + 3)^2$$

$$= 0$$

so that $\lambda_1 = \lambda_2 = -3$. For this particular value it is easily shown that

$$\begin{pmatrix} 1 \\ 1/3 \end{pmatrix}$$

is an eigenvector, and so one solution of the system is

$$\mathbf{X}_1 = \begin{pmatrix} 1 \\ 1/3 \end{pmatrix} e^{-3t}.$$

However, if we assume the solution vector

$$\mathbf{X}_2 = \begin{pmatrix} k_1 \\ k_2 \end{pmatrix} te^{-3t}$$

then

$$x = k_1 te^{-3t}$$
$$y = k_2 te^{-3t}.$$

Differentiating and substituting these equations into the original system gives

$$-3k_1 te^{-3t} + k_1 e^{-3t} = 3k_1 te^{-3t} - 18k_2 te^{-3t}$$
$$-3k_2 te^{-3t} + k_2 e^{-3t} = 2k_1 te^{-3t} - 9k_2 te^{-3t}.$$

Dividing out e^{-3t} and rearranging then yields

$$(6k_1 - 18k_2)t - k_1 = 0$$
$$(2k_1 - 6k_2)t - k_2 = 0.$$

Since this latter set of equations is to be zero for all t, we must have

$$6k_1 - 18k_2 = 0$$
$$-k_1 = 0$$
$$2k_1 - 6k_2 = 0$$
$$-k_2 = 0.$$

Thus it is clear that the only solution is the trivial solution $k_1 = 0, k_2 = 0$.

The second solution

The formal, correct procedure is slightly more complicated than that just outlined. When $\lambda_1 = \lambda_2$ we must assume a second solution of the form

$$\mathbf{X}_2 = \begin{pmatrix} k_1 + k_2 t \\ k_3 + k_4 t \end{pmatrix} e^{\lambda_1 t} = \begin{pmatrix} k_1 \\ k_3 \end{pmatrix} e^{\lambda_1 t} + \begin{pmatrix} k_2 \\ k_4 \end{pmatrix} te^{\lambda_1 t}.$$

In practice it is probably easier to use directly

$$x = (k_1 + k_2 t)e^{\lambda_1 t}$$
$$y = (k_3 + k_4 t)e^{\lambda_1 t}.$$

EXAMPLE

Find the general solution of

$$\frac{dx}{dt} = 3x - 18y$$
$$\frac{dy}{dt} = 2x - 9y. \tag{20}$$

Solution: From the foregoing discussion we already know that $\lambda_1 = \lambda_2 = -3$ and

$$\mathbf{X}_1 = \begin{pmatrix} 1 \\ 1/3 \end{pmatrix} e^{-3t}.$$

Now after substituting

$$x = (k_1 + k_2 t)e^{-3t}$$
$$y = (k_3 + k_4 t)e^{-3t}$$

into the equations of (20), we find

$$-3k_1 e^{-3t} - 3k_2 t e^{-3t} + k_2 e^{-3t} = 3(k_1 + k_2 t)e^{-3t} - 18(k_3 + k_4 t)e^{-3t}$$
$$-3k_3 e^{-3t} - 3k_4 t e^{-3t} + k_4 e^{-3t} = 2(k_1 + k_2 t)e^{-3t} - 9(k_3 + k_4 t)e^{-3t}.$$

Dividing by e^{-3t} and grouping by powers of t then gives

$$(6k_2 - 18k_4)t + 6k_1 - k_2 - 18k_3 = 0$$
$$(2k_2 - 6k_4)t + 2k_1 - k_4 - 6k_3 = 0$$

and so

$$6k_2 - 18k_4 = 0$$
$$2k_2 - 6k_4 = 0$$
$$6k_1 - k_2 - 18k_3 = 0$$
$$2k_1 - k_4 - 6k_3 = 0. \tag{21}$$

Since the solution vector $\mathbf{X}_2$ will eventually be multiplied by an arbitrary constant, we are interested in *any* specific, but nontrivial, set of constants k_1, k_2, k_3, k_4 satisfying (21). Notice that the first two equations are satisfied when $k_2 = 3$ and $k_4 = 1$. For this choice of k_2 and k_4 the last two equations then become

$$6k_1 - 18k_3 = 3$$
$$2k_1 - 6k_3 = 1.$$

Since this last system is obviously equivalent to one equation, we have an infinite number of choices for k_1 and k_3. For example, by picking $k_1 = 1$, we then find $k_3 = 1/6$. However, for simplicity we shall choose $k_1 = 1/2$ so that $k_3 = 0$. Hence $x = 1/2 + 3t$, $y = 0 + t$, and

$$\mathbf{X}_2 = \begin{pmatrix} x(t) \\ y(t) \end{pmatrix} = \begin{pmatrix} 1/2 + 3t \\ t \end{pmatrix} e^{-3t}.$$

Thus the general solution of (20) is

$$\mathbf{X} = c_1 \begin{pmatrix} 1 \\ 1/3 \end{pmatrix} e^{-3t} + c_2 \begin{pmatrix} 1/2 + 3t \\ t \end{pmatrix} e^{-3t}.$$

CASE III. Complex Conjugate Eigenvalues

Formally there is no difference between this last case and Case I. The only problem is, if

$$\lambda_1 = a + bi \qquad \text{and} \qquad \lambda_2 = a - bi$$

are the eigenvalues of the coefficient matrix **A**, we can then certainly expect their corresponding eigenvectors to have complex entries.

For example, the characteristic equation of the system

$$\frac{dx}{dt} = 6x - y$$

$$\frac{dy}{dt} = 5x + 4y$$

(22)

is

$$\begin{vmatrix} 6 - \lambda & -1 \\ 5 & 4 - \lambda \end{vmatrix} = (6 - \lambda)(4 - \lambda) + 5$$

$$= \lambda^2 - 10\lambda + 29$$

$$= 0.$$

From the quadratic formula we find

$$\lambda_1 = 5 + 2i, \qquad \lambda_2 = 5 - 2i.$$

Now for $\lambda_1 = 5 + 2i$ we must solve

$$(1 - 2i)k_1 - k_2 = 0$$

$$5k_1 - (1 + 2i)k_2 = 0.$$

Since $k_2 = (1 - 2i)k_1$ it follows, after choosing $k_1 = 1$, that one eigenvector is

$$\begin{pmatrix} 1 \\ 1 - 2i \end{pmatrix}.$$

Similarly, for $\lambda_2 = 5 - 2i$, we find the other eigenvector to be*

$$\begin{pmatrix} 1 \\ 1 + 2i \end{pmatrix}.$$

Thus the general solution of (22) is

$$\mathbf{X} = c_1 \begin{pmatrix} 1 \\ 1 - 2i \end{pmatrix} e^{(5 + 2i)t} + c_2 \begin{pmatrix} 1 \\ 1 + 2i \end{pmatrix} e^{(5 - 2i)t}.$$

(23)

---

*For matrices with real entries, it can be shown that the complex conjugate of the eigenvector corresponding to a complex eigenvalue $\lambda = a + bi$ is an eigenvector for $\bar{\lambda} = a - bi$.

It is desirable, and relatively easy to rewrite a solution such as (23) in terms of real functions. Since

$$x = c_1 e^{(5+2i)t} + c_2 e^{(5-2i)t}$$
$$y = c_1(1 - 2i)e^{(5+2i)t} + c_2(1 + 2i)e^{(5-2i)t}$$

it follows from Euler's formula that

$$x = e^{5t}[c_1 e^{2it} + c_2 e^{-2it}]$$
$$= e^{5t}[(c_1 + c_2)\cos 2t + (c_1 i - c_2 i)\sin 2t]$$
$$y = e^{5t}[(c_1(1 - 2i) + c_2(1 + 2i))\cos 2t$$
$$+ (c_1 i(1 - 2i) - c_2 i(1 + 2i))\sin 2t]$$
$$= e^{5t}[(c_1 + c_2) - 2(c_1 i - c_2 i)]\cos 2t$$
$$+ e^{5t}[2(c_1 + c_2) + (c_1 i - c_2 i)]\sin 2t.$$

If we replace $c_1 + c_2$ by C_1 and $c_1 i - c_2 i$ by C_2, then

$$x = e^{5t}[C_1 \cos 2t + C_2 \sin 2t]$$
$$y = e^{5t}[C_1 - 2C_2]\cos 2t + e^{5t}[2C_1 + C_2]\sin 2t,$$

or, in terms of vectors,

$$\mathbf{X} = \begin{pmatrix} x(t) \\ y(t) \end{pmatrix}$$
$$= C_1 \begin{pmatrix} \cos 2t \\ \cos 2t + 2\sin 2t \end{pmatrix} e^{5t} + C_2 \begin{pmatrix} \sin 2t \\ -2\cos 2t + \sin 2t \end{pmatrix} e^{5t}. \qquad (24)$$

Here, of course, it can be verified that each vector in (24) is a solution of (22). In addition, since the solutions are linearly independent, we may further assume that C_1 and C_2 are completely arbitrary and real.

Alternative method   Rather than using Euler's formula, we could also obtain the solution (24) by making the assumption

$$\mathbf{X} = \begin{pmatrix} c_1 \\ c_2 \end{pmatrix} e^{5t} \sin 2t + \begin{pmatrix} c_3 \\ c_4 \end{pmatrix} e^{5t} \cos 2t$$

and then substituting $x(t)$ and $y(t)$ into one of the equations of the original system. This procedure, which is basically that of Section 8.1, is illustrated in the next example.

EXAMPLE   Solve

$$\frac{dx}{dt} = x + 2y$$

$$\frac{dy}{dt} = -\tfrac{1}{2}x + y. \tag{25}$$

Solution: The solutions of the characteristic equation

$$\begin{vmatrix} 1 - \lambda & 2 \\ -\tfrac{1}{2} & 1 - \lambda \end{vmatrix} = (1 - \lambda)^2 + 1$$

$$= \lambda^2 - 2\lambda + 2$$

$$= 0$$

are $\lambda_1 = 1 + i$ and $\lambda_2 = 1 - i.$

Since the complex form of the solution would involve in this case $e^{(1 + i)t} = e^t(\cos t + i \sin t)$, we now make the assumption

$$\mathbf{X} = \begin{pmatrix} c_1 \\ c_2 \end{pmatrix} e^t \sin t + \begin{pmatrix} c_3 \\ c_4 \end{pmatrix} e^t \cos t$$

or $x = c_1 e^t \sin t + c_3 e^t \cos t$

$$y = c_2 e^t \sin t + c_4 e^t \cos t.$$

Substituting x and y back into the first equation of the given system (25) yields

$$(c_3 + 2c_2)e^t \sin t + (-c_1 + 2c_4)e^t \cos t = 0$$

or $c_3 = -2c_2$

$$c_4 = \tfrac{1}{2}c_1.$$

Therefore, $\mathbf{X} = \begin{pmatrix} c_1 \\ c_2 \end{pmatrix} e^t \sin t + \begin{pmatrix} -2c_2 \\ \tfrac{1}{2}c_1 \end{pmatrix} e^t \cos t$

$$= c_1 \begin{pmatrix} \sin t \\ \tfrac{1}{2}\cos t \end{pmatrix} e^t + c_2 \begin{pmatrix} -2\cos t \\ \sin t \end{pmatrix} e^t. \tag{26}$$

Larger systems   The procedures of the foregoing cases can be adapted to larger first-order systems in normal form.

EXAMPLE   Solve

$$\frac{dx}{dt} = x + 2y + z$$

$$\frac{dy}{dt} = 6x - y \tag{27}$$

$$\frac{dz}{dt} = -x - 2y - z.$$

Solution: To obtain the characteristic equation we can expand the determinant

$$\begin{vmatrix} 1 - \lambda & 2 & 1 \\ 6 & -1 - \lambda & 0 \\ -1 & -2 & -1 - \lambda \end{vmatrix}$$

by the cofactors of the second row. It follows that

$$-\lambda^3 - \lambda^2 + 12\lambda = 0 \quad \text{or} \quad \lambda(\lambda + 4)(\lambda - 3) = 0.$$

Hence the eigenvalues are $\lambda_1 = 0$, $\lambda_2 = -4$, $\lambda_3 = 3$. We must now determine three eigenvectors

$$\begin{pmatrix} k_1 \\ k_2 \\ k_3 \end{pmatrix}$$

by solving the algebraic system

$$\begin{aligned} (1 - \lambda)k_1 + & \quad 2k_2 + & k_3 = 0 \\ 6k_1 - (1 + \lambda)k_2 & & = 0 \\ -k_1 - & \quad 2k_2 - (1 + \lambda)k_3 = 0 \end{aligned} \tag{28}$$

three times corresponding to the three distinct values of λ.

For $\lambda_1 = 0$, (28) becomes

$$\begin{aligned} k_1 + 2k_2 + k_3 &= 0 \\ 6k_1 - k_2 &= 0 \\ -k_1 - 2k_2 - k_3 &= 0. \end{aligned}$$

Choosing $k_1 = 1$ immediately gives $k_2 = 6$ and $k_3 = -13$. Hence the first eigenvector is

$$\begin{pmatrix} 1 \\ 6 \\ -13 \end{pmatrix}. \tag{29}$$

For $\lambda_2 = -4$, (28) becomes

$$5k_1 + 2k_2 + k_3 = 0$$
$$6k_1 + 3k_2 = 0$$
$$-k_1 - 2k_2 + 3k_3 = 0.$$

Choosing $k_1 = 1$ gives $k_2 = -2$ and $k_3 = -1$. The second eigenvector is then

$$\begin{pmatrix} 1 \\ -2 \\ -1 \end{pmatrix}. \tag{30}$$

Finally, when $\lambda_3 = 3$, the system (28) becomes

$$-2k_1 + 2k_2 + k_3 = 0$$
$$6k_1 - 4k_2 = 0$$
$$-k_1 - 2k_2 - 4k_3 = 0.$$

The usual choice of $k_1 = 1$ leads to $k_2 = 3/2$ and $k_3 = -1$ so that the third eigenvector is

$$\begin{pmatrix} 1 \\ 3/2 \\ -1 \end{pmatrix}. \tag{31}$$

Multiplying the vectors (29), (30), and (31) by e^{0t}, e^{-4t}, and e^{3t}, respectively, yields three linearly independent solutions of (27). It follows from the superposition principle that the general solution of the system is

$$\mathbf{X} = c_1 \begin{pmatrix} 1 \\ 6 \\ -13 \end{pmatrix} + c_2 \begin{pmatrix} 1 \\ -2 \\ -1 \end{pmatrix} e^{-4t} + c_3 \begin{pmatrix} 1 \\ 3/2 \\ -1 \end{pmatrix} e^{3t}. \tag{32}$$

Remark: Matrices can be utilized in an entirely different manner to solve a homogeneous system (2). Recall that the simple linear first-order differential equation

$$x' = ax, \tag{33}$$

where a is a constant, possesses the general solution

$$x = ce^{at}. \tag{34}$$

By analogy, it seems natural then to ask whether the first-order system $\mathbf{X}' = \mathbf{AX}$, where $\mathbf{A}$ is an $n \times n$ matrix of constants, has a solution

$$\mathbf{X} = e^{\mathbf{A}t}\mathbf{C}, \tag{35}$$

where **C** is a column matrix of arbitrary constants.* While a solution of (2) can always be found in the form given in (35), the development of the complete meaning of the exponential function $e^{\mathbf{A}t}$ would necessitate a more thorough investigation of matrix algebra. We leave this particular theory to an advanced course or a course in linear algebra. One means of computing $e^{\mathbf{A}t}$ is given in Problem 16. The application of equation (35), in solving special 2×2 systems of linear first-order differential equations, is given in Problem 17.

EXERCISES 8.5

Answers to odd-numbered problems begin on page A-26 of the Appendix.
In Problems 1–12 find the general solution of the given system.

1. $\dfrac{dx}{dt} = x + 2y$

$\dfrac{dy}{dt} = 4x + 3y$

2. $\dfrac{dx}{dt} = 2y$

$\dfrac{dy}{dt} = 8x$

3. $\dfrac{dx}{dt} = 3x - y$

$\dfrac{dy}{dt} = 9x - 3y$

4. $\dfrac{dx}{dt} = \dfrac{1}{2}x + 9y$

$\dfrac{dy}{dt} = \dfrac{1}{2}x + 2y$

5. $\dfrac{dx}{dt} = -x + 3y$

$\dfrac{dy}{dt} = -3x + 5y$

★6. $\dfrac{dx}{dt} = x + y$

$\dfrac{dy}{dt} = -2x - y$

7. $\dfrac{dx}{dt} = 6x - y$

$\dfrac{dy}{dt} = 5x + 2y$

8. $\dfrac{dx}{dt} = -6x + 2y$

$\dfrac{dy}{dt} = -3x + y$

9. $\mathbf{X}' = \begin{pmatrix} 10 & -5 \\ 8 & -12 \end{pmatrix}\mathbf{X}$

★10. $\mathbf{X}' = \begin{pmatrix} 1 & -8 \\ 1 & -3 \end{pmatrix}\mathbf{X}$

11. $\dfrac{dx}{dt} = x + y - z$

$\dfrac{dy}{dt} = 2y$

$\dfrac{dz}{dt} = y - z$

12. $\dfrac{dx}{dt} = z$

$\dfrac{dy}{dt} = -z$

$\dfrac{dz}{dt} = y$

---

* It turns out that $e^{\mathbf{A}t}$ is another $n \times n$ matrix. The product $\mathbf{C}e^{\mathbf{A}t}$ is not defined.

13.   Solve the system

$$\frac{dx_1}{dt} = -\frac{2}{25}x_1 + \frac{1}{50}x_2$$

$$\frac{dx_2}{dt} = \frac{2}{25}x_1 - \frac{2}{25}x_2$$

subject to $x_1(0) = 25$, $x_2(0) = 0$.

★14.   Solve $$\mathbf{X}' = \begin{pmatrix} 1 & 0 \\ 0 & 1 \end{pmatrix}\mathbf{X}.$$

15.   Show that two of the eigenvalues of the system

$$\frac{dx}{dt} = 3x - y - z$$

$$\frac{dy}{dt} = x + y - z$$

$$\frac{dz}{dt} = x - y + z$$

are the same but that we can find three linearly independent solution vectors of form (1).

★16.   From calculus recall that

$$e^x = 1 + \frac{x}{1!} + \frac{x^2}{2!} + \frac{x^3}{3!} + \cdots + .$$

Similarly, for a 2×2 matrix $\mathbf{A}$ we define*

$$e^{\mathbf{A}t} = I + \frac{\mathbf{A}}{1!}t + \frac{\mathbf{A}^2}{2!}t^2 + \frac{\mathbf{A}^3}{3!}t^3 + \cdots + ,$$

where $I = \begin{pmatrix} 1 & 0 \\ 0 & 1 \end{pmatrix}$, and $\mathbf{A}^2 = \mathbf{A}\mathbf{A}, \mathbf{A}^3 = \mathbf{A}(\mathbf{A}^2)$, and so on. (See Problem 26, Section 8.4.) Compute the matrices $e^{\mathbf{A}t}$ and $e^{-\mathbf{A}t}$ for

(a) $\mathbf{A} = \begin{pmatrix} 0 & 1 \\ 1 & 0 \end{pmatrix}$ **(b)** $\mathbf{A} = \begin{pmatrix} 1 & 0 \\ 0 & 2 \end{pmatrix}$

17.   If $$\mathbf{C} = \begin{pmatrix} c_1 \\ c_2 \end{pmatrix}$$

---

* We are of course assuming here that the infinite series of matrices defining $e^{\mathbf{A}t}$ *converges* to a matrix. Also, this particular definition holds for any $n \times n$ matrix $\mathbf{A}$.

use the results of Problem 16 and equation (35) to find the general solution to each of the following systems.

(a) $\mathbf{X}' = \begin{pmatrix} 0 & 1 \\ 1 & 0 \end{pmatrix} \mathbf{X}$ **(b)** $\mathbf{X}' = \begin{pmatrix} 1 & 0 \\ 0 & 2 \end{pmatrix} \mathbf{X}$

8.6   Nonhomogeneous Linear Systems

The complementary function

In the discussion of Section 8.4 we defined the general solution of a nonhomogeneous system

$$\frac{dx}{dt} = a_{11}x + a_{12}y + f_1(t)$$

$$\frac{dy}{dt} = a_{21}x + a_{22}y + f_2(t) \tag{1}$$

or

$$\frac{d\mathbf{X}}{dt} = \mathbf{A}\mathbf{X} + \mathbf{F}(t), \tag{2}$$

where $f_1(t)$ and $f_2(t)$ are continuous on some common interval $a \leq t \leq b$, to be the linear combination

$$\mathbf{X} = \mathbf{X}_c + \mathbf{X}_p. \tag{3}$$

The vector

$$\mathbf{X}_c = c_1\mathbf{X}_1 + c_2\mathbf{X}_2 \tag{4}$$

is the general solution of the related homogeneous system $\mathbf{X}' = \mathbf{A}\mathbf{X}$ and the vector $\mathbf{X}_p$ is any particular solution of (1). Consistent with the terminology of Chapter 4, we shall also call (4) the **complementary function** of the system.

8.6.1   Undetermined Coefficients

The techniques for determining a particular solution for a nonhomogeneous system are quite similar to those discussed in the context of second-order differential equations. We begin by illustrating the method of **undetermined coefficients**.

EXAMPLE

Solve the system

$$\frac{dx}{dt} = 6x + \ y + \ 6t$$

$$\frac{dy}{dt} = 4x + 3y - 10t + 4 \tag{5}$$

Solution: We first solve the homogeneous system

$$\frac{dx}{dt} = 6x + y$$

$$\frac{dy}{dt} = 4x + 3y$$

by the method of Section 8.5. The eigenvalues are determined from

$$\begin{vmatrix} 6 - \lambda & 1 \\ 4 & 3 - \lambda \end{vmatrix} = (6 - \lambda)(3 - \lambda) - 4$$

$$= \lambda^2 - 9\lambda + 14$$

$$= (\lambda - 2)(\lambda - 7)$$

$$= 0.$$

Thus $\lambda_1 = 2$ and $\lambda_2 = 7$. It is then easily verified that the respective eigenvectors of the coefficient matrix are

$$\begin{pmatrix} 1 \\ -4 \end{pmatrix} \quad \text{and} \quad \begin{pmatrix} 1 \\ 1 \end{pmatrix}$$

Consequently, the complementary function is

$$\mathbf{X}_c = c_1 \begin{pmatrix} 1 \\ -4 \end{pmatrix} e^{2t} + c_2 \begin{pmatrix} 1 \\ 1 \end{pmatrix} e^{7t}.$$

Now observe that the given system (5) can be written as

$$\mathbf{X}' = \begin{pmatrix} 6 & 1 \\ 4 & 3 \end{pmatrix} \mathbf{X} + \begin{pmatrix} 6 \\ -10 \end{pmatrix} t + \begin{pmatrix} 0 \\ 4 \end{pmatrix} \tag{6}$$

Proceeding in exactly the same manner as in Section 4.4, we then expect a particular solution to possess the form

$$\mathbf{X}_p = \begin{pmatrix} a_2 \\ b_2 \end{pmatrix} t + \begin{pmatrix} a_1 \\ b_1 \end{pmatrix} \tag{7}$$

where we must find specific values of the coefficients a_2, b_2, a_1, b_1. Substituting (7) in (6) gives

$$\mathbf{X}'_p = \begin{pmatrix} 6 & 1 \\ 4 & 3 \end{pmatrix} \mathbf{X}_p + \begin{pmatrix} 6 \\ -10 \end{pmatrix} t + \begin{pmatrix} 0 \\ 4 \end{pmatrix}$$

or
$$\begin{pmatrix} a_2 \\ b_2 \end{pmatrix} = \begin{pmatrix} 6 & 1 \\ 4 & 3 \end{pmatrix} \left[\begin{pmatrix} a_2 \\ b_2 \end{pmatrix} t + \begin{pmatrix} a_1 \\ b_1 \end{pmatrix} \right] + \begin{pmatrix} 6 \\ -10 \end{pmatrix} t + \begin{pmatrix} 0 \\ 4 \end{pmatrix}$$

$$\begin{pmatrix} 0 \\ 0 \end{pmatrix} = \begin{pmatrix} (6a_2 + b_2 + 6)t + 6a_1 + b_1 - a_2 \\ (4a_2 + 3b_2 - 10)t + 4a_1 + 3b_1 - b_2 + 4 \end{pmatrix}.$$

Hence we must have

$$6a_2 + \ b_2 + \ 6 = 0$$

$$4a_2 + 3b_2 - 10 = 0$$

$$6a_1 + \ b_1 - a_2 \qquad = 0 \tag{8}$$

$$4a_1 + 3b_1 - b_2 + 4 = 0.$$

Solving the first two equations of (8) simultaneously yields $a_2 = -2$ and $b_2 = 6$. Substituting these values into the last two equations of (8) and solving for a_1 and b_1 gives $a_1 = -4/7$, $b_1 = 10/7$. It follows therefore that a particular solution vector is

$$\mathbf{X}_p = \begin{pmatrix} -2 \\ 6 \end{pmatrix} t + \begin{pmatrix} -4/7 \\ 10/7 \end{pmatrix}$$

and so the general solution of (5) is

$$\mathbf{X} = \mathbf{X}_c + \mathbf{X}_p$$

$$= c_1 \begin{pmatrix} 1 \\ -4 \end{pmatrix} e^{2t} + c_2 \begin{pmatrix} 1 \\ 1 \end{pmatrix} e^{7t} + \begin{pmatrix} -2 \\ 6 \end{pmatrix} t + \begin{pmatrix} -4/7 \\ 10/7 \end{pmatrix} \tag{9}$$

EXAMPLE

To find a particular solution vector for

$$\frac{dx}{dt} = -x + 4y - 8$$

$$\frac{dy}{dt} = \ 5x + 2y + 3$$

or

$$\mathbf{X}' = \begin{pmatrix} -1 & 4 \\ 5 & 2 \end{pmatrix} \mathbf{X} + \begin{pmatrix} -8 \\ 3 \end{pmatrix}$$

we would assume a constant vector $\mathbf{X}_p = \begin{pmatrix} a_1 \\ b_1 \end{pmatrix}$. The reader should verify that this assumption leads to

$$-a_1 + 4b_1 - 8 = 0$$

$$5a_1 + 2b_1 + 3 = 0.$$

Solving the system gives $a_1 = -14/11$, $b_1 = 37/22$. Thus a particular solution vector is

$$\mathbf{X}_p = \begin{pmatrix} -14/11 \\ 37/22 \end{pmatrix}$$

A word of caution is in order here, the assumption of a constant vector $\mathbf{X}_p$ in the preceding example is actually predicated on prior knowledge that the complementary function $\mathbf{X}_c$ does not contain a constant vector (that is, $\lambda = 0$ is not an eigenvalue). You should recall from Rule II of Section 4.4 that when duplication occurs between the complementary function and the initial assumed form of the particular solution, then all, or parts, of that assumption must be multiplied by positive integral powers of t. For example, it is readily shown that the complementary function of the system

$$\mathbf{X}' = \begin{pmatrix} 1 & -1 \\ -1 & 1 \end{pmatrix} \mathbf{X} + \begin{pmatrix} 2 \\ -5 \end{pmatrix}$$

is

$$\mathbf{X}_c = c_1 \begin{pmatrix} 1 \\ 1 \end{pmatrix} + c_2 \begin{pmatrix} 1 \\ -1 \end{pmatrix} e^{2t}$$

But, because of the constant vector present in $\mathbf{X}_c$, it is not unexpected that we are unable to find a constant particular solution vector

$$\begin{pmatrix} a_1 \\ b_1 \end{pmatrix} \tag{10}$$

However, we leave it as an exercise to show that the natural alternative form

$$\begin{pmatrix} a_1 \\ b_1 \end{pmatrix} t \tag{11}$$

still does *not* yield a particular solution. We need *both* (10) and (11) (that is, the sum) to find $\mathbf{X}_p$.

EXAMPLE   Find the general solution of the system

$$\mathbf{X}' = \begin{pmatrix} 1 & -1 \\ -1 & 1 \end{pmatrix} \mathbf{X} + \begin{pmatrix} 2 \\ -5 \end{pmatrix} \tag{12}$$

Solution: From the foregoing discussion we shall seek a particular solution with four undetermined coefficients

$$\mathbf{X}_p = \begin{pmatrix} a_2 \\ b_2 \end{pmatrix} t + \begin{pmatrix} a_1 \\ b_1 \end{pmatrix} \tag{13}$$

Differentiating (13), substituting in (12), and gathering terms gives

$$(a_2 - b_2)t + a_1 - b_1 - a_2 + 2 = 0$$
$$(-a_2 + b_2)t - a_1 + b_1 - b_2 - 5 = 0$$

or
$$a_2 - b_2 = 0$$
$$a_1 - b_1 - a_2 + 2 = 0$$
$$-a_1 + b_1 - b_2 - 5 = 0.$$

Substituting $a_2 = b_2$ into the last two equations implies that we must solve the following system of two equations in three unknowns

$$a_1 - a_2 - b_1 = -2$$
$$-a_1 - a_2 + b_1 = 5.$$

This system yields a specific value of a_2 whereas a_1 can be expressed in terms of b_1:

$$a_1 = b_1 - \tfrac{7}{2}$$
$$a_2 = -\tfrac{3}{2}. \tag{14}$$

By choosing b_1 arbitrarily*, say $b_1 = 1$, we find $a_1 = -5/2$. Hence we conclude that a particular solution vector is

$$\mathbf{X}_p = \begin{pmatrix} -3/2 \\ -3/2 \end{pmatrix} t + \begin{pmatrix} -5/2 \\ 1 \end{pmatrix}$$

It follows that the general solution of (12) is

$$\mathbf{X} = \mathbf{X}_c + \mathbf{X}_p$$
$$= c_1 \begin{pmatrix} 1 \\ 1 \end{pmatrix} + c_2 \begin{pmatrix} 1 \\ -1 \end{pmatrix} e^{2t} + \begin{pmatrix} -3/2 \\ -3/2 \end{pmatrix} t + \begin{pmatrix} -5/2 \\ 1 \end{pmatrix} \tag{15}$$

It is of interest to observe that had we chosen b_1 in (14) to be some value other than $b_1 = 1$, we naturally would have found a *different* particular solution $\mathbf{X}_p$. For example, by picking $b_1 = 0$, we then find $a_2 = b_2 = -3/2$, $a_1 = -7/2$, and, therefore,

$$\mathbf{X}_p = \begin{pmatrix} -3/2 \\ -3/2 \end{pmatrix} t + \begin{pmatrix} -7/2 \\ 0 \end{pmatrix}$$

---

* It might help to think of two planes
$$x - y - z = -2$$
$$-x - y + z = 5$$
intersecting in a line in the plane $y = -3/2$. Any point on this line will satisfy the system.

Notice, too, that the constant vector

$$\begin{pmatrix} -5/2 \\ 1 \end{pmatrix}$$

in (15) cannot be combined with the vector

$$c_1 \begin{pmatrix} 1 \\ 1 \end{pmatrix}$$

since the latter is an eigenvector, but the sum of the two vectors is not an eigenvector of the coefficient matrix. However, if we designate the arbitrary parameter b_1 by α, we can then write the particular solution vector as

$$\mathbf{X}_p = \begin{pmatrix} -3/2 \\ -3/2 \end{pmatrix} t + \begin{pmatrix} \alpha - 7/2 \\ \alpha \end{pmatrix}$$

$$= \begin{pmatrix} -3/2 \\ -3/2 \end{pmatrix} t + \begin{pmatrix} -7/2 \\ 0 \end{pmatrix} + \alpha \begin{pmatrix} 1 \\ 1 \end{pmatrix}$$

In the sum $\mathbf{X}_c + \mathbf{X}_p$ we can obviously combine

$$c_1 \begin{pmatrix} 1 \\ 1 \end{pmatrix} \qquad \text{and} \qquad \alpha \begin{pmatrix} 1 \\ 1 \end{pmatrix}$$

as one vector.

8.6.2   Variation of Parameters

The method of undetermined coefficients is limited to systems where the entries of $\mathbf{F}(t)$ are finite sums and products of polynomials, exponential functions, and sines and cosines. As usual, the method of **variation of parameters** possesses no such restriction.

Suppose the general solution of the homogeneous system

$$\frac{dx}{dt} = a_{11}x + a_{12}y$$

$$\frac{dy}{dt} = a_{21}x + a_{22}y \tag{16}$$

is given by

$$\mathbf{X}_c = c_1\mathbf{X}_1 + c_2\mathbf{X}_2$$

$$\begin{pmatrix} x(t) \\ y(t) \end{pmatrix} = c_1 \begin{pmatrix} x_1(t) \\ y_1(t) \end{pmatrix} + c_2 \begin{pmatrix} x_2(t) \\ y_2(t) \end{pmatrix}$$

or

$$x = c_1 x_1 + c_2 x_2$$

$$y = c_1 y_1 + c_2 y_2. \tag{17}$$

Replacing the parameters c_1 and c_2 in each equation of 17 by the functions $u_1(t)$ and $u_2(t)$, respectively, we now try to find a particular solution vector

$$\mathbf{X}_p = \begin{pmatrix} x \\ y \end{pmatrix}$$

in which

$$x = u_1 x_1 + u_2 x_2$$
$$y = u_1 y_1 + u_2 y_2. \tag{18}$$

Since
$$x' = u_1 x_1' + x_1 u_1' + u_2 x_2' + x_2 u_2'$$
$$y' = u_1 y_1' + y_1 u_1' + u_2 y_2' + y_2 u_2'$$

it follows that (1) becomes

$$u_1 x_1' + x_1 u_1' + u_2 x_2' + x_2 u_2' = a_{11} u_1 x_1 + a_{11} u_2 x_2 + a_{12} u_1 y_1 + a_{12} u_2 y_2 + f_1$$
$$u_1 y_1' + y_1 u_1' + u_2 y_2' + y_2 u_2' = a_{21} u_1 x_1 + a_{21} u_2 x_2 + a_{22} u_1 y_1 + a_{22} u_2 y_2 + f_2$$

or

$$u_1 x_1' + u_2 x_2' + x_1 u_1' + x_2 u_2' = u_1 [\overbrace{a_{11} x_1 + a_{12} y_1}^{x_1'}]$$

$$+ u_2 [\overbrace{a_{11} x_2 + a_{12} y_2}^{x_2'}] + f_1$$

$$u_1 y_1' + u_2 y_2' + y_1 u_1' + y_2 u_2' = u_1 [\overbrace{a_{21} x_1 + a_{22} y_1}^{y_1'}]$$

$$+ u_2 [\overbrace{a_{21} x_2 + a_{22} y_2}^{y_2'}] + f_2.$$

But, since x_1, y_1 and x_2, y_2 are pairs of solutions of the homogeneous system (16), the preceding simplifies to

$$x_1 u_1' + x_2 u_2' = f_1$$
$$y_1 u_1' + y_2 u_2' = f_2. \tag{19}$$

Solving (19) by determinants gives

$$u_1' = \frac{\begin{vmatrix} f_1 & x_2 \\ f_2 & y_2 \end{vmatrix}}{\begin{vmatrix} x_1 & x_2 \\ y_1 & y_2 \end{vmatrix}}, \qquad u_2' = \frac{\begin{vmatrix} x_1 & f_1 \\ y_1 & f_2 \end{vmatrix}}{\begin{vmatrix} x_1 & x_2 \\ y_1 & y_2 \end{vmatrix}} \tag{20}$$

Observe that the denominator of each ratio in (20) is the Wronskian $W(\mathbf{X}_1, \mathbf{X}_2)$. Under the assumption that $\mathbf{X}_1$ and $\mathbf{X}_2$ are linearly independent solutions of (16) on some interval $a \le t \le b$, we know that $W \ne 0$ for every t in the interval.

In summary, a particular solution of (2) is

$$
\mathbf{X}_p = \begin{pmatrix} u_1 x_1 + u_2 x_2 \\ u_1 y_1 + u_2 y_2 \end{pmatrix}
$$

where the functions x_1, y_1 and x_2, y_2 are determined from the solution vectors $\mathbf{X}_1$ and $\mathbf{X}_2$, respectively, of the related homogeneous system, and u_1 and u_2 are functions of t found from

$$
u_1' = \frac{\begin{vmatrix} f_1 & x_2 \\ f_2 & y_2 \end{vmatrix}}{W} \quad \text{and} \quad u_2' = \frac{\begin{vmatrix} x_1 & f_1 \\ y_1 & f_2 \end{vmatrix}}{W}
$$

EXAMPLE

Find a particular solution of

$$
\frac{dx}{dt} = x + 2y
$$

$$
\frac{dy}{dt} = -\frac{1}{2}x + y + e^t \tan t. \tag{21}
$$

Solution: Note that the method of undetermined coefficients is inappropriate for this particular system. We have already seen in an example of the preceding section (page 386) that the eigenvalues are $\lambda_1 = 1 + i$ and $\lambda_2 = 1 - i$ and that the solution vectors of the related homogeneous system are

$$
\mathbf{X}_1 = \begin{pmatrix} x_1 \\ y_1 \end{pmatrix} = \begin{pmatrix} \sin t \\ \frac{1}{2}\cos t \end{pmatrix} e^t
$$

$$
\mathbf{X}_2 = \begin{pmatrix} x_2 \\ y_2 \end{pmatrix} = \begin{pmatrix} -2\cos t \\ \sin t \end{pmatrix} e^t
$$

Since $f_1(t) = 0$ and $f_2(t) = e^t \tan t$, the equations of (20) yield

$$
u_1' = \frac{\begin{vmatrix} 0 & -2e^t \cos t \\ e^t \tan t & e^t \sin t \end{vmatrix}}{\begin{vmatrix} e^t \sin t & -2e^t \cos t \\ \frac{1}{2}e^t \cos t & e^t \sin t \end{vmatrix}}
$$

$$= \frac{2e^{2t}\tan t \cos t}{e^{2t}}$$

$$= 2\sin t,$$

$$u_2' = \frac{\begin{vmatrix} e^t \sin t & 0 \\ \frac{1}{2}e^t \cos t & e^t \tan t \end{vmatrix}}{e^{2t}}$$

$$= \frac{e^{2t}\sin t \tan t}{e^{2t}}$$

$$= \frac{\sin^2 t}{\cos t}$$

$$= \frac{1 - \cos^2 t}{\cos t}$$

$$= \sec t - \cos t.$$

Integrating the preceding expressions for u_1' and u_2' yields

$$u_1 = -2\cos t$$

$$u_2 = \ln|\sec t + \tan t| - \sin t$$

and, therefore,

$$x = u_1 x_1 + u_2 x_2$$

$$= -2e^t \cos t \ln|\sec t + \tan t|$$

$$y = u_1 y_1 + u_2 y_2$$

$$= -e^t \cos^2 t + e^t \sin t \ln|\sec t + \tan t| - e^t \sin^2 t$$

$$= -e^t + e^t \sin t \ln|\sec t + \tan t|.$$

It follows that

$$\mathbf{X}_p = \begin{pmatrix} -2\cos t \ln|\sec t + \tan t| \\ -1 + \sin t \ln|\sec t + \tan t| \end{pmatrix} e^t \tag{22}$$

In Section 8.7 we shall consider an equivalent but purely matrix formulation of the method of variation of parameters.

Remark: The differential equation in a single variable $x(t)$

$$x' = ax + f(t) \tag{23}$$

where a is a constant, possesses the general solution

$$x = ce^{at} + e^{at} \int e^{-at} f(t) \, dt \tag{24}$$

(See equation (9) of Section 2.4.) Furthermore, we can write (24) as $x = x_c + x_p$ where $x_c = ce^{at}$ and $x_p = e^{at} \int e^{-at} f(t) \, dt$. Similarly, it can be shown that the general solution of the matrix equation $\mathbf{X}' = \mathbf{A}\mathbf{X} + \mathbf{F}(t)$ is then

$$\mathbf{X} = \mathbf{X}_c + \mathbf{X}_p$$

$$= e^{\mathbf{A}t} \mathbf{C} + e^{\mathbf{A}t} \int e^{-\mathbf{A}t} \mathbf{F}(t) \, dt. \tag{25}$$

(See Problem 13.)

EXERCISES 8.6   Answers to odd-numbered problems begin on page A-26 of the Appendix.
    In Problems 1–6 use the method of undetermined coefficients to solve the given system.

EXAMPLE   Determine the form of the particular solution vector $\mathbf{X}_p$ for

$$\frac{dx}{dt} = 5x - 3y - 2e^{2t} + 1$$

$$\frac{dy}{dt} = -x + y + e^{2t} - 5t + 7.$$

Solution: Write the system as

$$\mathbf{X}' = \begin{pmatrix} 5 & -3 \\ -1 & 1 \end{pmatrix} \mathbf{X} + \begin{pmatrix} -2 \\ 1 \end{pmatrix} e^{2t} + \begin{pmatrix} 0 \\ -5 \end{pmatrix} t + \begin{pmatrix} 1 \\ 7 \end{pmatrix}.$$

Now find the eigenvalues:

$$\begin{vmatrix} 5 - \lambda & -3 \\ -1 & 1 - \lambda \end{vmatrix} = (5 - \lambda)(1 - \lambda) + 3$$

$$= \lambda^2 - 6\lambda + 8$$

$$= (\lambda - 2)(\lambda - 4)$$

$$= 0$$

which implies $\lambda_1 = 2$ and $\lambda_2 = 4$. Because $\lambda_1 = 2$ is an eigenvalue, we know that both $\mathbf{X}_c$ and $\mathbf{F}(t)$ contain vectors with the multiple e^{2t}. Hence we must assume

$$\mathbf{X}_p = \begin{pmatrix} a_4 \\ b_4 \end{pmatrix} te^{2t} + \begin{pmatrix} a_3 \\ b_3 \end{pmatrix} e^{2t} + \begin{pmatrix} a_2 \\ b_2 \end{pmatrix} t + \begin{pmatrix} a_1 \\ b_1 \end{pmatrix}.$$

[8.6.1]   **1.** $\dfrac{dx}{dt} = 2x + 3y - 7$

$\dfrac{dy}{dt} = -x - 2y + 5$

2. $\dfrac{dx}{dt} = 4x + \dfrac{1}{3}y - 3e^{t}$

$\dfrac{dy}{dt} = 9x + 6y + 10e^{t}$

3. $\dfrac{dx}{dt} = x + 3y - 2t^{2}$

$\dfrac{dy}{dt} = 3x + y + t + 5$

★4. $\dfrac{dx}{dt} = 6x + 8y - 3$

$\dfrac{dy}{dt} = 3x + 4y + 10t$

5. $\mathbf{X'} = \begin{pmatrix} 5 & 1 \\ -8 & -4 \end{pmatrix} \mathbf{X} + \begin{pmatrix} -2 \\ 3 \end{pmatrix} e^{4t}$

6. $\mathbf{X'} = \begin{pmatrix} -1 & 5 \\ -1 & 1 \end{pmatrix} \mathbf{X} + \begin{pmatrix} \sin t \\ -2\cos t \end{pmatrix}$

[8.6.2]   In Problems 7–11 use variation of parameters to solve the given system.

7. $\mathbf{X'} = \begin{pmatrix} 3 & -5 \\ 3/4 & -1 \end{pmatrix} \mathbf{X} + \begin{pmatrix} 1 \\ -1 \end{pmatrix} e^{t/2}$

8. $\mathbf{X'} = \begin{pmatrix} 0 & 1 \\ -1 & 0 \end{pmatrix} \mathbf{X} + \begin{pmatrix} 1 \\ \cot t \end{pmatrix}, \quad 0 < t < \pi$

9. $\dfrac{dx}{dt} = 3x - 3y + 4$

$\dfrac{dy}{dt} = 2x - 2y - 1$

★10. $\dfrac{dx}{dt} = 2x - y + e^{2t}\sin 2t$

$\dfrac{dy}{dt} = 4x + 2y + 2e^{2t}\cos 2t$

11. $\dfrac{dx}{dt} = 2x - y$

$\dfrac{dy}{dt} = 3x - 2y + 4t$

12. Verify that particular solutions either of the form

$$\begin{pmatrix} a_1 \\ b_1 \end{pmatrix} \quad \text{or} \quad \begin{pmatrix} a_1 \\ b_1 \end{pmatrix} t$$

cannot be found for the system

$$\mathbf{X'} = \begin{pmatrix} 1 & -1 \\ -1 & 1 \end{pmatrix} \mathbf{X} + \begin{pmatrix} 2 \\ -5 \end{pmatrix}.$$

13. Use formula (25) and the results of Problem 16, Section 8.5, to find the general solution to each of the following systems.

(a) $\mathbf{X'} = \begin{pmatrix} 0 & 1 \\ 1 & 0 \end{pmatrix} \mathbf{X} + \begin{pmatrix} 1 \\ 1 \end{pmatrix}$

(b) $\mathbf{X}' = \begin{pmatrix} 0 & 1 \\ 1 & 0 \end{pmatrix} \mathbf{X} + \begin{pmatrix} \cosh t \\ \sinh t \end{pmatrix}$

(c) $\mathbf{X}' = \begin{pmatrix} 1 & 0 \\ 0 & 2 \end{pmatrix} \mathbf{X} + \begin{pmatrix} t \\ e^{4t} \end{pmatrix}$

[O]   8.7   A Fundamental Matrix and Variation of Parameters Revisited

Let us re-examine the method of variation of parameters for the non-homogeneous system

$$\mathbf{X}' = \mathbf{AX} + \mathbf{F}(t) \tag{1}$$

where $\mathbf{A}$ is a 2×2 matrix of constants, and $\mathbf{F}(t)$ is a column matrix whose component functions are continuous on a common interval $a \leq t \leq b$. If

$$\mathbf{X}_1 = \begin{pmatrix} x_1 \\ y_1 \end{pmatrix} \quad \text{and} \quad \mathbf{X}_2 = \begin{pmatrix} x_2 \\ y_2 \end{pmatrix}$$

are linearly independent solutions of $\mathbf{X}' = \mathbf{AX}$ on the interval $a \leq t \leq b$, then we saw in the preceding chapter that a particular solution vector of (1) was

$$\mathbf{X}_p = \begin{pmatrix} u_1 x_1 + u_2 x_2 \\ u_1 y_1 + u_2 y_2 \end{pmatrix}. \tag{2}$$

We note that by Definition 8.5 of Section 8.4 we can write (2) as a product of a 2×2 matrix and a column matrix:

$$\mathbf{X}_p = \begin{pmatrix} x_1 & x_2 \\ y_1 & y_2 \end{pmatrix} \begin{pmatrix} u_1 \\ u_2 \end{pmatrix} \tag{3}$$

or

$$\mathbf{X}_p = \mathbf{\Phi}(t)\mathbf{U}(t) \tag{4}$$

where

$$\mathbf{\Phi}(t) = \begin{pmatrix} x_1(t) & x_2(t) \\ y_1(t) & y_2(t) \end{pmatrix} \quad \text{and} \quad \mathbf{U}(t) = \begin{pmatrix} u_1(t) \\ u_2(t) \end{pmatrix}.$$

This leads us to the following definition.

Fundamental matrix

DEFINITION 8.12   Let $\mathbf{A}$ be a 2×2 matrix of constants and

$$\mathbf{X}_1 = \begin{pmatrix} x_1 \\ y_1 \end{pmatrix} \quad \text{and} \quad \mathbf{X}_2 = \begin{pmatrix} x_2 \\ y_2 \end{pmatrix}$$

be linearly independent solution vectors of the system $\mathbf{X}' = \mathbf{AX}$ on some interval $a \le t \le b$. The matrix

$$\Phi(t) = \begin{pmatrix} x_1 & x_2 \\ y_1 & y_2 \end{pmatrix}$$

is said to be a **fundamental matrix** of the system.

EXAMPLE

Find a fundamental matrix of the system

$$\mathbf{X}' = \begin{pmatrix} -3 & 1 \\ 2 & -4 \end{pmatrix} \mathbf{X}. \tag{5}$$

Solution: The characteristic equation of the coefficient matrix is

$$\begin{vmatrix} -3 - \lambda & 1 \\ 2 & -4 - \lambda \end{vmatrix} = (3 + \lambda)(4 + \lambda) - 2$$

$$= \lambda^2 + 7\lambda + 10$$

$$= (\lambda + 2)(\lambda + 5)$$

$$= 0.$$

The eigenvalues are $\lambda_1 = -2$ and $\lambda_2 = -5$. To determine the eigenvectors we must solve

$$(-3 - \lambda)k_1 + \qquad k_2 = 0$$
$$2k_1 + (-4 - \lambda)k_2 = 0 \tag{6}$$

for each value of λ.

For $\lambda_1 = -2$, each equation of (6) becomes $-k_1 + k_2 = 0$, which implies $k_2 = k_1$. The choice of $k_1 = 1$ leads to the corresponding eigenvector

$$\begin{pmatrix} 1 \\ 1 \end{pmatrix}.$$

Similarly, for $\lambda_2 = -5$ we find its related eigenvector is

$$\begin{pmatrix} 1 \\ -2 \end{pmatrix}.$$

The solution vectors of the system (5) are then

$$\mathbf{X}_1 = \begin{pmatrix} 1 \\ 1 \end{pmatrix} e^{-2t} = \begin{pmatrix} e^{-2t} \\ e^{-2t} \end{pmatrix}$$

and

$$\mathbf{X}_2 = \begin{pmatrix} 1 \\ -2 \end{pmatrix} e^{-5t} = \begin{pmatrix} e^{-5t} \\ -2e^{-5t} \end{pmatrix}.$$

Thus a fundamental matrix of (5) is

$$\Phi(t) = \begin{pmatrix} e^{-2t} & e^{-5t} \\ e^{-2t} & -2e^{-5t} \end{pmatrix}.$$

Before proceeding with variation of parameters, we need the following additional definitions from the general theory of matrix algebra.

Product of two 2 × 2 matrices

DEFINITION 8.13   If

$$A = \begin{pmatrix} a_{11} & a_{12} \\ a_{21} & a_{22} \end{pmatrix} \quad \text{and} \quad B = \begin{pmatrix} b_{11} & b_{12} \\ b_{21} & b_{22} \end{pmatrix}$$

then the **product AB** is defined by*

$$AB = \begin{pmatrix} a_{11}b_{11} + a_{12}b_{21} & a_{11}b_{12} + a_{12}b_{22} \\ a_{21}b_{11} + a_{22}b_{21} & a_{21}b_{12} + a_{22}b_{22} \end{pmatrix}, \tag{7}$$

and the **product BA** is defined by

$$BA = \begin{pmatrix} b_{11}a_{11} + b_{12}a_{21} & b_{11}a_{12} + b_{12}a_{22} \\ b_{21}a_{11} + b_{22}a_{21} & b_{21}a_{12} + b_{22}a_{22} \end{pmatrix}. \tag{8}$$

EXAMPLE

If

$$A = \begin{pmatrix} 3 & -4 \\ 5 & 7 \end{pmatrix} \quad \text{and} \quad B = \begin{pmatrix} -2 & -6 \\ 8 & -3 \end{pmatrix}$$

find **AB** and **BA**.

Solution: From Definition 8.13 we have

$$AB = \begin{pmatrix} 3(-2) + (-4)8 & 3(-6) + (-4)(-3) \\ 5(-2) + 7(8) & 5(-6) + 7(-3) \end{pmatrix}$$

$$= \begin{pmatrix} -38 & -6 \\ 46 & -51 \end{pmatrix}.$$

Similarly, we find

$$BA = \begin{pmatrix} -2(3) + (-6)5 & -2(-4) + (-6)7 \\ 8(3) + (-3)5 & 8(-4) + (-3)7 \end{pmatrix}$$

$$= \begin{pmatrix} -36 & -34 \\ 9 & -53 \end{pmatrix}.$$

In general, **AB** ≠ **BA**.

---

* See Problem 26 of Section 8.4.

Multiplicative inverse

DEFINITION 8.14   Let **A** be a 2 × 2 matrix. If there exists a 2 × 2 matrix **B** such that

$$\mathbf{AB} = \mathbf{BA} = \mathbf{I},$$

where

$$\mathbf{I} = \begin{pmatrix} 1 & 0 \\ 0 & 1 \end{pmatrix},$$

then **B** is said to be the **multiplicative inverse of A** and is denoted by **B** = $\mathbf{A}^{-1}$.

The matrix **I** in the foregoing definition is called the **multiplicative identity** since it is easily verified that for any 2 × 2 matrix **A**, **AI** = **IA** = **A**. (See Problem 11.)

THEOREM 8.4   The matrix

$$\mathbf{A} = \begin{pmatrix} a_{11} & a_{12} \\ a_{21} & a_{22} \end{pmatrix} \tag{9}$$

possesses a multiplicative inverse if and only if $a_{11}a_{22} - a_{12}a_{21} \neq 0$.

The reader should recognize the expression $a_{11}a_{22} - a_{12}a_{21}$ as the value of the determinant

$$\begin{vmatrix} a_{11} & a_{12} \\ a_{21} & a_{22} \end{vmatrix}.$$

This value is also written as det **A**.

THEOREM 8.5   If **A** is the 2 × 2 matrix (9) then

$$\mathbf{A}^{-1} = \frac{1}{\det \mathbf{A}} \begin{pmatrix} a_{22} & -a_{12} \\ -a_{21} & a_{11} \end{pmatrix} \tag{10}$$

provided det **A** ≠ 0.

The proof of Theorem 8.5, which is left as an exercise, is an immediate consequence of Definitions 8.13 and 8.14 and Definition 8.3 of Section 8.4.

We note that the entries a_{ij} of **A** and $\mathbf{A}^{-1}$ in Theorems 8.4 and 8.5 could be functions of t. Also, not every 2 × 2 matrix has a multiplicative inverse. For example, if

$$A = \begin{pmatrix} 2 & 2 \\ 3 & 3 \end{pmatrix}$$

then det $A = 2(3) - 2(3) = 0$. We conclude in this case that A^{-1} does not exist.

EXAMPLE

Find the multiplicative inverse for

$$A = \begin{pmatrix} 1 & 4 \\ 2 & 10 \end{pmatrix}.$$

Solution: Since det $A = 10 - 8 = 2 \neq 0$, it follows from Theorem 8.4 A^{-1} exists. From Theorem 8.5 we find

$$A^{-1} = \frac{1}{2} \begin{pmatrix} 10 & -4 \\ -2 & 1 \end{pmatrix}$$

$$= \begin{pmatrix} 5 & -2 \\ -1 & \frac{1}{2} \end{pmatrix}.$$

Check:

$$AA^{-1} = \begin{pmatrix} 1 & 4 \\ 2 & 10 \end{pmatrix} \begin{pmatrix} 5 & -2 \\ -1 & \frac{1}{2} \end{pmatrix} = \begin{pmatrix} 5-4 & -2+2 \\ 10-10 & -4+5 \end{pmatrix}$$

$$= \begin{pmatrix} 1 & 0 \\ 0 & 1 \end{pmatrix}.$$

$$A^{-1}A = \begin{pmatrix} 5 & -2 \\ -1 & \frac{1}{2} \end{pmatrix} \begin{pmatrix} 1 & 4 \\ 2 & 10 \end{pmatrix} = \begin{pmatrix} 5-4 & 20-20 \\ -1+1 & -4+5 \end{pmatrix} = \begin{pmatrix} 1 & 0 \\ 0 & 1 \end{pmatrix}.$$

We state the next theorem without proof.

THEOREM 8.6   Let A be a 2×2 matrix of constants. If $\Phi(t)$ is a fundamental matrix of the system $X' = AX$ then $\Phi^{-1}(t)$ exists for every value of t in the interval $a \leq t \leq b$.

EXAMPLE

For the system

$$X' = \begin{pmatrix} -3 & 1 \\ 2 & -4 \end{pmatrix} X$$

we have already seen that

$$\Phi(t) = \begin{pmatrix} e^{-2t} & e^{-5t} \\ e^{-2t} & -2e^{-5t} \end{pmatrix}.$$

By making the identifications $a_{11} = e^{-2t}$, $a_{12} = e^{-5t}$, $a_{21} = e^{-2t}$, and $a_{22} = -2e^{-5t}$, it follows

$$a_{11}a_{22} - a_{12}a_{21} = -3e^{-7t}.$$

Therefore, from Theorem 8.5 we find

$$\mathbf{\Phi}^{-1}(t) = \frac{1}{-3e^{-7t}} \begin{pmatrix} -2e^{-5t} & -e^{-5t} \\ -e^{-2t} & e^{-2t} \end{pmatrix}$$

$$= \begin{pmatrix} \frac{2}{3}e^{2t} & \frac{1}{3}e^{2t} \\ \frac{1}{3}e^{5t} & -\frac{1}{3}e^{5t} \end{pmatrix}.$$

We shall use the concepts of a fundamental matrix $\mathbf{\Phi}(t)$ and its multiplicative inverse $\mathbf{\Phi}^{-1}(t)$ in finding a particular solution of the nonhomogeneous system (1). First we note that if

$$\mathbf{X} = c_1\mathbf{X}_1 + c_2\mathbf{X}_2$$

$$= \begin{pmatrix} c_1 x_1 + c_2 x_2 \\ c_1 y_1 + c_2 y_2 \end{pmatrix} \tag{11}$$

is the general solution of the homogeneous system $\mathbf{X}' = \mathbf{AX}$, then (11) can be written as the matrix product

$$\mathbf{X} = \begin{pmatrix} x_1 & x_2 \\ y_1 & y_2 \end{pmatrix} \begin{pmatrix} c_1 \\ c_2 \end{pmatrix}$$

$$= \mathbf{\Phi}(t)\mathbf{C}. \tag{12}$$

Furthermore, to say that $\mathbf{X} = \mathbf{\Phi}(t)\mathbf{C}$ is a solution of $\mathbf{X}' = \mathbf{AX}$ we mean

$$\mathbf{\Phi}'(t)\mathbf{C} = \mathbf{A}\mathbf{\Phi}(t)\mathbf{C}$$

or $\qquad\qquad (\mathbf{\Phi}'(t) - \mathbf{A}\mathbf{\Phi}(t))\mathbf{C} = \mathbf{0} \tag{13}$

where $\qquad\qquad \mathbf{0} = \begin{pmatrix} 0 \\ 0 \end{pmatrix}.$

Since (13) is to hold for every t in the interval $a \le t \le b$ for every possible column matrix of constants $\mathbf{C}$, we must have

$$\mathbf{\Phi}'(t) - \mathbf{A}\mathbf{\Phi}(t) = \mathbf{0}$$

or $\qquad\qquad \mathbf{\Phi}'(t) = \mathbf{A}\mathbf{\Phi}(t). \tag{14}$

(See Problem 27, Section 8.4.) This result will be useful in the discussion that follows.

Variation of parameters   Suppose

$$\mathbf{X}_c = \mathbf{\Phi}(t)\mathbf{C} \tag{15}$$

is the complementary function for the nonhomogeneous system (1). We have seen that the particular solution is given by

$$\mathbf{X}_p = \mathbf{\Phi}(t)\mathbf{U}(t) \tag{16}$$

where

$$\mathbf{U}(t) = \begin{pmatrix} u_1(t) \\ u_2(t) \end{pmatrix}.$$

By the product rule* the derivative of (16) is

$$\mathbf{X}_p' = \mathbf{\Phi}(t)\mathbf{U}'(t) + \mathbf{\Phi}'(t)\mathbf{U}(t). \tag{17}$$

Substituting (16) and (17) into (1) gives

$$\mathbf{\Phi}(t)\mathbf{U}'(t) + \mathbf{\Phi}'(t)\mathbf{U}(t) = \mathbf{A}\mathbf{\Phi}(t)\mathbf{U}(t) + \mathbf{F}(t).$$

In view of equation (14), this last equation becomes

$$\mathbf{\Phi}(t)\mathbf{U}'(t) + \mathbf{A}\mathbf{\Phi}(t)\mathbf{U}(t) = \mathbf{A}\mathbf{\Phi}(t)\mathbf{U}(t) + \mathbf{F}(t).$$

Thus we obtain

$$\mathbf{\Phi}(t)\mathbf{U}'(t) = \mathbf{F}(t). \tag{18}$$

Multiplying both sides of equation (18) by $\mathbf{\Phi}^{-1}(t)$ gives

$$\mathbf{U}'(t) = \mathbf{\Phi}^{-1}(t)\mathbf{F}(t) \tag{19}$$

or

$$\mathbf{U}(t) = \int \mathbf{\Phi}^{-1}(t)\mathbf{F}(t)\,dt. \tag{20}$$

Hence, by the assumption (16), we conclude that a particular solution of (1) is given by

$$\boxed{\mathbf{X}_p = \mathbf{\Phi}(t) \int \mathbf{\Phi}^{-1}(t)\mathbf{F}(t)\,dt.} \tag{21}$$

To calculate the indefinite integral of the column matrix $\mathbf{\Phi}^{-1}(t)\mathbf{F}(t)$ in (21), we simply integrate each entry. It can be shown readily that equation (21) is equivalent to the equations in (18) and (20) of Section 8.6.

In conclusion, we note that the general solution of the system (1) can now be written as

---

* The proof that the product rule is valid here is left as an exercise. Note that the order of the products is very important. Since $\mathbf{U}(t)$ is a column matrix, the products $\mathbf{U}'(t)\mathbf{\Phi}(t)$ and $\mathbf{U}(t)\mathbf{\Phi}'(t)$ are not defined.

$$\mathbf{X} = \mathbf{X}_c + \mathbf{X}_p$$

or

$$\boxed{\mathbf{X} = \boldsymbol{\Phi}(t)\mathbf{C} + \boldsymbol{\Phi}(t)\int \boldsymbol{\Phi}^{-1}(t)\mathbf{F}(t)\,dt.}$$ (22)

EXAMPLE   Use formula (22) to find the general solution of the nonhomogeneous system

$$\mathbf{X}' = \begin{pmatrix} -3 & 1 \\ 2 & -4 \end{pmatrix}\mathbf{X} + \begin{pmatrix} 3t \\ e^{-t} \end{pmatrix}.$$ (23)

Solution: We have already seen that

$$\boldsymbol{\Phi}(t) = \begin{pmatrix} e^{-2t} & e^{-5t} \\ e^{-2t} & -2e^{-5t} \end{pmatrix} \quad \text{and} \quad \boldsymbol{\Phi}^{-1}(t) = \begin{pmatrix} \tfrac{2}{3}e^{2t} & \tfrac{1}{3}e^{2t} \\ \tfrac{1}{3}e^{5t} & -\tfrac{1}{3}e^{5t} \end{pmatrix}.$$

From (21) we then obtain

$$\mathbf{X}_p = \boldsymbol{\Phi}(t)\int \boldsymbol{\Phi}^{-1}(t)\mathbf{F}(t)\,dt$$

$$= \begin{pmatrix} e^{-2t} & e^{-5t} \\ e^{-2t} & -2e^{-5t} \end{pmatrix}\int \begin{pmatrix} \tfrac{2}{3}e^{2t} & \tfrac{1}{3}e^{2t} \\ \tfrac{1}{3}e^{5t} & -\tfrac{1}{3}e^{5t} \end{pmatrix}\begin{pmatrix} 3t \\ e^{-t} \end{pmatrix}\,dt$$

$$= \begin{pmatrix} e^{-2t} & e^{-5t} \\ e^{-2t} & -2e^{-5t} \end{pmatrix}\int \begin{pmatrix} 2te^{2t} + \tfrac{1}{3}e^{t} \\ te^{5t} - \tfrac{1}{3}e^{4t} \end{pmatrix}\,dt$$

$$= \begin{pmatrix} e^{-2t} & e^{-5t} \\ e^{-2t} & -2e^{-5t} \end{pmatrix}\begin{pmatrix} te^{2t} - \tfrac{1}{2}e^{2t} + \tfrac{1}{3}e^{t} \\ \tfrac{1}{5}te^{5t} - \tfrac{1}{25}e^{5t} - \tfrac{1}{12}e^{4t} \end{pmatrix}$$

$$= \begin{pmatrix} \tfrac{6}{5}t - \tfrac{27}{50} + \tfrac{1}{4}e^{-t} \\ \tfrac{3}{5}t - \tfrac{21}{50} + \tfrac{1}{2}e^{-t} \end{pmatrix}.$$

Hence from (22) the general solution of (23) is

$$\mathbf{X} = \begin{pmatrix} e^{-2t} & e^{-5t} \\ e^{-2t} & -2e^{-5t} \end{pmatrix}\begin{pmatrix} c_1 \\ c_2 \end{pmatrix} + \begin{pmatrix} \tfrac{6}{5}t - \tfrac{27}{50} + \tfrac{1}{4}e^{-t} \\ \tfrac{3}{5}t - \tfrac{21}{50} + \tfrac{1}{2}e^{-t} \end{pmatrix}$$

$$= c_1\begin{pmatrix} 1 \\ 1 \end{pmatrix}e^{-2t} + c_2\begin{pmatrix} 1 \\ -2 \end{pmatrix}e^{-5t} + \begin{pmatrix} \tfrac{6}{5} \\ \tfrac{3}{5} \end{pmatrix}t - \begin{pmatrix} \tfrac{27}{50} \\ \tfrac{21}{50} \end{pmatrix} + \begin{pmatrix} \tfrac{1}{4} \\ \tfrac{1}{2} \end{pmatrix}e^{-t}.$$

All of the procedures discussed in this section carry over to larger linear systems of differential equations in the normal form (1). However, from a practical viewpoint, finding the matrix $\boldsymbol{\Phi}^{-1}(t)$ can be somewhat tedious even in the case of 3×3 matrices. (See Problems 14 and 15.)

EXERCISES 8.7

Answers to odd-numbered problems begin on page A-26 of the Appendix.

In Problems 1–10 use the method of variation of parameters as formulated in this section to find the general solution of each of the given systems.

1. $X' = \begin{pmatrix} 0 & 2 \\ -1 & 3 \end{pmatrix} X + \begin{pmatrix} 1 \\ -1 \end{pmatrix} e^t$

★2. $X' = \begin{pmatrix} 0 & 2 \\ -1 & 3 \end{pmatrix} X + \begin{pmatrix} 2 \\ e^{-3t} \end{pmatrix}$

3. $X' = \begin{pmatrix} 1 & 8 \\ 1 & -1 \end{pmatrix} X + \begin{pmatrix} 12 \\ 12 \end{pmatrix} t$

4. $X' = \begin{pmatrix} 1 & 8 \\ 1 & -1 \end{pmatrix} X + \begin{pmatrix} e^{-t} \\ te^t \end{pmatrix}$

5. $X' = \begin{pmatrix} 3 & 2 \\ -2 & -1 \end{pmatrix} X + \begin{pmatrix} 2e^{-t} \\ e^{-t} \end{pmatrix}$

★6. $X' = \begin{pmatrix} 3 & 2 \\ -2 & -1 \end{pmatrix} X + \begin{pmatrix} 1 \\ 1 \end{pmatrix}$

7. $X' = \begin{pmatrix} 0 & -1 \\ 1 & 0 \end{pmatrix} X + \begin{pmatrix} \sec t \\ 0 \end{pmatrix}$

8. $X' = \begin{pmatrix} 1 & -1 \\ 1 & 1 \end{pmatrix} X + \begin{pmatrix} 3 \\ 3 \end{pmatrix} e^t$

9. $X' = \begin{pmatrix} 1 & -1 \\ 1 & 1 \end{pmatrix} X + \begin{pmatrix} \cos t \\ \sin t \end{pmatrix} e^t$

10. $X' = \begin{pmatrix} 2 & -2 \\ 8 & -6 \end{pmatrix} X + \begin{pmatrix} 1 \\ 3 \end{pmatrix} \dfrac{e^{-2t}}{t}$

11. If
$$A = \begin{pmatrix} a_{11} & a_{12} \\ a_{21} & a_{22} \end{pmatrix} \quad \text{and} \quad I = \begin{pmatrix} 1 & 0 \\ 0 & 1 \end{pmatrix},$$

show that $AI = IA = A$.

12. Prove that formula (10) of Theorem 8.5 satisfies $AA^{-1} = A^{-1}A = I$, where A is any 2×2 matrix for which $a_{11}a_{22} - a_{12}a_{21} \neq 0$.

13. If $A(t)$ is a 2×2 matrix of differentiable functions and $X(t)$ is a 2×1 column matrix of differentiable functions, prove the product rule

$$\frac{d}{dt} [A(t)X(t)] = A(t)X'(t) + A'(t)X(t).$$

★14. Provided the determinant

$$\det A = \begin{vmatrix} a_{11} & a_{12} & a_{13} \\ a_{21} & a_{22} & a_{23} \\ a_{31} & a_{32} & a_{33} \end{vmatrix} \neq 0$$

the multiplicative inverse of a 3×3 matrix

$$A = \begin{pmatrix} a_{11} & a_{12} & a_{13} \\ a_{21} & a_{22} & a_{23} \\ a_{31} & a_{32} & a_{33} \end{pmatrix}$$

is given by

$$A^{-1} = \frac{1}{\det A} \begin{pmatrix} A_{11} & A_{21} & A_{31} \\ A_{12} & A_{22} & A_{32} \\ A_{13} & A_{23} & A_{33} \end{pmatrix}$$

where the A_{ij} are the cofactors* of the entries a_{ij} of the determinant det $\mathbf{A}$. Use the preceding formula to find $\mathbf{A}^{-1}$ for

$$\mathbf{A} = \begin{pmatrix} 2 & 1 & 0 \\ -1 & 2 & 1 \\ 1 & 2 & 1 \end{pmatrix}.$$

15. **(a)** Find the eigenvalues and eigenvectors of

$$\mathbf{A} = \begin{pmatrix} 1 & 1 & 0 \\ 1 & 1 & 0 \\ 0 & 0 & 3 \end{pmatrix}.$$

(b) Find a fundamental matrix $\mathbf{\Phi}(t)$ for the homogeneous system

$$\mathbf{X}' = \begin{pmatrix} 1 & 1 & 0 \\ 1 & 1 & 0 \\ 0 & 0 & 3 \end{pmatrix} \mathbf{X}.$$

(c) Using the procedure outlined in Problem 14, find $\mathbf{\Phi}^{-1}(t)$.

(d) Use formulas (20) and (21) to find the general solution of the nonhomogeneous system

$$\mathbf{X}' = \begin{pmatrix} 1 & 1 & 0 \\ 1 & 1 & 0 \\ 0 & 0 & 3 \end{pmatrix} \mathbf{X} + \begin{pmatrix} e^t \\ e^{2t} \\ te^{3t} \end{pmatrix}.$$

16. Use the method outlined in Problem 15 to find the general solution of the system

$$\mathbf{X}' = \begin{pmatrix} 3 & -1 & -1 \\ 1 & 1 & -1 \\ 1 & -1 & 1 \end{pmatrix} \mathbf{X} + \begin{pmatrix} 0 \\ t \\ 2e^t \end{pmatrix}.$$

CHAPTER SUMMARY

Throughout this chapter we have considered systems, or simultaneous, **linear** differential equations possessing **constant coefficients**.

For linear systems, probably the most basic technique of solution consists of rewriting the entire system in **operator notation** and then using **systematic elimination** to obtain single differential equations in one dependent

---

*A cofactor is a *signed* minor: $A_{ij} = (-1)^{i+j} M_{ij}$ where M_{ij} is the 2×2 determinant obtained by removing the ith row and the jth column.

CHAPTER SUMMARY

variable which can be solved by the usual procedures. Also, a modified form of Cramer's rule can be used to accomplish the same result. Once all dependent variables have been determined, it is necessary to use the system itself to find various relationships between the parameters.

When initial conditions are specified, the **Laplace transform** can be used to reduce the system to simultaneous algebraic equations in the transformed functions. However, we must again use an elimination procedure to solve for these transformed variables.

A first-order system in **normal form** in two dependent variables is any system

$$\frac{dx}{dt} = a_{11}x + a_{12}y + f_1(t)$$

$$\frac{dy}{dt} = a_{21}x + a_{22}y + f_2(t)$$

(1)

where $f_1(t)$ and $f_2(t)$ are continuous on some common interval $a \le t \le b$. In general, the a_{ij} can be functions of t, but we are concerned only with the case of constant coefficients. When $f_1(t) = 0$, $f_2(t) = 0$, the system is said to be **homogeneous**, otherwise it is said to be **nonhomogeneous**. Any linear second-order differential equation can be expressed in this particular form. If $f_1(t)$ and $f_2(t)$ are differentiable, then the system (1) can be reduced to a single second-order differential equation.

If $\mathbf{X}$ denotes the column matrix, or **vector**,

$$\begin{pmatrix} x \\ y \end{pmatrix}$$

then the system (1) can be written compactly as

$$\frac{d\mathbf{X}}{dt} = \mathbf{A}\mathbf{X} + \mathbf{F}(t)$$

(2)

where

$$\mathbf{A} = \begin{pmatrix} a_{11} & a_{12} \\ a_{21} & a_{22} \end{pmatrix} \quad \text{and} \quad \mathbf{F}(t) = \begin{pmatrix} f_1(t) \\ f_2(t) \end{pmatrix}.$$

The **general solution of the homogeneous system**

$$\frac{d\mathbf{X}}{dt} = \mathbf{A}\mathbf{X}$$

(3)

is defined to be the linear combination

$$\mathbf{X} = c_1\mathbf{X}_1 + c_2\mathbf{X}_2$$

(4)

where $\mathbf{X}_1$ and $\mathbf{X}_2$ are **linearly independent** solution vectors of (3). The **general solution of the nonhomogeneous system** (2) is defined to be

$$\mathbf{X} = \mathbf{X}_c + \mathbf{X}_p$$

CHAPTER SUMMARY

where $\mathbf{X}_c$ is defined by (4) and $\mathbf{X}_p$ is *any* solution vector of (2).

To solve a homogeneous system (3) we must first determine the **eigenvalues** of the coefficient matrix $\mathbf{A}$ by solving the **characteristic equation**

$$\begin{vmatrix} a_{11} - \lambda & a_{12} \\ a_{21} & a_{22} - \lambda \end{vmatrix} = 0.$$

For each value of λ we must find the corresponding **eigenvector** by solving the algebraic system

$$\begin{pmatrix} a_{11} - \lambda & a_{12} \\ a_{21} & a_{22} - \lambda \end{pmatrix} \begin{pmatrix} x \\ y \end{pmatrix} = \begin{pmatrix} 0 \\ 0 \end{pmatrix}.$$

When the values of λ are distinct or complex, we can always find two different eigenvectors. In either of these cases a solution vector of (3) has the form

$$\mathbf{X}_i = \begin{pmatrix} k_1 \\ k_2 \end{pmatrix} e^{\lambda_i t}, \qquad i = 1, 2,$$

where

$$\begin{pmatrix} k_1 \\ k_2 \end{pmatrix}$$

is the eigenvector corresponding to λ_i. When $\lambda_1 = \lambda_2$, we generally can find only one eigenvector for the matrix $\mathbf{A}$. We then seek to find a second solution vector of (3) possessing the form

$$\mathbf{X} = \begin{pmatrix} k_1 + k_2 t \\ k_3 + k_4 t \end{pmatrix} e^{\lambda_1 t} = \begin{pmatrix} k_1 \\ k_3 \end{pmatrix} e^{\lambda_1 t} + \begin{pmatrix} k_2 \\ k_4 \end{pmatrix} t e^{\lambda_1 t}.$$

To solve a nonhomogeneous system we must first solve the associated homogeneous system. We determine a particular solution vector $\mathbf{X}_p$ of the nonhomogeneous system by using either **undetermined coefficients** or **variation of parameters**. The basic procedures, as well as the advantages and disadvantages of these two techniques, are quite similar to those for a single second-order differential equation.

A **fundamental matrix** of a homogeneous system (3) in two dependent variables is defined to be

$$\mathbf{\Phi}(t) = \begin{pmatrix} x_1 & x_2 \\ y_1 & y_2 \end{pmatrix}. \tag{5}$$

The x_i and y_i, $i = 1, 2$, in (5) are functions obtained from two linearly independent solution vectors

$$\mathbf{X}_1 = \begin{pmatrix} x_1 \\ y_1 \end{pmatrix} \quad \text{and} \quad \mathbf{X}_2 = \begin{pmatrix} x_2 \\ y_2 \end{pmatrix}$$

CHAPTER
SUMMARY

of (3). In terms of matrices, the method of variation of parameters leads to a particular solution given by:

$$\mathbf{X}_p = \mathbf{\Phi}(t) \int \mathbf{\Phi}^{-1}(t)\mathbf{F}(t)\,dt. \tag{6}$$

The general solution of (3) is then

$$\mathbf{X} = \mathbf{\Phi}(t)\mathbf{C} + \mathbf{\Phi}(t) \int \mathbf{\Phi}^{-1}(t)\mathbf{F}(t)\,dt, \tag{7}$$

where $\mathbf{C}$ is a column matrix containing two arbitrary constants. The matrix $\mathbf{\Phi}^{-1}(t)$ is called the **multiplicative inverse** of $\mathbf{\Phi}(t)$; the multiplicative inverse satisfies $\mathbf{\Phi}(t)\mathbf{\Phi}^{-1}(t) = \mathbf{\Phi}^{-1}(t)\mathbf{\Phi}(t) = \mathbf{I}$, where

$$\mathbf{I} = \begin{pmatrix} 1 & 0 \\ 0 & 1 \end{pmatrix}.$$

REVIEW
EXERCISES

Answers to odd-numbered problems begin on page A-27 of the Appendix.

[8.1]

1. Prove that the operators

$$(D - 1)(D^2 + 2D + 1) \qquad \text{and} \qquad (D + 1)(D^2 - 1)$$

are the same.

★2. Prove that

$$(D^2 - t^2) \neq (D + t)(D - t)$$
$$\neq (D - t)(D + t).$$

3. Write the following system in operator notation and then solve by elimination

$$x' + \ y' = 2x + 2y + 1$$
$$x' + 2y' = \ y + 3.$$

4. Solve by using determinants

$$(D + 2)x + (D + 1)y = \sin 2t$$
$$5x + (D + 3)y = \cos 2t.$$

[8.2]

5. Solve by using the Laplace transform

$$x' + y \ = t$$
$$4x + y' = 0$$
$$x(0) = 1, \qquad y(0) = 2.$$

[8.3] **6.** Write the differential equation

$$3y^{(4)} - 5y'' + 9y = 6e^t - 2t$$

as a system of first-order equations in linear normal form.

7. Write the system

$$(2D^2 + D)y - D^2x \qquad = \ln t$$
$$D^2y + (D + 1)x = 5t - 2$$

as a system of first-order equations in linear normal form.

[8.4]   ★**8.** Write as one column matrix

$$\frac{d}{dt}\begin{pmatrix} 3 & 1 & 1 \\ -1 & 2 & -1 \\ 0 & -2 & 4 \end{pmatrix}\begin{pmatrix} t \\ t^2 \\ t^3 \end{pmatrix} - \begin{pmatrix} 2 \\ -2 \\ -1 \end{pmatrix} + 2t\begin{pmatrix} 1 \\ 0 \\ 4 \end{pmatrix} + 2t^2\begin{pmatrix} 1 \\ -1 \\ 7 \end{pmatrix}.$$

9. Show that the general solution of the system

$$\frac{dx}{dt} = y$$

$$\frac{dy}{dt} = -x + 2y - 2\cos t$$

is

$$\mathbf{X} = c_1\begin{pmatrix} 1 \\ 1 \end{pmatrix}e^t + c_2\left\{\begin{pmatrix} 0 \\ 1 \end{pmatrix}e^t + \begin{pmatrix} 1 \\ 1 \end{pmatrix}te^t\right\} + \begin{pmatrix} \sin t \\ \cos t \end{pmatrix}.$$

[8.5]   Solve the following homogeneous systems of equations.

★**10.** $\dfrac{dx}{dt} = -4x + 2y$

$\dfrac{dy}{dt} = \quad 2x - 4y$

11. $\dfrac{dx}{dt} = 2x + y$

$\dfrac{dy}{dt} = -x$

12. $\dfrac{d\mathbf{X}}{dt} = \begin{pmatrix} -2 & 5 \\ -2 & 4 \end{pmatrix}\mathbf{X}$

13. $\mathbf{X}' = \begin{pmatrix} 1 & 2 \\ -2 & 1 \end{pmatrix}\mathbf{X}$

[8.6]   Solve the following nonhomogeneous systems of equations.

14. $\dfrac{dx}{dt} = 2x + \ y + \ t - 2$

$\dfrac{dy}{dt} = 3x + 4y - 4t$

15. $\mathbf{X}' = \begin{pmatrix} 2 & 1 \\ 3 & 4 \end{pmatrix} \mathbf{X} - \begin{pmatrix} 1 \\ 7 \end{pmatrix} e^t$

★16. $\dfrac{dx}{dt} = x + y + e^t \sec t$

$\dfrac{dy}{dt} = -x + y + e^t \csc t$

[**8.7**] Use the method of variation of parameters in the form (21) and (22) to find the general solution of each of the following systems.

17. $\mathbf{X}' = \begin{pmatrix} 2 & 8 \\ 1 & 4 \end{pmatrix} \mathbf{X} + \begin{pmatrix} 0 \\ 3te^{6t} \end{pmatrix}$

18. $\mathbf{X}' = \begin{pmatrix} 3 & 1 \\ -1 & 1 \end{pmatrix} \mathbf{X} + \begin{pmatrix} -2 \\ 1 \end{pmatrix} e^{2t}$

19. $\mathbf{X}' = \begin{pmatrix} -1 & 1 \\ -2 & 1 \end{pmatrix} \mathbf{X} + \begin{pmatrix} 1 \\ \cot t \end{pmatrix} \qquad 0 < t < \pi$

CHAPTER 9

Numerical Methods

Introduction

A differential equation does not have to possess a solution, or even if a solution exists, we need not always be able to find an explicit or implicit formula, containing elementary functions, satisfying the equation. In many instances, particularly in the study of nonlinear equations, we may have to be satisfied with obtaining only approximations to a solution. Assuming that a solution to a differential equation exists, it represents a locus of points (points connected by a smooth curve) in the Cartesian plane. Beginning in Section 9.2 we shall study methods that utilize the differential equation to obtain a sequence of discrete points which numerically approximate the points on the actual solution curve (see Figure 9.1).

Throughout this chapter we shall confine our attention to first-order equations $dy/dx = f(x, y)$. As we saw in the preceding chapter, higher order differential equations can always be reduced to a system of first-order equations. The numerical procedures that we shall study are then easily adaptable to this system of equations (see Section 9.5).

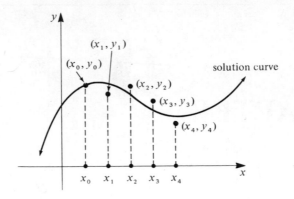

Figure 9.1

9.1   Direction Fields

Lineal elements

Suppose for the moment that we do not know the general solution of the simple equation $y' = y$. Specifically, the differential equation implies that the slope of the tangent line to a solution curve is given by the function $f(x, y) = y$. When $f(x, y)$ is held constant, that is, when

$$y = c \tag{1}$$

where c is any constant, we are in effect stating that the slope of the tangents to the solution curves is the same constant value along a horizontal line. For example, for $y = 2$ let us draw a sequence of short line segments, or **lineal elements**, each having slope 2 and its midpoint on the line. As shown in Figure 9.2 the solution curves pass through this horizontal line at every point tangent to the lineal elements.

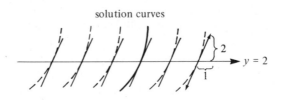

Figure 9.2

Isoclines and direction fields

Equation (1) represents a one-parameter family of horizontal lines. In general, any member of the family $f(x, y) = c$ is called an **isocline** which literally means a curve along which the inclination (of the tangents) is the same. As the parameter c is varied, we obtain a collection of isoclines on which the lineal elements are judiciously constructed. The totality of these lineal elements is called a **direction field**, **slope field**, or **lineal element field** of the differential equation $y' = f(x, y)$. As we see in Figure 9.3, the direction field suggests the "flow pattern" for the family of solution curves of the differential equation $y' = y$. In particular, if we want the one solution passing through the point $(0, 1)$, then, as indicated in Figure 9.4, we construct a curve through this point and passing through the isoclines with the appropriate slopes.

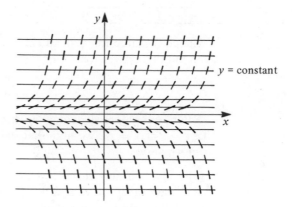

Figure 9.3

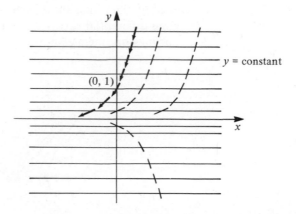

Figure 9.4

EXAMPLE   Determine the isoclines for the equation

$$\frac{dy}{dx} = 4x^2 + 9y^2.$$

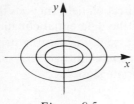

Figure 9.5

Solution: For $c > 0$ the isoclines are the curves

$$4x^2 + 9y^2 = c.$$

As Figure 9.5 shows, the curves are a concentric family of ellipses with major axis along the x-axis.

EXAMPLE

Sketch the direction field and indicate several possible members of the family of solution curves for

$$\frac{dy}{dx} = \frac{x}{y}.$$

Solution: Before sketching the direction field corresponding to the isoclines $x/y = c$ or $y = x/c$ we note that the differential equation gives the following information:

(a)   if a solution curve crosses the x-axis ($y = 0$), it does so tangent to a vertical lineal element at every point except possibly $(0, 0)$.

(b)   If a solution curve crosses the y-axis ($x = 0$), it does so tangent to a horizontal lineal element at every point except possibly $(0, 0)$.

(c)   The lineal elements corresponding to the isoclines $c = 1$ and $c = -1$ are collinear with the lines $y = x$ and $y = -x$, respectively. Indeed, it is easily verified that these isoclines are both particular solutions of the given differential equation. However, it should be noted that *in general* isoclines are themselves not solutions to a differential equation.†

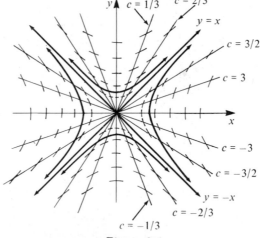

Figure 9.6

---

†When the isoclines are straight lines it is easy to determine which, if any, of these isoclines are also particular solutions of the differential equation. See Problems 16–20.

Figure 9.6 shows the direction field and several possible solution curves. Remember, on any particular isocline all the lineal elements are parallel. Also, the lineal elements may be drawn in such a manner as to suggest the flow of a particular curve.† In other words, imagine the isoclines so close together that if the lineal elements were connected, we would have a polygonal curve suggestive of the shape of a smooth curve.

EXAMPLE

The differential equation

$$y' = x^2 + y^2$$

cannot be solved in terms of elementary functions. Use a direction field to locate an approximate solution satisfying

$$y(0) = 1.$$

Solution: The isoclines are concentric circles defined by

$$x^2 + y^2 = c, \qquad c > 0.$$

By choosing $c = 1/4$, $c = 1$, $c = 9/4$, and $c = 4$, we obtain the circles with radii 1/2, 1, 3/2, and 2 shown in Figure 9.7. The lineal elements superimposed on each circle have slope corresponding to the particular value of c. It seems plausible from inspection of Figure 9.7 that a solution curve of the given initial-value problem might have the shape given in Figure 9.8. Unfortunately, we are not able to obtain any formula that describes this curve.

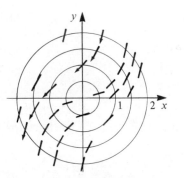

Figure 9.7

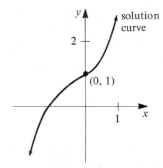

Figure 9.8

The concept of the direction field is used primarily to establish the existence and to possibly locate an approximate solution curve for a first-order differential equation which cannot be solved by the usual standard techniques.

---

† Alternatively, the lineal elements can be drawn uniformly spaced on the isocline.

However, the preceding discussion is of little value in determining specific values of a solution $y(x)$ at given points. For example, if we want to know the approximate value of $y(0.5)$ for the solution of

$$y' = x^2 + y^2$$

$$y(0) = 1,$$

then Figure 9.8 can do nothing more for us than to indicate that $y(0.5)$ may be in the same "ball park" as $y = 2$.

EXERCISES 9.1

Solutions to odd-numbered problems begin on page A-28 of the Appendix. In Problems 1–7 identify the isoclines for the given differential equation.

1. $y' = y - x^2$

★2. $y' = (x^2 + y^2)^{-1}$

3. $\dfrac{dy}{dx} = x^2 - y^2$

4. $y' = 2x + y$

5. $y' = \sqrt{x^2 + y^2 + 2y + 1}$

6. $y' = y + e^x$

7. $\dfrac{dy}{dx} = \dfrac{y - 1}{x - 2}$

In Problems 8–14 sketch the direction field for the given differential equation and indicate several possible solution curves.

8. $y\dfrac{dy}{dx} = -x$

9. $y' = x$

★10. $y' = x + y$

11. $y' = xy$

12. $\dfrac{dy}{dx} = \dfrac{1}{y}$

13. $y' = y - \cos\dfrac{\pi}{2}x$

14. $y' = 1 - \dfrac{y}{x}$

15. Formally show that the isoclines for the differential equation

$$\frac{dy}{dx} = \frac{\alpha x + \beta y}{\gamma x + \delta y}$$

are straight lines through the origin.

In Problems 16–20 find those isoclines which are also solutions of the given differential equation.

EXAMPLE

The isoclines of the differential equation

$$y' = 2x + y \tag{2}$$

are the straight lines

$$2x + y = c. \tag{3}$$

A line in this latter family will be a solution of the differential equation whenever its slope is the same as c. In other words, both the original equation and the line will satisfy $y' = c$. Since the slope of (3) is -2 if we choose $c = -2$, then $2x + y = -2$ is a solution of (2).

Check: Write the solution as

$$y = -2x - 2$$

and so

$$y' = -2$$

$$\overset{?}{=} 2x + y$$

$$= 2x + (-2x - 2)$$

$$= -2.$$

---

16. $y' = 3x + 2y$

17. $y' = \dfrac{2x}{y}$

★**18.** $\dfrac{dy}{dx} = \dfrac{2y}{x + y}$

19. $\dfrac{dy}{dx} = \dfrac{4x + 3y}{y}$

20. $y' = \dfrac{5x + 10y}{x + 2y}$

9.2   The Euler Methods

9.2.1   Euler's Method

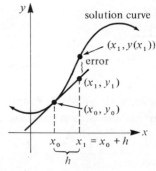

Figure 9.9

One of the simplest techniques for approximating solutions of differential equations is known as **Euler's method** or the method of **tangent lines**. Suppose we wish to approximate the solution of the equation

$$y' = f(x, y)$$

satisfying the initial condition

$$y(x_0) = y_0.$$

If h is a positive increment on the x-axis, then as Figure 9.9 shows, we can find a point $(x_1, y_1) = (x_0 + h, y_1)$ on the line tangent to the unknown solution curve at (x_0, y_0).

By the point-slope form of the equation of a line, we have

$$\frac{y_1 - y_0}{(x_0 + h) - x_0} = y'_0 \quad \text{or} \quad y_1 = y_0 + h y'_0$$

where $y_0' = f(x_0, y_0)$. If we label $x_0 + h$ by x_1, then the point (x_1, y_1) on the tangent line is an approximation to the point $(x_1, y(x_1))$ on the solution curve. That is, $y_1 \approx y(x_1)$. Of course, the accuracy of the approximation depends heavily on the size of the increment h. Usually we must choose this step size to be "reasonably small."

Assuming a uniform (constant) value of h, we can obtain a succession of points $(x_1, y_1), (x_2, y_2), \ldots, (x_n, y_n)$ which we hope are proximate to the points $(x_1, y(x_1)), (x_2, y(x_2)), \ldots, (x_n, y(x_n))$. (See Figure 9.10). Now using (x_1, y_1), we can obtain the value of y_2 which is the ordinate of a point on a new "tangent" line. We have

$$\frac{y_2 - y_1}{h} = y_1' \quad \text{or} \quad y_2 = y_1 + hy_1'$$

$$= y_1 + hf(x_1, y_1).$$

In general it follows that

$$\boxed{\begin{aligned} y_{n+1} &= y_n + hy_n' \\ &= y_n + hf(x_n, y_n) \end{aligned}} \tag{1}$$

where $x_n = x_0 + nh$.

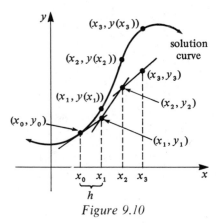

Figure 9.10

As an example, suppose we try the iteration scheme (1) on a differential equation for which we know the explicit solution; in this way we can compare the estimated values y_n and the true values $y(x_n)$.

EXAMPLE

Consider the initial-value problem

$$\frac{dy}{dx} = 2xy$$

$$y(1) = 1.$$

Use the Euler method to obtain an approximation to $y(1.5)$ using first $h = 0.1$ and then $h = 0.05$.

Solution: We first identify $f(x, y) = 2xy$ so that (1) becomes

$$y_{n+1} = y_n + h(2x_n y_n).$$

Then for $h = 0.1$ we find

$$y_1 = y_0 + (0.1)(2x_0 y_0)$$
$$= 1 + (0.1)[2(1)(1)]$$
$$= 1.2$$

which is an estimate to the value of $y(1.1)$. However, if we use $h = 0.05$ it takes *two* iterations to reach $x = 1.1$. We have

$$y_1 = 1 + (0.05)[2(1)(1)]$$
$$= 1.1,$$
$$y_2 = 1.1 + (0.05)[2(1.05)(1.1)]$$
$$= 1.2155.$$

Here we note that $y_1 \approx y(1.05)$ and $y_2 \approx y(1.1)$. The remainder of the calculations are summarized in Tables 9.1 and 9.2. Each entry is rounded to four decimal places.†

Table 9.1   Euler's Method with $h = 0.1$

x_n	y_n	True Value	Error	% Rel Error
1.00	1.0000	1.0000	0.0000	0.00
1.10	1.2000	1.2337	0.0337	2.73
1.20	1.4640	1.5527	0.0887	5.71
1.30	1.8154	1.9937	0.1784	8.95
1.40	2.2874	2.6117	0.3244	12.42
1.50	2.9278	3.4904	0.5625	16.12

---

† It is fairly easy to perform most of the calculations in this chapter on any scientific hand calculator. However, in each case a *Data General Nova 1200* computer was used.

Table 9.2 Euler's Method with $h = 0.05$

x_n	y_n	True Value	Error	% Rel Error
1.00	1.0000	1.0000	0.0000	0.00
1.05	1.1000	1.1079	0.0079	0.72
1.10	1.2155	1.2337	0.0182	1.47
1.15	1.3492	1.3806	0.0314	2.27
1.20	1.5044	1.5527	0.0483	3.11
1.25	1.6849	1.7551	0.0702	4.00
1.30	1.8955	1.9937	0.0982	4.93
1.35	2.1419	2.2762	0.1343	5.90
1.40	2.4311	2.6117	0.1806	6.92
1.45	2.7714	3.0117	0.2403	7.98
1.50	3.1733	3.4904	0.3171	9.08

In the preceding example the true values were calculated from the known solution $y = e^{x^2 - 1}$. Also, the percentage relative error is defined to be

$$\frac{|\text{true value} - \text{approximation}|}{\text{true value}} \times 100 = \frac{|\text{error}|}{\text{true value}} \times 100.$$

It should be apparent that in the case of the step size $h = 0.1$ a 16% relative error in the calculation of the approximation to $y(1.5)$ is totally unacceptable. At the expense of doubling the number of calculations a slight improvement in accuracy is obtained by halving the step size to $h = 0.05$.

Of course, in many instances we may not know the solution of a particular differential equation, or for that matter, whether a solution of an initial-value problem actually exists. The following nonlinear equation does possess a solution in closed form, but we leave it as an exercise for the reader to find it (see Problem 1).

EXAMPLE

Use the Euler method to obtain the approximate value of $y(0.5)$ for the solution of

$$y' = (x + y - 1)^2$$

$$y(0) = 2.$$

Solution: For $n = 0$ and $h = 0.1$ we have

$$y_1 = y_0 + (0.1)(x_0 + y_0 - 1)^2$$

$$= 2 + (0.1)(1)^2$$

$$= 2.1.$$

The remaining calculations are summarized in Tables 9.3 and 9.4 for $h = 0.1$ and $h = 0.05$, respectively.

Table 9.3 Euler's Method with $h = 0.1$

x_n	y_n
0.00	2.0000
0.10	2.1000
0.20	2.2440
0.30	2.4525
0.40	2.7596
0.50	3.2261

Table 9.4 Euler's Method with $h = 0.05$

x_n	y_n
0.00	2.0000
0.05	2.0500
0.10	2.1105
0.15	2.1838
0.20	2.2727
0.25	2.3812
0.30	2.5142
0.35	2.6788
0.40	2.8845
0.45	3.1455
0.50	3.4823

We may want greater accuracy than that displayed, say, in Table 9.2, and so we could try a step size even smaller than $h = 0.05$. However, rather than resorting to this extra labor, it probably would be more advantageous to employ an alternative numerical procedure. The Euler formula by itself, though attractive in its simplicity, is seldom used in serious calculations.

9.2.2 The Improved Euler Method

The formula

$$y_{n+1} = y_n + h \frac{f(x_n, y_n) + f(x_{n+1}, y_{n+1}^*)}{2}$$

where (2)

$$y_{n+1}^* = y_n + hf(x_n, y_n)$$

is known as the **improved Euler formula** or **Heun's formula**. The values $f(x_n, y_n)$ and $f(x_{n+1}, y_{n+1}^*)$ are approximations to the slope of the curve at $(x_n, y(x_n))$ and $(x_{n+1}, y(x_{n+1}))$ and consequently the ratio

$$\frac{f(x_n, y_n) + f(x_{n+1}, y_{n+1}^*)}{2}$$

can be interpreted as an average slope on the interval between x_n and x_{n+1}.

The equations in (2) can be readily visualized. In Figure 9.11 we have shown the case when $n = 0$. Note that

$$f(x_0, y_0) \qquad \text{and} \qquad f(x_1, y_1^*)$$

are slopes of the indicated straight lines passing through the points (x_0, y_0) and (x_1, y_1^*), respectively. By taking an average of these slopes, we obtain the slope of the dotted skew lines. Rather than advancing along the line with slope $m = f(x_0, y_0)$ to the point with ordinate y_1^* obtained by the usual Euler method, we advance instead along the line through (x_0, y_0) with slope m_{ave} until we reach x_1. It seems plausible from inspection of the figure that y_1 is an improvement over y_1^*.

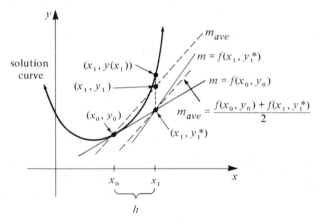

Figure 9.11

We might also say that the value of

$$y_1^* = y_0 + hf(x_0, y_0)$$

predicts a value of $y(x_1)$, whereas

$$y_1 = y_0 + h\frac{f(x_0, y_0) + f(x_1, y_1^*)}{2}$$

corrects this estimate.

EXAMPLE   Use the improved Euler formula to obtain the approximate value of $y(1.5)$ for the solution of

$$y' = 2xy$$
$$y(1) = 1.$$

Compare the results for $h = 0.1$ and $h = 0.05$.

Solution: For $n = 0$ and $h = 0.1$ we first compute

$$y_1^* = y_0 + (0.1)2x_0y_0$$
$$= 1.2.$$

Then from (2)

$$y_1 = y_0 + (0.1)\frac{2x_0y_0 + 2x_1y_1^*}{2}$$
$$= 1 + (0.1)\frac{2(1)(1) + 2(1.1)(1.2)}{2}$$
$$= 1.232.$$

The comparative values of the calculations for $h = 0.1$ and $h = 0.05$ are given in Tables 9.5 and 9.6, respectively.

Table 9.5   Improved Euler's Method with $h = 0.1$

x_n	y_n	True Value	Error	% Rel Error
1.00	1.0000	1.0000	0.0000	0.00
1.10	1.2320	1.2337	0.0017	0.14
1.20	1.5479	1.5527	0.0048	0.31
1.30	1.9832	1.9937	0.0106	0.53
1.40	2.5908	2.6117	0.0209	0.80
1.50	3.4509	3.4904	0.0394	1.13

Table 9.6 Improved Euler's Method with $h = 0.05$

x_n	y_n	True Value	Error	% Rel Error
1.00	1.0000	1.0000	0.0000	0.00
1.05	1.1077	1.1079	0.0002	0.02
1.10	1.2332	1.2337	0.0004	0.04
1.15	1.3798	1.3806	0.0008	0.06
1.20	1.5514	1.5527	0.0013	0.08
1.25	1.7531	1.7551	0.0020	0.11
1.30	1.9909	1.9937	0.0029	0.14
1.35	2.2721	2.2762	0.0041	0.18
1.40	2.6060	2.6117	0.0057	0.22
1.45	3.0038	3.0117	0.0079	0.26
1.50	3.4795	3.4904	0.0108	0.31

EXAMPLE

Use the improved Euler formula to obtain the approximate value of $y(0.5)$ for the solution of

$$y' = (x + y - 1)^2$$
$$y(0) = 2.$$

Solution: For $n = 0$ and $h = 0.1$, we have

$$y_1^* = y_0 + (0.1)(x_0 + y_0 - 1)^2$$
$$= 2.1$$

and so

$$y_1 = y_0 + (0.1)\frac{(x_0 + y_0 - 1)^2 + (x_1 + y_1^* - 1)^2}{2}$$

$$= 2 + (0.1)\frac{1 + 1.44}{2}$$

$$= 2.122.$$

The remaining calculations are summarized in Tables 9.7 and 9.8 for $h = 0.1$ and $h = 0.05$, respectively.

Table 9.7 Improved Euler's Method with $h = 0.1$

x_n	y_n
0.00	2.0000
0.10	2.1220
0.20	2.3049
0.30	2.5858
0.40	3.0378
0.50	3.8254

Table 9.8   Improved Euler's Method with $h = 0.05$

x_n	y_n
0.00	2.0000
0.05	2.0553
0.10	2.1228
0.15	2.2056
0.20	2.3075
0.25	2.4342
0.30	2.5931
0.35	2.7953
0.40	3.0574
0.45	3.4057
0.50	3.8840

A brief word of caution is in order here. We cannot compute all the values of y_n^* first and then substitute these values in the first formula of (2). In other words, we cannot use the data in Table 9.1 to help construct the values in Table 9.5. Why?

EXERCISES 9.2   Solutions to odd-numbered problems begin on page A-29 of the Appendix.

1. Solve the initial-value problem

$$y' = (x + y - 1)^2$$
$$y(0) = 2$$

in terms of elementary functions.

2. Let $y(x)$ be the solution of the initial-value problem given in Problem 1. Rounded to four decimal places, compute the exact values of $y(0.1)$, $y(0.2)$, $y(0.3)$, $y(0.4)$, and $y(0.5)$. Compare these values with the entries in Tables 9.3, 9.4, 9.7, and 9.8.

Given the initial-value problems in Problems 3–12. Use the Euler formula to obtain a four decimal approximation to the indicated value. First use **(a)** $h = 0.1$, and then **(b)** $h = 0.05$.

3. $y' = 2x - 3y + 1$, $y(1) = 5$; $y(1.5)$

4. $y' = 4x - 2y$, $y(0) = 2$; $y(0.5)$

5. $y' = 1 + y^2$, $y(0) = 0$; $y(0.5)$

6. $y' = x^2 + y^2$, $y(0) = 1$; $y(0.5)$

7. $y' = e^{-y}$, $y(0) = 0$; $y(0.5)$

8. $y' = x + y^2$, $y(0) = 0$; $y(0.5)$

9. $y' = (x - y)^2$, $y(0) = 0.5$; $y(0.5)$

10. $y' = xy + \sqrt{y}$, $y(0) = 1$; $y(0.5)$

11. $y' = xy^2 - \dfrac{y}{x}$, $y(1) = 1$; $y(1.5)$

★12. $y' = y - y^2$, $y(0) = 0.5$; $y(0.5)$

13. As parts **(a)**–**(j)** of this problem, repeat the calculations of Problems 3–12 using the improved Euler formula.

14. Derive the basic Euler formula by integrating both sides of the equation $y' = f(x, y)$ on the integral $x_n \leq x \leq x_{n+1}$. Approximate the integral of the right side by replacing the function $f(x, y)$ by its value at the left end point of the interval of integration.

15. By following the procedure outlined in Problem 14, derive the improved Euler formula. [*Hint:* Replace the integrand of the right side by the average of its values at the end points of the interval of integration.]

EXAMPLE

The improved Euler formula can be used to obtain a sequence of approximations to $y(x_n)$ at a *fixed value* of x_n. If the basic Euler formula is denoted by

$$y_{n+1,1} = y_n + hf(x_n, y_n) \tag{3}$$

then we can define

$$y_{n+1,k+1} = y_n + h\frac{f(x_n, y_n) + f(x_{n+1}, y_{n+1,k})}{2} \tag{4}$$

for $n \geq 0$, $k \geq 1$. For $n = 0$ and $k = 1, 2, 3, \ldots$ equations (3) and (4) yield the sequence of values

$$y_{1,1}, y_{1,2}, y_{1,3}, y_{1,4}, \ldots$$

which are all approximations to $y(x)$ at $x = x_1$. For example, $y_{1,2}$ corresponds to the *original* improved Euler formula given in (2) and

$$y_{1,3} = y_0 + h\frac{f(x_0, y_0) + f(x_1, y_{1,2})}{2}.$$

It might be conjectured that since an average of two slopes (formula (2)) yields an improved approximation to $y(x)$ at a point, that an average including an average (formula (4)) may even give better results. See Problem 16.

★**16.**   Consider the initial-value problem

$$y' = 2xy, \qquad y(1) = 1.$$

Convince yourself that "more" is not necessarily better by computing the values

$$y_{1,1}, y_{1,2}, y_{1,3}, y_{1,4}, y_{1,5}$$

with $h = 0.1$. By using the exact value of $y(1.1)$ (see Table 9.1), compute the percentage relative error at each step of the calculation.

17.   Although it may not be obvious from the differential equation, its solution could "behave badly" near a point x at which we wish to approximate $y(x)$. Numerical procedures may then give widely differing results near this point. Let $y(x)$ be the solution of the initial-value problem

$$y' = x^2 + y^3, \qquad y(1) = 1.$$

Using the step size $h = 0.1$, compare the results obtained from the Euler formula with the results from the improved Euler formula in the approximation of $y(1.4)$.

9.3   The Three-Term Taylor Method

The numerical method that we shall consider in this section is more of theoretical interest than of practical importance since the results obtained using formula (5) below will not differ substantially from those obtained using the improved Euler method.

In the study of numerical solutions of differential equations, many computational algorithms can be derived from a Taylor series expansion. Recall from calculus that the form of this expansion about a point $x = a$ is

$$y(x) = y(a) + y'(a)\frac{(x-a)}{1!} + y''(a)\frac{(x-a)^2}{2!} + \cdots \tag{1}$$

It is understood that the function $y(x)$ possesses derivatives of all orders and that the series (1) converges in some interval defined by $|x - a| < R$. Notice, in particular, that if we set $a = x_n$ and $x = x_n + h$, then (1) becomes

$$y(x_n + h) = y(x_n) + y'(x_n)h + y''(x_n)\frac{h^2}{2} + \cdots \tag{2}$$

The Euler method revisited

Furthermore, let us now assume that the function $y(x)$ is a solution of the first-order differential equation

$$y' = f(x, y).$$

If we then truncate the series (2) after, say, two terms we obtain the approximation

$$y(x_n + h) \approx y(x_n) + y'(x_n)h$$

or $$y(x_n + h) \approx y(x_n) + f(x_n, y(x_n))h.$$ (3)

Observe that we can obtain the Euler formula

$$y_{n+1} = y_n + hf(x_n, y_n)$$ (4)

of the preceding section by formally replacing $y(x_n + h)$ and $y(x_n)$ in (3) by their approximations y_{n+1} and y_n, respectively. The approximation symbol $\approx$ is replaced by an equality since we are defining the left side of (4) by the numbers obtained from the right-hand member.

The Taylor method

By retaining three terms in the series (2), we can write

$$y(x_n + h) \approx y(x_n) + y'(x_n)h + y''(x_n)\frac{h^2}{2}.$$

After using the replacements noted above, it follows that

$$y_{n+1} = y_n + y'_n h + y''_n \frac{h^2}{2}.$$ (5)

The second derivative y'' can be obtained by differentiating $y' = f(x, y)$.

At this point let us re-examine the two initial-value problems of the preceding section.

EXAMPLE

Use the three-term Taylor formula to obtain the approximate value of $y(1.5)$ for the solution of

$$y' = 2xy$$

$$y(1) = 1.$$

Compare the results for $h = 0.1$ and $h = 0.05$.

Solution: Since $y' = 2xy$ it follows by the product rule that $y'' = 2xy' + 2y$. Thus, for example, when $h = 0.1$, $n = 0$, we can first calculate

$$y'_0 = 2x_0 y_0$$

$$= 2(1)(1)$$

$$= 2,$$

and then

$$y_0'' = 2x_0 y_0' + 2y_0$$
$$= 2(1)(2) + 2(1).$$

Hence (5) becomes

$$y_1 = y_0 + y_0'(0.1) + y_0''\frac{(0.1)^2}{2}$$

$$= 1 + 2(0.1) + 6(0.005)$$

$$= 1.23.$$

The results of the iteration, along with the comparative exact values, are summarized in Tables 9.9 and 9.10.

Table 9.9   Three-Term Taylor Method with $h = 0.1$

x_n	y_n	True Value	Error	% Rel Error
1.00	1.0000	1.0000	0.0000	0.00
1.10	1.2300	1.2337	0.0037	0.30
1.20	1.5427	1.5527	0.0100	0.65
1.30	1.9728	1.9937	0.0210	1.05
1.40	2.5721	2.6117	0.0396	1.52
1.50	3.4188	3.4904	0.0715	2.05

Table 9.10   Three-Term Taylor Method with $h = 0.05$

x_n	y_n	True Value	Error	% Rel Error
1.00	1.0000	1.0000	0.0000	0.00
1.05	1.1075	1.1079	0.0004	0.04
1.10	1.2327	1.2337	0.0010	0.08
1.15	1.3788	1.3806	0.0018	0.13
1.20	1.5499	1.5527	0.0028	0.18
1.25	1.7509	1.7551	0.0041	0.23
1.30	1.9879	1.9937	0.0059	0.29
1.35	2.2681	2.2762	0.0081	0.36
1.40	2.6006	2.6117	0.0111	0.43
1.45	2.9967	3.0117	0.0150	0.50
1.50	3.4702	3.4904	0.0202	0.58

EXAMPLE   Use the three-term Taylor formula to obtain the approximate value of $y(0.5)$ for the solution of

$$y' = (x + y - 1)^2$$
$$y(0) = 2.$$

Solution: In this case we compute y'' by the power rule. We have

$$y'' = 2(x + y - 1)(1 + y').$$

The results are summarized in Tables 9.11 and 9.12 for $h = 0.1$ and $h = 0.05$, respectively.

Table 9.11   Three-Term Taylor Method with $h = 0.1$

x_n	y_n
0.00	2.0000
0.10	2.1200
0.20	2.2992
0.30	2.5726
0.40	3.0077
0.50	3.7511

Table 9.12   Three-term Taylor Method with $h = 0.05$

x_n	y_n
0.00	2.0000
0.05	2.0550
0.10	2.1222
0.15	2.2045
0.20	2.3058
0.25	2.4315
0.30	2.5890
0.35	2.7889
0.40	3.0475
0.45	3.3898
0.50	3.8574

A comparison of the last two examples with the corresponding results obtained from the improved Euler method shows no startling dissimilarities. However, the next example is of some interest.

EXAMPLE   Compare the approximate values of $y\,(1.5)$ for

$$y' = x + y - 1$$
$$y(1) = 5$$

using the three-term Taylor method and the improved Euler method with $h = 0.1$.

Solution: In this case the differential equation is linear in y so that it is readily shown that the exact solution is

$$y = -x + 6e^{x-1}.$$

The results of the respective iterations are given in Table 9.13.

Table 9.13   Comparison of Numerical Methods with $h = 0.1$

x_n	Improved Euler	Three-Term Taylor	True Value
1.00	5.0000	5.0000	5.0000
1.10	5.3000	5.5300	5.5310
1.20	6.1262	6.1262	6.1284
1.30	6.7954	6.7954	6.7992
1.40	7.5454	7.5454	7.5510
1.50	8.3847	8.3847	8.3923

The fact that the values obtained in the preceding example are the same for both methods is no accident in this case. The Taylor method gives the same values as the improved Euler when $f(x, y)$ is linear in x and y (see Problem 11).

EXERCISES 9.3   Answers to odd-numbered problems begin on page A-33 of the Appendix.
   Given the initial-value problems in Problems 1–10. Use the three-term Taylor formula to obtain a four decimal approximation to the indicated value. First use **(a)** $h = 0.1$, and then **(b)** $h = 0.05$.

1. $y' = 2x - 3y + 1, \quad y(1) = 5; \quad y(1.5)$

2. $y' = 4x - 2y, \quad y(0) = 2; \quad y(0.5)$

3. $y' = 1 + y^2, \quad y(0) = 0; \quad y(0.5)$

4. $y' = x^2 + y^2, \quad y(0) = 1; \quad y(0.5)$

5. $y' = e^{-y}, \quad y(0) = 0; \quad y(0.5)$

6. $y' = x + y^2, \quad y(0) = 0; \quad y(0.5)$

7. $y' = (x - y)^2, \quad y(0) = 0.5; \quad y(0.5)$

8. $y' = xy + \sqrt{y}, \quad y(0) = 1; \quad y(0.5)$

9. $y' = xy^2 - \dfrac{y}{x}, \quad y(1) = 1; \quad y(1.5)$

★10. $y' = y - y^2, \quad y(0) = 0.5; \quad y(0.5)$

11. Consider the differential equation $y' = f(x, y)$, where f is linear in x and y. In this case prove that the improved Euler formula is the same as the three-term Taylor formula. [*Hint:* Recall from calculus that a Taylor series for a function g of two variables is

$$g(a + h, b + k) = g(a, b) + g_x(a, b)h + g_y(a, b)k$$

$$+ \frac{1}{2}(h^2 g_{xx} + 2hk g_{xy} + k^2 g_{yy})\Big|_{(a,b)}$$

+ terms involving higher order derivatives.

Apply this result to $f(x_n + h, \ y_n + hf(x_n, y_n))$ in the improved Euler formula. Also use the fact that $y''(x) = \dfrac{d}{dx} y'(x) = f_x + f_y y',$]

★12. Let $y(x)$ be the solution of the initial-value problem

$$y' = x^2 + y^3, \qquad y(1) = 1.$$

Use $h = 0.1$ and the three-term Taylor formula to obtain an approximation to $y(1.4)$. Compare your answer with the results obtained in Problem 17 of Section 9.2.

9.4   The Runge–Kutta Method

Probably one of the most popular as well as accurate numerical procedures used in obtaining approximate solutions to differential equations is the **fourth-order Runge–Kutta method**.* As the name suggests there are Runge–Kutta methods of different orders.

For the moment let us consider a **second-order** procedure. This consists of finding constants a, b, α, and β such that the formula

$$y_{n+1} = y_n + ak_1 + bk_2, \tag{1}$$

---

* Carl Runge (1856–1927) and Wilhelm Kutta (1867–1944), German applied mathematicians.

where
$$k_1 = hf(x_n, y_n)$$
$$k_2 = hf(x_n + \alpha h, y_n + \beta k_1)$$

(2)

agrees with a Taylor series expansion to as many terms as possible. The obvious purpose is to achieve the accuracy of the Taylor method without the necessity of having to compute higher-order derivatives. Now it can be shown that whenever the constants satisfy

$$a + b = 1$$

$$b\alpha = \frac{1}{2}$$

$$b\beta = \frac{1}{2}$$

then (1) agrees with a Taylor expansion out to the h^2 or third term. It should be of interest to observe that when $a = 1/2, b = 1/2, \alpha = 1, \beta = 1$ then (1) *reduces to the improved Euler method*. Thus we can conclude that the three-term Taylor formula is essentially equivalent to the improved Euler formula. Also, the basic Euler method is a **first-order** Runge–Kutta procedure.

Notice, too, that the sum $ak_1 + bk_2, a + b = 1$, in equation (1) is simply a *weighted* average of k_1 and k_2. The numbers k_1 and k_2 are multiples of approximations to the slope at two different points.

The fourth-order Runge–Kutta formula

The **fourth-order** Runge–Kutta method consists of determining appropriate constants so that a formula such as

$$y_{n+1} = y_n + ak_1 + bk_2 + ck_3 + dk_4$$

agrees with a Taylor expansion out to h^4 or the fifth term. As in (2), the k_i are constant multiples of $f(x, y)$ evaluated at select points. The derivation of the actual method is tedious to say the least, so we state the results:

$$y_{n+1} = y_n + \tfrac{1}{6}(k_1 + 2k_2 + 2k_3 + k_4),$$
where
$$k_1 = hf(x_n, y_n)$$
$$k_2 = hf(x_n + \tfrac{1}{2}h, y_n + \tfrac{1}{2}k_1)$$
$$k_3 = hf(x_n + \tfrac{1}{2}h, y_n + \tfrac{1}{2}k_2)$$
$$k_4 = hf(x_n + h, y_n + k_3).$$

(3)

The reader is advised to look carefully at the formulas in (3); note that k_2 depends on k_1, k_3 depends on k_2, and so on. Also, k_2 and k_3 are approximations to the slope at the midpoint of the interval between x_n and $x_{n+1} = x_n + h$.

EXAMPLE   Use the Runge–Kutta method to obtain an approximation to $y(1.5)$ for the solution of

$$y' = 2xy$$
$$y(1) = 1.$$

Use $h = 0.1$.

Solution: For the sake of illustration let us compute the case when $n = 0$. From (3) we find

$$k_1 = (0.1)f(x_0, y_0)$$
$$= (0.1)2x_0y_0$$
$$= 0.2,$$

$$k_2 = (.01)f(x_0 + \tfrac{1}{2}(0.1), y_0 + \tfrac{1}{2}(0.2))$$
$$= (0.1)2(x_0 + \tfrac{1}{2}(0.1))(y_0 + \tfrac{1}{2}(0.2))$$
$$= 0.231,$$

$$k_3 = (0.1)f(x_0 + \tfrac{1}{2}(0.1), y_0 + \tfrac{1}{2}(0.231))$$
$$= (0.1)2(x_0 + \tfrac{1}{2}(0.1))(y_0 + \tfrac{1}{2}(0.231))$$
$$= 0.234255,$$

$$k_4 = (0.1)f(x_0 + 0.1, y_0 + 0.234255)$$
$$= (0.1)2(x_0 + 0.1)(y_0 + 0.234255)$$
$$= 0.2715361,$$

and, therefore,

$$y_1 = y_0 + \tfrac{1}{6}(k_1 + 2k_2 + 2k_3 + k_4)$$
$$= 1 + \tfrac{1}{6}(0.2 + 0.231) + 0.234255 + 0.2715361)$$
$$= 1.23367435.$$

Rounded to the usual four decimal places we obtain

$$y_1 = 1.2337.$$

The accompanying table should convince the student why the Runge–Kutta method is so popular. Of course, there is no need to use any smaller step size.

Table 9.14 Runge–Kutta Method with $h = 0.1$

x_n	y_n	True Value	Error	% Rel Error
1.00	1.0000	1.0000	0.0000	0.00
1.10	1.2337	1.2337	0.0000	0.00
1.20	1.5527	1.5527	0.0000	0.00
1.30	1.9937	1.9937	0.0000	0.00
1.40	2.6116	2.6117	0.0001	0.00
1.50	3.4902	3.4904	0.0001	0.00

EXAMPLE

Use the Runge–Kutta method to compute an approximation to $y(0.5)$ for the solution to

$$y' = (x + y - 1)^2$$

$$y(0) = 2.$$

Solution: The results of the calculations for the case when $h = 0.1$ are given in Table 9.15.

Table 9.15 Runge–Kutta Method with $h = 0.1$

x_n	y_n
0.00	2.0000
0.10	2.1230
0.20	2.3085
0.30	2.5958
0.40	3.0649
0.50	3.9078

The reader might be interested in inspecting Tables 9.16 and 9.17 at this point. These tables compare the results obtained from the various formulas that we have examined applied to the two specific problems

$$y' = 2xy, \quad y(1) = 1,$$
$$y' = (x + y - 1)^2, \quad y(0) = 2,$$

that we have considered throughout the last three sections.

Table 9.16 $y' = 2xy,$ $y(1) = 1$

Comparison of Numerical Methods with $h = 0.1$					
x_n	Euler	Improved Euler	3-Term Taylor	Runge–Kutta	True Value
1.00	1.0000	1.0000	1.0000	1.0000	1.0000
1.10	1.2000	1.2320	1.2300	1.2337	1.2337
1.20	1.4640	1.5479	1.5427	1.5527	1.5527
1.30	1.8154	1.9832	1.9728	1.9937	1.9937
1.40	2.2874	2.5908	2.5721	2.6116	2.6117
1.50	2.9278	3.4509	3.4188	3.4902	3.4904

Comparison of Numerical Methods with $h = 0.05$					
x_n	Euler	Improved Euler	3-Term Taylor	Runge–Kutta	True Value
1.00	1.0000	1.0000	1.0000	1.0000	1.0000
1.05	1.1000	1.1077	1.1075	1.1079	1.1079
1.10	1.2155	1.2332	1.2327	1.2337	1.2337
1.15	1.3492	1.3798	1.3788	1.3806	1.3806
1.20	1.5044	1.5514	1.5499	1.5527	1.5527
1.25	1.6849	1.7531	1.7509	1.7551	1.7551
1.30	1.8955	1.9909	1.9879	1.9937	1.9937
1.35	2.1419	2.2721	2.2681	2.2762	2.2762
1.40	2.4311	2.6060	2.6006	2.6117	2.6117
1.45	2.7714	3.0038	2.9967	3.0117	3.0117
1.50	3.1733	3.4795	3.4702	3.4903	3.4904

Table 9.17 $y' = (x + y - 1)^2,$ $y(0) = 2$

Comparison of Numerical Methods with $h = 0.1$					
x_n	Euler	Improved Euler	3-Term Taylor	Runge–Kutta	True Value
0.00	2.0000	2.0000	2.0000	2.0000	2.0000
0.10	2.1000	2.1220	2.1200	2.1230	2.1230
0.20	2.2440	2.3049	2.2992	2.3085	2.3085
0.30	2.4525	2.5858	2.5726	2.5958	2.5958
0.40	2.7596	3.0378	3.0077	3.0649	3.0650
0.50	3.2261	3.8254	3.7511	3.9078	3.9082

Table 9.17   *continued*

Comparison of Numerical Methods with $h = 0.05$					
x_n	Euler	Improved Euler	3-Term Taylor	Runge–Kutta	True Value
0.00	2.0000	2.0000	2.0000	2.0000	2.0000
0.05	2.0500	2.0553	2.0550	2.0554	2.0554
0.10	2.1105	2.1228	2.1222	2.1230	2.1230
0.15	2.1838	2.2056	2.2045	2.2061	2.2061
0.20	2.2727	2.3075	2.3058	2.3085	2.3085
0.25	2.3812	2.4342	2.4315	2.4358	2.4358
0.30	2.5142	2.5931	2.5890	2.5958	2.5958
0.35	2.6788	2.7953	2.7889	2.7998	2.7997
0.40	2.8845	3.0574	3.0475	3.0650	3.0650
0.45	3.1455	3.4057	3.3898	3.4189	3.4189
0.50	3.4823	3.8840	3.8574	3.9082	3.9082

EXERCISES 9.4

Answers to odd-numbered problems begin on page A-36 of the Appendix.
    Given the initial-value problems in Problems 1–10. Use the method of Runge–Kutta to obtain a four decimal approximation to the indicated value. Use $h = 0.1$.

1. $y' = 2x - 3y + 1$, $y(1) = 5$; $y(1.5)$

2. $y' = 4x - 2y$, $y(0) = 2$; $y(0.5)$

3. $y' = 1 + y^2$, $y(0) = 0$; $y(0.5)$

4. $y' = x^2 + y^2$, $y(0) = 1$; $y(0.5)$

5. $y' = e^{-y}$, $y(0) = 0$; $y(0.5)$

6. $y' = x + y^2$, $y(0) = 0$; $y(0.5)$

7. $y' = (x - y)^2$, $y(0) = 0.5$; $y(0.5)$

8. $y' = xy + \sqrt{y}$, $y(0) = 1$; $y(0.5)$

9. $y' = xy^2 - \dfrac{y}{x}$, $y(1) = 1$; $y(1.5)$

★10. $y' = y - y^2$, $y(0) = 0.5$; $y(0.5)$

11. Consider the differential equation $y' = f(x)$. In this case show that the fourth-order Runge–Kutta method reduces to Simpson's rule for the integral of $f(x)$ on the interval $x_n \le x \le x_{n+1}$.

★**12.**   Let $y(x)$ be the solution of the initial-value problem

$$y' = x^2 + y^3, \qquad y(1) = 1.$$

Determine whether the Runge–Kutta formula can be used to obtain an approximation for $y(1.4)$. Use $h = 0.1$.

[O]   9.5   Milne's Method, Second-Order Equations, Errors

There are many additional formulas which can be applied to obtain approximations to solutions of differential equations. Although it is not our intention to survey the vast field of numerical methods, one additional formula deserves mention. The **Milne method**, like the improved Euler formula, is a predictor-corrector method. By first using the *predictor*

$$y_{n+1}^* = y_{n-3} + \frac{4h}{3}(2y_n' - y_{n-1}' + 2y_{n-2}'), \tag{1}$$

where $n \geq 3$ and

$$y_n' = f(x_n, y_n)$$

$$y_{n-1}' = f(x_{n-1}, y_{n-1})$$

$$y_{n-2}' = f(x_{n-2}, y_{n-2})$$

we are then able to substitute the value of y_{n+1}^* into the *corrector*

$$y_{n+1} = y_{n-1} + \frac{h}{3}(y_{n+1}' + 4y_n' + y_{n-1}') \tag{2}$$

where $$y_{n+1}' = f(x_{n+1}, y_{n+1}^*).$$

Notice that formula (1) requires that we must know y_0, y_1, y_2, and y_3 in order to obtain y_4. Usually these last three values are computed by an accurate method such as the Runge–Kutta formula.

Since the Milne predictor-corrector formulas demand that we know more than just y_n to compute y_{n+1}, the procedure is called a **multistep** or **continuing** method. The Euler formulas, the three-term Taylor, and the Runge–Kutta formulas are examples of **single-step** or **starting** methods.

Higher order equations   The numerical procedures that we have discussed in this chapter we applied only to the first-order equation $dy/dx = f(x, y)$ subject to an initial condition $y(x_0) = y_0$. To approximate a solution to, say, a second-order equation

$$\frac{d^2y}{dx^2} = f(x, y, y') \tag{3}$$

we first reduce the equation to a system of first-order equations. If we let $y' = u$, equation (3) becomes

$$y' = u$$
$$u' = f(x, y, u). \tag{4}$$

We now apply a particular method to *each* equation in the resulting system. For example, the basic Euler formulas would be

$$y_{n+1} = y_n + hu_n$$
$$u_{n+1} = u_n + hf(x_n, y_n, u_n). \tag{5}$$

Errors

In a serious and detailed study of numerical solutions of differential equations we would have to pay close attention to the various sources of errors. For some kinds of computation, accumulation of errors might reduce the accuracy of an approximation to the point of being useless.

By using only three terms of a Taylor series to approximate the value of a function, the method itself naturally will be a source of error. As we have seen, the Euler formula is essentially two terms of a Taylor series expansion; by advancing along a tangent line, we do not necessarily get to a point on or even near the solution curve. The errors inherent to these methods are known as **truncation errors**.

Any calculator or computer can compute only to at most a finite number of decimal places. Suppose for the sake of illustration that we have a calculator that can display six digits while carrying eight digits internally. If we multiply two numbers, each having six decimals, then the product actually contains twelve decimal places. But the number that we see is rounded to six decimal places while the machine has stored a number rounded to eight decimal places. In one calculation such as this, the **round-off error** may not be deemed significant, but a problem could arise if many calculations are performed with rounded numbers. The effects of round-off can be minimized on a computer, provided it has double-precision capabilities.

When iterating a formula such as

$$y_{n+1} = y_n + hf(x_n, y_n)$$

we obtain a sequence of values

$$y_1, y_2, y_3, \ldots.$$

The value of y_1 is, of course, in error, and unfortunately, y_2 depends on y_1. Thus, y_2 must also be in error. In turn, y_3 inherits an error from y_2. The error resulting from the inheritance of errors in preceding calculations is known as **propagation error**. To make matters worse, formulas can be **unstable**. This means that errors occuring in the early stages of calculation are not only propagated but are also *compounded* at each step of the iteration. The error may grow so fast so as to completely overwhelm the subsequent approximations. Under certain circumstances the corrector formula in Milne's method is unstable.

Answers to odd-numbered problems begin on page A-38 of the Appendix.

EXAMPLE   Use the Euler method to obtain the approximate value of $y(0.2)$ where $y(x)$ is the solution of

$$y'' + xy' + y = 0$$

$$y(0) = 1, \qquad y'(0) = 2.$$

Solution: In terms of the substitution $y' = u$, the equation is equivalent to the system

$$y' = u$$

$$u' = -xu - y.$$

Thus from (5) we obtain

$$y_{n+1} = y_n + h\,u_n$$

$$u_{n+1} = u_n + h[-x_n u_n - y_n].$$

Using the step size $h = 0.2$, we find

$$y_1 = y_0 + (0.2)u_0$$

$$= 1 + (0.2)2$$

$$= 1.4,$$

$$u_1 = u_0 + (0.2)[-x_0 u_0 - y_0]$$

$$= 2 + (0.2)(-1)$$

$$= 1.8.$$

In other words, $y(0.2) \approx 1.4$ and $y'(0.2) \approx 1.8$.

---

1. Obtain an approximation to $y(0.2)$ of the preceding example using the step size $h = 0.1$.

2. Generalize the improved Euler formula to a system such as

$$y' = u$$

$$u' = f(x, y, u).$$

3. Use the improved Euler method to approximate $y(0.2)$ where $y(x)$ is the solution of the initial-value problem given in the preceding example. Use $h = 0.2$ and $h = 0.1$.

★4. Generalize the Euler method to systems of the form

$$x' = f(x, y, t)$$
$$y' = g(x, y, t).$$

Use the results to approximate the values of $x(0.2)$, $y(0.2)$ where $x(t)$ and $y(t)$ are solutions of

$$x' = x + y$$
$$y' = x - y,$$
$$x(0) = 1, \quad y(0) = 2.$$

Assume $h = 0.1$.

5. Use Milne's predictor-corrector method to approximate the value of $y(0.4)$ where $y(x)$ is solution of

$$y' = x + y - 1$$
$$y(0) = 1.$$

Obtain the values of y_1, y_2, and y_3 from the Runge–Kutta formula using $h = 0.1$.

★6. Consider the recurrence formula

$$y_{n+1} = k(1 - y_n)$$

where $n = 0, 1, 2, \ldots$, and k is a constant. Suppose that the initial value y_0 has an absolute error $\varepsilon = y_0 - y$, where y is the true value. Show that the formula is unstable for increasing n when $|k| > 1$ and stable when $|k| < 1$.

CHAPTER SUMMARY

A solution of a differential equation may exist and yet we may not be able to determine it in terms of the familiar elementary functions. A way of convincing oneself that a first-order equation

$$y' = f(x, y)$$

possesses a solution passing through a specific point

$$y(x_0) = y_0$$

is to sketch the **direction field** associated with the equation. The equation

$$f(x, y) = c$$

determines the **isoclines**, or curves of constant inclination. This means that every solution curve passing through a particular isocline does so with the same slope. The direction field is the totality of short line segments throughout

**CHAPTER
SUMMARY**

two-dimensional space which have midpoints on the isoclines and possessing slope equal to the value of the parameter c. A carefully plotted sequence of these **lineal elements** can suggest the shape of a solution curve passing through the given point (x_0, y_0).

At best, a direction field can give only the crudest form of an approximation to a numerical value of the solution $y(x)$ of the initial-value problem when x is close to x_0.

To obtain the approximate values of $y(x)$, we used **Euler's formula**:

$$y_{n+1} = y_n + hf(x_n, y_n);$$

The **improved Euler formula**:

$$y_{n+1} = y_n + h\frac{f(x_n, y_n) + f(x_{n+1}, y_{n+1}^*)}{2}$$

where

$$y_{n+1}^* = y_n + hf(x_n, y_n);$$

The **three-term Taylor formula**:

$$y_{n+1} = y_n + y_n'h + y_n''\frac{h^2}{2};$$

The **Runge–Kutta formula**:

$$y_{n+1} = y_n + \tfrac{1}{6}(k_1 + 2k_2 + 2k_3 + k_4),$$

where

$$k_1 = hf(x_n, y_n)$$

$$k_2 = hf(x_n + \tfrac{1}{2}h, y_n + \tfrac{1}{2}k_1)$$

$$k_3 = hf(x_n + \tfrac{1}{2}h, y_n + \tfrac{1}{2}k_2)$$

$$k_4 = hf(x_n + h, y_n + k_3);$$

The **Milne formulas**:

$$y_{n+1}^* = y_{n-3} + \frac{4h}{3}(2y_n' - y_{n-1}' + 2y_{n-2}')$$

$$y_{n+1} = y_{n-1} + \frac{h}{3}(y_{n+1}' + 4y_n' + y_{n-1}'),$$

where

$$y_{n+1}' = f(x_{n+1}, y_{n+1}^*).$$

In each of the above formulas, the number h is the length of a uniform step. In other words,

$$x_1 = x_0 + h, \ x_2 = x_1 + h = (x_0 + h) + h = x_0 + 2h, \dots, x_n = x_0 + nh.$$

Euler's method consists of approximating the solution curve by a sequence of straight lines. The improved Euler and Runge–Kutta methods use the idea of averaging slopes.

CHAPTER SUMMARY   The first four methods are known as **single step** or **starting methods** while Milne's method is an example of a **multi-step** or a **continuing method**. To use the latter method, we must first compute y_1, y_2, and y_3 by some starting method such as the improved Euler or the Runge–Kutta formulas. Euler's method is not generally used if we desire accuracy to several decimal places. The improved Euler and Milne formulas are also particular examples of a class of approximating formulas known as **predictor-corrector** formulas. For example, when using the improved Euler formula, the value y_{n+1}^* obtained from the basic Euler formula is the predicted value which is then corrected through the new formula.

To obtain numerical approximations to higher order differential equations, we can reduce the differential equation to a system of first-order equations. We then apply a particular numerical technique to each equation of the system.

REVIEW EXERCISES   **[9.1]**   Answers to odd-numbered problems begin on page A-38 of the Appendix.

In Problems 1–2 sketch the direction field for the given differential equation. Indicate several possible solution curves.

1. $ydx - xdy = 0$

2. $y' = 2x - y$

[9.2–9.4]   In Problems 3–6 construct a table comparing the indicated values of $y(x)$ using the Euler, improved Euler, three-term Taylor, and Runge–Kutta methods. Compute to four rounded decimal places. Use $h = 0.1$ and $h = 0.05$.

3. $y' = 2\ln xy, \quad y(1) = 2;$

$y(1.1), y(1.2), y(1.3), y(1.4), y(1.5)$

★4. $y' = \sin x^2 + \cos y^2, \quad y(0) = 0;$

$y(0.1), y(0.2), y(0.3), y(0.4), y(0.5)$

5. $y' = \sqrt{x + y}, \quad y(0.5) = 0.5$

$y(0.6), y(0.7), y(0.8), y(0.9), y(1.0)$

6. $y' = xy + y^2, \quad y(1) = 1$

$y(1.1), y(1.2), y(1.3), y(1.4), y(1.5)$

[9.5]   7. Use the Euler method to obtain the approximate value of $y(0.2)$ where $y(x)$ is the solution of the initial-value problem

$$y'' - (2x + 1)y = 0$$
$$y(0) = 3, \qquad y'(0) = 1.$$

First use one step with $h = 0.2$ and then repeat the calculations using $h = 0.1$.

★8.   Use Milne's predictor-corrector method to approximate the value of $y(0.4)$ where $y(x)$ is the solution of

$$y' = 4x - 2y$$

$$y(0) = 2.$$

Use the Runge–Kutta formula and $h = 0.1$ to obtain the values of y_1, y_2, and y_3. [See Problem 2 of Exercise 9.4.]

CHAPTER 10

Partial Differential Equations

Introduction

Throughout the preceding chapters, our attention has been focused on finding "general solutions" of ordinary differential equations. Also, we were primarily concerned with the theory and application of linear equations of order $n \leq 2$. In this chapter, we shall limit our consideration to a special kind of linear *partial differential equation*. However, we shall make no attempt to find, or even pursue, the concept of a general solution of such an equation. The emphasis will be on a specific procedure used in solving certain problems in the mathematical physics of temperature distributions and vibrations. These problems are described by relatively simple second-order partial differential equations subject to side conditions. As a matter of course, the solutions of these equations, and hence the physical problems, depend on solving associated ordinary differential equations.

451

10.1   Orthogonal Functions

Terminology   In this and the next two sections, we set the stage for the material in Section 10.4. Fundamental to the entire discussion is the notion of **orthogonal functions**.

> **DEFINITION 10.1**   Two functions f_1 and f_2 are said to be **orthogonal** on an interval $a \leq x \leq b$ if and only if
>
> $$\int_a^b f_1(x)f_2(x)\,dx = 0.* \tag{1}$$

EXAMPLE $f_1(x) = x^2$ and $f_2(x) = x^3$ are orthogonal on $-1 \leq x \leq 1$ since

$$\int_{-1}^1 f_1(x)f_2(x)\,dx = \int_{-1}^1 x^2 \cdot x^3\,dx$$

$$= \tfrac{1}{6}x^6 \Big|_{-1}^1$$

$$= \tfrac{1}{6}[1 - (-1)^6]$$

$$= 0.$$

> **DEFINITION 10.2**   An infinite set of real functions
>
> $$\phi_0(x), \quad \phi_1(x), \quad \phi_2(x), \ldots \tag{2}$$
>
> is said to be **orthogonal** on an interval $a \leq x \leq b$ if and only if
>
> $$\int_a^b \phi_m(x)\phi_n(x)\,dx \begin{cases} = 0, & m \neq n \\ \neq 0, & m = n. \end{cases} \tag{3}$$

The positive number

$$\|\phi_n(x)\|^2 = \int_a^b \phi_n^2(x)\,dx \tag{4}$$

is called the **square norm** and

$$\|\phi_n(x)\| = \sqrt{\int_a^b \phi_n^2(x)\,dx} \tag{5}$$

is the **norm** of the function $\phi_n(x)$. When $\|\phi_n(x)\| = 1$ for $n = 0, 1, 2, \ldots$, the set (2) is said to be **orthonormal** on the interval.

---

*The term *orthogonal* and condition (1) have no geometric significance.

EXAMPLE   Show that the set

$$1, \cos x, \cos 2x, \ldots,$$

is orthogonal on the interval $-\pi \leq x \leq \pi$.

Solution: If we make the identification $\phi_0(x) = 1$ and $\phi_n(x) = \cos nx$, we must then show $\int_{-\pi}^{\pi} \phi_0(x)\phi_n(x)\, dx = 0, n > 0$ and $\int_{-\pi}^{\pi} \phi_m(x)\phi_n(x)\, dx = 0,$ $m > 0, n > 0, m \neq n.$ We have in the first case

$$\int_{-\pi}^{\pi} \phi_0(x)\phi_n(x)\, dx = \int_{-\pi}^{\pi} \cos nx\, dx$$

$$= \frac{1}{n}\sin nx \Big|_{-\pi}^{\pi}$$

$$= \frac{1}{n}\Big[\sin n\pi - \sin(-n\pi)\Big]$$

$$= 0, \qquad n > 0,$$

and in the second,

$$\int_{-\pi}^{\pi} \phi_m(x)\phi_n(x)\, dx = \int_{-\pi}^{\pi} \cos mx \cos nx\, dx$$

$$= \frac{1}{2}\int_{-\pi}^{\pi}\Big[\cos(m+n)x + \cos(m-n)x\Big]dx$$

$$= \frac{1}{2}\Big[\frac{\sin(m+n)x}{m+n} + \frac{\sin(m-n)}{m-n}x\Big]_{-\pi}^{\pi}$$

$$= 0, \qquad m \neq n.$$

EXAMPLE   Find the norms of each function in the orthogonal set given in the preceding example.

Solution: For $\phi_0(x) = 1$, we have from (3)

$$\|\phi_0(x)\|^2 = \int_{-\pi}^{\pi} dx$$

$$= 2\pi$$

so that $\|\phi_0(x)\| = \sqrt{2\pi}$. For $\phi_n(x) = \cos nx, n > 0$, it follows that

$$\|\phi_n(x)\|^2 = \int_{-\pi}^{\pi} \cos^2 nx \, dx$$

$$= \frac{1}{2} \int_{-\pi}^{\pi} [1 + \cos 2nx] \, dx$$

$$= \pi.$$

Thus for $n > 0$, $\|\phi_n(x)\| = \sqrt{\pi}$.

Any orthogonal set of functions $\{\phi_n(x)\}, n = 0, 1, 2, \ldots$, can be **normalized**, that is, made into an orthonormal set, by dividing each function by its norm.

EXAMPLE

It follows from the first two examples that the set

$$\frac{1}{\sqrt{2\pi}}, \frac{\cos x}{\sqrt{\pi}}, \frac{\cos 2x}{\sqrt{\pi}}, \ldots,$$

is orthonormal on $-\pi \leq x \leq \pi$.

Generalized Fourier series

Suppose $\{\phi_n(x)\}$ is an infinite set of functions orthogonal on an interval $a \leq x \leq b$. We ask: If $y = f(x)$ is a function defined on the interval $a < x < b$, is it possible to determine a set of coefficients $c_n, n = 0, 1, 2, \ldots$, for which

$$f(x) = c_0\phi_0(x) + c_1\phi_1(x) + \cdots + c_n\phi_n(x) + \cdots ? \tag{6}$$

Multiplying (6) by $\phi_m(x)$ and integrating over the interval gives

$$\int_a^b f(x)\phi_m(x) \, dx = c_0 \int_a^b \phi_0(x)\phi_m(x) \, dx$$

$$+ c_1 \int_a^b \phi_1(x)\phi_m(x) \, dx + \cdots + c_n \int_a^b \phi_n(x)\phi_m(x) \, dx + \cdots$$

By orthogonality, each term on the right-hand side of the last equation is zero *except* when $m = n$. In this case we have

$$\int_a^b f(x)\phi_n(x) \, dx = c_n \int_a^b \phi_n^2(x) \, dx.$$

It follows that the required coefficients are

$$c_n = \frac{\int_a^b f(x)\phi_n(x) \, dx}{\int_a^b \phi_n^2(x) \, dx}, \qquad n = 0, 1, 2, \ldots.$$

In other words,

$$f(x) = \sum_{n=0}^{\infty} c_n \phi_n(x) \tag{7}$$

where

$$c_n = \frac{\int_a^b f(x)\phi_n(x)\, dx}{\|\phi_n(x)\|^2} \tag{8}$$

The series (7) with coefficients (8) is called a **generalized Fourier series**.

We note that the procedure outlined for determining the c_n was *formal*, that is, basic questions on whether a series expansion such as (7) is actually possible were ignored.

EXERCISES 10.1

Answers to odd-numbered problems begin on page A-41 of the Appendix. In Problems 1–6 show that the set of functions is orthogonal on the indicated interval.

1. $\sin x, \sin 3x, \sin 5x, \dots,\quad 0 \le x \le \dfrac{\pi}{2}$

2. $\cos x, \cos 3x, \cos 5x, \dots,\quad 0 \le x \le \dfrac{\pi}{2}$

3. $\{\sin nx\},\quad n = 1, 2, 3, \dots,\quad 0 \le x \le \pi$

4. $\left\{\sin \dfrac{n\pi}{p}x\right\},\quad n = 1, 2, 3, \dots,\quad 0 \le x \le p$

5. $\left\{1, \cos \dfrac{n\pi}{p}x\right\},\quad n = 1, 2, 3, \dots,\quad 0 \le x \le p$

★6. $\left\{1, \cos \dfrac{n\pi}{p}x, \sin \dfrac{m\pi}{p}x\right\},\quad n = 1, 2, 3, \dots,\quad m = 1, 2, 3, \dots,\quad -p \le x \le p$

7. Find the norm of each of the functions in the sets given in Problems 1–6.

A set of functions $\{\phi_n(x)\}, n = 0, 1, 2, \dots,$ is said to be **orthogonal with respect to a weight function** $w(x)$ on an interval $a \le x \le b$ if and only if

$$\int_a^b w(x)\phi_m(x)\phi_n(x)\, dx \begin{cases} = 0, & m \ne n \\ \ne 0, & m = n. \end{cases}$$

EXAMPLE

The set $\qquad\qquad 1, \cos x, \cos 2x, \dots,$

is orthogonal with respect to the constant weight function $w(x) = 1$ on the interval $0 \le x \le \pi$.

In Problems 8 and 9 verify by direct integration that the functions are orthogonal with respect to the indicated weight function on the given interval.

8. $L_0(x) = 1$, $L_1(x) = -x + 1$, $L_2(x) = \frac{1}{2}x^2 - 2x + 1$; $w(x) = e^{-x}$, $0 \le x < \infty$.

9. $H_0(x) = 1$, $H_1(x) = 2x$, $H_2(x) = 4x^2 - 2$; $w(x) = e^{-x^2}$, $-\infty < x < \infty$

10. Let p, q, r, r' be continuous on $a \le x \le b$ and $p(x) > 0, r(x) > 0$ for every x in $a < x < b$, and let y_m and y_n be solutions of the boundary value problem

$$\frac{d}{dx}\left[r(x)\frac{dy}{dx}\right] + [q(x) + \lambda p(x)]y = 0 \tag{9}$$

$$\begin{aligned}\alpha_1 y(a) + \beta_1 y'(a) &= 0 \\ \alpha_2 y(b) + \beta_2 y'(b) &= 0\end{aligned} \tag{10}$$

corresponding to distinct constants λ_m and λ_n. This is known as the

Sturm–Liouville problem.

(a) Show that y_m and y_n are orthogonal on the interval $a \le x \le b$ with respect to the weight function $p(x)$. [*Hint:* Multiply the differential equation for y_m by y_n, and multiply the differential equation for y_n by y_m. Subtract and integrate the result over the interval $a \le x \le b$ and then use (10).]
(b) Show that the boundary conditions (10) are not needed for orthogonality of y_m and y_n when $r(a) = r(b) = 0$.

11. Consider Legendre's differential equation

$$(1 - x^2)y'' - 2xy' + n(n + 1)y = 0, \quad n = 0, 1, 2, \ldots,$$

Use the result from part (b) of Problem 10 to show that the Legendre polynomials $P_n(x)$ are orthogonal with respect to the weight function $p(x) = 1$ on $-1 \le x \le 1$.

★12. Let
$$f(x) = \begin{cases} 0, & -1 < x < 0, \\ x, & 0 \le x < 1. \end{cases}$$

Use (8) and the Legendre polynomials given in (12) of Section 6.4 to find the first three coefficients in the expansion

$$f(x) = c_0 P_0(x) + c_1 P_1(x) + c_2 P_2(x) + \cdots$$

10.2 Trigonometric Series

10.2.1 Fourier Series

The set of functions

$$1, \cos\frac{\pi}{p}x, \cos\frac{2\pi}{p}x, \ldots, \sin\frac{\pi}{p}x, \sin\frac{2\pi}{p}x, \sin\frac{3\pi}{p}x, \ldots, \tag{1}$$

is orthogonal on the interval $-p \le x \le p$. (See Problem 6, Section 10.1.) Suppose f is a function defined on the interval $-p < x < p$ that can be represented by the trigonometric series

$$f(x) = \frac{a_0}{2} + \sum_{n=1}^{\infty} \left(a_n \cos\frac{n\pi}{p}x + b_n \sin\frac{n\pi}{p}x \right). \tag{2}$$

Then the coefficients $a_0, a_1, a_2, \ldots, b_1, b_2, \ldots$, can be determined as follows*. Integrating both sides of (2) from $-p$ to p gives

$$\int_{-p}^{p} f(x)\,dx = \frac{a_0}{2} \int_{-p}^{p} dx$$

$$+ \sum_{n=1}^{\infty} \left(a_n \int_{-p}^{p} \cos\frac{n\pi}{p}x\,dx + b_n \int_{-p}^{p} \sin\frac{n\pi}{p}x\,dx \right). \tag{3}$$

Since each function $\cos n\pi x/p$, $\sin n\pi x/p$, $n > 1$, is orthogonal to 1 on the interval the right side of the equation reduces to a single term and, consequently,

$$\int_{-p}^{p} f(x)\,dx = \frac{a_0}{2} \int_{-p}^{p} dx = \frac{a_0}{2}x \Big|_{-p}^{p} = pa_0.$$

Solving for a_0 yields

$$a_0 = \frac{1}{p} \int_{-p}^{p} f(x)\,dx. \tag{4}$$

Now multiply (2) by $\cos m\pi x/p$ and integrate:

$$\int_{-p}^{p} f(x)\cos\frac{m\pi}{p}x\,dx = \frac{a_0}{2} \int_{-p}^{p} \cos\frac{m\pi}{p}x\,dx$$

$$+ \sum_{n=1}^{\infty} \left(a_n \int_{-p}^{p} \cos\frac{m\pi}{p}x \cos\frac{n\pi}{p}x\,dx \right.$$

$$\left. + b_n \int_{-p}^{p} \cos\frac{m\pi}{p}x \sin\frac{n\pi}{p}x\,dx \right). \tag{5}$$

---

* We have chosen to write the coefficient of 1 in the series (1) as $a_0/2$ rather than a_0. This is for convenience only; the formula for a_n will then reduce to a_0 when $n = 0$.

Now
$$\int_{-p}^{p} \cos \frac{m\pi}{p} x \, dx = 0, \qquad m > 0,$$

$$\int_{-p}^{p} \cos \frac{m\pi}{p} x \cos \frac{n\pi}{p} x \, dx \quad \begin{cases} = 0, & m \neq n \\ = p, & m = n, \end{cases}$$

and
$$\int_{-p}^{p} \cos \frac{m\pi}{p} x \sin \frac{n\pi}{p} x \, dx = 0$$

so (5) reduces to
$$\int_{-p}^{p} f(x) \cos \frac{n\pi}{p} x \, dx = a_n p.$$

Therefore
$$a_n = \frac{1}{p} \int_{-p}^{p} f(x) \cos \frac{n\pi}{p} x \, dx. \tag{6}$$

Finally, if we multiply (2) by $\sin m\pi x/p$, integrate, and make use of the results

$$\int_{-p}^{p} \sin \frac{m\pi}{p} x \, dx = 0, \qquad m > 0$$

$$\int_{-p}^{p} \sin \frac{m\pi}{p} x \cos \frac{n\pi}{p} x \, dx = 0$$

$$\int_{-p}^{p} \sin \frac{m\pi}{p} x \sin \frac{n\pi}{p} x \, dx \quad \begin{cases} = 0, & m \neq n \\ = p, & m = n \end{cases}$$

we find that
$$b_n = \frac{1}{p} \int_{-p}^{p} f(x) \sin \frac{n\pi}{p} x \, dx. \tag{7}$$

The trigonometric series (1) with coefficients a_0, a_n, and b_n defined (4), (6), and (7), respectively, is said to be the **Fourier series** of the function f*. The coefficients are sometimes referred to as the **Euler coefficients**.

As in the discussion of generalized Fourier series in the preceding section, the underlying assumption that f can be represented by such series (1) and the subsequent determination of the coefficients corresponding to this assumption was strictly formal. We assumed that f was integrable on the interval and that (1), as well as the series obtained by multiplying (1) by $\cos m\pi x/p$ and $\sin m\pi x/p$, converged in such a manner as to permit term-by-term integration. Until (1) is shown to be convergent for a given function f, the equality sign is usually replaced by the symbol $\sim$. We summarize the above results.

---

* Named after the French mathematician, Joseph Fourier (1768–1830). Fourier used such series in his investigations into the theory of heat.

The **Fourier series** of a function f defined on the interval $-p < x < p$ is given by

$$f(x) \sim \frac{a_0}{2} + \sum_{n=1}^{\infty} \left(a_n \cos \frac{n\pi}{p} x + b_n \sin \frac{n\pi}{p} x \right) \tag{8}$$

where

$$a_0 = \frac{1}{p} \int_{-p}^{p} f(x) \, dx \tag{9}$$

$$a_n = \frac{1}{p} \int_{-p}^{p} f(x) \cos \frac{n\pi}{p} x \, dx \tag{10}$$

$$b_n = \frac{1}{p} \int_{-p}^{p} f(x) \sin \frac{n\pi}{p} x \, dx. \tag{11}$$

EXAMPLE

Expand

$$f(x) = \begin{cases} 0, & -\pi < x < 0 \\ \pi - x, & 0 < x < \pi \end{cases} \tag{12}$$

in a Fourier series.

Solution: The graph of f is given in Figure 10.1.

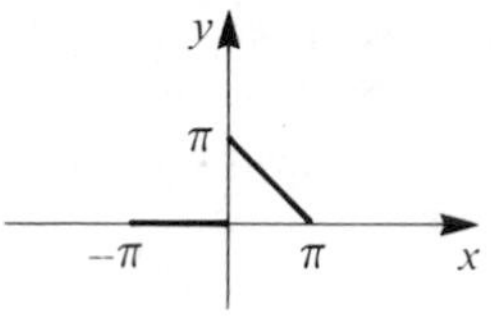

With $p = \pi$, we have from (9) and (10) that

$$a_0 = \frac{1}{\pi} \int_{-\pi}^{\pi} f(x) \, dx = \frac{1}{\pi} \left[\int_{-\pi}^{0} 0 \, dx + \int_{0}^{\pi} (\pi - x) \, dx \right]$$

$$= \frac{1}{\pi} \left[\pi x - \frac{x^2}{2} \right]_0^{\pi}$$

$$= \frac{\pi}{2},$$

$$a_n = \frac{1}{\pi} \int_{-\pi}^{\pi} f(x) \cos nx \, dx = \frac{1}{\pi} \left[\int_{-\pi}^{0} 0 \, dx + \int_{0}^{\pi} (\pi - x) \cos nx \, dx \right]$$

$$= \frac{1}{\pi} \left[(\pi - x) \frac{\sin nx}{n} \Big|_0^{\pi} + \frac{1}{n} \int_0^{\pi} \sin nx \, dx \right]$$

$$= -\frac{1}{n\pi} \frac{\cos nx}{n} \Big|_0^{\pi}$$

$$= \frac{-\cos n\pi + 1}{n^2 \pi}$$

$$= \frac{1 - (-1)^n}{n^2 \pi}.$$

y

π

$-\pi$ π x

Figure 10.1

In like manner we find from (11) that

$$b_n = \frac{1}{\pi} \int_0^\pi (\pi - x) \sin nx \, dx$$

$$= \frac{1}{n}$$

Therefore $f(x) \sim \dfrac{\pi}{4} + \displaystyle\sum_{n=1}^{\infty} \left[\dfrac{1 - (-1)^n}{n^2 \pi} \cos nx + \dfrac{1}{n} \sin nx \right].$ (13)

Note that a_n defined by (10) reduces to a_0 given by (9) when we set $n = 0$. But as the last example shows, this may not be the case *after* the integral for a_n is evaluated.

Convergence of a Fourier series

The following theorem gives sufficient conditions for convergence of a Fourier series to $f(x)$.

> **THEOREM 10.1** Let f and f' be piecewise continuous on $-p < x < p$, that is, let f and f' be continuous except at a finite number of points in the interval and have only finite discontinuities at these points. Then the Fourier series of f on the interval converges to $f(x)$ at a point of continuity. At a point of discontinuity, the Fourier series will converge to the average
>
> $$\frac{f(x+) + f(x-)}{2}$$
>
> where $f(x+)$ and $f(x-)$ denote the limit of f at x from the right and from the left, respectively.*

EXAMPLE

The function (12) given in the preceding example satisfies the conditions of Theorem 10.1. Thus for every x in $-\pi < x < \pi$, except at $x = 0$, the symbol $\sim$ in (13) can be replaced by an equality. At $x = 0$ the function is discontinuous and so the series (13) will converge to

$$\frac{f(0+) + f(0-)}{2} = \frac{\pi + 0}{2} = \frac{\pi}{2}.$$

---

* That is, for x a point in the interval and $h > 0$,

$$f(x+) = \lim_{h \to 0} f(x + h) \qquad f(x-) = \lim_{h \to 0} f(x - h).$$

Periodic extension

Observe that the functions in the basic set (1) have a common period $2p$. Hence the right side of (2) is periodic. We conclude that a Fourier series not only represents the function on the interval $-p < x < p$, but will also give the **periodic extension** of f outside this interval. We can now apply Theorem 10.1 to the periodic extension of f, or we may assume from the outset that the given function is periodic with period $2p$ (that is, $f(x + 2p) = f(x)$). When f is piecewise continuous and the right and left hand derivatives exist at $x = -p$ and $x = p$, respectively, then the series (8) will converge to the average $[f(p-) + f(-p+)]/2$ at these end points and to this value extended periodically to $\pm 3p$, $\pm 5p$, $\pm 7p$, and so on.

EXAMPLE

The Fourier series (13) converges to the periodic extension of (12) onto the entire x-axis. The solid dots given in Figure 10.2 represent the value

$$\frac{f(0+) + f(0-)}{2} = \frac{\pi}{2}$$

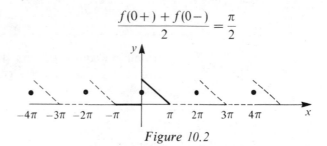

Figure 10.2

at 0, $\pm 2\pi$, $\pm 4\pi$,.... At $\pm \pi$, $\pm 3\pi$, $\pm 5\pi$,..., the series will converge to the value

$$\frac{f(\pi-) + f(-\pi+)}{2} = 0.$$

10.2.2   Cosine and Sine Series

Even and odd functions

The reader may recall that a function f is said to be **even** if

$$f(-x) = f(x).$$

Whereas, if

$$f(-x) = -f(x)$$

then f is said to be an **odd** function.

EXAMPLES

(a) $f(x) = x^2$ is even since

$$f(-x) = (-x)^2$$
$$= x^2$$
$$= f(x).$$

(b) $f(x) = x^3$ is odd since

$$f(-x) = (-x)^3$$
$$= -x^3$$
$$= -f(x)$$

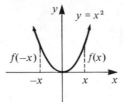

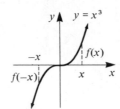

Figure 10.3   Figure 10.4

As illustrated in Figures 10.3 and 10.4, the graph of an even function is symmetric about the y-axis, and the graph of an odd function possesses symmetry about the origin.

EXAMPLE   Since $\cos(-x) = \cos x$ and $\sin(-x) = -\sin x$, the cosine and sine are even and odd functions, respectively.

Properties of even and odd functions

The proofs of the following properties are left as exercises.

  I.   The product of two even functions is even.
 II.   The product of two odd functions is even.
III. The product of an even function with an odd function is odd.
IV. If f is even, then $\int_{-a}^{a} f(x)\,dx = 2\int_{0}^{a} f(x)\,dx$.
 V.   If f is odd, then $\int_{-a}^{a} f(x)\,dx = 0$.

Cosine and sine series

If f is an even function on $-p < x < p$, then in view of the foregoing properties, the coefficients (9), (10), and (11) become

$$a_0 = \frac{1}{p}\int_{-p}^{p} f(x)\,dx = \frac{2}{p}\int_{0}^{p} f(x)\,dx$$

$$a_n = \frac{1}{p}\int_{-p}^{p} \underbrace{f(x)\cos\frac{n\pi}{p}x}_{\text{even}}\,dx = \frac{2}{p}\int_{0}^{p} f(x)\cos\frac{n\pi}{p}x\,dx$$

$$b_n = \frac{1}{p}\int_{-p}^{p} \underbrace{f(x)\sin\frac{n\pi}{p}x}_{\text{odd}}\,dx = 0.$$

Similarly, when f is odd on the interval,

$$a_n = 0, \quad n = 0, 1, 2, \dots,$$

$$b_n = \frac{2}{p} \int_0^p f(x) \sin \frac{n\pi}{p} x \, dx.$$

We summarize the results:

The Fourier series of an even function on the interval $-p < x < p$ is the **cosine series**

$$f(x) \sim \frac{a_0}{2} + \sum_{n=1}^{\infty} a_n \cos \frac{n\pi}{p} x \tag{14}$$

where

$$a_0 = \frac{2}{p} \int_0^p f(x) \, dx. \tag{15}$$

$$a_n = \frac{2}{p} \int_0^p f(x) \cos \frac{n\pi}{p} x \, dx. \tag{16}$$

The Fourier series of an odd function on the interval $-p < x < p$ is the **sine series**

$$f(x) \sim \sum_{n=1}^{\infty} b_n \sin \frac{n\pi}{p} x \tag{17}$$

where

$$b_n = \frac{2}{p} \int_0^p f(x) \sin \frac{n\pi}{p} x \, dx. \tag{18}$$

EXAMPLE

Expand

$$f(x) = x, \qquad -2 < x < 2, \tag{19}$$

in a Fourier series.

Solution: We expand f in a sine series since inspection of Figure 10.5 shows that the function is odd on the interval.

With the identification $2p = 4$, or $p = 2$, we can write (18) as

$$b_n = \int_0^2 x \sin \frac{n\pi}{2} x \, dx.$$

Integration by parts then yields

$$b_n = \frac{4(-1)^{n+1}}{n\pi}.$$

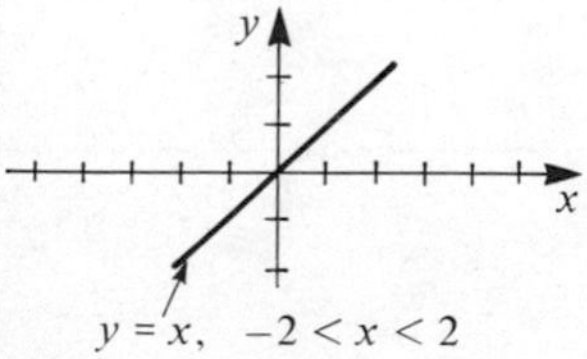

$y = x, \quad -2 < x < 2$

Figure 10.5

Therefore $$f(x) \sim \frac{4}{\pi} \sum_{n=1}^{\infty} \frac{(-1)^{n+1}}{n} \sin \frac{n\pi}{2} x.$$ (20)

EXAMPLE   The function (19) in the preceding example satisfies the conditions of Theorem 10.1. Hence the series (20) converges to the function on $-2 < x < 2$ and the periodic extension (of period 4) given in Figure 10.6.

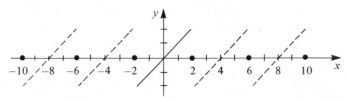

Figure 10.6

Half-range expansions   Throughout the preceding discussion it was understood that a function f was defined on an interval with the origin as midpoint, that is, $-p < x < p$. However, in many instances we are interested in representing a function that is defined only on $0 < x < L$ by a trigonometric series. This can be done in many different ways by supplying an arbitrary *definition* of the function to the interval $-L < x < 0$. For brevity we consider the two most important cases known as **half-range expansions**.

If $y = f(x)$ is defined on $0 < x < L$,

(i)   reflect the graph of the function about the y-axis onto $-L < x < 0$. The function is now even on $-L < x < L$. Use (14) with $p = L$. Or,

(ii)   reflect the graph of the function through the origin onto $-L < x < 0$. The function is now odd on $-L < x < L$. Use (17) with $p = L$.

Note that the coefficients of the series (14) and (17) utilize only the definition of the function on $0 < x < p$ (that is, half of the interval $-p < x < p$). Hence in practice there is no actual need to make the reflections described in (i) and (ii); if f is defined on $0 < x < L$, we simply identify the half-period p with the length L of the interval. The coefficient formulas and the series themselves will effect either an even or an odd periodic extension (of period $2L$) of the original function.

EXAMPLE   Expand $$f(x) = x^2, \quad 0 < x < L$$

(a)   in a cosine series,
(b)   in a sine series.

Solution: The graph of the function is given in Figure 10.7.

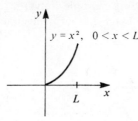

$y = x^2, \quad 0 < x < L$

Figure 10.7

(a)   We have

$$a_0 = \frac{2}{L} \int_0^L x^2 \, dx$$

$$= \tfrac{2}{3} L^2,$$

and, integrating by parts,

$$a_n = \frac{2}{L} \int_0^L x^2 \cos \frac{n\pi}{L} x \, dx$$

$$= \frac{2}{L} \left[\frac{L x^2 \sin \dfrac{n\pi}{L} x}{n\pi} \Bigg|_0^L - \frac{2L}{n\pi} \int_0^L x \sin \frac{n\pi}{L} x \, dx \right]$$

$$= -\frac{4}{n\pi} \left[-\frac{L x \cos \dfrac{n\pi}{L} x}{n\pi} \Bigg|_0^L + \frac{L}{n\pi} \int_0^L \cos \frac{n\pi}{L} x \, dx \right]$$

$$= \frac{4L^2 (-1)^n}{n^2 \pi^2}.$$

Thus

$$f(x) \sim \frac{L^2}{3} + \frac{4L^2}{\pi^2} \sum_{n=1}^{\infty} \frac{(-1)^n}{n^2} \cos \frac{n\pi}{L} x.$$

(b)   In this case

$$b_n = \frac{2}{L} \int_0^L x^2 \sin \frac{n\pi}{L} x \, dx.$$

After integrating by parts we find

$$b_n = \frac{2L^2 (-1)^{n+1}}{n\pi} + \frac{4L^2}{n^3 \pi^3} [(-1)^n - 1].$$

Thus

$$f(x) \sim \frac{2L^2}{\pi} \sum_{n=1}^{\infty} \left\{ \frac{(-1)^{n+1}}{n} + \frac{2}{n^3 \pi^2} [(-1)^n - 1] \right\} \sin \frac{n\pi}{L} x.$$

We note that the series in (a) and (b) of the foregoing example converge to the even periodic extension and the odd periodic extension of f given in Figures 10.8(a) and Figure 10.8(b), respectively.

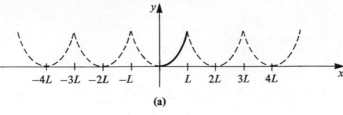

(a)

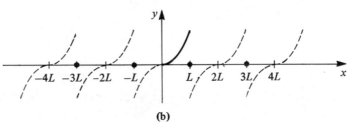

(b)

Figure 10.8

EXERCISES 10.2
[10.2.1]
Answers to odd-numbered problems begin on page A-41 of the Appendix. In Problems 1–14 find the Fourier series of f on the given interval.

1. $f(x) = \begin{cases} 0, & -\pi < x < 0 \\ 1, & 0 \le x < \pi \end{cases}$

2. $f(x) = \begin{cases} -1, & -\pi < x < 0 \\ 2, & 0 \le x < \pi \end{cases}$

3. $f(x) = \begin{cases} 1, & -1 < x < 0 \\ x, & 0 \le x < 1 \end{cases}$

★4. $f(x) = \begin{cases} 0, & -1 < x < 0 \\ x, & 0 \le x < 1 \end{cases}$

5. $f(x) = \begin{cases} 0, & -\pi < x < 0 \\ x^2, & 0 \le x < \pi \end{cases}$

6. $f(x) = \begin{cases} \pi^2, & -\pi < x < 0 \\ \pi^2 - x^2, & 0 \le x < \pi \end{cases}$

7. $f(x) = x + \pi, \quad -\pi < x < \pi$

8. $f(x) = 3 - 2x, \quad -\pi < x < \pi$

9. $f(x) = \begin{cases} 0, & -\pi < x < 0 \\ \sin x, & 0 \le x < \pi \end{cases}$

★10. $f(x) = \begin{cases} 0, & -\pi/2 < x < 0 \\ \cos x, & 0 \le x < \pi/2 \end{cases}$

11. $f(x) = \begin{cases} 0, & -2 < x < -1 \\ -2, & -1 \le x < 0 \\ 1, & 0 \le x < 1 \\ 0, & 1 \le x < 2 \end{cases}$

12. $f(x) = \begin{cases} 2 + x, & -2 < x < 0 \\ 2, & 0 \le x < 2 \end{cases}$

13. $f(x) = e^x, \quad -\pi < x < \pi$

14. $f(x) = \begin{cases} 0, & -\pi < x < 0 \\ e^x - 1, & 0 \le x < \pi \end{cases}$

15. **(a)** Use the result of Problem 5 to prove

$$\frac{\pi^2}{6} = 1 + \frac{1}{2^2} + \frac{1}{3^2} + \frac{1}{4^2} + \cdots \quad \text{and} \quad \frac{\pi^2}{12} = 1 - \frac{1}{2^2} + \frac{1}{3^2} - \frac{1}{4^2} + \cdots$$

(b) Find a series giving the numerical value of $\dfrac{\pi^2}{8}$.

★**16.**   **(a)** Use the result of Problem 7 to prove

$$\frac{\pi}{4} = 1 - \frac{1}{3} + \frac{1}{5} - \frac{1}{7} + \cdots$$

(b) Use the result of Problem 9 to prove

$$\frac{\pi}{4} = \frac{1}{2} + \frac{1}{1 \cdot 3} - \frac{1}{3 \cdot 5} + \frac{1}{5 \cdot 7} - \frac{1}{7 \cdot 9} + \cdots$$

In Problems 17 and 18 expand the given function in a Fourier series (8).

EXAMPLE $f(x) = x, \qquad 0 < x < 2\pi.$

Solution: Although f is not defined on an interval $-p < x < p$, nonetheless, we can *define* f to be periodic of period 2π and use the fact that the value of an integral of a periodic function is the same over any interval of length equal to the period. Thus with $p = \pi$, the coefficients (9), (10), and (11) are

$$a_0 = \frac{1}{\pi} \int_0^{2\pi} x \, dx = 2\pi,$$

$$a_n = \frac{1}{\pi} \int_0^{2\pi} x \cos nx \, dx = 0,$$

$$b_n = \frac{1}{\pi} \int_0^{2\pi} x \sin nx \, dx = -\frac{2}{n}.$$

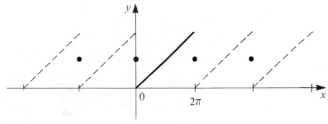

Figure 10.9

Hence

$$f(x) \sim \pi - 2 \sum_{n=1}^{\infty} \frac{1}{n} \sin nx.$$

Note that this is *not* a sine series since $a_0 \neq 0$. The series converges to the function whose graph is given in Figure 10.9.

---

17. $f(x) = x^2, \quad 0 < x < 2\pi$ **18.** $f(x) = 2 - x, \quad 0 < x < 2$

[**10.2.2**]   In Problems 19–30 expand the given function in an appropriate cosine or sine series.

19. $f(x) = \begin{cases} -1, & -\pi < x < 0 \\ 1, & 0 \le x < \pi \end{cases}$
    20. $f(x) = \begin{cases} 1, & -2 < x < -1 \\ 0, & -1 < x < 1 \\ 1, & 1 < x < 2 \end{cases}$

21. $f(x) = |x|, \quad -\pi < x < \pi$
    22. $f(x) = x, \quad -\pi < x < \pi$

23. $f(x) = x^2, \quad -1 < x < 1$
    ★**24.** $f(x) = x|x|, \quad -1 < x < 1$

25. $f(x) = \pi^2 - x^2, \quad -\pi < x < \pi$
    26. $f(x) = x^3, \quad -\pi < x < \pi$

27. $f(x) = \begin{cases} x - 1, & -\pi < x < 0 \\ x + 1, & 0 \le x < \pi \end{cases}$
    28. $f(x) = \begin{cases} x + 1, & -1 < x < 0 \\ x - 1, & 0 \le x < 1 \end{cases}$

29. $f(x) = |\sin x|, \quad -\pi < x < \pi$
    ★**30.** $f(x) = \cos x, \quad -\dfrac{\pi}{2} < x < \dfrac{\pi}{2}$

In Problems 31–38 find the half-range cosine and sine expansions of the given functions.

31. $f(x) = \begin{cases} 1, & 0 < x < \frac{1}{2} \\ 0, & \frac{1}{2} < x < 1 \end{cases}$
    ★**32.** $f(x) = \begin{cases} 0, & 0 < x < \frac{1}{2} \\ 1, & \frac{1}{2} < x < 1 \end{cases}$

33. $f(x) = \cos x, \quad 0 < x < \dfrac{\pi}{2}$
    34. $f(x) = \sin x, \quad 0 < x < \pi$

35. $f(x) = \begin{cases} x, & 0 < x < \dfrac{\pi}{2} \\ \pi - x, & \dfrac{\pi}{2} < x < \pi \end{cases}$
    36. $f(x) = \begin{cases} 0, & 0 < x < \pi \\ x - \pi, & \pi < x < 2\pi \end{cases}$

37. $f(x) = \begin{cases} x, & 0 < x < 1 \\ 1, & 1 < x < 2 \end{cases}$
    38. $f(x) = x(2 - x), \quad 0 < x < 2$

39. Prove Property I.
    40. Prove Property II.

41. Prove Property III.
    42. Prove Property IV.

43. Prove Property V.

10.3   Separable Partial Differential Equations

Linear equations

In this brief introduction to partial differential equations, we shall be interested in finding *particular* solutions of certain **linear** equations in two variables:

$$A(x, y)\frac{\partial^2 u}{\partial x^2} + B(x, y)\frac{\partial^2 u}{\partial x \partial y} + C(x, y)\frac{\partial^2 u}{\partial y^2} + D(x, y)\frac{\partial u}{\partial x}$$

$$+ E(x, y)\frac{\partial u}{\partial y} + F(x, y)u = G(x, y). \tag{1}$$

When $G(x, y) = 0$, the equation is said to be **homogeneous**, otherwise it is **nonhomogeneous**. Throughout this section and the next we shall consider only homogeneous equations.

Separation of variables

For a given linear partial differential equation, it is sometimes possible to find solutions in the form of a product

$$u(x, y) = X Y \tag{2}$$

where X is a function of x only, and Y is a function of y only. The use of the product (2), called the **method of separation of variables,*** may enable us to reduce a partial differential equation to several *ordinary* differential equations. To this end we note

$$\frac{\partial u}{\partial x} = X'Y, \qquad \frac{\partial u}{\partial y} = XY'$$

and

$$\frac{\partial^2 u}{\partial x^2} = X''Y, \qquad \frac{\partial^2 u}{\partial y^2} = XY''$$

where the primes denote ordinary differentiation.

EXAMPLE

Find product solutions of the equation

$$\frac{\partial^2 u}{\partial x^2} = 4\frac{\partial u}{\partial y}. \tag{3}$$

Solution: If $u = XY$, then (3) becomes

$$X''Y = 4XY'.$$

After dividing both sides by $4XY$, we have separated the variables:

$$\frac{X''}{4X} = \frac{Y'}{Y}. \tag{4}$$

Since the left-hand side of the last equation is independent of y and is identically equal to the right-hand side which is independent of x, we conclude that both sides must be a constant. (See Problem 19.) In practice it is convenient to write this real constant as either λ^2 or $-\lambda^2$. We distinguish the following cases.

---

* The procedure outlined in this section is not applicable to every linear equation nor does it yield a "general solution" of an equation.

CASE I   Using $\lambda^2 > 0$ the equalities

$$\frac{X''}{4X} = \frac{Y'}{Y} = \lambda^2$$

lead to $X'' - 4\lambda^2 X = 0$ and $Y' - \lambda^2 Y = 0$.

These latter equations have the general solutions

$$X = c_1 \cosh 2\lambda x + c_2 \sinh 2\lambda x \qquad \text{and} \qquad Y = c_3 e^{\lambda^2 y}$$

respectively.* Thus a particular solution of (3) is

$$
\begin{aligned}
u &= XY \\
&= (c_1 \cosh 2\lambda x + c_2 \sinh 2\lambda x)(c_3 e^{\lambda^2 y}) \\
&= A_1 e^{\lambda^2 y} \cosh 2\lambda x + B_1 e^{\lambda^2 y} \sinh 2\lambda x,
\end{aligned}
\tag{5}
$$

where $A_1 = c_1 c_3$ and $B_1 = c_2 c_3$.

CASE II   Using $-\lambda^2 < 0$ the equalities

$$\frac{X''}{4X} = \frac{Y'}{Y} = -\lambda^2$$

give $X'' + 4\lambda^2 X = 0$ and $Y' + \lambda^2 Y = 0$.

Since the solutions of these equations are

$$X = c_4 \cos 2\lambda x + c_5 \sin 2\lambda x \qquad \text{and} \qquad Y = c_6 e^{-\lambda^2 y}$$

respectively, another solution of (3) is

$$u = A_2 e^{-\lambda^2 y} \cos 2\lambda x + B_2 e^{-\lambda^2 y} \sin 2\lambda x \tag{6}$$

where $A_2 = c_4 c_6$ and $B_2 = c_5 c_6$.

CASE III   If $\lambda^2 = 0$ it follows that

$$X'' = 0 \qquad \text{and} \qquad Y' = 0.$$

In this case

$$X = c_7 x + c_8 \qquad \text{and} \quad Y = c_9$$

so that

$$u = A_3 x + B_3 \tag{7}$$

where $A_3 = c_7 c_9$ and $B_3 = c_8 c_9$.

---

* Recall X can be written in the alternative form $X = c_1 e^{-2\lambda x} + c_2 e^{2\lambda x}$

It is left as an exercise to verify that (5), (6), and (7) satisfy the given equation.

The superposition principle

The following theorem is analogous to Theorem 4.2 and is known as the **superposition principle**.

THEOREM 10.2 If $u_1, u_2, \ldots, u_k$ are solutions of a homogeneous linear partial differential equation, then the linear combination

$$u = c_1 u_1 + c_2 u_2 + \cdots + c_k u_k,$$

where the $c_i, i = 1, 2, \ldots, k$ are constants, is also a solution.

In the next section we shall make a formal assumption that whenever we have an infinite set

$$u_1, u_2, u_3, \ldots,$$

of solutions of a homogeneous linear equation that we can construct yet another solution u by forming the infinite series

$$u = \sum_{k=1}^{\infty} u_k.$$

EXERCISES 10.3

Answers to odd-numbered problems begin on page A-43 of the Appendix. In Problems 1–16 determine whether the method of separation of variables is applicable to the given equation. If so, find the product solutions.

1. $\dfrac{\partial u}{\partial x} = \dfrac{\partial u}{\partial y}$

★2. $\dfrac{\partial u}{\partial x} + 3\dfrac{\partial u}{\partial y} = 0$

3. $\dfrac{\partial u}{\partial x} + \dfrac{\partial u}{\partial y} = u$

4. $\dfrac{\partial u}{\partial x} = \dfrac{\partial u}{\partial y} + u$

5. $x\dfrac{\partial u}{\partial x} = y\dfrac{\partial u}{\partial y}$

6. $y\dfrac{\partial u}{\partial x} + x\dfrac{\partial u}{\partial y} = 0$

7. $\dfrac{\partial^2 u}{\partial x^2} + \dfrac{\partial^2 u}{\partial x \partial y} + \dfrac{\partial^2 u}{\partial y^2} = 0$

8. $y\dfrac{\partial^2 u}{\partial x \partial y} + u = 0$

9. $k\dfrac{\partial^2 u}{\partial x^2} - u = \dfrac{\partial u}{\partial t}, \quad k > 0$

10. $k\dfrac{\partial^2 u}{\partial x^2} = \dfrac{\partial u}{\partial t}, \quad k > 0$

11. $a^2\dfrac{\partial^2 u}{\partial x^2} = \dfrac{\partial^2 u}{\partial t^2}$

12. $a^2\dfrac{\partial^2 u}{\partial x^2} = \dfrac{\partial^2 u}{\partial t^2} - 2k\dfrac{\partial u}{\partial t}, \quad k > 0$

13. $\dfrac{\partial^2 u}{\partial x^2} + \dfrac{\partial^2 u}{\partial y^2} = 0$

★14. $x^2\dfrac{\partial^2 u}{\partial x^2} + \dfrac{\partial^2 u}{\partial y^2} = 0$

15. $\dfrac{\partial^2 u}{\partial x^2} + \dfrac{\partial^2 u}{\partial y^2} = u$

16. $a^2 \dfrac{\partial^2 u}{\partial x^2} - g = \dfrac{\partial^2 u}{\partial t^2}$, g a constant

17. Show that the equation

$$\frac{\partial u}{\partial t} = k\left(\frac{\partial^2 u}{\partial r^2} + \frac{1}{r}\frac{\partial u}{\partial r}\right), \qquad k > 0$$

possesses the product solution

$$u = e^{-k\lambda^2 t}\left(A_1 J_0(\lambda r) + B_2 J_0(\lambda r)\int \frac{dr}{r J_0^2(\lambda r)}\right).$$

18. Find a product solution of

$$\frac{\partial^2 u}{\partial t^2} = a^2\left(\frac{\partial^2 u}{\partial r^2} + \frac{1}{r}\frac{\partial u}{\partial r}\right).$$

19. Prove that each side of the separated form (4) of equation (3) is constant.

20. Verify that the products (5), (6), and (7) satisfy equation (3).

In Problems 21–23 find product solutions satisfying the given equation and the indicated conditions.

EXAMPLE

$$k\frac{\partial^2 u}{\partial x^2} = \frac{\partial u}{\partial t}, \qquad k > 0; \quad u(0,t) = 0, \quad u(L,t) = 0. \tag{8}$$

Solution: If $u = XT$, we can write the given equation as

$$\frac{X''}{X} = \frac{T'}{kT} = -\lambda^2 \tag{9}$$

which leads to

$$X'' + \lambda^2 X = 0 \tag{10}$$

$$T' + k\lambda^2 T = 0 \tag{11}$$

and

$$X_1 = c_1 \cos \lambda x + c_2 \sin \lambda x \tag{12}$$

$$T = c_3 e^{-k\lambda^2 t} \tag{13}$$

respectively. Now since

$$u(0,t) = X(0)T(t) = 0$$

$$u(L,t) = X(L)T(t) = 0$$

we must have $X(0) = 0$ and $X(L) = 0$. These are boundary conditions for equation (10). Applying the first of these conditions in (12) immediately gives $c_1 = 0$. Therefore

$$X = c_2 \sin \lambda x.$$

The second boundary condition now implies

$$X(L) = c_2 \sin \lambda L = 0.$$

If $c_2 = 0$ then $X = 0$ so that $u = 0$. To obtain a *nonzero* solution u, we must have $c_2 \neq 0$ and so the last equation is satisfied when

$$\sin \lambda L = 0.$$

This implies that $\lambda L = n\pi$ or $\lambda = n\pi/L$, $n = 1, 2, 3, \ldots$.

Thus

$$u = (c_2 \sin \lambda x)(c_3 e^{-k\lambda^2 t})$$

$$= A_n e^{-k(n^2\pi^2/L^2)t} \sin \frac{n\pi}{L} x$$

satisfies the given equation and both side conditions. The coefficient $c_2 c_3$ is rewritten as A_n to emphasize the fact that a different solution is obtained for each n.* The reader should verify that using $\lambda^2 \geq 0$ in (9) does not lead to a solution of (8).

---

21. $k\dfrac{\partial^2 u}{\partial x^2} = \dfrac{\partial u}{\partial t}$, $k > 0$; $\dfrac{\partial u}{\partial x}\Big|_{x=0} = 0, \dfrac{\partial u}{\partial x}\Big|_{x=5} = 0$

22. $a^2\dfrac{\partial^2 u}{\partial x^2} = \dfrac{\partial^2 u}{\partial t^2}$; $u(0, t) = 0, u(2, t) = 0, \dfrac{\partial u}{\partial t}\Big|_{t=0} = 0$

23. $\dfrac{\partial^2 u}{\partial x^2} + \dfrac{\partial^2 u}{\partial y^2} = 0$; $u(0, y) = 0,$ $u(x, 0) = 0,$ $u(x, 1) = 0$

★**24.** Consider the nonhomogeneous equation

$$\frac{\partial^2 u}{\partial x^2} + kx = \frac{\partial^2 u}{\partial t^2}, \qquad k > 0.$$

Find a function Ψ so that $v(x, t) = u(x, t) + \Psi(x)$ is a solution of the homogeneous equation

$$\frac{\partial^2 v}{\partial x^2} = \frac{\partial^2 v}{\partial t^2}.$$

Find particular solutions of the original equation.

---

* Note that when $n = 0$, $\sin 0 = 0$ so that $u = 0$. Also, if n is a negative integer, say, $n = -k$, $k = 1, 2, 3, \ldots$, we can use the trigonometric identity $\sin(-\theta) = -\sin\theta$ to rewrite $\sin(-k\pi x/L)$ as $-\sin k\pi x/L$. The factor of -1 can be absorbed in the arbitrary constant A_n. Thus, in this case, we need only consider the solutions obtained for the positive integers.

10.4   Boundary-Value Problems

Special equations   The following linear partial differential equations

$$k\frac{\partial^2 u}{\partial x^2} = \frac{\partial u}{\partial t}, \qquad k > 0, \tag{1}$$

$$a^2\frac{\partial^2 u}{\partial x^2} = \frac{\partial^2 u}{\partial t^2}, \tag{2}$$

$$\frac{\partial^2 u}{\partial x^2} + \frac{\partial^2 u}{\partial y^2} = 0 \tag{3}$$

play an important role in many areas of physics and engineering. Equations (1) and (2) are known as the **one-dimensional heat equation** and the **one-dimensional wave equation**, respectively. "One-dimensional" refers to the fact that x denotes a spatial dimension whereas t usually represents time. Equation (3) is called **Laplace's equation**.

We conclude this chapter by utilizing the method of separation of variables to solve several applied problems, each of which is described by one of the above equations along with certain side conditions. These side conditions consist of **boundary conditions**:

(a) u or $\partial u/\partial x$ specified at $x =$ constant; u or $\partial u/\partial y$ specified at $y =$ constant, and **initial conditions**:

(b) u at $t = 0$ for equation (1), or, u and $\partial u/\partial t$ at $t = 0$ for equation (2).

The collective mathematical description of such a problem is known as a **boundary-value problem**.

Equation (1) occurs in the theory of heat flow (that is, heat transferred by conduction) in a rod or a thin wire. The function $u(x, t)$ is temperature in the rod. Problems in mechanical vibrations often lead to the wave equation (2). For our purposes the solution $u(x, t)$ of (2) will represent the small displacements of an idealized vibrating string. Lastly, the solution $u(x, y)$ of Laplace's equation (3) can be interpreted as the steady-state (that is, time independent) temperature distribution in a thin flat plate. For a derivation of these equations in these three specific contexts, the reader is referred to any of the standard texts in engineering mathematics.*

Although we shall confine our attention to solving the problems described above, we note that the analysis of a wide variety of diverse phenomena yield equations (1), (2), or (3), or their generalizations involving a greater number of spatial variables. For example, (1) is sometimes called the **diffusion equation** since the diffusion of dissolved substances in solution is analogous to the flow of heat in a solid. The function $u(x, t)$ satisfying the partial differential equation in this case represents the concentration of the

---

** See C. R. Wylie, *Advanced Engineering Mathematics*, Fourth Edition, (N.Y.: McGraw-Hill Book Company, 1975).*

liquid. Similarly, equation (1) arises in the study of the flow of electricity in a long cable or a transmission line. In this particular setting, (1) is known as a **telegraph equation**. It can be shown that under certain assumptions the current and the voltage in the line are functions satisfying two equations identical in form with equation (1). The wave equation (2) also appears in the theory of high frequency transmission lines, fluid mechanics, acoustics, and elasticity. Laplace's equation (3) is encountered in engineering problems in static displacements of membranes, and most often, in problems dealing with potentials such as electrostatic, gravitational, and velocity potentials in fluid mechanics.

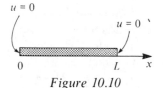

$u = 0$

$u = 0$

0 L x

Figure 10.10

10.4.1   The Heat Equation

Consider a thin rod of length L with an initial temperature of $f(x)$ throughout and whose ends are held at a constant temperature of zero degrees for all time. (See Figure 10.10.) If

(a)   the flow of heat takes place only in the x-direction,
(b)   no heat escapes from the lateral surface of the rod,
(c)   no heat is being generated in the rod,
(d)   the rod is homogeneous, that is, its density per length is constant,
(e)   its specific heat and thermal conductivity are constant,

then the temperature $u(x, t)$ in the rod is given by the solution of the boundary-value problem

$$k\frac{\partial^2 u}{\partial x^2} = \frac{\partial u}{\partial t}, \qquad k > 0, 0 < x < L, t > 0, \tag{4}$$

$$u(0, t) = 0, \qquad u(L, t) = 0, \quad t > 0, \tag{5}$$

$$u(x, 0) = f(x), \qquad 0 < x < L. \tag{6}$$

The constant k is proportional to the thermal conductivity and is called the diffusivity.

The solution

Using the product $u = XT$ and $-\lambda^2$ as a separation constant leads to

$$\frac{X''}{X} = \frac{T'}{kT} = -\lambda^2$$

and

$$X'' + \lambda^2 X = 0, \qquad X(0) = 0, X(L) = 0, \tag{7}$$

$$T' + k\lambda^2 T = 0. \tag{8}$$

We have already obtained the solution of equation (4) subject to the boundary conditions (5) by solving (7). (See Exercise 10.3, page 472.) It was seen that (7) possessed a nonzero solution only if the value of the parameter λ took on the values

$$\lambda = \frac{n\pi}{L}, \quad n = 1, 2, 3, \ldots. \tag{9}$$

The corresponding solutions of (7) were then

$$X = c_1 \sin \frac{n\pi}{L} x, \quad n = 1, 2, 3, \ldots. \tag{10}$$

Eigenvalues and eigenfunctions

The values (9) for which (7) possess a nontrivial solution are known as **characteristic values**, or more commonly, as **eigenvalues**. The solutions (10) are called **characteristic functions** or **eigenfunctions**. We note that for a choice of λ, other than those given in (9), the solution of (7) is the zero function $X \equiv 0$. In turn, this would imply that a function satisfying (4) and (5) is $u \equiv 0$. However, $u \equiv 0$ is *not* a solution of the original boundary-value problem when $f(x) \neq 0$. We naturally assume this last condition.

Since the solution of (8) is

$$T = c_3 e^{-k\lambda^2 t}$$
$$= c_3 e^{-k(n^2\pi^2/L^2)t}$$

the products

$$u_n = A_n e^{-k(n^2\pi^2/L^2)t} \sin \frac{n\pi}{L} x \tag{11}$$

satisfy the partial differential equation (4) and the boundary conditions (5) for each value of the positive integer n. For convenience we have replaced the constant $c_1 c_3$ by A_n. In order that the functions given in (11) satisfy the initial condition (6) we would have to choose the constant coefficients A_n in such a manner that

$$u(x, 0) = f(x) = A_n \sin \frac{n\pi}{L} x. \tag{12}$$

In general, we would not expect condition (12) to be satisfied for an arbitrary, but reasonable, choice of f. Therefore, we are forced to admit that (11) *is not a solution of the given problem*. However, by the superposition principle

$$u = \sum_{n=1}^{\infty} u_n$$
$$= \sum_{n=1}^{\infty} A_n e^{-k(n^2\pi^2/L^2)t} \sin \frac{n\pi}{L} x \tag{13}$$

must also, although formally, satisfy (4) and (5). Substituting $t = 0$ in (13) implies

$$u(x, 0) = f(x) = \sum_{n=1}^{\infty} A_n \sin \frac{n\pi}{L} x.$$

This last expression is the half-range expansion of f in a sine series. Thus, if we make the identification $A_n = b_n$, $n = 1, 2, 3, \ldots$, it follows from (18) of Section 10.2 that

$$A_n = \frac{2}{L} \int_0^L f(x) \sin \frac{n\pi}{L} x \, dx.$$

We conclude that the solution of the boundary-value problem described in (4), (5), and (6) is given by the infinite series

$$u(x, t) = \frac{2}{L} \sum_{n=1}^{\infty} \left(\int_0^L f(x) \sin \frac{n\pi}{L} x \, dx \right) e^{-k(n^2\pi^2/L^2)t} \sin \frac{n\pi}{L} x.$$

Insulated boundaries

In the problem described in Section 10.4.1, the ends or boundaries of the rod could be **insulated**. At an insulated boundary the normal derivative of the temperature is zero. This fact follows from an empirical law that states the flux of heat across a surface (the time rate of flow of heat per unit area) is proportional to the value of the directional derivative of the temperature normal (perpendicular) to the surface.

EXAMPLE

Give the boundary-value problem for the temperature u in a horizontal rod of length L if its ends are insulated and if its initial temperature throughout is given by $f(x)$, $0 < x < L$.

Solution: The ends of the rod are surfaces perpendicular to the x-axis and so $\partial u/\partial x = 0$ at both boundaries. Hence the temperature in the rod is given by the solution of

$$k \frac{\partial^2 u}{\partial x^2} = \frac{\partial u}{\partial t}, \qquad k > 0, \quad 0 < x < L, \qquad t > 0,$$

$$\left. \frac{\partial u}{\partial x} \right|_{x=0} = 0, \qquad \left. \frac{\partial u}{\partial x} \right|_{x=L} = 0, \qquad t > 0,$$

$$u(x, 0) = f(x), \qquad 0 < x < L.$$

The solution of the problem given in the foregoing example is left as an exercise. (See Problem 3.)

10.4.2   The Wave Equation

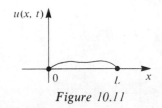

$u(x, t)$

0 L x

Figure 10.11

In the next example we consider the transverse vibrations of a string stretched between two points, say, $x = 0$ and $x = L$. As shown in Figure 10.11, the motion takes place in the xy-plane in such a manner that each point of the string moves in a direction perpendicular to the x-axis. If $u(x, t)$ denotes displacements of the string measured from the x-axis for $t > 0$, then u satisfies equation (2) under the following assumptions.

(a)   The string is perfectly flexible.
(b)   The string is homogeneous, that is, its mass per unit length is constant.
(c)   The displacements u are small compared to the length of the string.
(d)   The tension of the string is constant.
(e)   The tension is large compared with the force of gravity.
(f)   No other forces act on the string.

Thus a typical boundary-value problem is

$$a^2 \frac{\partial^2 u}{\partial x^2} = \frac{\partial^2 u}{\partial t^2}, \qquad 0 < x < L, \qquad t > 0, \tag{14}$$

$$u(0, t) = 0, \qquad u(L, t) = 0, \qquad t \geq 0, \tag{15}$$

$$u(x, 0) = f(x), \qquad \left.\frac{\partial u}{\partial t}\right|_{t=0} = g(x), \qquad 0 < x < L. \tag{16}$$

The boundary conditions (15) simply state that the string is secured at the end points for all time. At $t = 0$, the functions f and g given in (16) specify the initial configuration and the initial velocity of each point of the string, respectively. It is implicit in this context that f is continuous and $f(0) = 0$, $f(L) = 0$.

The solution

Separating variables in (14) gives

$$\frac{X''}{X} = \frac{T''}{a^2 T} = -\lambda^2$$

so that

$$X'' + \lambda^2 X = 0$$

$$T'' + \lambda^2 a^2 T = 0$$

and therefore

$$X = c_1 \cos \lambda x + c_2 \sin \lambda x$$

$$T = c_3 \cos \lambda at + c_4 \sin \lambda at.*$$

As before the boundary conditions (15) translate into $X(0) = 0$ and $X(L) = 0$. In turn we find

$$c_1 = 0 \qquad \text{and} \qquad c_2 \sin \lambda L = 0.$$

This last equation yields the eigenvalues $\lambda = n\pi/L$, $n = 1, 2, 3, \ldots$. The

---

*You should convince yourself that a different choice of separation constant does not lead to a solution.

corresponding eigenfunctions are

$$X = c_2 \sin \frac{n\pi}{L} x, \qquad n = 1, 2, 3, \ldots.$$

Thus solutions of equation (14) satisfying the boundary conditions (15) are

$$u_n = \left(A_n \cos \frac{n\pi a}{L} t + B_n \sin \frac{n\pi a}{L} t \right) \sin \frac{n\pi}{L} x,$$

and

$$u = \sum_{n=1}^{\infty} \left(A_n \cos \frac{n\pi a}{L} t + B_n \sin \frac{n\pi a}{L} t \right) \sin \frac{n\pi}{L} x. \tag{17}$$

Setting $t = 0$ in (17) gives

$$u(x, 0) = f(x) = \sum_{n=1}^{\infty} A_n \sin \frac{n\pi}{L} x$$

which we recognize again as a half-range expansion for f in a sine series. As in the discussion of the heat equation, we can write $A_n = b_n$,

$$A_n = \frac{2}{L} \int_0^L f(x) \sin \frac{n\pi}{L} x \, dx. \tag{18}$$

To determine B_n we differentiate (17) with respect to t and then set $t = 0$:

$$\frac{\partial u}{\partial t} = \sum_{n=1}^{\infty} \left(-A_n \frac{n\pi a}{L} \sin \frac{n\pi a}{L} t + B_n \frac{n\pi a}{L} \cos \frac{n\pi a}{L} t \right) \sin \frac{n\pi}{L} x$$

$$\left. \frac{\partial u}{\partial t} \right|_{t=0} = g(x) = \sum_{n=1}^{\infty} \left(B_n \frac{n\pi a}{L} \right) \sin \frac{n\pi}{L} x.$$

In order that this last series be the half-range sine expansion of g on the interval, the *total* coefficient $B_n n\pi a/L$ must be given by the form of (18) in Section 10.2. That is,

$$B_n \frac{n\pi a}{L} = \frac{2}{L} \int_0^L g(x) \sin \frac{n\pi}{L} x \, dx,$$

from which we obtain

$$B_n = \frac{2}{n\pi a} \int_0^L g(x) \sin \frac{n\pi}{L} x \, dx. \tag{19}$$

The formal solution of the problem consists of the series (17) with A_n and B_n defined by (18) and (19), respectively.

We note that when the string is released from *rest*, then $g(x) = 0$ for every x in $0 \le x \le L$ and, consequently, $B_n = 0$.

10.4.3   Laplace's Equation

Suppose we wish to find the steady-state temperature $u(x, y)$ in a rectangular plate with boundary conditions indicated in Figure 10.12. When no heat escapes from the lateral faces of the plate, the problem is

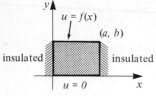

Figure 10.12

$$\frac{\partial^2 u}{\partial x^2} + \frac{\partial^2 u}{\partial y^2} = 0, \qquad 0 < x < a, \qquad 0 < y < b$$

$$\left.\frac{\partial u}{\partial x}\right|_{x=0} = 0, \qquad \left.\frac{\partial u}{\partial x}\right|_{x=a} = 0, \qquad 0 < y < b$$

$$u(x, 0) = 0, \qquad 0 < x < a$$

$$u(x, b) = f(x), \qquad 0 < x < a.$$

The solution

Separation of variables leads to

$$\frac{X''}{X} = -\frac{Y''}{Y} = -\lambda^2,$$

$$X'' + \lambda^2 X = 0 \tag{20}$$

$$Y'' - \lambda^2 Y = 0, \tag{21}$$

$$X = c_1 \cos \lambda x + c_2 \sin \lambda x \tag{22}$$

$$Y = c_3 \cosh \lambda y + c_4 \sinh \lambda y,^* \tag{23}$$

where $X'(0) = 0$, $X'(a) = 0$, and $Y(0) = 0$. Differentiating X and setting $x = 0$ implies $c_2 = 0$ and, therefore, $X = c_1 \cos \lambda x$. Differentiating again and then setting $x = a$ gives $-c_1 \lambda \sin \lambda a = 0$. This last condition is satisfied when $\lambda a = n\pi$, or $\lambda = n\pi/a$, $n = 0, 1, 2, \ldots$. Observe here that $\lambda = 0$ (when $n = 0$) is included as an eigenvalue since X is nonzero (constant) for this value. Thus the eigenfunctions are

$$X = c_1 \cos \frac{n\pi}{a} x, \qquad n = 0, 1, 2, \ldots.$$

Finally, the condition that $Y(0) = 0$ dictates that $c_3 = 0$ in (23) when $\lambda > 0$. However, when $\lambda = 0$ equation (21) becomes $Y'' = 0$; note that its general solution is the linear function $Y = c_3 + c_4 y$ rather than (23). Although $Y(0) = 0$ again implies $c_3 = 0$, the superposition principle forces us to assume a series solution of the form

$$u = A_0 y + \sum_{n=1}^{\infty} A_n \sinh \frac{n\pi}{a} y \cos \frac{n\pi}{a} x. \tag{24}$$

---

* There are problems where a solution in terms of real exponential functions is more useful. See Problem 17.

At $y = b$ we have

$$u(x, b) = f(x) = A_0 b + \sum_{n=1}^{\infty} \left(A_n \sinh \frac{n\pi}{a} b \right) \cos \frac{n\pi}{a} x$$

which, in this case, is a half-range expansion of f in a cosine series. If we make the identification $a_0 b = a_0/2$ and $A_n \sinh(n\pi b/a = a_n, n = 1, 2, 3, \ldots$, it follows from (15) and (16) of Section 10.2 that

$$2A_0 b = \frac{2}{a} \int_0^a f(x) \, dx$$

$$A_0 = \frac{1}{ab} \int_0^a f(x) \, dx, \tag{25}$$

and

$$A_n \sinh \frac{n\pi}{a} b = \frac{2}{a} \int_0^a f(x) \cos \frac{n\pi}{a} x \, dx$$

$$A_n = \frac{2}{a \sinh \dfrac{n\pi}{a} b} \int_0^a f(x) \cos \frac{n\pi}{a} x \, dx. \tag{26}$$

The formal solution of this problem consists of the series given in (24) where A_0 and A_n are defined by (25) and (26), respectively.

EXERCISES 10.4
[10.4.1]

Answers to odd-numbered problems begin on page A-44 of the Appendix. In Problems 1–4 solve the heat equation (1) subject to the given conditions. Assume rod of length L.

1. $u(0, t) = 0, \quad u(L, t) = 0$

$$u(x, 0) = \begin{cases} 1, & 0 < x < \dfrac{L}{2} \\[2mm] 0, & \dfrac{L}{2} < x < L \end{cases}$$

2. $u(0, t) = 0, \quad u(L, t) = 0$

$$u(x, 0) = x(L - x)$$

3. $\left. \dfrac{\partial u}{\partial x} \right|_{x=0} = 0, \quad \left. \dfrac{\partial u}{\partial x} \right|_{x=L} = 0$

$$u(x, 0) = f(x)$$

4. $\left. \dfrac{\partial u}{\partial x} \right|_{x=0} = 0, \quad \left. \dfrac{\partial u}{\partial x} \right|_{x=L} = 0$

$$u(x, 0) = \begin{cases} x, & 0 < x < \dfrac{L}{2} \\[2mm] 0, & \dfrac{L}{2} < x < L \end{cases}$$

5. Solve the boundary-value problem

$$k\frac{\partial^2 u}{\partial x^2} = \frac{\partial u}{\partial t} + hu, \quad h > 0, \quad k > 0, \quad 0 < x < L, \quad t > 0$$

$$\left.\frac{\partial u}{\partial x}\right|_{x=0} = 0, \quad \left.\frac{\partial u}{\partial x}\right|_{x=L} = 0$$

$$u(x, 0) = f(x).$$

This problem describes the temperature $u(x, t)$ in the rod when heat is escaping from the lateral surface into a medium of zero degrees.

★**6.** Solve the boundary-value problem consisting of equation (1) and the conditions

$$u(0, t) = 100, \qquad u(L, t) = 100$$

$$u(x, 0) = f(x), \qquad 0 < x < L.$$

[*Hint:*   Try to find a solution of the form $v = u - 100$.]

[10.4.2]   In Problems 7–10 solve the wave equation (2) subject to the given conditions. Assume a string stretched on the interval $0 \leq x \leq L$.

7. $u(0, t) = 0, \quad u(L, t) = 0$

$$u(x, 0) = \begin{cases} \dfrac{2hx}{L}, & 0 < x < \dfrac{L}{2} \\[2mm] 2h\left(1 - \dfrac{x}{L}\right), & \dfrac{L}{2} \leq x < L \end{cases}$$

$$\left.\frac{\partial u}{\partial t}\right|_{t=0} = 0$$

The constant h is positive but small compared to L. This is referred to as the "plucked string" problem.

8. $u(0, t) = 0, \quad u(L, t) = 0$

$$u(x, 0) = 0$$

$$\left.\frac{\partial u}{\partial t}\right|_{t=0} = x(L - x)$$

9. $u(0, t) = 0, \quad u(L, t) = 0$

$$u(x, 0) = 0$$

$$\left.\frac{\partial u}{\partial t}\right|_{t=0} = \sin\frac{\pi x}{L}$$

★**10.** $u(0, t) = 0, \quad u(L, t) = 0$

$u(x, 0)$ as specified in Figure 10.13.

$$\left.\frac{\partial u}{\partial t}\right|_{t=0} = 0$$

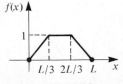

Figure 10.13

11. Solve the boundary-value problem

$$a^2 \frac{\partial^2 u}{\partial x^2} = \frac{\partial^2 u}{\partial t^2}, \quad 0 < x < L, t > 0$$

$$\left.\frac{\partial u}{\partial x}\right|_{x=0} = 0, \quad \left.\frac{\partial u}{\partial x}\right|_{x=L} = 0,$$

$$u(x,0) = x,$$

$$\left.\frac{\partial u}{\partial t}\right|_{t=0} = 0.$$

This problem could describe the longitudinal displacements $u(x, t)$ of a vibrating elastic rod with free ends.*

[10.4.3] In Problems 12–16 solve Laplace's equation (3) subject to the given conditions. Assume a flat plate such that $0 \le x \le a$ and $0 \le y \le b$.

12. $u(0, y) = 0, \quad u(a, y) = 0$

    $u(x, 0) = 0, \quad u(x, b) = f(x)$

13. $u(0, y) = 0, \quad u(a, y) = 0$

    $\left.\frac{\partial u}{\partial y}\right|_{y=0} = 0, \quad u(x, b) = f(x)$

★14. $u(0, y) = 0, \quad u(a, y) = 0$

    $u(x, 0) = f(x), \quad u(x, b) = 0$

15. $\left.\frac{\partial u}{\partial x}\right|_{x=0} = 0, \quad \left.\frac{\partial u}{\partial x}\right|_{x=a} = 0$

    $u(x, 0) = x, \quad u(x, b) = 0.$

★16. $u(0, y) = 0, \quad u(a, y) = 0$

    $u(x, 0) = f(x), \quad u(x, b) = g(x)$

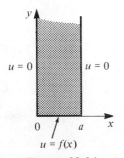

17. Consider a semi-infinite plate extending in the positive y-direction bounded by $x = 0$, $x = a$ and $y = 0$. Find the steady-state temperature $u(x, y)$ if the boundary conditions are as indicated in Figure 10.14. [*Hint:* Use exponential functions in solving for Y and the intuitive condition that $u \to 0$ as $y \to \infty$].

Figure 10.14

CHAPTER SUMMARY

A set of functions $\{\phi_n(x)\}, n = 0, 1, 3, \ldots$, is said to be **orthogonal** on an interval $a \le x \le b$ if and only if

$$\int_a^b \phi_m(x)\phi_n(x)\,dx \begin{cases} = 0, & m \ne n, \\ \ne 0, & m = n. \end{cases}$$

A function f defined on the interval $-p < x < p$ can formally be expanded in

---

* For a discussion of this theory see G. P. Tolstov, *Fourier Series*, Englewood Cliffs, N.J.: Prentice-Hall, 1962, pp. 275–82.

terms of the trigonometric functions in the orthogonal set

$$1, \cos\frac{\pi}{p}x, \cos\frac{2\pi}{p}x, \ldots, \sin\frac{\pi}{p}x, \sin\frac{2\pi}{p}x, \ldots.$$

We say
$$f(x) \sim \frac{a_0}{2} + \sum_{n=1}^{\infty}\left(a_n\cos\frac{n\pi}{p}x + b_n\sin\frac{n\pi}{p}x\right) \tag{1}$$

where
$$a_0 = \frac{1}{p}\int_{-p}^{p} f(x)\,dx \tag{2}$$

$$a_n = \frac{1}{p}\int_{-p}^{p} f(x)\cos\frac{n\pi}{p}x\,dx \tag{3}$$

$$b_n = \frac{1}{p}\int_{-p}^{p} f(x)\sin\frac{n\pi}{p}x\,dx. \tag{4}$$

is the **Fourier series** corresponding to f. The coefficients are obtained using the concept of orthogonality. If f is an even function on the interval then $b_n = 0$, $n = 1, 2, 3, \ldots$, and

$$a_0 = \frac{2}{p}\int_{0}^{p} f(x)\,dx \tag{5}$$

and
$$a_n = \frac{2}{p}\int_{0}^{p} f(x)\cos\frac{n\pi}{p}x\,dx. \tag{6}$$

Similarly, if f is odd on the interval then $a_n = 0$, $n = 0, 1, 2, 3, \ldots$,

and
$$b_n = \frac{2}{p}\int_{0}^{p} f(x)\sin\frac{n\pi}{p}x\,dx. \tag{7}$$

When f is defined on an interval $0 < x < L$ it can be neither even nor odd. Nonetheless we can expand f in a cosine or a sine series. By defining $p = L$, we obtain a cosine series by using the coefficients (5) and (6) and a sine series by using (7). Such series are known as **half-range expansions**.

A particular solution of a partial differential equation in two variables may be found by assuming a solution in the form of a product $u = XY$ where X is a function of x only, and Y is a function of y only. If applicable, this **method of separation of variables** leads to two ordinary differential equations.

A **boundary-value problem** consists of finding a function that satisfies a partial differential equation as well as side conditions consisting of perhaps both boundary conditions and initial conditions. We applied the method of separation of variables to obtain solutions of certain boundary-value problems involving the heat equation, the wave equation, and Laplace's equation. The procedure consisted of five basic steps.

CHAPTER
SUMMARY

(a) Separate the variables.

(b) Solve the separated ordinary differential equations and find the eigenvalues and eigenfunctions of the problem.

(c) Form the products u_n.

(d) Use the superposition principle to form an infinite series of the functions u_n.

(e) After using a boundary, or the initial condition(s), the coefficients in the series are obtained by making an appropriate identification with a half-range sine or cosine expansions.

REVIEW
EXERCISES

Answers to odd-numbered problems begin on page A-44 of the Appendix.

[**10.1**] 1. Show that the set

$$\sin \frac{\pi}{2L}x, \sin \frac{3\pi}{2L}x, \sin \frac{5\pi}{2L}x, \dots,$$

is orthogonal on the interval $0 \le x \le L$.

2. Find the norm of each function in Problem 1. Construct an orthonormal set.

[**10.2**] 3. Expand $f(x) = |x| - x$, $-1 < x < 1$, in a Fourier series.

4. Expand $f(x) = 2x^2 - 1$, $-1 < x < 1$, in a Fourier series.

5. Expand $f(x) = e^{-x}$, $0 < x < 1$, in a cosine series.

6. Expand the function given in Problem 5 in a sine series.

[**10.3**] 7. Show that the partial differential equation

$$\frac{\partial^2 u}{\partial x^2} + \frac{\partial^2 u}{\partial y^2} + k^2 (\cosh 2x - \cos 2y)u = 0$$

is separable. Do not try to solve the separated equations.

★8. Use separation of variables to find product solutions of

$$\frac{\partial^2 u}{\partial x^2} + \frac{\partial^2 u}{\partial y^2} + 2\frac{\partial u}{\partial x} + 2\frac{\partial u}{\partial y} = 0.$$

Is it possible to choose a constant of separation so that both X and Y are oscillatory functions?

9. Use separation of variables to find product solutions of

$$\frac{\partial^2 u}{\partial x \, \partial y} = u.$$

[10.4] ★10. Find the steady-state temperature $u(x, y)$ in the square plate shown in Figure 10.15. The boundary conditions are as indicated.

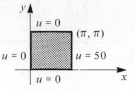

Figure 10.15

11. Find the steady-state temperature $u(x, y)$ in the semi-infinite plate of width π shown in Figure 10.16. The boundary conditions are as indicated.

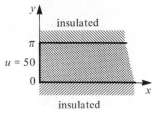

Figure 10.16

12. Solve Problem 11 if the boundaries $y = 0$ and $y = \pi$ are held at a constant zero degrees for all time.

APPENDIX

Answers to Odd-Numbered Problems

Note: Throughout the answer section, the indefinite integral

$$\int \frac{dx}{x}$$

is evaluated for convenience as

$$\ln x$$

rather than

$$\ln |x|.$$

Exercises 1.1, Page 9

1. linear, second-order
3. nonlinear, first-order
5. linear, fourth-order
7. nonlinear, second-order
9. linear, third-order

11. $y' - \dfrac{1}{x}y - 1 = 1 + \ln x - \ln x - 1 = 0$

13. $y' + y - \sin x$
$= \frac{1}{2}\cos x + \frac{1}{2}\sin x - 10e^{-x}$
$+ \frac{1}{2}\sin x - \frac{1}{2}\cos x + 10e^{-x} - \sin x = 0$

15. $y'' + y^2 = -\dfrac{1}{(x + c_1)^2} + \dfrac{1}{(x + c_1)^2} = 0$

17. $\dfrac{dy}{dt} + 20y - 24 = 24e^{-20t} + 24 - 24e^{-20t}$
$- 24 = 0$

19. $y' - 25 - y^2 = 25\sec^2 5x - 25(1 + \tan^2 5x)$
$= 25\sec^2 5x - 25\sec^2 5x$
$= 0$

21. $y''' - 3y'' + 3y' - y$
$= x^2 e^x + 6xe^x + 6e^x - 3x^2 e^x - 12xe^x$
$- 6e^x + 3x^2 e^x + 6xe^x - x^2 e^x = 0$

23. $y - 2xy' - y(y')^2 = y - 2x\dfrac{c_1}{2y} - y\dfrac{c_1^2}{4y^2}$

$$= \frac{y^2 - (c_1 x + (c_1^2/4))}{y}$$

$$= \frac{y^2 - y^2}{y} = 0$$

25. $y'' - 6y' + 13y = 5e^{3x}\cos 2x - 12e^{3x}\sin 2x$

$\qquad + 12e^{3x}\sin 2x - 18e^{3x}\cos 2x$

$\qquad + 13e^{3x}\cos 2x = 0$

27. $yx^2 = -1$ implies $d(yx^2) = 0$

$\qquad$ or $2yx\,dx + x^2\,dy = 0$

29. $\dfrac{d}{dt}\ln\dfrac{2-X}{1-X} = 1$

$$\left[\frac{-1}{2-X} + \frac{1}{1-X}\right]\frac{dX}{dt} = 1$$

$\qquad$ simplifies to $\dfrac{dX}{dt} = (2-X)(1-X)$

31. For $n = 2$

$\qquad (1 - x^2)T_2'' - xT_2' + 4T_2$

$\qquad\quad = (1 - x^2)4 - x(4x) + 4(2x^2 - 1) = 0$

33. For $n = 3$

$\qquad xL_3'' + (1 - x)L_3' + 3L_3$

$\qquad\quad = x(3 - x) + (1 - x)(-3 + 3x - \tfrac{1}{2}x^2)$

$\qquad\quad + 3(1 - 3x + \tfrac{3}{2}x^2 - \tfrac{1}{6}x^3) = 0$

35. $x > 3$ or $x < 1$

37. $y' - y^2 + 1$

$$= \frac{4ce^{2x}}{(1 - ce^{2x})^2} - \frac{(1 + ce^{2x})^2}{(1 - ce^{2x})^2} + 1$$

$$= -\frac{(1 - ce^{2x})^2}{(1 - ce^{2x})^2} + 1 = 0.$$

The solutions $y = 1$ and $y = -1$ are obvious; the former can be obtained from the general solution

by setting $c = 0$, but the latter is a singular solution.

39. No, c_1 and c_2 are not essential parameters.

41. $m = 2$, $m = -2$

43. $m = 0$, $m = -1$, $m = -2$

45. $m = \dfrac{1 \pm \sqrt{5}}{2}$

47. $m = -2$, $m = 2$, $m = 3$

49. $y - xy' - (y')^2 + \ln y'$

$\qquad = -t^2 - \ln t + 1 + 2t^2 - 1 - t^2$

$\qquad + \ln t = 0$

51. $\left(\dfrac{dy}{dx}\right)^3 + 2x\dfrac{dy}{dx} - 2y - 1$

$\qquad = t^3 - 3t^3 + 2t^3 + 1 - 1 = 0$

53. For $y = x^2$

$\qquad x^2 y'' - 4xy' + 6y = x^2(2) - 4x(2x) + 6x^2$

$\qquad\qquad\qquad\qquad\quad = 8x^2 - 8x^2 = 0;$

$\qquad$ for $y = x^3$

$\qquad x^2 y'' - 4xy' + 6y = x^2(6x) - 4x(3x^2) + 6x^3$

$\qquad\qquad\qquad\qquad\quad = 12x^3 - 12x^3 = 0;$

$\qquad$ yes; yes

Exercises 1.2, Page 23

1. $y \equiv 0$, $y = x^3$

3. The unique solution is $y \equiv 0$.

5. $xy' - y = x(c) - cx = 0$ for every c.
No, the given function is nondifferentiable at $x = 0$.

7. $y = \tfrac{3}{5}e^{4x} + \tfrac{2}{5}e^{-x}$

9. $xy'' - y' = x(2c_2) - (2c_2 x) = 0$.
$y(0) = 0$ is satisfied if $c_1 = 0$. Therefore $y = c_2 x^2$. But $y'(0) = 1$ leads to the contradictory statement $2c_2(0) = 1$. The problem here is $a_2(x) = x$ is zero at $x = 0$.

11. **(a)** $y = e^x \cos x - e^x \sin x$
    (b) no solution
    (c) $y = e^x \cos x + e^{-\pi/2} e^x \sin x$
    (d) $y = c_2 e^x \sin x$ where c_2 is arbitrary

13. $\lambda = n, \; n = 1, 2, 3, \ldots$

Exercises 1.3, Page 40

1. $xy' = y - 2$

3. $y'' - y' = 0$

5. $y'' - 8y' + 16y = 0$

7. $(x^2 - y)y' = xy$

9. $y'' + \omega^2 y = 0$

11. $x^2 y'' - xy' + y = 0$

13. $2xyy' = y^2 - x^2$

15. $2xyy' = y^2 - x^2 - 9$

17. $2xy' = y$

19. $\dfrac{dv}{dt} + \dfrac{k}{m} v^2 = g$

21. $\dfrac{dy}{dx} = -\dfrac{y}{\sqrt{s^2 - y^2}}$

23. $mx'' = -k \cos \theta \quad my'' = -mg - k \sin \theta$

$$= -k \cdot \dfrac{1}{v}\dfrac{dx}{dt} \qquad = -mg - k \cdot \dfrac{1}{v}\dfrac{dy}{dt}$$

$$= -|c|\dfrac{dx}{dt}, \qquad = -mg - |c|\dfrac{dy}{dt}$$

25. $\dfrac{dx}{dt} = r - kx, \, k > 0$

27. Using

$$\tan \phi = \dfrac{x}{y}, \qquad \tan\left(\dfrac{\pi}{2} - \theta\right) = \dfrac{dy}{dx},$$

$$\tan \theta = \dfrac{dx}{dy},$$

and $\quad \tan \phi = \tan 2\theta = \dfrac{2 \tan \theta}{1 - \tan^2 \theta}$

we obtain

$$x\left(\dfrac{dx}{dy}\right)^2 + 2y\dfrac{dx}{dy} = x.$$

29. By combining Newton's second law of motion with his law of gravitation we obtain

$$m\dfrac{d^2 y}{dt^2} = -k_1 \dfrac{mM}{y^2}$$

where M is the mass of the earth and k_1 is a constant of proportionality. Dividing by m gives

$$\dfrac{d^2 y}{dt^2} = -\dfrac{k}{y^2}$$

where $k = k_1 M$. The constant k is gR^2, where R is the radius of the earth. This follows from the fact that on the surface of the earth $y = R$ so that

$$k_1 \dfrac{mM}{R^2} = mg$$

$$k_1 M = gR^2$$

or $\qquad\qquad k = gR^2.$

If $t = 0$ is the time at which burnout occurs then

$$y(0) = R + y_B$$

where y_B is the distance from the earth's surface to the rocket at the time of burnout, and

$$y'(0) = V_B$$

is the corresponding velocity at that time.

Chapter 1 Review Exercises, Page 44

1. **(a)** $y = x^2$ **(b)** $y = \dfrac{x^2}{2}$

    (c) $y \equiv 0; y = e^x$ **(d)** $y \equiv 0; y = e^{5x}$

    (e) $y = 2$ **(f)** $y^2 = x$

3. $y' + 2xy - 2 - x^2 - y^2$

$$= 1 + \sec^2 x + 2x(x + \tan x) - 2 - x^2$$
$$\quad - (x + \tan x)^2$$

$$= 1 + \sec^2 x + 2x^2 + 2x \tan x - 2 - x^2$$
$$\quad - x^2 - 2x \tan x - \tan^2 x$$

$$= 0 \text{ since } \sec^2 x - 1 = \tan^2 x$$

5. $x < 0$ or $x > 1$

7. $y = -\cos(\ln x) + 4\sin(\ln x)$

9. If we substitute $x = 0, y = 1$ in the so-called general solution we encounter the contradictory statement $1 = 1 + 1/c$ or $0 = 1$. Thus no member of the given one-parameter family passes through the point $(0, 1)$. However, by inspection we see that the problem has the singular solution $y = 1$.

11. $2y'y''' = 3(y'')^2$

13. $(x - 2)y' = y - 1$

15. Water lost in time $\Delta t =$ change in volume of water

$$\tfrac{1}{4}\sqrt{2gh}\,\Delta t = -\pi r^2\,\Delta h$$

where Δh is the change in height for a small change in time Δt, and r is the radius of A_1. Dividing by Δt gives

$$\frac{\Delta h}{\Delta t} = -\frac{\sqrt{2gh}}{4\pi r^2}.$$

Now by similar triangles it follows that $r = 2h/5$ at any time. Thus as $t \to 0$

$$\frac{dh}{dt} = -\frac{25\sqrt{2g}}{16\pi}h^{-3/2}$$

Exercises 2.1, Page 53

1. $y = cx^4$

3. $-3 + 3x\ln x = xy^3 + cx$

5. $\dfrac{x^3}{3}\ln x - \dfrac{1}{9}x^3 = \dfrac{y^2}{2} + 2y + \ln y + c$

7. $(1 + x^3)(1 + y^3) = c$

9. $x^2(y - 1) = c(y + 1)(x + 1)^2$

11. $y^2 = x - \ln(x + 1) + c$

13. $y = \sin\!\left(\dfrac{x^2}{2} + c\right)$

15. $ty^2 = 2t^2 + ct - 2$

17. $y + y^2 = \tfrac{1}{2}(\ln x)^2 + c$

19. $\dfrac{P}{1 - P} = ce^t$ or $P = \dfrac{ce^t}{1 + ce^t}$

21. $(e^x + 1)^{-2} + 2(e^y + 1)^{-1} = c$

23. $y - 5\ln(y + 3) = x - 5\ln(x + 4) + c$

or $\left(\dfrac{y + 3}{x + 4}\right)^5 = c_1 e^{y - x}$

25. $y + \ln y - x\ln x + x = c$

27. $(1 + \cos x)(1 + e^y) = 4$

29. $y^2 = 4x^4 + 1$

31. $x = \tan(4y - 3\pi/4)$

33. $y = 3$

35. $y = -x - 1 + \tan(x + c)$

37. $4(y - 2x + 3) = (x + c)^2$

Exercises 2.2, Page 61

1. $x + y\ln x = cy$

3. $(x - y)\ln(x - y) = y + c(x - y)$

5. $e^{y/x}(y - x) = x\ln x + cx$

7. $4y^2\ln y = 2x^2\ln\dfrac{x}{y} - x^2 + cy^2$

9. $2y + x = cy^2$

11. $\ln(x^2 + y^2) + 2\tan^{-1}\dfrac{y}{x} = c$

13. $y^3 + 3x^3\ln x = 8x^3$

15. $y^2 = 4x(x + y)^2$

17. $\ln x = e^{y/x} - 1$

19. $4x\ln\dfrac{y}{x} + x\ln x + y - x = 0$

21. $3x^{3/2}\ln x + 3x^{1/2}y + 2y^{3/2} = 5x^{3/2}$

23. $(y + 1)^2 + 2(y + 1)(x - 2) - (x - 2)^2 = c$

25. By homogeneity the equation can be written as

$$M\!\left(\dfrac{x}{y}, 1\right)dx + N\!\left(\dfrac{x}{y}, 1\right)dy = 0.$$

With $v = x/y$, it follows that

$$M(v, 1)(v\,dy + y\,dv) + N(v, 1)\,dy = 0$$

$$[vM(v, 1) + N(v, 1)]\,dy + yM(v, 1)\,dv = 0$$

or $\qquad \dfrac{dy}{y} + \dfrac{M(v, 1)\,dv}{vM(v, 1) + N(v, 1)} = 0.$

Exercises 2.3, Page 69

1. $x^2y^2 - 3x + 4y = c$
3. not exact, but is homogeneous
5. $xy^3 + y^2 \cos x - \frac{1}{2}x^2 = c$
7. not exact
9. $xy - 2xe^x + 2e^x - 2x^3 = c$
11. $x + y + xy - 3\ln(xy) = c$
13. $x^3y^3 - \tan^{-1} 3x = c$
15. $-\ln(\cos x) + \cos x \sin y = c$
17. $y - 2x^2y - y^2 - x^4 = c$
19. $x^4y - 5x^3 - xy + y^3 = c$
21. $4xy + x^2 - 5x + 3y^2 - y = 8$
23. $y^2 \sin x - x^3y - x^2 + y\ln y - y = -1$

25. $M = ye^{xy} + y^2 - \dfrac{y}{x^2} + h(x)$

27. $\dfrac{\partial}{\partial x}[\mu N] = \mu\dfrac{\partial N}{\partial x} + N\dfrac{\partial \mu}{\partial x}$

$\dfrac{\partial}{\partial y}[\mu M] = \mu\dfrac{\partial M}{\partial y} + M\dfrac{\partial \mu}{\partial y}$

Equating and rearranging gives

$$N\dfrac{\partial \mu}{\partial x} - M\dfrac{\partial \mu}{\partial y} = \mu\dfrac{\partial M}{\partial y} - \mu\dfrac{\partial N}{\partial x}.$$

29. $M = -x^2y^2 \sin x + 2xy^2 \cos x$

$N = 2x^2y \cos x$

$\dfrac{\partial M}{\partial y} = -2x^2y \sin x + 4xy \cos x = \dfrac{\partial N}{\partial x}$

solution is $x^2y^2 \cos x = c$.

31. $M = 6xy^3$

$N = 4y^3 + 9x^2y^2$

$\dfrac{\partial M}{\partial y} = 18xy^2 = \dfrac{\partial N}{\partial x}$

solution is $3x^2y^3 + y^4 = c$

33. $M = \dfrac{x^2 + 2xy - y^2}{(x + y)^2}$

$N = \dfrac{y^2 + 2xy - x^2}{(x + y)^2}$

$\dfrac{\partial M}{\partial y} = -\dfrac{4xy}{(x + y)^3} = \dfrac{\partial N}{\partial x}$

solution is $\dfrac{x^2 + y^2}{x + y} = c$

35. The three resulting differential equations are equivalent to

$$d\left(\ln\dfrac{x}{y}\right) = 0, \; d\left(\dfrac{x}{y}\right) = 0, \; d\left(\tan^{-1}\dfrac{x}{y}\right) = 0.$$

Integrating and renaming the constants formally gives $y = cx$.

37. $\mu_1 = \dfrac{y^2}{x^4}, \quad \dfrac{y^3\,dx - y^2x\,dy}{x^4} = 0$

$\mu_2 = \dfrac{x^2}{y^4}, \quad \dfrac{x^2y\,dx - x^3\,dy}{y^4} = 0$

$\mu_3 = \dfrac{e^{x/y}}{y^2}, \quad \dfrac{ye^{x/y}\,dx - xe^{x/y}\,dy}{y^2} = 0$

Exercises 2.4, Page 79

1. $y = \frac{1}{10} + ce^{-5x}$
3. $y = \frac{1}{3} + ce^{-x^3}$
5. $y = x^{-1}\ln x + cx^{-1}$
7. $x = -\frac{4}{5}y^2 + cy^{-1/2}$
9. $xy = -x\cos x + \sin x + c$
11. $y = \sin x + c\cos x$
13. $y = \frac{1}{7}x^3 - \frac{1}{5}x + cx^{-4}$
15. $y = \frac{5}{3}(x + 2)^{-1} + c(x + 2)^{-4}$
17. $y = \sec x + c\csc x$
19. $y = \frac{1}{2}x^2 - \frac{1}{2} + ce^{-x^2}$
21. $y = 2 + ce^{-t^2 + t}$

C H A P T E R 2

23. $x = 2y^6 + cy^4$

25. $y = e^{-x}\ln(e^x + e^{-x}) + ce^{-x}$

27. $i(t) = \dfrac{E}{R} + \left(i_0 - \dfrac{E}{R}\right)e^{-Rt/L}$

29. $y = \sin x \cos x - \cos x$

31. $(x + 1)y = x\ln x - x + 21$

33. $x^3y^3 = 2x^3 - 9\ln x + c$

35. $e^y = -e^{-x}\cos x + ce^{-x}$

37. $y^2\ln x = ye^y - e^y + c$

39. $y = \begin{cases} \frac{1}{2}(1 - e^{-2x}), & 0 \le x \le 3, \\ \frac{1}{2}(e^6 - 1)e^{-2x}, & x > 3 \end{cases}$

41. $y = \begin{cases} \frac{1}{2} + \frac{3}{2}e^{-x^2}, & 0 \le x < 1 \\ (\frac{1}{2}e + \frac{3}{2})e^{-x^2}, & x \ge 1 \end{cases}$

Exercises 2.5, Page 83

1. The equation

$$\frac{dy}{dx} + P(x)y = f(x)y^n$$

can be written as

$$y^{-n}\frac{dy}{dx} + P(x)y^{1-n} = f(x).$$

Now since $w = y^{1-n}$ we have $dw/dx = (1 - n)y^{-n}\,dy/dx$ so that

$$\frac{1}{1 - n}\frac{dw}{dx} + P(x)w = f(x)$$

or $\dfrac{dw}{dx} + (1 - n)P(x)w = (1 - n)f(x).$

3. $y^3 = 1 + cx^{-3}$

5. $y^{-3} = -\frac{9}{5}x^{-1} + \frac{49}{5}x^{-6}$

7. If $y = y_1 + u$, then $y' = y_1' + u'$ and so $dy/dx = P(x) + Q(x)y + R(x)y^2$ becomes

$$y_1' + u' = P + Q(y_1 + u) + R(y_1 + u)^2$$

$$\begin{aligned} y_1' + u' &= P + Qy_1 + Ry_1^2 + Qu + 2y_1Ru \\ &\quad + Ru^2. \end{aligned}$$

Since y_1 is a solution of the Ricatti equation we obtain

$$u' - (Q + 2y_1R)u = Ru^2$$

Now the last equation is a Bernoulli equation in u so we let $w = u^{-1}$ which then implies $w' = -u^{-2}u'$. Finally it follows that

$$w' + (Q + 2y_1R)w = -R.$$

9. $y = 2 + \dfrac{1}{ce^{-3x} - 1/3}$

11. $y = \dfrac{2}{x} + \dfrac{1}{cx^{-3} - x/4}$

13. $y = -2 + \dfrac{1}{ce^{-x} - 1}$

15. If $y = \dfrac{w'}{w}$ then $y' = \dfrac{ww'' - (w')^2}{w^2}$ and so

$$y' + y^2 - Q(x)y - P(x) = 0$$

becomes

$$\frac{ww'' - (w')^2}{w^2} + \frac{(w')^2}{w^2} - Q\frac{w'}{w} - P = 0.$$

The last equation simplifies to

$$w'' - Qw' - Pw = 0.$$

17. $y = cx + 1 - \ln c;$ $y = 2 + \ln x$

19. $y = cx - c^3;$ $27y^2 = 4x^3$

21. $y = cx - e^c;$ $y = x\ln x - x$

Exercises 2.6, Page 89

1. $x^2e^{2y} = 2x\ln x - 2x + c$

3. $e^{-x} = y\ln y + cy$

5. $-e^{-y/x^4} = x^2 + c$

7. $x^2 + y^2 = x - 1 + ce^{-x}$

9. $\ln(\tan y) = x + cx^{-1}$

11. $y = \ln[\cos(c_1 - x)] + c_2$

13. $y = -\dfrac{1}{c_1}(1 - c_1^2x^2)^{1/2} + c_2$

15. The given equation is a Clairaut equation in $w = y'$. The solution is $y = c_1 x^2/2 + x + c_1^3 x + c_2$.

Chapter 2 Review Exercises, Page 92

1. (a) linear in x
  (b) homogeneous, exact, linear in y
  (c) Clairaut
  (d) Bernoulli in x
  (e) separable
  (f) separable, Ricatti
  (g) linear in x
  (h) homogeneous
  (i) Bernoulli
  (j) homogeneous, exact, Bernoulli
  (k) exact, linear in y
  (l) Clairaut
  (m) Ricatti
  (n) separable

3. $2y^2 \ln y - y^2 = 4xe^x - 4e^x - 1$

5. $2y^2 + x^2 = 9x^6$

7. $e^{xy} - 4y^3 = 5$

9. $y = \frac{1}{4} - 320(x^2 + 4)^{-4}$

11. $y = \dfrac{1}{x^4 - x^4 \ln x}$

13. $x^2 - \sin \dfrac{1}{y^2} = c$

Exercises 3.1, Page 100

1. $x^2 + y^2 = c_2^2$

3. $2y^2 + x^2 = c_2$

5. $y^2 = 2x + c_2$

7. $x^3 + y^3 = c_2$

9. $y^2 \ln y + x^2 = c_2 y^2$

11. $2y^2 = 2 \ln x + x^2 + c_2$

13. $2y^3 = 3x^2 + c_2$

15. $y^{5/3} = x^{5/3} + c_2$

17. $y = 2 - x + 3e^{-x}$

19. $r = c_2 \sin \theta$

21. $r^2 = c_2 \cos 2\theta$

23. $r = c_2 \csc \theta$

25. Let β be the angle of inclination, measured from the positive x-axis, of the tangent line to a member of the given family, and ϕ the angle of inclination of the tangent to a trajectory. At the point where the curves intersect, the angle between the tangents is α. From the following figures we conclude that there exist two possible cases, and that $\phi = \beta \pm \alpha$. Thus the slope of the tangent line to a trajectory is

$$\frac{dy}{dx} = \tan \phi = \tan(\beta \pm \alpha)$$
$$= \frac{\tan \beta \pm \tan \alpha}{1 \mp \tan \beta \tan \alpha}$$
$$= \frac{f(x, y) \pm \tan \alpha}{1 \mp f(x, y) \tan \alpha}.$$

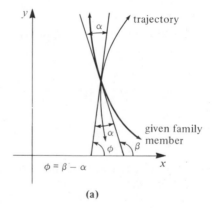

(a)

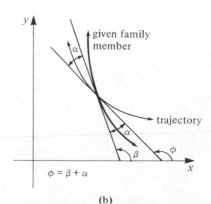

(b)

C
H
A
P
T
E
R
3

Exercises 3.2, Page 112

1. 7.9 years; 10 years

3. $P_1 = P_0 e^{kt_1}$ and $P_2 = P_0 e^{kt_2}$ so that

$$\frac{P_1}{P_0} = e^{kt_1} \quad \text{and} \quad \frac{P_2}{P_0} = e^{kt_2}.$$

Thus

$$\left(\frac{P_1}{P_0}\right)^{t_2} = e^{kt_1 t_2} \quad \text{and} \quad \left(\frac{P_2}{P_0}\right)^{t_1} = e^{kt_2 t_1}.$$

The result follows by equating $e^{kt_1 t_2}$ with $e^{kt_2 t_1}$.

5. (a) $P(t) = P_0 e^{(k_1 - k_2)t}$
   (b) $k_1 > k_2$, births surpass deaths so population increases.
   $k_1 = k_2$, a constant population since number of births equals the number of deaths.
   $k_1 < k_2$, deaths surpass births so population decreases.

7. 136.5 hours

9. $I(15) = 0.000098 I_0$ or $I(15)$ is approximately 0.1% of I_0.

11. 15,600 years

13. $T(1) = 36.67$ degrees; approximately 3.06 minutes

15. $i(t) = \frac{3}{5} - \frac{3}{5} e^{-500t}$; $t \to \frac{3}{5}$ as $t \to \infty$.

17. $A(t) = 200 - 170 e^{-t/50}$

19. The differential equation for the number of pounds of salt $A(t)$ is

$$\frac{dA}{dt} + \frac{4}{100 + 2t} A = 3;$$

$$A(30) = 64.38 \text{ lb}$$

21. $v(t) = \frac{mg}{k} + \left(v_0 - \frac{mg}{k}\right) e^{-kt/m};$

$v \to \frac{mg}{k}$ as $t \to \infty$;

$s(t) = \frac{mg}{k} t - \frac{m}{k}\left(v_0 - \frac{mg}{k}\right) e^{-kt/m}$

$\quad + \frac{m}{k}\left(v_0 - \frac{mg}{k}\right) + s_0$

Exercises 3.3, Page 123

1. 1834; 2000

3. 1,000,000; 52.9 months

5. (a) Separating variables gives

$$\frac{dP}{P(a - b \ln P)} = dt$$

so that

$$-\frac{1}{b} \ln (a - b \ln P) = t + c_1$$

$$a - b \ln P = c_2 e^{-bt} \qquad (e^{-bc_1} = c_2)$$

$$\ln P = \frac{a}{b} - ce^{-bt} \qquad \left(\frac{c_2}{b} = c\right)$$

$$P(t) = e^{a/b} \cdot e^{-ce^{-bt}}$$

(b) If $P(0) = P_0$ then

$$P_0 = e^{a/b} e^{-c} = e^{a/b - c}$$

and so $\quad \ln P_0 = \frac{a}{b} - c$

$$c = \frac{a}{b} - \ln P_0.$$

7. 29.3 grams; $X \to 60$ as $t \to \infty$; 0 grams of A and 30 grams of B.

9. For $\alpha \neq \beta$ the differential equation separates as

$$\frac{1}{\alpha - \beta}\left[-\frac{1}{\alpha - X} + \frac{1}{\beta - X}\right] dX = k \, dt.$$

It follows immediately that

$$\frac{1}{\alpha - \beta} [\ln (\alpha - X) - \ln (\beta - X)] = kt + c$$

or $\quad \frac{1}{\alpha - \beta} \ln \frac{\alpha - X}{\beta - X} = kt + c.$

For $\alpha = \beta$ the equation can be written as

$$(\alpha - X)^{-2} dX = k \, dt.$$

It follows that

$$(\alpha - X)^{-1} = kt + c$$

or $\qquad X = \alpha - \dfrac{1}{kt + c}.$

11. $v^2 = \dfrac{2gR^2}{y} + v_0^2 - 2gR.$

We note that as y increases v decreases. In particular, if $v_0^2 - 2gR < 0$ then there must be some value of y for $v = 0$; the rocket stops and returns to earth under the influence of gravity. However, if $v_0^2 - 2gR \geq 0$ then $v > 0$ for all values of y. Hence we should have $v_0 \geq \sqrt{2gR}$. Using the values $R = 4000$ miles, $g = 32\,\text{ft/sec}^2$, $1\,\text{ft} = 1/5280\,\text{mi}$, $1\,\text{sec} = 1/3600\,\text{hr}$, it follows that $v_0 \geq 25{,}067\,\text{mi/hr}$.

13. Using the condition $y'(1) = 0$ we find
$$\frac{dy}{dx} = \frac{1}{2}[x^{v_1/v_2} - x^{-v_1/v_2}].$$
Now if $v_1 = v_2$, $y = \frac{1}{4}x^2 - \frac{1}{2}\ln x - \frac{1}{4}$; if $v_1 \neq v_2$ then
$$y = \frac{1}{2}\left[\frac{x^{1+(v_1/v_2)}}{1 + \dfrac{v_1}{v_2}} - \frac{x^{1-(v_1/v_2)}}{1 - \dfrac{v_1}{v_2}}\right] + \frac{v_1 v_2}{v_2^2 - v_1^2}$$

15. $2h^{1/2} = -\frac{1}{25}t + 2\sqrt{20};\quad t = 50\sqrt{20}\,\text{sec}$

17. To evaluate the indefinite integral of the left side of
$$\frac{\sqrt{100 - y^2}}{y}\,dy = -dx$$
we use the substitution $y = 10\cos\theta$. It follows that
$$x = 10\ln\left(\frac{10 + \sqrt{100 - y^2}}{y}\right) - \sqrt{100 - y^2}.$$

19. Under the substitution $w = x^2$ the differential equation becomes
$$w = y\frac{dw}{dy} + \frac{1}{4}\left(\frac{dw}{dy}\right)^2$$
which is Clairaut's equation. The solution is
$$x^2 = cy + \frac{c^2}{4},$$

If $2c_1 = c$, then we recognize
$$x^2 = 2c_1 y + c_1^2$$
as describing a family of parabolas.

21. $-\gamma \ln y + \delta y = \alpha \ln x - \beta x + c$

Chapter 3 Review Exercises, Page 128

1. $2y^2 + 3x^2 = c_2$

3. $2(y - 2)^2 + (x - 1)^2 = c_2^2$

5. $P(45) = 8.99$ billion

7. $x(t) = \dfrac{\alpha c_1 e^{\alpha k_1 t}}{1 + c_1 e^{\alpha k_1 t}},$

$\qquad y(t) = c_2(1 + c_1 e^{\alpha k_1 t})^{k_2/k_1}$

Exercises 4.1, Page 145

1. **(a)** dependent
   (b) dependent
   (c) dependent
   (d) independent
   (e) dependent
   (f) independent
   (g) independent
   (h) independent
   (i) dependent

3. **(a)** The results follow from Theorems 4.1 and 4.2.
   (b) (i) dependent
   (ii) independent
   (iii) independent
   (iv) dependent
   (v) dependent
   (vi) independent

5. **(a)** The graphs on page A-10 show that y_1 and y_2 are not multiples of one another. Also,
$$x^2 y_1'' - 3x y_1' + 3y_1 = x^2(6x)$$
$$- 3x(3x^2) + 3x^3$$
$$= 9x^3 - 9x^3$$
$$= 0.$$

C
H
A
P
T
E
R

4

For $x \geq 0$ the demonstration that y_2 is a solution of the equation is exactly as given above for y_1. For $x < 0$, $y_2 = -x^3$ and so

$$x^2 y_2'' - 3x y_2' + 3y_2 = x^2(-6x)$$
$$- 3x(-3x^2)$$
$$+ 3(-x^3)$$
$$= -9x^3 + 9x^3$$
$$= 0.$$

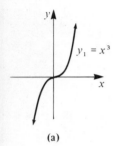

(a)

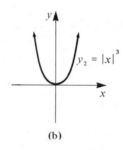

(b)

(b) For $x \geq 0$

$$W(y_1, y_2) = \begin{vmatrix} x^3 & x^3 \\ 3x^2 & 3x^2 \end{vmatrix}$$
$$= 3x^5 - 3x^5 = 0.$$

For $x < 0$

$$W(y_1, y_2) = \begin{vmatrix} x^3 & -x^3 \\ 3x^2 & -3x^2 \end{vmatrix}$$
$$= -3x^5 + 3x^5 = 0$$

Thus $W(y_1, y_2) = 0$ for every real value of x.

(c) No, $a_2(x) = x^2$ is zero at $x = 0$.

7. $x^2 y_1'' - 7x y_1' + 25 y_1$
$$= x^2(3x^2 \cos(3 \ln x) - 21x^2 \sin(3 \ln x))$$
$$- 7x(-3x^3 \sin(3 \ln x))$$
$$+ 4x^3 \cos(3 \ln x))$$
$$+ 25x^4 \cos(3 \ln x) = 0,$$

$$x^2 y_2'' - 7x y_2' + 25 y_2$$
$$= x^2(3x^2 \sin(3 \ln x) + 21x^2 \cos(3 \ln x))$$
$$- 7x(3x^3 \cos(3 \ln x)$$
$$+ 4x^3 \sin(3 \ln x))$$
$$+ 25x^4 \sin(3 \ln x) = 0.$$

At $x = 1$,

$$W(y_1(1), y_2(1)) = \begin{vmatrix} 1 & 0 \\ 4 & 3 \end{vmatrix} = 3$$

and so y_1 and y_2 are linearly independent on $x > 0$.

9. (a) Since y_1 and y_2 are solutions of the given differential equation we have

$$a_2(x) y_1'' + a_1(x) y_1' + a_0(x) y_1 = 0$$

and $a_2(x) y_2'' + a_1(x) y_2' + a_0(x) y_2 = 0$.

Now multiply the first equation by y_2 and the second by y_1 and subtract the first from the second:

$$a_2(x)[y_1 y_2'' - y_2 y_1'']$$
$$+ a_1(x)[y_1 y_2' - y_2 y_1'] = 0.$$

Now it is easily verified that

$$\frac{dW}{dx} = \frac{d}{dx}(y_1 y_2' - y_2 y_1')$$
$$= y_1 y_2'' - y_2 y_1''$$

and so it follows that

$$a_2(x) \frac{dW}{dx} + a_1(x) W = 0.$$

(b) Since this last equation is a linear first-order differential equation the integrating factor is

$$e^{\int (a_1(x)/a_2(x)) \, dx}.$$

Therefore from

$$\frac{d}{dx}[e^{\int (a_1(x)/a_2(x)) \, dx} W] = 0$$

we obtain

$$W = c e^{-\int (a_1(x)/a_2(x)) \, dx}.$$

(c)   Substituting $x = x_0$ in the given result we find $c = W(x_0)$.

(d)   Since an exponential function is never zero, when $W(x_0) \neq 0$ it follows from part (c) that $W \neq 0$. On the other hand, if $W(x_0) = 0$ we have immediately that $W = 0$.

11.   From part (c) of Problem 9 we have

$$W(y_1, y_2) = W(y_1(x_0), y_2(x_0)) e^{-\int_{x_0}^{x} dt/t}$$

$$= \begin{vmatrix} k_1 & k_3 \\ k_2 & k_4 \end{vmatrix} e^{-\ln(x/x_0)}$$

$$= (k_1 k_4 - k_3 k_2) \cdot \frac{x_0}{x}$$

13. (a)   general solution
   (b)   general solution
   (c)   general solution
   (d)   not a general solution
   (e)   general solution

Exercises 4.2, Page 152

1. $y_2 = e^{-4x}$

3. $y_2 = xe^{2x}$

5. $y_2 = \sinh x$

7. $y_2 = xe^{2x/3}$

9. $y_2 = x^4 \ln x$

11. $y_2 = x^2 + x + 2$

13. $y_2 = x \cos(\ln x)$

15. $y_2 = x$

17. $y_2 = x \ln x$

19. $y_2 = x^2$

21. $y_2 = \frac{1}{2}[\tan x \sec x + \ln(\sec x + \tan x)]$

Exercises 4.3, Page 160

1. $y = c_1 + c_2 e^{x/3}$

3. $y = c_1 \cos 3x + c_2 \sin 3x$

5. $y = c_1 e^{-4x} + c_2 x e^{-4x}$

7. $y = c_1 e^{(-3+\sqrt{29})x/2} + c_2 e^{(-3-\sqrt{29})x/2}$

9. $y = c_1 e^{-6x} + c_2 e^{7x}$

11. $y = e^{2x}(c_1 \cos x + c_2 \sin x)$

13. $y = c_1 + c_2 e^{-x} + c_3 e^{5x}$

15. $y = c_1 + c_2 x$

$$+ e^{-x/2}\left(c_3 \cos \frac{\sqrt{3}}{2}x + c_4 \sin \frac{\sqrt{3}}{2}x \right)$$

17. $y = c_1 e^{-x/2} + e^{2x}(c_2 \cos 2x + c_3 \sin 2x)$

19. $y = c_1 \cos \frac{\sqrt{3}}{2}x + c_2 \sin \frac{\sqrt{3}}{2}x$

$$+ c_3 x \cos \frac{\sqrt{3}}{2}x$$

$$+ c_4 x \sin \frac{\sqrt{3}}{2}x$$

21. $\dfrac{d^3 y}{dx^3} + 6\dfrac{d^2 y}{dx^2} - 15\dfrac{dy}{dx} - 100y = 0$

23. $y = 2\cos 4x - \frac{1}{2}\sin 4x$

25. $y = -\frac{3}{4}e^{-5x} + \frac{3}{4}e^{-x}$

27. $y = -e^x \cos x + e^x \sin x$

29. $y = \frac{5}{36} - \frac{5}{36}e^{-6x} + \frac{1}{6}xe^{-6x}$

31. $y = 2 - 2e^x + 2xe^x - \frac{1}{2}x^2 e^x$

33. $y \equiv 0$

35. $y = e^{2(x-1)} - e^{x-1}$

Exercises 4.4, Page 172

1. $y_p = Ax^2 \sin 3x + Bx^2 \cos 3x + Cx \sin 3x$
$$+ Dx \cos 3x$$

3. $y_p = Axe^{-x} + Be^{2x} + Cx^4 + Dx^3 + Ex^2$

5. $y_p = Axe^x \sin x + Bxe^x \cos x + Ce^x \sin x$
$$+ De^x \cos x$$

7. $y = c_1 \cos x + c_2 \sin x + x^2 - 2$

9. $y = c_1 e^x + c_2 xe^x + x^3 + 6x^2 + 22x + 32$

11. $y = c_1 \cos 2x + c_2 \sin 2x - \frac{1}{8}x \cos 2x$

13. $y = c_1 + c_2 x + c_3 e^{3x} - \frac{1}{15}x^5 - \frac{1}{6}x^4$
$$- \frac{2}{9}x^3 - \frac{2}{9}x^2$$

15. $y = c_1 + c_2e^{-2x} + c_3xe^{-2x} - xe^{-x} + e^{-x}$

$\qquad - \frac{4}{25}\cos x + \frac{3}{25}\sin x$

17. $y = c_1 + c_2e^{-x} + \frac{1}{4}x^4 + \frac{3}{2}x^2 - 2x$

19. $y = c_1e^x + c_2e^{3x} - \frac{1}{3}x^2 - \frac{2}{9}x - \frac{2}{27} + \frac{3}{2}xe^x$

21. $y = c_1e^{x/2} + c_2e^{-x/2} + c_3\cos\dfrac{x}{2} + c_4\sin\dfrac{x}{2}$

$\qquad + \frac{1}{8}xe^{x/2}$

23. $y = c_1e^{-3x} + c_2xe^{-3x} + \frac{1}{4}x^2e^{-x} - \frac{1}{2}xe^{-x}$

$\qquad + \frac{3}{8}e^{-x} + \frac{4}{9}x - \frac{8}{27}$

25. $y = c_1e^x + c_2xe^x + c_3x^2e^x + \frac{1}{6}x^3e^x$

$\qquad + x - 13$

27. $y = -\frac{41}{125} + \frac{41}{125}e^{5x} - \frac{1}{10}x^2 + \frac{9}{25}x$

29. $y = -\pi\cos x - \frac{11}{3}\sin x - \frac{8}{3}\cos 2x$

$\qquad + 2x\cos x$

31. $y = 2e^{2x}\cos 2x - \frac{3}{64}e^{2x}\sin 2x + \frac{1}{8}x^3$

$\qquad + \frac{3}{16}x^2 + \frac{3}{32}x$

Exercises 4.5, Page 179

1. $y = c_1\cos x + c_2\sin x + x\sin x$

$\qquad + \cos x\ln(\cos x)$

3. $y = c_1\cos x + c_2\sin x + \frac{1}{2}\sin x - \frac{1}{2}x\cos x$

$\qquad = c_1\cos x + c_3\sin x - \frac{1}{2}x\cos x$

5. $y = c_1\cos x + c_2\sin x + \frac{1}{2} - \frac{1}{6}\cos 2x$

7. $y = c_1e^{2x} + c_2e^{-2x}$

$\qquad + \dfrac{1}{4}\left(e^{2x}\ln x - e^{-2x}\displaystyle\int\dfrac{e^{4x}}{x}\,dx\right)$

9. $y = c_1e^{-2x} + c_2e^{-x} - e^{-2x}\sin e^x$

11. $y = c_1e^x + c_2xe^x - \frac{1}{2}e^x\ln(1+x^2)$

$\qquad + xe^x\tan^{-1}x$

13. $y = c_1e^{-x} + c_2xe^{-x} + \frac{1}{2}x^2e^{-x}\ln x$

$\qquad - \frac{3}{4}x^2e^{-x}$

15. $y = c_1e^{x/2} + c_2xe^{x/2} + \frac{8}{9}e^{-x} + x + 4$

17. $y = \frac{3}{8}e^{-x} + \frac{5}{8}e^x + \frac{1}{4}x^2e^x - \frac{1}{4}xe^x$

19. $y = \frac{4}{9}e^{-4x} + \frac{25}{36}e^{2x} - \frac{1}{4}e^{-2x} + \frac{1}{9}e^{-x}$

21. $y = c_1x + c_2x\ln x + \frac{2}{3}x(\ln x)^3$

23. $y = c_1 + c_2e^x + c_3e^{-x} + \frac{1}{4}x^2e^x - \frac{3}{4}xe^x$

Chapter 4 Review Exercises, Page 183

1. **(a)** linearly dependent
    (b) linearly independent
    (c) linearly dependent
    (d) linearly independent
    (e) linearly dependent
    (f) linearly independent

3. $y_2 = \sin 2x$

5. $y = c_1e^{(1+\sqrt{3})x} + c_2e^{(1-\sqrt{3})x}$

7. $y = c_1 + c_2e^{-5x} + c_3xe^{-5x}$

9. $y = c_1e^{-x/3}$

$\qquad + e^{-3x/2}\left[c_2\cos\dfrac{\sqrt{7}}{2}x + c_3\sin\dfrac{\sqrt{7}}{2}x\right]$

11. $y = e^{3x/2}\left[c_1\cos\dfrac{\sqrt{11}}{2}x + c_2\sin\dfrac{\sqrt{11}}{2}x\right]$

$\qquad + \frac{4}{5}x^3 + \frac{36}{25}x^2 + \frac{46}{125}x - \frac{222}{625}$

13. $y = c_1 + c_2e^{2x} + c_3e^{3x} + \frac{1}{5}\sin x - \frac{1}{5}\cos x$

$\qquad + \frac{4}{3}x$

15. $y = e^x[c_1\cos x + c_2\sin x]$

$\qquad - e^x\cos x\ln(\sec x + \tan x)$

Exercises 5.1, Page 192

1. $x(t) = 2\sqrt{2}\sin\left(5t - \dfrac{\pi}{4}\right)$

3. $x(t) = \sqrt{5}\sin(\sqrt{2}t + 3.6052)$

5. A weight of 4 lb ($\frac{1}{8}$ slug), attached to a spring, is released from a point 3 units above the equilibrium position with an initial upward velocity of 2 ft/sec. The spring constant is 3 lb/ft.

7. 8 lb

9. $x(t) = 2\sqrt{2}\cos\left(5t + \dfrac{5\pi}{4}\right)$

11. $x(t) = -\frac{1}{4}\cos 4\sqrt{6}t$

13. (a) $x(\pi/12) = -1/4;\quad x(\pi/8) = -1/2;$

$\qquad\quad x(\pi/6) = -1/4;\quad x(\pi/4) = 1/2;$

$\qquad\quad x(9\pi/32) = \sqrt{2}/4$

(b) 4 ft/sec; downward

(c) $t = (2k+1)\dfrac{\pi}{16}, k = 0, 1, 2, \dots.$

15. $x(t) = \frac{1}{2}\cos 2t + \frac{3}{4}\sin 2t$

$\qquad = \dfrac{\sqrt{13}}{4}\sin(2t + 0.5880)$

17. $t = \dfrac{\pi}{6} + \dfrac{2k\pi}{3},\quad k = 0, 1, 2, \dots,\quad$ and

$\quad t = -\dfrac{7\pi}{18} + \dfrac{2k\pi}{3},\quad k = 1, 2, 3, \dots.$

Exercises 5.2, Page 203

1. A 2-lb weight is attached to a spring whose constant is 1 lb/ft. The system is damped with a resisting force numerically equal to 2 times the instantaneous velocity. The weight starts from the equilibrium position with an upward velocity of 1.5 ft/sec.

3. $\frac{1}{4}$ sec; $\frac{1}{2}$ sec, $x(\frac{1}{2}) = e^{-2}$, that is, the weight is approximately 0.14 ft below the equilibrium position.

5. (a) The weight does not pass through the equilibrium position. The maximum displacement occurs at $t = 0$.

(b) The weight passes through the equilibrium position at $t = 0.153$ sec. The maximum displacement occurs at $t = 0.384$ sec. At this time the weight is 0.232 ft above the equilibrium position.

7. (a) $x(t) = e^{-2t}[-\cos 4t - \frac{1}{2}\sin 4t]$

(b) $x(t) = \dfrac{\sqrt{5}}{2}e^{-2t}\sin(4t + 4.249)$

(c) $t = 1.294$ sec.

9. Suppose $\delta = \sqrt{\omega^2 - \lambda^2}$ then the derivative of $x(t) = Ae^{-\lambda t}\sin(\delta t + \phi)$ is

$x'(t) = Ae^{-\lambda t}[\delta\cos(\delta t + \phi)$

$\qquad\qquad -\lambda\sin(\delta t + \phi)].$

So $x'(t) = 0$ implies

$$\tan(\delta t + \phi) = \frac{\delta}{\lambda}$$

from which it follows that

$$t = \frac{1}{\delta}\left[\tan^{-1}\frac{\delta}{\lambda} + k\pi - \phi\right].$$

The difference between the t values between two successive maxima (or minima) is then

$$t_{k+2} - t_k = (k+2)\frac{\pi}{\delta} - k\frac{\pi}{\delta}$$

$$= \frac{2\pi}{\delta}.$$

11. The intercepts are $t_k = 3\pi/4,\ 7\pi/4,\ 11\pi/4,$ $15\pi/4,\dots.$ Also $\sin(t + \pi/4) = \pm 1$ for $t_k^* = \pi/4,\ 5\pi/4,\ 9\pi/4,\ 13\pi/4,\dots.$ Note that the average of two successive t_k^* gives a value of t_k. However, the values of t for which $x(t)$ attains its extrema are $t = 0,\ \pi,\ 2\pi,\ 3\pi,\dots.$

Exercises 5.3, Page 212

1. $x(t) = e^{-t/2}\left[-\dfrac{4}{3}\cos\dfrac{\sqrt{47}}{2}t\right.$

$\qquad\qquad\left. -\dfrac{64}{3\sqrt{47}}\sin\dfrac{\sqrt{47}}{2}t\right]$

$\qquad\quad + \dfrac{10}{3}[\cos 3t + \sin 3t]$

3. (a) $g'(\gamma) = 0$ implies $\gamma(\gamma^2 - \omega^2 + 2\lambda^2) = 0$ so that either $\gamma = 0$ or $\gamma = \sqrt{\omega^2 - 2\lambda^2}$. The first derivative test can be used to verify that $g(\gamma)$ is a maximum at the latter value.

(b) $g(\sqrt{\omega^2 - 2\lambda^2}) = F_0/2\lambda\sqrt{\omega^2 - \lambda^2}$

5. $x_p = -5\cos 2t + 5\sin 2t$

$\qquad = 5\sqrt{2}\sin\left(2t - \dfrac{\pi}{4}\right)$

C
H
A
P
T
E
R

5

7. $m\dfrac{d^2x}{dt^2} = -k(x-h) - \beta\dfrac{dx}{dt}$

or

$\dfrac{d^2x}{dt^2} + 2\lambda\dfrac{dx}{dt} + \omega^2 x = \omega^2 h(t),$

where

$2\lambda = \dfrac{\beta}{m}$ and $\omega^2 = \dfrac{k}{m}.$

9. (a) $x(t) = x_c + x_p$

$= c_1\cos\omega t + c_2\sin\omega t$

$+ \dfrac{F_0}{\omega^2 - \gamma^2}\cos\gamma t$

where the initial conditions imply that $c_1 = -F_0/(\omega^2 - \gamma^2)$ and $c_2 = 0$.

(b) By L'Hôpital's rule the given limit is the same as

$\displaystyle\lim_{\gamma\to\omega}\dfrac{F_0(-t\sin\gamma t)}{-2\gamma} = \dfrac{F_0}{2\omega}t\sin\omega t.$

11. (a) Recall that

$\cos(u-v) = \cos u\cos v + \sin u\sin v$

$\cos(u+v) = \cos u\cos v - \sin u\sin v.$

Subtracting gives

$\sin u\sin v = \tfrac{1}{2}[\cos(u-v)$

$-\cos(u+v)].$

Setting $u = \tfrac{1}{2}(\gamma - \omega)t$ and $v = \tfrac{1}{2}(\gamma + \omega)t$ then gives

$\sin\tfrac{1}{2}(\gamma - \omega)t\sin\tfrac{1}{2}(\gamma + \omega)t$

$= \tfrac{1}{2}[\cos\omega t - \cos\gamma t]$

from which the result follows.

(b) For small $\varepsilon, \gamma \approx \omega$ so $\gamma + \omega \approx 2\gamma$ and therefore

$\dfrac{-2F_0}{(\omega + \gamma)(\omega - \gamma)}\sin\dfrac{1}{2}(\gamma - \omega)t\sin\dfrac{1}{2}(\gamma + \omega)t$

$\approx \dfrac{F_0}{2\gamma\varepsilon}\sin\varepsilon t\sin\tfrac{1}{2}(2\gamma)t.$

(c) By L'Hôpital's rule the given limit is the same as

$\displaystyle\lim_{\varepsilon\to 0}\dfrac{F_0 t\cos\varepsilon t\sin\gamma t}{2\gamma} = \dfrac{F_0}{2\gamma}t\sin\gamma t = \dfrac{F_0}{2\omega}t\sin\omega t.$

13. $x(t) = -\cos 2t - \tfrac{1}{8}\sin 2t + \tfrac{3}{4}t\sin 2t$
$+ \tfrac{5}{4}t\cos 2t$

Exercises 5.4, Page 217

1. Differentiate equation (1) with respect to t and use the fact that $dq/dt = i$. For example,

$$\dfrac{d^2q}{dt^2} = \dfrac{d}{dt}\left(\dfrac{dq}{dt}\right) = \dfrac{di}{dt}.$$

3. $i_p = \dfrac{1200k}{100 - k^2}\cos kt$

5. $q(t) = -\tfrac{1}{2}e^{-10t}(\cos 10t + \sin 10t) + \tfrac{3}{2};$
$\tfrac{3}{2}$ coulombs

Chapter 5 Review Exercises, Page 219

1. $\dfrac{2\sqrt{3}}{\pi}$

3. $\dfrac{\sqrt{13}}{6}$

5. $x(t) = -\tfrac{2}{3}e^{-2t} + \tfrac{1}{3}e^{-4t}$

7. $0 < m \le 2$

9. $\gamma = \dfrac{8\sqrt{3}}{3}$

11. $x(t) = e^{-4t}$

$\times\left[\dfrac{26}{17}\cos 2\sqrt{2}t + \dfrac{28\sqrt{2}}{17}\sin 2\sqrt{2}t\right]$

$+ \dfrac{8}{17}e^{-t}$

Exercises 6.1, Page 230

1. $y = c_1 x^{-1} + c_2 x^2$

3. $y = c_1 + c_2\ln x$

5. $y = c_1\cos(2\ln x) + c_2\sin(2\ln x)$

7. $y = x[c_1 \cos(\ln x) + c_2 \sin(\ln x)]$

9. $y = x^{-1/2}$

$$\times \left[c_1 \cos\left(\frac{\sqrt{3}}{6}\ln x\right) + c_2 \sin\left(\frac{\sqrt{3}}{6}\ln x\right) \right]$$

11. $y = c_1 x^3 + c_2 \cos(\sqrt{2}\ln x)$
     $+ c_3 \sin(\sqrt{2}\ln x)$

13. $y = c_1(x-1)^{-1} + c_2(x-1)^4$

15. $y = c_1 x^{-1} + c_2 x^{-8} + \frac{1}{30}x^2$

17. $y = x^2[c_1 \cos(3\ln x) + c_2 \sin(3\ln x)] + \frac{4}{13}$
     $+ \frac{3}{10}x$

19. $y = c_1 x^2 + c_2 x^{-10} - \frac{1}{7}x^{-3}$

21. $y = c_1 + c_2 \ln x + \frac{x^2}{4}$

23. $y = c_1 x^{-1/2} + c_2 x^{-1} + \frac{1}{15}x^2 - \frac{1}{6}x$

25. $y = c_1 x + c_2 x \ln x + x(\ln x)^2$

27. A natural assumption would be

$$y_p = Axe^x + Be^x$$

from which

$$y'_p = Axe^x + Ae^x + Be^x.$$

$$y''_p = Axe^x + 2Ae^x + Be^x.$$

Therefore,

$$x^2 y''_p - 2y_p = Ax^3 e^x + 2Ax^2 e^x + Bx^2 e^x$$
$$- 2Axe^x - 2Be^x.$$

No choice of A and B will result in this last expression equaling xe^x identically.

Exercises 6.2, Page 240

1. $y = c_0 e^{-x}$; $y = c_0 \sum_{n=0}^{\infty} \frac{(-1)^k}{k!}x^k$

3. $y = c_0 \cosh x + c_1 \sinh x$ (alternative solutions e^x and e^{-x} are obtained by letting $c_0 = c_1 = 1$ and $c_0 = 1$, $c_1 = -1$, respectively);

$$y = c_0 \sum_{n=0}^{\infty} \frac{1}{(2n)!}x^{2n}$$
$$+ c_1 \sum_{n=0}^{\infty} \frac{1}{(2n+1)!}x^{2n+1}$$

5. $y = c_0 \cos x + c_1 \sin x$;

$$y = c_0 \sum_{n=0}^{\infty} \frac{(-1)^n}{(2n)!}x^{2n}$$
$$+ c_1 \sum_{n=0}^{\infty} \frac{(-1)^n}{(2n+1)!}x^{2n+1}$$

7. $y_1(x) = c_0 \left[1 - \frac{1}{2}x^2 - \frac{3}{4!}x^4 - \frac{21}{6!}x^6 - \cdots \right]$

$y_2(x) = c_1 \left[x + \frac{1}{3!}x^3 + \frac{5}{5!}x^5 + \frac{45}{7!}x^7 + \cdots \right]$

9. $y_1(x) = c_0 \left[1 - \frac{1}{3!}x^3 + \frac{4^2}{6!}x^6 \right.$

$$\left. - \frac{7^2 \cdot 4^2}{9!}x^9 + \cdots \right]$$

$y_2(x) = c_1 \left[x - \frac{2^2}{4!}x^4 + \frac{5^2 \cdot 2^2}{7!}x^7 \right.$

$$\left. - \frac{8^2 \cdot 5^2 \cdot 2^2}{10!}x^{10} + \cdots \right]$$

11. $y_1(x) = c_0$; $y_2(x) = c_1 \sum_{n=1}^{\infty} \frac{1}{n}x^n$

13. $y_1(x) = c_0[1 + \frac{1}{2}x^2 + \frac{1}{6}x^3 + \frac{1}{6}x^4 + \cdots]$
     $y_2(x) = c_1[x + \frac{1}{2}x^2 + \frac{1}{2}x^3 + \frac{1}{4}x^4 + \cdots]$

15. $y_1(x) = c_0 \sum_{n=0}^{\infty} x^{2n}$; $y_2(x) = c_1 \sum_{n=0}^{\infty} x^{2n+1}$

17. $y_1(x) = c_0 \left[1 + \frac{1}{4}x^2 - \frac{7}{4 \cdot 4!}x^4 \right.$

$$\left. + \frac{23 \cdot 7}{8 \cdot 6!}x^6 - \cdots \right]$$

$y_2(x) = c_1 \left[x - \frac{1}{6}x^3 + \frac{14}{2 \cdot 5!}x^5 \right.$

$$\left. - \frac{34 \cdot 14}{4 \cdot 7!}x^7 - \cdots \right]$$

C H A P T E R 6

19. $y_1(x) = c_0[1 - \frac{1}{2}x^2 + \frac{1}{6}x^3 - \frac{1}{40}x^5 + \cdots]$

$y_2(x) = c_1[x - \frac{1}{6}x^3 + \frac{1}{12}x^4 - \frac{1}{60}x^5 + \cdots]$

21. $y_1(x) = c_0[1 + \frac{1}{2}x^2 - \frac{1}{6}x^3 - \frac{1}{120}x^5 + \cdots]$

$y_2(x) = c_1[x - \frac{1}{2}x^2 + \frac{1}{6}x^3 - \frac{1}{24}x^4 + \cdots]$

23. $y_1(x) = c_0\Big[1 + \frac{1}{3!}x^3 + \frac{4}{6!}x^6$

$\qquad\qquad + \frac{7 \cdot 4}{9!}x^9 + \cdots\Big]$

$\qquad + c_1\Big[x + \frac{2}{4!}x^4 + \frac{5 \cdot 2}{7!}x^7$

$\qquad\qquad + \frac{8 \cdot 5 \cdot 2}{10!}x^{10} + \cdots\Big]$

$\qquad + \frac{1}{2!}x^2 + \frac{3}{5!}x^5 + \frac{6 \cdot 3}{8!}x^8$

$\qquad\qquad + \frac{9 \cdot 6 \cdot 3}{11!}x^{11} + \cdots$

Exercises 6.3, Page 262

1. $x = 0$, irregular singular point

3. $x = -3$, regular singular point; $x = 3$, irregular singular point

5. $x = 0, 2i, -2i$, regular singular points

7. $x = -3, 2$, regular singular points

9. $r_1 = \frac{3}{2}, r_2 = 0$;

$y(x) = C_1 x^{3/2}\Big[1 - \frac{2}{5}x + \frac{2^2}{7 \cdot 5 \cdot 2}x^2$

$\qquad\qquad - \frac{2^3}{9 \cdot 7 \cdot 5 \cdot 3!}x^3 + \cdots\Big]$

$\qquad + C_2\Big[1 + 2x - 2x^2$

$\qquad\qquad + \frac{2^3}{3 \cdot 3!}x^3 - \cdots\Big]$

11. $r_1 = \frac{7}{8}, r_2 = 0$;

$y(x) = C_1 x^{7/8}\Big[1 - \frac{2}{15}x + \frac{2^2}{23 \cdot 15 \cdot 2}x^2$

$\qquad\qquad - \frac{2^3}{31 \cdot 23 \cdot 15 \cdot 3!}x^3 + \cdots\Big]$

$\qquad + C_2\Big[1 - 2x + \frac{2^2}{9 \cdot 2}x^2$

$\qquad\qquad - \frac{2^3}{17 \cdot 9 \cdot 3!}x^3 + \cdots\Big]$

13. $r_1 = \frac{1}{3}, r_2 = 0$;

$y(x) = C_1 x^{1/3}\Big[1 + \frac{1}{3}x + \frac{1}{3^2 \cdot 2}x^2$

$\qquad\qquad + \frac{1}{3^3 \cdot 3!}x^3 + \cdots\Big]$

$\qquad + C_2\Big[1 + \frac{1}{2}x + \frac{1}{5 \cdot 2}x^2$

$\qquad\qquad + \frac{1}{8 \cdot 5 \cdot 2}x^3 + \cdots\Big]$

15. $r_1 = \frac{5}{2}, r_2 = 0$;

$y(x) = C_1 x^{5/2}\Big[1 + \frac{2 \cdot 2}{7}x + \frac{2^2 \cdot 3}{9 \cdot 7}x^2$

$\qquad\qquad + \frac{2^3 \cdot 4}{11 \cdot 9 \cdot 7}x^3 + \cdots\Big]$

$\qquad + C_2\Big[1 + \frac{1}{3}x - \frac{1}{6}x^2 - \frac{1}{6}x^3 - \cdots\Big]$

17. $r_1 = \frac{2}{3}, r_2 = \frac{1}{3}$,

$y(x) = C_1 x^{2/3}[1 - \frac{1}{2}x + \frac{5}{28}x^2 - \frac{1}{21}x^3 + \cdots]$

$\qquad + C_2 x^{1/3}[1 - \frac{1}{2}x + \frac{1}{5}x^2 - \frac{7}{120}x^3 + \cdots]$

19. $r_1 = 0, r_2 = -1$;

$y(x) = C_1 x^{-1} \displaystyle\sum_{n=0}^{\infty} \frac{1}{(2n)!}x^{2n}$

$$+ C_2 x^{-1} \sum_{n=0}^{\infty} \frac{1}{(2n+1)!} x^{2n+1}$$

$$= \frac{1}{x} [C_1 \cosh x + C_2 \sinh x]$$

21. $r_1 = 4, r_2 = 0$;

$$y(x) = C_1 \left[1 + \frac{2}{3} x + \frac{1}{3} x^2 \right]$$

$$+ C_2 \sum_{n=0}^{\infty} (n+1) x^{n+4}$$

23. $r_1 = r_2 = 0$;

$$y(x) = C_1 y_1(x) + C_2 \left[y_1(x) \ln x + y_1(x) \right.$$

$$\left. \times \left(-x + \frac{1}{4} x^2 - \frac{1}{3 \cdot 3!} x^3 + \frac{1}{4 \cdot 4!} x^4 - \cdots \right) \right],$$

where $y_1(x) = \sum_{n=0}^{\infty} \frac{1}{n!} x^n = e^x$

25. $r_1 = r_2 = 0$;

$$y(x) = C_1 y_1(x) + C_2 [y_1(x) \ln x + y_1(x)$$

$$\times (2x + \tfrac{5}{4} x^2 + \tfrac{23}{27} x^3 + \cdots)],$$

where $y_1(x) = \sum_{n=0}^{\infty} \frac{(-1)^n}{(n!)^{2n}} x^n$

27. $r_1 = r_2 = 1$;

$$y(x) = C_1 x e^{-x} + C_2 x e^{-x}$$

$$\times \left[\ln x + x + \frac{1}{4} x^2 + \frac{1}{3 \cdot 3!} x^3 + \cdots \right]$$

29. $r_1 = 2, r_2 = 0$;

$$y(x) = C_1 x^2 + C_2 \left[\frac{1}{2} x^2 \ln x - \frac{1}{2} + x \right.$$

$$\left. - \frac{1}{3!} x^3 + \cdots \right]$$

31. The method of Frobenius yields only the trivial solution $y(x) \equiv 0$.

33. There is a regular singular point at ∞.

35. There is a regular singular point at ∞.

Exercises 6.4, Page 271

1. (a) $\Gamma(1 + \alpha) = \displaystyle\int_0^{\infty} t^{\alpha} e^{-t} \, dt$

$$= - e^{-t} t^{\alpha} \Big|_0^{\infty}$$

$$+ \alpha \int_0^{\infty} t^{\alpha-1} e^{-t} \, dt$$

$$= \alpha \Gamma(\alpha) \text{ for } \alpha > 0$$

(b) $\Gamma(1) = \displaystyle\int_0^{\infty} e^{-t} \, dt = 1$

(c) $\Gamma(1 + n) = n \Gamma(n)$

$\Gamma(2) = 1 \cdot \Gamma(1) = 1$

$\Gamma(3) = 2 \cdot \Gamma(2) = 2 \cdot 1 = 2!$

$\Gamma(4) = 3 \cdot \Gamma(3) = 3 \cdot 2! = 3!$

and so on. The result can be proved by induction.

3. Using the hint we can write

$$x J_v'(x) = - v \sum_{n=0}^{\infty} \frac{(-1)^n}{n! \Gamma(1+v+n)} \left(\frac{x}{2} \right)^{2n+v}$$

$$+ 2 \sum_{n=0}^{\infty} \frac{(-1)^n (n+v)}{n! (n+v) \Gamma(n+v)} \left(\frac{x}{2} \right)^{2n+v}$$

$$= - v \sum_{n=0}^{\infty} \frac{(-1)^n}{n! \Gamma(1+v+n)} \left(\frac{x}{2} \right)^{2n+v}$$

$$+ x \sum_{n=0}^{\infty} \frac{(-1)^n}{n! \Gamma(n+v)} \left(\frac{x}{2} \right)^{2n+v-1}$$

$$= - v J_v(x) + x J_{v-1}(x).$$

5. Subtracting the equations

$$x J_v'(x) = v J_v(x) - x J_{v+1}(x)$$

$$x J_v'(x) = - v J_v(x) + x J_{v-1}(x)$$

gives $2v J_v(x) = x J_{v+1}(x) + x J_{v-1}(x)$.

7. The result from the given example

$$x J_v'(x) - v J_v(x) = - x J_{v+1}(x)$$

is a linear first-order differential equation in $J_v(x)$. Dividing by x we find the integrating factor is $x^{-\nu}$. It follows from this theory that after multiplying both sides of the equation by the integrating factor we must have

$$\frac{d}{dx}[x^{-\nu}J_\nu(x)] = -x^{-\nu}J_{\nu+1}(x).$$

9. $J_{-1/2}(x) = \sqrt{\dfrac{2}{\pi x}}\cos x$

11. If we let $t = \lambda x$, the differential equation becomes

$$t^2 y'' + t y' + (t^2 - \nu^2)y = 0.$$

Since the solution of the last equation is

$$y = c_1 J_\nu(t) + c_2 J_{-\nu}(t)$$

we find

$$y = c_1 J_\nu(\lambda x) + c_2 J_{-\nu}(\lambda x), \quad \nu \neq \text{integer.}$$

13. After using the change of variables, the differential equation becomes

$$x^2 v'' + x v' + (\lambda^2 x^2 - \tfrac{1}{4})v = 0.$$

Since the solution of the last equation is

$$v = c_1 J_{1/2}(\lambda x) + c_2 J_{-1/2}(\lambda x)$$

we find

$$y = c_1 x^{-1/2} J_{1/2}(\lambda x) + c_2 x^{-1/2} J_{-1/2}(\lambda x).$$

15. After using the change of variables, the differential equation becomes

$$xy'' + (1 + 2n)y' + xy$$

$$= x^{-n-1}[x^2 J_n'' + x J_n' + (x^2 - n^2)J_n]$$

$$= x^{-n-1} \cdot 0 = 0.$$

17. (a) $y = x J_1(x)$
     (b) $y = x^{-1} J_1(x)$
     (c) $y = x^3 J_3(x)$

19. (a) $P_5(x) = \tfrac{1}{8}(63x^5 - 70x^3 + 15x)$

$$P_6(x) = \tfrac{1}{16}(231x^6 - 315x^4$$
$$+ 105x^2 - 5)$$

     (b) $y = P_5(x)$ satisfies $(1 - x^2)y'' - 2xy'$
     $+ 30y = 0$.
     $y = P_6(x)$ satisfies $(1 - x^2)y'' - 2xy'$
     $+ 42y = 0$.

21. If $x = \cos\theta$ then $\dfrac{dy}{d\theta} = \dfrac{dy}{dx}\dfrac{dx}{d\theta} = -\sin\theta\dfrac{dy}{dx}$

and $\dfrac{d^2y}{d\theta^2} = \sin^2\theta\dfrac{d^2y}{dx^2} - \cos\theta\dfrac{dy}{dx}$. Now the original equation can be written as

$$\frac{d^2y}{d\theta^2} + \frac{\cos\theta}{\sin\theta}\frac{dy}{d\theta} + n(n+1)y = 0$$

and so

$$\sin^2\theta\frac{d^2y}{dx^2} - 2\cos\theta\frac{dy}{dx} + n(n+1)y = 0.$$

since $x = \cos\theta$ and $\sin^2\theta = 1 - \cos^2\theta = 1 - x^2$ we obtain

$$(1 - x^2)\frac{d^2y}{dx^2} - 2x\frac{dy}{dx} + n(n+1)y = 0.$$

23. By the binomial theorem we have formally

$$(1 - 2xt + t^2)^{-1/2} =$$
$$1 + \frac{1}{2}(2xt - t^2) + \frac{1\cdot 3}{2^2 2!}$$
$$\times (2xt - t^2)^2 + \cdots.$$

Grouping by powers of t, we then find

$$(1 - 2xt + t^2)^{-1/2} = 1 \cdot t^0 + x \cdot t$$
$$+ \tfrac{1}{2}(3x^2 - 1)t^2 + \cdots$$
$$= P_0(x)t^0 + P_1(x)t$$
$$+ P_2(x)t^2 + \cdots.$$

25. For $k = 1$, $P_2(x) = \tfrac{1}{2}[3xP_1(x) - P_0(x)]$
$$= \tfrac{1}{2}(3x^2 - 1).$$

For $k = 2$, $P_3(x) = \tfrac{1}{3}[5xP_2(x) - 2P_1(x)]$
$$= \tfrac{1}{3}[5x \cdot \tfrac{1}{2}(3x^2 - 1)$$
$$- 2x]$$
$$= \tfrac{1}{2}(5x^3 - 3x).$$

For $k = 3$, $P_4(x) = \tfrac{1}{4}[7xP_3(x) - 3P_2(x)]$
$$= \tfrac{1}{4}[7x \cdot \tfrac{1}{2}(5x^3 - 3x)$$
$$- \tfrac{3}{2}(3x^2 - 1)]$$
$$= \tfrac{1}{8}(35x^4 - 30x^2 + 3).$$

27. For $n = 0, 1, 2, 3$, the value of the integral is 2, 2/3, 2/5, and 2/7, respectively. In general

$$\int_{-1}^{1} P_n^2(x)\,dx = \frac{2}{2n+1}, \quad n = 0, 1, 2, \ldots$$

29. $c_0 = 0$, $c_1 = 3/5$, $c_2 = 0$, $c_3 = 2/5$

31. (a) The equation becomes

$$r^2 R''\Theta + 2rR'\Theta = -R\Theta''$$
$$- \frac{\cos\theta}{\sin\theta}R\Theta'.$$

By dividing both sides by $R\Theta$ we obtain

$$r^2\frac{R''}{R} + 2r\frac{R'}{R} = -\frac{\Theta''}{\Theta} - \frac{\cos\theta}{\sin\theta}\frac{\Theta'}{\Theta}$$

(b) If both sides of the equation are equal to $n(n+1)$, then the left side simplifies to

$$r^2 R'' + 2rR' - n(n+1)R = 0$$

whereas the right side simplifies to

$$\sin\theta\,\Theta'' + \cos\theta\,\Theta' + n(n+1)\Theta = 0.$$

(c) The first equation in (b) is a Cauchy–Euler differential equation with general solution

$$R = c_1 r^{-n-1} + c_2 r^n.$$

By problem 21, a particular solution of the second equation in part (b) is

$$\Theta = P_n(\cos\theta).$$

Chapter 6 Review Exercises, Page 279

1. $y(x) = c_1 x^{-3} + c_2 x^{-3}\ln x + c_3 x^{-1/2}$

3. $y(x) = c_1 x^2 + c_2 x^3 + x^4 - x^2\ln x$

5. $y_1(x) = c_0\left[1 - \frac{1}{3\cdot 2}x^3 + \frac{1}{6\cdot 5\cdot 3\cdot 2}x^6\right.$

$$\left. - \frac{1}{9\cdot 8\cdot 6\cdot 5\cdot 3\cdot 2}x^9 + \cdots\right]$$

$$y_2(x) = c_1\left[x - \frac{1}{4\cdot 3}x^4 + \frac{1}{7\cdot 6\cdot 4\cdot 3}x^7\right.$$

$$\left. - \frac{1}{10\cdot 9\cdot 7\cdot 6\cdot 4\cdot 3}x^{10} + \cdots\right]$$

7. $y_1(x) = c_0[1 + \frac{3}{2}x^2 + \frac{1}{2}x^3 + \frac{5}{8}x^4 + \cdots]$

$y_2(x) = c_1[x + \frac{1}{2}x^3 + \frac{1}{4}x^4 + \cdots]$

9. $r_1 = 1, r_2 = -\frac{1}{2}$;

$$y(x) = C_1 x\left[1 + \frac{1}{5}x + \frac{1}{7\cdot 5\cdot 2}x^2\right.$$

$$\left. + \frac{1}{9\cdot 7\cdot 5\cdot 3\cdot 2}x^3 + \cdots\right]$$

$$+ C_2 x^{-1/2}\left[1 - x - \frac{1}{2}x^2\right.$$

$$\left. - \frac{1}{3^2\cdot 2}x^3 - \cdots\right]$$

11. $r_1 = 3, r_2 = 0$;

$$y(x) = C_1 y_1(x)$$

$$+ C_2\left[-\frac{1}{36}y_1(x)\ln x + y_1(x)\right.$$

$$\left. \times \left(-\frac{1}{3}\frac{1}{x^3} + \frac{1}{4}\frac{1}{x^2} + \frac{1}{16}\frac{1}{x} + \cdots\right)\right]$$

13. $r_1 = r_2 = 0$; $y(x) = C_1 e^x + C_2 e^x\ln x$

15. Given $y = \sqrt{x}J_v(ax)$, we have

$$y' = a\sqrt{x}J_v'(ax)$$

$$+ \frac{1}{2}x^{-1/2}J_v(ax),$$

and $y'' = a^2\sqrt{x}J_v''(ax)$

$$+ ax^{-1/2}J_v'(ax)$$

$$- \frac{1}{4}x^{-3/2}J_v(ax).$$

Then

$$4x^2 y'' + (4a^2 x^2 - 4v^2 + 1)y$$

$$= 4a^2 x^{5/2}J_v''(ax) + 4ax^{3/2}J_v'(ax)$$

$$- x^{1/2}J_v(ax) + 4a^2 x^{5/2}J_v(ax)$$

$$- 4v^2 x^{1/2}J_v(ax) + x^{1/2}J_v(ax)$$

$$= 4x^{1/2}[a^2x^2J_\nu''(ax) + axJ_\nu'(ax)$$
$$+ (a^2x^2 - v^2)J_\nu(ax)$$
$$= 4\sqrt{x}[(ax)^2J_\nu''(ax) + (ax)J_\nu'(ax)$$
$$+ ((ax)^2 - v^2)J_\nu(ax)] = 0,$$

since

$$(ax)^2J_\nu''(ax) + (ax)J_\nu'(ax)$$
$$+ ((ax)^2 - v^2)J_\nu(ax)$$

is Bessel's equation in *ax*.

17. $y(x) = C_1\sqrt{x}J_{1/2}(x) + C_2\sqrt{x}J_{-1/2}(x)$

19. $c_0 = -9, c_1 = 37/5, c_2 = -2, c_3 = 8/5$

(b) $\dfrac{1}{2}\left(\dfrac{s}{s^2 + 1} - \dfrac{s}{s^2 + 9}\right)$

(c) $\dfrac{1}{2}\left(\dfrac{3}{s^2 + 9} - \dfrac{1}{s^2 + 1}\right)$

19. $1 + 3t + \frac{3}{2}t^2 + \frac{1}{6}t^3$

21. $\frac{1}{4}e^{-t/4}$ 23. $\cos\dfrac{t}{2}$

25. $\frac{1}{3} - \frac{1}{3}e^{-3t}$

27. $-\frac{1}{3}e^{-t} + \frac{8}{15}e^{2t} - \frac{1}{5}e^{-3t}$

29. $\frac{1}{2}e^t - \frac{1}{2}\cos t + \frac{1}{2}\sin t$

31. $\frac{1}{8}e^{2t} - \frac{1}{8}e^{-2t} + \frac{1}{2}te^{-2t}$

33. **(a)** $\dfrac{1}{s}$ **(b)** $\dfrac{1}{s - 3}$

Exercises 7.1, Page 295

1. $\dfrac{2}{s}e^{-s} - \dfrac{1}{s}$

3. $\dfrac{1}{s^2} - \dfrac{1}{s^2}e^{-s}$

5. $\dfrac{1}{s^2 + 2s + 2}$

7. $\dfrac{2}{s^2 + 16}$

9. Use $\sinh kt = \dfrac{e^{kt} - e^{-kt}}{2}$ to show that

$$\mathcal{L}\{\sinh kt\} = \dfrac{k}{s^2 - k^2}$$

11. $\dfrac{8}{s^3} - \dfrac{15}{s^2 + 9}$

13. $\dfrac{8}{s(s^2 - 4)}$

15. $\dfrac{s^2 + 8}{s(s^2 + 16)}$

17. **(a)** $\dfrac{1}{2}\left(\dfrac{s}{s^2 + 9} + \dfrac{s}{s^2 + 1}\right)$

Exercises 7.2, Page 309

1. $\dfrac{1}{(s - 10)^2}$

3. $\dfrac{3}{(s - 1)^2 + 9}$

5. $\dfrac{3}{(s - 5)^2 - 9}$

7. $\frac{1}{2}te^{-2t}$

9. $e^{-2t}\cos t - 2e^{-2t}\sin t$

11. $5 - t - 5e^{-t} - 4te^{-t} - \frac{3}{2}t^2e^{-t}$

13. $e^{-t} - te^{-t}$

15. $\dfrac{s + 1}{s[(s + 1)^2 + 1]}$

17. $\dfrac{e^{-2s}}{s + 1}$

19. $\dfrac{e^{-s}}{s^2} + \dfrac{e^{-s}}{s}$

21. $\frac{1}{2}(t - 2)^2\mathscr{U}(t - 2)$

23. $\dfrac{s^2 - 4}{(s^2 + 4)^2}$

25. $\dfrac{6s^2 + 2}{(s^2 - 1)^3}$

27. $\dfrac{1}{(s - 2)^2} + \dfrac{2}{(s - 3)^2} + \dfrac{1}{(s - 4)^2}$

29. $\dfrac{4}{s^2 + 64}$

31. $\frac{1}{2} t e^{-t} \sin t$

33. $-\frac{1}{3} e^{-t} + \frac{1}{3} e^{2t}$

35. $1 - \cos t$

37. $\frac{1}{4} t \sin 2t$

39. $\dfrac{e^{-t} - e^{3t}}{t}$

41. $\dfrac{\sin 2t}{t}$

43. $\ln \dfrac{s + 1}{s - 1}$

45. (a) $\dfrac{1}{(s - 2)(s^2 + 1)}$

(b) $\dfrac{48}{s^8}$

(c) $\dfrac{s - 1}{(s + 1)(s^2 - 2s + 2)}$

47. By periodicity of $f(t)$, we have $f(t) = f(t - T)$ and so

$$\mathcal{L}\{f(t)\} = \int_0^T e^{-st} f(t)\, dt$$

$$+ \int_T^\infty e^{-st} f(t - T)\, dt$$

$$= \int_0^T e^{-st} f(t)\, dt$$

$$+ \int_T^\infty e^{-st} f(t - T)\, dt$$

(letting $u = t - T$)

$$= \int_0^T e^{-st} f(t)\, dt$$

$$+ e^{-sT} \int_0^\infty e^{-su} f(u)\, du$$

$$= \int_0^T e^{-st} f(t)\, dt + e^{-sT} \mathcal{L}\{f(t)\}.$$

Solving for $\mathcal{L}\{f(t)\}$ gives

$$(1 - e^{-sT}) \mathcal{L}\{f(t)\} = \int_0^T s^{-st} f(t)\, dt$$

$$\mathcal{L}\{f(t)\} = \dfrac{1}{1 - e^{-sT}} \int_0^T e^{-st} f(t)\, dt.$$

49. $f(t) = t^2 \mathcal{U}(t - 1)$

$$= (t - 1)^2 \mathcal{U}(t - 1) + 2(t - 1)\mathcal{U}(t - 1)$$

$$+ \mathcal{U}(t - 1);$$

$$\mathcal{L}\{f(t)\} = \dfrac{e^{-s}}{s^3} + 2\dfrac{e^{-s}}{s^2} + \dfrac{e^{-s}}{s}$$

51. $f(t) = e^t \mathcal{U}(t - 2)$

$$= e^2 e^{t-2} \mathcal{U}(t - 2);$$

$$\mathcal{L}\{f(t)\} = e^2 \cdot \dfrac{e^{-2s}}{s - 1}$$

Exercises 7.3, Page 319

1. $y = \frac{4}{3} e^{-t} - \frac{1}{3} e^{-4t}$

3. $y = \frac{1}{9} t + \frac{2}{27} - \frac{2}{27} e^{3t} + \frac{10}{9} t e^{3t}$

5. $y = \frac{1}{20} t^5 e^{2t}$

7. $y = \cos t - \frac{1}{2} \sin t - \frac{1}{2} t \cos t$

9. $y = \frac{1}{2} - \frac{1}{2} e^t \cos t + \frac{1}{2} e^t \sin t$

11. $y = \cos t$

13. $y = \frac{1}{3} t^3 + \frac{1}{2} c t^2$

15. $y = c \displaystyle\sum_{n=0}^\infty \dfrac{(-1)^n t^{2n}}{2^{2n}(n!)^2}$, the student may recognize this as the Bessel function $J_0(t)$.

17. $\mathcal{L}\{t^2 y'' - 2ty' + 2y\}$

$$= s^2 Y''(s) + 6s Y'(s) + 6Y$$

which would result in another Cauchy–Euler equation.

C.
H
A.
P
T
E
R
7

19. $y = -\frac{1}{4} + \frac{1}{2}t + \frac{1}{4}e^{-2t} - \frac{1}{4}\mathcal{U}(t-1)$

$\qquad - \frac{1}{2}(t-1)\mathcal{U}(t-1)$

$\qquad + \frac{1}{4}e^{-2(t-1)}\mathcal{U}(t-1)$

21. $y = \cos 2t - \frac{1}{6}\sin 2(t-2\pi)\mathcal{U}(t-2\pi)$

$\qquad + \frac{1}{3}\sin(t-2\pi)\mathcal{U}(t-2\pi)$

23. $f(t) = \sin t$

25. $f(t) = -\frac{1}{8}e^{-t} + \frac{1}{8}e^{t} + \frac{3}{4}te^{t} + \frac{1}{4}t^2 e^{t}$

27. $f(t) = e^{-t}$

29. $f(t) = \frac{3}{8}e^{2t} + \frac{1}{8}e^{-2t} + \frac{1}{2}\cos 2t + \frac{1}{4}\sin 2t$

31. $y = \sin t - \frac{1}{2}t\sin t$

33. $i(t) = \dfrac{1}{101}e^{-10t} - \dfrac{1}{101}\cos t + \dfrac{10}{101}\sin t$

$\qquad - \dfrac{10}{101}e^{-10(t-3\pi/2)}\mathcal{U}\left(t - \dfrac{3\pi}{2}\right)$

$\qquad + \dfrac{10}{101}\cos\left(t - \dfrac{3\pi}{2}\right)\mathcal{U}\left(t - \dfrac{3\pi}{2}\right)$

$\qquad + \dfrac{1}{101}\sin\left(t - \dfrac{3\pi}{2}\right)\mathcal{U}\left(t - \dfrac{3\pi}{2}\right)$

35. $q(t) = \frac{3}{5}e^{-10t} + 6te^{-10t} - \frac{3}{5}\cos 10t;$

$\qquad i(t) = -60te^{-10t} + 6\sin 10t;$

$\qquad$ steady-state current is $6\sin 10t$

37. $x(t) = -\dfrac{3}{2}e^{-7t/2}\cos\dfrac{\sqrt{15}}{2}t$

$\qquad - \dfrac{7\sqrt{15}}{10}e^{-7t/2}\sin\dfrac{\sqrt{15}}{2}$

Chapter 7 Review Exercises Page 325

1. $\dfrac{2}{s^3} - \dfrac{2}{s^2} + \dfrac{1}{s}$

3. $\dfrac{1}{s^2} - \dfrac{2}{s^2}e^{-s}$

5. $\dfrac{8}{s^2 + 64} - \dfrac{1}{(s-3)^2} + \dfrac{8}{(s+2)^3}$

7. $\dfrac{e^{-3s}}{s+1}$

9. $e^{3t}\cos 4t + \frac{3}{4}e^{3t}\sin 4t$

11. $\dfrac{e^{-4t}\sin t}{t}$

13. $\dfrac{1}{4}\dfrac{s}{s^2+1} - \dfrac{1}{4}\dfrac{s}{s^2+9}$

15. $y = 5te^{t} + \frac{1}{2}t^2 e^{t}$

17. $y = 1 + t + \frac{1}{2}t^2$

19. $q(t) = \frac{1}{10} - \frac{1}{10}e^{-10t}\cos 10t$

$\qquad - \frac{1}{10}e^{-10t}\sin 10t - \frac{1}{10}\mathcal{U}(t-5)$

$\qquad + \frac{1}{10}e^{-10(t-5)}\cos 10(t-5)\mathcal{U}(t-5)$

$\qquad + \frac{1}{10}e^{-10(t-5)}\sin 10(t-5)\mathcal{U}(t-5)$

Exercises 8.1, Page 338

1. $(D+3)(2D-1)y = (D+3)(2y' - y)$

$\qquad = 2y'' - y' + 6y' - 3y$

$\qquad = 2y'' + 5y' - 3y$

$\qquad (2D-1)(D+3)y = (2D-1)(y' + 3y)$

$\qquad = 2y'' + 6y' - y' - 3y$

$\qquad = 2y'' + 5y' - 3y$

3. $(D-1)(D^2 + D + 1)(D+1)$

$\qquad\qquad \times (D^2 - D + 1)y = 0$

5. $x = c_1\cos t + c_2\sin t + t + 1$

$\qquad y = c_1\sin t - c_2\cos t + t - 1$

7. $x = c_1 e^{t} + c_2 te^{t}$

$\qquad y = (c_1 - c_2)e^{t} + c_2 te^{t}$

9. $x = \frac{1}{2}c_1\sin t + \frac{1}{2}c_2\cos t - 2c_3\sin\sqrt{6}t$

$\qquad - 2c_4\cos\sqrt{6}t$

$\qquad y = c_1\sin t + c_2\cos t + c_3\sin\sqrt{6}t$

$\qquad + c_4\cos\sqrt{6}t$

11. $x = c_1 e^{2t} + c_2 e^{-2t} + c_3 \sin 2t$
$\quad + c_4 \cos 2t + \frac{1}{5}e^t$
$y = c_1 e^{2t} + c_2 e^{-2t} - c_3 \sin 2t$
$\quad - c_4 \cos 2t - \frac{1}{5}e^t$

13. $x = c_1 - c_2 \cos t + c_3 \sin t + \frac{17}{15}e^{3t}$
$y = c_1 + c_2 \sin t + c_3 \cos t - \frac{4}{15}e^{3t}$

15. $x = c_1 e^{4t} + \frac{4}{3}e^t$
$y = -\frac{3}{4}c_1 e^{4t} + c_2 + 5e^t$

17. $x = c_1 + c_2 t + c_3 e^t + te^t$
$y = -c_1 - c_2 - c_2 t - c_3 e^t - te^t + e^t$

19. $x = c_1 e^t + c_2 e^{-t/2} \sin \dfrac{\sqrt{3}}{2}t$

$\quad + c_3 e^{-t/2} \cos \dfrac{\sqrt{3}}{2}t$

$y = c_1 e^t + \left(-\dfrac{1}{2}c_2 - \dfrac{\sqrt{3}}{2}c_3\right) e^{-t/2} \sin \dfrac{\sqrt{3}}{2}t$

$\quad + \left(\dfrac{\sqrt{3}}{2}c_2 - \dfrac{1}{2}c_3\right) e^{-t/2} \cos \dfrac{\sqrt{3}}{2}t$

$z = c_1 e^t + \left(-\dfrac{1}{2}c_2 + \dfrac{\sqrt{3}}{2}c_3\right) e^{-t/2} \sin \dfrac{\sqrt{3}}{2}t$

$\quad + \left(-\dfrac{\sqrt{3}}{2}c_2 - \dfrac{1}{2}c_3\right) e^{-t/2} \cos \dfrac{\sqrt{3}}{2}t$

21. $x = -6c_1 e^{-t} - 3c_2 e^{-2t} + 2c_3 e^{3t}$
$y = c_1 e^{-t} + c_2 e^{-2t} + c_3 e^{3t}$
$z = 5c_1 e^{-t} + c_2 e^{-2t} + c_3 e^{3t}$

23. $Dx - Dy = 0$
$(D-1)x - y = 0$

Exercises 8.2, Page 347

1. $x = -\frac{1}{3}e^{-2t} + \frac{1}{3}e^t$
$y = \frac{1}{3}e^{-2t} + \frac{2}{3}e^t$

3. $x = -\cos 3t - \frac{5}{3}\sin 3t$
$y = 2\cos 3t - \frac{7}{3}\sin 3t$

5. $x = -2e^{3t} + \frac{5}{2}e^{2t} - \frac{1}{2}$
$y = \frac{8}{3}e^{3t} - \frac{5}{2}e^{2t} - \frac{1}{6}$

7. $x = -\frac{1}{2}t - \frac{3}{4}\sqrt{2}\sin \sqrt{2}t$
$y = -\frac{1}{2}t + \frac{3}{4}\sqrt{2}\sin t$

9. $x = 8 + \dfrac{2}{3!}t^3 + \dfrac{1}{4!}t^4$

$y = -\dfrac{2}{3!}t^3 + \dfrac{1}{4!}t^4$

11. $x = \frac{1}{2}t^2 + t + 1 - e^{-t}$
$y = -\frac{1}{3} + \frac{1}{3}e^{-t} + \frac{1}{3}te^{-t}$

13. $x_1 = \dfrac{3}{5}\sin t + \dfrac{\sqrt{6}}{15}\sin \sqrt{6}t + \dfrac{2}{5}\cos t$

$\quad - \dfrac{2}{5}\cos \sqrt{6}t$

$x_2 = \dfrac{6}{5}\sin t - \dfrac{\sqrt{6}}{30}\sin \sqrt{6}t + \dfrac{4}{5}\cos t$

$\quad + \dfrac{1}{5}\cos \sqrt{6}t$

15. $i_2 = \frac{100}{9} - \frac{100}{9}e^{-900t}$
$i_3 = \frac{80}{9} - \frac{80}{9}e^{-900t}$
$i_1 = 20 - 20e^{-900t}$

17. $i_1(t) = \frac{6}{5} - \frac{6}{5}e^{-100t}\cos 100t$
$i_2(t) = \frac{6}{5} - \frac{6}{5}e^{-100t}\cos 100t$
$\quad - \frac{6}{5}e^{-100t}\sin 100t$

19. $i_2 = -\frac{20}{13}e^{-2t} + \frac{375}{1469}e^{-15t} + \frac{145}{113}\cos t$
$\quad + \frac{85}{113}\sin t$
$i_3 = \frac{30}{13}e^{-2t} + \frac{250}{1469}e^{-15t} - \frac{280}{113}\cos t$
$\quad + \frac{810}{113}\sin t$

21. $\theta_1(t) = \dfrac{1}{4}\cos\dfrac{2}{\sqrt{3}}t + \dfrac{3}{4}\cos 2t$

$\theta_2(t) = \dfrac{1}{2}\cos\dfrac{2}{\sqrt{3}}t - \dfrac{3}{2}\cos 2t$

Exercises 8.3, Page 356

1. $x_1' = x_2$
$x_2' = -4x_1 + 3x_2 + \sin t$

3. $x_1' = x_2$
$x_2' = x_3$
$x_3' = 10x_1 - 6x_2 + 3x_3 + t^2 + 1$

5. $x_1' = x_2$
$x_2' = x_3$
$x_3' = x_4$
$x_4' = -x_1 - 4x_2 + 2x_3 + t$

7. $x_1' = x_2$
$x_2' = x_3$
$x_3' = -x_1^2 + x_1x_3 + 2t - 1$

9. $\dfrac{d^2y}{dt^2} - 7\dfrac{dy}{dt} + 13y = 3t$

11. $Dx = t^2 + 5t - 2$
$Dy = -x + 5t - 2$

13. The system is degenerate.

15. $Dx = u$
$Dy = v$
$Du = w$
$Dv = 10t^2 - 4u + 3v$
$Dw = 4x + 4v - 3w$

17. $\dfrac{dx_1}{dt} = 6 - \dfrac{2}{25}x_1 + \dfrac{1}{50}x_2$

$\dfrac{dx_2}{dt} = \dfrac{2}{25}x_1 - \dfrac{2}{25}x_2$

Exercises 8.4, Page 372

1. $\begin{pmatrix} -14 \\ 1 \end{pmatrix}$

3. $\begin{pmatrix} -38 \\ -2 \end{pmatrix}$

5. $\begin{pmatrix} 0 \\ 0 \end{pmatrix}$

7. $\dfrac{d}{dt}\begin{pmatrix} x \\ y \\ z \end{pmatrix} = \begin{pmatrix} 1 & -1 & 0 \\ 1 & 0 & 2 \\ -1 & 0 & 1 \end{pmatrix}\begin{pmatrix} x \\ y \\ z \end{pmatrix}$

9. $\dfrac{d}{dt}\begin{pmatrix} x \\ y \end{pmatrix} = \begin{pmatrix} -3 & 4 \\ 5 & 9 \end{pmatrix}\begin{pmatrix} x \\ y \end{pmatrix} + \begin{pmatrix} \sin 2t \\ 4\cos 2t \end{pmatrix}e^{-t}$

11. $\dfrac{d\mathbf{X}}{dt} = \begin{pmatrix} -5e^{-5t} \\ -10e^{-5t} \end{pmatrix}$

$\begin{pmatrix} 3 & -4 \\ 4 & -7 \end{pmatrix}\mathbf{X} = \begin{pmatrix} 3-8 \\ 4-14 \end{pmatrix}e^{-5t} = \begin{pmatrix} -5 \\ -10 \end{pmatrix}e^{-5t}$

$= \dfrac{d\mathbf{X}}{dt}$

13. $\dfrac{d\mathbf{X}}{dt} = \begin{pmatrix} 0 \\ 0 \\ 0 \end{pmatrix}$

$\begin{pmatrix} 1 & 2 & 1 \\ 6 & -1 & 0 \\ -1 & -2 & -1 \end{pmatrix}\mathbf{X} = \begin{pmatrix} 1+12-13 \\ 6-6 \\ -1-12+13 \end{pmatrix}$

$= \begin{pmatrix} 0 \\ 0 \\ 0 \end{pmatrix} = \dfrac{d\mathbf{X}}{dt}$

15. $\dfrac{d\mathbf{X}}{dt} = \begin{pmatrix} 5e^t\cos t - 5e^t\sin t \\ 2e^t\cos t - 4e^t\sin t \end{pmatrix}$

$\begin{pmatrix} -2 & 5 \\ -2 & 4 \end{pmatrix}\mathbf{X} =$

$= \begin{pmatrix} -10e^t\cos t + 15e^t\cos t - 5e^t\sin t \\ -10e^t\cos t + 12e^t\cos t - 4e^t\sin t \end{pmatrix}$

$= \begin{pmatrix} 5e^t\cos t - 5e^t\sin t \\ 2e^t\cos t - 4e^t\sin t \end{pmatrix} = \dfrac{d\mathbf{X}}{dt}$

17. $\dfrac{d\mathbf{X}_p}{dt} = \begin{pmatrix} 2 \\ -1 \end{pmatrix}$

$\begin{pmatrix} 1 & 4 \\ 3 & 2 \end{pmatrix}\mathbf{X}_p + \begin{pmatrix} 2 \\ -4 \end{pmatrix}t - \begin{pmatrix} 7 \\ 18 \end{pmatrix}$

$\qquad = \begin{pmatrix} (2-4)t + 9 + 2t - 7 \\ (6-2)t + 17 - 4t - 18 \end{pmatrix}$

$\qquad = \begin{pmatrix} 2 \\ -1 \end{pmatrix} = \dfrac{d\mathbf{X}_p}{dt}$

19. $\mathbf{X}_p' = \begin{pmatrix} 2e^t + te^t \\ -te^t \end{pmatrix}$

$\begin{pmatrix} 2 & 1 \\ 3 & 4 \end{pmatrix}\mathbf{X}_p - \begin{pmatrix} 1 \\ 7 \end{pmatrix}e^t = \begin{pmatrix} 3e^t + te^t - e^t \\ 7e^t - te^t - 7e^t \end{pmatrix}$

$\qquad = \begin{pmatrix} 2e^t + te^t \\ -te^t \end{pmatrix} = \dfrac{d\mathbf{X}_p}{dt}$

21. Let $\mathbf{X}_1 = \begin{pmatrix} 6 \\ -1 \\ -5 \end{pmatrix}e^{-t}$, $\mathbf{X}_2 = \begin{pmatrix} -3 \\ 1 \\ 1 \end{pmatrix}e^{-2t}$,

$\mathbf{X}_3 = \begin{pmatrix} 2 \\ 1 \\ 1 \end{pmatrix}e^{3t}$, and

$\mathbf{A} = \begin{pmatrix} 0 & 6 & 0 \\ 1 & 0 & 1 \\ 1 & 1 & 0 \end{pmatrix}$. Then

$\mathbf{A}\mathbf{X}_1 = \begin{pmatrix} -6 \\ 1 \\ 5 \end{pmatrix}e^{-t} = \mathbf{X}_1'$,

$\mathbf{A}\mathbf{X}_2 = \begin{pmatrix} 6 \\ -2 \\ -2 \end{pmatrix}e^{-2t} = \mathbf{X}_2'$,

$\mathbf{A}\mathbf{X}_3 = \begin{pmatrix} 6 \\ 3 \\ 3 \end{pmatrix}e^{3t} = \mathbf{X}_3'$

and

$W(\mathbf{X}_1, \mathbf{X}_2, \mathbf{X}_3) = \begin{vmatrix} 6e^{-t} & -3e^{-2t} & 2e^{3t} \\ -e^{-t} & e^{-2t} & e^{3t} \\ -5e^{-t} & e^{-2t} & e^{3t} \end{vmatrix}$

$\qquad = 20 \neq 0.$

Therefore $\mathbf{X}_1, \mathbf{X}_2, \mathbf{X}_3$ are linearly independent solutions of $\mathbf{X}' = \mathbf{A}\mathbf{X}$ on $-\infty < t < \infty$ and $\mathbf{X} = c_1\mathbf{X}_1 + c_2\mathbf{X}_2 + c_3\mathbf{X}_3$, by definition, is its general solution.

23. $W(\mathbf{X}_1, \mathbf{X}_2, \mathbf{X}_3) = \begin{vmatrix} 1 & e^{-4t} & 2e^{3t} \\ 6 & -2e^{-4t} & 3e^{3t} \\ -13 & -e^{-4t} & -2e^{3t} \end{vmatrix}$

$\qquad = -84e^{-t} \neq 0.$

Therefore, $\mathbf{X}_1, \mathbf{X}_2, \mathbf{X}_3$ are linearly independent on $-\infty < t < \infty$.

25. $W(\mathbf{X}_1, \mathbf{X}_2, \mathbf{X}_3) =$

$\qquad = \begin{vmatrix} 1+t & 1 & 3+2t \\ -2+2t & -2 & -6+4t \\ 4+2t & 4 & 12+4t \end{vmatrix}$

$\qquad = 0$ for every t.

The solution vectors are linearly dependent on $-\infty < t < \infty$. Note that

$$\mathbf{X}_3 = 2\mathbf{X}_1 + \mathbf{X}_2.$$

27. The system $\mathbf{A}\mathbf{C} = \mathbf{0}$ is equivalent to

$a_{11}c_1 + a_{12}c_2 = 0$

$a_{21}c_1 + a_{22}c_2 = 0.$

Note that if

$$\mathbf{C} = \begin{pmatrix} 1 \\ -1 \end{pmatrix}$$

then $\mathbf{A}\mathbf{C} = \mathbf{0}$ is satisfied for $a_{11} = a_{12}$ and $a_{21} = a_{22}$. But $\mathbf{A}\mathbf{C} = \mathbf{0}$ is to be satisfied for *any* choice of $\mathbf{C}$. In particular if we choose

$$\mathbf{C} = \begin{pmatrix} 0 \\ 1 \end{pmatrix}$$

then $a_{12} = 0$, $a_{22} = 0$. Similarly if

$$C = \begin{pmatrix} 1 \\ 0 \end{pmatrix}$$

then it follows that $a_{11} = 0$, $a_{21} = 0$. Thus

$$A = \begin{pmatrix} 0 & 0 \\ 0 & 0 \end{pmatrix}$$

is the only matrix satisfying $AC = 0$ for every C.

Exercises 8.5, Page 389

1. $X = c_1 \begin{pmatrix} 1 \\ 2 \end{pmatrix} e^{5t} + c_2 \begin{pmatrix} 1 \\ -1 \end{pmatrix} e^{-t}$

3. $X = c_1 \begin{pmatrix} 1 \\ 3 \end{pmatrix} + c_2 \left\{ \begin{pmatrix} 1 \\ -1 \end{pmatrix} + \begin{pmatrix} 4 \\ 12 \end{pmatrix} t \right\}$

5. $X = c_1 \begin{pmatrix} 1 \\ 1 \end{pmatrix} e^{2t} + c_2 \left\{ \begin{pmatrix} -1 \\ 0 \end{pmatrix} e^{2t} + \begin{pmatrix} 3 \\ 3 \end{pmatrix} te^{2t} \right\}$

7. $X = c_1 \begin{pmatrix} \cos t \\ 2\cos t + \sin t \end{pmatrix} e^{4t}$

$\quad + c_2 \begin{pmatrix} \sin t \\ 2\sin t - \cos t \end{pmatrix} e^{4t}$

9. $X = c_1 \begin{pmatrix} 5 \\ 2 \end{pmatrix} e^{8t} + c_2 \begin{pmatrix} 1 \\ 4 \end{pmatrix} e^{-10t}$

11. $X = c_1 \begin{pmatrix} 1 \\ 0 \\ 0 \end{pmatrix} e^t + c_2 \begin{pmatrix} 2 \\ 3 \\ 1 \end{pmatrix} e^{2t} + c_1 \begin{pmatrix} 1 \\ 0 \\ 2 \end{pmatrix} e^{-t}$

13. $X = \begin{pmatrix} \frac{25}{2} \\ -25 \end{pmatrix} e^{-3t/25} + \begin{pmatrix} \frac{25}{2} \\ 25 \end{pmatrix} e^{-t/25}$

15. $X = c_1 \begin{pmatrix} 1 \\ 1 \\ 1 \end{pmatrix} e^t + c_2 \begin{pmatrix} 1 \\ 1 \\ 0 \end{pmatrix} e^{2t} + c_3 \begin{pmatrix} 1 \\ 0 \\ 1 \end{pmatrix} e^{2t}$

17. (a) $X = \begin{pmatrix} \cosh t & \sinh t \\ \sinh t & \cosh t \end{pmatrix} \begin{pmatrix} c_1 \\ c_2 \end{pmatrix}$

    (b) $X = \begin{pmatrix} e^t & 0 \\ 0 & e^{2t} \end{pmatrix} \begin{pmatrix} c_1 \\ c_2 \end{pmatrix}$

Exercises 8.6, Page 400

1. $X = c_1 \begin{pmatrix} -1 \\ 1 \end{pmatrix} e^{-t} + c_2 \begin{pmatrix} -3 \\ 1 \end{pmatrix} e^t + \begin{pmatrix} -1 \\ 3 \end{pmatrix}$

3. $X = c_1 \begin{pmatrix} 1 \\ -1 \end{pmatrix} e^{-2t} + c_2 \begin{pmatrix} 1 \\ 1 \end{pmatrix} e^{4t} + \begin{pmatrix} -\frac{1}{4} \\ \frac{3}{4} \end{pmatrix} t^2$

$\quad + \begin{pmatrix} \frac{1}{4} \\ -\frac{1}{4} \end{pmatrix} t + \begin{pmatrix} -2 \\ \frac{3}{4} \end{pmatrix}$

5. $X = c_1 \begin{pmatrix} 1 \\ -8 \end{pmatrix} e^{-3t} + c_2 \begin{pmatrix} 1 \\ -1 \end{pmatrix} e^{4t}$

$\quad + \begin{pmatrix} -\frac{13}{7} \\ \frac{13}{7} \end{pmatrix} te^{4t} + \begin{pmatrix} 0 \\ \frac{1}{7} \end{pmatrix} e^{4t}$

7. $X = c_1 \begin{pmatrix} 2 \\ 1 \end{pmatrix} e^{t/2} + c_2 \begin{pmatrix} 10 \\ 3 \end{pmatrix} e^{3t/2}$

$\quad - \begin{pmatrix} \frac{13}{2} \\ \frac{13}{4} \end{pmatrix} te^{t/2} - \begin{pmatrix} \frac{15}{2} \\ \frac{9}{4} \end{pmatrix} e^{t/2}$

9. $X = c_1 \begin{pmatrix} 1 \\ 1 \end{pmatrix} + c_2 \begin{pmatrix} 3 \\ 2 \end{pmatrix} e^t - \begin{pmatrix} 11 \\ 11 \end{pmatrix} t - \begin{pmatrix} 15 \\ 10 \end{pmatrix}$

11. $X = c_1 \begin{pmatrix} 1 \\ 1 \end{pmatrix} e^t + c_2 \begin{pmatrix} 1 \\ 3 \end{pmatrix} e^{-t} + \begin{pmatrix} 4 \\ 8 \end{pmatrix} t + \begin{pmatrix} 0 \\ -4 \end{pmatrix}$

13. (a) $X = c_1 \begin{pmatrix} \cosh t \\ \sinh t \end{pmatrix} + c_2 \begin{pmatrix} \sinh t \\ \cosh t \end{pmatrix} - \begin{pmatrix} 1 \\ 1 \end{pmatrix}$

    (b) $X = c_1 \begin{pmatrix} \cosh t \\ \sinh t \end{pmatrix} + c_2 \begin{pmatrix} \sinh t \\ \cosh t \end{pmatrix}$

    $\quad + \begin{pmatrix} \cosh t \\ \sinh t \end{pmatrix} t$

    (c) $X = c_1 \begin{pmatrix} 1 \\ 0 \end{pmatrix} e^t + c_2 \begin{pmatrix} 0 \\ 1 \end{pmatrix} e^{2t} + \begin{pmatrix} -t-1 \\ \frac{1}{2}e^{4t} \end{pmatrix}$

Exercises 8.7, Page 410

1. $X = c_1 \begin{pmatrix} 2 \\ 1 \end{pmatrix} e^t + c_2 \begin{pmatrix} 1 \\ 1 \end{pmatrix} e^{2t} + \begin{pmatrix} 3 \\ 3 \end{pmatrix} e^t + \begin{pmatrix} 4 \\ 2 \end{pmatrix} te^t$

3. $X = c_1 \begin{pmatrix} 4 \\ 1 \end{pmatrix} e^{3t} + c_2 \begin{pmatrix} -2 \\ 1 \end{pmatrix} e^{-3t} + \begin{pmatrix} -12 \\ 0 \end{pmatrix} t$

$\quad - \begin{pmatrix} \frac{4}{3} \\ \frac{4}{3} \end{pmatrix}$

5. $\mathbf{X} = c_1 \begin{pmatrix} 1 \\ -1 \end{pmatrix} e^t + c_2 \begin{pmatrix} t \\ \frac{1}{2} - t \end{pmatrix} e^t + \begin{pmatrix} \frac{1}{2} \\ -2 \end{pmatrix} e^{-t}$

7. $\mathbf{X} = c_1 \begin{pmatrix} \cos t \\ \sin t \end{pmatrix} + c_2 \begin{pmatrix} \sin t \\ -\cos t \end{pmatrix} + \begin{pmatrix} \cos t \\ \sin t \end{pmatrix} t$

$\quad + \begin{pmatrix} -\sin t \\ \cos t \end{pmatrix} \ln (\cos t)$

9. $\mathbf{X} = c_1 \begin{pmatrix} e^t \cos t \\ e^t \sin t \end{pmatrix} + c_2 \begin{pmatrix} e^t \sin t \\ -e^t \cos t \end{pmatrix}$

$\quad + \begin{pmatrix} \cos t \\ \sin t \end{pmatrix} te^t$

11. $\begin{pmatrix} 1 & 0 \\ 0 & 1 \end{pmatrix} \begin{pmatrix} a_{11} & a_{12} \\ a_{21} & a_{22} \end{pmatrix}$

$\quad = \begin{pmatrix} 1 \cdot a_{11} + 0 \cdot a_{21} & 1 \cdot a_{12} + 0 \cdot a_{22} \\ 0 \cdot a_{11} + 1 \cdot a_{21} & 0 \cdot a_{12} + 1 \cdot a_{22} \end{pmatrix}$

$\quad = \begin{pmatrix} a_{11} & a_{12} \\ a_{21} & a_{22} \end{pmatrix}$

$\begin{pmatrix} a_{11} & a_{12} \\ a_{21} & a_{22} \end{pmatrix} \begin{pmatrix} 1 & 0 \\ 0 & 1 \end{pmatrix}$

$\quad = \begin{pmatrix} a_{11} \cdot 1 + a_{12} \cdot 0 & a_{11} \cdot 0 + a_{12} \cdot 1 \\ a_{21} \cdot 1 + a_{22} \cdot 0 & a_{21} \cdot 0 + a_{22} \cdot 1 \end{pmatrix}$

$\quad = \begin{pmatrix} a_{11} & a_{12} \\ a_{21} & a_{22} \end{pmatrix}$

13. $\dfrac{d}{dt} \begin{pmatrix} a_{11}(t) & a_{12}(t) \\ a_{21}(t) & a_{22}(t) \end{pmatrix} \begin{pmatrix} x_1(t) \\ x_2(t) \end{pmatrix}$

$\quad = \dfrac{d}{dt} \begin{pmatrix} a_{11}(t)x_1(t) + a_{12}(t)x_2(t) \\ a_{21}(t)x_1(t) + a_{22}(t)x_2(t) \end{pmatrix}$

$= \begin{pmatrix} a_{11}(t)x_1'(t) + a_{11}'(t)x_1(t) + a_{12}(t)x_2'(t) + a_{12}'(t)x_2(t) \\ a_{21}(t)x_1'(t) + a_{21}'(t)x_1(t) + a_{22}(t)x_2'(t) + a_{22}'(t)x_2(t) \end{pmatrix}$

$= \begin{pmatrix} a_{11}(t)x_1'(t) + a_{12}(t)x_2'(t) + a_{11}'(t)x_1(t) + a_{12}'(t)x_2(t) \\ a_{21}(t)x_1'(t) + a_{22}(t)x_2'(t) + a_{21}'(t)x_1(t) + a_{22}'(t)x_2(t) \end{pmatrix}$

$= \begin{pmatrix} a_{11}(t) & a_{12}(t) \\ a_{21}(t) & a_{22}(t) \end{pmatrix} \begin{pmatrix} x_1'(t) \\ x_2'(t) \end{pmatrix} + \begin{pmatrix} a_{11}'(t) & a_{12}'(t) \\ a_{21}'(t) & a_{22}'(t) \end{pmatrix} \begin{pmatrix} x_1(t) \\ x_2(t) \end{pmatrix}$

$= \mathbf{A}(t)\mathbf{X}'(t) + \mathbf{A}'(t)\mathbf{X}(t)$

15. **(a)** The eigenvalues are $\lambda_1 = 0$, $\lambda_2 = 2$, and $\lambda_3 = 3$. The respective eigenvectors are

$$\begin{pmatrix} 1 \\ -1 \\ 0 \end{pmatrix}, \begin{pmatrix} 1 \\ 1 \\ 0 \end{pmatrix}, \begin{pmatrix} 0 \\ 0 \\ 1 \end{pmatrix}.$$

(b)

$$\Phi(t) = \begin{pmatrix} 1 & e^{2t} & 0 \\ -1 & e^{2t} & 0 \\ 0 & 0 & e^{3t} \end{pmatrix}$$

(c)

$$\Phi^{-1}(t) = \begin{pmatrix} \frac{1}{2} & -\frac{1}{2} & 0 \\ \frac{1}{2}e^{-2t} & \frac{1}{2}e^{2t} & 0 \\ 0 & 0 & e^{-3t} \end{pmatrix}$$

(d)

$$\mathbf{X} = c_1 \begin{pmatrix} 1 \\ -1 \\ 0 \end{pmatrix} + c_2 \begin{pmatrix} 1 \\ 1 \\ 0 \end{pmatrix} e^{2t} + c_3 \begin{pmatrix} 0 \\ 0 \\ 1 \end{pmatrix} e^{3t}$$

$$+ \begin{pmatrix} -\frac{1}{4}e^{2t} + \frac{1}{2}te^{2t} \\ -e^t + \frac{1}{4}e^{2t} + \frac{1}{2}te^{2t} \\ \frac{1}{2}t^2 e^{3t} \end{pmatrix}$$

Chapter 8 Review Exercises, Page 414

1. Let $w = (D^2 + 2D + 1)y$ then

$(D - 1)w = Dw - w$

$\quad = D(D^2 + 2D + 1)y$

$\quad - (D^2 + 2D + 1)y$

$\quad = D^3 y + 2D^2 y + Dy - D^2 y$

$\quad - 2Dy - Dy$

$\quad = D^3 y + D^2 y - Dy - y.$

Now if $w = (D^2 - 1)y$ then

$(D + 1)w = Dw + w$

$\quad = D(D^2 - 1)y + (D^2 - 1)y$

$\quad = D^3 y - Dy + D^2 y - y$

$\quad = D^3 y + D^2 y - Dy - y.$

3. $x = -c_1e^t - \frac{3}{2}c_2e^{2t} + \frac{5}{2}$

$y = \quad c_1e^t + \quad c_2e^{2t} - 3$

5. $x = -\frac{1}{4} + \frac{9}{8}e^{-2t} + \frac{1}{8}e^{2t}$

$y = t + \frac{9}{4}e^{-2t} - \frac{1}{4}e^{2t}$

7. $Dx = u$

$Dy = v$

$Du = -2u + v - 2x - \ln t + 10t - 4$

$Dv = -\quad u \quad - \quad x \quad + 5t - 2$

9. $\mathbf{X}_c = c_1\mathbf{X}_1 + c_2\mathbf{X}_2$

$= c_1\begin{pmatrix} 1 \\ 1 \end{pmatrix}e^t + c_2\begin{pmatrix} te^t \\ e^t + te^t \end{pmatrix}$

is the complementary function of the homogeneous system

$\mathbf{X}' = \begin{pmatrix} 0 & 1 \\ -1 & 2 \end{pmatrix}\mathbf{X}$ since

$\mathbf{X}_1' = \begin{pmatrix} e^t \\ e^t \end{pmatrix}$ and $\begin{pmatrix} 0 & 1 \\ -1 & 2 \end{pmatrix}\mathbf{X}_1 = \begin{pmatrix} e^t \\ e^t \end{pmatrix}$,

$\mathbf{X}_2' = \begin{pmatrix} e^t + te^t \\ 2e^t + te^t \end{pmatrix}$ and $\begin{pmatrix} 0 & 1 \\ -1 & 2 \end{pmatrix}\mathbf{X}_2$

$= \begin{pmatrix} e^t + te^t \\ 2e^t + te^t \end{pmatrix}.$

The vectors $\mathbf{X}_1$ and $\mathbf{X}_2$ are linearly independent since $W(\mathbf{X}_1, \mathbf{X}_2) = e^{2t} \neq 0$ for every t.

Also, a particular solution vector is

$\mathbf{X}_p = \begin{pmatrix} \sin t \\ \cos t \end{pmatrix}$ since

$\mathbf{X}_p' = \begin{pmatrix} \cos t \\ -\sin t \end{pmatrix}$ and $\begin{pmatrix} 0 & 1 \\ -1 & 2 \end{pmatrix}\mathbf{X}_p$

$+ \begin{pmatrix} 0 \\ -2\cos t \end{pmatrix} = \begin{pmatrix} \cos t \\ -\sin t \end{pmatrix}.$

11. $\mathbf{X} = c_1\begin{pmatrix} 1 \\ -1 \end{pmatrix}e^t + c_2\left\{ \begin{pmatrix} 0 \\ 1 \end{pmatrix}e^t + \begin{pmatrix} 1 \\ -1 \end{pmatrix}te^t \right\}$

13. $\mathbf{X} = c_1\begin{pmatrix} e^t\cos 2t \\ -e^t\sin 2t \end{pmatrix} + c_2\begin{pmatrix} e^t\sin 2t \\ e^t\cos 2t \end{pmatrix}$

15. $\mathbf{X} = c_1\begin{pmatrix} 1 \\ -1 \end{pmatrix}e^t + c_2\begin{pmatrix} 1 \\ 3 \end{pmatrix}e^{5t} + \begin{pmatrix} \frac{1}{2} \\ \frac{3}{2} \end{pmatrix}e^t$

$+ \begin{pmatrix} 1 \\ -1 \end{pmatrix}te^t$

17. $\mathbf{X} = c_1\begin{pmatrix} -4 \\ 1 \end{pmatrix} + c_2\begin{pmatrix} 2 \\ 1 \end{pmatrix}e^{6t} + \begin{pmatrix} 2 \\ 1 \end{pmatrix}t^2e^{6t}$

$+ \begin{pmatrix} -\frac{2}{3} \\ \frac{1}{6} \end{pmatrix}te^{6t} + \begin{pmatrix} \frac{1}{9} \\ -\frac{1}{36} \end{pmatrix}e^{6t}$

19. $\mathbf{X} = c_1\begin{pmatrix} \cos t \\ \cos t - \sin t \end{pmatrix} + c_2\begin{pmatrix} \sin t \\ \sin t + \cos t \end{pmatrix}$

$- \begin{pmatrix} 1 \\ 1 \end{pmatrix} + \begin{pmatrix} \sin t \\ \sin t + \cos t \end{pmatrix}\ln(\csc t - \cot t)$

Exercises 9.1, Page 422

1. a family of parabolas $y = x^2 + c$

3. a family of hyperbolas $x^2 - y^2 = c$

5. a family of circles $x^2 + (y + 1)^2 = c^2$ with center at $(0, -1)$

7. a family of straight lines $y = c(x - 2) + 1$ passing through $(2,1)$

9.

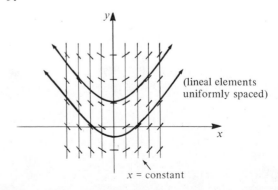

(lineal elements uniformly spaced)

$x = \text{constant}$

11.

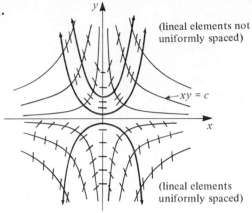

(lineal elements not uniformly spaced)

$xy = c$

(lineal elements uniformly spaced)

13.

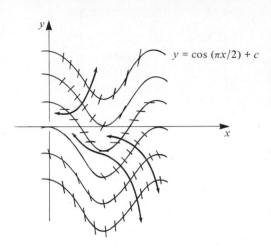

$y = \cos(\pi x/2) + c$

15. $y = \dfrac{\alpha - c\gamma}{c\delta - \beta} x$ **17.** $y = \pm\sqrt{2}x$ **19.** $y = 4x; \quad y = -x$

Exercises 9.2, Page 431

1. $y = 1 - x + \tan(x + \pi/4)$

3. (a)

x_n	y_n
1.00	5.0000
1.10	3.8000
1.20	2.9800
1.30	2.4260
1.40	2.0582
1.50	1.8207

(b)

x_n	y_n
1.00	5.0000
1.05	4.4000
1.10	3.8950
1.15	3.4707
1.20	3.1151
1.25	2.8179
1.30	2.5702
1.35	2.3647
1.40	2.1950
1.45	2.0557
1.50	1.9424

5. **(a)**

x_n	y_n
0.00	0.0000
0.10	0.1000
0.20	0.2010
0.30	0.3050
0.40	0.4143
0.50	0.5315

(b)

x_n	y_n
0.00	0.0000
0.05	0.0500
0.10	0.1001
0.15	0.1506
0.20	0.2018
0.25	0.2538
0.30	0.3070
0.35	0.3617
0.40	0.4183
0.45	0.4770
0.50	0.5384

7. **(a)**

x_n	y_n
0.00	0.0000
0.10	0.1000
0.20	0.1905
0.30	0.2731
0.40	0.3492
0.50	0.4198

(b)

x_n	y_n
0.00	0.0000
0.05	0.0500
0.10	0.0976
0.15	0.1429
0.20	0.1863
0.25	0.2278
0.30	0.2676
0.35	0.3058
0.40	0.3427
0.45	0.3782
0.50	0.4124

9. **(a)**

x_n	y_n
0.00	0.5000
0.10	0.5250
0.20	0.5431
0.30	0.5548
0.40	0.5613
0.50	0.5639

(b)

x_n	y_n
0.00	0.5000
0.05	0.5125
0.10	0.5232
0.15	0.5322
0.20	0.5395
0.25	0.5452
0.30	0.5496
0.35	0.5527
0.40	0.5547
0.45	0.5559
0.50	0.5565

11. (a)

x_n	y_n
1.00	1.0000
1.10	1.0000
1.20	1.0191
1.30	1.0588
1.40	1.1231
1.50	1.2194

(b)

x_n	y_n
1.00	1.0000
1.05	1.0000
1.10	1.0049
1.15	1.0147
1.20	1.0298
1.25	1.0506
1.30	1.0775
1.35	1.1115
1.40	1.1538
1.45	1.2057
1.50	1.2696

13. (a) $h = 0.1$

x_n	y_n
1.00	5.0000
1.10	3.9900
1.20	3.2545
1.30	2.7236
1.40	2.3451
1.50	2.0801

$h = 0.05$

x_n	y_n
1.00	5.0000
1.05	4.4475
1.10	3.9763
1.15	3.5751
1.20	3.2342
1.25	2.9452
1.30	2.7009
1.35	2.4952
1.40	2.3226
1.45	2.1786
1.50	2.0592

(c) $h = 0.1$

x_n	y_n
0.00	0.0000
0.10	0.1005
0.20	0.2030
0.30	0.3098
0.40	0.4234
0.50	0.5470

$h = 0.05$

x_n	y_n
0.00	0.0000
0.05	0.0501
0.10	0.1004
0.15	0.1512
0.20	0.2028
0.25	0.2554
0.30	0.3095
0.35	0.3652
0.40	0.4230
0.45	0.4832
0.50	0.5465

(e) $h = 0.1$

x_n	y_n
0.00	0.0000
0.10	0.0952
0.20	0.1822
0.30	0.2622
0.40	0.3363
0.50	0.4053

$h = 0.05$

x_n	y_n
0.00	0.0000
0.05	0.0488
0.10	0.0953
0.15	0.1397
0.20	0.1823
0.25	0.2231
0.30	0.2623
0.35	0.3001
0.40	0.3364
0.45	0.3715
0.50	0.4054

(g) $h = 0.1$

x_n	y_n
0.00	0.5000
0.10	0.5215
0.20	0.5362
0.30	0.5449
0.40	0.5490
0.50	0.5503

$h = 0.05$

x_n	y_n
0.00	0.5000
0.05	0.5116
0.10	0.5214
0.15	0.5294
0.20	0.5359
0.25	0.5408
0.30	0.5444
0.35	0.5469
0.40	0.5484
0.45	0.5492
0.50	0.5495

(i) $h = 0.1$

x_n	y_n
1.00	1.0000
1.10	1.0095
1.20	1.0404
1.30	1.0967
1.40	1.1866
1.50	1.3260

$h = 0.05$

x_n	y_n
1.00	1.0000
1.05	1.0024
1.10	1.0100
1.15	1.0228
1.20	1.0414
1.25	1.0663
1.30	1.0984
1.35	1.1389
1.40	1.1895
1.45	1.2526
1.50	1.3315

15. From the fundamental theorem of calculus we have

$$\int_{x_n}^{x_{n+1}} y'\,dx = y(x)\Big|_{x_n}^{x_{n+1}} = y(x_{n+1}) - y(x_n).$$

Taking

$$f(x,y) \approx \frac{f(x_n,y_n) + f(x_{n+1},y_{n+1})}{2}$$

for $x_n \le x_{n+1}$ we have

$$\int_{x_n}^{x_{n+1}} f(x,y)\,dx \approx (x_{n+1} - x_n)$$

$$\times \frac{f(x_n,y_n) + f(x_{n+1},y_{n+1})}{2}$$

$$= h\frac{f(x_n,y_n) + f(x_{n+1},y_{n+1})}{2}.$$

Using $y' = f(x,y)$ gives

$$\int_{x_n}^{x_{n+1}} y'\,dx = \int_{x_n}^{x_{n+1}} f(x,y)\,dx$$

$$\times\ y(x_{n+1}) - y(x_n) \approx h\frac{f(x_n,y_n) + f(x_{n+1},y_{n+1})}{2}$$

$$\times\ y(x_{n+1}) \approx y(x_n) + h\frac{f(x_n,y_n) + f(x_{n+1},y_{n+1})}{2}.$$

We write this as

$$y_{n+1} = y_n + h\frac{f(x_n,y_n) + f(x_{n+1},y_{n+1}^*)}{2},$$

where

$$y_{n+1}^* = y_n + hf(x_n,y_n).$$

17.

x_n	Euler	Improved Euler
1.0	1.0000	1.0000
1.1	1.2000	1.2469
1.2	1.4938	1.6668
1.3	1.9711	2.6427
1.4	2.9060	8.7989

Exercises 9.3, Page 437

1. (a)

x_n	y_n
1.00	5.0000
1.10	3.9900
1.20	3.2545
1.30	2.7236
1.40	2.3451
1.50	2.0801

(b)

x_n	y_n
1.00	5.0000
1.05	4.4475
1.10	3.9763
1.15	3.5751
1.20	3.2342
1.25	2.9452
1.30	2.7009
1.35	2.4952
1.40	2.3226
1.45	2.1786
1.50	2.0592

3. (a)

x_n	y_n
0.00	0.0000
0.10	0.1000
0.20	0.2020
0.30	0.3082
0.40	0.4211
0.50	0.5438

(b)

x_n	y_n
0.00	0.0000
0.05	0.0500
0.10	0.1003
0.15	0.1510
0.20	0.2025
0.25	0.2551
0.30	0.3090
0.35	0.3647
0.40	0.4223
0.45	0.4825
0.50	0.5456

5. (a)

x_n	y_n
0.00	0.0000
0.10	0.0950
0.20	0.1818
0.30	0.2617
0.40	0.3357
0.50	0.4046

(b)

x_n	y_n
0.00	0.0000
0.05	0.0488
0.10	0.0952
0.15	0.1397
0.20	0.1822
0.25	0.2230
0.30	0.2622
0.35	0.2999
0.40	0.3363
0.45	0.3714
0.50	0.4053

7. (a)

x_n	y_n
0.00	0.5000
0.10	0.5213
0.20	0.5355
0.30	0.5438
0.40	0.5475
0.50	0.5482

(b)

x_n	y_n
0.00	0.5000
0.05	0.5116
0.10	0.5213
0.15	0.5293
0.20	0.5357
0.25	0.5406
0.30	0.5441
0.35	0.5466
0.40	0.5480
0.45	0.5487
0.50	0.5490

9. **(a)**

x_n	y_n
1.00	1.0000
1.10	1.0100
1.20	1.0410
1.30	1.0969
1.40	1.1857
1.50	1.3226

(b)

x_n	y_n
1.00	1.0000
1.05	1.0025
1.10	1.0101
1.15	1.0229
1.20	1.0415
1.25	1.0663
1.30	1.0983
1.35	1.1387
1.40	1.1891
1.45	1.2518
1.50	1.3301

11. Let $f(x, y) = \alpha x + \beta y$. Then $f_x(x, y) = \alpha$, $f_y(x, y) = \beta$ and all higher derivatives are 0. Thus, using the Taylor series expansion for $f(x, y)$, we have

$$f(x_{n+1}, y_{n+1}^*) = f(x_n + h, y_n + hf(x_n, y_n))$$
$$= f(x_n, y_n) + f_x(x_n, y_n)h$$
$$+ f_y(x_n, y_n)hf(x_n, y_n) + 0$$
$$= f(x_n, y_n) + \alpha h$$
$$+ \beta hf(x_n, y_n).$$

Now $f(x_n, y_n) = y_n'$ and $\alpha + \beta y_n' = y_n''$. Hence the improved Euler formula may be written

$$y_{n+1} = y_n + \frac{h}{2}[f(x_n, y_n)$$
$$+ f(x_{n+1}, y_{n+1}^*)]$$
$$= y_n + \frac{h}{2}[f(x_n, y_n) + f(x_n, y_n) + \alpha h$$
$$+ \beta hf(x_n, y_n)]$$
$$= y_n + \frac{h}{2}[2y_n' + h(\alpha + \beta y_n')]$$
$$= y_n + hy_n' + \frac{h^2}{2}y_n''.$$

Exercises 9.4, Page 443

1. (a)

x_n	y_n
1.00	5.0000
1.10	3.9724
1.20	3.2284
1.30	2.6945
1.40	2.3163
1.50	2.0533

(b)

x_n	y_n
1.00	5.0000
1.05	4.4452
1.10	3.9723
1.15	3.5700
1.20	3.2283
1.25	2.9389
1.30	2.6944
1.35	2.4886
1.40	2.3162
1.45	2.1724
1.50	2.0532

3. (a)

x_n	y_n
0.00	0.0000
0.10	0.1003
0.20	0.2027
0.30	0.3093
0.40	0.4228
0.50	0.5463

(b)

x_n	y_n
0.00	0.0000
0.05	0.0500
0.10	0.1003
0.15	0.1511
0.20	0.2027
0.25	0.2553
0.30	0.3093
0.35	0.3650
0.40	0.4228
0.45	0.4831
0.50	0.5463

5. (a)

x_n	y_n
0.00	0.0000
0.10	0.0953
0.20	0.1823
0.30	0.2624
0.40	0.3365
0.50	0.4055

(b)

x_n	y_n
0.00	0.0000
0.05	0.0488
0.10	0.0953
0.15	0.1398
0.20	0.1823
0.25	0.2231
0.30	0.2624
0.35	0.3001
0.40	0.3365
0.45	0.3716
0.50	0.4055

7. (a)

x_n	y_n
0.00	0.5000
0.10	0.5213
0.20	0.5358
0.30	0.5443
0.40	0.5482
0.50	0.5493

(b)

x_n	y_n
0.00	0.5000
0.05	0.5116
0.10	0.5213
0.15	0.5294
0.20	0.5358
0.25	0.5407
0.30	0.5443
0.35	0.5467
0.40	0.5482
0.45	0.5490
0.50	0.5493

9. (a)

x_n	y_n
1.00	1.0000
1.10	1.0101
1.20	1.0417
1.30	1.0989
1.40	1.1905
1.50	1.3333

(b)

x_n	y_n
1.00	1.0000
1.05	1.0025
1.10	1.0101
1.15	1.0230
1.20	1.0417
1.25	1.0667
1.30	1.0989
1.35	1.1396
1.40	1.1905
1.45	1.2539
1.50	1.3333

11. Simpson's rule on $[x_n, x_n + h]$ is

$$\int_{x_n}^{x_n+h} f(x)\,dx \approx \frac{h/2}{3}\left[f(x_n) + 4f\left(x_n + \frac{1}{2}h\right) \right.$$

$$\left. + f(x_n + h) \right].$$

For $f(x, y) = f(x)$ the Runge–Kutta method gives

$$k_1 = hf(x_n), \qquad k_3 = hf(x_n + \tfrac{1}{2}h),$$
$$k_2 = hf(x_n + \tfrac{1}{2}h), \qquad k_4 = hf(x_n + h),$$

and

$$y_{n+1} = y_n + \frac{h}{6}\left[f(x_n) + 4f\left(x_n + \frac{1}{2}h\right) + f(x_n + h) \right].$$

Exercises 9.5, Page 446

1. $y(0.2) \approx 1.39$

3. $h = 0.2$; $y(0.2) \approx 1.38$

$h = 0.1$:

x_n	y_n	u_n
0.0	1.0000	2.0000
0.1	1.1950	1.8808
0.2	1.3762	1.7254

5.

x_n	y_n
0.0	1.0000
0.1	1.0052
0.2	1.0214
0.3	1.0499
0.4	1.0918

Chapter 9 Review Exercises, Page 449

1. All isoclines $y = cx$ are solutions of the differential equation.

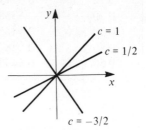

3.

Comparison of Numerical Methods with $h = 0.1$				
x_n	Euler	Improved Euler	3-Term Taylor	Runge–Kutta
1.00	2.0000	2.0000	2.0000	2.0000
1.10	2.1386	2.1549	2.1556	2.1556
1.20	2.3097	2.3439	2.3453	2.3454
1.30	2.5136	2.5672	2.5694	2.5695
1.40	2.7504	2.8246	2.8277	2.8278
1.50	3.0201	3.1157	3.1198	3.1197

Comparison of Numerical Methods with $h = 0.05$				
x_n	Euler	Improved Euler	3-Term Taylor	Runge–Kutta
1.00	2.0000	2.0000	2.0000	2.0000
1.05	2.0693	2.0735	2.0735	2.0736
1.10	2.1469	2.1554	2.1556	2.1556
1.15	2.2329	2.2459	2.2462	2.2462
1.20	2.3272	2.3450	2.3454	2.3454
1.25	2.4299	2.4527	2.4532	2.4532
1.30	2.5410	2.5689	2.5695	2.5695
1.35	2.6604	2.6937	2.6944	2.6944
1.40	2.7883	2.8269	2.8278	2.8278
1.45	2.9245	2.9686	2.9696	2.9696
1.50	3.0690	3.1187	3.1198	3.1197

5.

			Comparison of Numerical Methods with $h = 0.1$	
x_n	Euler	Improved Euler	3-Term Taylor	Runge–Kutta
0.50	0.5000	0.5000	0.5000	0.5000
0.60	0.6000	0.6048	0.6050	0.6049
0.70	0.7095	0.7191	0.7195	0.7194
0.80	0.8283	0.8427	0.8433	0.8431
0.90	0.9559	0.9752	0.9759	0.9757
1.00	1.0921	1.1163	1.1172	1.1169

			Comparison of Numerical Methods with $h = 0.05$	
x_n	Euler	Improved Euler	3-Term Taylor	Runge–Kutta
0.50	0.5000	0.5000	0.5000	0.5000
0.55	0.5500	0.5512	0.5512	0.5512
0.60	0.6024	0.6049	0.6049	0.6049
0.65	0.6573	0.6609	0.6610	0.6610
0.70	0.7144	0.7193	0.7194	0.7194
0.75	0.7739	0.7800	0.7802	0.7801
0.80	0.8356	0.8430	0.8431	0.8431
0.85	0.8996	0.9082	0.9083	0.9083
0.90	0.9657	0.9755	0.9757	0.9757
0.95	1.0340	1.0451	1.0453	1.0452
1.00	1.1044	1.1168	1.1170	1.1169

7. $h = 0.2$: $y(0.2) \approx 3.2000$

$h = 0.1$:

x_n	y_n	u_n
0.0	3.0000	1.0000
0.1	3.1000	1.3000
0.2	3.2300	1.6720

Exercises 10.1, Page 455

1. $\displaystyle\int_0^{\pi/2} \sin(2m+1)x \sin(2n+1)x\,dx$

$\displaystyle = \frac{1}{2}\int_0^{\pi/2} [\cos 2(m-n)x$

$\qquad - \cos 2(m+n+1)x]\,dx$

$\displaystyle = \frac{1}{4}\left[\frac{\sin 2(m-n)x}{m-n} - \frac{\sin 2(m+n+1)x}{m+n+1}\right]_0^{\pi/2}$

$= 0, \quad m \neq n$

3. $\displaystyle\int_0^{\pi} \sin mx \sin nx\,dx$

$\displaystyle = \frac{1}{2}\int_0^{\pi} [\cos(m-n)x - \cos(m+n)x]\,dx$

$\displaystyle = \frac{1}{2}\left[\frac{\sin(m-n)x}{m-n} - \frac{\sin(m+n)x}{m+n}\right]_0^{\pi}$

$= 0, \quad m \neq n$

5. $\displaystyle\int_0^{p} \cos\frac{n\pi}{p}x\,dx = \frac{p}{n\pi}\sin\frac{n\pi}{p}x\Big|_0^{p} = 0, \; n \neq 0;$

$\displaystyle\int_0^{p} \cos\frac{m\pi}{p}x \cos\frac{n\pi}{p}x\,dx$

$\displaystyle = \frac{1}{2}\int_0^{p}\left[\cos\frac{(m-n)\pi}{p}x + \cos\frac{(m+n)\pi}{p}x\right]dx$

$\displaystyle = \frac{p}{2\pi}\left[\frac{\sin\dfrac{(m-n)\pi}{p}x}{m-n} + \frac{\sin\dfrac{(m+n)\pi}{p}x}{m+n}\right]_0^{p}$

$= 0, \quad m \neq n$

7. (1) $\displaystyle\frac{\sqrt{\pi}}{2},$ (3) $\displaystyle\sqrt{\frac{\pi}{2}},$

(5) $\|1\| = \sqrt{p}, \; \left\|\cos\dfrac{n\pi}{p}x\right\| = \sqrt{\dfrac{p}{2}}$

9. For example

$\displaystyle\int_{-\infty}^{\infty} e^{-x^2}H_0(x)H_1(x)\,dx = \int_{-\infty}^{\infty} e^{-x^2}(2x)\,dx$

$\displaystyle = -\int_{-\infty}^{0} e^{-x^2}(-2x\,dx) - \int_0^{\infty} e^{-x^2}(-2x\,dx)$

$\displaystyle = -e^{-x^2}\Big|_{-\infty}^{0} - e^{-x^2}\Big|_0^{\infty}$

$= -1 - (-1) = 0.$

The results

$\displaystyle\int_{-\infty}^{\infty} e^{-x^2}H_0(x)H_2(x)\,dx = 0$

and $\displaystyle\int_{-\infty}^{\infty} e^{-x^2}H_1(x)H_2(x)\,dx = 0$

follow from integration by parts.

11. Legendre's equation can be written in the form

$$\frac{d}{dx}\left[(1-x^2)\frac{dy}{dx}\right] + n(n+1)y = 0.$$

With the identification $r(x) = 1 - x^2$, we see $r(-1) = r(1) = 0$. Since the weight function is $p(x) = 1, q(x) = 0, \lambda = n(n+1)$ it follows from part (b) of Problem 10 that

$$\int_{-1}^{1} P_m(x)P_n(x)\,dx = 0, \quad m \neq n.$$

Exercises 10.2, Page 466

1. $\displaystyle f(x) \sim \frac{1}{2} + \frac{1}{\pi}\sum_{n=1}^{\infty}\frac{1-(-1)^n}{n}\sin nx$

3. $\displaystyle f(x) \sim \frac{3}{4} + \sum_{n=1}^{\infty}\left[\frac{(-1)^n-1}{n^2\pi^2}\cos n\pi x\right.$

$\displaystyle\left. - \frac{1}{n\pi}\sin n\pi x\right]$

5. $f(x) \sim \dfrac{\pi^2}{6} + \displaystyle\sum_{n=1}^{\infty} \left\{ \dfrac{2(-1)^n}{n^2} \cos nx \right.$

$\left. + \left(\dfrac{(-1)^{n+1}\pi}{n} + \dfrac{2}{\pi n^3}[(-1)^n - 1] \right) \sin nx \right\}$

7. $f(x) \sim \pi + 2 \displaystyle\sum_{n=1}^{\infty} \dfrac{(-1)^{n+1}}{n} \sin nx$

9. $f(x) \sim \dfrac{1}{\pi} + \dfrac{1}{2} \sin x + \dfrac{1}{\pi} \displaystyle\sum_{n=2}^{\infty} \dfrac{(-1)^n + 1}{1 - n^2} \cos nx$

11. $f(x) \sim \dfrac{3}{4} + \dfrac{1}{\pi} \displaystyle\sum_{n=1}^{\infty} \left[-\dfrac{1}{n} \sin \dfrac{n\pi}{2} \cos \dfrac{n\pi}{2} x \right.$

$\left. + \dfrac{3}{n} \left(1 - \cos \dfrac{n\pi}{2} \right) \sin \dfrac{n\pi}{2} x \right]$

13. $f(x) \sim \dfrac{2 \sinh \pi}{\pi} \left[\dfrac{1}{2} + \displaystyle\sum_{n=1}^{\infty} \dfrac{(-1)^n}{1 + n^2} (\cos nx \right.$

$\left. - n \sin nx) \right]$

15. (a) At the endpoint $x = \pi$ the series will converge to

$$\dfrac{f(\pi -) + f(-\pi +)}{2} = \dfrac{\pi^2}{2}.$$

Substituting $x = \pi$ into the series gives

$$\dfrac{\pi^2}{6} + 2 \displaystyle\sum_{n=1}^{\infty} \dfrac{1}{n^2}.$$

Equating the two results then yields

$$\dfrac{\pi^2}{6} = \displaystyle\sum_{n=1}^{\infty} \dfrac{1}{n^2} = 1 + \dfrac{1}{2^2} + \dfrac{1}{3^2} + \dfrac{1}{4^2} + \cdots$$

Now at $x = 0$ the series converges to

$$f(0) = 0 = \dfrac{\pi^2}{6} + \displaystyle\sum_{n=1}^{\infty} \dfrac{2(-1)^n}{n^2}$$

This implies

$$\dfrac{\pi^2}{12} = \displaystyle\sum_{n=1}^{\infty} \dfrac{(-1)^{n+1}}{n^2} = 1 - \dfrac{1}{2^2} + \dfrac{1}{3^2}$$

$$- \dfrac{1}{4^2} + \cdots$$

(b) The value of $\pi^2/8$ is obtained by adding the two series given in part (a):

$$\dfrac{\pi^2}{8} = 1 + \dfrac{1}{3^2} + \dfrac{1}{5^2} + \dfrac{1}{7^2} + \cdots$$

17. $f(x) \sim \dfrac{4\pi^2}{3} + 4 \displaystyle\sum_{n=1}^{\infty} \left[\dfrac{1}{n^2} \cos nx - \dfrac{\pi}{n} \sin nx \right]$

19. $f(x) \sim \dfrac{2}{\pi} \displaystyle\sum_{n=1}^{\infty} \dfrac{1 - (-1)^n}{n} \sin nx$

21. $f(x) \sim \dfrac{\pi}{2} + \dfrac{2}{\pi} \displaystyle\sum_{n=1}^{\infty} \dfrac{(-1)^n - 1}{n^2} \cos nx$

23. $f(x) \sim \dfrac{1}{3} + \dfrac{4}{\pi^2} \displaystyle\sum_{n=1}^{\infty} \dfrac{(-1)^n}{n^2} \cos n\pi x$

25. $f(x) \sim \dfrac{2\pi^2}{3} + 4 \displaystyle\sum_{n=1}^{\infty} \dfrac{(-1)^{n+1}}{n^2} \cos nx$

27. $f(x) \sim \dfrac{2}{\pi} \displaystyle\sum_{n=1}^{\infty} \dfrac{1 - (-1)^n(1 + \pi)}{n} \sin nx$

29. $f(x) \sim \dfrac{2}{\pi} + \dfrac{2}{\pi} \displaystyle\sum_{n=2}^{\infty} \dfrac{1 + (-1)^n}{1 - n^2} \cos nx$

31. $f(x) \sim \dfrac{1}{2} + \dfrac{2}{\pi} \displaystyle\sum_{n=1}^{\infty} \dfrac{\sin \dfrac{n\pi}{2}}{n} \cos n\pi x$

$f(x) \sim \dfrac{2}{\pi} \displaystyle\sum_{n=1}^{\infty} \dfrac{1 - \cos \dfrac{n\pi}{2}}{n} \sin n\pi x$

33. $f(x) \sim \dfrac{2}{\pi} + \dfrac{4}{\pi} \displaystyle\sum_{n=1}^{\infty} \dfrac{(-1)^n}{1 - 4n^2} \cos 2nx$

$f(x) \sim \dfrac{8}{\pi} \displaystyle\sum_{n=1}^{\infty} \dfrac{n}{4n^2 - 1} \sin 2nx$

35. $f(x) \sim \dfrac{\pi}{4} + \dfrac{2}{\pi} \displaystyle\sum_{n=1}^{\infty} \dfrac{2 \cos \dfrac{n\pi}{2} - (-1)^n - 1}{n^2} \cos nx$

$f(x) \sim \dfrac{4}{\pi} \displaystyle\sum_{n=1}^{\infty} \dfrac{\sin \dfrac{n\pi}{2}}{n^2} \sin nx$

37. $f(x) \sim \dfrac{3}{4} + \dfrac{4}{\pi^2} \displaystyle\sum_{n=1}^{\infty} \dfrac{\cos\dfrac{n\pi}{2} - 1}{n^2} \cos\dfrac{n\pi}{2}x$

$f(x) \sim \displaystyle\sum_{n=1}^{\infty} \left\{ \dfrac{4}{n^2\pi^2} \sin\dfrac{n\pi}{2} - \dfrac{2}{n\pi}(-1)^n \right\} \sin\dfrac{n\pi}{2}x$

39. Let f and g be even functions. Define

$$h(x) = f(x)g(x).$$

Then

$$h(-x) = f(-x)g(-x) = f(x)g(x) = h(x).$$

41. Let f be an even function and g be an odd function. Define

$$h(x) = f(x)g(x).$$

Then

$$h(-x) = f(-x)g(-x)$$

$$= f(x)[-g(x)] = -f(x)g(x)$$

$$= -h(x).$$

43. Let f be an odd function. Then

$$\int_{-a}^{a} f(x)\,dx = \int_{-a}^{0} f(x)\,dx$$

$$+ \int_{0}^{a} f(x)\,dx = I_1 + I_2.$$

In I_1 let $-x = t$ and $-dx = dt$ so that

$$I_1 = \int_{a}^{0} f(-t)(-dt)$$

$$= \int_{0}^{a} f(-t)\,dt$$

$$= -\int_{0}^{a} f(t)\,dt$$

$$= -I_2.$$

Therefore $I_1 + I_2 = 0$.

Exercises 10.3, Page 471

1. The possible cases can be summarized in one form $u = c_1 e^{c_2(x+y)}$ where c_1 and c_2 are constants.

3. $u = c_1 e^{y + c_2(x-y)}$

5. $u = c_1(xy)^{c_2}$

7. Not separable

9. $u = e^{-t}[A_1 e^{k\lambda^2 t} \cosh \lambda x + B_1 e^{k\lambda^2 t} \sinh \lambda x]$

$u = e^{-t}[A_2 e^{-k\lambda^2 t} \cos \lambda x + B_2 e^{-k\lambda^2 t} \sin \lambda x]$

$u = (c_7 x + c_8)(-t + c_9)$

11. $u = (c_1 \cosh \lambda x + c_2 \sinh \lambda x)(c_3 \cosh at + c_4 \sinh at)$

$u = (c_5 \cos \lambda x + c_6 \sin \lambda x)(c_7 \cos at + c_8 \sin at)$

$u = (c_9 x + c_{10})(c_{11} t + c_{12})$

13. $u = (c_1 \cosh \lambda x + c_2 \sinh \lambda x)(c_3 \cos \lambda y + c_4 \sin \lambda y)$

$u = (c_5 \cos \lambda x + c_6 \sin \lambda x)(c_7 \cosh \lambda y + c_8 \sinh \lambda y)$

$u = (c_9 x + c_{10})(c_{11} y + c_{12})$

15. For $\lambda^2 > 0$ there are three possibilities:

$u = (c_1 \cosh \lambda x$

$\qquad + c_2 \sinh \lambda x)(c_3 \cosh \sqrt{1 - \lambda^2}\, y$

$\qquad + c_4 \sinh \sqrt{1 - \lambda^2}\, y),\ \lambda^2 < 1,$

$u = (c_1 \cosh \lambda x$

$\qquad + c_2 \sinh \lambda x)(c_3 \cos \sqrt{\lambda^2 - 1}\, y$

$\qquad + c_4 \sin \sqrt{\lambda^2 - 1}\, y),\ \lambda^2 > 1,$

$u = (c_1 \cosh x + c_2 \sinh x)$

$\qquad \times (c_3 y + c_4),\ \lambda^2 = 1.$

The results for the case $-\lambda^2 < 0$ are similar. For $\lambda^2 = 0$ we have

$u = (c_9 x + c_{10})(c_{11} \cosh y + c_{12} \sinh y).$

17. Using $-\lambda^2$ as a separation constant we obtain

$$T' + k\lambda^2 T = 0$$

$$rR'' + R' + \lambda^2 rR = 0.$$

This last equation can be written as

$$r^2 R'' + r R' + \lambda^2 r^2 R = 0$$

which we recognize as Bessel's equation with $v = 0$. The general solutions of the respective equations are as indicated in the problem.

Exercises 10.4 Page 481

1. $u(x,t) =$

$$= \frac{2}{\pi} \sum_{n=1}^{\infty} \left(\frac{-\cos\frac{n\pi}{2} + 1}{n} \right) e^{-k(n^2\pi^2/L^2)t} \sin\frac{n\pi}{L}x$$

3. $u(x,t) = \dfrac{1}{L} \displaystyle\int_0^L f(x)\,dx$

$$+ \frac{2}{L} \sum_{n=1}^{\infty} \left(\int_0^L f(x)\cos\frac{n\pi}{L}x\,dx \right)$$

$$\times\, e^{-k(n^2\pi^2/L^2)t}\cos\frac{n\pi}{L}x$$

5. $u(x,t) = e^{-ht}\left[\dfrac{1}{L} \displaystyle\int_0^L f(x)\,dx \right.$

$$+ \frac{2}{L} \sum_{n=1}^{\infty} \left(\int_0^L f(x)\cos\frac{n\pi}{L}x\,dx \right)$$

$$\left. \times\, e^{-k(n^2\pi^2/L^2)t}\cos\frac{n\pi}{L}x \right]$$

7. $u(x,t) = \dfrac{8h}{\pi^2} \displaystyle\sum_{n=1}^{\infty} \dfrac{\sin\frac{n\pi}{2}}{n^2} \sin\frac{n\pi}{L}x\cos\frac{n\pi a}{L}t$

9. $u(x,t) = \dfrac{L}{\pi a} \sin\dfrac{\pi}{L}x\sin\dfrac{\pi a}{L}t$

11. $u(x,t) = \dfrac{L}{2} - \dfrac{2L}{\pi^2} \displaystyle\sum_{n=1}^{\infty}$

$$\times \frac{1-(-1)^n}{n^2}\cos\frac{n\pi}{L}x\cos\frac{n\pi a}{L}t$$

13. $u(x,y) = \dfrac{2}{a} \displaystyle\sum_{n=1}^{\infty} \left(\int_0^a f(x)\sin\frac{n\pi}{a}x\,dx \right)$

$$\times \frac{\cosh\dfrac{n\pi}{a}y}{\cosh\dfrac{n\pi}{a}b} \sin\frac{n\pi}{a}x$$

15. $u(x,y) = \dfrac{a}{2b}(b-y)$

$$+ \frac{2a}{\pi^2} \sum_{n=1}^{\infty} \frac{(-1)^n - 1}{n^2} \frac{\sinh\dfrac{n\pi}{a}(b-y)}{\sinh\dfrac{n\pi}{a}b}\cos\frac{n\pi}{a}x$$

Here we have used the identity
$$\sinh(\alpha - \beta) = \sinh\alpha\cosh\beta - \cosh\alpha\sinh\beta.$$

17. $u(x,y)$

$$= \sum_{n=1}^{\infty} \left(\frac{2}{a} \int_0^a f(x)\sin\frac{n\pi}{a}x\,dx \right) e^{-n\pi y/a}\sin\frac{n\pi}{a}x$$

19. Differentiate each side with respect to x:

$$\frac{d}{dx}\left[\frac{X''}{4X}\right] = \frac{d}{dx}\left[\frac{Y'}{Y}\right].$$

Since the right-hand side is zero we have

$$\frac{d}{dx}\left[\frac{X''}{4X}\right] = 0.$$

This implies $X''/4X$ is a constant. Similarly, if we differentiate both sides with respect to y we can show that Y'/Y is a constant.

21. $u = A_n e^{-k(n^2\pi^2/25)t}\cos\dfrac{n\pi}{5}x,\ n = 0,1,2,\dots$

23. $u = A_n \sinh n\pi x \sin n\pi y,\ n = 1,2,3,\dots$

Chapter 10 Review Exercises, Page 485

1. $\displaystyle\int_0^L \sin\frac{(2m+1)\pi}{2L}x\sin\frac{(2n+1)\pi}{2L}x\,dx$

$$= \frac{1}{2} \int_0^L \left[\cos\frac{(m-n)\pi}{L}x \right.$$

$$\left. - \cos\frac{(m+n+1)\pi}{L}x \right] dx$$

$$= \frac{L}{2\pi}\left[\frac{\sin\dfrac{(m-n)\pi}{L}x}{m-n} \right.$$

$$\left. - \frac{\sin\dfrac{(m+n+1)\pi}{L}x}{m+n+1} \right]_0^L$$

$$= 0, \quad m \neq n.$$

3. $f(x) \sim \dfrac{1}{2} + \dfrac{2}{\pi} \displaystyle\sum_{n=1}^{\infty} \left\{ \dfrac{1}{n^2\pi} [(-1)^n - 1] \cos n\pi x \right.$

$\left. + \dfrac{2}{n}(-1)^n \sin n\pi x \right\}$

5. $f(x) \sim 1 - e^{-1} + 2 \displaystyle\sum_{n=1}^{\infty} \dfrac{1 - (-1)^n e^{-1}}{1 + n^2\pi^2} \cos n\pi x$

7. The given equation can be written as

$$\frac{X''}{X} + k^2 \cosh 2x = -\frac{Y''}{Y} + k^2 \cos 2y = \lambda^2$$

so that

$$X'' - (\lambda^2 - k^2 \cosh 2x)X = 0$$

$$Y'' + (\lambda^2 - k^2 \cos 2y)Y = 0.$$

9. $u = c_1 e^{(c_2 x + y/c_2)}$

11. $u = 50$

INDEX

Abel's formula, 147
Amplitude, 190
Analytic function, 235
Applications of differential equations
  atomic physics, 103, 105–107
  biology, 35–36, 103–104, 115–116, 118–119
  chemistry, 120–123
  electric circuits, 32–33, 109–110, 215–216, 315–316, 344–347
  geometric problems, 26–31, 95–100
  problems in mechanics, 32–35, 37–40, 125, 185–217, 314–315, 477–479
  mixtures, 111–112, 355–356
  temperature distributions, 108–109, 475–477, 480–481
Auxiliary equation, 155, 225

Beats, 215
Bernoulli's equation, 83–84
Bessel's equation, 264–265
  solution of, 265–266
Bessel functions of first kind, 267
  spherical, 273
Boundary-value problem, 20, 474–483

Canonical form of linear system of equations, 350
Carbon dating, 106–107
Catenary, 39
Cauchy-Euler differential equation, 224–229
Characteristic equation, 155, 378
Characteristic roots, 155–156, 377
Characteristic vectors, 378
Chebyshev's equation, 10
Clairaut's equation, 86
Complementary function, 143, 391
Continuing method, 444
Continuous compound interest, 36–37
Convergence of a Fourier series, 460
Convolution integral, 307
Convolution theorem, 306
Critical damping, 196

Damped motion, 194–203
Decay, radioactive, 102–106
Degenerate system of equations, 354
Differential operator, 328
Diffusion equation, 474
Direction field, 418–419

Eigenfunctions, 476
Eigenvalues of a matrix, 377
  of a boundary value problem, 476
Eigenvectors of a matrix, 378
Electrical networks, 344–347
Epidemics, 118–119
Equidimensional equation, 224
Equilibrium position, 34, 186
Escape velocity, 125
Essential parameters, 7
Euler coefficients, 458
Even function, 461
Exact differential, 63
Exact differential equation, 63–69
Existence and uniqueness of a solution, 15–19
Expansion of a function
  in a cosine series, 463
  in a Fourier series, 457–459
  in a sine series, 463
  in terms of orthogonal functions, 454–455
Exponential order, 284
Exponents of a singularity, 248

First-order chemical reactions, 120
First-order differential equations
  applications of, 95–128
  solutions of, 47–91
First translation theorem, 297
Forced motion, 205–212
Fourier series
  generalized, 454
  trigonometric, 457–459
Fourier cosine series, 462–463

Fourier sine series, 462–463
Free motion
  damped, 195
  undamped, 187
Frequency, 187
Frobenius, method of, 245–246
Fundamental matrix, 402–403

Gamma function, 266, 271, 295
General solution
  of a differential equation, 7, 140, 144
  of a linear system, 369, 371
Generalized Fourier series, 455
Generating function, 275
Gompertz curve, 120
Growth and decay, 102–106

Half-life, 105–106
Half-range expansions, 464
Hanging cable, 37–38
Heat equation, 474–475
Hermites equation, 10
Homogeneous differential equations, 56, 131, 469
  functions of degree n, 56–58
  linear systems, 350, 364, 376–389
Hooke's law, 33, 39, 185–186

Identity matrix, 405
Implicit solution, 4
Improved Euler method, 427–431
Indicial equation, 248
Indicial roots, 248
Initial value problem, 14–17
Insulated boundaries, 477
Integral equation, 321–322
Integrating factor, 68–69, 70, 74–75
Integrodifferential equation, 315–316
Inverse Laplace transform, 289–290
Inverse matrix, 405, 410
Irregular singular point, 243
  at ∞, 264
Isoclines, 418
Isogonal trajectories, 102

Kirchoff's laws, 32–33, 215, 315, 344–345

Laguerre's equation, 10
Laplace's equation, 474, 480
Laplace transform, 281–325
  convolution, 306–307
  definition of, 282

existence of, 284
inverse, 289–294
linearity of, 283
operational properties, 296–309
tables of, 323–324
translation theorems, 297, 300–301
Law of Malthus, 129
Law of mass action, 123
Legendre's equation, 264–265
  solution of, 268–270
Legendre polynomials, 270
Lineal elements, 418
Linear dependence, 134
  of functions, 134, 137
  of solution vectors, 367
Linear independence, 134
  of functions, 136–137
  of solutions, 139–140
  of solution vectors, 367–368
Linear ordinary differential equations, 2, 73, 131–180, 224
  applications of, 102–112, 185–217
  complementary solution of, 143–144
  general solution of, 140, 144
  particular solution of, 143
Linear operation, 281
Linear systems, 328
  degenerate, 354
  in matrix form, 362–363
  in normal form, 350
Linear partial differential equations, 468
Logarithmic decrement, 204
Logistic equation, 36, 115–116
Lotka and Volterra, equations of, 127–128

Matrices, 358–388, 402–409
  addition of two vectors, 359–360
  column, 359
  definition of, 358
  derivative of, 361
  eigenvalues of, 377
  eigenvectors of, 377–378
  form of a linear system, 362
  fundamental, 402–403
  multiples of, 359
  multiplicative identity, 405
  multiplicative inverse
    for a 2×2 matrix, 405
    for a 3×3 matrix, 410
  product of 2×2 matrices, 404
  product of, with a vector, 360

Mechanical resonance, 208–212
Method of Frobenius, 245–262
Milne's method, 444
Mixtures, 111–112, 355–358
Multistep method, 444

Newton's law of cooling, 36, 108–109
Newton's second law of motion, 33, 186
Nonhomogeneous linear differential equation, 131
Nonhomogeneous linear systems of differential equations, 350, 363
Nonlinear differential equations, 2–3
Normal form, 350
Norm, 452
Normalized set of functions, 454
Numerical methods, 423–449
    Euler's method, 424
    Heun's formula, 428
    Improved Euler method, 427
    Milne's method, 444
    Runge-Kutta methods, 438–439
    Three-term Taylor method, 434

Odd function, 461
Operator, differential, 328
Order of a differential equation, 2
Ordinary differential equation, definition of, 2
Ordinary point, 235
Origins of differential equations, 25–43
Orthogonal functions, 452
    with respect to a weight function, 455
Orthogonal trajectories, 98–100
Orthonormal set of functions, 452
Overdamped motion, 196

Parametric Bessel equation, 273
Partial differential equation, 2
    homogeneous, 469
    linear, 468
    nonhomogeneous, 469
    separable, 469
Particular solution, 7, 143
Pendulum motion, 34–35, 192, 349
Periodic extension, 461
Periodic functions, Laplace transform of, 311
Phase angle, 190
Piecewise continuous function, 284
Power series solutions, 232–240
Population growth, 103, 115
Predator-prey, 127
Predictor-corrector methods, 428, 444

Propagation error, 445
Pure resonance, 208–209

Quasi-period, 202

Radioactive decay, 103, 105–107
Recurrence relation, 233
Reduction of order, 148–149
Regular singular point, 243
    at ∞, 264
Resonance, 208–212
Resonance curve, 213
Ricatti's equation, 84–85
Rocket motion, 125
Rodrigues' formula, 276
Round-off error, 445
Runge-Kutta methods, 438–439

Second-order chemical reactions, 121
Second translation theorem, 300–301
Separable equations
    ordinary, 47
    partial, 469
Separation constant, 469
Series, Fourier, 457–459
Series solutions, of ordinary differential equations, 232–271
    around an ordinary point, 234–240
    around a regular singular point, 245–264
Simple harmonic motion, 187
Singular point of a differential equation, 235
    irregular, 243
    regular, 243
    at ∞, 264
Singular solution, 7
Slope field, 418
Solution of a differential equation, 3
Spherical Bessel functions, 273
Spread of a disease, 35–36
Square norm, 452
Stability, 445
Starting methods, 444
Steady-state, current, 110
    solution, 207
    temperature, 480
Stefan's law of radiation, 126
Sturm-Liouville problem, 456
Superposition principle, 133, 366, 471

Telegraph equation, 475
Third-order chemical reaction, 125

Three-term Taylor method, 434
Total differential, 62
Tractrix, 41, 127
Trajectories, 98, 101–102
Transient, current, 110
  term, 207
Translation theorems, for Laplace transform, 297,
    300–301
Trivial solution, 3
Truncation error, 445
Twisted shaft, 216

Underdamped motion, 196
Undetermined coefficients, 162–172
  for systems, 391–396
Unit step function, 299

Variables, separable, 47–53, 469
Variation of parameters, 173–179
  for systems, 396–399, 408–409
Vectors, 359
  linear independence of, 367
  solutions of systems, 364
Verhulst, P.F., 115
Vibrations, spring-mass systems, 33–34, 39–40,
    185–215, 342–344
Vibrating string, 477–479

Wave equation, 474, 477–479
Wronskian, 136, 368
  Abel's formula for, 147

Table I. Transforms of Some Basic Functions

$f(t)$	$\mathscr{L}\{f(t)\} = F(s)$
1. 1	$\dfrac{1}{s}$
2. t^n, $n = 1, 2, 3, \ldots$	$\dfrac{n!}{s^{n+1}}$
3. e^{at}	$\dfrac{1}{s-a}$
4. $\sin kt$	$\dfrac{k}{s^2 + k^2}$
5. $\cos kt$	$\dfrac{s}{s^2 + k^2}$
6. $\sinh kt$	$\dfrac{k}{s^2 - k^2}$
7. $\cosh kt$	$\dfrac{s}{s^2 - k^2}$